Business Applications and Computational Intelligence

Kevin E. Voges, University of Canterbury, New Zealand

Nigel K. Ll. Pope, Griffith University, Australia

Acquisitions Editor: Michelle Potter
Development Editor: Kristin Roth
Senior Managing Editor: Amanda Appicello
Managing Editor: Jennifer Neidig
Copy Editor: Bernard J. Kieklak, Jr.
Typesetter: Jennifer Neidig
Cover Design: Lisa Tosheff
Printed at: Integrated Book Technology

Published in the United States of America by
Idea Group Publishing (an imprint of Idea Group Inc.)
701 E. Chocolate Avenue
Hershey PA 17033
Tel: 717-533-8845
Fax: 717-533-8661
E-mail: cust@idea-group.com
Web site: http://www.idea-group.com

and in the United Kingdom by
Idea Group Publishing (an imprint of Idea Group Inc.)
3 Henrietta Street
Covent Garden
London WC2E 8LU
Tel: 44 20 7240 0856
Fax: 44 20 7379 0609
Web site: http://www.eurospanonline.com

Library of Congress Cataloging-in-Publication Data

Business applications and computational intelligence / Kevin Voges and Nigel Pope, editors.
p. cm.
Summary: "This book deals with the computational intelligence field, particularly business applications adopting computational intelligence techniques"--Provided by publisher.
Includes bibliographical references and index.
ISBN 1-59140-702-8 (hardcover) -- ISBN 1-59140-703-6 (softcover) -- ISBN 1-59140-704-4 (ebook)
1. Business--Data processing. 2. Computational intelligence.
I. Voges, Kevin, 1952- . II. Pope, Nigel.
HF5548.2.B7975 2006
658'.0563--dc22

2005023881

British Cataloguing in Publication Data
A Cataloguing in Publication record for this book is available from the British Library.

Business Applications and Computational Intelligence

Table of Contents

Section VI: Financial Applications

Section VII: Postscript

Preface

Computational intelligence (also called artificial intelligence) is a branch of computer science that explores methods of automating behavior that can be categorized as intelligent. The formal study of topics in computational intelligence (CI) has been under way for more than 50 years. Although its intellectual roots can be traced back to Greek mythology, the modern investigation into computational intelligence can be traced back to the start of the computer era, when Alan Turing first asked if it would be possible for "machinery to show intelligent behaviour." Modern CI has many subdisciplines, including reasoning with uncertain or incomplete information (Bayesian reasoning, fuzzy sets, rough sets), knowledge representation (frames, scripts, conceptual graphs, connectionist approaches including neural networks), and adaptive and emergent approaches (such as evolutionary algorithms and artificial immune systems).

CI has a long history in business applications. Expert systems have been used for decision support in management, neural networks and fuzzy logic have been used in process control, a variety of techniques have been used in forecasting, and data mining has become a core component of Customer Relationship Management (CRM) in marketing. More recently developed agent-based applications have involved the use of intelligent agents — Web-based shopping advisors, modelling in organizational theory and marketing, and scenario-based planning in strategic management. Despite the obvious benefits of CI to business and industry - benefits of modeling, forecasting, process control and financial prediction to name only a few - practitioners have been slow to take up the methods available.

Business practitioners and researchers tend to read and publish in scholarly journals and conference proceedings in their own discipline areas. Consequently, they can be unaware of the range of publications exploring the interaction between business and computational intelligence. This volume addresses the need for a compact overview of the diversity of applications of CI techniques in a number of business disciplines. The volume consists of open-solicited and invited chapters written by leading international researchers in the field of business applications of computational intelligence. All papers were peer reviewed by at least two recognised reviewers. The book covers some foundational material on computational intelligence in business, as well as technical expositions of CI techniques. The book aims to deepen understanding of the area by providing examples of the value of CI concepts and techniques to both theoretical frameworks and practical applications in business. Despite the variety of application areas and techniques, all chapters provide practical business applications.

This book reflects the diversity of the field — 43 authors from 13 countries contributed the 22 chapters. Most fields of business are covered — marketing, data mining, e-commerce, production and operations, finance, decision-making, and general management. Many of the standard techniques from computational intelligence are also covered in the following chapters — association rules, neural networks, support vector machines, evolutionary algorithms, fuzzy systems, reinforcement learning, artificial immune systems, self-organizing maps, and agent-based approaches.

The 22 chapters are categorized into the following seven sections:

Section I: Introduction

Section II: Marketing Applications

Section III: Production and Operations Applications

Section IV: Data Mining Applications

Section V: Management Applications

Section VI: Financial Applications

Section VII: Postscript

Section I contains three chapters, which provide introductory material relating to CI applications in business. Chapter I provides an overview of the field through a cross-sectional review of the literature. It provides access to the vast and scattered literature by citing reviews of many important CI techniques, including expert systems, artificial neural networks, fuzzy systems, rough sets, evolutionary algorithms, and multi-agent systems. Reviews and cited articles cover many areas in business, including finance and economics, production and operations, marketing, and management. Chapter II identifies important conceptual, cultural and technical barriers preventing the successful commercial application of CI techniques, describes the different ways in which they affect both the business user and the CI practitioner, and suggests a number of ways in which these barriers may be overcome. The chapter discusses the practical consequences for the business user of issues such as non-linearity and the extrapolation of prediction into untested ranges. The aim is to highlight to technical and business readers how their different expectations can affect the successful outcome of a CI project. The hope is that by enabling both parties to understand each other's perspective, the true potential of CI in a commercial project can be realized. Chapter III presents an innovative use of CI as a method for collecting survey-type data in management studies, designed to overcome "questionnaire fatigue." The agent-based simulation approach makes it possible to exploit the advantages of questionnaires, experimental designs, role-plays, and scenarios, gaining a synergy from a combination of methodologies. The chapter discusses and presents a behavioral simulation based on the agent-based simulation life cycle, which is supported by Web technology. An example simulation is presented for researchers and practitioners to understand how the technique is implemented.

Section II consists of four chapters illustrating marketing applications of CI (Chapters IV to VII). Chapter IV develops a heuristic genetic algorithm for product portfolio planning. Product portfolio planning is a critical business process in which a company strives for an optimal mix of product offerings through various combinations of products and/or attribute levels. The chapter develops a practical solution method that can find near optimal solutions and can assist marketing managers in product portfolio decision-making. Chapter V reviews some classical methods for modeling customer brand choice behavior, and then discusses newly developed customer behavior models, based on boosting and stacking neural network models. The new models are applied to a scanner data set of liquid detergent purchases, and their performance is compared with previously published results. The models are then used to predict the effect of different pricing schemes upon market share. The main advantage of these new methods is a gain in the ability to predict expected market share. Chapter VI reviews several fields of research that are attempting to solve a problem of knowledge management related to the retrieval and integration of data from different electronic sources. These research fields include information gathering and multi-agent technologies. The chapter uses a specific information gathering multi-agent system called MAPWeb to build new Web agent-based systems that can be incorporated into business-to-consumer activities. The chapter shows how a multi-agent system can be redesigned using a Web-services-oriented architecture, which allows the system to utilize Web-service technologies. A sample example using tourism information is presented. Chapter VII uses a data-mining information retrieval technique to create a Web-mining system. It describes how an off-line process is used to cluster users according to their characteristics and preferences, which then enables the system to effectively provide appropriate information. The system uses a fuzzy c-means algorithm and information retrieval techniques that can be used for text categorization, clustering and information integration. The chapter describes how this system reduces the online response time in a practical test case of a service Web site selling mobile phones. The case shows how the proposed information retrieval technique leads to a query-response containing a reasonable number of mobile phones purchase suggestions that best matched a user's preferences.

Section III contains three chapters illustrating CI applications in the general field of production and operations (Chapters VIII to X). Chapter VIII discusses the various techniques, such as artificial neural networks, wavelet decomposition, support vector machines, and data mining, that can be used for the forecasting of market demand and price in a deregulated electricity market. The chapter argues that the various techniques can offer different advantages in providing satisfactory demand and price signal forecast results, depending on the specific forecasting needs. The techniques can be applied to traditional time-series-based forecasts when the market is reasonably stable, and can also be applied to the analysis of price spikes, which are less common and hence more difficult to predict. Chapter IX presents a hybrid-agent model for Belief-Desire-Intention agents that uses CI and interactive learning methods to handle multiple events and intention reconsideration. In the model, the agent has knowledge of all possible options at every state, which helps the agent to compare and switch between options quickly if the current intention is no longer valid. The model uses a new Adaptive Neuro-Fuzzy Inference System (ANFIS) to simulate vessel berthing in container terminals. The chapter shows how the agents are used to provide autonomous decision making capabilities that lead to an enhancement of the productivity of the terminal. Chapter X describes a new CI algorithm called Horizon Scan, a heuristic-based technique designed to search for optimal solutions in non-linear space. Horizon Scan is a variant of the Hill-Climbing technique. The chapter describes an application of the technique to finding the optimal solution for the scheduling-pricing-dispatch problem in the Australian deregulated electricity market. The approach outlined is general enough to be applied to a range of optimization problems.

Section IV consists of five chapters in the general area of data mining (Chapters XI to XV). Chapter XI argues that data-mining algorithms often generate a large number of rules describing relationships in the data, but often many of the rules generated are not of practical use. The chapter presents a new technique that integrates visualization into the process of generating association rules. This enables users to apply their knowledge to the mining process and be involved in finding interesting association rules through an interactive visualization process. Chapter XII suggests using association rule data-mining techniques to assist manufacturing companies with customer requirement analysis, one of the principal factors in the process of product development. Product development is an important activity in an organization's market expansion strategy. In situations where market segments are already established and product platforms have been installed, the methodology can improve the efficiency and quality of the customer requirement analysis process by integrating information from both the customer and design viewpoints. The chapter argues that generating a product portfolio based on knowledge already available in historical data helps to maintain the integrity of existing product platforms, process platforms, and core business competencies. A case study of vibration motors for mobile phones is used to demonstrate the approach. Chapter XIII suggests that, while association rules mining is useful in discovering items that are frequently found together, rules with lower frequencies are often of more interest to the user. The chapter presents a technique for overcoming the rare-item problem by grouping association rules. The chapter proposes a method for clustering this categorical data based on the conditional probabilities of association rules for data sets with large numbers of attributes. The method uses a combination of a Kohonen Self-Organizing Map and a non-linear optimisation approach, combined with a graphical display, to provide non-technical users with a better understanding of patterns discovered in the data set.

Chapter XIV provides a brief historical background of inductive learning and pattern recognition. It then presents an introduction to Support Vector Machines, which belong to a general class of problem solving techniques known as kernel methods. The chapter includes a comparison with other approaches. As the chapter points out, the basic concept underlying Support Vector Machines is quite simple and intuitive, and involves separating out two classes of data from one another using a linear function that is the maximum possible distance from the data. While free and easy-to-use software packages are available, the actual use of the approach is often impeded by the poor results obtained by novices. The chapter aims at reducing this problem by providing a basic understanding of the theory and practice of Support Vector Machines. Chapter XV presents an overview of one of the oldest and most fundamental areas in data mining, that of association rule mining. It also introduces the maximum sub-array problem, an approach that is gaining importance as a data-mining technique. A number of other data-mining algorithms, covering decision trees, regression trees, clustering, and text mining, are also briefly overviewed. The chapter provides pseudo-code to demonstrate the logic behind these fundamental approaches to data mining, and gives online access to code to enable CI practitioners to incorporate the algorithms into their own software development.

Section V considers management applications, particularly tools and support for decision-making, in three chapters (Chapters XVI to XVIII). Chapter XVI introduces a new deliberative process to enhance group decision-making within organizations, by allowing for and against propositions in a discussion to be explicitly articulated. The approach is called ConSULT (Consensus based on a Shared Understanding of a Leading Topic), and provides a computer-mediated framework to allow for asynchronous and anonymous argumentation, collection and evaluation of discussions, and group decision-making. The approach can be used in conjunction with any CI technique to enhance the outcome of group decision-making. Chapter VII describes an uncertain–reasoning-based technique called NCaRBS (N state Classification and Ranking Belief Simplex), an extension of the CaRBS system developed from Dempster-Shafer theory, The chapter shows how the technique can be used to categorize the strategic stance (Prospector, Defender, or Reactor) of U.S. states in relation to the public provision of long-term care. The approach also has the advantage of treating missing values, which are very common in most public sector data, as ignorant evidence rather than attempting to transform them through imputation. The system displays the results graphically, which the authors argue helps the elucidation of the uncertain reasoning-based analysis, and which should help move public management research towards better benchmarking and more useful examinations of the relationship between strategy and performance. Chapter XVIII argues that simple multi-criteria decisions are made by first deriving priorities of importance for the criteria in terms of a goal, and then priorities of the alternatives in terms of the criteria identified. Benefits, opportunities, cost and risks are also often considered in the decision-making process. The chapter shows how to derive priorities from pair-wise comparison judgments from theories of prioritisation and decision-making using the Analytic Hierarchy Process (AHP) and the Analytic Network Process (ANP), both developed by the author. The techniques are illustrated with a number of examples, including an estimation of market share.

Section VI contains three chapters demonstrating financial applications (Chapters XIX to XXI). Chapter XIX introduces artificial immune system algorithms, inspired by the workings of the natural immune system and, to date, not widely applied to business problems. The authors point out that the natural immune system can be considered as a distributed, self-organising, classification system that operates in a dynamic environment and, as such, has characteristics that make its simulated equivalent very suitable for offering solutions to business problems. The chapter provides an example of how the algorithm can be used to develop a classification system for predicting corporate failure. The chapter reports that the system displays good out-of-sample classification accuracy up to two years prior to failure. Chapter XX presents an intelligent trading system, using a hybrid genetic algorithm and reinforcement learning system that emulates trader behaviour on the Foreign Exchange market and finds the most profitable trading strategy. The chapter reports the process of training and testing on historical data, and shows that the system is capable of achieving moderate gains over the period tested. The chapter also reports the development of real-time software capable of replacing a human trader. Chapter XXI provides an overview of recent online portfolio selection strategies for financial markets. The aim of the strategies is to choose a portfolio of stocks to hold in each trading period, using information collected from the past history of the market. The chapter presents experimental results that compare the performance of these strategies with respect to a standard sequence of historical data, and that demonstrate future potential of the algorithms for online portfolio selection. The chapter suggests that investment companies are starting to recognize the usefulness of online portfolios trading for long-term investment gains.

Finally, in Section VII, after the technical material of the preceding chapters, the postscript (Chapter XXII) presents a non-technical topic, a brief overview of the history of mathematics-based approaches to problem solving and analysis. Despite the tremendous gains in our theoretical understanding and practical use of statistics and data analysis over the last half century, the discipline remains grounded in the work of early pioneers of statistical thought. The chapter shows the human dimension of these early developments from pre-history through to the beginning of the 20th century.

This book will be useful to business academics and practitioners, as well as academics and researchers working in the computational intelligence field who are interested in the business applications of their areas of study.

Acknowledgments

We would like to acknowledge the help of all those involved in the collation and review process of this book, without whose support the project could not have been completed. Most of the authors of the chapters in this volume also served as referees for articles written by other authors. There were also a number of external reviewers who kindly refereed submissions. Thanks go to all who provided comprehensive constructive reviews and comments. A special note of thanks goes to the staff at Idea Group Publishing, whose contributions throughout the whole process from inception to publication have been invaluable.

We would like to thank the authors for their excellent contributions to this volume. We would also like to thank Senior Editor Dr. Mehdi Khosrow-Pour, Managing Director Jan Travers, and Development Editors, Michele Rossi and Kristin Roth at Idea Group Publishing. Finally, we wish to thank out families for their support during the project.

Kevin E. Voges, PhD and Nigel K. Ll. Pope, PhD
Editors

Section I

Introduction

Chapter I

Computational Intelligence Applications in Business: A Cross-Section of the Field

Kevin E. Voges, University of Canterbury, New Zealand

Nigel K. Ll. Pope, Griffith University, Australia

Abstract

We present an overview of the literature relating to computational intelligence (also commonly called artificial intelligence) and business applications, particularly the journal-based literature. The modern investigation into artificial intelligence started with Alan Turing who asked in 1948 if it would be possible for "machinery to show intelligent behaviour." The computational intelligence discipline is primarily concerned with understanding the mechanisms underlying intelligent behavior, and consequently embodying these mechanisms in machines. The term "artificial intelligence" first appeared in print in 1955. As this overview shows, the 50 years of research since then have produced a wide range of techniques, many of which have important implications for many business functions, including finance, economics, production, operations, marketing, and management. However, gaining access to the literature can prove difficult for both the computational intelligence researcher and the business practitioner, as the material is contained in numerous journals and discipline areas. The chapter provides access to the vast and scattered literature by citing reviews of the main computational intelligence techniques, including expert systems, artificial neural networks, fuzzy systems, rough sets, evolutionary algorithms, and multi-agent systems.

Introduction

Although its intellectual roots can be traced back to Greek mythology (McCorduck, 2004), the modern investigation into artificial intelligence started at the beginning of the computer era, when Alan Turing (1948, 1950) first investigated the question "as to whether it is possible for machinery to show intelligent behaviour" (Turing, 1948, p. 1). Many of Turing's insights in that remarkable (unpublished) 1948 manuscript became central concepts in later investigations of machine intelligence. Some of these concepts, including networks of artificial neurons, only became widely available after reinvention by other researchers. For those new to the field, there are many excellent introductions to the study of computational intelligence (Callan, 2003; Engelbrecht, 2002; Hoffmann, 1998; Konar, 2000; Luger & Stubblefield, 1998; Munakata, 1998; Negnevitsky, 2002; Poole, Mackworth, & Goebel, 1998).

Artificial intelligence can be defined as "the scientific understanding of the mechanisms underlying thought and intelligent behavior and their embodiment in machines" (American Association for Artificial Intelligence, n.d.). The term "artificial intelligence" first appeared in print in 1955, in conjunction with a research program at Dartmouth College (McCarthy, Minsky, Rochester, & Shannon, 1955). Recently the term "computational intelligence" has been proposed as more appropriate for this field of study (Poole et al., 1998). As they state, "[t]he central scientific goal of computational intelligence is to understand the principles that make intelligent behavior possible, in natural or artificial systems" (Poole et al., 1998, p. 1).

Poole et al. (1998) feel that "artificial intelligence" is a confusing term for a number of reasons: artificial implies "not real," but the field of study looks at both natural and artificial systems; artificial also "connotes simulated intelligence" (p. 2), but the goal is not to simulate intelligence, but to "understand real (natural or synthetic) intelligent systems by synthesizing them" (p. 2). As they state: "[a] simulation of an earthquake isn't an earthquake; however, we want to actually create intelligence, as you could imagine creating an earthquake. The misunderstanding comes about because most simulations are now carried out on computers. However … the digital computer, the archetype of an interpreted automatic, formal, symbol-manipulation system, is a tool unlike any other: It can produce the real thing" (p. 2). Computational intelligence also has the advantage of making the "computational hypothesis explicit in the name" (p. 2). For these reasons, we prefer (and use) the term computational intelligence (CI).

Debates about terminology aside, 50 years of study into "the principles of intelligent behavior" have led to the development of a wide range of software tools with applications relevant for most business disciplines. The chapter provides references to the many reviews of CI applications available in the literature. This cross-section of the field (as opposed to a comprehensive review) will briefly outline some of the different "tools of intelligence" and show examples of their applications across a broad spectrum of business applications.

Tools of Intelligence

The study of computational intelligence has led to a number of techniques, many of which have had immediate practical applications, even though they fall far short of the type of intelligent behavior envisaged by early enthusiastic artificial intelligence practitioners and popular fiction. Some of the CI techniques derive from abstract systems of symbol processing (e.g., frame-based systems, rule-based systems, logic-based systems, the event calculus, predicate calculus, fuzzy logic, and rough sets). More recent techniques have emulated natural processes (e.g., neural networks, evolutionary algorithms, auto-immune systems, ant colony optimisation, and simulated annealing). Just to add to the confusion of terminology, some of these latter techniques are also referred to as "soft computing" (Tikk, Kóczy, & Gedeon, 2003). In addition, a specific sub-branch of CI is referred to as machine learning (Flach, 2001). This section provides a brief overview of some of these tools of intelligence, with references to the literature for those readers interesting in pursuing some of the techniques in depth. The next section will then briefly look at the literature from the perspective of specific business disciplines, and show the application of some of these techniques to practical business problems.

Expert Systems

The field of expert systems (ES), which appeared in the mid-1960s, is considered to be the first commercial application of CI research. Expert knowledge is considered to be a combination of a theoretical understanding of the problem and a collection of heuristic problem-solving rules that experience has shown to be effective in solving the problem — these two components form the basis of most ES. While ES have found a number of applications within business and industry, problems have been identified that reduce its value in computational intelligence research generally. For example, the lack of general applicability of the rules generated makes most ES very problem-domain specific. In addition, most expert systems have very limited abilities for autonomous learning from experience — knowledge acquisition depends on the intervention of a programmer. The development of hybrids — combinations of ES with other techniques such as neural networks and fuzzy systems — are attempts to overcome these problems. We will return to hybrid systems later in this section.

A number of general reviews of ES are available, including a recent review of methodologies and applications (Liao, 2005). Older reviews include the use of ES in businesses in the UK (Coakes & Merchant, 1996), and applications in business generally (Eom, 1996; Wong & Monaco, 1995). More specialised reviews of ES applications to specific business disciplines have also been published, including production planning and scheduling (Metaxiotis, Askounis, & Psarras, 2002), new product development (Rao, Nahm, Shi, Deng, & Syamil, 1999), and finance (Nedovic & Devedzic, 2002; Zopounidis, Doumpos, & Matsatsinis, 1997).

As an example of possible applications, a review of the use of expert systems in finance undertaken by Nedovic and Devedzic (2002) identified four different areas: financial analysis of firms, analyzing the causes of successful or unsuccessful business development, market analysis, and management education. Expert systems have also been applied in other business areas — for example, human resource management (Lawler & Elliot, 1993; Yildiz & Erdogmus, 1999), and marketing (Sisodia, 1991; Steinberg & Plank, 1990; Wright & Rowe, 1992), to name just a few.

Artificial Neural Networks

Artificial Neural Networks (ANN) are powerful general-purpose software tools based on abstract simplified models of neural connections. The concept was first proposed in the 1940s (McCulloch & Pitts, 1943; Turing, 1948), made limited progress in the 1950s and 1960s (Rosenblatt, 1958), and experienced a resurgence in popularity in the 1980s (Rumelhart & McClelland, 1986). Since then, ANN have generated considerable interest across a number of disciplines, as evidenced by the number of published research papers. Approximately 22,500 journal articles and 13,800 conference papers were published in the field during the period 1999 to 2003, primarily investigating neural networks in such fields as fluid dynamics, psychology, engineering, medicine, computer science and business (Gyan, Voges, & Pope, 2004).

ANN have been widely applied to a variety of business problems, and in some fields such as marketing, they are the most widely applied computational intelligence technique. A number of reviews of ANN applications in business and management have appeared (Krycha & Wagner, 1999; Vellido, Lisboa, & Vaughan, 1999; Wong, Bodnovich, & Selvi, 1997; Wong, Lai, & Lam, 2000). One of the most common themes in the literature is the effectiveness of ANN, often in comparison with other techniques — Adya and Collopy (1998) review this literature. Most ANN implementations are software-based, however, a review of hardware implementations is also available (Dias, Antunes, & Mota, 2004).

Other more specific discipline-based reviews have appeared in auditing (Koskivaara, 2004), finance (Chatterjee, Ayadi, & Boone, 2000; Wong & Selvi, 1998), manufacturing (Dimla, Lister, & Leighton, 1997; Hussain, 1999; Sick, 2002), management (Boussabaine, 1996), and resource management (Kalogirou, 1999, 2001; Maier & Dandy, 2000).

Artificial neural networks have been applied in other business areas, such as new product development (Thieme, Song, & Calantone, 2000), and marketing (Lin & Bruwer, 1996; Venugopal & Baets, 1994). The *Journal of Retailing and Consumer Services* has produced a special issue dedicated to ANN (Mazenec & Moutinho, 1999).

Krycha and Wagner (1999) surveyed a range of marketing, finance and production applications of ANN within management science. They commented on the broad range of problems addressed by the technique, and reported that many of the studies surveyed suggest using ANN as a data analysis technique as an alternative to traditional statistical methods such as classification, forecasting, and optimisation. However they point out that "[t]he discrimination between ... models is based mainly on very elementary statistical considerations and is not performed by means of adequate model-discrimination criteria" (Krycha & Wagner, 1999, p. 200). This suggests that the level of sophistication in assessing the effectiveness of ANN in business applications still has some way to go.

In finance, Wong and Selvi (1998) report that during the period 1990 to 1996, ANN were mainly used for the prediction bankruptcy in banks and firms, and the prediction of stock selection and performance. ANN techniques are able to analyze the relationships between large numbers of variables, even if the variables are highly correlated. Artificial neural networks are effective because "the environment where these diverse variables exist is constantly changing. Therefore, the effectiveness of a model depends on how well it reflects the operating environment of the industry in terms of adjusting itself, as new observations are available. Neural networks not only accumulate, store, and recognize patterns of knowledge based on experience, but also constantly reflect and adapt to new environmental situations while they are performing predictions by constantly retraining and relearning" (Wong & Selvi, 1998, p. 130).

Fuzzy Logic, Fuzzy Sets, and Fuzzy Systems

Fuzzy logic (Zadeh, 1965) is a form of multi-valued logic that allows intermediate values between the two values of conventional bi-valued logic (such as true/false, black/white, etc.). This multi-valued logic enables "fuzzy" concepts such as warm or cold to be defined by mathematical formulations, and hence makes them amenable to computational processing. In fuzzy sets the same multi-valued logic concept is applied to set descriptions. More generally, a fuzzy system is a process that establishes a mapping relationship between fuzzy sets (Kosko, 1994). A basic introduction to fuzzy logic is available in Bauer, Nouak, and Winkler (1996).

A limited number of reviews of fuzzy system applications in the business literature are available. These reviews cover production and operations (Sárfi, Salama, & Chikhani, 1996; Vasant, Nagarajan, & Yaacob, 2004), Web mining (Arotaritei & Mitra, 2004), and portfolio selection (Inuiguchi & Ramik, 2000). Fuzzy systems have also been applied in other business areas, such as determining credit rating (Baetge & Heitmann, 2000) and market research (Varki, Cooil, & Rust, 2000). More general reviews of machine learning techniques, which include fuzzy systems and neural networks, are also available (Du & Wolfe, 1995; Quiroga & Rabelo, 1995).

In marketing, Casabayo, Agell, and Aguado, (2004) used a fuzzy system to identify customers who are most likely to defect to a different grocery retailer when a new retailer establishes itself in the same area. As they state, the value added by such techniques to customer relationship management is the "ability to transform customer data into real useful knowledge for taking strategic marketing decisions" (Casabayo et al., 2004, p. 307).

Rough Sets

The concept of a rough or approximation set was developed by Pawlak (1982, 1991). A rough set is formed from two sets, referred to as the lower approximation and upper approximation. The lower approximation contains objects that are definitely in the set, and the complement of the upper approximation contains objects that are definitely not in the set. Those objects whose set membership is unknown constitute the boundary region. The union of the lower approximation and the boundary region make up the upper approximation (Pawlak, 1991). This simple insight of defining a set in terms of two sets has generated a substantial literature. Numerous edited books and conferences have extended Pawlak's original insight into new areas of application and theory (e.g., Lin & Cercone, 1997; Polkowski & Skowron, 1998; Polkowski, Tsumoto, & Lin, 2000; Wang, Liu, Yao, & Skowron, 2003; Zhong, Skowron, & Ohsuga, 1999). Most of the published applications of rough sets have concentrated on classification problems, where there is a known sub-grouping within the data set that can be identified by a grouping variable (Pawlak, 1984). The rough sets technique has also been extended to clustering problems, where there are no predetermined sub-groups (do Prado, Engel, & Filho, 2002; Voges, Pope & Brown, 2002).

In a business context, rough sets has been applied to a number of areas of application, including business failure prediction (Dimitras, Slowinski, Susmaga, & Zopounidis, 1999), accounting (Omer, Leavins, & O'Shaughnessy, 1996), data mining (Kowalczyk & Piasta, 1998), and marketing (Au & Law, 2000; Beynon, Curry, & Morgan, 2001; Kowalczyk & Slisser, 1997; Van den Poel & Piasta, 1998; Voges, 2005; Voges, Pope, & Brown, 2002).

Evolutionary Algorithms

Evolutionary algorithms (EA) derive their inspiration from highly abstracted models of the mechanics of natural evolution (Bäck, 1996; Davis, 1991; Fogel, 1995). A number of different approaches to EA have been independently developed, including genetic algorithms (Goldberg, 1989; Holland, 1975), evolution strategies (Rechenberg, 1994; Schwefel, 1995), genetic programming (Koza, 1992), evolutionary programming (Fogel, Owens, & Walsh, 1966), and the global method of data handling (Ivakhnenko & Ivakhnenko, 1974).

Evolutionary algorithms have been applied to many different business applications, including control systems (Fleming & Purshouse, 2002), design (Gen & Kim, 1999), scheduling (Cheng, Gen, & Tsujimura, 1996; Cheng, Gen & Tsujimura, 1999), optimisation (Coello, 2000), information retrieval (Cordón, Herrera-Viedma, López-Pujalte, Luque, & Zarco, 2003), management (Biethahn & Nissen, 1995), and marketing (Bhattacharyya, 2003; Hurley, Moutinho, & Stephens, 1995; Voges, 1997; Voges & Pope, 2004).

Hybrids and Other Techniques

Many of the techniques described in the previous subsections can be combined together in various ways to form hybrid techniques. Examples of such hybrids in the business literature are neural networks and expert systems in manufacturing (Huang & Zhang, 1995), neural networks, fuzzy systems and expert systems in marketing (Li, 2000; Li, Davies, Edwards, Kinman, & Duan, 2002), rough sets and evolutionary algorithms in marketing (Voges & Pope, 2004), and fuzzy neural networks and genetic algorithms in a sales forecasting system (Kuo, 2001). A number of the chapters in the present volume report the use of hybrid approaches.

The review has considered a range of techniques, but is by no means exhaustive. For example, one increasingly popular approach yet to find its way into the wider business literature (although referred to in a number of chapters in the current volume), is support vector machines, more generally known as kernel methods (Campbell, 2002).

Multi-Agent Systems

A programming approach growing in importance is agent-oriented programming (Muller, 1996; Schleiffer, 2005), often considered an extension of object-oriented programming. An agent is a software entity that is situated in an (usually dynamic) environment. The agent is able to sense the characteristics of the environment and act autonomously within it to achieve a goal. Most agents are endowed with some form of intelligence, usually through one of the techniques described above, including in many cases hybrid systems. Populations of agents are referred to as multi-agent systems (Wooldridge, 1999, 2000, 2002).

This approach is growing rapidly in use and application area, and warrants a separate review to do it justice. Representative business areas include factory control (Baker, 1998), technological innovation (Ma & Nakamori, 2005), environmental management (Deadman, 1999), organizational theory (Lomi & Larsen, 1996), economic modelling (Caldas & Coelho, 1994; Chaturvedi, Mehta, Dolk, & Ayer, 2005; Holland & Miller, 1991; Terna, 1997), computational finance (LeBaron, 2000), retail modeling (Chang & Harrington, 2000; McGeary & Decker, 2001), marketing analysis (Schwartz, 2000), competitive intelligence (Desouza, 2001), and database searching (Ryoke & Nakamori, 2005).

Business Applications

The previous section has identified many references relating to business applications of CI, categorized by the CI technique used. There are also many reviews and papers covering business applications that refer to CI in general, rather than reporting on a specific technique. To avoid repeating early citations, only references not previously mentioned will be discussed here.

As recognition of the growing interest in, and importance of, computational intelligence techniques in business, some scholarly journals have produced special issues. For example, the journal *Information Sciences* has published a special issue covering CI in economics and finance (Chen & Wang, 2005), including a review of Herbert Simon's early contributions to this cross-disciplinary area (Chen, 2005). A book on computational intelligence in economics and finance has also recently been published (Chen & Wang, 2004).

Perhaps not surprisingly, because of the technical nature of most CI techniques, they have figured prominently in a wide range of production and operations applications, such as design, planning, manufacturing, quality control, energy systems and scheduling. There are extensive reviews giving access to the diverse literature available (Årzén, 1996; Aytug, Bhattacharyya, Koehler, & Snowdon, 1994; Du & Sun, in press; Herroelen & Leus, 2005; Kalogirou, 2003; Metaxiotis, Kagiannas, Askounis, & Psarras, 2003; Park & Kim, 1998; Power & Bahri, 2005; Proudlove, Vadera, & Kobbacy, 1998; Ruiz & Maroto, 2005; Wiers, 1997). A book has also been published on the application of computational intelligence to control problems (Mohammadian, Sarker, & Yao, 2003).

The marketing literature covers a range of problem areas, including forecasting retail sales (Alon, Qi, & Sadowski, 2001), decision-making (Amaravadi, Samaddar, & Dutta, 1995; Suh, Suh, & Lee, 1995), market analysis and optimization (Anand & Kahn, 1993), and classification (Montgomery, Swinnen, & Vanhoof, 1997).

Other business areas that have produced published papers relating to CI implementations include specific industries such as the food industry (Corney, 2002), and general business topics such as management (Crerar, 2001), organizational design (Prem, 1997) and decision support (Dutta, 1996). In addition, many CI techniques have entered the business environment through the approach known popularly as Data Mining, although Knowledge Discovery in Databases (KDD) is probably the more technically correct term, with Data Mining being one component of the overall KDD process (Facca & Lanzi, 2005; Goethals & Siebes, 2005; Lee & Siau 2001; Peacock, 1998; Zhou, 2003).

Conclusion

This necessarily brief review of computational intelligence applications in business aims to provide any interested CI researcher or business practitioner access to the extensive literature available. In particular, the cited reviews provide comprehensive lists of references in a wide range of business disciplines. The chapters that follow in this edited volume also provide access to the literature in a diverse range of techniques and application areas.

References

Adya, M., & Collopy, F. (1998). How effective are neural networks at forecasting and prediction? A review and evaluation. *Journal of Forecasting, 17*(5/6), 481-495.

Alon, I., Qi, M., & Sadowski, R. (2001). Forecasting aggregate retail sales: A comparison of artificial neural networks and traditional methods. *Journal of Retailing and Consumer Services, 8*(3), 147-156.

Amaravadi, C. S., Samaddar, S., & Dutta, S. (1995). Intelligent marketing information systems: Computerized intelligence for marketing decision making. *Marketing Intelligence and Planning, 13*(2), 4-13.

American Association for Artificial Intelligence. (n.d.). *Welcome to AI topics: A dynamic library of introductory information about artificial intelligence.* Retrieved May 5, 2005, from http://www.aaai.org/AITopics/index.html

Anand, T., & Kahn, G. (1993, August). Focusing knowledge-based techniques on market analysis, *IEEE Expert*, 19-24.

Arotaritei, D., & Mitra, S. (2004). Web mining: a survey in the fuzzy framework. *Fuzzy Sets and Systems, 148*(1), 5-19.

Årzén, K.-E. (1996). AI in the feedback loop: a survey of alternative approaches. *Annual Reviews in Control, 20*, 71-82.

Au, N., & Law, R. (2000, August). The application of rough sets to sightseeing expenditures. *Journal of Travel Research, 39*, 70-77.

Aytug, H., Bhattacharyya, S., Koehler, G. J., & Snowdon, J. L. (1994). A review of machine learning in scheduling. *IEEE Transactions on Engineering Management, 41*(2), 165-171.

Bäch, T. (1996). *Evolutionary algorithms in theory and practice: Evolution strategies, evolutionary programming, genetic algorithms.* New York: Oxford University.

Baetge, J., & Heitmann, C. (2000). Creating a fuzzy rule-based indicator for the review of credit standing. *Schmalenbach Business Review, 52*(4), 318-343.

Baker, A. D. (1998). A survey of factory control algorithms that can be implemented in a multi-agent heterarchy: Dispatching, scheduling, and pull. *Journal of Manufacturing Systems, 17*(4), 297-319.

Bauer, P., Nouak, S., & Winkler, R. (1996). *A brief course in fuzzy logic and fuzzy control.* Energy Systems Research Unit, Department of Mechanical Engineering. University of Strathclyde. Retrieved May 10, 2005, from http://www.esru.strath.ac.uk/Reference/concepts/fuzzy/fuzzy.htm

Beynon, M., Curry, B., & Morgan, P. (2001). Knowledge discovery in marketing: An approach through rough set theory. *European Journal of Marketing, 35*(7/8), 915-933.

Bhattacharyya, S. (2003). Evolutionary computation for database marketing. *Journal of Database Management, 10*(4), 343- 352.

Biethahn, J., & Nissen, V. (Eds.). (1995). *Evolutionary algorithms in management applications*. Berlin: Springer-Verlag.

Boussabaine, A. H. (1996). The use of artifical neural networks in construction management: A review. *Construction Management and Economics*, *14*(5), 427-436.

Caldas, J. C., & Coelho, H. (1994). Strategic interaction in oligopolistic markets — Experimenting with real and artificial agents. In C. Castelfranchi & E. Werner (Eds.), *Artificial Social Systems: 4th European Workshop on Modelling Autonomous Agents in a Multi-Agent World* (pp. 147-163). Berlin: Springer-Verlag.

Callan, R. (2003). *Artificial intelligence*. Basingstoke, UK: Palgrave Macmillan.

Campbell, C. (2002). Kernel methods: A survey of current techniques. *Neurocomputing*, *48*(1-4), 63-84.

Casabayo, M., Agell, N., & Aguado, J. C. (2004). Using AI techniques in the grocery industry: Identifying the customers most likely to defect. *International Review of Retail, Distribution and Consumer Research*, *14*(3), 295-308.

Chang, M-H., & Harrington, J. E. (2000). Centralization vs. decentralization in a multi-unit organization: A computational model of a retail chain as a multi-agent adaptive system. *Management Science*, *46*(11), 1427-1440.

Chatterjee, A., Ayadi, O. F., & Boone, B. E. (2000). Artificial neural network and the financial markets: A survey. *Managerial Finance*, *26*(12), 32-44.

Chaturvedi, A., Mehta, S., Dolk, D., & Ayer, R. (2005). Agent-based simulation for computational experimentation: Developing an artificial labor market. *European Journal of Operational Research*, *166*, 694-716.

Chen, S.-H. (2005). Computational intelligence in economics and finance: Carrying on the legacy of Herbert Simon. *Information Sciences*, *170*(1), 121-131.

Chen, S.-H., & Wang, P. P. (2004). *Computational intelligence in economics and finance*. Berlin: Springer.

Chen, S.-H., & Wang, P. (2005). Editorial — Special issue on computational intelligence in economics and finance. *Information Sciences*, *170*(1), 1-2.

Cheng, R., Gen, M., & Tsujimura, Y. (1996). A tutorial survey of job-shop scheduling problems using genetic algorithms: Part I. Representation. *Computers and Industrial Engineering*, *30*(4), 983-997.

Cheng, R., Gen, M., & Tsujimura, Y. (1999). A tutorial survey of job-shop scheduling problems using genetic algorithms: Part II. Hybrid genetic search strategies. *Computers and Industrial Engineering*, *37*(1-2), 51-55.

Coakes, E., & Merchant, K. (1996). Expert systems: A survey of their use in UK business. *Information & Management*, *30*(5), 223-230.

Coello, C. A. (2000). An updated survey of GA-based multiobjective optimization techniques. *ACM Computing Surveys*, *32*(2), 109-143.

Cordón, O., Herrera-Viedma, E., López-Pujalte, C., Luque, M., & Zarco, C. (2003). A review on the application of evolutionary computation to information retrieval. *International Journal of Approximate Reasoning*, *34*(2-3), 241-264.

Corney, D. (2002). Food bytes: Intelligent systems in the food industry. *British Food Journal*, *104*(10/11), 787-805.

Crerar, A. (2001, May/June). Artificial intelligence — coming of age? *The British Journal of Administrative Management*, 25, 18-19.

Davis, L. (Ed.). (1991). *Handbook of genetic algorithms*. New York: Van Nostrand Reinhold.

Deadman, P. J. (1999). Modelling individual behaviour and group performance in an intelligent agent-based simulation of the tragedy of the commons. *Journal of Environmental Management*, *56*, 159-172.

Desouza, K. C. (2001). Intelligence agents for competitive intelligence: Survey of applications. *Competitive Intelligence Review*, *12*(4), 57-65.

Dias, F. M., Antunes, A., & Mota, A. M. (2004). Artificial neural networks: A review of commercial hardware. *Engineering Applications of Artificial Intelligence*, *17*, 945-952.

Dimitras, A. I., Slowinski, R., Susmaga, R., & Zopounidis, C. (1999). Business failure prediction using rough sets. *European Journal of Operational Research*, *114*, 263-280.

Dimla, D. E. Jr., Lister, P. M., & Leighton, N. J. (1997). Neural network solutions to the tool condition monitoring problem in metal cutting — A critical review of methods. *International Journal of Machine Tools and Manufacture*, *37*(9), 1219-1241.

do Prado, H. A., Engel, P. M., & Filho, H. C. (2002). Rough clustering: An alternative to find meaningful clusters by using the reducts from a dataset. In J. J. Alpigini, J. F. Peters, A. Skowron, & N. Zhong (Eds.), *Rough Sets and Current Trends in Computing, Third International Conference RSCTC 2002 LNCS 2475* (pp. 234-238). Berlin: Springer-Verlag.

Du, C.-J., & Sun, D.-W. (In Press). Learning techniques used in computer vision for food quality evaluation: A review. *Journal of Food Engineering*.

Du, T. C.-T., & Wolfe, P. M. (1995). The amalgamation of neural networks and fuzzy logic systems — A survey. *Computers and Industrial Engineering*, *29*(1-4), 193-197.

Dutta, A. (1996). Integrating AI and optimization for decision support: A survey. *Decision Support Systems*, *18*(3,4), 217-226.

Engelbrecht, A. P. (2002). *Computational intelligence: An introduction*. Chichester, UK: John Wiley.

Eom, S. B. (1996). A survey of operational expert systems in business (1980-1993). *Interfaces*, *26*(5), 50-71.

Facca, F. M., & Lanzi, P. L. (2005). Mining interesting knowledge from weblogs: A survey. *Data and Knowledge Engineering*, *53*(3), 225-241.

Flach, P. A. (2001). On the state of the art in machine learning: A personal review. *Artificial Intelligence*, *131*(1-2), 199-222.

Fleming, P. J., & Purshouse, R. C. (2002). Evolutionary algorithms in control systems engineering: a survey. *Control Engineering Practice*, *10*(11), 1223-1241.

Fogel, D. B. (1995). *Evolutionary computation: Toward a new philosophy of machine intelligence*. New York: IEEE.

Fogel, L. J., Owens, A. J., & Walsh, M. J. (1966). *Artificial intelligence through simulated evolution*. New York: Wiley.

Gen, M., & Kim, J. R. (1999). GA-based reliability design: State-of-the-art survey. *Computers and Industrial Engineering*, *37*(1-2), 151-155.

Goethals, B., & Siebes, A. (Eds.). (2005). *Knowledge Discovery in Inductive Databases: Third International Workshop, KDID 2004, LNCS 3377*. Berlin: Springer.

Goldberg, D. E. (1989). *Genetic algorithms in search, optimization, and machine learning*. Reading, MA: Addison-Wesley.

Gyan, B., Voges, K. E., & Pope, N. K. (2004, November 29 - December 1). Artificial neural networks in marketing from 1999 to 2003: A region of origin and topic area analysis. In *Proceedings of ANZMAC2004: Australian and New Zealand Marketing Academy Conference, Victoria University of Wellington*. Wellington, New Zealand: ANZMAC.

Herroelen, W., & Leus, R. (2005). Project scheduling under uncertainty: Survey and research potentials. *European Journal of Operational Research*, *165*(2), 289-306.

Hoffmann, A. G. (1998). *Paradigms of artificial intelligence: A methodological and computational analysis*. Singapore: Springer.

Holland, J. H. (1975). *Adaptation in natural and artificial systems*. Ann Arbor: University of Michigan.

Holland, J. H., & Miller, J. H. (1991, May). Artificial adaptive agents in economic theory. *AEA Papers and Proceedings: Learning and Adaptive Economic Behavior*, *81*(2), 365-370.

Huang, S. H., & Zhang, H.-C. (1995). Neural-expert hybrid approach for intelligent manufacturing: A survey. *Computers in Industry*, *26*(2), 107-126.

Hurley, S., Moutinho, L., & Stephens, N. M. (1995). Solving marketing optimization problems using genetic algorithms. *European Journal of Marketing*, *29*(4), 39-56.

Hussain, M. A. (1999). Review of the applications of neural networks in chemical process control — Simulation and online implementation. *Artificial Intelligence in Engineering*, *13*(1), 55-68.

Inuiguchi, M., & Ramik, J. (2000). Possibilistic linear programming: A brief review of fuzzy mathematical programming and a comparison with stochastic programming in portfolio selection problem. *Fuzzy Sets and Systems*, *111*, 3-28.

Ivakhnenko, A. G., & Ivakhnenko, N. A. (1974). Long-term prediction by GMDH algorithms using the unbiased criterion and the balance-of-variables criterion. *Soviet Automatic Control*, *7*(4), 40-45.

Kalogirou, S. A. (1999). Applications of artificial neural networks in energy systems: A review. *Energy Conversion and Management*, *40*(10), 1073-1087.

Kalogirou, S. A. (2001). Artificial neural networks in renewable energy systems applications: a review. *Renewable and Sustainable Energy Reviews*, *5*(4), 373-401.

Kalogirou, S. A. (2003). Artificial intelligence for the modeling and control of combustion processes: A review. *Progress in Energy and Combustion Science, 29*(6), 515-566.

Konar, A. (2000). *Artificial intelligence and soft computing: Behavioral and cognitive modeling of the human brain.* Boca Raton, FL: CRC.

Koskivaara, E. (2004). Artificial neural networks in analytical review procedures. *Managerial Auditing Journal, 19*(2), 191-223.

Kosko, B. (1994). *Fuzzy thinking: The new science of fuzzy logic.* London: Flamingo.

Kowalczyk, W., & Piasta, Z. (1998). Rough-set inspired approach to knowledge discovery in business databases. In X. Wu, R. Kotagiri, & K. B. Korb (Eds.), *Research and development in knowledge discovery and data mining* (pp. 186-197). Berlin: Springer.

Kowalczyk, W., & Slisser, F. (1997). Modelling customer retention with rough data models. In J. Komorowski & J. Zytkow (Eds.), *Principles of data mining and knowledge discovery* (pp. 7-13). Berlin: Springer.

Koza, J. R. (1992). *Genetic Programming: On the programming of computers by means of natural selection.* Cambridge, MA: MIT.

Krycha, K. A., & Wagner, U. (1999). Applications of artificial neural networks in management science: A survey. *Journal of Retailing and Consumer Services, 6*(4), 185-203.

Kuo, R. J. (2001). A sales forecasting system based on fuzzy neural network with initial weights generated by genetic algorithm. *European Journal of Operational Research, 129*, 496-517.

Lawler, J. J., & Elliot, R. (1993). Artificial Intelligence in HRM: An experimental study of an expert system. In *Proceedings of the 1993 Conference on Computer Personnel Research* (pp. 473-480). New York: ACM.

LeBaron, B. (2000). Agent-based computational finance: Suggested readings and early research. *Journal of Economic Dynamics and Control, 24*, 679-702.

Lee, S. J., & Siau, K. (2001). A review of data mining techniques. *Industrial Management and Data Systems, 101*(1), 41-46.

Li, S. (2000). The development of a hybrid intelligent system for developing marketing strategy. *Decision Support Systems, 27*, 395-409.

Li, S., Davies, B., Edwards, J., Kinman, R., & Duan, Y. (2002). Integrating group Delphi, fuzzy logic and expert systems for marketing strategy development: The hybridization and its effectiveness. *Marketing Intelligence and Planning, 20*(4/5), 273-284.

Liao, S-H. (2005). Expert system methodologies and applications — a decade review from 1995 to 2004. *Expert Systems with Applications, 28*(1), 93-103.

Lin, B., & Bruwer, J. (1996). Neural network applications in marketing. *Journal of Computer Information Systems, 36*(2), 15-20.

Lin, T. Y., & Cercone, N. (Eds.) (1997). *Rough sets and data mining: Analysis of imprecise data.* Boston: Kluwer.

Lomi, A., & Larsen, E. R. (1996). Interacting locally and evolving globally: A computational approach to the dynamics of organizational populations. *Academy of Management Journal, 39*(4), 1287-1321.

Luger, G. F., & Stubblefield, W. A. (1998). *Artificial intelligence: Structures and strategies for complex problem solving* (3rd ed.). Reading, MA: Addison Wesley Longman.

Ma, T., & Nakamori, Y. (2005). Agent-based modeling on technological innovation as an evolutionary process. *European Journal of Operational Research, 166*(3), 741-755.

Maier, H. R., & Dandy, G. C. (2000). Neural networks for the prediction and forecasting of water resources variables: A review of modelling issues and applications. *Environmental Modelling and Software, 15*(1), 101-124.

Mazenec, J. A., & Moutinho, L. (1999). Why it is timely to publish a JRCS Special Issue on neural networks. *Journal of Retailing and Consumer Services, 6*, 183-184.

McCarthy, J., Minsky, M. L., Rochester, N., & Shannon, C.E. (1955, August 31). *A proposal for the Dartmouth Summer Research Project on Artificial Intelligence.* Retrieved May 2, 2005, from http://www-formal.stanford.edu/jmc/history/dartmouth/dartmouth.html

McCorduck, P. (2004). *Machines who think: A personal inquiry into the history and prospects of artificial intelligence.* Natick, MA: A.K. Peters.

McCulloch, W. S., & Pitts, W. (1943). A logical calculus of ideas immanent in nervous activity. *Bulletin of Mathematical Biophysics, 5*, 115-133.

McGeary, F., & Decker, K. (2001). Modeling a virtual food court using DECAF. In S. Moss & P. Davidsson (Eds.), *Multi-agent-based simulation* (pp. 68-81). Berlin: Springer.

Metaxiotis, K. S., Askounis, D., & Psarras, J. (2002). Expert systems in production planning and scheduling: A state-of-the-art survey. *Journal of Intelligent Manufacturing, 13*(4), 253-260.

Metaxiotis, K., Kagiannas, A., Askounis, D., & Psarras, J. (2003). Artificial intelligence in short term electric load forecasting: a state-of-the-art survey for the researcher. *Energy Conversion and Management, 44*(9), 1525-1534.

Mohammadian, M., Sarker, R. A., & Yao, X. (2003). *Computational intelligence in control.* Hershey, PA: Idea Group.

Montgomery, D., Swinnen, G., & Vanhoof, K. (1997). Comparison of some AI and statistical classification methods for a marketing case. *European Journal of Operational Research, 103*, 312-325.

Muller, J. P. (1996). *The design of intelligent agents: A layered approach.* Berlin: Springer-Verlag.

Munakata, T. (1998). *Fundamentals of the new artificial intelligence: Beyond traditional paradigms.* New York: Springer-Verlag.

Nedovic, L., & Devedzic, V. (2002). Expert systems in finance – a cross section of the field. *Expert Systems with Applications, 23*, 49-66.

Negnevitsky, M. (2002). *Artificial intelligence: A guide to intelligent systems.* Harlow, NY: Pearson/Addison.

Omer, K., Leavins, J., & O'Shaughnessy, J. (1996). A rough set approach to dealing with ambiguity in the peer review process in public accounting. *Managerial Finance, 22*(11), 30-42.

Park, K. S., & Kim, S. H. (1998). Artificial intelligence approaches to determination of CNC machining parameters in manufacturing: a review. *Artificial Intelligence in Engineering, 12*(1-2), 127-134.

Pawlak, Z. (1982). Rough sets. *International Journal of Information and Computer Sciences, 11*(5), 341-356.

Pawlak, Z. (1984). Rough classification. *International Journal of Man-Machine Studies, 20*, 469-483.

Pawlak, Z. (1991). *Rough sets: Theoretical aspects of reasoning about data.* Boston: Kluwer.

Peacock, P. R. (1998, Winter). Data mining in marketing: Part 1. *Marketing Management*, 9-18.

Polkowski, L., & Skowron, A. (Eds.) (1998). *Rough Sets and Current Trends in Computing (First International Conference, RSCTC98).* Berlin: Springer.

Polkowski, L., Tsumoto, S., & Lin, T. Y. (Eds.) (2000). *Rough set methods and applications: New developments in knowledge discovery in information systems.* New York: Physica-Verlag.

Poole, D., Mackworth, A., & Goebel, R. (1998). *Computational intelligence: A logical approach.* New York: Oxford University.

Power, Y., & Bahri, P. A. (2005). Integration techniques in intelligent operational management: a review. *Knowledge-Based Systems, 18*(2-3), 89-97.

Prem, E. (1997). The behavior-based firm: Application of recent AI concepts to company management. *Applied Artificial Intelligence, 11*, 173-195.

Proudlove, N. C., Vadera, S., & Kobbacy, K. A. H. (1998). Intelligent management systems in operations: A review. *The Journal of the Operational Research Society, 49*(7), 682-699.

Quiroga, L. A., & Rabelo, L. C. (1995). Learning from examples: A review of machine learning, neural networks and fuzzy logic paradigms. *Computers and Industrial Engineering, 29*(1-4), 561-565.

Rao, S. S., Nahm, A., Shi, Z., Deng, X., & Syamil, A. (1999). Artificial intelligence and expert systems applications in new product development — a survey. *Journal of Intelligent Manufacturing, 10*(3-4), 231-244.

Rechenberg, I. (1994). *Evolutionsstrategie.* Stuttgart: Fromman-Holzboog.

Rosenblatt, F. (1958). The Perceptron: A probabilistic model for information storage and organization in the brain. *Psychological Review, 65*, 386-408.

Ruiz, R., & Maroto, C. (2005). A comprehensive review and evaluation of permutation flowshop heuristics. *European Journal of Operational Research, 165*(2), 479-494.

Rumelhart, D. E., & McClelland, J. L. (1986). *Parallel distributed processing: Explorations in the microstructure of cognition.* Cambridge, MA: MIT.

Ryoke, M., & Nakamori, Y. (2005). Agent-based approach to complex systems modeling. *European Journal of Operational Research, 166*, 717-725.

Sárfi, R. J., Salama, M. M. A., & Chikhani, A. Y. (1996). Applications of fuzzy sets theory in power systems planning and operation: a critical review to assist in implementation. *Electric Power Systems Research, 39*(2), 89-101.

Schleiffer, R. (2005). An intelligent agent model. *European Journal of Operational Research, 166*, 666-693.

Schwartz, D. G. (2000). Concurrent marketing analysis: A multi-agent model for product, price, place and promotion. *Marketing Intelligence and Planning, 18*(1), 24-29.

Schwefel, H-P. (1995). *Evolution and optimum seeking.* New York: Wiley.

Sick, B. (2002). On-line and indirect tool wear monitoring in turning with artificial neural networks: A review of more than a decade of research. *Mechanical Systems and Signal Processing, 16*(4), 487-546.

Sisodia, R. S. (1991). Expert systems for services marketing — Prospects and payoffs. *Journal of Services Marketing, 5*(3), 37-54.

Steinberg, M., & Plank, R. E. (1990). Implementing expert systems into business-to-business marketing practice. *Journal of Business and Industrial Marketing, 5*(2), 15-26.

Suh, C.-K., Suh, E.-H., & Lee, D.-M. (1995). Artificial intelligence approaches in model management systems: A survey. *Computers & Industrial Engineering, 28*(2), 291-299.

Terna, P. (1997). A laboratory for agent based computational economics: The self-development of consistency in agents' behaviour. In R. Conte, R. Hegselmann, & P. Terno (Eds.), *Simulating social phenomena* (pp. 73-88). Berlin: Springer.

Thieme, R. J., Song, M., & Calantone, R. J. (2000). Artificial neural network decision support systems for new product development project selection. *Journal of Marketing Research, 37*(4), 499-507.

Tikk, D., Kóczy, L. T., & Gedeon, T. D. (2003). A survey on universal approximation and its limits in soft computing techniques. *International Journal of Approximate Reasoning, 33*(2), 185-202.

Turing, A. (1948). *Intelligent machinery.* (Unpublished report) Retrieved May 2, 2005, from http://www.alanturing.net/turing_archive/archive/l/l32/L32-001.html

Turing, A. (1950). Computing machinery and intelligence. *Mind, 59*, 433-460.

Van den Poel, D., & Piasta, Z. (1998). Purchase prediction in database marketing with the ProbRough system. In L. Polkowski & A. Skowron (Eds.), *Rough sets and current trends in computing* (pp. 593-600). Berlin: Springer.

Varki, S., Cooil, B., & Rust, R. T. (2000, November). Modeling fuzzy data in qualitative marketing research. *Journal of Marketing Research, 37*, 480-489.

Vasant, P., Nagarajan, R., & Yaacob, S. (2004). Decision making in industrial production planning using fuzzy linear programming. *IMA Journal of Management Mathematics, 15*(1), 53-65.

Vellido, A., Lisboa, P. J. G., & Vaughan, J. (1999). Neural networks in business: A survey of applications (1992-1998). *Expert Systems with Applications, 17*(1), 51-70.

Venugopal, V., & Baets, W. (1994). Neural networks and their applications in marketing management. *Journal of Systems Management, 45*(9), 16-21.

Voges, K. E. (1997). Using evolutionary algorithm techniques for the analysis of data in marketing. *Cyber-Journal of Sport Marketing*, 1(2), 66-82.

Voges, K. E. (2005). Cluster analysis using rough clustering and k-means clustering. In M. Khosrow-Pour (Ed.), *Encyclopedia of Information Science and Technology* (pp. 435-438). Hershey, PA: Idea Group.

Voges, K. E., & Pope, N. K. (2004). Generating compact rough cluster descriptions using an evolutionary algorithm. In K. Deb et al. (Eds.), *GECCO2004: Genetic and Evolutionary Algorithm Conference - LNCS 3103* (pp. 1332-1333). Berlin: Springer-Verlag.

Voges, K. E., Pope, N. K., & Brown, M. R. (2002). Cluster analysis of marketing data examining on-line shopping orientation: A comparison of k-means and rough clustering approaches. In H. A. Abbass, R. A. Sarker, & C. S. Newton (Eds.), *Heuristic and Optimization for Knowledge Discovery* (pp. 207-224). Hershey, PA: Idea Group Publishing.

Wang, G., Liu, Q., Yao, Y., & Skowron, A. (Eds.). (2003). Rough sets, fuzzy sets, data mining, and granular computing. *Proceedings Ninth International Conference, RSFDGrC 2003*. New York: Springer.

Wiers, V. C. S. (1997). A review of the applicability of OR and AI scheduling techniques in practice. *Omega, 25*(2), 145-153.

Wooldridge, M. (1999). *Multiagent systems: A modern approach to distributed artificial intelligence*. Cambridge, MA: MIT.

Wooldridge, M. (2000). *Reasoning about rational agents*. Cambridge, MA: MIT.

Wooldridge, M. (2002). *An introduction to multi-agent systems*. New York: John Wiley.

Wong, B. K., Bodnovich, T. A., & Selvi, Y. (1997). Neural network applications in business: A review and analysis of the literature (1988-1995). *Decision Support Systems, 19*(4), 301-320.

Wong, B. K., Lai, V. S., & Lam, J. (2000). A bibliography of neural network business applications research: 1994 to 1998. *Computers and Operations Research, 27*, 1045-1076.

Wong, B. K., & Monaco, J. A. (1995). Expert system applications in business: A review and analysis of the literature (1977–1993). *Information and Management, 29*(3), 141-152.

Wong, B. K., & Selvi, Y. (1998). Neural network applications in finance: A review and analysis of literature (1990–1996). *Information and Management, 34*(3), 129-139.

Wright, G., & Rowe, G. (1992). Expert systems in marketing: Current trends and an alternative scenario. *Marketing Intelligence and Planning*, *10*(6), 24-30.

Yildiz, G., & Erdogmus, N. (1999, September). Expert system development in HRM: A case study in retailing. *Knowledge Engineering and Management*, 203-209.

Zadeh, L. A. (1965). Fuzzy sets. *Information and Control*, *8*, 338-353.

Zhong, N., Skowron, A., & Ohsuga, S. (Eds.) (1999). *New directions in rough sets, data mining, and granular-soft computing*. Berlin: Springer.

Zhou, Z.-H. (2003). Three perspectives of data mining. *Artificial Intelligence*, *143*(1), 139-146.

Zopounidis, C., Doumpos, M., & Matsatsinis, N. F. (1997). On the use of knowledge-based decision support systems in financial management: A survey. *Decision Support Systems*, *20*(3), 259-277.

Chapter II

Making Decisions with Data: Using Computational Intelligence within a Business Environment

Kevin Swingler, University of Stirling, Scotland

David Cairns, University of Stirling, Scotland

Abstract

This chapter identifies important barriers to the successful application of Computational Intelligence (CI) techniques in a commercial environment and suggests a number of ways in which they may be overcome. It identifies key conceptual, cultural and technical barriers and describes the different ways in which they affect both the business user and the CI practitioner. The chapter does not provide technical detail on how to implement any given technique, rather it discusses the practical consequences for the business user of issues such as non-linearity and extrapolation. For the CI practitioner, we discuss several cultural issues that need to be addressed when seeking to find a commercial application for CI techniques. The authors aim to highlight to technical and business readers how their different expectations can affect the successful outcome of a CI project. The authors hope that by enabling both parties to understand each other's perspective, the true potential of CI can be realized.

Introduction

Computational Intelligence (CI) appears to offer new opportunities to a business that wishes to improve the efficiency of their operations. It appears to provide a view into the future, answering questions such as, "What will my customers buy?", "Who is most likely to file a claim on an insurance policy?", and "What increase in demand will follow an advertising campaign?" It can filter good prospects from bad, the fraudulent from the genuine and the profitable from the loss-making.

These abilities should bring many benefits to a business, yet the adoption of these techniques has been slow. Despite the early promise of expert systems and neural networks, the application of computational intelligence has not become mainstream. This might seem all the more odd when one considers the explosion in data warehousing, loyalty card data collection and online data driven commerce that has accompanied the development of CI techniques (Hoss, 2000).

In this chapter, we discuss some of the reasons why CI has not had the impact on commerce that one might expect, and we offer some recommendations for the reader who is planning to embark on a project that utilizes CI. For the CI practitioner, this chapter should highlight cultural and conceptual business obstacles that they may not have considered. For the business user, this chapter should provide an overview of what a CI system can and cannot do, and in particular the dependence of CI systems on the availability of relevant data.

Given the right environment the technology has been shown to work effectively in a number of fields. These include financial prediction (Kim & Lee, 2004; Trippi & DeSieno, 1992; Tsaih, Hsu, & Lai, 1998), process control (Bhat & McAvoy, 1990; Jazayeri-Rad, 2004; Yu & Gomm, 2002) and bio-informatics (Blazewicz & Kasprzak, 2003). This path to successful application has a number of pitfalls and it is our aim to highlight some of the more common difficulties that occur during the process of applying CI and suggest methods for avoiding them.

Background

Computational Intelligence is primarily concerned with using an analytical approach to making decisions based on prior data. It normally involves applying one or more computationally intensive techniques to a data set in such a way that meta-information can be extracted from these data. This meta-information is then used to predict or classify the outcome of new situations that were not present in the original data. Effectively, the power of the CI system derives from its ability to generalize from what it has seen in the past to make sensible judgements about new situations.

A typical example of this scenario would be the use of a computational intelligence technique such as a neural network (Bishop, 1995; Hecht-Neilsen, 1990; Hertz, Krogh, & Palmer, 1991) to predict who might buy a product based on prior sales of the product.

A neural network application would process the historical data set containing past purchasing behaviour and build up a set of weighted values which correlate observed input patterns with consequent output patterns. If there was a predictable consistency between a buyer's profile (e.g., age, gender, income) and the products they bought, the neural network would extract the salient aspects of this consistency and store it in the meta-information represented by its internal weights. A prospective customer could then be presented to the neural network which would use these weights to calculate an expected outcome as to whether the prospect is likely to become a customer or not (Law, 1999).

Although neural networks are mentioned above, this process is similar when used with a number of different computational intelligence approaches. Even within the neural network field, there are a large number of different approaches that could be used (Haykin, 1994). The common element in this process is the extraction and use of information from a prior data set. This information extraction process is completely dependent upon the quality and quantity of the available data. Indeed it is not always clear that the available data are actually relevant to the task at hand — a difficult issue within a business environment when a contract has already been signed that promises to deliver a specific result.

Being Commercial

This chapter makes two assumptions. The first is that the reader is interested in applying CI techniques to commercial problems. The second is that the reader has not yet succeeded in doing so to any great extent. The reader may therefore be a CI practitioner who thoroughly understands the computational aspects and is having difficulties with the business aspects of selling CI, or a business manager who would like to use CI but would like to be more informed about the requirements for applying it. In this chapter we offer some observations we have made when commercializing CI techniques, in the hope that the reader will find a smoother route to market than they might otherwise have taken.

If you are hoping to find commercial application for your expertise in CI, then it is probably for one or more of the following reasons:

- You want to see your work commercially applied.
- Commercialization is stipulated in a grant you have won.
- You want to earn more money.

Many technologists with an entrepreneurial eye will have heard the phrase, "When you have invented a hammer, everything looks like a nail." Perhaps the most common mistake made by any technologist looking to commercialize their ideas for the first time is to concentrate too much on the technology and insufficiently on the needs of their customers (Moore, 1999). The more tied you are to a specific technique, the easier this mistake is to make. It is easy to concentrate on the technological aspects of an applied project, particularly if that is where your expertise lies.

Conceptual, Cultural, and Technical Barriers

We believe that Computational Intelligence has a number of barriers that impede its general use in business. We have broken these down into three key areas: conceptual, cultural and technical barriers. On the surface, it may appear that technical barriers would present the greatest difficulties, however, it is frequently the conceptual and cultural barriers that stop a project dead in its tracks. The following sections discuss each of these concepts in turn. We first discuss some of the main foundations of CI under the heading of "Conceptual Barriers," this is followed by a discussion of the business issues relating to CI under the topic of "Cultural Barriers" and we finish off by covering the "nuts and bolts" of a CI project in a section on "Technical Barriers."

Conceptual Barriers

CI offers a set of methods for making decisions based on calculations made from data. These calculations are normally probabilities of possible outcomes. This is not a concept that many people are familiar with. People are used to the idea of a computer giving definitive answers — the value of sales for last year, for example. They are less comfortable with the idea that a computer can make a judgement that may turn out to be wrong.

The end user of a CI system must understand what it means to make a prediction based on data, the effect of errors and non-linearity and the requirements for the right kind of data if a project is to be successful. Analysts will understand these points intuitively, but if managers and end users do not understand them, problems will often arise.

Core Concepts

In this section, we will define and explain some of the mathematical concepts that everybody involved in a CI project will need to understand. If you are reading this as a CI practitioner, it may seem trivial and somewhat obvious. This unfortunately is one of the first traps of applying CI — there will be people who do not understand these concepts or perhaps have an incomplete understanding, which may lead them to expect different outcomes. These differences in understanding must be resolved in order for a project to succeed. We highlight these mathematical concepts because they are what makes CI different from the type of computing many people find familiar. They are conceptual barriers because their consequences have a material impact on the operation of a CI-based system.

Systems, Models, and The Real World

First, let us define some terms in order to simplify the text and enhance clarity. A system is any part of the real world that we can measure or observe. Generally, we will want to predict its future behaviour or categorize its current state. The system will have inputs: values we can observe and often control, that lead to outputs that we cannot directly control. Normally the only method available to us if we want to change the values of the outputs is to modify the inputs. Our goal is usually to do this in a controlled and predictable manner.

In the purchasing example used above, our inputs would be the profile of the buyer (their age, gender, income, etc.) and the outputs would be products that people with a given profile have bought before. We could then run a set of possible customers through the model of the system and record those that are predicted to have the greatest likelihood of buying the product we are trying to sell.

Given that a CI system is generally derived from data collected from a real-world system, it is important to determine what factors or variables affect the system and what can safely be ignored. It is often quite difficult to estimate in advance all the factors or variables that may affect a system and even if it were, it is not always possible to gather data about those factors.

The usual approach, forced on CI modelers through pragmatism, is to use all the variables that are available and then exclude variables that are subsequently found to be irrelevant. Time constraints frequently do not allow for data on further variables to be collected. It is important to acknowledge that this compromise is present since a model with reduced functionality will almost certainly be produced. From a business point of view, it is essential that a client is made aware that the limitations of the model are attributable to the limitations of their data rather than the CI technique that has been used. This can often be a point of conflict and therefore needs to be clarified at the very outset of any work.

Related to this issue of collecting data for all the variables that could affect a system is the collection of sufficient data that span the range of all the values a variable might take with respect to all the other variables in the system. The goal here is to develop a model that accurately links the patterns in the input data to corresponding output patterns and ideally this model would be an exact match to the real-world system. Unfortunately, this is rarely the case since it is usually not possible to gather sufficient data to cover all the possible intricacies of the real-world system.

The client will frequently have collected the data before engaging the CI expert. They will have done this without a proper knowledge of what is likely to be required. A significant part of the CI practitioner's expertise is concerned with the correct collection of the right data. This is a complex issue and is discussed in detail in Baum and Haussler (1989).

A simple example of this might be the collection of temperature readings for a chemical process. Within the normal operation of this process, the temperature may remain inside a very stable range, barely moving by a few degrees. If regular recordings of the system state are being made every 5 seconds then the majority of the data that are collected will record this temperature measurement as being within its stable range. An analyst may however be interested in what happens to the system when it is perturbed outside its normal behaviour or perhaps what can be done to make the system optimal. This may involve temperature variations that are relatively high or low compared to the norm.

Unless the client is willing to perturb their system such that a large number of measurements of high and low temperatures can be obtained then it will not be possible to make queries about how the system will react to novel situations.

This lack of relevant data over all the "space" that a system might cover will lead to a model that is only an approximation to the real world. The model has regions where it maps very well to the real world and produces accurate predictions, but it will also have regions where data were sparse or noisy and its approximations are consequently very poor.

Inputs and Outputs

Input and output values are characterized by variables — a variable describes a single input or output, for example "temperature" or "gender." Variables take values — temperature might take values from 0 to 100 and gender would take the values "male" or "female." Values for a given variable can be numeric like those for a temperature range or symbolic like those of "gender." It is rare that a variable will have values that are in part numeric and in part symbolic. The general approach in this case is to force the variable to be regarded as symbolic if any of its values are symbolic. Fuzzy systems can impose an order on symbolic data, for example we can say that "cold" is less than "warm" which is less than "hot." This enables us to combine the two concepts.

Numbers have an order and allow distances to be calculated between them, symbolic variables do not, although they may have an implied scale such as "small," "medium" or "large." Ignoring the idea of creating an artificial distance metric for symbolic variables, a Computational Intelligence system cannot know, for example, that blue and purple are closer than blue and yellow. This information may be present in the knowledge of a user, but it is not obvious from just looking at the symbolic values "blue" and "yellow."

Coincidence and Causation

If two things reliably coincide, it does not necessarily follow that one caused the other. Causation cannot be established from data alone. We can observe that A always occurs when B occurs, but we cannot say for sure that A causes B (or indeed, that B causes A). If we observe that B always follows A, then we can rule out B causing A, but we still can't conclude that A causes B from the data alone. If A is "rain" and B is "wet streets" then we can infer that there is a causal effect, but if A is "people sending Christmas cards" and B is "snow falling" then we know that A does not cause B nor B cause A, yet the two factors are associated. Generally, however, if A always occurs when B occurs, then we can use that fact to predict that B will occur if we have seen A. Spotting such co-occurrences and making proper use of them is at the heart of many CI techniques.

Non-Linearity

Consider any system in which altering an input leads to a change in an output. Take the relationship between the price of a product and the demand for that product. If an increase in price of $1 always leads to a decrease in demand of 50 units regardless of the current price then the relationship is said to be linear. If, however, the change in demand following a $1 increase varies depending on the current price, then the system is non-linear. This is the standard demand curve and is an example of non-linearity for a single input variable.

Adding further input variables can introduce non-linearity, even when each individual variable produces a linear effect if it alone is changed. This occurs when two or more input variables interact within the system such that the effect of one is dependent upon the value of the other (and vice versa). An example of such a situation would be the connection between advertising spend, price of the product and the effect these two input variables might have on the demand for the product. For example, adding $1 to the price of the product during an expensive advertising campaign may cause less of a drop in demand compared with the same increase when little has been spent on advertising.

Non-linearity has a number of major consequences for trying to predict a future outcome from data. Indeed, it is these non-linear effects that drove much of the research into the development of the more sophisticated neural networks. It is also this aspect of computational intelligence that can cause significant problems in understanding how the system works. A client will frequently request a simplified explanation of how a CI system is deriving its answer. If the CI model requires a large number of parameters (e.g., the weights of a neural network) to capture the non-linear effects, then it is usually not possible to provide a simplified explanation of that model. The very act of simplifying it removes the crucial elements that encode the non-linear effects.

This directly relates to one of the more frequently requested requirements of a CI system — the decision-making process should be traceable such that a client can look at a suggested course of action and then examine the rationale behind it. This can frequently lead to simple, linear CI techniques being selected over more complex and effective non-linear approaches because linear processes can be queried and understood more easily.

A further consequence of non-linearity is that it makes it impossible to answer a question such as "How does x affect y?" with a general all encompassing answer. The answer would have to become either, "It depends on the current value of x" in the case of x having a simple non-linear relationship with y, and "It depends on z" in cases where the presence of one or more other variables introduce non-linearity.

Here is an example based on a CI system that calculates the risk of a person making a claim on a motor insurance policy. Let us say we notice that as people grow older, their risk increases, but that it grows more steeply once people are over 60 years of age. That is a non-linearity as growing older by one year will have a varying effect on risk depending on the current age.

Now let us assume that the effect of age is linear, but that for males risk gets lower as they grow older and for females the risk gets higher with age. Now, we cannot know the effect of age without knowing the gender of the person in question. There is a non-linear effect produced by the interaction of the variables "age" and "gender." It is possible for several inputs to combine to affect an output in a linear fashion. Therefore, the presence of several inputs is not a sufficient condition for non-linearity.

Classification

A classification system takes the description of an object and assigns it to one class among several alternatives. For example, a classifier of fruit would see the description "yellow, long, hard peel" and classify the fruit as a banana. The output variable is "class of fruit," the value is "banana." It is tempting to see classification as a type of prediction. Based on a description of an object, you predict that the object will be a banana. Under normal circumstances, that makes sense but there are situations where that does not make sense, and they are common in business applications of CI.

A CI classification system is built by presenting many examples of the descriptions of the objects to be classified to the classifier-building algorithm. Some algorithms require the user to specify the classes and their members in this data. Other algorithms (referred to as clustering algorithms) work out suitable classes based on groups of objects that are similar enough to each other but different enough from other things to qualify for a class of their own.

A common application of CI techniques in marketing is the use of an existing customer database to build a CI system capable of classifying new prospects as belonging to either the class "customer" or "non-customer." Classifying a prospect as somebody who resembles a customer is not the same as predicting that the person will become a customer. Such systems are built by presenting examples of customers and non-customers. When they are being used, they will be presented with prospective customers (i.e., those who do not fall into the class of customer at the moment since they have not bought anything). Those prospects that are classified by the CI system as "customer" are treated as good prospects as they share sufficient characteristics with the existing customers.

It must be remembered, however, that they currently fall into the non-customer category, so the use of the classification to predict that they would become customers if approached is erroneous. What the system will have highlighted is that they have a greater similarity to existing customers than those classified as "non-customer." It does not indicate that they definitely will become a "customer."

For example, if such a system were used to generate a mailing list for a direct-mail campaign, you would choose all the current non-customers who were classified as potential customers by the CI system and target them with a mail shot. If a random mailing produced a 1% response rate and you doubled that to 2% with your CI approach, the client should be more than satisfied. However, if you treated your classification of customers as a prediction that those people would respond to the mailing, you would still have been wrong on 98% of your predictions.

Prospect list management is increasingly seen as an important part of Customer Relationship Management (CRM) and it is in that aspect that CI can offer real advantages. Producing a list of 5,000 prospects and predicting that they will all become customers is a sure way of producing scepticism in the client at best, and at worst of failing to deliver.

Dealing with Errors and Uncertainty

Individual predictions from a CI system have a level of error associated with them. The level of error may depend on the values of the inputs for the current situation, with some situations being more predictable than others. This lack of certainty can be caused by noise in the data, inconsistencies in the behaviour of the system under consideration or by the effects of other variables that are not available to the analysis. Dealing with this uncertainty is an important part of any CI project. It is important both in technical terms — measuring and acting on different levels of certainty — and conceptual levels — ensuring that the client understands that the uncertainty is present. (See Jepson, Collins, & Evans, 1993; Srivastava & Weigend, 1994 for different methods for measuring errors.)

We have stated that a classification can be seen as a label of a class that a new object most closely resembles, as opposed to being a prediction of a class of behaviour. A consequence of this is that a CI system can make a prediction or a classification that turns out to be wrong. In the broadest sense, this would be defined as an error but could also be seen as a consequence of the probabilistic nature of CI systems. For example, if a CI system predicts that an event will occur with a probability of 0.8 and that event does not occur for a given prediction, then the prediction and its associated probability could still be seen as being correct. It is just that in this instance the most probable outcome did not occur. In order to validate the system, you must look at all the results for the all the predictions. If a CI model assigns a probability of 0.8 to an event, it should occur 8 times out of 10 for the system to be valid but you should still expect it to misclassify 2 out of 10 events.

For example, if a given insurance claim is assigned a probability of being fraudulent of 0.8 then one would expect 8 out of 10 identical claims to be fraudulent. If this turned out not to be the case, for example only 6 out 10 turned out to be fraudulent, then the CI system would be considered to be wrong.

Returning to the customer-prospecting example, it is clear that the individual cost of a wrong classification in large campaigns is small. If we have made it clear that the prospects were chosen for looking most like previous customers and that no predictions are made about a prospect actually converting, the job of the CI system becomes to increase the response rate to a campaign.

There are many cases where it is necessary to introduce the concept of the CI system being able to produce an "I don't know" answer. Such cases are defined as any prediction or classification with a confidence score below a certain threshold. By refusing to make a judgement on such cases, it is possible to reduce the number of errors made in all other cases.

The authors have found that neural network based systems are very useful for the detection of fraudulent insurance claims. A system was developed that could detect fraudulent claims with reasonable accuracy. However, the client did not want to investigate customers whose claims looked fraudulent but were not. By introducing the ability of the system to indicate when it was uncertain about a given case, we were able to significantly reduce the number of valid claims that were investigated.

The two aspects that had to be considered when looking at the pattern of errors within the above example were the cost of a false positive and the cost of a false negative. An example of a false positive would be a situation where an insurance fraud detection system classified a claim as "positive" for fraud (i.e., fraudulent) but subsequent investigation indicated the claim to be valid. In the case of a false negative, the insurance fraud system might indicate that a claim is "negative" for fraud when in fact it was actually fraudulent. In the latter case you would not know that you had paid out on a fraudulent claim unless you explicitly investigated every claim while validating the fraud detection system.

False positives and false negatives have a cost associated with them in any specific application. The key to dealing with these errors lies in the cost-benefit ratio for each type of error. A false positive in the above case may cost two days work for an investigator. A false negative (i.e., paying out on a missed fraudulent claim) may cost many thousands of dollars.

Interpolation vs. Extrapolation

Many users want a model that they can use to make predictions about uncharted territory. This involves either interpolation within the current model or extrapolation into regions outside the data set from which the model was built. This might happen in a case where the user asks the system to make a prediction for the outcome of a chemical process when one of the input variables, such as temperature, is higher than any example provided in the recorded data set.

Without a measure of the non-linearity in the system, it can be difficult to estimate how accurate such predictions are likely to be. For example, interpolation within a data-rich area of the variable space is likely to produce accurate results unless the system is highly non-linear. Conversely, interpolation within a data-poor area is likely to produce almost random answers unless the system is very linear in the region of the interpolation. The problem with many computational systems is that it is often not obvious when the model has strayed outside its "domain knowledge."

A good example comes from a current application being developed by the authors. We are using a neural network to predict sales levels of newly released products to allow distributors and retailers to choose the right stocking levels. The effect on sales of the factors that we can measure is non-linear, which means that we do not know how those factors would lead to sales levels that were any higher than those we have seen already. The system is constrained to predicting sales levels up to the maximum that it has already seen. If a new product is released in the future, and sells more than the best selling product that we have currently seen, we will fall short in our prediction.

In the case of interpolation, the simplest method for ensuring that non-linearity is accurately modelled is to gather as much data as possible. This is because the more data we have, the more likely it is that areas of non-linearity within the system will have sample data points indicating the shape of the parameter space. If there were insufficient data in a non-linear part of the system, then a CI method would tend to model the area as though it were linear.

In the extreme, you only need two data points to model a linear relationship. As soon as a line becomes a curve then we need a multitude of data points along the curve to map out its correct shape. Figure 1 (a) shows a simple case of identifying a linear relationship in a system with two variables. With only two points available, the most obvious conclusion to draw would be that the system is linear. Figure 1 (b) highlights what would happen if we were to obtain more data points. Our initial assumptions would be shown to be potentially invalid. We would now have a case for suspecting that the system is non-linear or perhaps very noisy. A CI model would adapt to take account of the new data points and produce an estimate of the likely shape of the curve that would account for the shape of the points (Figure 1 (c)).

It can be seen from Figure 1 (c) that if we had interpolated between the original two points shown in Figure 1 (a) then we would have made an incorrect prediction. By ensuring that we had adequate data, the non-linearity of the system would be revealed and the CI technique would adapt its model accordingly.

Related to this concept is the possibility of extrapolating from our current known position in order to make predictions about areas outside the original data set used to build the model. Extrapolation of the linear system in Figure 1 (a) would be perfectly acceptable if we knew the system was actually linear. However, if we know the system is non-linear, this approach becomes very error prone. An example of the possible shape of the curve is shown in Figure 1 (c), however, we have no guarantee that this is actually where the curve goes. Further data collection in the extremes of the system (shown by black squares) might reveal that the boundaries of the curve are actually quite a different shape to the one we have extrapolated (Figure 1 (d)). While we remained in the data-rich central area of the curve, our prediction would have remained accurate. However, as soon as we went to the extremes, errors would have quickly crept in.

Given that we have the original data set at our disposal, it is possible to determine how well sampled a particular region is that we wish to make a prediction in. This should enable us to provide a measure of uncertainty about the prediction itself. With regards to extrapolation, we usually know what the upper and lower bounds are for the data used to build the model. We will therefore know that we have set a given input variable to a value outside the range on which the data used to build the model was limited to. For anything but the simplest of systems, this should start ringing alarm bells. It is important that a client using a CI system understands the implications of what they are asking for under each of these situations and where possible, steer away from trying to use such information.

Figure 1 (a) A simple linear system derived from 2 points. (b) The addition of further data reveals non-linearity. (c) A CI system fits a curve to the available data. (d) The shape of the estimated curve showing how further data produces a new shape — extrapolation would fail in these regions.

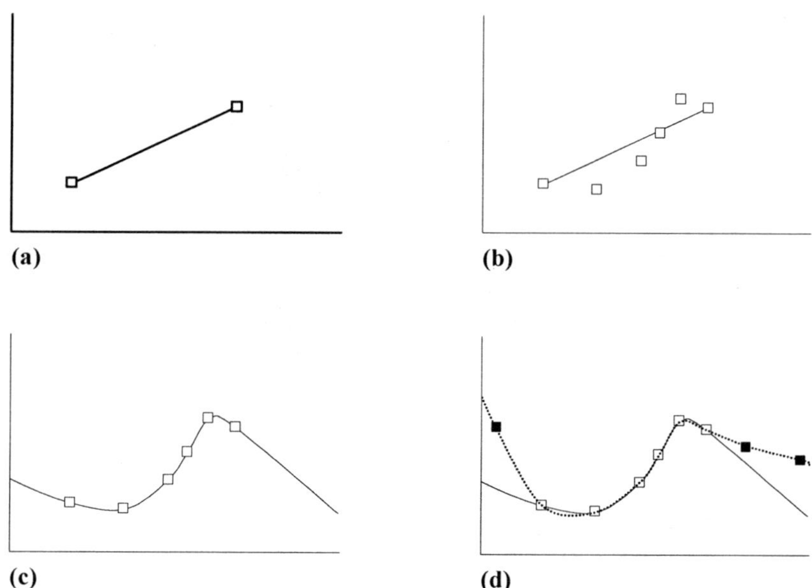

Generalization

This leads us to the concept of generalization — an important issue in the development of an actual CI system. Generalization is concerned with avoiding the construction of a CI system that is very accurate when tested with data that has been used to build it, but performs very poorly when presented with novel data. With regard to the previous section, generalization deals with the ability of a non-linear system to accurately interpolate between points from the data used to construct it.

An idealized goal for a CI system is that it should aim to produce accurate predictions for data that it has not seen before. With a poorly constructed CI system that may have been built with unrepresentative data, the system is likely to perform well when making predictions in the region of this unrepresentative data and very poorly when tested with novel data that is more representative of the typical operating environment. In simple terms, the system attempts to build a predictive system that very closely follows all the observed historical data to the detriment of new data.

If all the data used to build a system completely captured the behaviour of the system then generalization would not be an issue. This is almost never the case, as it is very difficult to capture all the data describing the state of a system and furthermore data usually have some degree of noise associated with them. The CI practitioner will understand these limitations and will attempt to minimize their effects on the performance of the CI system. For the business manager interested in applying CI with the assistance of the practitioner, this will generally present itself as a need for a significant amount of data in an attempt to overcome the noise within it and ensure that a representative sample of the real-world system has been captured.

Cultural Barriers

CI's apparent power lies in its ability to address issues at the heart of a business: choosing prospects, pricing insurance, or warning that a machine needs servicing. These are high-level decisions that a business trusts experts to perform. Can you go into a business and challenge the expertise of their marketing team, their underwriters, or their engineers in the same way that production line robots have replaced car assembly workers? We look at these cultural barriers and the ways in which they have been successfully overcome. Whether you are an external consultant selling to a client or an internal manager selling an idea to the board, you will need to understand how to win acceptance for this new and challenging approach if your project is to succeed.

People who are experts at their job do not like to think that a computer can do it better. In general, computers are regarded as dumb tools — there to help the human experts with the tedious aspects of their work. Robots and simple machines have successfully replaced a lot of manual labor. There have been barriers to this replacement — protests from unions and doubts about quality for example — but automation of manual labor is now an integral aspect of the industrialized world.

Computational Intelligence might be vaunted as offering a modern computational revolution where machines are able to replace human decision-making processes. This replacement process should free up people to focus on special cases that require thought and knowledge of context that the computer may be lacking. Given these positive aspects, there are still many reasons why this shift might not come about. In the first instance, there is the position of power held by the people to be replaced. The people who make the decisions are less than happy with the idea that they might be replaceable and that they might be called upon to help build the systems that might replace them. Manual workers have little say in the running of an organization. However, marketing executives and underwriters are higher up a company's decision-making chain — replacing them with a computer is consequently a more difficult prospect.

Next there is the issue of trust. I might not believe that a machine can build a car, but show me one that does and I have to believe you. If I do not believe that a computer can understand my customers better than me, you can show me an improved response to a mail campaign for a competing company, but I will still believe that my business is different and it will require a lot of evidence before I will change my mind.

Related to the issue of trust is that of understanding. This is a problem on two levels — first people do not always understand how they themselves do something. For example, we interviewed experts in spotting insurance fraud, who said things like, "You can just tell when a claim is dodgy — it doesn't look right." You can call it intuition or experience, but it is hard to persuade somebody that it is the result of a set of non-linear equations served up by their subconscious. The brain is a mysterious thing and people find the idea that in some areas it can be improved upon by a computer very hard to swallow.

The second problem is that people have difficulty believing that a computer can learn. If a person does not understand the concepts of computer learning and how it is possible to use data to make a computer learn, then it is hard for them to make the conceptual leap required to believe that a computer could be good at something that they see as a very human ability.

Here is an example to illustrate the point. A printing company might upgrade from an old optical system to a complete state-of-the-art digital system. In the process they would replace the very core of their business with a new technology, perhaps with the result that their old skills become obsolete. A graphic designer, however, would not want to buy a system that could automatically produce logos from a written brief, no matter how clever the technology.

Our experience has shown that many of these problems can be overcome if the right kind of simplification is applied to the sales pitch. That is not to say that technical details should be avoided or that buyers should be considered stupid. It means choosing the right level of technical description and, more importantly, setting the strength of claims being made about the technology on offer.

We shall use the task of building a CI system for use in motor insurance as an example. We developed a system that could calculate the risk associated with a new policy better than most underwriters. It could spot fraud more effectively than most claims handlers and it could choose prospective customers for direct marketing better than the marketing department. Insurance could be revolutionized by the use of CI (Viaene, Derrig, Baesens, & Dedene, 2003), but the industry has so far resisted.

An insurance company would never replace its underwriters, so if we are to help them with a CI system, it must be clearly positioned as a tool — something that helps them do their job better without doing it for them. Even though you could train a neural network to predict the probability associated with a new policy leading to a claim better than the underwriter can, it would do too much of his or her job to be acceptable.

Our experience has shown us that approximately 90% of motor insurance policies carry a similar, low probability of leading to a claim. There are 5% that have a high risk associated with them and 5% that have a very low risk. A system for spotting people who fall into the interesting 10% in order to avoid the high risks and increase the low risk policies would leave the underwriters still doing their job on the majority of policies and give them an extra tool to help avoid very high risks. The CI system becomes the basis of a portfolio management system and the sale is then about better portfolio management and not about intelligent computing — a much easier prospect to sell.

Within the context of the insurance fraud example, investigators spent a considerable amount of their time looking at routine cases. Each case took a brief amount of time to review but, due to the large number of them, this took up the majority of their time. If you put forward the argument that the investigators would be better spending their time on the more complex cases where their skills could truly be used, then you can make a case for installing a CI system that does a lot of the routine work for them and only presents the cases that it regards as suspicious.

Another barrier to the successful commercialization of CI techniques is, to put it bluntly, a lack of demand. It is easy to put this lack of demand down to a lack of awareness, but it should be stated with more strength than that: CI is not in the commercial consciousness. Perhaps if prospective customers understood the power of CI techniques, then they would be easily sold on the idea. To an extent, of course, that is true. But to find the true reason behind a lack of demand, we must look at things from a customer's point of view. Will CI be on the customer's shopping list? Will there be a budget allocated? Are there pressing reasons for a CI system to be implemented? If the answer to these questions is no, then there is no demand. There is only, at best, the chance to persuade a forward-thinking visionary in the company who has the time, resources and security to risk a CI approach.

To use our e-commerce example again, a company building an online shop will need to worry about secure servers, an e-commerce system, order processing, delivery and promotion of the site. Those things will naturally be on their shopping list. An intelligent shop assistant to help the customer choose what to buy might be the only thing that would make a new e-commerce site stand out. It might be a perfect technical application of CI, and it might double sales, but it will not be planned, nor budgeted for. That makes the difference between you having to sell and the customer wanting to buy.

Technical Barriers

It has been our experience that the most common and fundamental technical barrier to most CI applications concerns access to source data of the correct type and quality. Obviously, if there is no data available relating to a given application, then no data-driven CI technique will be of use. A number of more common problems arise, however, when a client initially claims to have adequate data.

Is the client able to extract the data in electronic form? Some database systems actually do not have a facility for dumping entire table contents, compelling the user to make selections one-at-a-time. Some companies still maintain paper-only storage systems and some companies have a policy against data leaving their premises. It is also well worth remembering that the appropriate data will not only need to be available at the time of CI system development, but at run time, too. A typical use of CI in marketing is to make predictions about the buying behaviour of customers. It is easy to append lifestyle data to a customer database off-line ready for analysis, but will that same data be available online when a prediction is required for any given member of the population as a whole?

Does the data reflect the task you intend to perform and does it contain the information required to do so? Ultimately, finding the answer to this question is the job of the CI expert, but this is only true when the data appears to reflect the application well. It can be worth establishing early on that the data at least appears useful.

There are also technical aspects of a CI project that will have an impact on the contractual arrangements between you and the client. These are consequences of the fact that it is not always possible to guarantee the success of a CI project since the outcome depends on the quality of the data.

If the client does not have suitable data but is willing to collect some, it is important to be clear about what is to be collected and when that data will be delivered. If your contract with the client sets out a time table, be sure that delays in the data collection (which are not uncommon) allow your own milestones to be moved. Be clear that your work cannot start until the data are delivered. You may also want to be clear that the data must meet a certain set of criteria.

You also need to make it very clear what the client is buying. Most clients will be used to the idea that if they have a contract with (say) a software company to develop a bespoke solution, then that solution will be delivered, working as agreed upon in the specification. If it is not, then the contract will usually allow for payment to be reduced or withheld. It should be made clear to the client that their data, and whether or not it contains the information required to allow the CI approach to work, will be the major contributing factor to the success or otherwise of the project. The client must understand that success cannot be guaranteed. It has been our experience that the client often does not see it this way — the failure of the CI model to accurately predict who their customers are is seen as a failure of CI, not their carefully collected data.

Another consequence of the lack of available data at the start of a project is the difficulty it presents if you plan to demonstrate your approach to a prospective client. You can generate mock data that carries the information you hope to find in your client's database, but this proves little to the client as it is clearly invented by you. You can talk about (and possibly even demonstrate) what you have done for similar, anonymous clients, but each company's situation is usually different and CI models are very specific to each customer. The difficulty of needing data therefore remains.

There are many specific technical problems including choosing the right CI technique and using it to produce the best results. Each CI technique has its own particular requirements and issues. It is beyond the scope of this chapter to cover such topics — we have focussed on the elements that occur generally across the diverse set of CI approaches. Further chapters in this book address technique specific issues.

Future Trends

We believe that CI technology is currently at a stage of development where weaknesses in the techniques are not the major barriers to immediate commercial exploitation. We have identified what we consider to be the main cultural, conceptual and technical barriers to commercialization of CI and the reader may have noticed that the technical barriers did not include any shortcomings of the CI methods themselves.

There is a large gap between the power of the techniques available and the problems that are currently being solved by those techniques. Unusually, however, it is the technology that is ahead. One can easily imagine impressive applications of CI techniques that are yet to be perfected — Web agents that can write you an original essay on any topic you choose, robot cars capable of negotiating the worst rush hour traffic at high speeds, and intelligent CCTV cameras that can recognize that a crime is taking place and alert the police. None of these applications are possible today and they are likely to remain difficult for a long time to come. The small improvements to the techniques that are possible in commercially viable time scales will not bring about a step change in the types of applications to which the techniques may be applied.

Our view of the near future of the commercial exploitation of CI, therefore, is concentrated on the methods of delivery of existing techniques and not the development or improvement of those techniques. Of course, the development of CI techniques is important, but it is the commercialization that must catch up with the technology, and not the converse. The consequence of this observation is, we believe, that the near future of the commercial exploitation of CI techniques requires little further technical research. The current techniques can do far more than they are being asked to do.

We expect to see a shift away from selling the idea of the techniques themselves and towards selling a product or service improved by the techniques without reference to those techniques. The search engine Google is a good example. People do not care about the clever methods behind it. They just know it works as a very good search engine. Another good example of underplayed technology comes from the world of industrial control. Most industrial control is done using a technique known as PID. Many university engineering departments have produced improvements to the PID controller and very few of them have found their way into an industrial process. One reason for this is that everybody in the industry understands and trusts PID controllers. Nobody wants to open the Pandora's box of new and challenging techniques that might fragment the industry and its expertise.

One company developed an improvement to the PID controller and did not even admit to its existence. They simply embedded it in a new product and sold it as a standard PID controller. It worked just that bit better than all the others. Nobody really knew why it was better, but it was. The controller sold very well, nobody was threatened by the new technique, and there was no technical concept to sell. It just worked better.

An alternative and related example is the use of CI systems to spot fraudulent credit card behaviour. It is simply not practical for investigators to analyze every single credit card transaction. A CI system can be used to monitor activity for each user and determine when it has become unusual. At this point an investigator is alerted who can contact the owner of the card to verify their spending behaviour. People are generally not aware that CI systems are behind such applications, and for all practical purposes, this does not matter. The important issue is the benefits they bring rather than their technical sophistication.

The authors have put this approach into practice. Having spent several years selling CI technology to direct marketing agencies with little success, they have recently launched a Web-based direct marketing system that is driven by CI techniques. The service allows clients to upload their current customer database to a Web server. It then appends lifestyle data to the names in the database, which is then used to generate a new list of prospects for the client to download.

The primary selling point of the service is that it is easy to use and inexpensive (the techniques are automated). These are far easier concepts to sell because they are clearly demonstrable — the client can see our prices and visit our Web site to see how easy the process is to use. Having got a foot in the door of the mailing list market, our system quietly uses some very straightforward CI techniques to produce prospect lists that yield response rates up to four times better than the industry standard.

Our approach is proving successful and it is based on the following points:

- We selected a market where there was clearly money to be made from delivering an improvement to the existing, inefficient norm.
- The main selling point of the product is not technical, thus all problems associated with explaining and selling the CI concept are avoided.
- We deliver a service that the customer needs, already has budgeted for, and understands perfectly.
- The data we receive are always in the same format (names and addresses) and we provide all the additional data required. Consequently, we never have a problem with data quality.

This approach has a number of advantages. It removes the need for the client to worry that they are taking a risk by using a new technology. It removes the need for us to try and sell the idea of the technology, and it allows us to sell to a mature market.

Summary

We have seen that there are a number of barriers to the successful commercialization of CI techniques. There is a lack of awareness and understanding from potential customers. Their mathematical nature and the fact that the success of a project depends on the quality of the data it uses can make the concept hard to sell. The lack of awareness also means that companies are not actively looking for CI solutions and are consequently unlikely to have budgets in place with which to buy them.

CI techniques face cultural barriers to their adoption as they could potentially replace existing human expertise. The existing human experts are often in a powerful position to prevent even the risk of this replacement and their unwillingness to change should not be underestimated. We have also touched upon technical barriers, such as accessing the correct data both at design and run-time, and the problems of specifying, demonstrating and prototyping a system based on data.

We have suggested a number of approaches designed to overcome the barriers discussed in this chapter. These approaches can be summarized by the notion of putting yourself in your prospective customer's position. Ask yourself what the customer needs, not what you can offer. Think about how much change a customer is likely to accept and whether or not they could cope with that change. Ask yourself whether you are making more work for the customer or making their life easier. Think about whether the customer is likely to have a budget for what you offer. If not, can you present it as something they do have budget for? Find out what level of technical risk the customer is likely to be comfortable with. Are they early adopters or conservative followers?

We believe that the future success of CI will rely on keeping your customer on board and giving them what they want, not impressing them with all the clever tricks that you can perform. The key element is for both you and the client to maintain the same point of view of the problem you are both trying to solve. This will primarily mean that if you are the provider of the CI solution, you will need to adapt your perspective to fit that of the client. It is, however, important that the client understands the conceptual limits of CI as discussed in the early parts of this chapter. In order to maintain a positive working relationship with a client, it is important that they understand both the benefits and limitations of Computational Intelligence and therefore know, at least in principle, what can and cannot be done.

References

Baum, E.B., & Haussler, D. (1989). What net size gives valid generalisation? *Neural Computation, 1*(1), 151-160.

Bhat, N., & McAvoy, T. J. (1990). Use of neural nets for dynamic modelling and control of chemical process systems. *Computer Chemical Engineering, 14*(4/5), 573-583.

Bishop, C. M. (1995). *Neural networks for pattern recognition.* Oxford, UK: Oxford University.

Blazewicz, J., & Kasprzak, M. (2003). Determining genome sequences from experimental data using evolutionary computation. In G. G. Fogel & D. W. Corne (Eds.), *Evolutionary computation in bioinformatics* (pp. 41-58). San Francisco: Morgan Kaufmann.

Haykin, S. (1994). *Neural networks, a comprehensive foundation.* New York: Macmillan.

Hecht-Nielsen, R. (1990). *Neurocomputing.* Reading, MA: Addison Wesley.

Hertz, J., Krogh, A., & Palmer, R. G. (1991). *Introduction to the theory of neural computation.* Redwood City, CA: Addison Wesley

Hoss, D. (2000). The e-business explosion: Strategic data solutions for e-business success. *DM Review*, *10*(8), 24-28.

Jazayeri-Rad, H. (2004). The nonlinear model-predictive control of a chemical plant using multiple neural networks. *Neural Computing and Applications*, *13*(1), 2-15.

Jepson, B., Collins, A., & Evans, A. (1993). Post-neural network procedure to determine expected prediction values and their confidence limits. *Neural Computing and Applications*, *1*(3), 224-228.

Kim, K., & Lee, W. B. (2004). Stock market prediction using artificial neural networks with optimal feature transformation. *Neural Computing and Applications*, *13*(3), 255-260.

Law, R. (1999). Demand for hotel spending by visitors to Hong Kong: A study of various forecasting techniques. *Journal of Hospitality and Leisure Marketing*, *6*(4), 17-29.

Moore, G. (1999). *Crossing the chasm: Marketing and selling high-tech products to mainstream customers*. Oxford, UK: Capstone.

Srivastava, A. N., & Weigend, A. S. (1994). Computing the probability density in connectionist regression. In M. Marinara & G. Morasso (Eds.), *Proceedings ICANN, 1* (pp. 685-688). Berlin: Springer-Verlag.

Trippi, R. R., & DeSieno, D. (1992). Trading equity index futures with a neural-network. *Journal of Portfolio Management*, *19,* 27-33.

Tsaih, R., Hsu, Y., & Lai, C. C. (1998). Forecasting S & P 500 stock index futures with a hybrid AI system. *Decision Support Systems*, *23*(2), 161-174.

Viaene, S., Derrig, R. A., Baesens, B., & Dedene, G. (2003). A comparison of state-of-the-art classification techniques for expert automobile insurance claim fraud detection. *Journal of Risk and Insurance*, *69*(3), 373-421.

Yu, D. L., & Gomm, J. B. (2002). Enhanced neural network modelling for a real multi-variable chemical process. *Neural Computing and Applications*, 10(4), 289-299.

Chapter III

Computational Intelligence as a Platform for a Data Collection Methodology in Management Science

Kristina Risom Jespersen, Aarhus School of Business, Denmark

Abstract

With an increased focus in management science on how to collect data close to the real world of managers, we consider how agent-based simulations have interesting prospects that are usable for the design of business applications aimed at the collection of data. As an example of a new generation of data collection methodologies, this chapter discusses and presents a behavioral simulation founded in the agent-based simulation life cycle and supported by Web technology. With agent-based modeling the complexity of the method can be increased without limiting the research as a result of limited technological support. This makes it possible to exploit the advantages of a questionnaire, an experimental design, a role-play and a scenario, gaining the synergy of a combination of these methodologies. At the end of the chapter an example of a simulation is presented for researchers and practitioners to study. [1]

Introduction

As the complexity of problems and the speed of changes increase for companies, the accuracy of management science relies on measuring behavior as close to the real world as possible. The methodological tradition in management science has been the self-administered questionnaire and case analysis. Though these are valid research strategies, the retrospective nature of the collected data is a weakness, because the accuracy of respondents' recollection of events can be questioned. Recent reviews of various research fields of the social sciences have pointed to the need for more interactive data collection methods (Englis & Solomon, 2000; Zaltman, 1997). It is here computational intelligence, specifically agent-based simulations, has a great deal to offer researchers in the design of business applications for the collection of data.

The use of computers for data collection is well known. The first computerized experiment was launched as early as the 1970s. Within the field of decision-making, experiments have been computer-interactive from quite early on (Connolly & Thorn, 1987). For research purposes the computational intelligence available through the Web is still by and large an unexplored territory in management science (Birnbaum, 2000; Englis & Solomon, 2000; Jespersen, 2004; Klassen & Jacobs, 2001; Reips, 2000; Stanton, 1998). Images are presented or exchanged with ease, and communication is taking place without the significant delay that comes through other mediums, such as film. Complex structures in search machines or on home pages present a simple interface to users. These exciting developments in Web technology bring with them new ways of investigating scientific questions, by offering the opportunity to extend traditional data collection methods into behavioral simulations. Extensions of data collection methodologies can learn from and build on agent-based simulations developed within the field of computational intelligence. An advantage of computational models of human behavior is that, like humans, agents are able to learn in the simulations, and hence the models exhibit computational intelligence (Boer, Ebben, & Sitar, 2003; Potgieter & Bishop, 2002; Wahle, Bazzan, Klügl, & Schrenkenberg, 2002). Therefore, with simulations it is possible to collect data on how decision-makers operate in companies. One such interactive data collection methodology is a Web-based behavioral simulation, which monitors the actions of human agents in a virtual decision process as known from computer games (Jespersen, 2005).

The purpose of this chapter is to demonstrate that computational intelligence can aid the collection of data through the design of a Web-based behavioral simulation. Specifically, an agent-based simulation can be a vehicle for the collection of real-time data concerned with managerial decision-making. The chapter begins with a discussion of the platform used in agent-based simulations and the benefits of Web technology. This is followed by a discussion of the agent-based simulation life-cycle as a data collection vehicle and an example of such a business application. Finally, implications and future challenges are presented.

Agent-Based Simulation as a Platform for Data Collection

Looking at the history of agent-based computational economic models, the connection to managerial decision-making is obvious. The first agent-based computational economic models were influenced by experimental economics, which focused on markets and games composed of real human agents (Chen, 2004). The focus was on the optimization of decision-making. A criticism of experimental economic studies of information utility is that utility functions do not necessarily resemble the true utilities of information. This is because human agents are subject to biases, errors, and misconceptions (Chaturvedi, Mehta, Dolk, & Ayer, 2004; Einhorn & Hogarth, 1981; Feldman & March, 1981). Parallel to this, behavioral economic research showed that the biases creating interference in experimental economics were similar to those in real life. Humans optimize their behavior as assumed in experimental economics, but from a satisficing criterion because humans are bounded rational beings (Bettman, Payne, & Johnson, 1993; March & Simon, 1993; Newell & Simon, 1972). To help the understanding of the effect of bounded rationality in economic models, the research area of agent-based simulations emerged as a way to observe actual behavior as opposed to behavior deduced from a set of axioms (Chen, 2005). It is this objective to observe actual behavior of agents that makes agent-based simulations a useful platform to collect real-time data in management science.

Benefits of Web Technology

Building an agent-based simulation on Web technology enhances the possibilities of agent-based simulations as a data-collection vehicle because Web technology can carry out the large database structure upholding the simulation active and dynamic. Therefore, the possibilities made available with an agent-based simulation as a platform for data collection are closely linked to the use of Web technology.

Being new, the Web-based approach may eliminate, at least temporarily, declining response rates. Other possible reasons why a response rate may actually increase when using a Web-based approach are: (i) the minimization of response time for participants, (ii) the ease and flexibility of participation (since the Internet is available 24 hours a day, seven days a week), and (iii) lower cost for participants (Birnbaum, 2000). Though compelling, early experiences show that e-mail response rates are lower than a mailed, paper-and-pencil survey, that e-mails are more often and more easily ignored, and that the drop-out rate is slightly higher (Reips, 2000; Sheehan, 2001; Stanton, 1998). One explanation may be that users of the Internet are expecting easily comprehensible Web pages. Hence, the design of a Web-based methodology has to be very user-oriented. If the design becomes too heavy or too boring, participants will drop out. For a behavioral simulation, Web technology represents a known medium for playing games and seeking information and can therefore be expected to increase the willingness to participate.

Another important issue of data collection is item completion. Here Web technology has a strong advantage. Item completion can be simplified through the use of pull-down menus, check boxes, radio button scales, and drop-down scales. These options really make the Web-based approach user-friendly. Furthermore, pages can be programmed to check whether all items have been completed before continuing to the next page, thereby eliminating missing values. Additional advantages of Web technology can be: (i) the ease of modifying the research instrument or creating multiple experimental versions, (ii) the automated data collection eliminates coding errors, (iii) reduction of experimenter effects, and (iv) the ability to reach a larger and more diverse subject pool. But also, two disadvantages are apparent: (i) the potential for systematic bias and measurement error and, (ii) the unwillingness of respondents to provide sensitive information over what they view as insecure lines (Birnbaum, 2000). Thus, as with any data collection methodology, care and consideration should be demonstrated in order to maintain data validity.

Agent-Based Simulation Life Cycle as a Data Collection Vehicle

The development of a behavioral simulation for data collection purposes in management science is anchored in the agent-based simulation life cycle (Chaturvedi et al., 2004; Ma & Nakamori, 2004). The life cycle proceeds clockwise through the phases in Figure 1, starting at the definition of the system and its objectives and ending with the simulation results. The two paths in Figure 1 are the solid lines representing the process and the dotted lines represent the verification, validation and testing (V-V-T) considerations. The agent-based simulation involves two segments: the model where the body of the simulation is defined, and the simulation stating how the model is run for analysis and decision-making. The transition between the two segments of the life cycle is represented by the design of the use of the model (design of experiments). Each aspect of the simulation life cycle is discussed below in relation to the creation of a data-collecting behavioral simulation.

Definition of System and Objectives

The first phase of the life cycle is the definition of systems and objectives for the agent-based simulation. When the agent-based simulation is used as a data collection vehicle, the system is a managerial decision-making process, and the objective is to collect real-time data on human behavior within this decision-making process. In general, the use of behavioral simulations for the collection of data could apply to any type of decision process.

Figure 1. Basic agent-based simulation life cycle

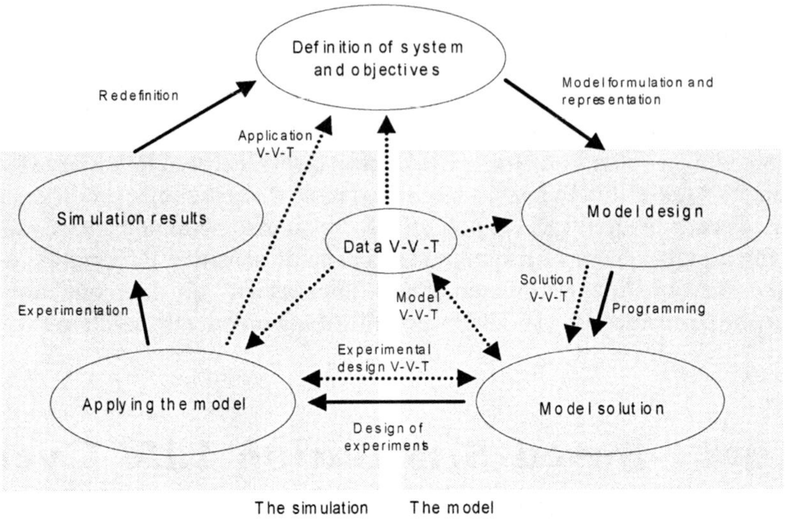

The author's conception on basis of Chaturvedi et al. (2005).

Model Formulation and Representation

The first part of the simulation life cycle focuses on the design and creation of the virtual environment in which the simulation takes place. The first step is the formulation and representation of the conceptual model under investigation. This is the specification of the decision-making process under investigation and the context framing it through analysis of the normative theory. For the design of the model, the conceptual model has to depict the behavioral traits of the virtual and human agents.

Model Design

The model design phase is the most time-consuming task of the simulation, since it focuses on the realization of all the parts in the conceptual model. With the objective of collecting data in real-time, the model design is the phase where the pieces of the virtual decision process are created. The basic requirements for the model are the specification of: (i) the agents, (ii) the decision parameters controlled by the agent, (iii) exogenous factors, and (iv) the behavior of artificial agents with respect to the decision-making process and the rules of engagement in the process (Chaturvedi et al., 2004; Hare & Deadman, 2004). As the objective is to collect reliable and valid data, these basic requirements must be coupled with sound data collection methods. Therefore, the model design synthesizes data collection methods such as questionnaire, experimental design, role-play, and scenarios. Questionnaires and experimental design are the more commonly

Table 1. Basic design principles for role-playing

- The role-players should be similar to those being represented. Meaning that a role-player should act as him/herself.
- Role-players should read instructions for their roles before reading about the situation.
- The administrator:
  - (i) provides short, yet comprehensive descriptions and
  - (ii) creates realistic surroundings in order to provide a realistic enactment of the situation.

* *(Jespersen, 2004; Armstrong 2000)*

applied data collection methods whereas role-playing and scenarios are not as wide-spread when collecting empirical management data.

The aim of the questionnaire is two-fold: (i) ensuring that information about decision behavior in companies is retained and, (ii) validating the observed behavior of the agents in the simulation. Hence, the decision parameters of the agents are confirmed by the questionnaire. Where the questionnaire represents the scope, an experiment focuses on depth by offering a standardized and controlled presentation of the decision situation (Perkins & Rao, 1990). So, the experiment introduces activity and dynamics - though the setting is more simplified than the "real world." Exogenous factors can be specified and controlled in the model through experimental design.

Traditionally, role-playing has been used to forecast decisions in conflict situations among interacting groups, but it can also be used in predicting decisions by an individual not interacting directly with others (Armstrong, 2000). More importantly, the similarity between laboratory research and role-playing is well documented (Dabholkar, 1994). The advantage of role-playing is that the role influences a person's perception of a situation. Participants are asked to engage in the role description and then either to imagine their actions or to act them out - in both cases as they would in fact do - that is, managers should not play customers or vice-versa. The key is to make the role realistic (Armstrong, 2000; Eroglu, 1987). Therefore, with role-play the agent of the agent-based simulations can be specified. Table 1 provides some basic design principles.

The scenario is the situation in which the role-play is acted out by the participants and is therefore the heart of the simulation. The strength of using scenarios as frames for the decision-making process is that it makes the respondents relate more directly to the posed subjects, and to a high degree this results in more accurate responses (Eroglu, 1987). The ability of a scenario is threefold in that it: (i) increases interest in participation, (ii) makes it possible to create a realistic context, and (iii) provides all respondents with a standard stimulus (Frederickson, 1984, 1985; White, Varadarajan, & Dacin, 2002). In addition, when respondents are presented with a scenario before decision-making, their attention is guided to the relevant problem area. The key is to structure the scenario in accordance with the decision process under investigation in order to maintain the realism of the simulation (Jespersen, 2004). From this viewpoint, the scenario can successfully complement the experimental design by maintaining control of the decision-making process being investigated. Thus, the scenario defines the behavior of the artificial agents in the model.

Programming and Model Solution

The programming and model solution phase of the life cycle addresses the software implementation. For data collection, a Web-based ASP environment will easily handle the virtual execution environment and collect data for further analysis. The virtual execution environment is comprised of a browser-based software interface with an extensive database layer that handles storage and retrieval of Web pages. The research protocol is administered on a client-server platform. The base system is designed to function as a remote server linked to the agent through an Internet connection. In this configuration, all Web-page components reside on the database server and are reassembled into Web pages through the ASP-server interface. The formation of the Web pages is contingent on the data input to the database-server, because data consists of the continuous tracking of the behavior of the human agent at the browser. The Web application is a mix of three languages — ASP, Javascript and HTML. HTML is the standard for generating application layout as it appears on the Internet. The ASP is the dynamic part of the Web site and controls the interface with the human agent and makes sure that the human agent is guided to the right Web pages and that the Web pages have the appropriate content. It is also the ASP that makes the experimental design work. The Javascript is used to validate the answers and choices made by the participants on each Web page. Behind this architecture is an Access 2000 database that contains all the information on the agents.

Sampling: The Transition between the Model and the Simulation

At this point the use of the agent-based simulation life cycle significantly alters its focus from actions to observations in that the model is not producing data through simulated actions of agents but through an observation of the behavior of human agents. The sampling design when collecting data is equally as important as the design of strategies is in computational modeling. Without proper attention to the selection of human agents, the validity of the data obtained through the simulation will suffer severely. Furthermore, the analysis of managerial decision-making assumes that human agents are individual decision-makers familiar with the management decision-making process under analysis. Thus, great attention should be attached to this part of the data collection life cycle.

Collecting and Analyzing Data

The second part of the life cycle is the execution of the model. Here focus is on the collection and analysis of data. The first part of the simulation is the application of the model, that is, the collection of data. This phase of the life cycle is perhaps where the agent-based simulation life cycle and the data-collection cycle depart most radically. In the simulation context, applying the model implies the processing of data for each planned experiment. In the data collection context, this phase of the life cycle is the interactive part where human agents run through the simulation thereby ensuring real-

Figure 2. Data-collection, agent-based simulation life cycle

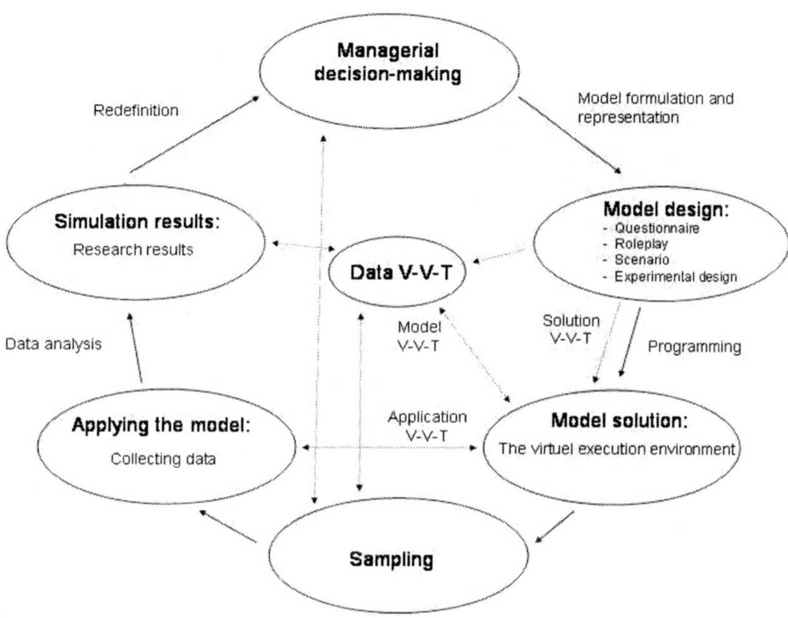

**The author's own conception.*

time data for further analysis of the dynamics of decision-making. Though the perspectives are different, this is also where the use of computational intelligence for data collection becomes most obvious. The application of the model has the same goal: to gather information about human decision behavior, but the means are different as a natural consequence of the different research perspectives. Data having been collected, the next step is the data analysis and the preparation of research results that ends the life cycle. Figure 2 summarizes the data-collection agent-based simulation life cycle.

Challenges with Simulation as a Data Collecting Tool

Despite a behavioral simulation's potential there are four critical concerns that a project must address explicitly. First, the external validity of data collected with simulations is essential for generalization of the results. Despite the many benefits of a simulation, it is a constructed reality that the respondents enter. This constrains the results of the analysis and introduces the possibility of explaining nothing but the behavior within the simulation. To counter this criticism several validation questions must be designed into the simulation to observe whether the simulated managerial decision-making process resembles the actual decision-making processes in the participating companies. Additionally, a starting questionnaire must be developed to ensure that the collected data connects the behavior within the simulations to environmental and company characteristics. Still, it must be expected that some results can be explained by the behavior of the human agents being influenced by the simulation.

Secondly, combining simulations and Web technology introduces a new type of validity known in agent-based modeling as solution validity (Chaturvedi et al., 2005; Jespersen, 2004). Solution validity ensures compatibility between the empirical data collection methods and the model solution in order to secure reliable and valid data. This means restraining the technological possibilities. Though a model of a real decision process, some constraints have to be imposed on Web technology. A simple example is the habitually used back and forward buttons on the Internet. If these are not locked, the respondents would be able to go back and alter decisions without the researcher's knowledge. Such a simple design consideration can jeopardize data validity.

The third major concern is the assumption that company characteristics are reflected by the individual behavior of participants in a simulation. This concern is related to the similarity between the virtual new product development (NPD) in the presented behavioral simulation (below) and NPD in the participating companies. To address this concern about the realism of the behavioral simulation, interviews with companies in the sampling frame would be beneficial. Furthermore, company, environmental, or decision-process characteristics should be varied in an experimental design in order to analyze differences in behavior caused by familiarity with the scenario in the simulation.

The concern about realism touches upon the fourth concern regarding a simulation as a data collection tool-time. Designing a simulation takes time, as does the design of a questionnaire (especially if a pilot test is performed). True, a simulation is not a quick fix to get data, but if the researcher seeks new insights and wants to collect real-time data, then care and consideration for the design of the data collection method is needed. Though the design of a simulation can seem overwhelming, the case example presented in the following had a development time of only six month before it was ready for the collection of data. Considering the benefits in the form of real-time data, high validity, and a high response rate, time should not be a barrier for the use of a simulation in the collection of data.

CASE: Info@performance.NPD

The example of using a behavioral simulation as the data collection instrument has been developed for a study of NPD decision-making (Jespersen, 2004). The aim was to gain greater insights concerning the value of information when new products are screened in the various phases of the NPD process. The analysis of the value of information was two-dimensional, including both the value-for-money and the decision-value of information. Hence, the behavioral simulation focused on the information processing cycle of decision-makers, that is, whether information was acquired, and whether the acquired information was used for the screening decisions.

The Model: A Virtual New Product Development Process

A virtual NPD process was created in which the participants were asked to acquire information for the evaluation of a new product idea as the product idea moved through the NPD process from idea to market planning. Hence, the simulation ended with the decision whether to launch or not. Because the game scenario used the Internet as medium, it was named Info@performance.NPD. Figure 3 depicts the structure of the simulation.

The starting questionnaire contained questions on new product development in the companies related to market orientation, strategy, budget, new product evaluation and information use. Then, the participants were asked to play the role of the new product development manager in the company MacVic[2] and were given a job description. Then there followed a brief account of the new product development situation in MacVic followed by an introduction of the virtual company. The description of MacVic focused on the external environmental conditions under which MacVic conducts business. As part of the simulation, the human agents were given a monetary budget, as they would have in their actual companies. The budget ensured that the human agents had to decide

Figure 3. Simulation structure

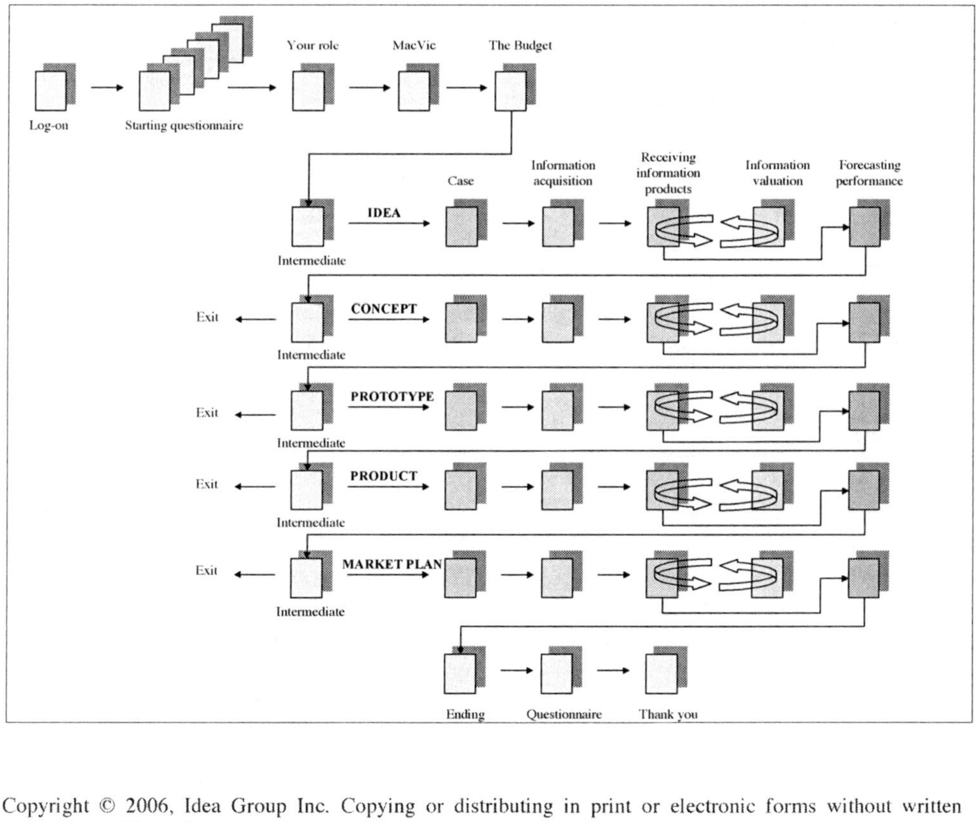

among the different information products, since it was only large enough to cover two-thirds of all the information products in the simulation. The size and use of the budget were validated with a cross-analysis of questions from the starting questionnaire.

The simulated NPD process in the game scenario contained a thorough description of the status of the product idea in the five phases of the development process (idea, concept, prototype, product, and market planning) along with a total of 36 information products available at different points in the product development process. The available information products that the participants could acquire were designed in accordance with the "best practices" guidelines developed by research on NPD success and failure (Benedetto, 1999; Booz, Allen, & Hamilton, 1968; Brown & Eisenhardt, 1995; Cooper, 1999; Cooper & Kleinschmidt, 1987, 1995; Crawford, 1997; Henard & Szymanski, 2001; Montoya-Weiss & Calantone, 1994; Souder, 1989). Hence, the information products were different in each phase of the NPD process, but always represented the four information types - secondary market information, primary market information, secondary technical information, and primary technical information. Furthermore, the information products were given a realistic touch through discussions of content, format and costs with professional market research companies. Additionally, the level of competitive stress facing MacVic, and consequently the human agents, were designed experimentally and regulated at three levels — low, medium, and high. The human agents encountered competitive stress in the concept and the prototype phases. To measure whether the acquired information was useful to the decision-making, each phase ended with the participants evaluating the potential of the new product idea in the simulation on a scale from zero to 100.

The Simulation

To illustrate Info@performance.NPD, Figure 4 shows the concept phase of the NPD process in the simulation. From these Web pages it should be possible to get an idea of how the simulation worked. The first Web page is a description of the product development in the concept phase (Picture 1) — what had happen to the product idea since the idea phase. Then the participant could choose from a list of information products (Picture 2). The participant rated each information product on an importance scale. The participant then received the ordered product (Pictures 3 and 4), and rated the value of each (Picture 5). Finally, the participant was asked to evaluate the product idea (Picture 6).

Sampling

The sample was drawn from international companies having their R&D units in Denmark. The targeted companies develop either high- or low-technology products for the consumer market. Low-technology products were represented by the food industry whereas high-technology products were represented more diversely by industries such as telecommunications, personal computers, kitchen hardware, speakers, washing machines, tumblers, and headphones. The selection criterion was that the company did

Figure 4. Concept phase simulated in Info@performance.NPD

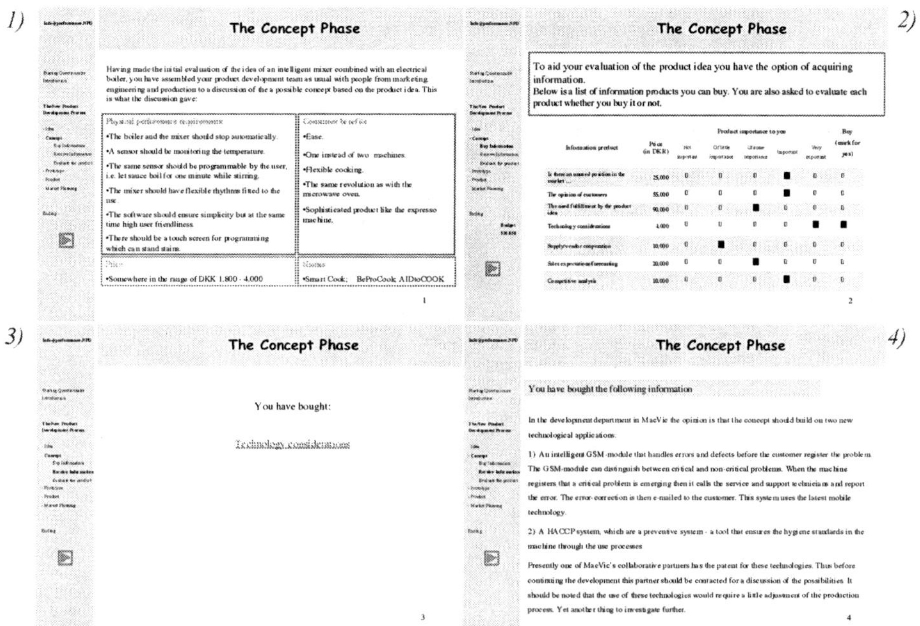

product development of consumer products in Denmark. This reduced tremendously the population of high-technology companies, and introduced another constraint on the low-technology companies. The food companies had to be of a reasonable size. The participating human agents were found either on basis of job title as R&D Manager/ Director or through the organizational structure chart, from which it was possible to determine whether it was a marketing, engineering or project manager that was the relevant contact person. A total of 42 companies used the simulation, giving a response rate of 68%.

Data Validity

Two important aspects of the simulation as data collection methodology are data validity and the judgment by the participating companies. Data validity were found through analyses of: (i) the budget, which showed that the human agents used the same amount of money in the simulation as they would have in their companies, (ii) the price on the different information products, where the relation between importance and the acquisition of an information product demonstrated a reasonable pricing in the simulation, and (iii) the information utility of the individual information products. With high average ratings for all information products on the dimensions — relevance, quality and novelty

Figure 5. Appeal of the behavioral simulation

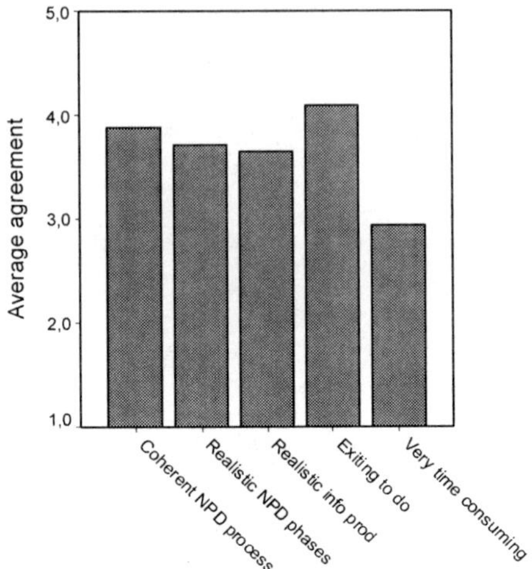

— the information products did not obscure the decision-making process. The human agents evaluated the simulation on four dimensions — coherent and easily comprehended new product development process, realistic content, exiting participation, and time consumption (see Figure 5). In general the simulation was found enjoyable and very realistic. The only negative aspect was, as expected, the time used in participation. Though the measured time for participation was 60 minutes, with the possibility of breaking this time down into minor intervals, this reaction from the participants was expected. Despite this, several participants expressed their positive experience of research going in new directions. The positive comments seem promising for behavioral simulations as a new methodological technique.

Conclusion

Methodologically, agent-based simulation proved to be a sound platform for data collection. Simulations are an interesting new approach to the collection of data given the technological development of the Internet. They provide high interaction with respondents and immediate payback through learning for the time invested in participation. Also, the combination of several methodological traditions is beneficial for future development and collaborations. Of course, behavioral simulations need to be used with extreme care in both design and sampling in order to ensure validity and generalization of results. The current rate of technological development imposes a great challenge on researchers and as such behavioral simulation as a data collection can expect to be a process of continuous development.

References

Armstrong, J. S. (2000). Role playing: A method to forecast decisions. In J. S. Armstrong (Ed.), *Principles of forecasting: A handbook for researchers and practitioners*. Norwell, MA: Kluwer Academic.

Benedetto, C. A. D. (1999). Identifying the key success factors in a new product launch. *Journal of Product Innovation Management*, *16*, 530-544.

Bettman, J. R., Payne, J., & Johnson, E. J. (1993). *The adaptive decision maker*. Cambridge, NY: Cambridge University.

Birnbaum, M. H. (Ed.). (2000). *Psychological experiments on the Internet*. San Diego, CA: Academic.

Boer, L. D., Ebben, M., & Sitar, C. P. (2003). Studying purchasing specialization in organizations: A multi-agent simulation approach. *Journal of Purchasing and Supply Management*, *9*, 199-206.

Booz, Allen, & Hamilton. (1968). *Management of new products*. New York: Booz, Allen and Hamilton.

Brown, S. L., & Eisenhardt, K. M. (1995). Product development: past research, recent findings and future directions. *Academy of Management Review*, *20*(2), 343-378.

Chaturvedi, A., Mehta, S., Dolk, D., & Ayer, R. (2004). Agent-based simulation for computational experimentation: Developing an artificial labor market. *European Journal of Operational Research*, *166*(3), 694-716.

Chen, S.-H. (2004). Computational intelligence in economics and finance: Carrying on the legacy of Herbert Simon. *Information Sciences*, *170*(1), 121-131.

Connolly, T., & Thorn, B. K. (1987). Predecisional information acquisition: Effects of task variables on suboptimal search strategies. *Organizational Behavior and Human Decision Processes*, *39*, 397-416.

Cooper, R. G. (1999). From experience: The invisible success factors in product development. *Journal of Product Innovation Management*, *16*, 115-133.

Cooper, R. G., & Kleinschmidt, E. J. (1987). Success factors in product innovation. *Industrial Marketing Management*, *16*, 215-223.

Cooper, R. G., & Kleinschmidt, E. J. (1995). New product performance: Keys to success, profitability and cycle time reduction. *Journal of Marketing Management*, *11*, 315-337.

Crawford, C. M. (1997). *New products management*. London: Irwin.

Dabholkar, P. A. (1994). Incorporating choice into an attitudinal framework: Analyzing models of mental comparison processes. *Journal of Consumer Research*, *21*, 100-118.

Einhorn, H., & Hogarth, R. (1981). Behavioral decision theory: Processes of judgement and choice. *Annual Review of Psychology*, *32*, 53-88.

Englis, B. G., & Solomon, M. R. (2000). LIFE/STYLE ONLINE: A web-based methodology for visually-oriented consumer research. *Journal of Interactive Marketing*, *14*(1), 2-14.

Eroglu, S. (1987). *The scenario method: A theoretical, not theatrical, approach.* American Marketing Association: Educators Proceedings.

Feldman, M. S., & March, J. G. (1981). Information in organizations as signal and symbol. *Administrative Science Quarterly, 26*, 171-186.

Frederickson, J. W. (1984). The comprehensiveness of strategic decision processes: Extension, observation, future directions. *Academy of Management Journal, 27*(3), 445-466.

Frederickson, J. W. (1985). Effects of decision motive and organizational performance level on strategic decision processes. *Academy of Management Journal, 28*(4), 821-843.

Hare, M., & Deadman, P. (2004). Further towards a taxonomy of agent-based simulation models in environmental management. *Mathematics and Computers in Simulation, 64*, 25-40.

Henard, D. H., & Szymanski, D. M. (2001). Why some new products are more successful than others. *Journal of Marketing Research, 38*, 362-375.

Jespersen, K. R. (2004). *Information and new product development decision-making.* Department of Marketing, Informatics and Statistics. Denmark: The Aarhus School of Business.

Jespersen, K. R. (2005). *Collecting real-time data with a behavioral simulation: A new methodological trait.* Paper presented at ECRM2005: Fourth European Conference on Research Methods in Business and Management, Universite Paris-Dauphine, Paris.

Klassen, R. D., & Jacobs, J. (2001). Experimental comparison of web, electronic and mail survey technologies in operations management. *Journal of Operations Management, 19*, 713-728.

Ma, T., & Nakamori, Y. (2005). Agent-based modeling on technological innovation as an evolutionary process. *European Journal of Operational Research, 166*(3), 741-755.

March, J. G., & Simon, H. A. (1993). *Organizations* (2nd ed.). Cambridge, MA: Blackwell.

Montoya-Weiss, M. M., & Calantone, R. (1994). Determinants of new product performance: A review and meta-analysis. *Journal of Product Innovation Management, 11*(5), 397-417.

Newell, A., & Simon, H. A. (1972). *Human problem solving.* Englewood Cliffs, NJ: Prentice-Hall.

Perkins, S. W., & Rao, R. C. (1990). The role of experience in information use and decision making by marketing managers. *Journal of Marketing Research, 27*, 1-10.

Potgieter, A., & Bishop, J. (2002). Bayesian agencies in control. In M. Mohammadian (Ed.), *Computational intelligence in control.* Hershey, PA: Idea Group Publishing.

Reips, U.-D. (2000). The web experiment method: Advantages, disadvantages, and solutions. In M. H. Birnbaum (Ed.), *Psychological experiments on the Internet.* San Diego, CA: Academic.

Sheehan, K. (2001). E-mail survey response rates: A review. *Journal of Computer Mediated Communication*, *6*(2), 1-19.

Souder, W. E. (1989). *Managing new product innovations*. Lexington, MA: Lexington Books.

Stanton, J. M. (1998). An empirical assessment of data collection using the Internet. *Personnel Psychology*, *51*(3), 709-725.

Wahle, J., Bazzan, A. L. C., Klügl, F., & Schrenkenberg, M. (2002). The impact of real-time information in a two-route scenario using agent-based simulation. *Transportation Research Part C*, *10*, 399-417.

White, J. C., Varadarajan, P. R., & Dacin, P. A. (2003). Marketing situation interpretation and response: The role of cognitive style, organizational culture, and information use. *Journal of Marketing*, *67*(3), 63-80.

Zaltman, G. (1997). Rethinking market research: Putting people back in. *Journal of Marketing Research*, *34*, 424-437.

Endnotes

[1] I want to thank the two blind reviewers for their useful and very constructive comments that helped improve this chapter.

[2] MacVic is a fully imaginary company invented for the simulation.

Section II

Marketing Applications

Chapter IV

Heuristic Genetic Algorithm for Product Portfolio Planning

Jianxin (Roger) Jiao, Nanyang Technological University, Singapore

Yiyang Zhang, Nanyang Technological University, Singapore

Yi Wang, Nanyang Technological University, Singapore

Abstract

This chapter applies the Genetic Algorithm to help manufacturing companies plan their product portfolio. Product portfolio planning (PPP) is a critical decision faced by companies across industries and is very important in helping manufacturing companies keep their competitive advantage. PPP has been classified as a combinatorial optimization problem, in that each company strives for the optimality of its product offerings through various combinations of products and/or attribute levels. Towards this end, this chapter develops a heuristic genetic algorithm (HGA) for solving the PPP problem. The objective of this chapter is to develop a practical method that can find near optimal solutions and assist marketing managers in product portfolio decision-making.

Introduction

To compete in the marketplace, manufacturers seek ways to expand their product lines and differentiate their product offerings, based on the intuitively appealing belief that large product variety will stimulate sales and thus be conducive to revenue growth (Ho & Tang, 1998). While a high variety strategy may offer effective means for companies to differentiate themselves from their competitors, it unavoidably leads to high complexity and costs in product fulfillment (Child, Diederichs, Sanders, & Wisniowski, 1991). Moreover, making a wide variety of products available and letting customers vote "on the shelf" may cause customers to be overwhelmed by the huge assortment offered or frustrated by the complexity involved in making a choice (Huffman & Kahn, 1998). Therefore, it becomes imperative for the manufacturer to determine how to offer the "right" product variety to the target market. Such decisions on the optimal number of product offerings to provide generally draw upon the general wisdom suggested in the Boston Consulting Group's notion of product portfolio strategy (Henderson, 1970). While representing the spectrum of a company's product offerings, the product portfolio must be carefully set up, planned and managed so as to match customer needs in the target market (Warren, 1983).

Product portfolio planning has been traditionally dealt with in the management and marketing fields, with a focus on portfolio optimization based on customer preferences. The objective is to maximize profit, share of choices, or sales (Urban & Hauser, 1993). Consequently, measuring customer preferences among multi-attribute alternatives has been a primary concern in marketing research. Of the many methods developed, conjoint analysis has turned out to be one of the most popular preference-based techniques for identifying and evaluating new product concepts (Green & Krieger, 1985). A number of conjoint-based models have been developed by those with particular interests in mathematical modelling techniques for optimal product line design (for example, Dobson & Kalish, 1993). These models seek to determine optimal product concepts using customers' idiosyncratic or segment-level part-worth (i.e., customer-perceived value of a particular level of an attribute) preference functions that are estimated within a conjoint framework (Steiner & Hruschka, 2002). While many methods offer the ability to determine optimal, or near-optimal, product designs from conjoint data, traditional conjoint analysis is limited to considering input from the customers only, rather than analyzing distinct conjoint data from both customers and engineering concerns.

In the engineering community, product portfolio decisions have been extensively studied with the primary focus on costs and flexibility issues associated with product variety and mix (for example, Lancaster, 1990). However the effect of product lines on the profit side of the equation has been seldom considered (Yano & Dobson, 1998). Few industries have developed an effective set of analysis techniques to manage the profit from variety and the costs from complexity simultaneously in product portfolio decision-making (Otto, Tang, & Seering, 2003). It is imperative to take into account the combined effects of multiple product offerings on both profit and engineering costs (Krishnan & Ulrich, 2001). Therefore, product portfolio planning should be positioned on the crossroad of engineering and marketing, where the interaction between the customer and engineering concerns is the linchpin (Markus & Váncza, 1998). In particular, portfolio decisions with customer-engineering interaction need to address the trade-offs between economies of scope in profit from the customers and markets and diseconomies of scope in design, production, and distribution at the backend of product fulfillment (Yano & Dobson, 1998).

Towards this end, this chapter examines the benefits of integrating the marketing implications of product portfolio planning with the engineering implications. A comprehensive methodology for product portfolio planning is developed, aiming at leveraging both customer and engineering concerns. A case study of notebook computer product portfolio planning is also reported.

Background Review

Various approaches to product line design have been reported in the literature. Most literature on product line design tackles the optimal selection of products by maximizing the surplus — the margin between the customer-perceived utility and the price of the product (Kaul & Rao, 1995). Other objectives widely used in selecting products among a large set of potential products include maximization of profit (Monroe, Sunder, Wells, & Zoltners, 1976), net present value (Li & Azarm, 2002), a seller's welfare (McBride & Zufryden, 1988), and market share within a target market (Kohli & Krishnamurti, 1987).

While numerous papers in the marketing literature deal with the selection problem using various objectives based on profit, few of them explicitly model the costs of manufacturing and engineering design (Yano & Dobson, 1998). Dobson and Kalish (1993) introduced per-product fixed costs, but more recent product line design models allow for more complex cost structures. Raman and Chhajed (1995) have observed that, in addition to choosing which products to produce, one must also choose the process by which these products are manufactured. Morgan, Daniels and Kouvelis (2001) have examined the benefits of integrating marketing implications of product mix with more detailed manufacturing cost implications, which sheds light on the impact of alternative manufacturing environment characteristics on the composition of the optimal product line.

Product line design involves two basic issues: generation of a set of feasible product alternatives and the subsequent selection of promising products from this reference set to construct a product line (Li & Azarm, 2002). Existing approaches to product line design can be classified into two categories (Steiner & Hruschka, 2002). One-step approaches aim at constructing product lines directly from part-worth preference and cost/return functions. On the other hand, two-step approaches first reduce the total set of feasible product profiles to a smaller set, and then select promising products from this smaller set to constitute a product line. Most literature follows the two-step approach with emphasis on the maximization of profit contributions in the second step (Dobson & Kalish, 1993; McBride & Zufryden, 1988). The determination of a product line from a reference set of products is thereby limited to partial models due to the underlying assumption that the reference set is given *apriori*. Following the two-step approach, Green and Krieger (1989) have introduced several heuristic procedures considering how to generate a reference set appropriately. On the other hand, Nair, Thakur, and Wen (1995) have adopted the one-step approach, in which product lines are constructed directly from part-worth data rather than by enumerating potential product designs. In general, the one-step approach is preferable, as the second step of enumerating utilities and profits of a large number of reference set items can be eliminated (Steiner & Hruschka, 2002). Only when the reference set contains a small number of product profiles can the two-step approach work well. As a result, few papers in marketing literature allow for a large number of attributes for describing a product (Yano & Dobson, 1998).

Problem Description

The product portfolio planning problem has the goal of maximizing an expected surplus from both the customer and engineering perspectives. More specifically, we consider a scenario with a large set of product attributes, $A \equiv \{a_k \mid k = 1, \cdots, K\}$, given that the firm has the capabilities (both design and production) to produce all these attributes. Each attribute possesses a few levels, discrete or continuous, that is, $A_k^* \equiv \{a_{kl}^* \mid l = 1, \cdots, L_k\}$. One advantage of using discrete levels is that it does not presume linearity with respect to the continuous variables (Train, 2003).

A set of potential product profiles, $Z \equiv \{\bar{z}_j \mid j = 1, \cdots, J\}$, is generated by choosing one of the levels for certain attributes, subjective to satisfying certain configuration constraints. Each product is defined as a vector of specific attribute levels, that is, $\bar{z}_j = \left[a_{kl_j}^* \right]_K$, where any $a_{kl_j}^* = \varnothing$ indicates that product $\bar{z}_j$ does not contain attribute a_k; and any $a_{kl_j}^* \neq \varnothing$ represents an element of the set of attribute levels that can be assumed by product $\bar{z}_j$. A product portfolio, Λ, is a set consisting of a few selected product profiles, i.e., $\Lambda \equiv \{\bar{z}_j \mid j = 1, \cdots, J^\dagger\} \subseteq Z$, $\exists J^\dagger \in \{1, \cdots, J\}$, denotes the number of products contained in the product portfolio.

Every product is associated with certain engineering costs, denoted as $\{C_j\}_J$. The manufacturer must make decisions to select what products to offer as well as their respective prices, $\{p_j\}_J$. As for portfolio decisions, the manufacturer must also determine what combinations of attributes and their levels should be introduced or should be discarded from a consideration of product offerings. This is different from traditional product line design, which involves the selection of products only, yet leaves the sets of attributes and their levels intact, and assumes the products are generated *a priori* by enumerating all possible attribute levels. In this sense, a one-step approach is adopted to the optimal product line design problem, because it excels in simultaneously optimizing product generation and selection facing a large number of combinations of attributes and their levels (Steiner & Hruschka, 2002).

There are multiple market segments, $S \equiv \{s_i \mid i = 1, \cdots, I\}$, each containing homogeneous customers, with a size, Q_i. The customer-engineering interaction is embodied in the decisions associated with customers' choices of different products. Various customer preferences on diverse products are represented by respective utilities, $\{U_{ij}\}_{I \cdot J}$. Product demands or market shares, $\{P_{ij}\}_{I \cdot J}$, are described by the probabilities of customers' choosing products, denoted as customer or segment-product pairs, $\{(s_i, \vec{z}_j)\}_{I \cdot J} \in S \times Z$.

Model Development

In customer preference or seller value-focused approaches, the objective functions widely used for solving the selection problem are formulated by measuring the consumer surplus — the amount that customers benefit by being able to purchase a product for a price that is less than they would be willing to pay. With more focus on engineering concerns, the selection problem is approached by measuring the producer surplus — the amount that producers benefit by selling at a market price that is higher than they would be willing to sell for. Considering the customer-engineering interaction in product portfolio planning, the above economic surpluses should be leveraged from both the customer and engineering perspectives. A shared surplus is proposed to leverage both the customer and engineering concerns. Then the model can be formulated as the following:

$$Maximize \quad E[V] = \sum_{i=1}^{I} \sum_{j=1}^{J} \left(\frac{U_{ij}}{\beta e^{\frac{3\sigma_j^T}{\mu_j^T - LSL^T}}} \right) \left(\frac{e^{\mu U_{ij}}}{\sum_{n=1}^{N} e^{\mu U_{in}}} \right) Q_i y_j , \qquad \textbf{(1a)}$$

$$\text{s.t.} \quad U_{ij} = \sum_{k=1}^{K+1} \sum_{l=1}^{L_k} \left(w_{jk} u_{ikl} x_{jkl} + \pi_j \right) + \varepsilon_{ij}, \quad \forall i \in \{1, \cdots, I\}, \forall j \in \{1, \cdots, J\}, \qquad \textbf{(1b)}$$

$$\sum_{l=1}^{L_k} x_{jkl} = 1, \qquad \forall j \in \{1, \cdots, J\}, \forall k \in \{1, \cdots, K+1\}, \qquad \textbf{(1c)}$$

$$\sum_{k=1}^{K+1} \sum_{l=1}^{L_k} \left| x_{jkl} - x_{j'kl} \right| > 0, \qquad \forall j, j' \in \{1, \cdots, J\}, j \neq j', \qquad \textbf{(1d)}$$

$$\sum_{j=1}^{J} y_j \leq J^{\dagger}, \qquad \forall J^{\dagger} \in \{1, \cdots, J\}, \qquad \textbf{(1e)}$$

$$x_{jkl}, y_j \in \{0,1\}, \qquad \forall j \in \{1, \cdots, J\}, \forall k \in \{1, \cdots, K+1\}, \forall l \in \{1, \cdots, L_k\}. \qquad \textbf{(1f)}$$

where u_{ikl} is the part-worth utility of segment s_i for the l-th level of attribute a_k (i.e., a_{kl}^{*}) individually, w_{jk} is the utility weights among attributes, $\{a_k\}_K$, contained in product $\vec{z}_j$, π_j is a constant associated with the derivation of a composite utility from part-worth utilities with respect to product $\vec{z}_j$, ε_{ij} is an error term for each segment-product pair,

x_{jkl} is a binary variable such that x_{jkl}=1 if the l-th level of attribute a_k is contained in product $\tilde{z}_j$ and x_{jkl}=0 otherwise, β is a constant indicating the average dollar cost per variation of process capabilities, LSL^T denotes the baseline of cycle times for all product variants to be produced within the process platform, μ_j^T and σ_j^T are the mean and the standard deviation of the estimated cycle time for product $\tilde{z}_j$, respectively.

Objective function (1a) is designed to maximize the expected shared surplus by offering a product portfolio consisting of products, $\{\tilde{z}_j\}_J$, to customer segments, $\{s_i\}_I$, each with size Q_i. Market potential, $\{Q_i\}_I$, can be given exogenously at the outset or estimated through a variety of techniques based on historical data or test markets (Lilien, Kotler, & Moorthy, 1992). Constraint (1b) refers to conjoint analysis — ensures that the composite utility of segment s_i for product $\tilde{z}_j$ can be constructed from part-worth utilities of individual attribute levels. Constraint (1c) suggests an exclusiveness condition — this enforces that exactly one and only one level of each attribute can be chosen for each product. Constraint (1d) denotes a divergence condition — requires that several products to be offered must pair-wise differ in at least one attribute level. Constraint (1e) indicates a capacity condition — limits the maximal number of products that can be chosen by each segment. It can be in an inequality or an equality form. In the case of an inequality constraint, $J^\dagger$ is the upper bound on the number of products that the manufacturer wants to introduce to a product portfolio, whereas, with an equality constraint, $J^\dagger$ is the exact number of products contained in a product portfolio. Constraint (1f) represents the binary restriction with regard to the decision variables of the optimization problem.

GA-Based Solution

In the above mathematical problem, there are two types of decision variables involved, that is, x_{jkl} and y_j, representing two layers of decision-making in portfolio planning, respectively. As a result, an optimal product portfolio, $\Lambda^\dagger \equiv \{\tilde{z}_j^\dagger \mid j = 1, \cdots, J^\dagger\}$ is yielded as a combination of selected products corresponding to $\{y_j \mid \forall j\}$, where each selected product, $\tilde{z}_j^\dagger$, comprises a few selected attributes and the associated levels corresponding to $\{x_{jkl} \mid \forall j, k, l\}$. As the number of attributes and levels associated with a product increases, so does the number of combinations of products. A product with nine attributes of three levels each may produce 3^9 = 19683 possible variants. A product portfolio consisting of a maximum of three such products may yield $(3^9)^3 + (3^9)^2 + (3^9)^1 = 7.62598 \times 10^{12}$ possible combinations. Complete enumeration to obtain optimal product selections in portfolio planning becomes prohibitive (Tarasewich & Nair, 2001). Comparing with traditional calculus-based or approximation optimization techniques, genetic algorithms (GA) have been proven to excel in solving combinatorial optimization problems (Steiner & Hruschka, 2002). The GA approach adopts a probabilistic search technique based on the principle of natural selection, (survival of the fittest) on the basis of objective function information, and thus is easily adjustable to different objectives with little algorithmic modification (Holland, 1992). Hence, a GA approach is employed in this chapter to solve the mixed integer program in Equations (1a) to (1f). A heuristic genetic algorithm is formulated below.

Generic Encoding

The first step in the implementation of a heuristic GA involves the representation of a problem to be solved with a finite-length string called a chromosome. A generic strategy for encoding the portfolio planning problem is illustrated in Figure 1. A product portfolio is represented by a chromosome consisting of a string. Each fragment of the chromosome (i.e., substring) represents a product contained in the portfolio. Each element of the string (gene) indicates an attribute of the product. The value assumed by a gene (allele) represents an index of the attribute level instantiated by an attribute. A portfolio (chromosome) consists of one to many products (fragments of chromosome), exhibiting a type of composition (AND) relationship. Likewise, each product (fragment of chromosome) comprises one to many attributes (genes). Nevertheless, each attribute (gene) can assume one and only one out of many possible attribute levels (alleles), suggesting an exclusive or (XOR) instantiation.

Given $J^{\dagger} \leq J$ products to be selected for a product portfolio, $\Lambda = \{\bar{z}_j\}_{J^{\dagger}}$, and $K+1$ attributes in each product, $\bar{z}_j$, a generic string of the chromosome is defined to be composed of J substrings, with $J - J^{\dagger}$ empty substrings corresponding to those unselected products, and contains a total number of $J \cdot (K+1)$ genes, with each substring consisting of $K+1$ genes.

Implementation Issues

Following the basic GA procedures (Gen & Cheng, 2000), the product portfolio planning problem in Equations (1a) to (1f) is solved iteratively, as depicted below.

(1) **Initialization:** Initialization involves generating initial solutions to the problem. The initial solutions can be generated either randomly or using some heuristic methods (Obitko, 2003). Considering the feasibility of product configurations, an initial population of product portfolios of size M, $\{\Lambda_m\}_M$, is determined *a priori* and accordingly M chromosome strings are encoded. Each chromosome string is assigned a fitness value in lieu of its expected shared surplus obtained by calculating Equation (1a).

(2) **Handling of configuration constraints:** In order to obtain feasible solutions, each chromosome must satisfy certain configuration constraints on the product genera-

Figure 1. Generic encoding for product portfolio

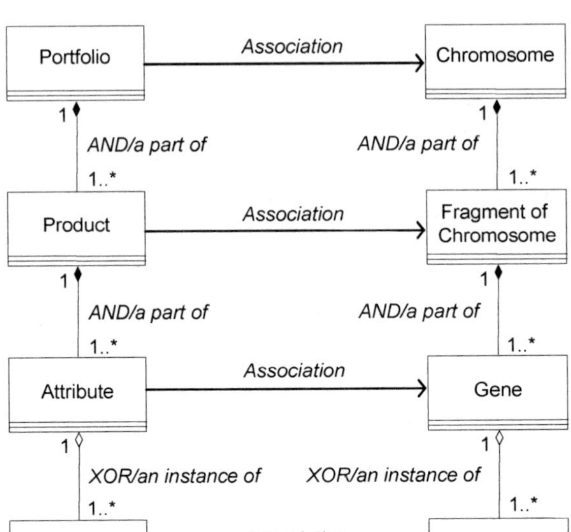

tion from combinations of attribute levels. These constitute two types of constraints: compatibility constraints and selection constraints. Compatibility constraints refer to the restrictions on choices of attribute levels (e.g., size compatible) and are generally described as IF THEN rules (Du, Jiao, & Tseng, 2001). Selection constraints refer to those conjoint, exclusiveness, divergence and capacity conditions as postulated in Equations (1b) to (1f). The chapter adopts a rejecting strategy. Whenever a new chromosome is generated, a constraint check is conducted with respect to all types of constraints, and only valid chromosomes are kept in the population.

(3) **Selection and reproduction:** The GA starts with the parent selection and reproduction process. Parent selection is a process that allocates reproductive opportunities throughout the chromosome population. While there are many selection rules available (Obitko, 2003), this chapter adopts the roulette wheel selection process. A reproduction probability is assigned to each chromosome based on its fitness value. Then the roulette wheel is filled using the respective cumulative probabilities of every chromosome. The areas of sections on the wheel depend on the fitness values of the associated chromosomes, with fitter chromosomes occupying larger areas in this biased roulette wheel, thus increasing their chances of survival. The roulette wheel selection can be implemented by generating random numbers between 0 and 1 in accordance with the cumulative reproduction probabilities (Obitko, 2003).

(4) **Crossover:** After reproduction, each two of the parent strings in the mating pool are picked randomly and each pair of strings undergoes crossover with a certain

probability. Cross-over requires two individual chromosomes to exchange parts of their genetic compositions. The offspring thus inherits some genes from both parents. While a number of cross-over operators are available for specific encoding schemes (Obitko, 2003), this chapter adopts a single-point random cross-over operator. Within a generic encoding chromosome, one cross-over point can be randomly located among genes (attributes) without causing conflict to product variety generation by configuring various attributes. With single-point cross-over, the integer string of an offspring is first copied from the first parent from the beginning until the cross-over point. Then the rest is added by copying from the second parent from the cross-over point to the end. The order of combination is reversed for the other offspring. In regard to the generic chromosome, there are $J \cdot (K+1) - 1$ cutting points.

(5) **Mutation:** Mutation is applied to each offspring individually after cross-over. The process randomly picks a gene within each string with a small probability (referred to as the mutation rate) and alters the corresponding attribute level at random. This process enables a small amount of random search, thus ensuring that the GA search does not quickly converge at a local optimum. But mutation should not occur very often, otherwise the GA becomes a purely random search method (Holland, 1992). While reproduction reduces the diversity of chromosomes in a population, mutation maintains a certain degree of heterogeneity of solutions, which is necessary to avoid premature convergence of the GA process (Steiner & Hruschka, 2002).

(6) **Termination:** The processes of cross-over and reproduction are repeated until the population converges or reaches a pre-specified number of generations. The number of generations has a direct consequence on the performance of the algorithm. A maximum number can be set ex ante at a large number. However, the algorithm may have found a solution before this number is ever reached. Then extra computations may be performed even after the solution has been found. Balakrishnan and Jacob (1996) have developed a moving average rule that can provide a good indication of convergence to a solution. Specifically, the GA process terminates if the average fitness of the best three strings of the current generation has increased by less than a threshold (the convergence rate) as compared with the average fitness of the best three strings over three immediate previous generations.

To reduce possible problems of termination by using either convergence or maximum number of generations alone, this chapter adopts a two-step stopping rule to incorporate both. A moving average rule is used for the first stopping check, and the maximum number of generations is specified as the criterion for the second stopping check. If the search is very complex (for example, in the case of a very tight convergence rate), the second stopping criterion helps avoid running the GA process infinitely. If the model can converge at the optimal solution within a few generations, then there is no need to run the maximum number of generations.

Case Study

The proposed framework has been applied to the notebook computer portfolio planning problem for a world-leading computer manufacturing company. Based on existing technologies, product offerings of notebook computers manifest themselves through various forms of a number of functional attributes. For illustrative simplicity, a set of key attributes and available attribute levels are listed in Table 1.

It is interesting to observe the importance of product portfolio planning in this case problem. Taking the "processor" attribute as an example, existing micro-electronics technologies have made it possible to achieve CPU performance ranging from Centrino 1.4 GHz up to Centrino 2.0 GHz. As a matter of fact, one of two existing competitors of the company does offer its products with a very finely discriminated product portfolio, including Centrino 1.4 GHz, 1.5 GHz, 1.6 GHz, 1.7 GHz, 1.8 GHz, and 2.0 GHz. On the other hand, the other competitor only offers Centrino 1.4 GHz, 1.8 GHz, and 2.0 GHz. It then becomes imperative to justify the most appropriate variety possible for the company's product portfolio, regardless of the fact that all of these attribute levels are technologically feasible.

Conjoint analysis starts with the construction of product profiles. A total number of 30 customers were selected to act as the respondents. Each respondent was asked to evaluate all 81 orthogonal profiles one-by-one by giving a mark based on a 9-point scale, where "9" means the customer prefers a product most and "1" least. This results in 30×81 groups of data. Based on these data, cluster analysis was run to find customer segments based on the similarity among customer preferences. Three customer segments were formed: s_1, s_2, and s_3, suggesting home users, regular users, and professional/business users, respectively. For each respondent in a segment, 81 regression equations were obtained by interpreting the original choice data as a binary instance of each part-worth utility. Each regression corresponds to a product profile and indicates the composition of the customer's original preference in terms of part-worth utilities according to Equation (1b). With these 81 equations, the part-worth utilities for this respondent were derived. Averaging the part-worth utility results of all respondents belonging to the same segment, a segment-level utility is obtained for each attribute level as shown in columns 2 to 4 in Table 2.

Table 2 also shows the part-worth standard times for all attribute levels. The company fulfilled customer orders through assembly-to-order production while importing all components and parts via global sourcing. The part-worth standard time of each attribute level was established based on work and time studies of the related assembly and testing operations. With assembly-to-order production, the company has identified and established standard routings as basic constructs of its process platform. Based on empirical studies, costing parameters are known as $LSL^T = 45$ (second) and $\beta = 0.004$.

To determine an optimal notebook computer portfolio for the target three segments, the GA procedure was applied to search for a maximum expected shared surplus among all attribute, product, and portfolio alternatives. Assume that each portfolio may consist of a maximal number of $J^{\dagger} = 5$ products. Then the chromosome string comprises 9×5 = 45

Table 1. List of attributes and their feasible levels for notebook computers

Attribute		Attribute Levels		
a_k	Description	a^*_{kl}	Code	Description
a_1	Processor	a^*_{11}	A1-1	Pentium 2.4 GHz
		a^*_{12}	A1-2	Pentium 2.6 GHz
		a^*_{13}	A1-3	Pentium 2.8 GHz
		a^*_{14}	A1-4	Centrino 1.4 GHz
		a^*_{15}	A1-5	Centrino 1.5 GHz
		a^*_{16}	A1-6	Centrino 1.6 GHz
		a^*_{17}	A1-7	Centrino 1.7 GHz
		a^*_{18}	A1-8	Centrino 1.8 GHz
		a^*_{19}	A1-9	Centrino 2.0 GHz
a_2	Display	a^*_{21}	A2-1	12.1" TFT XGA
		a^*_{22}	A2-2	14.1" TFT SXGA
		a^*_{23}	A2-3	15.4" TFT XGA/UXGA
a_3	Memory	a^*_{31}	A3-1	128 MB DDR SDRAM
		a^*_{32}	A3-2	256 MB DDR SDRAM
		a^*_{33}	A3-3	512 MB DDR SDRAM
		a^*_{34}	A3-4	1 GB DDR SDRAM
a_4	Hard Disk	a^*_{41}	A4-1	40 GB
		a^*_{42}	A4-2	60 GB
		a^*_{43}	A4-3	80 GB
		a^*_{44}	A4-4	120 GB
a_5	Disk Drive	a^*_{51}	A5-1	CD-ROM
		a^*_{52}	A5-2	CD-RW
		a^*_{53}	A5-3	DVD/CD-RW Combo
a_6	Weight	a^*_{61}	A6-1	Low (below 2.0 KG with battery)
		a^*_{62}	A6-2	Moderate (2.0 - 2.8 KG with battery)
		a^*_{63}	A6-3	High (2.8 KG above with battery)
a_7	Battery Life	a^*_{71}	A7-1	Regular (around 6 hours)
		a^*_{72}	A7-2	Long (7.5 hours above)
a_8	Software	a^*_{81}	A8-1	Multimedia package
		a^*_{82}	A8-2	Office package
a_9	Price	a^*_{91}	A9-1	Less than $800
		a^*_{92}	A9-2	$800 - $1.3K
		a^*_{93}	A9-3	$1.3K - $1.8K
		a^*_{94}	A9-4	$1.8K - $2.5K
		a^*_{95}	A9-5	$2.5K above

genes. Each substring is as long as 9 genes and represents a product that constitutes the portfolio.

During the reproduction process, new product and portfolio alternatives keep being generated through cross-over and mutation operations. Using a constraint check, only valid chromosomes are passed on for further evaluation. For every generation, a population size of $M = 20$ is maintained, meaning that only the top 20 fit product portfolios are kept for reproduction.

Table 2. Part-worth utilities and part-worth standard times

Attribute Level	Part-worth Utility (Customer Segment)			Part-worth Standard Time (Assembly & Testing Operations)	
	s_1	s_2	s_3	μ^t (second)	σ^t (second)
A1-1	0.75	0.65	0.62	497	9.5
A1-2	0.77	0.83	0.82	536	11
A1-3	0.81	0.78	1.18	563	12
A1-4	0.74	0.66	0.61	512	10.5
A1-5	0.77	0.86	0.89	556	11.8
A1-6	0.78	0.77	1.16	589	21
A1-7	0.81	0.79	1.18	598	21.1
A1-8	0.83	0.82	1.21	615	22.3
A1-9	0.84	0.85	1.22	637	24
A2-1	1.18	1.05	0.75	739	35
A2-2	1.21	1.47	1.18	819	37
A2-3	1.25	1.49	1.38	836	39
A3-1	1.02	0.5	0.4	659	24.5
A3-2	1.09	0.9	0.65	699	26.5
A3-3	1.12	1.15	0.93	725	32
A3-4	1.14	1.18	1.11	756	36
A4-1	1.33	0.97	0.63	641	26
A4-2	1.38	1.08	0.78	668	28
A4-3	1.52	1.13	1.08	707	29
A4-4	1.56	1.19	1.22	865	40
A5-1	0.86	0.93	0.78	293	4.4
A5-2	0.88	1.11	0.82	321	5.1
A5-3	0.92	1.35	0.83	368	5.5
A6-1	0.7	0.2	0.3	215	3.8
A6-2	0.9	0.7	0.8	256	4.0
A6-3	1.1	0.9	0.9	285	4.1
A7-1	0.7	0.6	0.3	125	1.6
A7-2	0.8	0.9	1.2	458	19.1
A8-1	1.2	1.1	1.2	115	1.55
A8-2	0.5	0.8	1.0	68	0.95
A9-1	0	0	0	N.A.	N.A.
A9-2	-1.75	-0.35	-0.2		
A9-3	-2.25	-0.65	-0.47		
A9-4	-2.75	-2.48	-0.6		
A9-5	-3.5	-3.3	-0.95		

The results of the GA solution are presented in Figure 2. As shown in Figure 2, the fitness value continues to improve through the reproduction process generation by generation. Certain local optima (e.g., around 100 generations) are successfully overcome. The saturation period (350-500 generations) is quite short, indicating the GA search is efficient. This proves that the moving average rule is a reasonable convergence measure. It helps avoid the potential problem that the GA procedure may run unnecessarily long for as many as 1,000 generations. Upon termination at the 495th generation, the GA solver returns the optimal result, which achieves an expected shared surplus of 802K, as shown in Table 3.

As shown in Table 3, the optimal product portfolio consists of two products, $\bar{z}_1^1$ and $\bar{z}_2^1$. From the specifications of attribute levels, we can see they basically represent the low-end and high-end notebook computers, respectively. With such a two-product portfolio, all home, regular and professional/business users can be served with an optimistic expectation of maximizing the shared surplus. While low-end notebook computer $\bar{z}_1^1$ includes all available attributes, high-end notebook computer $\bar{z}_2^1$ does not contain the "software" attribute. This may reflect the fact that most professionals prefer to install

Figure 2. Shared surpluses among generations

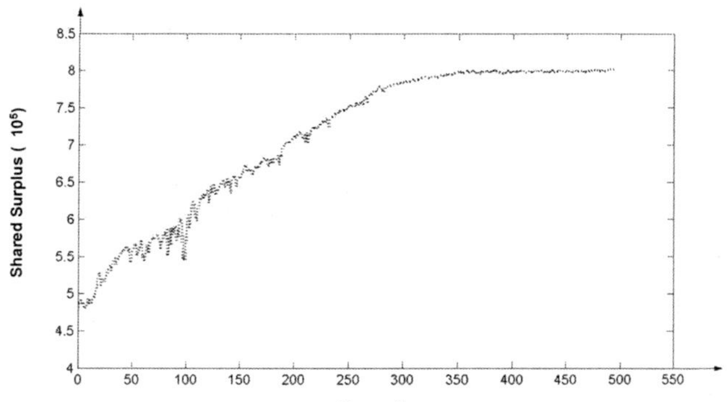

Table 3. Optimal solution of notebook computer portfolio

Product Portfolio $\Lambda^{\dagger}$	$\Lambda^{\dagger} = [1,2,1,1,1,3,1,1,2;8,3,3,3,3,1,2,0,4;0,0,0,0,0,0,0,0,0;0,0,0,0,0,0,0,0,0;0,0,0,0,0,0,0,0,0]$			
Constituent Products $\{\bar{z}_j^{\dagger}\}_{J^{\dagger}}$	$\bar{z}_1^{1} = [1,2,1,1,1,3,1,1,2]$		$\bar{z}_2^{1} = [8,3,3,3,3,1,2,0,4]$	
Attributes $\{a_k^{\dagger}\}_{(K+1)^{\dagger}}$ Attribute Levels $\{a_{kl}^{*}\}_{(K+1)^{\dagger}}$	$a_k^{\dagger}$	a_{kl}^{*}	$a_k^{\dagger}$	a_{kl}^{*}
	Processor	Pentium 2.4 GHz	Processor	Centrino 1.8 GHz
	Display	14.1" TFT SXGA	Display	15.4" TFT XGA/UXGA
	Memory	128 MB DDR SDRAM	Memory	512 MB DDR SDRAM
	Hard Disk	40 GB	Hard Disk	80 GB
	Disk Drive	CD-ROM	Disk Drive	DVD/CD-RW Combo
	Weight	High (2.8 KG above)	Weight	Low (below 2.0 KG)
	Battery Life	Regular (around 6 hours)	Battery Life	Long (7.5 hours above)
	Software	Multimedia package	$\varnothing$	Nil
	Price	$800 - $1.3K	Price	$1.8K - $2.5K
Expected Shared Surplus $E[V^{\dagger}]$	802K			

software authorized by their business organizations for the purpose of, for example, systems maintenance and technical support.

Conclusion

This chapter describes a process that allows products to be constructed directly from attribute-level, part-worth utilities and costs. The shared surplus model accounts both for diverse customer preferences across market segments and engineering costs that vary with the composition of a product portfolio. By integrating marketing inputs with detailed cost information obtained through coordinated product and process platforms, the model captures the trade-offs between the benefits derived from providing variety to the marketplace, and the cost savings that can be realized by selecting a mix of products that can be produced efficiently within a company's manufacturing capabilities.

A heuristic genetic algorithm was developed and applied to solve the combinatorial optimization problem involved in product portfolio planning. The study indicates that the GA works efficiently in searching for optimal product portfolio solutions. Although the model was used to solve a seller's problem of introducing a new product portfolio with the objective of maximal shared surplus, the proposed framework could easily be adjusted to handle such complex problems as maximizing share-of-choices and extending an existing product portfolio by allowing for already existing items developed by the seller. This is supported by the flexibility of the GA procedure that merely uses objective function information and, therefore, is capable of accommodating different fitness criteria without any substantial modification of the algorithm.

As shown in the case study, the strength of the GA lies in its ability to carry out repeated iterations without major changes of parameter values or defining different initial populations, thus improving the chance of finding an optimal or at least a near-optimal solution. It is also possible to insert solutions obtained from other techniques into the initial population. Hence, rather than testing all of the alternatives of the initial population at random, the GA can use prior knowledge about potential optima to arrange the initial population or improve on an existing solution. This can perform as a kind of lower bound or benchmark for GA performance.

In the case study, we tested the performance of the proposed heuristic GA on a small- to medium-sized problem. Although we do not know how well the heuristic GA would perform on large problems in an absolute sense, we believe, given the popularity of high performance computation, what is important is not the computational efficiency of GA, but the quality of solutions returned by the GA procedure. The heuristic GA can also provide high flexibility with regard to the final decision making of a product portfolio. For example, the decision-maker may be provided with quite a number of solutions using similar high fitness values that reach his or her expectations. In this way, the decision-maker can select additional fitness criteria to select the best product portfolio.

References

Balakrishnan, P. V. S., & Jacob, V. S. (1996). Genetic algorithms for product design. *Management Science*, *42*, 1105-1117.

Child, P., Diederichs, R., Sanders, F. H., & Wisniowski, S. (1991). SMR forum: The management of complexity. *Sloan Management Review*, *33*, 73-80.

Dobson, G., & Kalish, S. (1993). Heuristics for pricing and positioning a product-line using conjoint and cost data. *Management Science*, *39*, 160-175.

Du, X., Jiao, J., & Tseng, M. M. (2001). Architecture of product family: Fundamentals and methodology. *Concurrent Engineering: Research and Application*, *9*, 309-325.

Gen, M., & Cheng, R. (2000). *Genetic algorithms and engineering optimization*. New York: John Wiley.

Green, P. E., & Krieger, A. M. (1985). Models and heuristics for product line selection. *Marketing Science*, *4*, 1-19.

Green, P. E., & Krieger, A. M. (1989). Recent contributions to optimal product positioning and buyer segmentation. *European Journal of Operational Research*, *41*, 127-141.

Henderson, B. D. (1970). *The product portfolio*. Boston: Boston Consulting Group.

Ho, T. H., & Tang, C. S. (1998). *Product variety management: Research advances*. London: Kluwer Academic.

Holland, J. H. (1992). *Adaptation in natural and artificial systems*. Cambridge, MA: MIT.

Huffman, C., & Kahn, B. (1998). Variety for sale: Mass customization or mass confusion. *Journal of Retailing*, *74*, 491-513.

Kaul, A., & Rao, V. R. (1995). Research for product positioning and design decisions: An integrative review. *International Journal of Research in Marketing*, *12*, 293-320.

Kohli, R., & Krishnamurti, R. (1987). A heuristic approach to product design. *Management Science*, *33*, 1523-1533.

Krishnan, V., & Ulrich, K. (2001). Product development decisions: a review of the literature. *Management Science*, *47*, 1-21.

Lancaster, K. (1990). The economics of product variety: A survey. *Marketing Science*, *9*, 189-211.

Li, H., & Azarm, S. (2002). An approach for product line design selection under uncertainty and competition. *Transactions of the ASME Journal of Mechanical Design*, *124*, 385-392.

Lilien, G. L., Kotler, P., & Moorthy, K. S. (1992). *Marketing models*. NJ: Prentice-Hall.

Markus, A., & Váncza, J. (1998). Product line development with customer interaction. *CIRP Annals*, *47*, 361-364.

McBride, R. D., & Zufryden, F. S. (1988). An integer programming approach to the optimal product line selection problem. *Marketing Science, 7*, 126-140.

Monroe, K., Sunder, S., Wells, W. A., & Zoltners, A. A. (1976). A multi-period integer programming approach to the product mix problem. In K. L. Bernhardt (Ed.), *Marketing 1776-1976 and Beyond: 1976 Educator Proceedings, Series #39* (pp. 493-497). Chicago: American Marketing Association.

Morgan, L. O., Daniels, R. L., & Kouvelis, P. (2001). Marketing/manufacturing tradeoffs in product line management. *IIE Transactions*, *33*(11), 949-962.

Nair, S. K., Thakur, L. S., & Wen, K. (1995). Near optimal solutions for product line design and selection: beam search heuristics. *Management Science*, *41*, 767-785.

Obitko, M. (2003). *Introduction to genetic algorithms*. Retrieved May 15, 2005, from http://cs.felk.cvut.cz/~xobitko/ga/

Otto, K., Tang, V., & Seering, W. (2003). *Establishing quantitative economic value for features and functionality of new products and new services*. MIT PDMA Toolbook II, Retrieved May 15, 2005, from http://hdl.handle.net/1721.1/3821

Raman, N., & Chhajed, D. (1995). Simultaneous determination of product attributes and prices and production processes in product-line design. *Journal of Operations Management*, *12*, 187-204.

Steiner, W. J., & Hruschka, H. (2002). A probabilistic one-step approach to the optimal product line design problem using conjoint and cost data. *Review of Marketing Science Working Papers, 1*, Working Paper 4. Retrieved May 15, 2005, from http://www.bepress.com/roms/vol1/iss4/paper4

Tarasewich, P., & Nair, S. K. (2001). Designer-moderated product design. *IEEE Transactions on Engineering Management, 48*, 175-188.

Train, K. E. (2003). *Discrete choice methods with simulation*. Cambridge, UK: Cambridge University.

Urban, G. L., & Hauser, J. R. (1993). *Design and marketing of new products*. Englewood Cliffs, NJ: Prentice-Hall.

Warren, A. A. (1983). *Optimal control of the product portfolio*. Unpublished doctoral dissertation, University of Texas at Austin.

Yano, C., & Dobson, G. (1998). Profit optimizing product line design, selection and pricing with manufacturing cost considerations. In T. H. Ho (Ed.), *Product variety management: Research advances* (pp. 145-176). London: Kluwer Academic.

Chapter V

Modeling Brand Choice Using Boosted and Stacked Neural Networks

Rob Potharst, Erasmus University Rotterdam, The Netherlands

Michiel van Rijthoven, Oracle Nederland BV, The Netherlands

Michiel C. van Wezel, Erasmus University Rotterdam, The Netherlands

Abstract

Starting with a review of some classical quantitative methods for modeling customer behavior in the brand choice situation, some new methods are explained which are based on recently developed techniques from data mining and artificial intelligence: boosting and/or stacking neural network models. The main advantage of these new methods is the gain in predictive performance that is often achieved, which in a marketing setting directly translates into increased reliability of expected market share estimates. The new models are applied to a well-known data set containing scanner data on liquid detergent purchases. The performance of the new models on this data set is compared with results from the marketing literature. Finally, the developed models are applied to some practical marketing issues such as predicting the effect of different pricing schemes upon market share.

Introduction

A classical topic in marketing is modeling brand choice. This amounts to setting up a predictive model for the following situation: to purchase a specific product available in *k* brands, a consumer or household chooses one of these brands; the prediction of this choice is based on a number of household characteristics (such as income), product factors (such as price) and situational factors (such as whether or not the product is on display at purchase time). In the past, numerous different models have been proposed for brand choice problems. The best known models are the conditional and multinomial logit models (Franses & Paap, 2001; McFadden, 1973).

During the last decade, methods from computational intelligence, such as neural networks, have been proposed as an alternative to these classical models (Hruschka, 1993; West, Brockett, & Golden, 1997). A recent contribution to the neural networks for brand choice literature is a paper by Vroomen, Franses, and van Nierop (2004) in which neural networks are used to model a two-stage brand choice process: first a household chooses a so-called consideration set (i.e., a sub-set of the available brands which are most interesting for the consumer), and then the household selects a brand from this consideration set (Roberts & Lattin, 1997).

Another line of research which became very popular during the last decade, both in the statistics and in the computational intelligence community, is the use of ensemble methods such as boosting, bagging and stacking (Hastie, Tibshirani, & Friedman, 2001; Rijthoven, 2004; Schwenk & Bengio, 2000; Tibshirani, Friedman, & Hastie, 2000). These methods work by building not one model for a particular problem, but a whole series (ensemble) of models. These models are subsequently combined to give the final model that is to be used. The main advantage of these ensemble techniques is the sometimes spectacular increase in predictive performance that can be achieved. The predictive performance of a marketing model is a crucial factor for its successful application, since an increase in prediction accuracy causes increased reliability of market share estimates, which may have a substantial effect on the expected turnover of competing firms. In marketing, ensemble methods are proposed in a forthcoming paper by two of the authors of this chapter (van Wezel & Potharst, 2005). Stacked neural networks for customer choice modeling were also applied in Hu and Tsoukalas (2003). The use of boosted neural networks in another application area (character recognition) is described in Schwenk and Bengio (2000).

In this chapter we will explain some of these ensemble methods (especially boosting and stacking) and use them by combining the results of a series of neural networks for a specific brand choice problem. All methods presented will be demonstrated on an existing set of scanner data which has been extensively analyzed in the marketing literature: the A.C. Nielsen household scanner panel data on purchases of liquid detergents in a Sioux Falls, South Dakota, market. This dataset contains 3,055 purchases concerning 400 households of six different brands of liquid detergent: Tide, Wisk, Eraplus, Surf, Solo and All. In addition, possible use of these methods by marketing managers is demonstrated in a special section on market share simulations.

Summarizing, this chapter contains:

- a brief description of classical models for brand choice in the next section;
- a detailed description of how neural networks with one hidden layer may be used to model a brand choice problem, including a discussion of the features to be selected as explaining characteristics in the third section;
- an explanation of how the concept of a consideration set can be modeled using a specific kind of hidden layer for the neural network, also in the third section;
- a description of the real life scanner data set that is used as the running example in the fourth section;
- an exposition on the ensemble methods of boosting and stacking, applied to the neural network models considered above in the fifth section;
- demonstrations of all methods described, including a discussion on the adaptations that were devised within the framework of this particular marketing problem, and a comparison of the performance of all models, in the sixth section;
- a number of market share simulations that make use of the developed models to show how marketing managers might employ the proposed methods, in the seventh section; and
- a concluding section which also contains an outline of some possible future trends.

Modeling Brand Choice: Classical Models

A classical problem in marketing is the so-called *brand choice* problem: trying to model the purchase behavior of a consumer given a number of explanatory variables. At purchase occasion i a consumer is faced with a choice between J brands $1, 2, \ldots, J$ of a product he or she is going to buy. The final choice Y_i (which must be one of the brands $1,\ldots, J$) depends on three kinds of variables. The first kind of variable depends on the consumer or the purchase occasion, but not on the brand, for instance consumer income. We will denote such a variable by a capital X, so for instance the income of the consumer that purchases on occasion i is denoted by X_i. The second kind of variable depends only on brand, not on purchase time and consumer. We will denote such a variable by a capital Z, so for instance the brand awareness of brand j is Z_j. The third group of variables depends both on consumer/purchase occasion and on brand. These variables are denoted by capital W, so for instance the price of the product of brand j that the consumer has to pay on purchase occasion i is W_{ij}.

Many models have been proposed for the brand choice problem in the marketing literature. In this section four representative models will be described. We start with the *multinomial logit* model. According to this model, $\Pr[Y_i = j \mid X_i]$, the probability that on occasion i a consumer chooses brand j, given the value of the explanatory variable X_i, has the following hypothesized functional form: for $j = 1, \ldots, J-1$ we have

$$\Pr[Y_i = j \mid X_i] = \frac{\exp(\alpha_j + \beta_j X_i)}{1 + \sum_{j=1}^{J-1} \exp(\alpha_j + \beta_j X_i)}$$

and

$$\Pr[Y_i = J \mid X_i] = \frac{1}{1 + \sum_{j=1}^{J-1} \exp(\alpha_j + \beta_j X_i)}.$$

Note that, whatever the values of the parameters α_j and β_j and whatever the value of X_i, the sum of these probabilities over all brands equals one. Note further that only variables of type X play a role in this type of model, variables of type W or Z are excluded. When purchase data is given, one may estimate the parameters α_j and β_j of this model by maximum likelihood methods.

The second kind of model we will mention is the *conditional logit* model, originally proposed by McFadden (1973). For this model the probability that brand j is chosen equals, for j = 1, … , J

$$\Pr[Y_i = j \mid W_{i1},\dots,W_{iJ}] = \frac{\exp(\alpha_j + \beta W_{ij})}{\sum_{j=1}^{J} \exp(\alpha_j + \beta W_{ij})}.$$

Note again that the sum over all probabilities equals one, and in this type of model we have only variables of type W; here variables of type X and Z are excluded. Note also that parameter β does not have an index: the sensitivity for price-changes is supposed to be equal for all brands. This constraint may be relaxed using the model discussed next. Again, the parameters may be estimated using maximum likelihood.

The third model is the *general logit* model in which all three variable types (X, W and Z) may play a role. For this model the probability that brand j is chosen equals,

for j = 1, … , J

$$\Pr[Y_i = j \mid X_i, W_{i1},\dots,W_{iJ}, Z_1,\dots,Z_J] = \frac{\exp(\alpha_j + \beta_j X_i + \gamma_j W_{ij} + \delta Z_j)}{\sum_{j=1}^{J} \exp(\alpha_j + \beta_j X_i + \gamma_j W_{ij} + \delta Z_j)}.$$

Note that not only all three variable types are incorporated in this model, but also variable W has a brand-specific coefficient, which relaxes the mentioned constraint of the conditional logit model.

Modeling Brand Choice: Neural Network Models

In addition to the statistical models introduced in the previous section, brand choice can also be modeled using neural networks. This is a technique that was put forward at the end of the 1980s in the machine learning community, and its popularity soon grew in many very diverse fields, from linguistics to engineering, from marketing to medicine. Neural network models have been proposed for the brand choice problem by several authors (Dasgupta, Dispensa, & Ghose, 1994; Hruschka, 1993; Hruschka, Fettes, Probst, & Mies, 2002; Hu, Shanker, & Hung, 1999; Vroomen et al., 2004; West et al., 1997). The neural network methodology is clearly explained in the first chapter of the introductory book by Smith and Gupta (2002). This work also contains a number of other applications of neural network methodology to marketing problems, such as Potharst, Kaymak, and Pijls (2002).

We will introduce neural network modeling for the brand choice problem on the basis of a recently proposed neural network model that makes use of so-called *consideration sets* (Vroomen et al., 2004). Let us first review the theory on considerations sets. To this purpose, the process of choosing a product of a particular brand is viewed as consisting of two stages. In the first stage, the consumer reduces the set of available brands to a smaller sub-set: this sub-set is the consideration set that will exclusively be considered when the consumer makes his or her final choice. In the second stage the consumer picks his or her final choice from the brands that reside in the consideration set (Roberts & Lattin, 1997). Vroomen et al. (2004) make use of a neural network with one hidden layer to model this two-stage process. Their model can be visualized as follows:

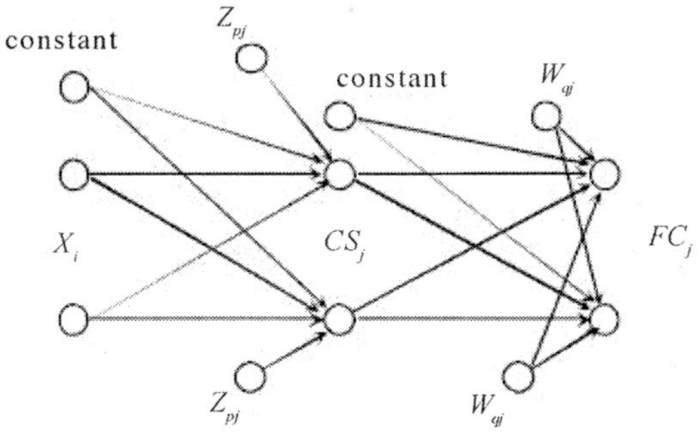

As can be seen from this graph the network consists of three layers of nodes; roughly spoken, there is an input layer, followed by a hidden layer in which the consideration set (*CS*) is modeled, and an output layer that models the probability of the final choice for a brand (*FC*). Three types of input variables are used: household characteristics (X_i) such as size of household or income level, brand characteristics (Z_{pj}) such as price, promotion and advertising, and finally choice- and brand-specific characteristics (W_{qj}) such as the observed price at the purchase occasion. Let the number of X-type variables be I, the number of Z-type variables P and the number of W-type variables Q. For each of the J brands there is a sigmoidal hidden node CS_j, that determines the probability that brand j is in the consideration set, as follows. For $j = 1,\ldots, J$

$$CS_j = G(\alpha_{0j} + \sum_{i=1}^{I} \alpha_{ij} X_i + \sum_{p=1}^{P} \beta_{pj} Z_{pj})$$

where the coefficients α_{0j}, α_{ij} and β_{pj} are parameters that must be estimated from the data and G is the logistic (or sigmoidal) function

$$G(x) = \frac{1}{1+e^{-x}}.$$

Next, in the second part of the network model, the probability of the final choice (FC_j) is determined using the consideration set, as follows. For $j = 1,\ldots, J$

$$FC_j = \frac{\exp(\gamma_{0j} + \sum_{k=1}^{J} \gamma_{kj} CS_k + \sum_{q=1}^{Q} \delta_{qj} W_{qj})}{\sum_{m=1}^{J} \exp(\gamma_{0m} + \sum_{k=1}^{J} \gamma_{km} CS_k + \sum_{q=1}^{Q} \delta_{qm} W_{qm})},$$

where again the coefficients γ_{0j}, γ_{kj} and δ_{qj} are parameters that must be estimated from the data. The final outcome of the neural network is the brand j that gets the largest probability FC_j. In (Vroomen et al., 2004) all these parameters are estimated (or, in the usual idiom, the network is trained) by using the back-propagation algorithm, which is based on gradient descent.

The Data Set: Scanner Data for Six Liquid Detergent Brand

The data set we use to test our methods is the data set also used by Vroomen et al. (2004), which is described by Chintagunta and Prasad (1998). This data set is freely available on the Internet. It consists of scanner data on 3,055 purchases of a liquid detergent of six possible brands: Tide, Wisk, Eraplus, Surf, Solo and All. These purchases concern 400 different households. For each purchase, the values of four different household-specific variables (X_i) are available ($I = 4$), furthermore there are four brand-specific variables (Z_{pj}, so $P = 4$) and three extra variables (W_{qj}, so $Q = 3$) Specifically, we have the following set of variables:

X_1 = the total volume the household purchased on the previous purchase occasion
X_2 = the total expenditure of the household on non-detergents
X_3 = the size of the household
X_4 = the inter-purchase time
Z_{1j} = the price of brand j in cents per ounce
Z_{2j} = 1 or 0 according to whether brand j was on feature promotion or not
Z_{3j} = 1 or 0 according to whether brand j was on display promotion or not
Z_{4j} = an indication of how recently brand j was purchased (between 0 and 1)
W_{1j} = 1 or 0 according to whether the household bought brand j on the previous purchase occasion, or not
W_{2j} = 1 or 0 according to whether brand j was the brand most purchased over all previous purchase occasions, or not
W_{3j} = the fraction of recent purchases of brand j by the household divided by the total of all recent purchases of any detergent by the household

For a complete description of these variables, see Vroomen et al. (2004). Because of incompleteness of some of the records, we eliminated 798 of them, so we have 3,055-798 = 2,257 complete records available. All non-binary variables were scaled to the [0, 1] interval in order to make all scales comparable.

Ensemble Methods: Bagging, Boosting, and Stacking

In recent years there has been a growing interest in the data mining and statistics communities in so-called ensemble methods. These methods, also known as committee

Figure 1. Effect of combining models on the prediction accuracy

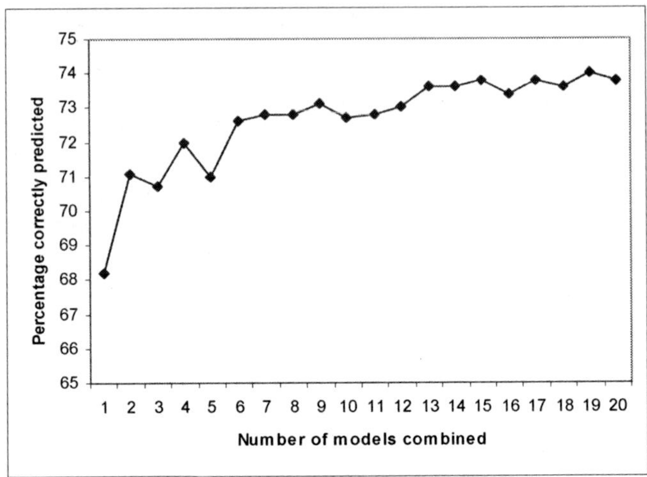

methods or opinion pools, work by combining different individual models (also called *base* models) for the same problem. A great advantage of these methods is the gain in predictive performance that is often achieved by applying them. We illustrate this argument with the following example (see Figure 1), based on a credit scoring data set which is freely available on the Internet. The problem which is addressed is to predict at the time of application for a loan whether the loan would ever be repaid or not. As can be seen from the graph below the error rate of such predictions drops from 32% when only one model is used to 25% when a combination of 20 models is used to predict the outcome.

Three of the best-known ensemble methods are bagging, boosting and stacking (Hastie et al., 2001). *Bagging* is shorthand for "bootstrap aggregating" and it works roughly as follows: from the data set we draw a random sample[1] (of the same size as the original data set) with replacement and build a model using only the data from this sample. A second model is built using only the data from a second random sample drawn from the original data set, and so on. In this manner we arrive at a number of base models which are subsequently combined by casting votes. For instance, for an ensemble of 10 models, if for a certain input vector, 5 of the models predict brand 3, 2 models predict brand 1 and the remaining three models predict brand 2, the combined model predicts brand 3 (the majority of the votes). Since we will not use this method in this chapter we will not outline the exact algorithm for this method.

The second method we consider is *boosting*. The general idea of boosting is to create a sequence of models, where each model is trained on a re-weighted version of the original data set. Each training example in the data set is assigned a weight and these weights are dynamically adjusted: when the model in a certain iteration of the algorithm makes an error in the classification of the n-th training pattern, the weight associated with this pattern is increased. This causes the model of the next iteration to focus on the patterns that were misclassified earlier. Continuing this way, an ensemble of models is created. The final model is a weighted majority vote of all the models from the ensemble.

The original boosting algorithm is called AdaBoost (Freund & Schapire, 1996), and we will now give an exact description of this algorithm. The original version of this algorithm is meant for two-class problems, where the classes are called −1 and +1. Since in the case of the brand choice problem we will not work with only two brands but with any number (J) of brands, we will have to adapt this algorithm to our needs. This adaptation will be described in the next section. Let us assume we have a dataset consisting of N data pairs (x_i, y_i), where x_i is a vector of input values and y_i the corresponding class value (either +1 or −1). In the description of the algorithm we will use the following notation: w_i is the weight of the i-th data pair, M is the number of boosting iterations (so the ensemble will consist of M models), $\chi(A)$ is an indicator function for Boolean arguments A, which equals 1 if A is true and 0 if A is false. The function $\text{sgn}(x) = 1$ if $x \geq 0$ and -1 if $x < 0$. Note further that $F_m(x)$ can be any model based on the data, whether it be a statistical model, a neural network or a decision tree.

Here is the AdaBoost algorithm:

1. Initialize the boosting weights: for $i = 1, \ldots, N$

$$w_i = \frac{1}{N}$$

2. For $m = 1$ to M perform each of the following:

   (a) Train the base-model $F_m(x)$ on the dataset with weights $\{w_i : i = 1, \ldots, N\}$

   (b) Compute

$$err_m = \sum_{i=1}^{N} w_i \chi(y_i \neq F_m(x_i))$$

   (c) Compute

$$\alpha_m = \log\left(\frac{1 - err_m}{err_m}\right) \quad (1)$$

(d) Redefine the weights w_i : for $i = 1, \ldots, N$

$$w_i = w_i \exp(\alpha_m \chi(y_i \neq F_m(x_i)))$$

(e) Normalize the weights w_i : for $i = 1, \ldots, N$

$$w_i = \frac{w_i}{\sum_{k=1}^{N} w_k}$$

3. Output the final combined model:

$$O(x) = \text{sgn}(\sum_{m=1}^{M} \alpha_m F_m(x)) \tag{2}$$

Let us take a look at this algorithm somewhat more closely to see how it works. First of all, in step 2(a), it is assumed that we are able to train a model on a data set containing observations (purchases!) that each have a different weight. This can be implemented in several ways. We used the so-called resampling method which will be explained below. In step 2(b) the error rate err_m of the model built in the previous step is calculated. This is the in-sample training error rate that allows for different weights in the dataset. Using this error rate, in step 2(c) the α_m coefficient is calculated. Provided the error rate < 0.5 (which it should be if the model does better than random guessing), this coefficient will be a positive number that increases if the error rate decreases. This α_m coefficient will be used in step 3 to weigh the votes from different models: the votes of models with lower error rates get a higher weight than those from models that perform less well. In step 2(d) the weights of the samples in the data set are updated: for each sample that is classified incorrectly its weight is increased with the same factor that involves the α_m coefficient. The weights of correctly classified samples remain unchanged. In step 2(e) the weights are normalized (they should sum to one). Finally, in step 3 the whole ensemble of models developed is combined using the weighted voting scheme as described.

The third ensemble method we consider is *stacking*. This term is usually referred to when there are two levels of learning involved: on the first level several models are trained on the data set. These may be models of different types. Next, the models are combined, not via a fixed voting scheme, but by learning an optimal combination method from the data. This is the second level of learning involved. Of course, such a stacking scheme can be implemented in many different ways. We will use a simple stacking scheme (designed by us) that is built on top of our boosting procedure: instead of combining the models from the boosting ensemble directly via Step 3, we will learn an optimal sequence of α_m coefficients from the data using the following algorithm:

1. Use the sequence of α_m coefficients that is constructed by the boosting algorithm as starting values
2. For iteration $k = 1$ to K perform the following steps:

   (a) for observation $i = 1$ to N do

      i. determine the output $O(x_i)$ using equation (2)
      ii. if $O(x_i) \neq y_i$ increase all coefficients α_m that belong to a model that gives the correct prediction y_i with a constant factor c: $\alpha_m = c*\alpha_m$.

   (b) determine the error rate of the new combined model (2) on the *validation set*; if it is lower than the best error rate so far, store this sequence of α_m's.

3. Output the final model (2) with the optimal sequence of α_m's.

Here K is the number of training iterations, and c is the constant update factor. (We will use $K = 50$ and $c = 1.01$.) The validation set is a data set that is completely independent of our training set. How we construct such a validation set will be explained in the next section.

Comparing Performance

Now that we have introduced the methods we are going to use and the brand choice data set we will apply these methods to, we are in a position to knot things together. What we would like is make a comparison of the performance on the liquid detergent sales dataset of the methods we have introduced. Particularly, we would like to see the performance of Vroomen's model in comparison with boosting and stacking. As to performance, we are especially interested in the predictive performance of the different models (since the claim is that it can be improved using ensemble methods). So, in this section we will be concerned with the predictive performance of the three methods we want to test.

In order to apply the boosting algorithm to the brand choice data set there are a number of decisions to be made and problems to be solved. First of all, it has to be decided what kind of models we take as our base models, to serve as members of the ensemble. Since we want to make a comparison with Vroomen's model, it would be a good idea to use his model as our base model. Next, it should be decided what method we will use build a model on a data set with weighted instances. We decided to use the so-called *resampling* method: we draw N times a random instance from the data set (with replacement) giving each instance i a weight w_i. Thus, we get a data set of the same size as the original data set, which contains however multiple copies of some instances with large weights while some instances with small weights might have disappeared from this new data set. With this new data set we build a model, which is thus based on a weighted data set. One disadvantage of this method is that the generated model has a stochastic nature, since it is based on a random sample from the data set. Another disadvantage is that some records just disappear from some of these randomly chosen data sets. However, this loss is fully compensated by the fact that we don't need to adapt the original model building method to the case of a data set with weighted instances.

The most important adaptation we had to make regards the fact that we want our methods to work for any J brands, not just for two brands. If we call the brands we consider 1, ..., J, it follows that for the instance pairs (x_i, y_i) in our data set we have $y_i \in \{1, \ldots, J\}$. Also, for each x, $F_m(x)$ (the output of the neural network) must be an integer in the range 1, ..., J. With this situation in mind, it is not hard to see that the generalization of equation (2) to the situation of J brands should be replaced by the following:

$$O(x) = \arg\max_{1 \le j \le J} \sum_{m=1}^{M} \alpha_m \chi(F_m(x) = j) \qquad \textbf{(3)}$$

This equation expresses the procedure to cast a weighted vote for the brands among the M models (with weights α_m) and to pick the brand that got the largest number of (weighted) votes.

Another important adaptation also had to be devised, regarding the situation of J instead of two brands. In equation (1), for the situation of two brands, we have seen that a positive coefficient is delivered provided the error rate err_m does not exceed 0.5. In the case of two brands this is an acceptable state of affairs, since random guessing between two brands results in an error rate of 0.5. So the only requirement that a model should meet, would be to be better than random guessing. However, in the situation of J brands, random guessing results in an error rate of $(J-1)/J$ since there are J-1 possibilities for an incorrect guess. Thus, if we set a comparable requirement to the formula for calculating the α_m coefficients as in the case of two brands, we should demand that α_m be positive as long as the error rate err_m does not exceed $(J-1)/J$. This is the case, if we define α_m according to the following equation:

$$\alpha_m = \frac{1}{J-1} \log\left(\frac{1-err_m}{err_m} \cdot (J-1)\right) \qquad \textbf{(4)}$$

The other important property, namely that α_m increases when the error rate err_m decreases remains true with this definition and it is equivalent to (1) in case $J = 2$. For these reasons, we used (4) to replace (1) in our boosting procedure.

Thus, the complete boosting algorithm we used for the brand choice problem is the Adaboost algorithm described in the previous section, with equation (1) replaced by (3) and equation (2) replaced by (4). Both of these changes will not be found in the standard literature on boosting (as far as the authors know) and were devised by the authors.

Since we now have a complete description of the methods we used on the detergent data set, we will now describe the experiments that we performed and their results. In order to get a fair view of the performance of a model, it should be tested on a completely independent test set. By the same token, a validation set, that is used to get an optimal sequence of α_m coefficients using the stacking algorithm, should be completely independent of both the training set and the test set. We used the following procedure to arrive at completely independent training, validation and test sets and an associated experimental cycle:

1. Split the 400 households randomly into a three groups, one of size 200 (training households, TR), and two groups each of size 100 (validation households and test households, VA and TE).
2. Training set = all purchases in the original data set of 2,257 records of the households from TR; validation set = all purchases of the households from VA; test set = all purchases of the households from TE.
3. Using the back propagation algorithm on the training set, a Vroomen model was created, and the accuracy of this model on the training set, the validation set, and the test set was determined.
4. Using the boosting algorithm on the training set a whole ensemble of Vroomen models + a combined model was built. The accuracy of the combined model was determined for the training set, the validation set and the test set.
5. Using the stacking algorithm, starting from the ensemble of step 4 and making use of the validation set, an optimal sequence of α_m coefficients was trained for a new combined model. For this model the accuracy on training, validation, and test set was determined.

This complete cycle was repeated ten times. The resulting mean accuracies over these ten runs, together with their standard deviations are displayed in the following table:

	Vroomen	Boosting	Stacking
training accuracy	80.7 ± 1.5	81.3 ± 1.9	81.8 ± 1.9
validation accuracy	76.4 ± 2.8	79.4 ± 2.3	79.3 ± 2.6
test accuracy	75.9 ± 1.8	78.6 ± 2.1	79.1 ± 2.5

We conclude from this table that the use of boosting and stacking results in a clear increase in performance, especially on validation data and completely independent test data. A stacked model predicts on average 3.2% better on unseen data than a Vroomen model. Actually, both boosting and stacking perform better than Vroomen on the test set in all of our ten runs. With boosting the increase varies from 0.6% to 4.5% and with stacking from 0.7% tot 5.5%. So the expected increase in predictive performance is confirmed on the detergent data set.

Another remarkable outcome of these experiments is that in our experiments the Vroomen model does better than reported in Vroomen et al. (2003) on the same data set: they report an accuracy of 73.9% on an independent test set, whereas we get 75.9% on average. One reason for this difference might be that we use three extra variables in the second stage of the model (the W_{qj} variables) while they use only one extra variable, namely price. Another difference is that we repeat the whole experiment ten times, whereas they reported only one experiment. Their random split of the data set into training, validation and test set might just have been an unlucky one. By repeating the experiment ten times we get a fair idea of the stability of our results on this data set.

Market Share Simulations

In this section we will demonstrate the use of the models built in the previous sections by applying them to the problem of calculating market share for various price setting scenarios. The idea behind this is the following: if we have a well-performing predictive model for the brand choice problem, we may use this model as an oracle that predicts a brand for any combination of household/brand/purchase values that is offered to the model. Using this idea we may perform a simulation study as follows:

1. Select one of the models that has been developed for the problem at hand. As an example, we select a model built by the stacking method (accuracy = 79.1% on average).
2. Select a brand, for instance brand j_0. In the examples below we will select Tide, Wisk and Surf, consecutively.
3. Fix the price Z_{1j} of brand j_0 to p
4. Set the prices of all brands $\neq j_0$ to their respective averages and set all the variables Z_{2j} and Z_{3j} to their default values 0.
5. For all households h in the data set separately:
    a. Set all X, Z and W variables that have not been set in step 3 and 4 to their respective values in the data set.
    b. Calculate the brand Y_h predicted by the model picked in step 1.
    c. Let Q_h be the total amount of liquid detergent, bought by household h in the observed period, in ounces. Then the predicted revenue for brand j caused by household h will be estimated by

$$r_{hj} = Z_{1j} Q_h \chi(Y_h = j)$$

6. Calculate the total revenue R_j for each brand j as $R_j = \sum_h r_{hj}$

Figure 2. Predicted market shares of all brands with varying prices of Tide

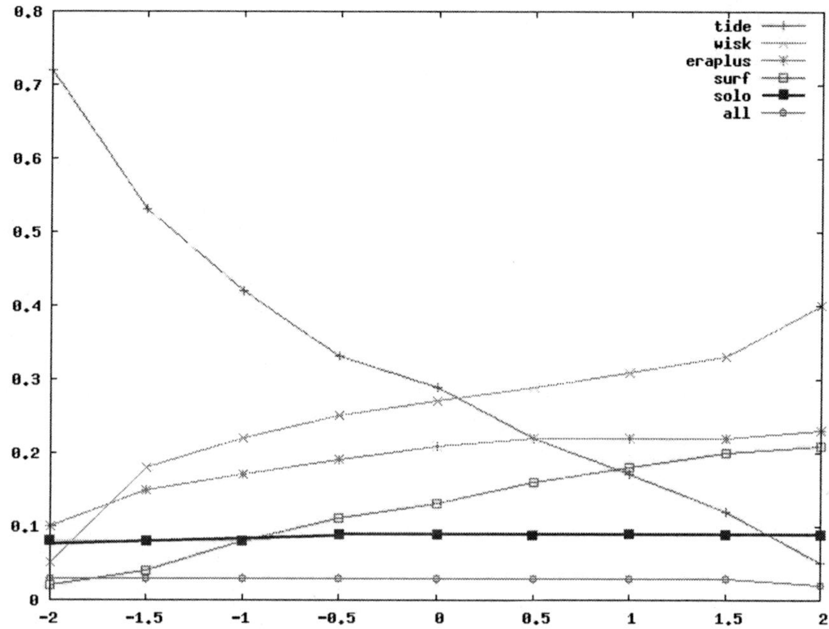

7. Calculate the market shares M_j for each brand j as $M_j = R_j / \sum_i R_i$

8. Repeat steps 3 through 7 for a number of different prices p.

The result of such a simulation will be a graph that shows the markets shares of all brands as a function of the price of one brand, with all other brands set on their average prices. Of course, the accuracy of these estimated market share values depend on the accuracy of the underlying model. Thus, the predictive performance of the proposed models, as determined in the previous section, is extremely valuable for the confidence one can have in these simulation results.

Simulation studies like the one described above were performed for the Tide, Wisk and Surf brands. For each of these brands, the different prices p that were tested (in line 3 of the above algorithm) ranged two standard deviations around the average price for each brand. Also, to enhance the reliability of our results, in step 1 of the simulation algorithm we consecutively selected all ten stacked models developed (see the previous section). Next, the market share results were averaged over these ten models. The outcomes of these simulations resulted in the graphs of Figure 2 to Figure 4.

Figure 3. Predicted market shares of all brands with varying prices of Wisk

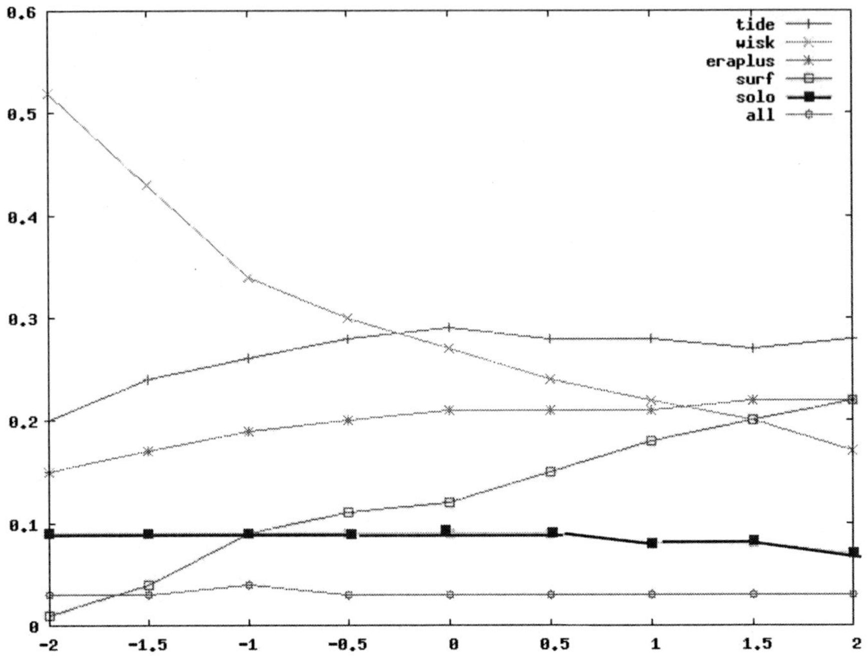

Figure 2 shows that the market share of the Tide brand is heavily dependent on its price. Wisk and Eraplus are strong competitors when the price of Tide is around average. Surf and Wisk profit most by an increase of the price of Tide. However, when the price of Tide is set at a lower than average level, it quickly becomes by far the market leader, reducing the market share of the competitors to below 10%. Remarkably, the market share of the Solo and All brands, though very small players in this market, are almost unaffected by any price changes of Tide. Customer loyalty seems to be very high for these brands.

Figure 3 tells a different story. Changes in the price of Wisk do not nearly have the effect that changes in the price of Tide have. Wisk is less price dependent than Tide, especially in the average price range. Households seem to be quite loyal to Wisk. However, when they switch to another brand, they choose Surf, and not the big competitors Tide and Eraplus. But that also means that if Wisk lowers its price, the market share of Surf will decrease quickly.

The story for Surf is different again, as can be seen from Figure 4. Surf seems to be just as heavily price dependent as Tide. However, we also see the surprising outcome that the price of Surf is very significant for the market share of only Tide. The other competitors seem to suffer much less from price changes of Surf, even for extreme values of the price of Surf.

Figure 4. Predicted market shares of all brands with varying prices of Surf

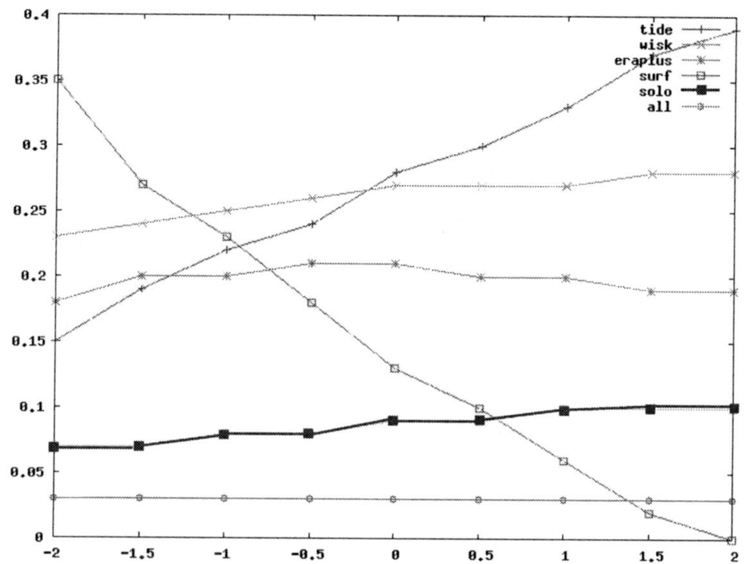

These findings may be summarized for each of the brands separately, as follows:

- Tide is very dependent on its own price and the price of Surf; the price of Wisk does not matter so much for the market share of Tide.
- Wisk is as dependent on the price of Tide as on its own price. Surf is not important for Wisk.
- Surf is dependent on the prices of Tide and Wisk and on its own price. It does not have many loyal customers, so with too high a price, market share will drop to zero.
- Eraplus has loyal and quite constant customers. The graph with varying prices of Eraplus is not displayed here, but showed no big shifts in market share.
- Solo and All are small players in this market, with a very loyal group of households. However, the evidence for these two products is based on only a small number of entries in the data set, which makes it somewhat less trustworthy.

Finally, one other simulation study was performed using the same model that was used in the previous studies. For this last simulation, the object was to study the behavior of the market in a situation in which all prices drop simultaneously, as when a price war is raging. In fact, instead of fixing all brand prices except one to their averages and allowing one price to vary, for this simulation all brand prices are fixed on their averages minus a varying discount percentage p. So we replace steps 2, 3 and 4 of the simulation algorithm by the following steps:

Figure 5. Predicted market shares of all brands if all prices are cut with a fixed percentage

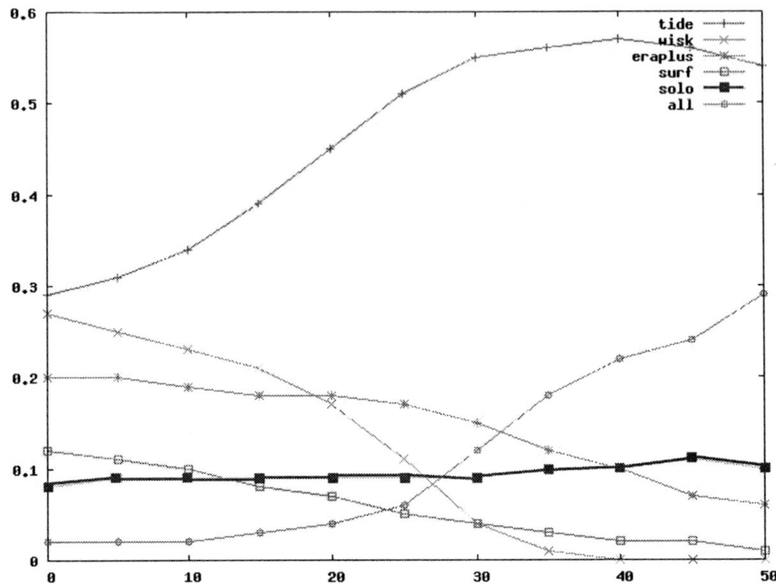

2. Select a fixed discount percentage p
3. Fix the price Z_{1j} of all brands j to $(1 - p/100)$ times the average price of brand j
4. Set all the variables Z_{2j} and Z_{3j} to their default values 0.

And the last step is replaced by:

8. Repeat steps 2 through 7 for a number of different discount percentages p.

The results are shown in Figure 5. Clearly, Tide is the winner of this price war in this market, and the biggest loser is Wisk. Surf and Eraplus will also lose market share, but at a more gradual rate. When discounts rise above 20%, All is a surprising winner: it becomes second in the market, with a market share that is well beyond its usual level. Again, Solo's market share does not respond to price changes. Marketers will have no problem in making conclusions on the basis of these simulation outcomes. For instance, if Tide uses an aggressive pricing strategy in this market, they will surely win market share.

These simulations are just an example of the use of the marketing models based on boosting and stacking that were presented in this chapter. Many more applications could be devised using these models.

Trends and Conclusion

In this chapter we showed how some new methods from the field of computational intelligence (ensemble methods such as boosting and stacking) could be used for a traditional marketing problem such as brand choice. We found that indeed the predictive performance of the models based on the ensemble techniques improved even compared to the most sophisticated existing model that we found in the literature. Although predictive performance is one aspect that candidate models should be judged on, there are more aspects that should be taken into consideration. One aspect that has not been considered here is the interpretability of the generated model. Since models built by ensemble methods consist of a combination of different (sometimes many) base models, the complexity of the final model is usually high, making it difficult to interpret. This is one of the themes that should be taken into account by future serious work into this direction.

References

Chintagunta, P. K., & Prasad, A. R. (1998). An empirical investigation of the dynamic McFadden model of purchase timing and brand choice: Implications for market structure. *Journal of Business and Economic Statistics*, *16*, 2-11.

Dasgupta, C. G., Dispensa, G. S., & Ghose, S. (1994). Comparing the predictive performance of a neural network model with some traditional market response models. *International Journal of Forecasting*, *10*, 235-244.

Franses, P. H., & Paap, R. (2001). *Quantitative models in marketing research.* Cambridge, UK: Cambridge University.

Freund, Y., & Schapire, R. (1996). Experiments with a new boosting algorithm. In L. Saitta (Ed.), *Proceedings of the Thirteenth International Conference on Machine Learning* (pp. 148-156). San Francisco: Morgan Kaufmann.

Hastie, T., Tibshirani, R., & Friedman, J. (2001). *The elements of statistical learning.* New York: Springer-Verlag.

Hruschka, H. (1993). Determining market response functions by neural network modeling: A comparison to econometric techniques. *European Journal of Operational Research*, *66*, 27-35.

Hruschka, H., Fettes, W., Probst, M., & Mies, C. (2002). A flexible brand choice model based on neural net methodology. A comparison to the linear utility multinomial logit model and its latent class extension. *OR Spectrum*, *24*, 127-143.

Hu, M. Y., Shanker, M., & Hung, M. S. (1999). Estimation of posterior probabilities of consumer situational choices with neural network classifiers. *International Journal of Research in Marketing*, *16*, 307-317.

Hu, M. Y., & Tsoukalas, C. (2003). Explaining consumer choice through neural networks: The stacked generalization approach. *European Journal of Operational Research, 146*, 650-660.

McFadden, D. (1973). Conditional logit analysis of qualitative choice behavior. In P. Zarembka (Ed.), *Frontiers in econometrics* (pp. 105-142). New York: Academic.

Potharst, R., Kaymak, U., & Pijls, W. (2002). Neural networks for target selection in direct marketing. In K. Smith & J. Gupta (Eds.), *Neural networks in business: Techniques and applications* (pp. 89-110). Hershey, PA: Idea Group Publishing.

Rijthoven, M. P. S. van (2004). *The use of neural network boosting in a marketing environment.* Masters Thesis, Erasmus University.

Roberts, J. H., & Lattin, J. M. (1997). Consideration: Review of research and prospects for future insights. *Journal of Marketing Research, 34*, 406-410.

Schwenk, H., & Bengio, Y. (2000). Boosting neural networks. *Neural Computation, 12*, 1869-1887.

Smith, K., & Gupta, J. (Eds.). (2002). *Neural networks in business: Techniques and applications*. Hershey, PA: Idea Group Publishing.

Tibshirani, R., Friedman, J., & Hastie, T. (2000). Additive logistic regression: a statistical view of boosting. *Annals of Statistics*, 28, 337-407.

Vroomen, B., Franses, P. H., & van Nierop, E., (2004). Modeling consideration sets and brand choice using artificial neural networks. *European Journal of Operational Research, 154*, 206-217.

West, P. M., Brockett, P. L., & Golden, L. L. (1997). A comparative analysis of neural networks and statistical methods for predicting consumer choice. *Marketing Science, 16*(4), 370-391.

Wezel, M. van, & Potharst, R. (2005). *Improved customer choice predictions using ensemble methods.* Technical Report, Erasmus University, Econometric Institute EI2005-08.

Chapter VI

Applying Information Gathering Techniques in Business-to-Consumer and Web Scenarios

David Camacho, Universidad Autónoma de Madrid, Spain

Abstract

The last decade has shown the e-business community and computer science researchers that there can be serious problems and pitfalls when e-companies are created. One of the problems is related to the necessity for the management of knowledge (data, information, or other electronic resources) from different companies. This chapter will focus on two important research fields that are currently working to solve this problem — Information Gathering (IG) techniques and Web-enabled Agent technologies. IG techniques are related to the problem of retrieval, extraction and integration of data from different (usually heterogeneous) sources into new forms. Agent and Multi-Agent technologies have been successfully applied in domains such as the Web. This chapter will show, using a specific IG Multi-Agent system called MAPWeb, how information gathering techniques have been successfully combined with agent technologies to build new Web agent-based systems. These systems can be migrated into Business-to-

Consumer (B2C) scenarios using several technologies related to the Semantic Web, such as SOAP, UDDI or Web services.

Introduction

The aim of this chapter is to show how several Computational Intelligence (CI) techniques have evolved to allow the implementation of intelligent Business-to-Consumer (B2C) applications using new technologies related to the Semantic Web. The evolution of these applications is made possible by several CI techniques (such as Machine Learning or Planning) that allow users to represent, integrate, and manage information and resources available in electronic repositories. It is also made possible by the evolution of the World Wide Web and its associated technologies (such as XML or RDF). In addition, Web services are emerging as a major technology for achieving automated interactions between distributed and heterogeneous applications. Various technologies constitute the backbone of this achievement, for example WSDL, UDDI, and SOAP. These technologies aim at supporting the definition of services, their advertisement, and their binding for triggering purposes. The advantages of Web services have already been demonstrated and highlight their capacity to be combined into high-level business processes. These business processes are composites that consist of several component services. It is argued that composition via service interconnection allows more sophisticated services and applications to be hierarchically constructed from primitive ones (Curbera, Duftler, Khalaf, Nagy, Mukhi, & Weerawarana, 2002; McIlraith, Son, & Zeng, 2002; WWW Consortium, 2002).

Computational intelligence techniques allow for the implementation of robust, adaptable, and reliable applications, and these characteristics are needed for a successful deployment of B2C applications. CI techniques are therefore important in promoting and developing B2C solutions on the Web. Many B2C applications have now been deployed as Web applications with considerable repercussions for e-business. These new kinds of Web sites allow consumers to rent a car, book a hotel, schedule travel, buy music, books, etc. It is obvious that new Web-based B2C applications are flourishing in the commercial sphere of the Internet.

The Semantic Web (Berners-Lee, Hendler, & Lassila, 2001) with its tools and related technologies, (including Ontology, WSDL, UDDI, SOAP) and Web services are likely to fall short of realizing the complete automation often envisioned by e-business practitioners. The evolution from the current Web to the Semantic Web has created new business possibilities that go beyond what traditional Information Retrieval (Baeza-Yates & Ribeiro-Neto, 1999; Jones & Willett, 1997), or Information Searching (Chen, Chung, Ramsey, & Yang, 2001; Howe & Dreilinger, 1997; Lieberman, 1995) techniques provide. Some of those possibilities arise because new problems can be solved using the available information from several electronic sources. These problems need to use multiple information sources to obtain a solution or solutions. The large number of available electronic sources and the opportunity to find any type of information makes it possible to think about building systems that can retrieve, reason and finally reuse the stored information to obtain new solutions, much like a person does when consulting those same Web sources. These types of systems need to use techniques that allow not only the retrieval of a set of documents, but also to integrate the knowledge stored in those documents using automated reasoning. To build this kind of systems it is necessary to deal with several problems such as:

- How to represent the problems to be solved or the knowledge sources that store useful information for them;
- How to implement the necessary mechanisms to retrieve the information;
- When useful information is found in different knowledge sources, how to integrate these into a common solution;
- Finally, if several electronically distributed sources are considered, how to build a robust and flexible system that allows for the addition of new sources or the modification of existing ones.

Previous techniques can be defined as *Information Gathering* (IG) (Fan & Gauch, 1999). IG tries to integrate a set of different information sources with the aim of querying them as if they were a single information source. IG systems are able to extract knowledge from documents by analyzing their contents looking for a particular structure. So a document is seen by these systems as having some kind of inner structure (usually called semi-structured information). Because of the amount of information available, efficiency considerations become very important, such as, selecting which information sources will be queried, and even the order in which they will be queried. In order to both integrate and select the relevant information sources different techniques can be used, such as Case-Based Reasoning (CBR) (Daniels & Rissland, 1995; Ricci, Arslan, Mirzadeh, & Venturini, 2002), planning (Camacho, Borrajo, Molina, & Aler, 2001; Carranza, Muñoz-Avila, Weberskirch, & Bergmann, 1998; Hüllen, Bergmann, & Weberskirch, 1999), and workflow (Ambite, Genevieve, Gordon, Pan, & Bharracharjee, 2002). These (and many other) CI techniques are used to build intelligent systems that implement characteristics such as adaptability, autonomy, or reasoning skills.

The distributed nature of the electronic resources available in networks like the Internet suggest a distributed software application to manage them, and consequently gain better performance and reliability in the behaviour of those systems. Multi-Agent technologies have defined and implemented several techniques that enable the building of intelligent, adaptable, and reliable systems (Chavez, Dreilinger, Guttman, & Maes, 1997; Decker, Sycara, & Williamson, 1997; Petrie, 1996; Sycara, 1989). This chapter shows how a Multi-Agent system can be designed using a Web service oriented architecture. If Multi-Agent systems are Web services-enabled, there is a natural way to share their information product with other agent-based systems, or with other business applications. Therefore, the main contribution of this chapter is in the demonstration of how, through the utilization of a particular IG multi-agent system, IG techniques can be combined with agent-based technologies to build new Web agent-based systems that can be migrated to Business-to-Consumer (B2C) scenarios. The chapter analyzes how a multi-agent system (MAS) can be redesigned using a Web services-oriented architecture. This new design perspective allows MAS to utilize Web services-enabled technologies, and provides a natural way to share information products with other business-to-consumer (B2C) applications.

The chapter is structured as follows. The next section provides a brief introduction to some basic concepts related with Agents and Web Services technologies. The third section describes some deployed systems that are able to integrate and manage information extracted from the Web. The fourth section describes a specific B2C application, MAPWeb, that has been designed to gather and reuse Web information into a common general solution using CI techniques. The fifth section shows how this B2C Information Gathering application can be migrated into a new Web Services-oriented architecture. The last section provides the conclusions of this work.

Agents and Web Services Technologies: A Brief Introduction

There is a considerable literature relating to Intelligent Agents and Web Services technologies. This section provides a brief introduction to the basic concepts of both technologies.

Intelligent Agents and Multi-Agent Systems

Several researchers have proposed formal definitions for agents and multi-agent systems, to define the concept of intelligent, or autonomous agents we use the following: "An autonomous agent is a system situated within and a part of an environment that senses that environment and acts on it, over time, in pursuit of its own agenda and so as to effect what it senses in the future" (Franklin & Graesser, 1996, p. 5). An agent can be characterized by the following properties (Ferber, 1999; Wooldridge & Jennings, 1995):

- **Autonomy:** agents work without the direct intervention of humans or others, and have some kind of control over their actions and internal state.
- **Social ability:** agents interact or communicate with other agents.
- **Reactivity:** agents perceive their environment (which may be the physical world, a user via a graphical user interface, a collection of other agents, the Internet, or perhaps all of these combined), and responds in a timely fashion to changes that occur in it.
- **Pro-activity:** agents do not simply act in response to their environment, they are able to exhibit goal-directed behaviour by taking the initiative. An agent is capable of handling complex, high-level tasks. The decision as to how such tasks are best

split up into smaller sub-tasks, and in which order and way the sub-tasks are best performed, should be made by the agent itself.

- **Temporal continuity:** agents are continuously running processes.
- **Mobility:** an agent has the ability to transport itself from one machine to another, retaining its current state.

An MAS is a system composed of a population of autonomous agents, which cooperate with each other to reach common objectives, while simultaneously pursuing individual objectives (Wooldridge, 2002). In order to solve common problems coherently, the agents must communicate amongst themselves and coordinate their activities. Coordination and communication are central to MAS, for without it, any benefits of interaction vanish and a group of agents quickly degenerates into a collection of individuals with chaotic behaviour. In the most general case, agents will be acting on behalf of users with different goals and motivations. The characteristics of any MAS can be summarized as follows (Sycara, 1998):

- every agent has incomplete information or capabilities for solving the problem and, thus, has a limited viewpoint;
- there is no global control;
- data are decentralized;
- computation is asynchronous.

Web Services Technologies

Web services have emerged as the next generation of Web-based technology for exchanging information. Web services are modular, self-describing, self-contained applications that are accessible over the Internet. Based on open standards, Web services allow the implementation of Web-based applications using any platform, object model, or programming language.

Web services are services offered via the Web. In a typical Web-services scenario, a business application sends a request to a service at a given URL using the SOAP (Simple Object Access Protocol) protocol over HTTP, and uses XML (eXtensible Markup Language) as the base language. The service receives the request, processes it and returns a response. A well-known example of a Web service is that of a stock quote service (i.e., a book store), in which the request asks for the current price of a specified book in stock, and the response gives the price. This is one of the simplest forms of a Web service in that the request is filled almost immediately, with the request and response being parts of the same method call.

Where the current Web enables users to connect to applications, the Web-services architecture enables applications to connect to other applications. Web services is therefore a key technology in enabling business models to move from B2C (Business to Consumer) to B2B (Business to Business). An enterprise can be the provider of Web

Figure 1. Web Services architecture

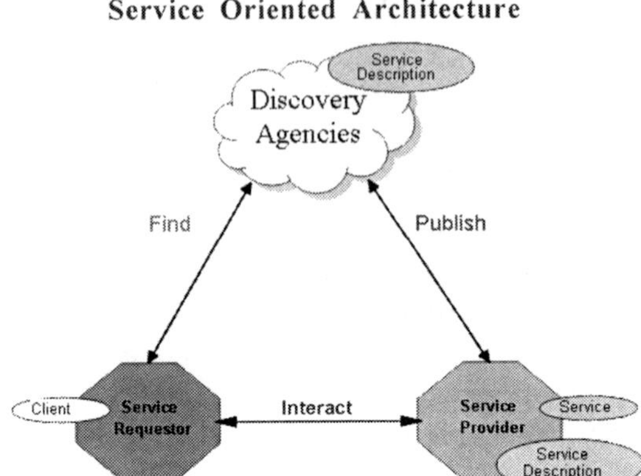

services and also the consumer of other Web Services. Also, Web Services are based on a set of standardized rules and specifications, making it more portable. The generic Web-Services architecture is shown in Figure 1, this architecture shows the infrastructure required to support Web services in terms of three roles: service provider, service requestor and service registry, and the necessary transactions and interactions between them: publish, find, and bind. A *service provider* publishes a service description to a service registry, a *service requester* then finds the service description via the service registry. Finally, the services description contains sufficient information for the service requestor to bind to the service provider to use the service (Berners-Lee, 2003; Gardner, 2001). Binding is the process that allows an application to connect to a Web service at a particular Web location and start interacting with it.

Using Web services there are three important technologies that are necessary to be familiar with (Gardner, 2001):

- **Web Services Description Language (WSDL):** WSDL is the metadata language of Web services. It acts as a "user's manual" for Web services, defining how service providers and requesters communicate with each other about Web services. Similar to XML, WSDL is extensible to allow the description of endpoints and their messages, regardless of what message formats or network protocols are used for communicating. Typically, if somebody wants to create an application that communicates with a particular Web service, it is only necessary to describe that service's WSDL in a file (WSDL, 2001).
- **Simple Object Access Protocol (SOAP):** SOAP is an XML-based protocol for exchanging information in a decentralized, distributed environment. It defines a mechanism to pass commands and parameters between clients and servers. Like Web services as a whole, SOAP is independent of the platform, object model, and programming language being used (SOAP, 2003).

- **Universal Description, Discovery, and Integration (UDDI):** UDDI is the meeting place for Web services. An information database of Web services, a UDDI registry stores descriptions about companies and the services they offer in a common XML format. Web-based applications interact with a UDDI registry using SOAP messages. Conceptually, the data in a UDDI registry can be divided into three different types of directories: a white-pages section that provides business contact information, a yellow-pages section that categorizes businesses and services, and a green-pages section that provides technical information about the services that a business offers (OASIS-UDDI, 2005).

Related Work

This section provides a brief description of several Web Information Gathering Systems that currently have been designed and deployed to work with the information stored in the Web. These systems use different CI techniques and Web technologies to integrate the retrieved information. The following is a brief description of some of those systems:

- **WebPlan** (Hüllen et al., 1999): is a Web assistant for domain-specific search on the Internet that is based on dynamic planning and plan execution techniques. The existing planning system CAPlan has been extended in different ways in order to deal with incomplete information, information seeking operators, user interaction, and interleaving planning and execution. WebPlan specializes in finding specific PC software on the Internet. Planning is used in this system to select the most appropriate sources to look for information.
- **SIMS/Ariadne** (Knoblock et al., 2000). This system includes a set of tools to construct wrappers that make Web sources look like relational databases. Planning and mediation techniques are used, both to access the distributed information, and to integrate the information found.
- **Heracles** (Ambite, Barish, Knoblock, Muslea, Oh, & Minton, 2002). This framework is used to develop different information assistant systems that employ a set of information agents (Ariadne, Theseus, Electric Elves). A dynamic hierarchical constraint propagation network (CPN) is used to integrate the different information sources. Two assistant systems have been implemented: The Travel Planning Assistant (specialized in assisting tourists to plan their trips) and The WorldInfo Assistant (for a user-specified location, the system integrates information from different information sources such as weather, news, holidays, maps, airports, etc.). In this framework the integration of the retrieved information is made by a CPN.
- **Argos** (Dynamic Composition of Web Services for Goods Movement Analysis and Planning). The Argos project is developing a new approach to automatic generation of scientific workflows based on Web services. There are three main objectives:

- To advance computer science research by developing an expressive Web services description language and techniques for dynamically composing Web services.
- To develop and conduct test applications of an intra-metropolitan goods movement flow model using Web services in cooperation with government partners.
- To use the model to conduct social science research on intra-metropolitan economic linkages and spatial structure. Although the focus is on the specific topic of urban goods movement, the approach to Web service composition is general and can be applied to other scientific data gathering and analysis tasks. (Ambite et al., 2002; Ambite et al., 2004)

- **SAMAP** (Multiagent Context-sensitive Adaptive Planning System). The main objective of SAMAP is the analysis, design and implementation of a multi-agent system with the ability to perform hierarchical, temporal, and resource planning and scheduling in the area of ubiquitous computing. The system will also be dynamic in that it will be able to learn from past problem solving experiences, as well as automatically acquiring a user model.
- **Intelligent Travel Recommendation** (ITR) (Ricci et al., 2002). ITR is a Web-based recommender system that enables the user to select travel locations, activities and attractions, and supports the building of a personalized travel plan. In this system the user is asked explicitly about his or her needs and constraints. The system, combining content-based filtering technologies, interactive query management, and variations of the collaborative-filtering approach or case-based reasoning, ranks suggestions extracted from structured catalogues. Travel plans are stored in a memory of cases, which is obtained from ranking travel items extracted from catalogues.

MAPWeb: Multi-Agent Planning on the Web

This section describes in detail a B2C application called MAPWeb (**M**ulti-**A**gent **P**lanning on the **Web**) that is able to gather and reuse information from Web sources to integrate partial information into a common solution (Camacho, Aler, Borrajo, & Molina, 2005; Camacho, Borrajo, & Molina, 2001).

MAPWeb Architecture

Any Multiagent System (MAS) defined using MAPWeb can be implemented using one or several teams. A specialized agent, CoachAgent (CCH), manages every team. To manage the different teams it is necessary to use a single ManagerAgent (*MNG*). This agent (known as Agent Name Server, *ANS*, in other architectures) is used to manage the insertion and deletion of other agents in/from the MAS. Therefore, in MAPWeb (as in other MAS frameworks), any system implemented will need at least the following agents to work properly:

- **Control Agents:** manage the different agents in the system. There are two types:
  - **ManagerAgent (MNG):** This agent is similar to any ANS that can perform the following roles in the system: responsible for adding and removing other agents from the system; controls which agents are active in the agent society; groups agents in teams. When any agent requests to be inserted in the society, the MNG determines which teams require this agent.
  - **CoachAgent (CCH):** Controls a team of agents, guaranteeing stability and smooth operation of the active agents. These agents report problems to the MNG. When a new agent is required for the team, they guarantee that the yellow pages of the team members are coherent.
- **Execution Agents:** These agents are responsible for achieving different goals within the system. To coordinate different teams of agents it is possible to include a new skill in the control module of the agents. Currently, there exist different kinds of execution agents, including those that are able to use a planner to solve problems (PlannerAgents), information agents that can retrieve Web data (WebAgents), agents that can interact with the RoboSoccer simulator, etc.

Figure 2 shows the general architecture for any MAS in MAPWeb. The main characteristics of any MAS implemented in this way can be summarized as:

Figure 2. MAPWeb multi-agent architecture

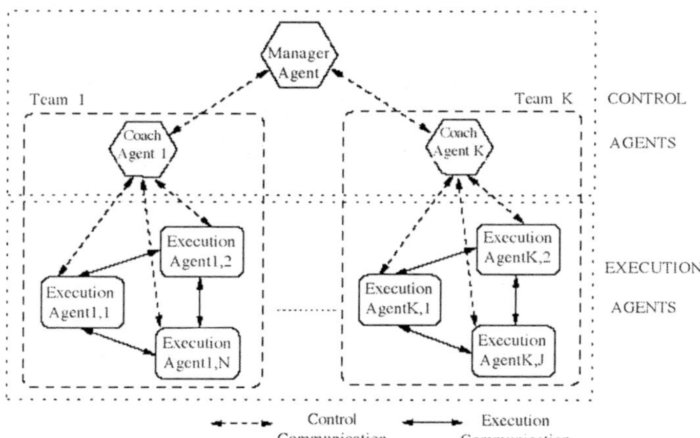

- Agents in the system use message-passing to communicate with other agents.
- All the agents have the same architecture and are specialized in different tasks through the implementation of different skills.
- Although the communication language is the same for all the agents in MAPWeb, it is possible to distinguish two different types of communication messages. On one hand, there are control messages whose main goal is to manage the behaviour of the system (control communication in Figure 2). On the other hand, execution messages are used to share knowledge and tasks among the agents, to achieve desired goals (execution communication).

To establish the MAS, it is necessary to perform the following steps:

1. First, the *MNG* is executed.
2. Agents in the system need to register themselves with the *MNG*. Once a *CCH* has registered, the *MNG* will select the necessary execution agents from its white pages and will build an operative team. If there are not enough agents, the *CCH* will wait for them. To build a team the *MNG* selects the execution agents and provides the necessary information to the *CCH*. Once the information on the agents has been stored in the *CCH*'s yellow pages, it updates the yellow pages of its execution agents. To select the necessary agents to build a group, the *MNG* uses the Ontology of the *CCH* agent.
3. Once a team is built, the execution agents can only communicate with the agents belonging to its team or with its CCH.

MAPWeb Application Domain

Although the agent and multi-agent architecture proposed in MAPWeb has been successfully applied in other domains (such as robo soccer and genetic programming), the architecture was initially designed to gather and reuse information extracted from heterogeneous Web sources. The first application domain of MAPWeb was related to the problem of planning user travel.

The high number of companies connected to tourism activities, such as hotels, car rental, transport (flights, train, buses...), museums, theatres, etc., ..., that have used the World Wide Web as a communication gateway between their resources and potential users, has changed the concept of traditional tourism. In fact "...travel and tourism represents the leading application in B2C (business-to-consumer) e-commerce" (Fodor, Dell'Erba, Ricci, & Werthner, 2002, p. 1).

The tourism domain is complex and heterogeneous. It is possible to find heterogeneous information such as maps, textual information (about places to visit), schedule and fare information about hotels, transports, etc., ... It is possible for any user to consult (and even to buy) anything that he or she could need in their travel experience. All of this information needs to be appropriately managed and integrated to provide useful information. Different systems have been implemented to deal with the tourism information in the Web, such as intelligent electronic tourist guides (e.g., GUIDE — Cheverst, Davies, Mitchell, Friday, & Efstratiou, 2000; cyberguide — Abowd, Atkeson, Hong, Long, Kooper, & Pinkerton, 1997), travel assistants (Ambite et al., 2002; Yang, Yang, Denecke, & Waibel, 1999), and context-aware systems for tourism (Zipf, 2002).

Although other CI techniques such as Case-Based Reasoning or Information Retrieval have been successfully used in this domain, we have modelled the tourism domain as a planning domain, where the user needs to create a plan to travel between several places. This modification allows us to use classical planning techniques, both to manage access to the Web companies that provide the information, and to look for heterogeneous solutions (integrating into a common solution the retrieved information from the Web). The main goal of this approach is to allow the integration of CI techniques, such as learning or planning, with Information Gathering techniques into a real and complex domain.

Our MAS model uses a set of deliberative and cooperative software agents which integrate CI techniques and the Web to gather information (Camacho et al., 2005). The reasoning techniques used by those agents are planning (planning agents), and Case-Based Reasoning (Web agents and planning agents). The e-tourism domain has been modeled as a planning domain and has been included as part of the knowledge (ontology) shared by the agents. This domain uses a set of operators to work with the different topics in tourism such as hire rental car, book room, obtain flight tickets, etc. Using previous operators, specialized agents build skeletal plans that represents the different steps that may be executed by the user. The agent uses this skeletal solution to achieve several goals:

- To coordinate other agents (user, planner, and Web agents). The planning agent uses the skeletal plan (abstract solution) as a template to decide what agent will be requested for help.
- To share the information stored in different agents (old plans in other planning agents, or records retrieved by Web agents).
- The use the skeletal plan as the integration structure to build the final solution to the travel problem. The heterogeneous information provided by Web agents are integrated into specific solutions using the skeletal plan.
- To cooperate in the solving process with other planning agents. The planner agent can divide the initial problem into sub-problems with lower complexity (i.e., a problem with three independent goals can be divided into three one-goal problems), and request help from other planning agents.

Figure 3 shows one possible MAPWeb topology, or configuration, when the system is applied in the tourism domain. Two operative teams managed by a *MNG* build this configuration, and every team is locally managed by a CCH. *Team_1* has the minimum set of agents to be operative, whereas *Team_2* is built by *K* UserAgents, *P* PlannerAgents and *J* WebAgents. In addition, the following execution agents are needed:

Figure 3. MAPWeb e-tourism topology

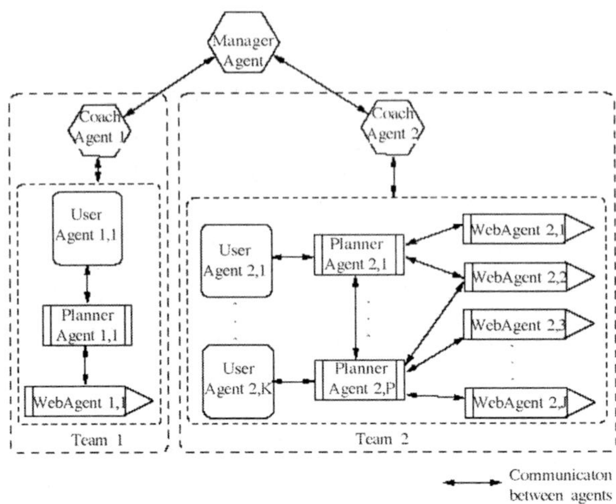

- UserAgents are the bridge between the users and the system. They only implement basic input/output skills to acquire problem descriptions from users and to show the solutions found to them.
- PlannerAgents are able to solve planning problems using the information gathered from the Web.
- WebAgents are able to provide the requested Web information such as a set of relational records to the PlannerAgents using wrapping techniques. These agents use caching techniques to optimize the access to the Web.

Although MAPWeb is a generic architecture that combines Web information retrieval with planning, its skills are better understood in a particular domain. In this section, we will use the e-tourism domain, where the goal is to assist a user in planning his or her trip. MAPWeb's processes can be described as follows. First, the user interacts with the UserAgent to input their query. The query captures information such as the departure and return dates and cities, one way or return trip, maximum number of transfers, and some preference criteria. This information is sent to the PlannerAgent, which transforms it into a planning problem. This planning problem retains only those parts that are essential for the planning process — this is called the *abstract representation* of the user query. Then, the agent generates several abstract solutions for the user query. The planning steps in the abstract solutions need to be completed and validated with actual information that is retrieved from the Web. To accomplish this, the PlannerAgent sends information queries to specialized WebAgents that return several records for every information query. Then, the PlannerAgent integrates and validates the solutions and returns the data to the UserAgent, which in turn displays it to the user. A detailed description about both the utilization of CI techniques, such as planning or machine learning, used by PlannerAgents to reason with the retrieved information, and the coordination processes among different agents in MAPWeb through message passing can be found in Camacho, Borrajo, Molina and Aler (2001) and Camacho et al. (2005).

Currently, MAPWeb is able to access, gather, and reuse information from the following Web sources:

- **Flight companies:** Iberia Airlines, Avianca Airlines, Amadeus flights, 4Airlines flights.
- **Train companies:** Renfe, BritRail, RailEurope.
- **Rental Car companies:** Avis, Hertz, Amadeus car rental, 4Airlines car rental.
- **Hotel companies:** Amadeus hotels, 4Airlines hotels.

These Web sources can be classified into two main groups: Meta-search systems such as Amadeus, 4Airlines, BritRail and RailEurope, which extract information from several companies, and individual sources which belong to a particular company (Iberia, Avianca, Renfe, etc.).

Agents' Characteristics

The previous section has described the roles of control and execution agents used in MAPWeb, this section provides a description about the specific characteristics of these agents. Table 1 provides the specific characteristics of the control agents. Table 1 shows how it is only necessary to implement in the *MNG* agent simple acts such as insert or delete, because the main role of this agent is to manage the correct insertion and deletion of the agents into the system.

This agent distributes the agents into operative teams (it tries to implement teams with at least one operative agent). However, the number and type of agents that implement a particular team could change in time. For instance, a particular WebAgent might not be operative for network problems (the Web server is down), so the *CCH* could suspend temporally the agent, and resume again when the problems has disappeared. The act: [Ask-for-agent] is used by the *CCH* agent to ask for the particular type of agent that is necessary for the correct work of the team. Finally, the Knowledge Base and the Yellow Pages of the agents stores all related information with the managed agents.

The skills implemented in the *MNG* agent allows it to modify (in number and type) any team of agents. This agent uses a policy to distribute new agents and to build the teams, or to share a particular agent in several teams (by providing its direction to the CoachAgents of the teams). The skills implemented for the *CCH* agents allow those agents to manage a team, and to request help from the *MNG* if any agent (PlannerAgent, WebAgent, UserAgent) is necessary for the team to work correctly.

Table 2 provides a description about the characteristics of the execution agents in MAPWeb. As Table 2 shows, the implemented UserAgent is the most simple execution agent, it has only a set of graphical interfaces to allow communication between the user and the system. The most remarkable characteristic in these agents is the implementation

Table 1. Specific attributes for control agents

	Skills	Knowledge Base	Communication Module
ManagerAgent (*MNG*)	- Insert new agent - Delete agent - Team management policy	Stores the information about all the agents in the system, naming information, skills, teams, etc…	Is implemented using the Kqml-ACL language and TCP/IP protocol
CoachAgent (*CCH*)	- Insert new agent in the team - Delete agent in the team - Suspend a particular agent - Resume a particular agent - Ask for new agent	Their KB stores the specific information about their execution agents and the contact address of the *MNG*	Kqml-ACL language and TCP/IP protocol

Table 2. Specific attributes for execution agents

	Skills	Knowledge Base	Communication Module
WebAgent	- ***Automatic-Web-access.*** It allows access, retrieval and translation into an relational format the data found in the Web sources. - A ***caching technique.*** It has been implemented using a database of retrieved records (only stored those records that are finally sent to the PlannerAgents)	This module is built with the context information necessary to access and manage their related Web sources, and by a Case-Base of records retrieved from these sources	Kqml-ACL language and TCP/IP protocol
PlannerAgent	- ***Case-Based Planning.*** It allows storage, retrieval and retention of old successful plans that can be used later by this agent (or by other PlannerAgents in the team) - ***Planning.*** Permit the use of planners (we actually use Prodigy 4.0) as main reasoning module - ***Cooperation.*** Allows to request help in the solving process to other PlannerAgents	The information to translate the user problem into an standard representation, the definition of the planning domain (e-tourism), and the Plan Base is stored, and managed, by these agents	Kqml-ACL language and TCP/IP protocol
UserAgent	- ***User/system communication.*** It allows to provide the problems, user characteristics (profile), and to show the solutions found - ***Fuzzy classification.*** A fuzzy algorithm is used to sort appropriately the solutions found by the system	Store information about the users (they can adapt the behaviour of the system defining his/her profiles), and information about the PlannerAgents that can help to solve a problem	Kqml-ACL language and TCP/IP protocol

of a fuzzy skill that is used like a classifier to select and order the most promising solutions found (this algorithm uses some characteristics provided by the users in their profiles, or a predefined pattern which uses characteristics such time of travel or cost). The main goal of the PlannerAgents is to reason and deal with the Web information gathered by the WebAgents and build solutions for the given problems. For this reason, several techniques such as Planning and Case-Base Planning have been implemented. The cooperation among PlannerAgents is also allowed. Finally, the main characteristics of the WebAgents are the Automatic-Web-access and the Caching technique implemented. The automatic Web access is implemented through a set of specialized *Wrappers* that allows those agent to access, retrieve and store in a standard format the information stored in the Web sources. In addition, the implementation of a Case Base allows those agents to minimize the number of times they need to access the Web.

From MAPWeb to MAPWeSC

This section describes how our specific B2C Information gathering application (MAPWeb) can be migrated into a new Web Services oriented architecture called MAPWeSC (**M**ulti-**A**gent **P**lanning through **We**b **S**ervice **C**omposition) to adapt an old agent-based Information Gathering application into current Web technologies.

Problems and Pitfalls in MAPWeb

When any Web Information Gathering MAS system, such as MAPWeb is deployed several problems (related to their domain application) need to be dealt with. Some of those problems can be briefly summarized as follows:

- There exist several problems related to important characteristics such as, *proactiveness, security* or *robustness*, in those Multi-agent systems. Although several CI techniques (such as Machine Learning or planning) are used to improve on previous characteristics it is necessary to study (using the current Web technologies) how to ask the following questions:
  - What happens when several Web sources are temporally down?
  - How could any agent be proactive in the Web?
- There are important problems related to the *management* of the information retrieved from the Web sources. Two main problems need to be solved - how to extract the information from several Web sites, and how represent this information in a coherent way. Therefore, for any IG Web systems it will be necessary:
  - To apply several information extraction techniques that allow the agents to automatically gather information from a particular Web site.
  - To represent (using a standard format) the information gathered from the Web, to allow this information to be shared between different information agents in the system.

Although previous problems have been traditionally solved using techniques such as Wrapper technologies or Machine learning (to automatically extract the information), ontologies (to represent the information), etc., the implementation of new Web technologies (such as XML, SOAP, Web services) provide a new frameworks that could be used to design new solutions to old problems. The previous problems could be solved using Web services technologies as follows:

- Robustness and security characteristics can be improved using the Web services security features that provide message integrity, authentication and confidentiality, message session security, etc.
- Proactiveness in a multi-agent system can be improved using the facilities of Web services discovery. The Universal Description Discovery and Integration Protocol (UDDI) specifies a protocol for querying and updating a common directory of Web service information. The directory includes information about service providers, the services they host, and the protocols those services implement. The directory also provides mechanisms to add meta-data to any registered information. Therefore, this protocol can be used by information agents (or Web agents) to automatically discover new Web sources.
- The problem of Web knowledge representation can be reduced using the XML standard representation provided by the Web service.
- The extraction of the information could be automatically learned using the provided Web service representation. If this representation is modified, it is possible to use the new data and meta-data information to build a new wrapper that is able to extract information.

Using these new set of technologies, our previous B2C Web system can be designed to adapt its functionalities to new Web services technologies.

MAPWeSC Architecture

From our initial MAPWeb architecture, the skills of several agents need to be modified to adapt them to the new Web services characteristics. Agents will be considered as Web services inside the system. Therefore some architectural characteristics will be modified:

- **Control Agents:** The ManagerAgent and CoachAgent basic skills will not be modified because they are responsible for the management of the different agents in the system. The communication processes is adapted to allow a request to the different Web service agent for a particular service (i.e., suspend a particular agent, insert or delete an agent from a particular team) to be managed as a Web service.
- **Execution Agents:** The main modifications are achieved in the information agents (or Web agents) that are adapted to the Web service. These modifications will be described in detail in the next section.

The new architecture of MAPWeSC is shown in Figure 4. This new architecture has been modified to allow the sharing of information between agents using the protocols provided by Web services such as SOAP.

Figure 4. MAPWeSC Web service-oriented architecture

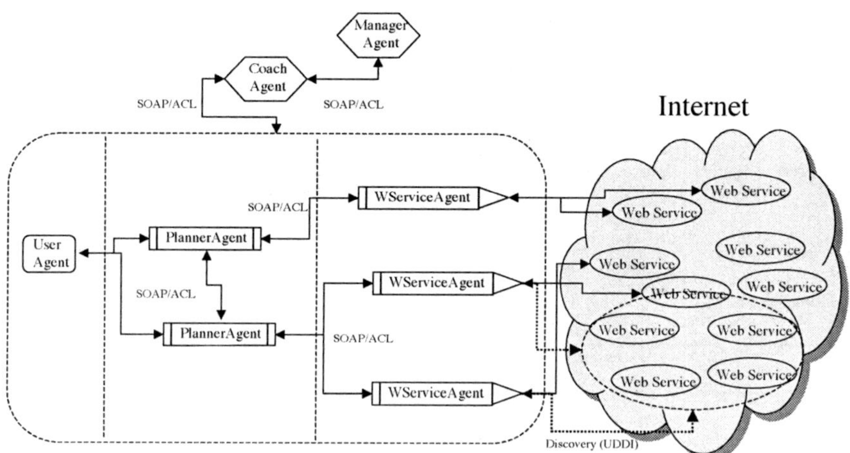

An infrastructure agent that registers a Web service agent's service as a Web service in the UDDI registry would be useful. The necessary UDDI advertisement information should be accessible in the FIPA Service Description and contain a tag to indicate the Web service agent's intent to offer its service as a Web service. A UDDI registering agent could harvest the information on such services from the Directory Facilitator and dynamically register them in the appropriate UDDI registry. The UDDI registry could be used by different agents (such as WebService agents in Figure 4) to "discover" new (potential) Web services. The suggested infrastructure elements are shown in Table 3.

Agent's Characteristics in MAPWeSC

To have a software agent access an external Web service for its own use or to offer its service to other agents is relatively straightforward. A mapping between the Web service

Table 3. Necessary elements to support agent-based Web services

Element	Functionality
Web Service Agent	Agent offers a Web service to other clients. The Web service is an exposed service of the MAS at useful level of granularity
UDDI Registering capability	Dynamically harvest descriptions of agent-based Web services and register them in the UDDI registry
Service description and translation services	Provide support for describing agent-based Web services according to FIPA, or KQML, standards and translating, where possible, to alternative descriptions of Web Services (e.g., DAML-S and WSDL, UDDI entries)

Table 4. Agent features modification to facilitate use of external Web services in MAPWeSC

	Roles	Skills	Communication Module
WebServiceAgent	- Automatic access to external Web services - Proxy external Web service agent - SOAP-Binding - Transport -- HTTP - Binding exemplar	- Interface of Web service, endpoints (WSDL file), UDDI descriptive info - Knowledge of SOAP binding to HTTP or other transport - Caching technique	SOAP/ACL
PlannerAgent	- Web services composition - Data integration	- CBP - Planning - WS querying, discovering (WS agents)	SOAP/ACL
UserAgent	- User/system interaction	- WS querying, discovering (planners)	SOAP/ACL

descriptions and the basic agent skills must be done. Table 4 presents agent roles and skills necessary to proxy an external (non-agent system) Web service.

Agents within the MAS that offer services to other agents should have the option of having these services offered as Web services for the potential use of non-agent clients. Our approach requires a new layer of software agents that have the task of offering these services. They have been modified from our old Web agents, called Web service agents (Figure 4). Other agent clients can continue to interact with the original service-offering agents in the same ACL (Agent Communication Language) Interaction protocol-based manner (i.e., FIPA, KQML). As an example, consider an agent in the MAS that has as part of its knowledge base the most recent flight ticket price. The Web service report contains information such as departure and arrival date and time, price, flight duration, number of transfers, etc. Other agents within the MAS will interact with this SearchFlights agent in pursuit of their individual goals as part of an overall agent-based application. Part of this flight information can be offered to non-agent clients through a Web Services framework. The exposure of the MAS services can be done at various levels of granularity by adjusting the information that the Web service agents offer.

Although communication between agents in any MAS is intrinsically asynchronous, a Web browser (and any Web service) typically expects a synchronous response. We have implemented in MAPWeSC asynchronous communications embedded in a synchronous communication module.

Finally, The Web service software agent must advertise its service. It must have its service advertised in the UDDI registry (for non-agent clients) and with the Directory Facilitator (for agent clients, in our approach this service needs to be advertised to the CoachAgent). The Web service software agent must describe its service on the agent platform. Since this is the same service that is being offered to non-agent clients, the service information content would also be useful for its entries in the UDDI registry and in its WSDL file. A mapping is needed. The UDDI registry entry for a Web service must contain at least one pointer to a WSDL access file, in addition to any descriptive information. Information on where the WSDL access file is hosted must be provided to the agent platform.

Conclusion

This chapter has analyzed how a Multi-Agent System can be redesigned using a Web services oriented architecture. This new design perspective allows any MAS to utilize Web services technologies, and provides a natural way to share their information product with other business-to-consumer (B2C) applications.

Two alternatives can be considered for empowering Web services with agents' properties. One is to implement a wrapper that turns a current Web service into an agent-like entity. The other alternative is to capture all the functionalities of a Web Service and embed them into an existing software agent in a MultiAgent System. While the first approach is quite straightforward it doesn't guarantee a large-scale usage. The second approach requires considering a reconfiguration of the new agent as a Web Service. To do so, we have described and redesigned a new kind of information agent, called a Web service agent, to make it advertisable in a UDDI registry, and accessible through the SOAP communication protocol.

Using our previous multi-agent approach, we have obtained several advantages. On one hand, we allow the building of active, autonomous, cooperative and context-aware Web service agents. On the other hand, these agents can coordinate their work with other agents (i.e., planner agents) to allow an automatic service composition, through the utilization of other CI techniques such as planning (Camacho & Aler, in press; Camacho et al., 2005).

References

Abowd, G., Atkeson, C., Hong, J., Long, S., Kooper, R., & Pinkerton, M. (1997). Cyberguide: A mobile context-aware tour guide. *ACM Wireless, 3*, 421-433.

Ambite, J. L., Barish, G., Knoblock, C. A., Muslea, M., Oh, J., & Minton, S. (2002). Getting from here to there: Interactive planning and agent execution for optimizing travel. In S. Chien & J. Riedl (Eds.), *Proceedings of the Fourteenth Innovative Applications of Artificial Intelligence Conference (IAAI)*. Edmonton, Canada: AAAI.

Ambite, J. L., Genevieve, G., Gordon, P., Pan, Q., & Bharracharjee, S. (2002). Integrating heterogeneous data sources for better freight flow analysis and planning. In *Proceedings of the Second National Conference on Digital Government Research*. Redondo Beach, CA: Digital Government Research Center. Retrieved May 8, 2005, from http://www.dgrc.org/conferences/2002_proceedings.jsp

Ambite et al. (2004). ARGOS: Dynamic composition of Web services for goods movement analysis. In *Proceedings of the National Conference on Digital Government Research*. Redondo Beach, CA: Digital Government Research Center. Retrieved May 8, 2005, from http://dgrc.org/dgo2004/

Baeza-Yates, R., & Ribeiro-Neto, B. (1999). *Modern information retrieval*. London: Addison-Wesley Longman.

Berners-Lee, T. (2003). *Web services. Program integration across application and organization boundaries.* Retrieved July 24, 2003, from http://www.w3.org/DesignIssues/WebServices.html

Berners-Lee, T., Hendler, J., & Lassila, O. (2001, May). The semantic Web. *Scientific American, 284*(5), 34-43.

Camacho, D., & Aler, R. (2005). Software and performance measures for evaluating multi-agent frameworks. *Applied Artificial Intelligence, 19*(6), 645-657.

Camacho, D., Aler, R., Borrajo, D., & Molina, J. M. (2005). A multi-agent architecture for intelligent gathering systems. *AI Communications: The European Journal on Artificial Intelligence, 18*(1), 1-19.

Camacho, D., Borrajo, D., & Molina, J. M. (2001). Intelligent travel planning: A multi-agent planning system to solve Web problems in the e-tourism domain. *International Journal on Autonomous Agents and Multiagent Systems*, *4*(4), 387-392.

Camacho, D., Borrajo, D., Molina, J. M., & Aler, R. (2001, September). Flexible integration of planning and information gathering. In A. Cesta & D. Borrajo (Eds.), *Proceedings of the European Conference on Planning (ECP-01),* Spain (pp. 73-84). Berlin: Springer-Verlag.

Carranza, C., Muñoz-Avila, H., Weberskirch, F., & Bergmann, R. (1998). Proposal for a planning approach for information seeking. In R. Bergmann & A. Kott (Eds.), *AIPS'98 Workshop on Integrating Planning, Scheduling and Execution in Dynamic and Uncertain Environments*. Pittsburgh, PA: AAAI.

Chavez, A., Dreilinger, D., Guttman, R., & Maes, P. (1997, April). A real-life experiment in creating an agent marketplace. In *Proceedings of the Second International Conference on the Practical Application of Intelligent Agents and Multi-Agent Technology (PAAM'97)*. London.

Chen, H., Chung, Y., Ramsey, M., & Yang, C. (2001). A smart itsy bitsy spider for the Web. *Journal of the American Society for Information Science*, *49*(7), 604-618.

Cheverst, K., Davies, N., Mitchell, K., Friday, A., & Efstratiou, C. (2000). Developing a context-aware electronic tourist guide: Some issues and experiences. In J. M. Carroll & P. P. Tanner (Eds.), *Conference on Human-Computer Interaction* (pp. 17-24). The Hague, The Netherlands: ACM.

Curbera, F., Duftler, M., Khalaf, R., Nagy, W., Mukhi, N., & Weerawarana, S. (2002). Unravelling the Web services Web: An introduction to SOAP, WSDL, and UDDI. *IEEE Internet Computing*, *6*(2), 86-93.

Daniels, J. J., & Rissland, E. L. (1995). A case-based approach to intelligent information retrieval. In *Proceedings of the Eighteenth Annual International ACM SIGIR*

Conference on Research and Development in Information Retrieval (pp. 238-245). Seattle, WA: ACM.

Decker, K., Sycara, K., & Williamson, M. (1997). Middle-agents for the Internet. In *Proceedings of the Thirteenth International Joint Conference on Artificial Intelligence (IJCAI-97)*. Nagoya, Japan. Retrieved May 8, 2005, from http://citeseer.ist.psu.edu/decker97middleagents.html

Fan, Y., & Gauch, S. (1999). Adaptive agents for information gathering from multiple, distributed information sources. *Proceedings of 1999 AAAI Symposium on Intelligent Agents in Cyberspace*. Stanford University, AAAI Press. Retrieved May 8, 2005, from http://www.ittc.ku.edu/~sgauch/papers/AAAI99.html

Ferber, J. (1999). *Multi-agent systems: An introduction to distributed artificial intelligence*. London: Addison-Wesley Professional.

FIPA-org. (1997) Agent communication language. *Technical report, Foundation for intelligent physical agents*. Retrieved May 8, 2005, from http://www.fipa.org

Fodor, O., Dell'Erba, M., Ricci, F., & Werthner, H. (2002, October 7-9). Harmonise: A solution for data interoperability. In *Proceedings of the Second IFIP Conference on E-Commerce, E-Business and E-Government* (pp. 1-13). Lisbon, Portugal. Retrieved May 8, 2005, from http://ectrl.itc.it:8080/home/publications/2002/Harmonise_IFIP02-5.pdf

Franklin, S., & Graesser, A. (1996). Is it an agent, or just a program? A taxonomy for autonomous agents. In J. P. Müller, M. Wooldridge, & N. R. Jennings (Eds.), *Proceedings of the Third International Workshop on Agent Theories, Architectures, and Languages* (pp. 21-35). London: Springer-Verlag.

Gardner, T. (2001, October). An introduction to Web services. *Ariadne, 29*. Retrieved May 8, 2005, from http://www.ariadne.ac.uk/issue29/gardner/intro.html

Howe, A. E., & Dreilinger, D. (1997). Savvysearch. A metasearch engine that learns which search engines to query. *AI Magazine*, *18*(2), 19-25.

Hüllen, J., Bergmann, R., & Weberskirch, F. (1999). WebPlan: Dynamic planning for domain-specific search in the Internet. In *Proceedings of the Workshop Planen und Konfigurieren (PuK-99)*.

Jones, K. S., & Willett, P. (1997). *Readings in information retrieval*. San Francisco: Morgan Kaufmann.

Knoblock et al. (2000). The Ariadne approach to Web-based information integration. *International Journal on Cooperative Information Systems (IJCIS) Special Issue on Intelligent Information Agents: Theory and Applications*, *10*(1-2), 145-169.

Lieberman, H. (1995). Letizia: An agent that assists Web browsing. In C. S. Mellish (Ed.), *International Joint Conference on Artificial Intelligence (IJCAI95) Montreal, Canada* (pp. 924-929). San Mateo, CA: Morgan Kaufmann.

McIlraith S., Son T. C., & Zeng, H. (2002). Semantic Web services, *IEEE Intelligent Systems, Special Issue on the Semantic Web*, *16*(2), 46-53.

OASIS-UDDI. (2005). *Advancing Web services discovery standard, UDDI version 3.0.2*. Retrieved May 8, 2005, from http://uddi.org/pubs/uddi_v3.htm

Petrie, C. (1996). Agent-based engineering, the Web, and intelligence. *IEEE Expert, 11*(6), 24-29.

Ricci F., Arslan B., Mirzadeh N., & Venturini A. (2002, September 4-7). ITR: A case-based travel advisory system. In S. Craw & A. D. Preece (Eds.), *Proceedings of the Sixth European Conference on Case Based Reasoning (ECCBR 2002),* Aberdeen, Scotland (pp. 613-627). LNCS 2416. Berlin: Springer Verlag.

SOAP. (2003). *Simple Object Access Protocol 1.1*. Retrieved May 8, 2005, from http://www.w3.org/TR/soap/

Sycara, K. P. (1998). Multiagent systems. *AI Magazine, 19*(2), 79-92.

Sycara, K. P. (1989). Multiagent compromise via negotiation. In M. Huhns (Ed.),. *Distributed artificial intelligence, Volume II* (pp. 119-138). San Mateo, CA: Morgan Kaufmann.

Wooldridge, M. (2002). *An introduction to multi-agent systems.* Chichester, UK: John Wiley.

Wooldridge, M., & Jennings, N. R. (1995), Agent theories, architectures, and languages: A survey. In M. Wooldridge & N. R. Jennings (Eds.), *Intelligent agents* (pp. 1-22). Berlin: Springer-Verlag.

WSDL. (2001). *Web services description language 1.1.* W3C Note 15 March 2001. Retrieved May 8, 2005, from http://www.w3.org/TR/wsdl

WWW Consortium. (2002). *Semantic Web services.* Retrieved May 8, 2005, from http://www.w3.org/2002/ws

Yang, J., Yang, W., Denecke, M., & Waibel, A. (1999). Smart sight: A tourist assistant system. In *International Software Web Conference* (pp. 73-78).

Zipf, A., (2002). User-adaptive maps for location-based services (lbs) for tourism. In *Proceedings of the Ninth International Conference for Information and Communication Technologies in Tourism, ENTER 2002.* Berlin: Springer Verlag. Retrieved May 8, 2005, from http://www2.geoinform.fh-mainz.de/~zipf/ENTER2002.pdf

Chapter VII

Web Mining System for Mobile-Phone Marketing

Miao-Ling Wang, Minghsin University of Science & Technology, Taiwan, ROC

Hsiao-Fan Wang, National Tsing Hua University, Taiwan, ROC[1]

Abstract

With the ever-increasing and ever-changing flow of information available on the Web, information analysis has never been more important. Web text mining, which includes text categorization, text clustering, association analysis and prediction of trends, can assist us in discovering useful information in an effective and efficient manner. In this chapter, we have proposed a Web mining system that incorporates both online efficiency and off-line effectiveness to provide the "right" information based on users' preferences. A Bi-Objective Fuzzy c*-Means algorithm and information retrieval technique, for text categorization, clustering and integration, was employed for analysis. The proposed system is illustrated via a case involving the Web site marketing of mobile phones. A variety of Web sites exist on the Internet and a common type involves the trading of goods. In this type of Web site, the question to ask is:* If we want to establish a Web site that provides information about products, how can we respond quickly and accurately to queries? *This is equivalent to asking:* How can we design a flexible search engine according to users' preferences? *In this study, we have applied data mining techniques to cope with such problems, by proposing, as an example, a Web site providing information on mobile phones in Taiwan. In order to efficiently provide useful information, two tasks were considered during the Web design phase. One related to off-line analysis: this was done by first carrying out a survey of frequent Web users, students between 15 and 40 years of age, regarding their preferences, so that Web customers' behavior could be characterized. Then the survey data, as well as the products offered, were classified into different demand and preference groups. The other task was related to online query: this was done through the application of an information retrieval technique that responded to users' queries. Based on the ideas above the remainder of the chapter is organized as follows: first, we present a literature review, introduce some concepts and review existing methods relevant to our study, then, the proposed Web mining system is presented, a case study of a mobile-phone marketing Web site is illustrated and finally, a summary and conclusions are offered.*

Literature Review

Over 150 million people, worldwide, have become Internet users since 1994. The rapid development of information technology and the Internet has changed the traditional business environment. The Internet has enabled the development of Electronic Commerce (e-commerce), which can be defined as selling, buying, conducting logistics, or other organization-management activities, via the Web (Schneider, 2004). Companies are finding that using the Web makes it easier for their business to communicate effectively with customers. For example, Amazom.com, an online bookstore that started up in 1998, reached an annual sales volume of over $1 billion in 2003 (Schneider, 2004). Much research has focused on the impact and mechanisms of e-commerce (Angelides, 1997; Hanson, 2000; Janal, 1995; Mohammed, Fisher, Jaworski, & Paddison, 2004; Rayport & Jaworski, 2002; Schneider, 2004). Although many people challenge the future of e-commerce, Web site managers must take advantage of Internet specialties which potentially enable their companies to make higher profits and their customers to make better decisions. Given that the amount of information available on the Web is large and rapidly increasing, determining an effective way to help users find useful information has become critical. Existing document retrieval systems are mostly based on the Boolean Logic model. Such systems' applications can be rather limited because they cannot handle ambiguous requests. Chen and Wang (1995) proposed a knowledge-based fuzzy information retrieval method, using the concept of fuzzy sets to represent the categories or features of documents. Fuzzy Set Theory was introduced by Zadeh (1965), and is different from traditional Set Theory, as it uses the concept of membership functions to deal with questions that cannot be solved by two-valued logic. Fuzzy Set Theory concepts have been applied to solve special dynamic processes, especially those observations concerned with linguistic values.

Because the Fuzzy concept has been shown to be applicable when coping with linguistic and vague queries, Chen and Wang's method is discussed below. Their method is based on a concept matrix for knowledge representation and is defined by a symmetric relation matrix as follows:

$$A = \begin{matrix} A_1 \\ A_2 \\ \vdots \\ A_n \end{matrix} \begin{bmatrix} a_{11} & a_{12} & \cdots & a_{1n} \\ a_{21} & a_{22} & & \vdots \\ \vdots & & \ddots & \vdots \\ a_{n1} & a_{n2} & \cdots & a_{nn} \end{bmatrix} \quad (1)$$

$$0 \le a_{ij} \le 1, \quad 1 \le i \le n, \quad 1 \le j \le n$$

where n is the number of concepts, and a_{ij} represents the relevant values between concepts A_i and A_j with $a_{ii} = 1$, $\forall\, i$. It can be seen that this concept matrix can reveal the relationship between properties used to describe objects, which has benefits for product identification, query solving, and online sales development. For effective analysis, these properties, determined as the attributes of an object, should be independent of each other; however this may not always be so. Therefore a transitive closure matrix A^* must be obtained from the following definition.

Definition 1: Let A be a concept matrix as shown in Equation (1), define:

$$A^2 = A \otimes A$$

$$= \begin{bmatrix} \bigvee_{i=1,\cdots,n} (a_{1i} \wedge a_{i1}) & \bigvee_{i=1,\cdots,n} (a_{1i} \wedge a_{i2}) & \cdots & \bigvee_{i=1,\cdots,n} (a_{1i} \wedge a_{in}) \\ \bigvee_{i=1,\cdots,n} (a_{2i} \wedge a_{i1}) & \bigvee_{i=1,\cdots,n} (a_{2i} \wedge a_{i2}) & \cdots & \bigvee_{i=1,\cdots,n} (a_{2i} \wedge a_{in}) \\ \vdots & \vdots & \ddots & \vdots \\ \bigvee_{i=1,\cdots,n} (a_{ni} \wedge a_{i1}) & \bigvee_{i=1,\cdots,n} (a_{ni} \wedge a_{i2}) & \cdots & \bigvee_{i=1,\cdots,n} (a_{ni} \wedge a_{in}) \end{bmatrix} \quad (2)$$

where $\otimes$ is the max-min composite operation with "$\vee$" being the maximum operation and "$\wedge$" being the minimum operation. If there exists an integer $p \le n - 1$ such that $A^p = A^{p+1} = A^{p+2} = \ldots$, $A^* = A^p$ is called the Transitive Closure of the concept matrix A.

Matrix A^* is an equivalent matrix which satisfies reflexive, symmetric and transitive properties.

To identify each object by its properties, a document descriptor matrix D is constructed in the following form:

$$D = \begin{array}{c} \\ D_1 \\ D_2 \\ \vdots \\ D_m \end{array} \begin{array}{c} \begin{array}{cccc} A_1 & A_2 & \cdots & A_n \end{array} \\ \begin{bmatrix} d_{11} & d_{12} & \cdots & d_{1n} \\ d_{21} & d_{22} & \cdots & d_{2n} \\ \vdots & \vdots & \ddots & \vdots \\ d_{m1} & d_{m2} & \cdots & d_{mn} \end{bmatrix} \end{array} \tag{3}$$

$$0 \leq d_{ij} \leq 1$$

where d_{ij} represents the degree of relevance of document D_i with respect to concept A_j and m is the number of documents in general terms. By applying the max-min composite operation $\otimes$ to D and A^*, we have matrix $B = D \otimes A^* = [b_{ij}]_{m\times n}$ where b_{ij} represents the relevance of each document D_i with respect to a particular concept A_j.

The implication of this approach for Web mining is: when we classify objects by their properties, if we can also cluster people according to their properties and preferences, then when a query is made, matching a user's properties to retrieval of the corresponding concept matrices of each cluster will speed up online response.

Clustering is fundamental to data mining. Clustering algorithms are used extensively, not only to organize and categorize data, but also for data compression and model construction. There are two major types of clustering algorithms: hierarchical and partitioning. A hierarchical algorithm produces a nested series of patterns with similarity levels at which groupings change. A partitioning algorithm produces only one partition by optimizing an objective function, for example, squared-error criterion (Chen, 2001). Using clustering methods, a data set can be partitioned into several groups, such that the degree of similarity within a group is high, and similarity between the groups is low. There are various kinds of clustering methods (Chen, 2001; Jang, Sun, & Mizutani, 1997; Wang, Wang, & Wu, 1994). In this study, we applied the forward off-line method in order to group people according to their properties and preferences.

The *c*-Means algorithm (Tamura, Higuchi, & Tanaka, 1971) also called Hard *c*-Means (HCM), is a commonly used objective-clustering method, which finds the center of each cluster and minimizes the total spread around these cluster centers. By defining the distance from each datum to the center (a measure of Euclidean distance), the model ensures that each datum is assigned to exactly one cluster. However, in this case in contrast to the HCM, there is vague data and elements may belong to several clusters, with different degrees of belonging. For such situations, Bezdek (1973) developed an algorithm called the Fuzzy *c*-Means (FCM) algorithm for fuzzy partitioning, such that one datum can belong to several groups with degrees of belonging, specified by membership values between 0 and 1. Obviously, the FCM is more flexible than the HCM, when determining data related to degrees of belonging.

Because of the vague boundaries of fuzzy clusters, Wang et al. (1994) showed that it is not sufficient to classify a fuzzy system simply by minimizing the within-group variance. Instead, the maximal between-group variance also had to be taken into account. This led to a Bi-objective Fuzzy c-Means Method (BOFCM) as shown below, in which the performance of clustering can be seen to be improved:

$$\text{(BOFCM):}\quad \begin{aligned} &Min \quad Z(U;V)=\sum_{i=1}^{c}\sum_{k=1}^{K}(\mu_{ik})^2\|x_k - v_i\|^2 \\ &Max \quad L(U;V)=\sum_{i=1}^{c}\sum_{j<i}\|v_i - v_j\|^2 \\ &\text{subject to} \quad \sum_{i=1}^{c}\mu_{ik}=1, \quad \forall k=1,\dots,K \\ &\qquad \mu_{ik}\geq 0, \quad \forall i=1,..,c, k=1,\dots,K \end{aligned}, \tag{4}$$

where c is number of the clusters, $\|\cdot\|$ is an inner product norm, x_k, $k = 1, \dots, K$, denote K elements, v_i, $i = 1, \dots, c$ is the center of Cluster i and μ_{ik}, $i = 1, \dots, c$; $k = 1, \dots, K$ are the membership values of x_k belonging to Cluster i.

The Web Mining System

When looking at Web site development, it needs to be appreciated that Web users can be quite capricious, given the multitude of Web sites available on the Internet. The question arises: how should a Web site be set up so that it provides the right product information to the right customers? And specifically, how can the query response time be speeded up?

Clustering types of users with their preferences is one solution. From the above discussion, it can be seen that we may use the BOFCM algorithm for this purpose. After introducing the weights $\alpha, \beta, \alpha+\beta = 1$ for the objectives, Model (4) was transformed into a single objective nonlinear problem. The following lemmas provide the basis for solving it:

Lemma 1 (Wang et al., 1994): The solution set of Model (4) can be found by:

$$v_i = \frac{\beta\sum_{k=1}^{K}\mu_{ik}^2 x_k}{\beta\sum_{k=1}^{K}\mu_{ik}^2 - \alpha c} - \frac{\alpha\sum_{s=1}^{c}\frac{\beta\sum_{k=1}^{K}\mu_{sk}^2 x_k}{\beta\sum_{k=1}^{K}\mu_{sk}^2 - \alpha c}}{\left(\beta\sum_{k=1}^{K}\mu_{ik}^2 - \alpha c\right)\left(1+\alpha\sum_{s=1}^{c}\frac{1}{\beta\sum_{k=1}^{n}\mu_{sk}^2 - \alpha c}\right)}, \tag{5}$$

$$\mu_{ik} = \frac{\left(\frac{1}{\left\|x_k - v_i\right\|^2}\right)^{1/f-1}}{\sum_{s=1}^{c}\left(\frac{1}{\left\|x_k - v_s\right\|^2}\right)^{1/f-1}}. \tag{6}$$

Then, the solution procedures can be summarized as:

Step 1. Fix c. Give the initial membership value of each datum to each cluster, that is, the membership matrix $U^{(0)} = [\mu_{ik}^{(0)}]$ is constructed. Assign an allowed perturbed value τ and set $\delta = \tau, f=2$, and $l=0$.

Step 2. Calculate α and β by using $U^{(l)}$, $\alpha = \min_i \left\{ \frac{\sum_{k=1}^{K} (\mu_{ik}^{(0)})^2}{\sum_{k=1}^{K} (\mu_{ik}^{(0)})^2 + c - 1} \right\} - \delta$ and

$$\beta = \max_i \left\{ \frac{c-1}{\sum_{k=1}^{K} (\mu_{ik}^{(0)})^2 + c - 1} \right\} + \delta.$$

Step 3. Calculate $\{v_i^{(l)}\}$ with Equation (5) and $U^{(l)}$.

Step 4. Calculate the new membership matrix $U^{(l+1)}$ by using $\{v_i^{(l)}\}$ and Equation (6), if $x_k \neq v_i^{(l)}$; else set $\mu_{jk}^{(l+1)} = \begin{cases} 1, \text{for} & j = i \\ 0, \text{for} & j \neq i \end{cases}$.

Step 5. Let $\delta = \tau + \delta$ and go to Step 2 if $\{\mu_{ik}^{(l+1)}\}$ does not satisfy $\alpha < \min_i \left\{ \frac{\sum_{k=1}^{K} (\mu_{ik}^{(l+1)})^2}{\sum_{k=1}^{K} (\mu_{ik}^{(l+1)})^2 + c - 1} \right\}$

and $\beta > \max_i \left\{ \frac{c-1}{\sum_{k=1}^{K} (\mu_{ik}^{(l+1)})^2 + c - 1} \right\}$.

Step 6. Calculate $\Delta = \left\| \widetilde{U}^{(l+1)} - \widetilde{U}^{(l)} \right\|$. If $\Delta > \varepsilon$ set $l=l+1$ and go to Step 3. If $\Delta \le \varepsilon$ stop.

From the above analysis, we can obtain the clustered data within each center.

To speed up the process, the documents can also be grouped according to their degrees of similarity, as defined by Jaccard's coefficient as follows:

$$r_{ij} = \frac{\sum_{s=1}^{m} \min[b_{is}, b_{js}]}{\sum_{s=1}^{m} \max[b_{is}, b_{js}]}, \quad 0 \le b_{is}, b_{js} \le 1, \tag{7}$$

where r_{ij} is the similarity between document D_i and document D_j. b_{iS}, b_{jS} from matrix B are the relevant values with respect to documents D_i, D_k and documents D_j, D_k. So we can obtain the document fuzzy relationship matrix R:

$$R = \begin{array}{c} \\ D_1 \\ D_2 \\ \vdots \\ D_m \end{array} \begin{array}{c} \begin{array}{cccc} D_1 & D_2 & \cdots & D_m \end{array} \\ \begin{bmatrix} r_{11} & r_{12} & \cdots & r_{1m} \\ r_{21} & r_{22} & \cdots & r_{1m} \\ \vdots & \vdots & \ddots & \vdots \\ r_{m1} & r_{m2} & \cdots & r_{mm} \end{bmatrix} \end{array} \tag{8}$$

Again a transitive closure R^* of R must be obtained. Then by defining an acceptable level of λ by the mean of the upper triangular matrix R^*, i.e., $\lambda = \dfrac{\sum_{i=1}^{m-1} \sum_{j>i}^{m} r_{ij}}{\left(m(m-1) \big/ 2 \right)}$, we have an λ-threshold partition of documents into clusters. Based on the document descriptor of each document, we can obtain a cluster-concept matrix B':

$$B' = \begin{array}{c} \\ Group\ 1 \\ Group\ 2 \\ \vdots \\ Group\ u \end{array} \begin{array}{c} \begin{array}{cccc} A_1 & A_2 & \cdots & A_n \end{array} \\ \begin{bmatrix} b'_{11} & b'_{12} & \cdots & b'_{1n} \\ b'_{21} & b'_{22} & \cdots & b'_{2n} \\ \vdots & \vdots & \ddots & \vdots \\ b'_{u1} & b'_{u2} & \cdots & b'_{un} \end{bmatrix} \end{array}, \tag{9}$$

where u is the number of clusters of documents.

Figure 1. Framework of the Web mining system

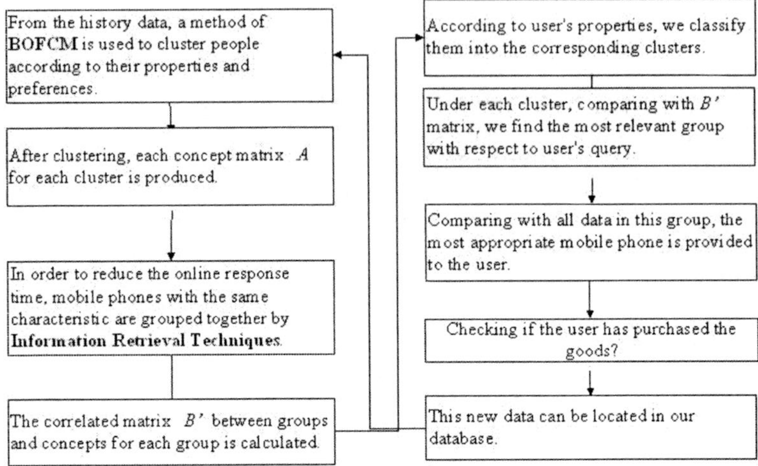

With the results of above off-line analysis, a user can take advantage of the clustered documents to improve response time when making an online query. By comparing the matrix B' with the user's query vector, the most relevant cluster(s) are selected. Then, by searching the documents within the selected cluster(s), the documents may be retrieved more efficiently. The framework of the proposed Web mining system (Lin, 2002), with both online and off-line operations, is shown in Figure 1.

A Case Study of the Web Mining System

In order to demonstrate the proposed system, a Web site, called veryMobile-Phone (http://203.68.224.196/verymobile/), was constructed in Chinese, in order to catch the behavior of local customers in Taiwan. The online operation procedure, based on the information provided from an off-line established database, is shown in Figure 2.

This initial database was established based on a survey of 800 individuals. The respondents were full- and part-time students, ranging from 15 to 35 years of age, at the Minghsin University of Science and Technology and full-time students, ranging from 20 to 30 years of age, at the Tsing Hua University. A total of 638 questionnaires were returned. After deleting invalid questionnaires, we had 562 valid responses. In this questionnaire, personal data, such as *Sex — male or female*; *Age — under 15, 16~18, 19~22, 23~30 or over 30*; *Education — senior high school, college, university, masters, Ph.D. or others*; *Average Income — none, under NTS 18,000, 18,000~30,000, 30,000~45,000 or over 45,000* were recorded, along with their preferences in purchasing

Figure 2. Flow diagram of verymobile-phone system

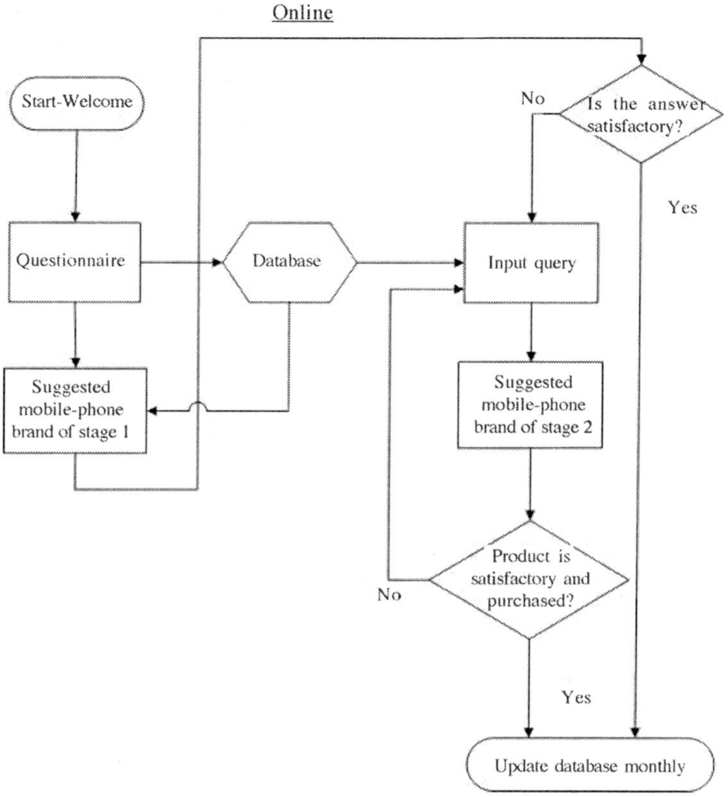

a mobile phone, with features made up of A_1:*brand*, A_2:*external*, A_3:*price*, A_4:*service*, A_5:*function*, A_6:*ease of use*, A_7:*special offer*, etc. Via the BOFCM, users were classified into c=4 groups. The mobile phones, in stock, were also grouped by their features, according to the concepts defined for information retrieval. Below, we demonstrate how the proposed mechanism can be used to suggest the appropriate mobile phone brand for each user, by responding to his or her query, based on his or her features and preferences.

Off-Line Phase

The off-line analysis is used mainly to establish the initial database features, including user categories and preferences, as well as mobile phone clusters. The users' data were grouped by applying the BOFCM. Four clusters were obtained and stored. For each group of users, the concept matrix was calculated, as shown below, to describe the preference relationships obtained among the mobile phones features:

$$A1 = \begin{array}{r} \\ \\ \text{brand} \\ \text{external} \\ \text{price} \\ \text{service} \\ \text{function} \\ \text{ease of use} \\ \text{special offer} \end{array} \begin{array}{c} \begin{array}{ccccccc} \text{brand} & \text{external} & \text{price} & \text{service} & \text{function} & \text{ease of use} & \text{special offer} \end{array} \\ \begin{bmatrix} 1 & 0.11 & 0.12 & 0.1 & 0.07 & 0.11 & 0 \\ 0.11 & 1 & 0.1 & 0.08 & 0.06 & 0.09 & 0 \\ 0.12 & 0.12 & 1 & 0.09 & 0.07 & 0.11 & 0 \\ 0.1 & 0.08 & 0.09 & 1 & 0.05 & 0.1 & 0 \\ 0.07 & 0.06 & 0.07 & 0.05 & 1 & 0.06 & 0 \\ 0.11 & 0.09 & 0.11 & 0.1 & 0.06 & 1 & 0 \\ 0 & 0 & 0 & 0 & 0 & 0 & 1 \end{bmatrix} \end{array};$$

$$A2 = \begin{array}{r} \\ \\ \text{brand} \\ \text{external} \\ \text{price} \\ \text{service} \\ \text{function} \\ \text{ease of use} \\ \text{special offer} \end{array} \begin{array}{c} \begin{array}{ccccccc} \text{brand} & \text{external} & \text{price} & \text{service} & \text{function} & \text{ease of use} & \text{special offer} \end{array} \\ \begin{bmatrix} 1 & 0.12 & 0.15 & 0.1 & 0.09 & 0.15 & 0 \\ 0.12 & 1 & 0.11 & 0.08 & 0.07 & 0.1 & 0 \\ 0.15 & 0.11 & 1 & 0.1 & 0.08 & 0.12 & 0 \\ 0.1 & 0.08 & 0.1 & 1 & 0.06 & 0.09 & 0 \\ 0.09 & 0.07 & 0.08 & 0.06 & 1 & 0.07 & 0 \\ 0.15 & 0.1 & 0.12 & 0.09 & 0.07 & 1 & 0 \\ 0 & 0 & 0 & 0 & 0 & 0 & 1 \end{bmatrix} \end{array};$$

$$A3 = \begin{array}{r} \\ \\ \text{brand} \\ \text{external} \\ \text{price} \\ \text{service} \\ \text{function} \\ \text{ease of use} \\ \text{special offer} \end{array} \begin{array}{c} \begin{array}{ccccccc} \text{brand} & \text{external} & \text{price} & \text{service} & \text{function} & \text{ease of use} & \text{special offer} \end{array} \\ \begin{bmatrix} 1 & 0.13 & 0.15 & 0.12 & 0.1 & 0.13 & 0.05 \\ 0.13 & 1 & 0.11 & 0.1 & 0.08 & 0.1 & 0.04 \\ 0.15 & 0.11 & 1 & 0.12 & 0.09 & 0.12 & 0.05 \\ 0.12 & 0.1 & 0.12 & 1 & 0.08 & 0.1 & 0.04 \\ 0.1 & 0.08 & 0.09 & 0.08 & 1 & 0.08 & 0.03 \\ 0.13 & 0.1 & 0.12 & 0.1 & 0.08 & 1 & 0.04 \\ 0.05 & 0.04 & 0.05 & 0.04 & 0.03 & 0.04 & 1 \end{bmatrix} \end{array};$$

$$A4 = \begin{array}{r} \\ \\ \text{brand} \\ \text{external} \\ \text{price} \\ \text{service} \\ \text{function} \\ \text{ease of use} \\ \text{special offer} \end{array} \begin{array}{c} \begin{array}{ccccccc} \text{brand} & \text{external} & \text{price} & \text{service} & \text{function} & \text{ease of use} & \text{special offer} \end{array} \\ \begin{bmatrix} 1 & 0.12 & 0.14 & 0.12 & 0.08 & 0.13 & 0.04 \\ 0.12 & 1 & 0.11 & 0.1 & 0.07 & 0.11 & 0.03 \\ 0.14 & 0.11 & 1 & 0.11 & 0.08 & 0.12 & 0.04 \\ 0.12 & 0.1 & 0.11 & 1 & 0.07 & 0.11 & 0.04 \\ 0.08 & 0.07 & 0.06 & 0.07 & 1 & 0.08 & 0.03 \\ 0.13 & 0.11 & 0.12 & 0.11 & 0.08 & 1 & 0.04 \\ 0.04 & 0.03 & 0.04 & 0.04 & 0.03 & 0.04 & 1 \end{bmatrix} \end{array}.$$

Taking Cluster 2 as an example, the transitive closure of the concept matrix $A2$ is shown in the following analysis:

$A2^* =$

	brand	external	price	service	function	ease of use	special offer
brand	1	0.12	0.15	0.1	0.09	0.15	0
external	0.12	1	0.12	0.1	0.09	0.12	0
price	0.15	0.12	1	0.1	0.09	0.1	0
service	0.1	0.1	0.1	1	0.09	0.1	0
function	0.09	0.09	0.09	0.09	1	0.09	0
ease of use	0.15	0.12	0.15	0.1	0.09	1	0
special offer	0	0	0	0	0	0	1

In the meantime, the document descriptor matrix was generated by 14 mobile-phone brands versus 7 concepts:

$D =$

	brand	external	price	service	function	ease of use	special offer
BenQ	0	0.14	0.29	0	0.14	0	0.43
ALCATEL	0.13	0.38	0.25	0	0.06	0	0.19
Sony ERICSSON	0.17	0.27	0.08	0.06	0.27	0.04	0.12
Kyocera	0	0.80	0.07	0	0.07	0	0.07
Mitsubishi	0.20	0.40	0	0	0.20	0	0.20
MOTOROLA	0.17	0.30	0.11	0.03	0.21	0.06	0.12
NEC	0.17	0.39	0.22	0.04	0.17	0	0.00
NOKIA	0.22	0.27	0.19	0.02	0.21	0.03	0.06
Panasonic	0.10	0.54	0.10	0	0.17	0	0.08
PHILIPS	0	0.33	0.50	0	0	0	0.17
SAGEM	0.14	0.21	0.14	0.07	0.11	0	0.32
SIEMENS	0.04	0.17	0.25	0	0.33	0	0.21
BOSCH	0	0	0.67	0	0	0	0.33
Others	0	0	1.00	0	0	0	0.00

To obtain the document-concept matrix, the D and $A2^*$ matrix was composed.

$B2 = D \otimes A2^* =$

	brand	external	price	service	function	ease of use	special offer
BenQ	0.15	0.14	0.29	0.10	0.14	0.15	0.43
ALCATEL	0.15	0.38	0.25	0.10	0.09	0.15	0.19
Sony ERICSSON	0.17	0.27	0.15	0.10	0.27	0.15	0.12
Kyocera	0.12	0.80	0.12	0.10	0.09	0.12	0.07
Mitsubishi	0.20	0.40	0.15	0.10	0.20	0.15	0.20
MOTOROLA	0.17	0.30	0.15	0.10	0.21	0.15	0.12
NEC	0.17	0.39	0.22	0.10	0.17	0.15	0.00
NOKIA	0.22	0.27	0.19	0.10	0.21	0.15	0.06
Panasonic	0.12	0.54	0.12	0.10	0.17	0.12	0.08
PHILIPS	0.15	0.33	0.50	0.10	0.09	0.15	0.17
SAGEM	0.14	0.21	0.14	0.10	0.11	0.14	0.32
SIEMENS	0.15	0.17	0.25	0.10	0.33	0.15	0.21
BOSCH	0.15	0.12	0.67	0.10	0.09	0.15	0.33
Others	0.15	0.12	1.00	0.10	0.09	0.15	0.00

From the matrix $B2$, the relationship between each mobile phone is calculated.

$R2 =$

	BenQ	ALCATEL	Sony ERICSSON	Kyocera	Mitsubishi	MOTOROLA	NEC	NOKIA	Panasonic	PHILIPS	SAGAM	SIEMENS	BOSCH	Others
BenQ	1.00	0.65	0.57	0.37	0.58	0.58	0.53	0.56	0.45	0.61	0.74	0.70	0.69	0.43
ALCATEL	0.65	1.00	0.68	0.58	0.81	0.73	0.77	0.67	0.65	0.79	0.69	0.70	0.56	0.42
Sony ERICSSON	0.57	0.68	1.00	0.51	0.79	0.93	0.71	0.84	0.65	0.61	0.67	0.75	0.45	0.37
Kyocera	0.37	0.58	0.51	1.00	0.57	0.54	0.56	0.51	0.77	0.48	0.47	0.40	0.32	0.28
Mitsubishi	0.58	0.81	0.79	0.57	1.00	0.84	0.77	0.77	0.72	0.65	0.68	0.68	0.47	0.34
MOTOROLA	0.58	0.73	0.93	0.54	0.84	1.00	0.76	0.86	0.70	0.65	0.69	0.70	0.46	0.37
NEC	0.53	0.77	0.71	0.56	0.77	0.76	1.00	0.78	0.71	0.63	0.55	0.60	0.42	0.42
NOKIA	0.56	0.67	0.84	0.51	0.77	0.86	0.78	1.00	0.64	0.60	0.62	0.67	0.44	0.40
Panasonic	0.45	0.65	0.65	0.77	0.72	0.70	0.71	0.64	1.00	0.54	0.55	0.51	0.36	0.31
PHILIPS	0.61	0.79	0.61	0.48	0.65	0.65	0.63	0.60	0.54	1.00	0.60	0.61	0.70	0.56
SAGEM	0.74	0.69	0.67	0.47	0.68	0.69	0.55	0.62	0.55	0.60	1.00	0.67	0.61	0.36
SIEMENS	0.70	0.70	0.75	0.40	0.68	0.70	0.60	0.67	0.51	0.61	0.67	1.00	0.56	0.41
BOSCH	0.69	0.56	0.45	0.32	0.47	0.46	0.42	0.44	0.36	0.70	0.61	0.56	1.00	0.66
Others	0.43	0.42	0.37	0.28	0.34	0.37	0.42	0.40	0.31	0.56	0.36	0.41	0.66	1.00

Then the transitive closure of the concept matrix $R2$ can be obtained, as shown below, which is an equivalent matrix that can be used for clustering, according to the desired level of similarity, λ.

$R2^* =$

	BenQ	ALCATEL	Sony ERICSSON	Kyocera	Mitsubishi	MOTOROLA	NEC	NOKIA	Panasonic	PHILIPS	SAGAM	SIEMENS	BOSCH	Others
BenQ	1.00	0.70	0.70	0.70	0.70	0.70	0.70	0.70	0.70	0.70	0.74	0.70	0.70	0.66
ALCATEL	0.70	1.00	0.81	0.72	0.81	0.81	0.78	0.81	0.72	0.79	0.70	0.75	0.70	0.66
Sony ERICSSON	0.70	0.81	1.00	0.72	0.84	0.93	0.78	0.86	0.72	0.79	0.70	0.75	0.70	0.66
Kyocera	0.70	0.72	0.72	1.00	0.72	0.72	0.72	0.72	0.77	0.72	0.70	0.72	0.70	0.66
Mitsubishi	0.70	0.81	0.84	0.72	1.00	0.84	0.78	0.84	0.72	0.79	0.70	0.75	0.70	0.66
MOTOROLA	0.70	0.81	0.93	0.72	0.84	1.00	0.78	0.86	0.72	0.79	0.70	0.75	0.70	0.66
NEC	0.70	0.78	0.78	0.72	0.78	0.78	1.00	0.78	0.72	0.78	0.70	0.75	0.70	0.66
NOKIA	0.70	0.81	0.86	0.72	0.84	0.86	0.78	1.00	0.72	0.79	0.70	0.75	0.70	0.66
Panasonic	0.70	0.72	0.72	0.77	0.72	0.72	0.72	0.72	1.00	0.72	0.70	0.72	0.70	0.66
PHILIPS	0.70	0.79	0.79	0.72	0.79	0.79	0.78	0.79	0.72	1.00	0.70	0.75	0.70	0.66
SAGEM	0.74	0.70	0.70	0.70	0.70	0.70	0.70	0.70	0.70	0.70	1.00	0.70	0.70	0.66
SIEMENS	0.70	0.75	0.75	0.72	0.75	0.75	0.75	0.75	0.72	0.75	0.70	1.00	0.70	0.66
BOSCH	0.70	0.70	0.70	0.70	0.70	0.70	0.70	0.70	0.70	0.70	0.70	0.70	1.00	0.66
Others	0.66	0.66	0.66	0.66	0.66	0.66	0.66	0.66	0.66	0.66	0.66	0.66	0.66	1.00

In our system, a default value of λ is defined by taking the mean value of all elements of the upper triangle. That is, $\lambda = 0.73$ is the clustering threshold of $R2^*$ and with such λ-cut operation, $R2^*$ can be transformed into a 0/1 matrix.

$R2^*_{\lambda=0.73} =$

	BenQ	ALCATEL	Sony ERICSSON	Kyocera	Mitsubishi	MOTOROLA	NEC	NOKIA	Panasonic	PHILIPS	SAGAM	SIEMENS	BOSCH	Others
BenQ	1	0	0	0	0	0	0	0	0	0	1	0	0	0
ALCATEL	0	1	1	0	1	1	1	1	0	1	0	1	0	0
Sony ERICSSON	0	1	1	0	1	1	1	1	0	1	0	1	0	0
Kyocera	0	0	0	1	0	0	0	0	1	0	0	0	0	0
Mitsubishi	0	1	1	0	1	1	1	1	0	1	0	1	0	0
MOTOROLA	0	1	1	0	1	1	1	1	0	1	0	1	0	0
NEC	0	1	1	0	1	1	1	1	0	1	0	1	0	0
NOKIA	0	1	1	0	1	1	1	1	0	1	0	1	0	0
Panasonic	0	0	0	1	0	0	0	0	1	0	0	0	0	0
PHILIPS	0	1	1	0	1	1	1	1	0	1	0	1	0	0
SAGEM	1	0	0	0	0	0	0	0	0	0	1	0	0	0
SIEMENS	0	1	1	0	1	1	1	1	0	1	0	1	0	0
BOSCH	0	0	0	0	0	0	0	0	0	0	0	0	1	0
Others	0	0	0	0	0	0	0	0	0	0	0	0	0	1

In consequence, 5(u=5) groups of mobile-phone types can be obtained from the 14 available brands, as follows:

$Group\ 1 = \{\text{BenQ, SAGEM}\},$

$Group\ 2 = \{$ALCATEL, Sony ERICSSON, Mitsubishi, MOTOROLA, NEC, NOKIA, PHILIPS, SIEMENS$\}$,

$Group\ 3 = \{\text{Kyocera, Panasonic}\},$

$Group\ 4 = \{\text{BOSCH}\},$

$Group\ 5 = \{\text{Others}\}$

Based on the document descriptor of each document, we obtained the group-concept matrix $B2'$, which extensively reduces the data dimension and thus speeds up the information retrieval process.

$$B2' = \begin{array}{r} \\ \\ Group\ 1 \\ Group\ 2 \\ Group\ 3 \\ Group\ 4 \\ Group\ 5 \end{array} \begin{array}{ccccccc} \text{brand} & \text{external} & \text{price} & \text{service} & \text{function} & \text{ease} & \text{special} \\ & & & & & \text{of use} & \text{offer} \\ 0.15 & 0.17 & 0.21 & 0.10 & 0.13 & 0.15 & 0.38 \\ 0.17 & 0.31 & 0.23 & 0.10 & 0.20 & 0.15 & 0.13 \\ 0.12 & 0.67 & 0.12 & 0.10 & 0.13 & 0.12 & 0.08 \\ 0.15 & 0.12 & 0.67 & 0.10 & 0.09 & 0.15 & 0.33 \\ 0.15 & 0.12 & 1.00 & 0.10 & 0.09 & 0.15 & 0.00 \end{array}$$

With the same procedure, we can calculate the document-concept matrices *B1, B3, B4* for each set of clustered users, respectively; this clustering information is also stored in the database. This completes the off-line phase.

Online Phase

If a Web user wants to buy a mobile phone, and signs into the Web site, he or she is asked to provide basic data. If, say, the user is *female*, *22 years old*, *university* educated and earns *NTS 30,000~45,000 Income*, and emphasized *external* as her top preference in purchasing a mobile phone, then this information will allow the system to classify the user into user-cluster 2, and with lexicographic ordering of the components, corresponding

Figure 3. Result of the case study

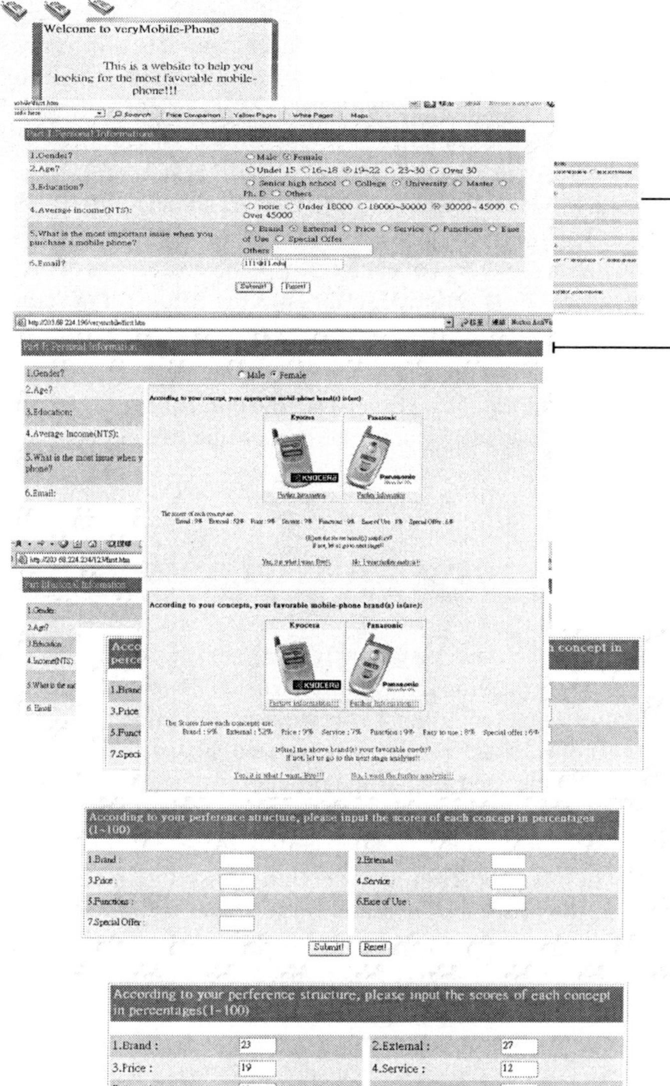

to the concept "*external*" of $B2'$, the system will provide { Kyocera, Panasonic } of *Group* 3 with the scores of each concept in percentages of (9,50,9,7,10,9,6). The corresponding scores come up with *brand*: 12, *external*: 67, *price*: 12, *service*: 10, *function*: 13, *ease of use*: 12, and *special offer*: 8 for reference.

If she is not satisfied, the system will ask for her preference structure with reference to the above scores. If she replies with the scores of (23, 27, 19, 12, 11, 4, 4), comparing vector Q with the matrix B', we can find that the most compatible group of mobile phone is the second one, *Group* 2 = {ALCATEL, Sony ERICSSON, Mitsubishi, MOTOROLA, NEC, NOKIA, PHILIPS, SIEMENS} and then suggest that this user purchase the most relevant mobile phone. The result, shown below, has been translated into English for ease of understanding (see Figure 3). Different types of users map into different users' clusters and the system provides the most appropriate information corresponding to different clusters of documents. For example, if a *male* user, *18 years old*, *college* educated, with *no Income*, and an emphasis on *function*, he would be classified into Cluster 4. The documents would be grouped as *Group* 1: {BenQ, SAGEM}; *Group* 2: {ALCATEL, Sony ERICSSON, Kyocera, Mitsubishi, MOTOROLA, NEC, NOKIA, PHILIPS, SIEMENS}, *Group* 3: {Panasonic}, *Group* 4: {BOSCH} and *Group* 5: {Others}. The system will provide {Panasonic} with the scores of each concept in percentages of (11, 13, 18, 8, 25, 9, 15). Furthermore, if he is not satisfied, after entering a new set of scores, the system will provide a new suggestion.

If the users referred to above purchased the mobile phones recommended, their data would be used to update the database, otherwise the database will not be changed. Due to the billing system, such updating processes would be carried out once a month.

Summary and Discussion

Internet technology has developed rapidly in recent years and one of the primary current issues is how to effectively provide information to users. In this study, we utilized a data mining information retrieval technique to create a Web mining system. Since existing retrieval methods do not consider user preferences and hence do not effectively provide appropriate information, we used an off-line process to cluster users, according to their features and preferences, using a bi-criteria BOFCM algorithm. By doing so, the online response time was reduced in a practical test case when a user sent a query to the Web site. The case study in this chapter (a service Web site selling mobile phones) demonstrated that by using the proposed information retrieval technique, a query-response containing a reasonable number, rather than a huge number, of mobile phones could be provided which best matched a users' preferences. Furthermore, it was shown that a single criterion for choosing the most favorable mobile-phone brand was not sufficient. Thus, the scores provided for the suggested group could be used as a reference for overall consideration. This not only speeds up the query process, but can also effectively support purchase decisions. In system maintenance, counterfeit information causes aggravation for Web site owners. Our proposed system updates the database only if the purchase action is actually carried out, which reduces the risk of false data. Further study into how a linguistic query may be transformed into a numerical query is necessary to allow a greater practical application of this proposal.

References

Angelides, M. C. (1997). Implementing the Internet for business: A global marketing opportunity. *International Journal of Information Management*, *17*(6), 405-419.

Bedeck, J. C. (1973). *Fuzzy mathematics in pattern classification*. Unpublished doctoral dissertation, Applied Mathematics Center, Cornell University, Ithaca.

Chen, S. M., & Wang, J. Y. (1995). Document retrieval using knowledge-based fuzzy information retrieval techniques. *IEEE Transactions on Systems, Man and Cybernetics*, *25*(5), 793-802.

Chen, Z. (2001). *Data mining and uncertain reasoning*. New York: John Wiley.

Hanson, W. (2000). *Principles of Internet marketing*. Sydney: South-Western College.

Janal, D. S. (1995). *Online marketing handbook: How to sell, advertise, publicize and promote your product and services on Internet and commercial online systems*. New York: Van Nostrand Reinhold.

Jang, J. S., Sun, C. T., & Mizutani, E. (1997). *Neuro-fuzzy and soft computing: A computational approach to learning and machine intelligence*. Upper Saddle River, NJ: Prentice-Hall.

Lin, C. L. (2002). *Web mining based on fuzzy means for service web site*. Unpublished master's dissertation, Tsing Hua University, Taiwan.

Mohammed, R. A., Fisher, R. J., Jaworski, B. J., & Paddison, G. J. (2004). *Internet marketing - Building advantage in a networked economy*. Boston: McGraw Hill / Irwin.

Schneider, G. P. (2004). *Electronic commerce: The second wave*. Australia: Thomson Learning.

Rayport, C., & Jaworski, H. (2002). *E-commerce marketing: Introduction to e-commerce*. Boston: McGraw Hill / Irwin.

Tamura, S., Higuchi, K., & Tanaka, K. (1971). Pattern classification based on fuzzy relations. *IEEE Transactions on Systems, Man and Cybernetics*, *1*, 61-66.

Wang, H. F., Wang, C., & Wu, G. Y. (1994). Multicriteria fuzzy C-means analysis. *Fuzzy Sets and Systems*, *64*, 311-319.

Zadeh, L. A. (1965). Fuzzy sets. *Information and Control*, *8*, 338-353.

Endnote

[1] This study is supported by National Science Council, Taiwan, ROC, with project number NSC91-2213-E-007-075.

Section III

Production and Operations Applications

Chapter VIII

Artificial Intelligence in Electricity Market Operations and Management

Zhao Yang Dong, The University of Queensland, Australia

Tapan Kumar Saha, The University of Queensland, Australia

Kit Po Wong, The Hong Kong Polytechnic University, Hong Kong

Abstract

This chapter introduces advanced techniques such as artificial neural networks, wavelet decomposition, support vector machines, and data-mining techniques in electricity market demand and price forecasts. It argues that various techniques can offer different advantages in providing satisfactory demand and price signal forecast results for a deregulated electricity market, depending on the specific needs in forecasting. Furthermore, the authors hope that an understanding of these techniques and their application will help the reader to form a comprehensive view of electricity market data analysis needs, not only for the traditional time-series based forecast, but also the new correlation-based, price spike analysis.

Introduction

Power systems worldwide have experienced significant deregulation and reorganization in the past decade. The objective of deregulation is to enhance competition among electricity energy suppliers, to provide electricity consumers' with a choice of providers and to maximize overall social welfare. As a result the vertically integrated power industry has been deregulated into generation companies, transmission companies and distribution companies. The transmission services still operate under different regulations because of their natural monopoly characteristic within the regulatory system. Generation and distribution companies are market participants in either pool, bilateral, or more popular, hybrid type markets supporting both pool transactions and bilateral contracts. The electricity market has several unique features that differentiate it from other markets. A key feature is that electricity needs to be traded immediately after being generated in order to maintain a supply and demand balance. A further limitation is that the delivery of energy has to follow the physical constraints of the power system. Deregulation may appear quite straightforward and economically attractive. However, there have been a number of difficulties in the process, with the most significant ones being reliable market operations and planning to meet the increasing demands for electricity through the competitive electricity market. The introduction of the electricity market to traditional power systems has, in many cases, pushed the power system to run close to the limit of reliable and secure supply, creating numerous new challenges to the power industry in operations and management. Since its introduction, there have been continuing discussions on how to achieve profit maximization objectives from the generation companies while maintaining the system security and reliability in the electricity market. Numerical market rules and designs have been proposed and tested in the major electricity markets worldwide. The essential issues for power systems in a deregulated environment are power system operations, management and planning. These tasks require the system to be reliable and secure while satisfying the market objective of profit maximization for generation companies or social welfare maximization for the system operator. Forecasting of system demand and price is at the foundation of these tasks in a competitive electricity market. From the market operations point of view, proper demand and price forecasting is essential for development of risk management plans for the participating companies in the electricity market. In a competitive market, a generation company may lose its whole year's revenue because of unexpected events (Wu & Varaiya, 1999). Market participants use different instruments to control and minimize the risks because of market clearing price volatility. In Victoria, Australia, generators and retailers can use vesting contracts and contestable contracts to hedge against pool price volatility risks (Wolak, 1998). With better estimates of electricity market demand and clearing price prediction, generators and retailers can reduce their risks and maximize their outcomes further.

The significance of proper forecasting is equally important for planning within the electricity market. Recent major blackouts, attracting attention to electricity market operations and management, caused demands for solutions to the various problems concerning the power industry. In August 2003, the power grid of North America, including parts of Canada, experienced the most serious blackout in the history of power supply so far (Sweet, 2003). Subsequent blackouts in the UK and Italy further illustrated the challenges and significance of deregulation on power market operations and management. The reasons for these blackouts cover a wide variety of issues. However, the main causes for the North America blackout was insufficient capacity of the power grid to meet the demand given underestimated demand growth, which resulted in under-investment in the power system through system planning. This fact clearly reflects the importance of accurate market forecasting for efficient and reliable market operations.

Traditionally, econometric regression models and the least-cost approach are employed in power system demand forecasting and planning. However, the regression approach relies on historical data and uses mostly linear models. The technique is limited when emerging factors in the electricity market impact upon demand and/or price, but there is limited historical data to demonstrate possible impacts upon demand and/or price signals. Regression models such as ARMA have been widely used in demand forecasting. However the natural nonlinearity and complexity of the demand and price signals in a competitive electricity market often introduce significant errors to traditional forecasting methods.

Electricity market operations and management is a very complex problem and covers a large number of aspects. It is impossible to cover all the major issues of market operations and management in a single chapter with reasonable detail. It has been identified both in regulated and deregulated power industries that forecasting is a key issue for market operations and management. Other tasks such as risk management, bidding strategy and system planning all depend on reliable and accurate market forecasts. Accordingly, we will focus on forecasting techniques in this chapter.

Forecasting of electricity market signals includes demand and price over the long, mid- and short-terms. In addition to historical electricity data, long-term forecasts also require extensive data from social and economical domains. Short-term forecasts have more direct impacts on market operations and in realizing the objective of profit maximization for generation companies. Most of the advances in demand and price forecasting are in the area of short-term forecasting.

Short-term demand or load forecast is the prediction of future electricity demands based on information such as historical data and predicted weather conditions (Bunn, 2000; Papalexopoulos & Hesterberg, 1990; Ranaweera, Karady, & Farmer, 1996). Short-term electricity market clearing price forecasts provide market participants with price signals for the future to help them form optimal operational plans that lead to maximal market returns (Sansom & Saha, 1999). Electricity demand follows certain yearly, seasonal, weekly and daily patterns. The load profile can be used to form the load duration curve, which is very important in system reliability assessment and hence system planning. Research into demand forecasting and analysis are more or less well established, with a variety of mathematical and economical techniques. Compared with demand signals, electricity market price signals are much more volatile through a competitive market mechanism. Sometimes the price signal skyrockets to hundreds of times higher than expected within a very short time. Consequently, electricity price forecasting is much more complex and difficult than demand forecasting and will become more and more important with deregulation.

For both traditional techniques and recent advances in forecasting, it is necessary to provide a level of confidence with every forecast (Makridakis, Wheelwright, & Hyndman, 1998; Sanders, 1999). Sometimes such levels of confidence are represented by forecast errors, which have considerable implications for profits, market shares and shareholder values in a deregulated electricity market (Bunn, 2000).

There has been much work done on electricity demand and price forecasting over recent years (Contreras, Espinola, Nogales, & Conejo, 2003; Guo & Luh, 2003; Nogales, Contreras, Conejo, & Espinola, 2002; Zhang & Dong, 2001; Zhang, Luh, & Kasiviswanathan, 2003). Various techniques have been used in the literature for demand and price forecasting. An efficient way to forecast is by using regression models including ARMA and Fuzzy-Neural Autoregressive models (Contreras et al., 2003). Newer techniques are based on the learning capability of artificial neural networks (ANN) and support vector machines (SVM) trained with historical data (Guo & Luh, 2003). Time-series analysis is another important attempt in this direction with promising results (Nogales et al., 2002). Signal processing techniques have been used in time-series-based demand and price forecast with ANN learning modules to discover the hidden dynamics and trends in the data series in order to improve forecast performance (Zhang & Dong, 2001). Efforts in forecasting price spikes have been illustrated in the literature as well, (Lu, Dong, & Li, 2005; Xu, Dong, & Liu, 2003).

In this chapter, we will discuss advanced forecasting techniques for power system demand and price data in a deregulated environment, to develop a framework for comprehensive market data forecasting of both demand and prices. Compared with other techniques, the accuracy of demand forecasting is enhanced and price forecasting is more comprehensive. A difference from other forecasting models is that the price forecasting module of the framework presented in this chapter is able to process both normal range price signals (e.g., $20-50 /MWhr) and price spikes (e.g., $9,000/MWhr depending on the definition of Value of Lost Load (VoLL) and relevant market regulations in a market).

The chapter is arranged as follows: We first review existing forecasting techniques, followed by an overview of artificial intelligence techniques and their applications in this area. Then time-series analysis techniques for electricity market demand forecast with neural networks and wavelets are discussed in the next section. Support vector machines are then presented in the third section as a powerful tool for both demand and price forecasting. In the fourth section, data-mining techniques are added to the previously discussed techniques to form a forecasting framework that can forecast demand series and price series in both normal ranges and as price spikes. Finally, we present some case studies for electricity demand and price forecasts using these advanced techniques in the fifth section, before the conclusion.

Short-Term Demand Forecast with Neural Network and Wavelet Decomposition Techniques

Power system demand forecast is normally based on time-series information from historical data including demand, weather information and other relevant information, which has been identified as having a certain level of impact on the electricity or energy demand. Based on the time series, the first step is to extract information, which can be forecasted by regression models such as the trend and periodic components. The remaining information is normally stochastic time-series data, which requires time-series analysis techniques for further forecasts. This regression-model-based approach has been used to forecast demand in the long term (15-30 years ahead). In the following sections, we focus on short-term forecasting with neural networks, support vector machines and data-mining techniques. We introduce these techniques in the context of application in market data analysis. Detailed mathematical foundations of such techniques can be found in appropriate references listed at the end of the chapter.

Neural Networks

Artificial neural networks are well established and among the most popular techniques for short-term forecasts (Pham & Karaboga, 1999; Poggio & Girosi, 1990; Rice, 1964). They are composed of interconnected neurons as processing units and are associated with some training algorithms, such as back propagation (BP). A neural network can have one or more hidden layers, and it can be a network without internal feedback paths — feed-forward networks, or a recurrent network with internal feedback paths. Previous research has concluded that with a sufficient number of hidden neurons, a multilayer neural network with at least one hidden layer can approximate any continuous nonlinear function arbitrarily over a compact set (Poggio & Girosi, 1990; Rice, 1964). The recurrent neural networks can represent any n-th order dynamic system but may have difficulty in being trained with a BP algorithm (Pham & Karaboga, 1999). With their approximation and generalization abilities, neural networks have been used for short-term demand forecasting. The most commonly used Multilayer Perceptron neural networks (MLPs) are employed as the basic forecasting units in the forecast models.

Demand and price signals are among the most import signals for the operation and planning of an electricity market. Accordingly, time series representing demand and electricity prices become more difficult to forecast with neural networks alone. Considering the risk management requirements in the electricity market, more accurate forecasting techniques are needed. In order to provide more accurate and reliable forecasts, we have worked out several plans to enhance the demand and price forecast based on neural networks. These include wavelet decomposition, evolutionary-computation-based neural network training, and using recurrent networks, to capture the dynamics in the demand and price series.

Discrete Wavelet Transform

Extreme values in a time series (such as in the demand series) are removed after data preprocessing. The resulting time series can then be treated as a discrete signal ready for further analysis. A signal can be decomposed by Wavelet decomposition in both time and frequency domains. Discrete wavelet transform (DWT) provides a time and frequency representation of the signal in discrete time. The DWT of a discrete signal $f(k)$ can be defined by Equation (1) (Misiti, Misiti, Oppenheim, & Poggi, 1996; Xu et al., 2003).

$$DWT(m,n) = \sum_{k}^{K} f(k) \frac{1}{\sqrt{2^m}} g\left(\frac{k - n2^m}{2^m} \right) \quad (1)$$

where m is the scaling (stretching, or decomposition level), n is an integer and k is the shifting (translating) constant. The function $g\left(\frac{k - n2^m}{2^m} \right)$ is the scaled, shifted wavelet function given the mother wavelet function of $g(k)$. The discrete feature of time series (either demand or price) makes DWT a very useful tool for decomposition. With DWT the time localization of spectral components can be obtained. Using the DWT technique, a very large proportion of the coefficients of the transformation can be set to zero without appreciable loss of information. This property holds even for signals that contain occasional abrupt changes of level or other dynamic behavior such as price spikes in electricity market price signal series. Traditional decomposition techniques such as the Fourier analysis require the signal to be stationary. However, the demand and price signals are mostly non-stationary signals and therefore make the DWT application more appropriate (Tran, Nguyen, & Shihabi, 1999). An example of electricity price signal decomposed with DWT is given in Figure 1. As we can see from Figure 1, the original time-series signal is decomposed into different levels of series, which consequently reveal more characteristics of the original time series and enable the application of advanced forecasting methods to generate better results than using the original series alone.

EC-Enhanced Recurrent Neural Networks for Forecasting

After the DWT decomposition, each decomposed series can be forecasted using a neural network. Given that some of the decomposed signals are still rich in dynamics, recurrent neural networks are needed for such signals. However, as pointed out earlier by Elman (1990), the conventional BP algorithm may face difficulties in training such recurrent networks, we use evolutionary computing algorithms to train the networks.

Evolutionary computation includes stochastic search and optimization algorithms whose origins are in natural evolution principles. These algorithms are robust and have been applied to a variety of problems requiring search and optimization tasks. Different from the traditional Newton-type optimization techniques, evolutionary algorithms are based on a population of encoded tentative solutions. Such solutions or individuals are processed with evolutionary operators such as cross-over or mutation to find reasonably good solutions, if not the global optimum.

Genetic Algorithms (GAs), Evolutionary Programming (EP), and Evolutionary Strategies (ES) are the three main algorithms for evolutionary computation (EC) proposed as early as in the 1950s (Bremermann, 1962; Fogel, Owens, & Walsh, 1966; Fraser, 1957; Goldberg, 1989; Holland, 1975; Wong & Li, 2002). These algorithms operate following the rules of

Figure 1. Wavelet decomposition of electricity price signals (selected from March 2004 Queensland market record from The National Electricity Market Management Company Limited — NEMMCO — Web site). It clearly demonstrates the approximation (a) and different levels of details of the original price signal (s) after wavelet decomposition ($d_1 - d_5$) using Daubechies wavelet filters.

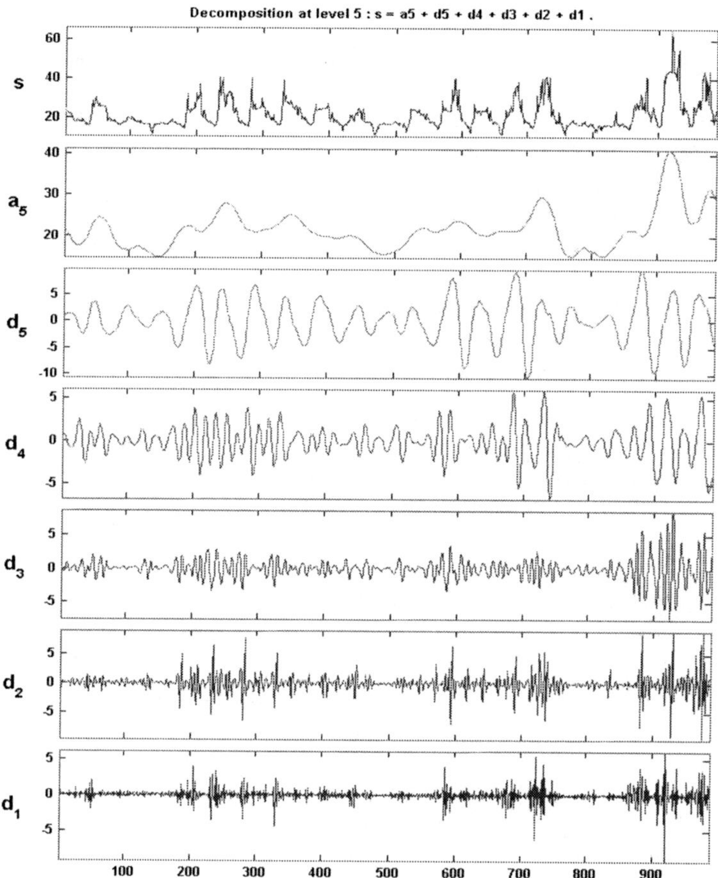

the natural evolution and do not require the optimization problem to be continuous, convex and differentiable. These rules form the basis of the advantage of EC over class optimization techniques, which normally require differentiate operation and the problem be convex. These properties determine that the application of EC to recurrent neural network training is appropriate, instead of the BP algorithm.

In Xu, Dong, and Tay (2004), a GA-based recursive neural network is developed and applied when analyzing the demand and price signals in an electricity market. It is able to overcome the difficulties faced by BP algorithms when optimizing the weights of a recurrent neural network. Elman neural networks are used in Xu et al. (2004) as a local recurrent network for forecasting. Elman neural networks were first proposed by Elman (1990) to solve language problems. Since then they have been applied widely in the fields of identification, prediction and control. Elman networks are used to capture the complex, nonlinear correlations among the time series to enhance the demand and price forecast accuracy.

A Time-Series-Based Signal Forecast Model

Given the characteristics of wavelet decomposition and the learning capabilities of neural networks, a wavelet enhanced neural network forecast model is proposed in Zhang and Dong (2001), Xu et al. (2004), and Low and Dong (2002) (see Figure 2). Both MLP and recurrent networks can be used in such a model depending on the dynamics of the time series to be predicted. The model includes three stages (Geva, 1998): (i) the time series signal decomposition, (ii) a separate neural network forecast at each scale after decomposition; and (iii) the original time series is predicted by another neural network (NN) using the different scale's prediction. A wavelet reconstruction is needed to form a uniform forecast after the individual forecast at each level.

Time-series forecast can be one-step ahead or k-step ahead. Suppose we have a time series $\boldsymbol{Y} = \{y(1), y(2), \ldots y(N)\}$ as the training data set. For 1 step forecast, we want to use the data to train the network to predict the value at point n with the values at n-1, n-2, … n-m, where $m<n\leq N$:

$$\hat{y}(n) = NN[y(n-1), y(n-2), \ldots, y(n-m)] \tag{2}$$

where $\hat{y}$ is the predicted value, and y is the real value of the series $\boldsymbol{Y}$.

Figure 2. Forecasting framework model (w$_1$, …, w$_k$ *are wavelet coefficients,* c *is the residual coefficient series)*

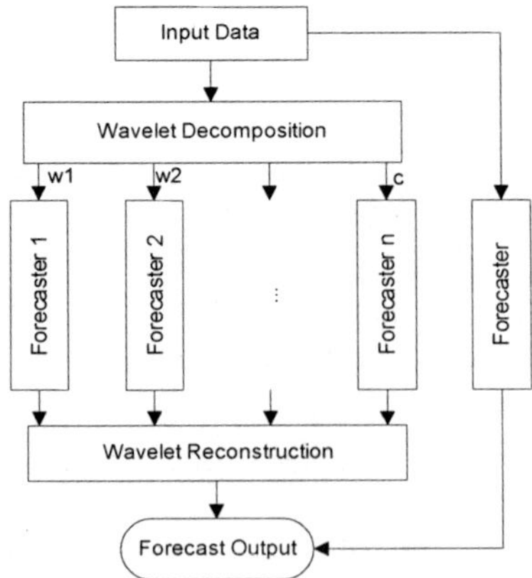

The objective of NN training is to minimize the errors resulting from the difference between the NN output and the real values using the training data. In the case of highly dynamic data, recurrent networks are used with GA training instead of the BP algorithm. To convert this NN training minimization problem into a maximization problem as a fitness function for the GA, the following fitness function weight adjustment module can be used (Low & Dong, 2002):

$$f = \frac{1}{\left|Y^{*}(k) - Y(k)\right| + \eta} \quad \textbf{(3)}$$

where $|Y^{*}(k)-Y(k)|$ is the error between neural network output and the real data from the training set, and $\eta \in \mathbf{R}^{+}$ is a small positive constant number to avoid the possible singularity in the fitness function.

Support Vector Machines in Demand and Price Forecasting

Support Vector Machines

The Support Vector Machine (SVM) is a nonlinear generalization of the Generalized Portrait algorithm developed in the 1960s (Smola & Schölkopf, 1998; Vapnik, 1995) (see Figure 3). The algorithm is based on statistical learning theory or Vapnik-Chervonenkis (VC) theory, which ensures the good performance of SVM on training data and good generalization on testing data. This property is attractive for many machine-learning problems (Xu et al., 2003).

The SVM has been applied to regression and time-series prediction recently (Smola & Schölkopf, 1998; Xu et al., 2003). SVM regression is used to map the data X into a high dimensional feature space Γ via a nonlinear mapping function ϕ to enable linear regression in this space, with b as the threshold.

$$f(x) = (\omega \cdot \phi(x)) + b \quad with\, \phi : R^{n} \rightarrow \Gamma, \omega \in \Gamma \quad \textbf{(4)}$$

For ε-SVM regression, the objective is to find a $f(x)$ that has at most -deviation from the actually obtained Y_i for all training data $\{(X_1, Y_1), (X_2, Y_2), \ldots, (X_m, Y_m)\} \subset \boldsymbol{X} \times \boldsymbol{R}$, and is as flat as possible (Smola & Schölkopf, 1998; Vapnik, 1995). The regression is an optimization problem minimizing a risk function,

$$R_{reg}[f] = R_{emp}[f] + \frac{\lambda}{2}\|\omega\|^2 \tag{5}$$

where is a cost function penalizing the prediction errors based on the empirical data X. is the flatness index of (Smola & Schölkopf, 1998). The regression quality is controlled by factors including , the cost error, cost function, the mapping function and the flatness index. The radial basis function is used as the mapping function. More details about SVM and its application can be found in Vapnik (1995), Smola and Schölkopf (1998), and Rüping (2002).

Compared to NN, SVM have fewer obvious tuneable parameters than NN and the choice of parameter values may be relatively less crucial for good forecasting results compared with NN. The SVM is designed to systematically optimize its structure based on the input training data. SVM training is a quadratic optimization problem, which has one unique solution and does not involve the random initialization of weights as NN training does. As a result, SVM with the same parameter settings trained on identical data will give identical results. This increases the repeatability of SVM forecasts and therefore significantly reduces the amount of training time.

Interaction among Demand, Generation, and Price

In a PoolCo-type electricity market, such as the Australian NEM, a large volume of market information is available to market participants. Under the competitive market conditions, the ability to predict the market demand and prices naturally gives significant advantages to market participants as well as the system operator. Traditionally, load forecasting includes econometric regression model forecasts, end-use forecasts and, for the short term, time-series forecasting techniques. Given the fact that (i) demand forecast techniques have been established for decades and (ii) the supply and demand relationship is the fundamental relationship in a microeconomic sense for a competitive electricity market, it is naturally understood that the relationship between electricity demand and the market price will contribute to the market price forecast (Ramsay, 1995; Sapeluk, 1994). However, the exact contribution of the demand forecast to price forecast needs further investigation. More discussion can be found in the next section using data-mining approaches. Compared with the demand series, electricity prices are more volatile and therefore require more advanced techniques in forecasting.

SVM Forecasting Model with the PASA Data

NEMMCO publicizes the short-term Projected Assessment of System Adequacy (PASA) Data every two hours (Sansom, Downs, & Saha, 2003). These data files provide projected half-hourly data for the next six days starting at 04:30 the day after the PASA file was published. The relevant variables from the PASA data to improve the price and demand forecast includes:

- predicted capacity required
- predicted reserve required
- predicted reserve surplus
- predicted regional demand 10% Probability of Exceedence (POE) (NEMMCO, 2002)
- predicted regional demand 50% POE
- predicted regional demand 90% POE

The predicted capacity required is an approximation of the total regional generation capacity required for that half-hour. The capacity required is equal to 10% POE regional demand forecast plus a specific required reserve. The projected reserve required is the minimum level of reserve required in the region at approximately 5 to 7% of the expected total regional demand. Projected reserve surplus is the surplus or deficiency of available reserves (negative value) compared to the capacity required. The 10% POE regional demand forecast is the regional demand forecast produced with a 10% probability of being exceeded. Similarly, the 50% and 90% POE forecasts have 50% and 90% chance of being less than the actual demand at that half-hour.

In the Australian NEM, the regional reference price (RRP) for electricity is the result of a market clearing process, and is available through the NEMMCO Web site in the short-term PASA files. Econometric regression models indicate that inclusion of relevant information can improve the forecast accuracy. The PASA data provides more variables than simply the RRP and demand, and is considered to have a reasonably high correlation with the price signal. The PASA data is included in the SVM model for forecasting electricity demand and prices.

The SVM training and forecasts were performed with the mySVM program developed by Rüping (2002). The forecast model using SVM include SVM alone and a wavelet-SVM forecast model as shown in Figure 2, where the NN are replaced by SVM.

Given the useful data available from the PASA files, the electricity price forecast assumes the accuracy of demand forecast sufficient to cover the forecasting duration. In addition to the PASA data, the input to SVM also includes spot price, regional demand, daily half-hour and weekly half-hour demand information (Sansom et al., 2003). Detailed forecasting results and analysis are given in the following section.

Data Mining and a General Electricity Market Price Forecasting Framework

Price Spikes and Relationship with Demand and Other Factors

It is clear that there is a correlation between demand and price signals in an electricity market. Knowledge of such a relationship is useful for forecasting. However, it is difficult to measure due to the complexity of electricity markets. The complexity comes from the physical nature of the power grid behind the market, which requires that the demand be met by the continuous generation and the economic interactions following the demand-and-supply relationship in the market. Such a relationship can be used to assist price forecasting and needs to be identified.

It is noted that many of the existing price forecasting methods require a pre-processing stage to remove abnormal prices — price spikes before generating price forecasts. However, economically, such price spikes could be as important to market participants as that of the normal market prices. This is more important in a pool-type market such as the NEM of Australia where VOLL is as high as $10,000 per MWh. Under such a market, the price spikes are more influential to market participants, because even a short period with a high price spike could cost the annual profit of a company. With many of the existing techniques, the volatility of the price spikes in the price series may cause a very inaccurate price forecast if not filtered out of normal price forecasts. It is very useful for the market participants to have a forecasting model that can predict not only the normal price, but also the volatile price spikes.

A data-mining-based approach is presented in this section to explore the price spike forecasting based on some pioneer research in Lu et al. (2005). Lu et al. also proposed a framework of general price forecasting for both normal market price and price spikes. This model is able to handle the uncertainty of spike occurrence and difficult-to-predict characteristics such as forecasts of levels of spikes and confidence intervals for forecasts.

Framework of Electricity Price Forecasting

In order to forecast both the normal price signals and price spikes, a general price forecast model is given in Figure 5, which includes a normal price forecast module and a price spike forecast module (Lu et al., 2005). The original electricity price signal is separated into normal prices and price spikes, which are processed by the normal price forecast module, and the price spike forecast module respectively. The normal price forecast module is derived from those models described in previous sections with wavelet, neural networks and/or SVM. The price spike forecast module is based on data-mining techniques and uses historical price spike information for forecasting. A comprehensive price forecast can be realized with this model for both normal prices and price spikes.

The forecasting procedures are clearly illustrated in Figure 4 where the wavelet-NN module also predicts the possibility of price spikes at specific occasions. If a specific occasion is forecast to have a price-spike signal, then the price-spike forecast module is activated with reference to historical data in order to estimate the value of the price spikes, stage of the price spikes and level of confidence for the forecast. If needed, the forecast normal prices and price spikes are then reconstructed to form an overall (comprehensive) electricity price. Otherwise, each forecast is taken to provide useful information for the market participants. In order to use this method, threshold values for defining the price spikes are needed and are usually determined by experience. For example, in the Queensland (QLD) market, a threshold of $75/MWhr is defined as the

Figure 4. Flow chart of the comprehensive electricity price forecast model (Kantardzic, 2002; Lu et al., 2005)

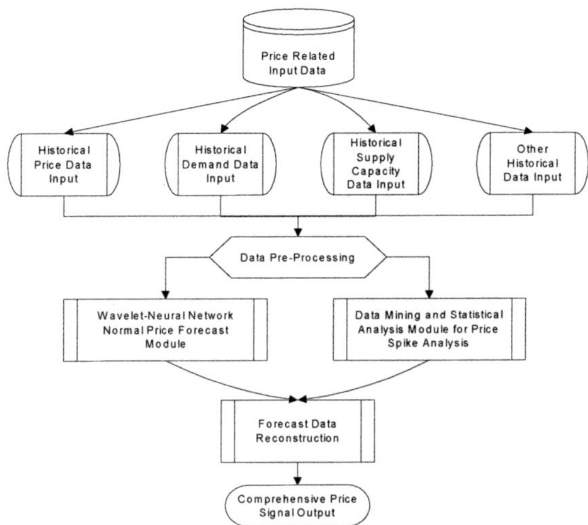

threshold to differentiate normal price ranges and price spikes, although this needs to be updated continuously with actual market price data.

Factors Affecting the Market Price and Price Spikes

Determined by market clearing processes, or bilateral trading, the electricity market price is affected by many factors including current demand, supply capacity, reserve capacity, network conditions, generation bids, seasonal impact and importantly, the demand/supply relationship. In Lu et al. (2005), several specific relationship factors are defined to assist in price-spike analysis, including factors relating RRP vs. Demand and RRP vs. Reserve. Basically, the higher the demand the higher the price. However, this relationship is hard to formulate accurately and requires more refinement from the point of view of reserve capacity. The reserve capacity is (approximately) inverse, proportional to the *RRP*. When the reserve capacity is sufficient, the electricity price is more likely to be in lower value ranges.

Ideally, price spikes only happen when the demand exceeds supply in a competitive market. In reality, most electricity markets are not perfectly competitive markets. Consequently, price spikes happen even when there is sufficient supply to meet the demand. Factors contributing to the occurrence of price spikes include: the exercise of market power, large generation reserves held by a large number of generation companies, system contingencies (such as extreme weather conditions), inadequacy in supply of electricity, supply scarcity, and transmission system congestions.

The Queensland electricity market has demonstrated a close relationship between the probability of price spikes and factors of demand (reserve and time). Specifically, the probability of price spikes is high when the demand is high, otherwise it is low. The reserve level has a close relation with price spikes, that is, the spike probability is high when generation reserve is smaller than a certain level. It is also observed that price spike probability is higher at daily peak hours and/or working days, and is lower at off-peak hours/weekends and public holidays. It should be noted that because of the uniqueness of different electricity markets, the factors affecting market prices differ and the main factors contributing to price spikes should be analyzed on a case-by-case basis considering the specific characteristics of each market.

Price Spike Forecast Model

It is clear that the market price has a close relationship with many factors. However, a single relationship is able to reflect only a fraction of the overall complex relationship for prices or price spikes. Lu et al. (2005) define two indices in order to consider the impact of demand data.

Supply-Demand Balance Index (SDI)

$$SDI = \frac{Reserve(i)}{Demand(i)} \times 100\% \tag{6}$$

Where *Demand*(i) and *Reserve*(i) are the market demand and electricity supply reserve capacity at time/occasion i respectively. SDI reflects the relationship between reserve and demand levels of a market.

Relative Demand Index (RDI)

$$RDI = \frac{Demand(i)}{Demand(0)} \times 100\% \tag{7}$$

Where *Demand*(0) is the demand value at the beginning of the trading day (04:30 for Australian NEM). RDI indicates the degree of current demand relative to the initial demand at the beginning of the trading day.

Predicting Electricity Price Spikes

Using these two indices, there are three steps to predict the electricity price spikes:

Forecasting the Occurrence of Price Spikes

Forecasting a price spike is achieved by measuring normal price forecast on RRP_i. If the forecast normal price RRP_i is greater than a threshold price value then a price spike may happen at that occasion i. Based on the statistical analysis for the Queensland market a \$75/MWhr threshold is used to define the occurrence of spikes by (8)

$$Spike(RRP_i) = \begin{cases} True & RRP_i > \$75/MWh \\ False & RRP_i <= \$75/MWh \end{cases} \quad (8)$$

A good estimation of the occurrence of price spikes can also be realized by comparing the trading information with that of the previous occasion.

Forecasting the Range of Price Spikes

Once the occurrence of price spikes is predicted, the range of the spike is predicted. Statistical analysis shows that the relationships between RRP and SDI or RRP and RDI are nonlinear. Price spikes are highly stochastic and, largely randomly distributed. The relationships of RRP vs. SDI and RRP vs. RDI during the price spike periods are of significance for price forecasting. These can be computed with historical data. The range of price spikes can be forecast based on the probabilistic distribution of RRP vs. SDI and RDI through data-mining techniques such as categorization algorithms. More specifically, the range of RRP can be predicted based on the SDI and RDI values.

Currently, there are many data-mining techniques that can be used for this purpose, such as the Judgment Tree categorization method, Bayesian categorization method, Neural Network categorization, correlation-based categorization, closest k-neighborhood categorization, reasoning-based categorization, Genetic-Algorithm-based categorization, and rough–set- and fuzzy-set-based categorization (Zhao, Dong, Li, & Wong, 2005). Bayesian categorization and SVM are used as the classification algorithm. The training data sample is collected through data mining from the database. With the training data sample, Bayesian method or SVM can be used to categorize those new unknown test data, or to predict the price spike ranges and associated level of confidence based on SDI and RDI (Lu et al., 2005).

Forecasting the Price Spike Values

After having determined the range of price spikes, the next step is to predict the actual values of the price spike within the predicted range. The k-nearer neighbor approach can be used for this task. From the training data samples, k-neighboring samples closest to the unknown sample are selected. Then the average value of the k-nearest samples is computed as the unknown sample's value. With $X=\{x_1, x_2, \ldots, x_n\}$ and $Y=\{y_1, y_2, \ldots, y_n\}$ representing two neighboring set of samples, the distance is defined in (9),

$$d(X,Y) = \sqrt{\sum_{i=1}^{n}((x_i - y_i)/(MAX_i - MIN_i))^2} \quad \textbf{(9)}$$

Given a threshold value for the neighbors in the sample space, then if all the points in this space with a distance to an unknown sample are less than the threshold they are regarded as neighbors of this unknown sample. Assuming there are k ($k \geq 1$) such neighboring samples, then the unknown sample's RRP value can be predicted as

$$\widehat{RRP} = \frac{1}{k}\sum_{i=1}^{k} RRP(i) \quad \textbf{(10)}$$

With the forecast of price spikes, we can claim a rather comprehensive forecast for electricity market prices, which covers both the normal prices and abnormal prices — price spikes. Case studies with market data from the NEM of Australia are given in the following section to illustrate the application of these forecast methods.

Case Studies

The Australian NEM was established in December of 1998 consisting of New South Wales, Victoria, South Australia and Queensland electricity markets, with Tasmania to

Figure 5. Australian National Electricity Market, where arrows indicate interregional links of power transmission (interconnectors)

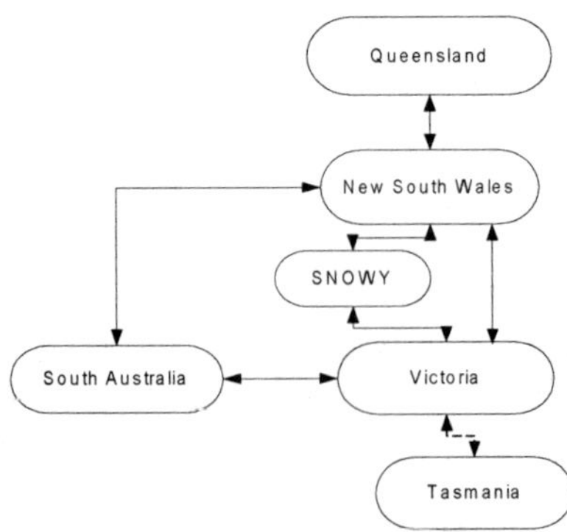

join soon. NEMMCO is the System Operator (SO) of the NEM. The electricity spot market of the NEM is cleared every half hour. As the largest market of the NEM, the New South Wales (NSW) electricity market has a recorded peak demand of 11,572 MW (recorded in 2000), annual average price vary from $28.88 (99/00) to $38.36 (00/01), with high volatility, especially in winter and summer. The data used in our case study was obtained from the NEMMCO Web site. Previous studies of the NSW market demand data of January 2001 using a wavelet-NN forecast model can be found in Low and Dong (2002), Xu et al. (2003) and Xu et al. (2004).

It is very important to have a clear performance measure for the different forecasting techniques. One such criterion is the absolute percentage error (APE) as defined in Equation (11).

$$\varepsilon_{APE}^{2} = 100\frac{|L^k - \hat{L}^k|}{|L^k|} \quad \textbf{(11)}$$

where L^k and $\hat{L}^k$ are the actual and forecast load at time k respectively. This APE error measure is more meaningfully represented as an average and standard deviation over the forecasting range of interests. Another important performance measure is the Root Mean Square (RMS) error ($\mathrm{Err}_{\mathrm{RMS}}$) defined in Equation (12)

$$Err_{RMS} = \sqrt{\frac{\sum_{n=1}^{N}(\hat{u}(n)-u(n))^2}{N}} \quad \textbf{(12)}$$

where $\hat{u}(n)$ is the forecast signal at step n; $u(n)$ is the actual signal at step n; and N is the total number of forecast steps. Both AEP and RMS are used as the primary criteria of performance measurement in the case study.

A detailed comparison of the results shows that the wavelet-NN model is able to generate the forecast with higher accuracy (maximum AEP = 0.89%) compared with the NN only model (maximum AEP = 3.44%) (see Table 1).

With less training data for the same NSW market, a recurrent neural network is used for demand forecasting. The recurrent network used an Elman network with Genetic Algorithm enhanced weight adjusting modules. The results show further improvement of forecast accuracy (Xu et al., 2004). More detailed simulation results are given for forecasts with SVM and data-mining techniques in the following sub-sections.

Table 1. Forecasting errors

Points ahead	APE %	
	Wavelet Forecast	Normal Forecast
1	0.1631	0.0918
2	0.0533	1.0396
3	0.1059	0.7312
4	0.8978	1.1556
5	0.0178	1.3441
6	0.0055	2.0125
7	0.0572	3.0819
8	0.3245	3.0765
9	0.8953	3.4439
10	0.3426	2.0583

SVM Price Forecasting

Measured by geographical distance, the QLD market is the largest in the NEM, with a power grid over 1,700 km in length. Half-hourly spot price, load and temperature data of the first two weeks of January 2001 in QLD market have been studied with SVM techniques (Xu et al., 2003). The price forecast results are shown in Figures 6 to 8.

Figure 6 shows the testing results of the second week of January, forecast data and the original data. The simulation is based on a single-step prediction.

The RMS error of the second January week forecast is 1.9476 and the corresponding APE is presented in Figure 7, where the average value of the APE is 6.4%. The results demonstrate that this SVM and wavelet approach can provide very good forecasting accuracy.

Figure 6. Single step forecast of January week in QLD market (Err_{rms}= 1.9476)

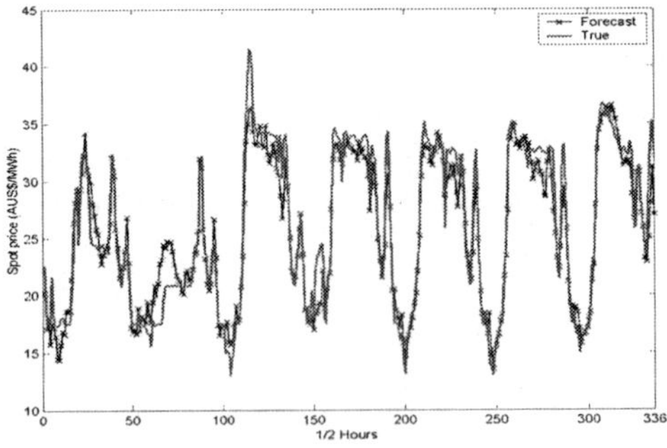

Figure 7. The APE of January week forecast in QLD market ($APE_{average}$ = 6.4%)

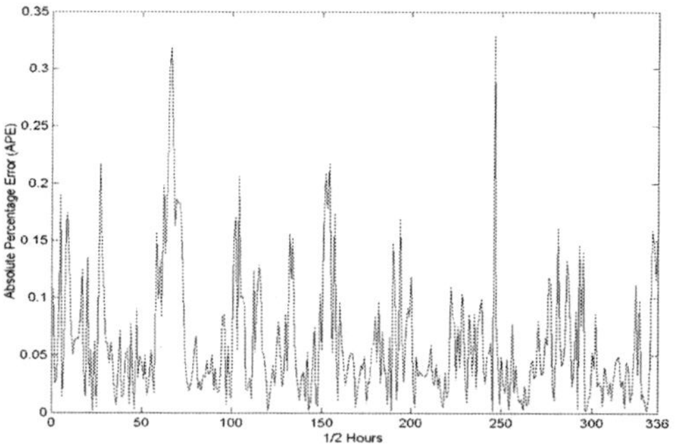

Figure 8. Single step forecast of January week in QLD market by SVM along (Err_{rms} = 3.8538 and $APE_{average}$ = 12.03%) (Lu, Dong, & Li, 2005)

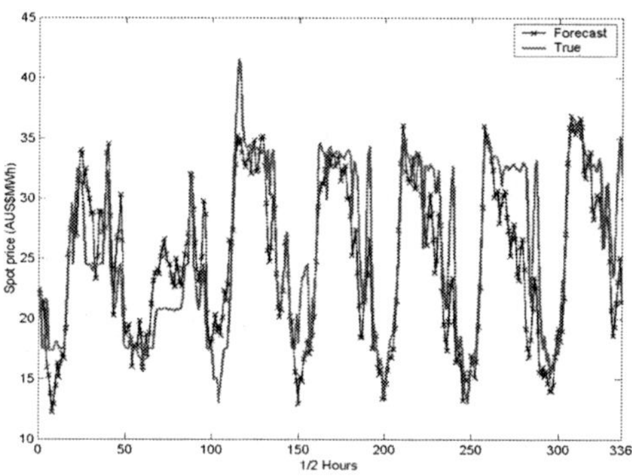

SVM PASA Data Forecasting

NEMMCO provides PASA data for the NEM of Australia. This case study has used a SVM forecast stage only (Sansom et al., 2003). A good accuracy week forecast of demand and price is shown in Figure 9, compared with a poor accuracy week forecast in Figure 10.

With SVM alone, forecasts without PASA data have total errors with a mean absolute error (MAE) of 28.6% and a RMS error of 251. The addition of PASA data offered some improvement in forecasting accuracy to MAE 28.0% and RMS 254. The plots of MAE and RMS are shown in Figure 9 and Figure 10. The plots for the model not using PASA data were almost identical to these plots shown (Sansom et al, 2003).

The PASA data proved only a small improvement in the accuracy of the SVM-alone price-forecasting model. This is partially solved with data-mining techniques in the next case study.

Figure 9. Price forecast on a good accuracy week

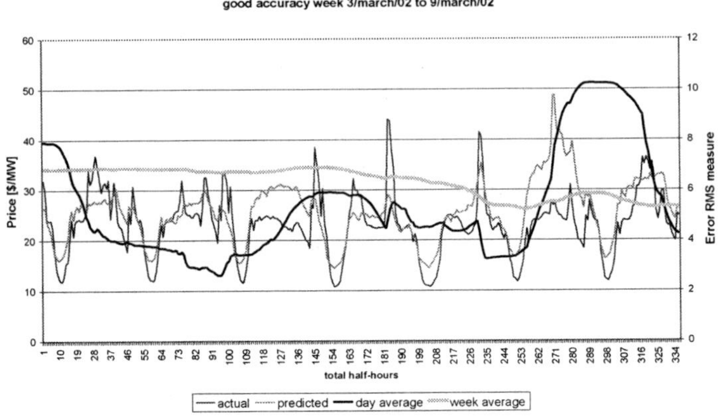

Figure 10. Price forecast on a poor accuracy week

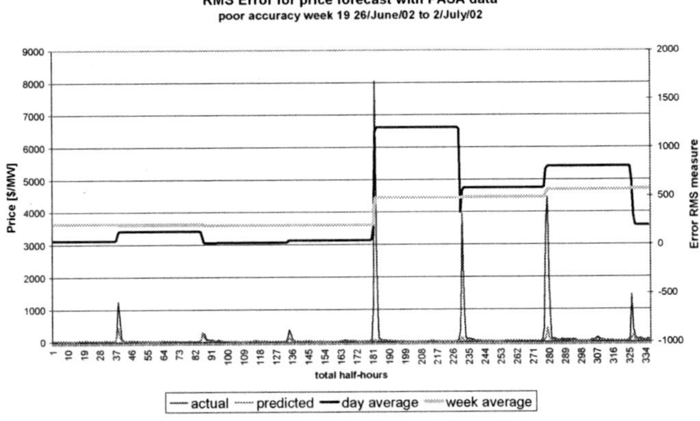

Price Spike Forecast Case Study

Price spike forecast for the Queensland electricity market is conducted with the general demand-price-price spike forecast model described in the previous section. The market RRP values, demand, generation reserve and other historical data of 01/2003-06/2003 are used for the training data sets. The data from the July-September 2003 period were used as test data with statistics on price spikes summarized in Table 2. The case study on price spike forecast has an accuracy rate of just over 50%. This is mainly because there was a less than 1% probability of price spikes during Jan-Sep 2003 in the Queensland Electricity Market. With more historical data, the performance will surely be improved. Moreover, given the highly stochastic nature of price spikes, the achieved forecast accuracy level is sufficiently good and useful for market participants. It is worth mentioning that with the wavelet-NN or wavelet-SVM forecast models the accuracy of

Table 2. Frequency and probability of price spike of Queensland Electricity Market during January - June 2003 (Lu, Dong, & Li, 2005)

Range of Price spike ($/MWh)	75 - 100	100 - 150	150 - 250	250 – 500	500 – 2000	>2000	Total
Frequency	22	22	11	10	11	2	78
Probability	$P(C_1)=$ 28.2%	$P(C_2)=$ 28.2%	$P(C_3)=$ 14.1%	$P(C_4)=$ 12.8%	$P(C_5)=$ 14.1%	$P(C_6)=$ 2.6%	100%

Figure 11. Electricity market price forecast of 1-15 Jun 2004 including both normal price range (<$75/MWhr) and price spikes (>$75/MWhr) (Zhao et al., 2005)

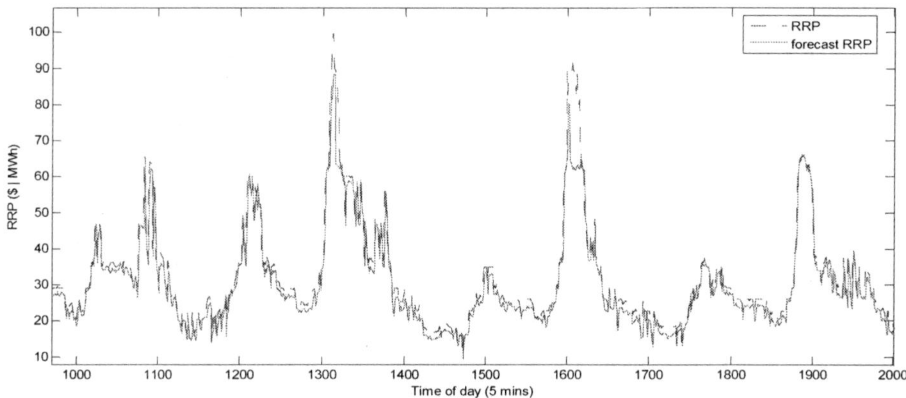

normal price (without spikes) forecast could be very high. By combining the normal price range forecast and the price spike forecast results, the model is able to provide comprehensive results with very useful and reliable information for an electricity market. Selected simulation results of composite price forecast are given in Figure 11.

Conclusion

This chapter presents the development and application of artificial-intelligence techniques in electricity market operations and management, especially in demand and price forecasting tasks. Because of the deregulation and highly complex nature of the electricity market and power system behind it, forecasting based on traditional regression models is no longer viewed as able to provide results to meet the requirements of the market participants. With learning and classification capabilities, artificial intelligence techniques are essential in providing solutions for market forecasting in a deregulated environment. Several forecasting models are discussed and tested with numerical data from the Australian NEM. These models are able to handle electricity demand and price forecasting with a high degree of accuracy. The general comprehensive forecast model given in the Data Mining section, based on time-series techniques, learning algorithms and data-mining techniques, is able to handle both normal price and price spike forecasts as well demand forecasts. All the forecast methods are able to provide an associated level of confidence to make the forecast realistically useful for market operations and management. The chapter presents techniques for electricity market price forecasts, which are clearly more complex and difficult than demand forecast. Among many different factors in an electricity market, the main factor affecting the market price is the demand-supply relationship. This relationship is the essential information used in price forecasting. In addition to the artificial intelligence techniques, traditional techniques such as Bayesian method and *k*-nearest neighbor method are used in the forecast model in this chapter. Through the detailed analysis and case studies, the chapter provides a general overview of a key issue in electricity market operations and management – market forecast and illustrates the successful application of artificial intelligence techniques in this area.

References

Bremermann, H. J. (1962). Optimisation through evolution and recombination. In M. C. Yovits, G. F. Jacobi, & G. D. Goldstine (Eds.), *Self-organizing systems* (pp. 93-106). Washington, DC: Spartan.

Bunn, D. W. (2000). Forecasting loads and prices in competitive power markets. *Proceedings of the IEEE, 88*(2), 163-169.

Contreras, J., Espinola, R., Nogales, F. J., & Conejo, A. J. (2003). ARIMA models to predict next-day electricity prices. *IEEE Transactions on Power Systems, 18*(3), 1014-1020.

Elman, J. L. (1990). Find structure in time. *Cognitive Science, 12*, 179-211.

Fogel, L. J., Owens, A. J., & Walsh, M. J. (1966). *Artificial intelligence through simulated evolution.* New York: Wiley.

Fraser, A. S. (1957). Simulation of genetic systems by automatic digital computers. *Australian Journal of Biological Science, 10*, 484-491.

Geva, A. B. (1998). ScaleNet — Multiscale neural-network architecture for time series prediction. *IEEE Transactions on Neural Networks, 9*(5), 1471-1482.

Goldberg, D. (1989). *Genetic algorithms in search, optimisation and machine learning.* Reading, MA: Addison-Wesley.

Guo, J.-J., & Luh, P. B. (2003). Selecting input factors for clusters of Gaussian radial basis function networks to improve market clearing price prediction. *IEEE Transactions on Power Systems, 18*(2), 665-672.

Holland, J. (1975). *Adaptation in natural and artificial systems.* Ann Arbor: University of Michigan.

Low, Y. F., & Dong, Z. Y. (2002, September 25-27). Enhancing neural network electricity load forecast with wavelet techniques. In Q.-G. Wang (Eds.). *Proceedings of IFAC and EUCA Asian Control Conference 2002,Singapore* (pp. 203-208). Singapore: Casual Productions.

Lu, X., Dong, Z. Y., & Li, X., (2005). Price spike forecasting with data mining techniques in a competitive electricity market. *International Journal of Electric Power Systems Research, 73*, 19-29.

Makridakis, S., Wheelwright, S. C., & Hyndman, R. J. (1998). *Forecasting methods and applications* (3rd ed.). New York: John Wiley.

Misiti, M., Misiti, Y., Oppenheim, G., & Poggi, J. M. (1996). *Wavelet toolbox for use with MATLAB*. Novi, MI: Math Works.

NEMMCO (2002). *NEMMCO Statement of Opportunities 2002*. Technical Report. Adelaide, Australia: National Electricity Market Management Company.

Nogales, F. J., Contreras, J., Conejo, A. J., & Espinola, R. (2002). Forecasting next-day electricity prices by time series models. *IEEE Transactions on Power Systems, 17*(2), 342-348.

Papalexopoulos, A. D., & Hesterberg, T. C. (1990). A regression-based approach to short-term system load forecasting. *IEEE Transactions on Power Systems, 5*(4), 1535-1547.

Pham, D. T., & Karaboga, D. (1999). Training Elman and Jordan networks for system identification using genetic algorithms. *Artificial Intelligence in Engineering, 13*, 107-117.

Poggio, T., & Girosi, F. (1990). Networks for approximation and learning. *Proceedings of the IEEE, 78*, 1481-1497.

Ramsay, B. (1995). *A neural network for predicting system marginal price in the UK power pool*. University of Dundee, UK.

Ranaweera, D. K., Karady, G. G., & Farmer, R. G. (1996). Effect of probabilistic inputs on neural network-based electric load forecasting. *IEEE Transactions on Neural Networks, 7*(6), 1528-1532.

Rice, J. R. (1964). *The approximation of functions*. Reading, MA: Addison Wesley.

Rüping, S. (2002). *mySVM software*. Retrieved July 10, 2002, from http://www.kernel-machines.org/

Sanders, N. R. (1999). Forecasting theory. In J. G. Webster (Ed.), *Wiley encyclopaedia of electrical and electronics engineering*. New York: Wiley-Interscience.

Sansom, D., Downs, T., & Saha, T. K. (2003, November 27-29). Support vector machine based electricity price forecasting for electricity markets utilising projected assessment of system adequacy data. In S. S. Choi & S. C. Soh (Eds.), *Proceedings of the Sixth International Power Engineering Conference (IPEC2003),* Singapore (Paper #2195). Singapore: JCS Office Services and Supplies.

Sansom, D., & Saha, T. K. (1999). Neural networks for forecasting electricity pool price in a deregulated electricity supply industry. In Y. D. Vashishtha, N. Trinne, P. Chandler, & D. Patterson (Eds.), *Proceedings Australasian Universities Power Engineering Conference, AUPEC'99. Darwin, Australia* (pp. 214-219). Darwin, NT, Australia: Northern Territory University.

Sapeluk, A. (1994). Pool price forecasting: A neural network application. In O. Gol (Ed.), *Proceedings Australasian Universities Power Engineering Conference, AUPEC'94.2* (pp. 840-846). Adelaide, SA, Australia: University of South Australia.

Smola, A. J., & Schölkopf, B. (1998). *A tutorial on support vector regression.* NeuroCOLT Technical Report NC-TR-98-030, Royal Holloway College, University of London.

Sweet, W. (2003). Tighter regional regulation needed of power grids — that is the unanimous conclusion of experts on the great 2003 blackout. *IEEE Spectrum, 40*(10) 12-13.

Tran, B. N., Nguyen, T. M., & Shihabi, M. M. (1999). Wavelets. In J. Webster (Ed.), *Wiley encyclopaedia of electrical and electronics engineering* (online). New York: John Wiley.

Vapnik, V. (1995). *The nature of statistical learning theory.* New York: Springer.

Wolak, F. A. (1998). *Market design and price behaviour in restructured electricity markets: An international comparison.* Retrieved May 1, 2005, from http://www.stanford.edu/~wolak

Wong, K. P., & Li, A. (2002). Virtual population and acceleration techniques for evolutionary power flow calculation in power systems. In R. Sarker, M. Mohammadian, & X. Yao (Eds.), *Evolutionary optimisation* (pp. 329-345). The Netherlands: Kluwer Academic.

Wu, F. F., & Varaiya, P. (1999). Coordinated multilateral trades for electric power networks: theory and implementation 1. *Electrical Power and Energy Systems, 21*, 75-102.

Xu, Z. Dong, Z. Y., & Liu, W. Q. (2003, May). Short-term electricity price forecasting using wavelet and SVM techniques. In X. Liu (Ed.), *Proceedings of the Third International DCDIS Conference on Engineering Applications and Computational Algorithms* (pp. 372-377), invited paper. Waterloo, Canada: Watam.

Xu, L. X., Dong, Z. Y., & Tay, A. (2004). Time series forecast with Elman neural networks and genetic algorithms. In K. C. Tan, M. H. Lim, X. Yao, & L. P. Wang (Eds.), *Recent advances in simulated evolution and learning* (pp. 747-768). World Scientific Series on Advances in Natural Computation. Singapore: World Scientific.

Zhang, B. L., & Dong, Z. Y. (2001). An adaptive neural-wavelet model for short term load forecasting. *International Journal of Electric Power Systems Research, 59*, 121-129.

Zhang, B. L., Luh, P. B., & Kasiviswanathan, K. (2003). Energy clearing price prediction and confidence interval estimation with cascaded neural networks. *IEEE Transactions on Power Systems, 18*(1), 99-105.

Zhao, J. H., Dong, Z. Y., Li, X., & Wong, K. P. (2005, June). A general method for price spike forecasting in a competitive electricity market. *Proceedings of the IEEE PES General Meeting 2005*, San Francisco.

Chapter IX

Reinforcement Learning-Based Intelligent Agents for Improved Productivity in Container Vessel Berthing Applications

Prasanna Lokuge, Monash University, Australia

Damminda Alahakoon, Monash University, Australia

Abstract

This chapter introduces the use of hybrid intelligent agents in a vessel berthing application. Vessel berthing in container terminals is regarded as a very complex, dynamic application, which requires autonomous decision-making capabilities to improve the productivity of the berths. In this chapter, the dynamic nature of the container vessel berthing system has been simulated with reinforcement learning theory, which essentially learns what to do by interaction with the environment. Other techniques, such as Belief-Desire-Intention (BDI) agent systems have also been implemented in many business applications. The chapter proposes a new hybrid agent model using an Adaptive Neuro Fuzzy Inference System (ANFIS), neural networks, and reinforcement learning methods to improve the reactive, proactive and intelligent behavior of generic BDI agents in a shipping application.

Introduction

Competition among container ports continues to increase as the worldwide container trade grows (Ryan, 1998). Managers in many container ports are trying to attract more vessel lines by automating the handling of equipment, and providing and speeding up various port-related services. One of the important applications in container terminals is the vessel berthing system, where system functionalities include the optimal allocation of berths to vessels, allocation of cranes, labor, and trucks of containers (loading and discharging) guaranteeing the high productivity of the container terminals.

The research described in this chapter is motivated by a berth assignment problem faced by terminal operators in large container hub ports. It aims to investigate the possibility of using intelligent agents for the efficient management of vessel berthing operations. In a dynamic environment, a vessel berthing system is a very complex dynamic application system, which requires dealing with various uncertainties to assure improved productivity and efficiency in the container terminals.

Numerous studies have been conducted in vessel and port-related operations in the past. Most of the research focuses on a static vessel berthing system, where the main issue is to find a good plan for assigning vessels. Brown, Lawphongpanich, and Thurman (1994) used an integer-programming model for assigning one berth to many vessels in a naval port. Operations and the dynamic nature of a container port are not considered in the vessel berthing program. Lim (1998) addressed the vessel planning problem with a fixed berthing time; Li, Cai, and Lee (1998) addressed the scheduling problem with a single processor and multiple jobs and assumed that vessels had already arrived; Chia, Lau, and Lim (1999) used an Ant Colony Optimization approach to solve the berthing system by minimizing the wharf length; Kim and Moon (2003) used simulated annealing in berth scheduling. We suggest that the use of experience with dynamic decision-making capabilities would help to ease the burden of operational complexities at container terminals. We argue that the application systems should always interact with the environment to observe changes at different time intervals and should react promptly by suggesting alternative solutions. These features would essentially improve the autonomous behavior of current vessel berthing and planning application systems.

The BDI agent model is possibly the best known and best studied model of practical reasoning for implementations (Georgeff, Pell, Pollack, & Wooldridge, 1998), for example, IRMA (Bratman, Israel, & Pollack, 1998) and the PRS-like systems and dMARS. In some instances the criticism regarding the BDI model has been that it is not well suited to certain types of behavior. In particular, the basic BDI model appears to be inappropriate for building complex systems that must learn and adapt their behaviors. Such systems are becoming increasingly important for business applications.

The hybrid BDI model suggested in this article discusses a new agent model to overcome some of the limitations of the generic BDI model. A hybrid-agent model for container terminals is introduced with only a few intelligent tools, such as neural networks and an adaptive neuro-fuzzy inference system (ANFIS). This greatly improves agent behavior in complex applications, such as a vessel berthing systems. Further, it enhances the capabilities of learning, social behavior, and adaptability in planning, especially in dynamically changing environments.

The research is being carried out at the School of Business Systems, Monash University, Australia, in collaboration with the Jaya Container Terminal at the port of Colombo, Sri Lanka and Patrick Terminals in Melbourne, Australia. The rest of the chapter is organized as follows: The second section provides an introduction to a generic berthing application in a container terminal. The third section describes the BDI agent architecture. The fourth section describes the proposed hybrid BDI agent architecture for vessel berthing applications in a container terminal. The main components of the *h*-BD[I] architecture are discussed in the fifth section. The sixth section outlines a case scenario and experimental results of the research work. The final section gives a conclusion.

Generic Berthing Application

Container terminals generally have many container berths for stevedoring operations (loading and discharging of containers). The speed and performance of the stevedoring operations in berths differ according to the facilities and performance of the equipment in respective berths. Terminal managers in many container ports attempt to improve the productivity of the berths by assuring efficient utilization of resources, meeting targets and deal lines, minimizing operational delays and increasing revenues.

In current operations, a shipping line indicates the expected time of arrival of a vessel three months prior to arrival. The shipping line then regularly updates the port about any changes to the original plan of arrival. An arrival declaration, sent by shipping lines to ports, generally contains the date of arrival, expected time of arrival, vessel details, number of containers to be discharged, number of containers to be loaded, remarks about cargo type, berthing and sailing draft requirements, the crane outreach required and air draft (Lokuge & Damminda, 2004b). When vessels are berthed, quay cranes unload the boxes and load them into prime movers. Transfer cranes in the yard area pick up the boxes from the prime movers and stack them in pre-defined locations in the yard. When the cargo is to be loaded, transfer cranes pick up the boxes in the yard and load them into prime movers. The boxes are then loaded, by quay cranes, to a pre-defined sequence at the berths. The terminal managers should be able to forecast the expected-time-of-berth, expected-completion-time, and the expected-berth-productivity for the calling vessels. The generic data used in the vessel berthing system are as follows:

cty^v -cargo type of the new vessel v: "N"-normal, "D"-dangerous or "P"-perishable cargo, nob^v - number of boxes in the new vessel v, vbd^v - vessel berth draft required for the new vessel v (meters), vsd^v -vessel sailing draft requirement (meters), vcr^v -crane length required to reach the boxes in the vessel v (meters), bdr_b -berth draft of the berth b (meters), len^i_{bj} -length of the cranes i in the berth bj (meters), $gcp^v_{i,j}$ -gross crane productivity of the crane i in berth j for vessel v (measured in number of boxes move per hour), gbp_j^i -average berth productivity which indicate the number of boxes handled by berth j for vessel i, eta^v -expected time of arrival of the new vessel v (hh:mm), etb^v_b -expected time of berth for the vessel v in berth b (hh:mm), etc^v_b - expected time of completion of the vessel v at berth b (hh:mm), odl_b^v -operational delays expected for the vessel v in berth b (hh:mm), ebp_b^v-expected berth productivity for vessel v in berth b in moves per hour (mph), eot^v_b-expected operation time required for vessel v in berth b (hh:mm), l_b-length of the berth b in meters and *noc* for the number of cranes in a berth, cob_j-crane outreach of the berth j, nov_j-number of vessel in the berth j, and gap_j-status of the distance between vessels in berth j.

The Port of Colombo has been used as the test bed for the comparison of results obtained from the proposed hybrid-agent architecture. It handles approximately 1.7 million container boxes annually and has been recognized as one of the more efficient ports in Asia. The main terminal is the "Jaya Container Terminal" *(JCT),* which has four main berths *(Jct1, Jct2, Jct3 and Jct4)* and two cross-berths for feeder vessels. We have only considered the four main berths in the JCT. Figure 1 shows the available berths and their drafts in the JCT terminal. The distance between vessel v_i and v_j in berth k is denoted as t^k_{ij}. It shows an example of a berthing scenario, which indicates the berth lengths and the drafts.

Constraints imposed in a generic vessel berthing system are described in the next subsection below (Lokuge & Damminda, 2004a). An agent should consider these constraints before a suitable berth is selected for the calling vessel in a container terminal.

Sailing and Berth Drafts

The sailing and the berthing drafts of the calling vessel (vbd^{vi} *and* vsd^{vi}) should be less than or equal to the draft of the respective berths (bdr_{bj}). The *nob* denotes the number of berths in the terminal.

$$\forall i, j: \left[\left(vbd^{vi} \leq bdr_{bj}\right) \wedge \left(vsd^{vi} \leq bdr_{bj}\right)\right] \quad Where,\ 1 \leq bj \leq nob. \qquad \textbf{(1)}$$

Outreach of Cranes in the Berths

All the cranes in the berths should be able to completely move across the vessel for loading and discharging containers. More formally,

Figure 1. Available berths and drafts in JCT

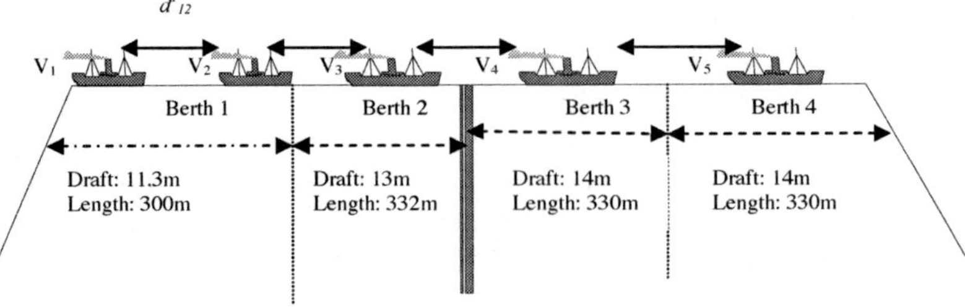

$$for\ all\ i\ and\ j\ :\left\{vcr^{vi} \le len^{i}_{bj}\right\} where\ 1 \le i \le 4,\ \ 1 \le j \le noc \qquad (2)$$

Minimum Waiting Time of a Vessel

The vessel waiting time for a berth is another very important factor to be considered in the system. If w^v denotes the minimum waiting time of the calling vessel v then

$$w^v = Min.\left\{eta^v - etb_{bi} \mid \forall\, bi \in [1..4]\right\} \qquad (3)$$

Average Crane Productivity of Berths

An individual berth should maximize the average crane productivity for calling vessels to gain the competitive advantage over other berths. The expected gross crane productivity of crane i in berth j for the new vessel vi is $gcp^{vi}_{i,j}$ as in

$$gcp^{vi}_{i,j} = \frac{nob^{vi}_i}{\left|\left(cmo^{vi}_{i,j} - cpo^{vi}_{i,j}\right)\right|} \qquad (4)$$

The average crane productivity of the berth j for the vessel vi is given as

$$acp^{vi}_j = \frac{1}{n}\sum_{i=1}^{n} gcp^{vi}_{i,j} \qquad (5)$$

where $cmo^{vi}_{i,j}$ and $cpo^{vi}_{i,j}$ indicates the commencement and completion times of crane *i* in berth *j* for the vessel *vi*, nob^{vi}_i and acp^{vi}_j indicates the number of boxes handled by crane *i* and the expected average crane productivity in berth *j* for vessel *vi*.

Distance Required for Vessel Berthing and Sailing

A recommended distance must always be kept between vessels in the berth (vessel distance requirement, vdr), which minimize the delays in vessel berthing and sailing. If d_l^{bi} and d_r^{bi} indicate the left- and right-side distance from the vessel to the berth ends and d^{bi}_{ij} is the distance between two vessels *i* and *j* in the same berth. Three different cases of vessel berthing scenarios are shown in Figure 2(a), 2(b) and 2(c). If occ_{bi} denotes the occupancy of the berth b_i in a terminal, then

Figure 2(a). Vessel is left side of the berth

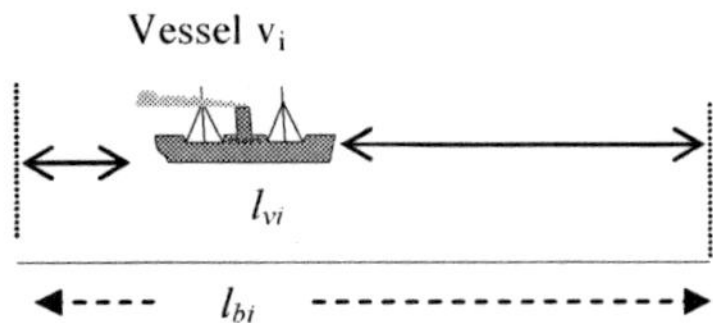

Figure 2(b). Vessel is right side of the berth

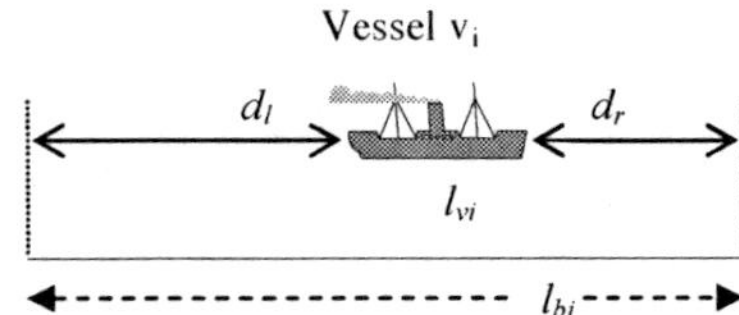

Figure 2(c). Two vessels at the berth

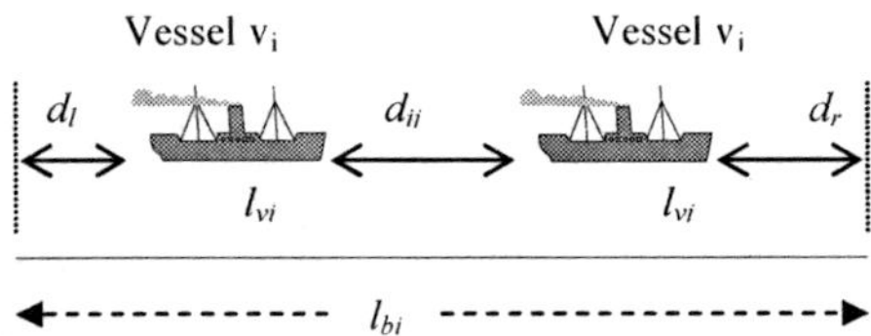

$$occ_{bi} = \begin{cases} 0 \text{ if number of vessels } = 0 \\ 1 \text{ if number of vessel } = 1 \\ 2 \text{ if number of vessel } = 2 \end{cases} \quad (6)$$

If the Boolean value for ls_{vi} indicates the side of the vessel *vi* in the berth, then

$$ls_{vi} = \begin{cases} 1 \text{ if vessel is at left end} \\ 0 \text{ otherwise} \end{cases} \quad (7)$$

If md_l^{bi} and md_r^{bi} are the minimum left- and right-side distances to be kept between a vessel and the left and right sides of the berths, md_{ij}^{bi} indicates the minimum distance between two vessels *i* and *j* in a berth. The minimum requirements (that is, Pre- and Post-conditions) that a terminal manger has to consider about the gaps to be kept between vessels and berth ends are given as:

$$\begin{aligned}&Case\,1\,(occ_{bi}=0)\\&\Pr e:\{l_{bi}\geq(l_{vi}+md_l^{bi}+md_r^{bi})\}\\&Post:\{(d_l\geq md_l^{bi})\wedge(d_r\geq md_r^{bi})\}\end{aligned} \tag{8}$$

Case 1 indicates a scenario where a berth has no vessels at the time of planning whereas Case 2 and 3 indicate scenarios where one vessel is already berthed at the time of planning the second vessel.

$$\begin{aligned}&Case\,2:((occ_{bi}=1)\wedge(ls_{vi}=1))\\&\Pr e:\left\{\begin{matrix}(d_l\geq md_l^{bi})\wedge(d_r\geq md_r^{bi})\wedge\\ [d_r\geq(md_{ij}^{bi}+l_{vi}+md_r^{bi})]\end{matrix}\right\}\\&Post:occ_{bi}=2\end{aligned} \tag{9}$$

$$\begin{aligned}&Case\,3:((occ_{bi}=1)\wedge(ls_{vi}=0))\\&\Pr e:\left\{\begin{matrix}(d_l\geq md_l^{bi})\wedge(d_r\geq md_r^{bi})\wedge\\ [d_l\geq(md_{ij}^{bi}+l_{vi}+md_l^{bi})]\end{matrix}\right\}\\&Post:occ_{bi}=2\end{aligned} \tag{10}$$

One of the aims is to build computer programs that can independently make good decisions about what action to perform. It is important to note that agents are the systems that are *situated* or *embodied* in some environment — thus they are not disembodied systems (Wooldridge, 2000).

An increasingly popular programming paradigm is that of *agent-oriented programming* (Muller, 1996). Often described as a natural successor to object-oriented programming, it is highly suited to applications which are embedded in complex dynamic environments (Ljungberg & Lucas, 1992). Agent technology has been used in areas such as air traffic control, automated manufacturing, and the space shuttle (Ljungberg & Lucas, 1992). An agent can be described as a computer system that is situated in some environment that is capable of autonomous action in this environment in order to meet its design objectives (Figure 3). The agent takes the sensory inputs from the environment, and produces as output actions that affect it. The interaction is usually ongoing and non-terminating (Wooldridge, 2002).

The next section describes the traditional BDI agent architecture.

Figure 3. Agent interaction between environments

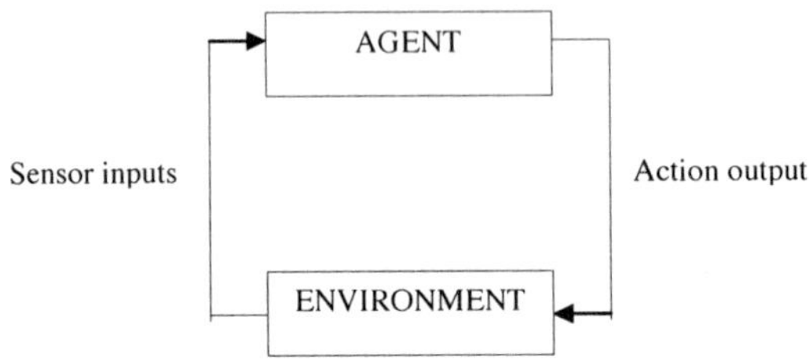

Belief-Desire-Intention (BDI) Agent Architecture

The role played by beliefs, desires and intentions in the design of rational agents has been well recognized in the philosophical and AI literature (Bratman, 1987; Bratman, Israel & Pollack, 1988; Georgeff & Ingrand, 1989). An approach to the study of rational agency, which has received a great deal of attention, is the so-called *Belief-Desire-Intention* (BDI) architecture developed by Rao and Georgeff (1992). This model is possibly the best-known and best-studied model of practical reasoning agents. It has its roots in the philosophical tradition of understanding *practical reasoning* in humans. Simply, practical reasoning is directed towards actions — the process of figuring out what to do (Wooldridge, 2000). Components of the BDI agent architecture are described in the next section.

Main Components in the BDI Model

Beliefs: information concerning the world is described in beliefs which are represented as data structures in the BDI model. *Desires:* a set of goals the agent could achieve. In the "real world" an agent would like all its desires to be achieved. *Intentions:* the desires that an agent is committed to achieve. The control loop of a generic BDI agent is shown in Figure 4 (Rao & Georgeff, 1992; Wooldridge, 2000).

In line 1, the beliefs, intentions and plans are initialized. In lines 2 and 3, the agent perceives and updates its beliefs. In line 5, the agent starts deliberation of possible desires, and in line 6, it commits to an intention to achieve. In line 7, the agent generates a plan to execute. The algorithm has many limitations, in particular, it assumes that the environment has not changed since it observed it at step 3 (Schut & Wooldridge, 2000; Wooldridge, 2000). Another limitation of the above algorithm is that the agent has over-committed to its intention. That is, all of the plans which belong to the committed intention will be executed by the agents regardless of environmental changes.

Figure 4. Generic BDI control loop

```
1.  B=B0; I=I0; π := null;
2.  While true do
3.    get next percept p;
4.    B:= update beliefs ;
5.    D:= option ( B,I) ; /* get desires */
6.    I:= select intentions ( B,D,I)
7.    π := plan ( B,I) /* plan to be executed */
8.    execute (π ) ;
9.  end while
```

Wooldridge (2000) has developed improvements designed to overcome the above limitations, but does not describe how to implement the intention reconsideration process. Schut and Wooldridge (2001) integrated meta-reasoning in a decision theoretic model (Russell & Wefald, 1992) for the deliberation process of the BDI agent architecture in the intention reconsideration process. But there are still limitations in the model, as the estimation of future environmental changes needs to be known in advance and, therefore, is static. A proposed hybrid-BDI architecture, designed to overcome these limitations, is described in the next section.

Hybrid-BDI Architecture ("*h*-BD[I]" Architecture)

Intelligent learning while interacting with the environment is one of our primary objectives in developing hybrid-BDI agents. This minimizes some of the limitations that exist with current BDI agents, especially when dealing with complex dynamic application systems. Questions raised by researchers on the use of BDI agents in a real environment are addressed in our proposed model.

Firstly, the present BDI execution cycle given in Figure 4 shows that the agent always observes only the next available event or input before it commences the intention reconsideration process. This is a limitation in the present architecture that leads to delays in making correct decisions quickly. The ability to capture all the available events related to a committed intention would help the agent to look forward many steps before it proceeds with the intention reconsideration process. Figure 5 indicates the advantage of observing all the related events in the event queue before an agent commences its intention reconsideration process.

The left side of Figure 5 indicates that the agent has committed to achieve the intention "*assign-berth (jct1)*" for the calling vessel at time t_0. Supposing that the agent begins executing plans at time t_0, the upper right hand side of Figure 5 shows that it will observe

Figure 5. Observation of events in Intention reconsideration process

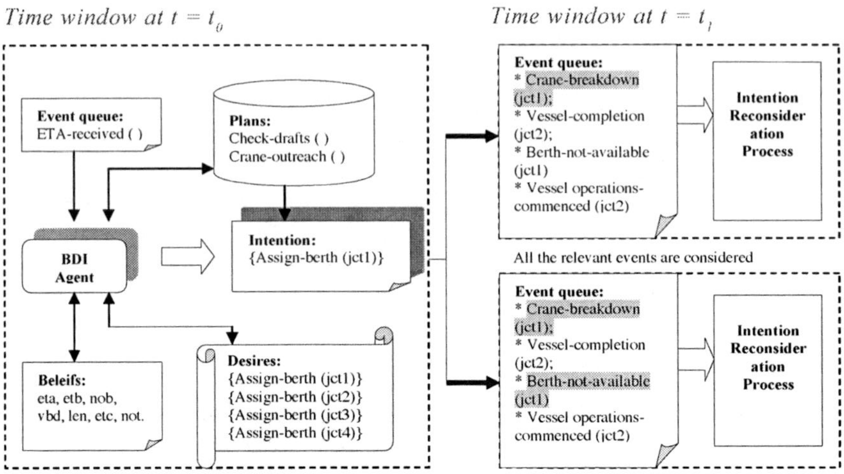

only the immediately available event in the intention reconsideration process. In this situation, the agent's knowledge of the environmental changes is limited, as it depends only on the immediate event in the event queue. Hence, the agent may not be able to find the optimal solution in the intention reconsideration process.

Observations of all relevant events for the currently committed intention are given in the lower right-hand side of Figure 5. Two events in the event queue, that is "*crane-breakdown (jct1)*" and "*berth-not-available (jct1)*" are considered in this situation. Since the "*berth-not-available (jct1)*" event causes a negative impact on the present committed "*assign-berth (jct1)*" intention, the agent may decide to drop it since it is now no longer relevant. But in the first case, limited knowledge of the world prevents the selection of the optimal decision in the early stage and would cause unnecessary computational cost in the intention reconsideration process. We propose an extended BDI execution cycle with a reinforcement learning technique to overcome the above limitation in the present BDI execution cycle.

Secondly, the present BDI execution cycle does not indicate how to adopt the previously dropped intentions in the present environment. For example, Figure 5 shows that at time t_0, the agent has committed to achieve "*assign-berth (jct1).*" Then, at time t_1, it observes the world has changed so that it should activate the intention reconsideration process. Assuming that the deliberation process suggested dropping the current intention committed, then agent should know the alternative options available for achieving its long-term goal. This is the novel feature we propose in our hybrid-BDI model.

A new *h*-BD[I] architecture is proposed to overcome the limitations in generic BDI agents in dealing with dynamic complex environments. The use of supervised neural networks and ANFIS are embedded in the generic BDI model, which is symbolized by an additional character "*h*" in front of the "BDI." Further, "[I]" is used to denote that the extended BDI architecture monitors the other alternative options recently dropped while processing

Figure 6. Main modules in the hybrid BDI model

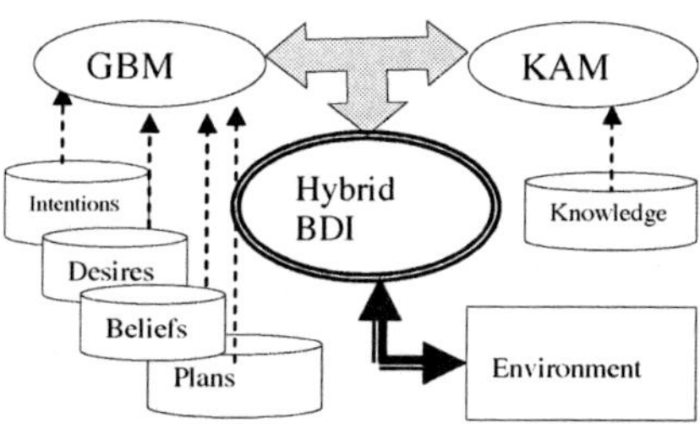

its intention reconsideration process. The next sub-section describes the main modules introduced in this hybrid-BDI model.

Main Modules in the "*h*-BD[I]" Architecture

The new hybrid architecture (as shown in Figure 6) consists of two modules to overcome the limitations in learning mechanism in the generic BDI model. "*Generic BDI Module*" *(GBM)* will execute the generic BDI interpreter as shown in Figure 4. "*Knowledge Acquisition Module*" *(KAM)* provides the necessary intelligence for the execution of plans (Lokuge & Damminda, 2004c). Intelligent behavior in the proposed model is assured with the use of supervised neural networks and adaptive neuro-fuzzy techniques in the *KAM* module.

Components of the *h*-BD[I] architecture are described in the next section.

Main Components of the h-BD[I] Architecture

The main components of the *h*-BD[I] architecture are shown in Figure 7. The EVENT-COMPOSER is primarily responsible for maintaining a queue of events occurring during the execution of plans in the environment. Events belonging to various intentions are stored in the EVENT–COMPOSER. The deliberation process typically indicates what options are available in the environment. INTELLIGENT-DELIBERATOR in the *KAM* module uses supervised neutral network based training in selecting the options available for the agent. Reinforcement learning techniques adopted in the INTENTION-DRIVER enable the agent to view many events occurring in the world and to recognize the effects of the changes to the committed intention and to alternative options. Further, our *h*-BD[I] model is capable of comparing the effect of change on the committed intention and alternative options. The ANFIS based IMPACT-ANALYZER component finally decides the intention reconsideration of the proposed *h*-BD[I] model.

Figure 7. Components of the h-BD[I] architecture

The Event-Composter Component

The EVENT-COMPOSER records a list of events it receives from the environment in chronological order. Beliefs about the environment are updated with the incoming events in the event queue. If $S = \{s_i | 1 \leq i \leq n\}$ denotes n number of states in the environment, any state s_i, is described as a set of beliefs bel_i^I for an intention I. Events in the EVENT-COMPOSER are described as $E = \{e_i^j | i = 1..N, 1 \leq j \leq nos\}$, where nos indicate the number of states in the environment. The effect of the ith event at state j in the environment is given as e_i^j. The EVENT-COMPOSER is responsible for updating the beliefs in states due to various events at different intervals of time. Sets of states and beliefs at a given time for achieving the agent desire, "*assign-berth*" are shown in Figure 8.

P1, P2 and *P3* show the plans to be executed in achieving the desire "*assign-berth.*" The execution of plans makes the agent move from one state to another in the environment. It would be interesting to investigate the degree of effect of the belief changes in different

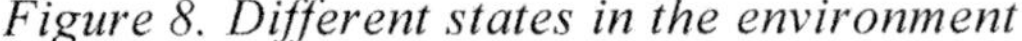

Figure 8. Different states in the environment

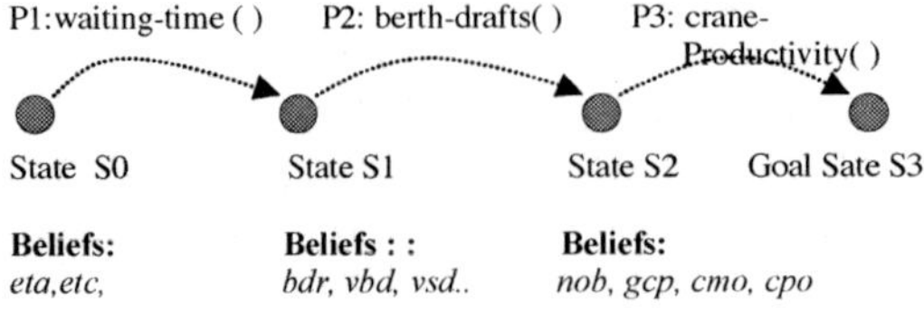

states. A Belief-Impact-Matrix (BIM) has been added to the proposed *h*-BD[I] architecture to analyze the effects of various belief changes on achieving the agent intention at different states, where *BIM* is defined as:

$$BIM = \begin{bmatrix} \alpha_{1,1}^{I,p} \ \alpha_{1,2}^{I,p} \cdots \alpha_{1,k}^{I,p} \\ \cdots\cdots \\ \alpha_{l,1}^{I,p} \ \alpha_{l,2}^{I,p} \cdots \alpha_{l,k}^{I,p} \end{bmatrix} \tag{11}$$

$\alpha_{i,j}^{I,p}$ ($0 \leq \alpha_{i,j}^{I,p} \leq 1$) shows the impact factor or influence of the jth belief in the state *i* in the execution of plan *p* for the intention *I*.

The Intelligent-Deliberator Component

The proposed INTELLIGENT-DELIBERATOR is capable of producing all the possible intentions or options available to achieve the final goal of the agent. The Goal Success Factor of the options (θ^{opt}), where ($0 \leq \theta^{opt} \leq 1$) will be produced from the trained neural network model in the INTELLIGENT-DELIBERATOR. Options with larger values in θ^{opt} indicate a high success rate if that option is selected by the agent. Beliefs, desires, intentions and events used in the supervised neural network to produce θ^{opt} are shown in Figure 9. Next, *h*-BD[I] should be able to filter the options generated by the neural network and commit to executing the highest success rate option as the intention.

The efficiency of the proposed model is dependent on the selection criteria used in the filtering process, which should decide how many alternative options should be consid-

Figure 9. Neural network in the INTELLIGENT-DELIBERATOR component

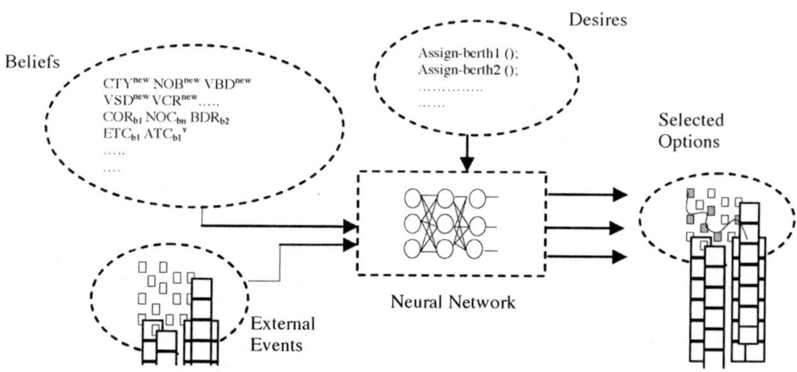

Figure 10. Algorithm for controlling the agent global view

1. Accept event from EVENT-COMPOSER;
2. Define option-control-factor ϑ;
3. $\theta^{opt} = \{\theta_i^{opt} | i = 1..N\}$
4. θ^{opt} = KAM-Intentions (beliefs, desires, options);
5. For i =1 to Max. number of options do
6. if ($\theta_i^{opt} \geq \theta_{max}^{opt}$) then
7. $\theta_{max}^{opt} = \theta_i^{opt}$;
8. End-loop
9. Select the committed intention θ_I^{opt};
10. For i =1 to max. number of options do
11. if $\left(\theta_I^{opt} - \theta_i^{opt}\right) \leq \vartheta$ then
12. selected-options[i] = θ_i^{opt};
13. end-loop

ered in achieving the long-term goal of the agent. The algorithm used in controlling the number of alternative options is described in Figure 10.

The selection of number of alternative options is controlled by the option-control-factor (ϑ), where ($0 \leq \vartheta \leq 1$), as defined in the agent model. The larger the values in ϑ, the more options to be considered in the intention reconsideration process. The INTENTION-DRIVER component is described in the next section.

The Intention-Driver Component

Reinforcement learning is learning what to do and how to map situations to actions so as to maximize a numerical reward signal (Sutton & Barto, 1988). Reinforcement learning involves learning while interacting with the environment. We propose the use of reinforcement learning techniques to compute the effects of the execution of plans and environmental changes for achieving the long-term goal of the agent. The reinforcement-learning technique adopted in computing the plan execution is described in the next section.

Execution of Plans in H-BD[I] Model Using Reinforcement Learning

Reinforcement learning is an approach to artificial intelligence that emphasizes learning by the individual from its interaction with its environment (Sutton & Barto, 1988). It has

Figure 11. Reinforcement leaning model for plans

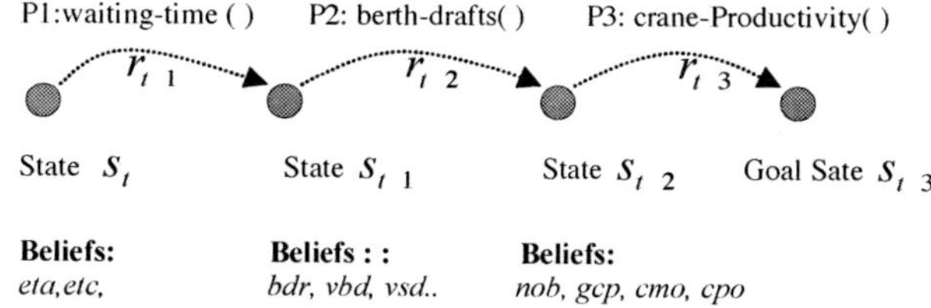

been applied to balancing an inverted pole (Anderson, 1988), optimizing elevator performance (Crites & Barto, 1996), playing backgammon (Tesauro, 1995) and many other applications. As described in the previous sections, a state is defined as a set of beliefs at a given time. The execution of a plan causes the agent to move from one state to another through the committed intention. Figure 11 indicates four states in a typical vessel berthing application in assigning a vessel to a particular berth. By executing plan P1 at time t, the agent moves from S0 to state S1, receiving a reward r_{t+1}.

If the sequence of rewards received after time-step t is denoted as $r_{t+1}, r_{t+2}, r_{t+3}, \ldots$, then the total return expected in executing all the plans in achieving the intention is:

$$R^I{}_t = r_{t+1} + r_{t+2} + r_{t+3} + \cdots r_T \qquad \textbf{(12)}$$

where T is the final goal step in the committed intention. The additional concept introduced in reinforcement learning is discounting. The discount rate determines the present value of future rewards. The discounted rewards that an agent could determine during the execution of plans for an intention is given as:

$$R^I{}_t = r_{t+1} + \gamma r_{t+2} + \gamma^2 r_{t+3} + \ldots = \sum_{k=0}^{\infty} \gamma^k r_{t+k+1} \qquad \textbf{(13)}$$

where the discount factor, γ, is $(0 \le \gamma \le 1)$, r and R denote the rewards and sum of the rewards. A reward receiving k time-steps in the future is worth only γ^{k-1} times what it would be worth if it were received immediately (Sutton & Barto, 1988). The value of state s under policy p, denoted as $V^\pi(s)$, is the expected return when starting in s and following p is given in equation 14.

$$V^\pi(s) = E_\pi\{R_t | s_t = s\} = E_\pi\left\{\sum_{k=0}^{\infty} \gamma^k r_{t+k+1} | s_t = s\right\} \qquad \textbf{(14)}$$

The state values can be updated using iterative policy evaluation when executing plans for achieving an intention:

$$V'(s_t) = r_{t+1} + V(s_{t+1}) \quad \textbf{(15)}$$

This shows that the value of the current state is the value of the next estimated state plus the rewards during the transition due to the execution of the current plan for an intention. The value of executing a plan p in a state s for achieving the intention I under a policy p, denoted as $V_I^{\pi}(s,p)$ is the expected return starting from state s, executing plan p and thereafter following policy p:

$$V_I^{\pi}(s,p) = E^I_{\pi}\{R_t | s_t = s, p_t = p\} = E^I_{\pi}\left\{\sum_{k=0}^{\infty} \gamma^k r_{t+k+1} | s_t = s, p_t = p\right\} \quad \textbf{(16)}$$

The equation shown above could be used to compute the expected value from state s to goal state for all the other alternative options in the h-BD[I] agent model.

Most of the dynamic complex application systems are model-free and non-deterministic, where the probability of state transition is not predictable. In such situations, the agent should interact with the environment in deciding the optimal solution. Temporal difference learning is a method used in model free environments to approximate the value function (Barnard, 1993). The value of the present state can be expressed using the next immediate reinforcement and the value of the next state. The standard temporal difference update is shown in Equation 17.

$$V'(s_t) \leftarrow V(s_t) + \alpha[r_{t+1} + \gamma V(s_{t+1}) - V(s_t)] \quad \textbf{(17)}$$

where $\alpha\{0 \le \alpha \le 1\}$ is the learning rate and γ is the discount factor.

The calculation of the rewards in the execution of plans in state s, assuming, $E^{m}_{(s,p)}$ is the ideal value expected in the execution. $A^{m}_{(s,p)}$ is the actual value computed from the execution of plans p in state s. $A^{I,t}_{(s,p)}$ is the actual distance or reward computed based on the beliefs in the environment for plans p in state s for achieving the intention I and, finally, $E^{I,t}_{(s,p)} (0 \le E^{I,t}_{(s,p)} \le 1)$ is the expected distance or reward allocated according to the expected value in state s for the plan p. The actual reward or distance due to the execution of a plan p in state s for a given intention I is given in Equation 18.

$$A_{(s,p)}^{I,t} = r_{t+1} = \left\{ \frac{E_{(s,p)}^{I,t}}{E_{(s,p)}^{m}} \times A_{(s,p)}^{m} \middle| s_t = s,\ p_t = p \right\} \quad \textbf{(18)}$$

The sequence of rewards is then computed for all the plans in the various options identified from the INTELLIGENT-DELIBERATOR. The option that has the highest initial state value is considered to be the optimal option in the agent model. For example, $A_{(s,p)}^{m}$ is computed based on the beliefs at different states and the maximum value for $E_{(s,p)}^{m}$ has been pre-defined for all the individual options produced from the INTELLIGENT-DELIBERATOR. A normalized value between one and zero has been defined as $E_{(s,p)}^{I,t}$ in the execution of plans.

The value estimate for a state or its distance from a goal state is updated on the basis of the rewards obtained, with a simple transition from it to the immediately following state, plus the next state estimate, as shown in Equation 19.

$$V^{I}(s_t) \leftarrow V^{I}(s_t) + \alpha \left[A_{t+1}^{I,t} + \gamma V^{I}(s_{t+1}) - V^{I}(s_t) \right] \quad \textbf{(19)}$$

$V^{I}(s_t)$ indicates the state value or the total distance computed from state s to the goal state. The reward received at state *s* for executing plan *p*, for achieving the intention I, $A_{(s,p)}^{I,t}$, is calculated as shown in Equation 18. A simple temporal difference method is based on the one next reward, using the value of the state one step later as a proxy for the remaining rewards.

$$R_t^{(n)} = r_{t+1} + \gamma r_{t+2} + \gamma^2 r_{t+3} + \cdots + \gamma^{n-1} r_{t+n} + \gamma^n V_t(s_{t+n}) \quad \textbf{(20)}$$

An *n-step backup* is defined as a backup of values towards *n-step* return (Sutton & Barto, 1988), as shown in Equation 20. The *n-step backup* method is used in capturing the value change to the state, which considers all the changes that occurred due to the events in the environment. The value change of state *s* due to all the relevant events is given as:

$$\Delta V_t(s_t) = \alpha \left[R_t^{n} - V_t(s_t) \right], \quad \textbf{(21)}$$

where, R^{n}_{t} is the *n-step* return due to events observed for an intention. For example, if an agent observes that there are *n* events that may have some impact on the committed intention, then Equation 21 is used to compute the expected value change in state *s*. Individual rewards in states are computed using Equation 18. Figure 12 shows a simple scenario observed by the *h*-BD[I] agent in a typical vessel berthing application. If we

Figure 12. Committed intention and an alternative option in the h-BD[I] model

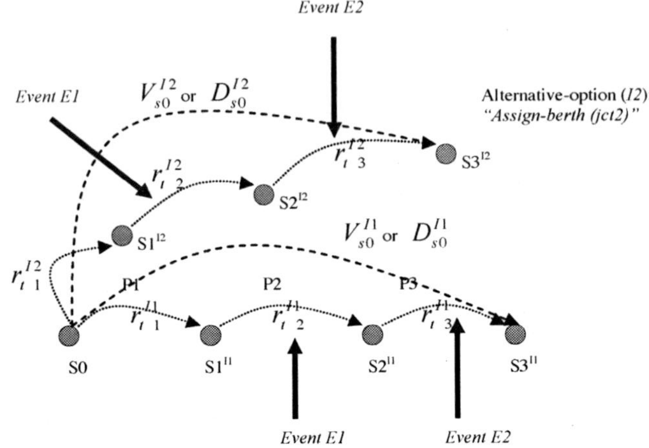

assume that the INTELLIGENT-DELIBERATOR component has chosen "*assign-berth (jct1)*" as the intention *(I1)* and "*assign-berth (jct2)*" as an alternative option *(I2)* in assigning a berth to the calling vessel *v1,* the agent has three plans namely P1: "*find-waiting-time ( )*", "P2: "*get-berth-draft ( )*" and p3: "*find-crane-productivity ( )*" to achieve the final goal or desire to assign the optimal berth to the calling vessel *v1*.

When the vessel declaration is received, INTENTION-DRIVER uses the incremental reinforcement learning method with the available data until the method converges upon an answer. The state values produced by the reinforcement learning based INTENTION-DRIVER is sent to the ANFIS based IMPACT-ANALYZER for making the final decision of the intention reconsideration. A brief description of the ANFIS based IMPACT-ANALYZER component is given in the next section.

The Impact-Analyzer Component

Jang (1993) proposed an interesting architectures for fuzzy neural nets, which is a fuzzy inference system implemented in the framework of an adaptive neuro-fuzzy inference system (ANFIS). ANFIS implements a Takagi-Sugeno-Kang (TSK) fuzzy inference system in which the conclusion of the fuzzy rule is constituted by a weighted linear combination of the crisp inputs (Jang, 1993). Figure 13 shows the TSK fuzzy inference system when two membership functions are each assigned to the two inputs (x and y).

Figure 14 shows the ANFIS architecture (Jang, 1993) used in the IMPACT-ANALYZER component. A brief description of the layers is given:

Figure 13. TSK type fuzzy inference system

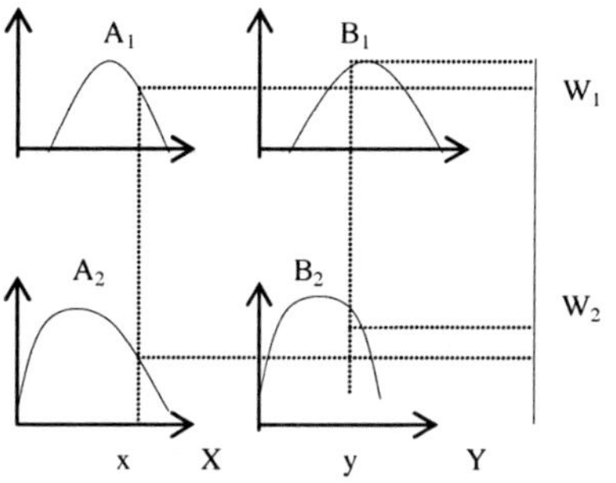

$$f_1 = p_1 x + q_1 y + r_1 \qquad f = \frac{w_1 f_1 + w_2 f_2}{w_1 + w_2} \tag{22}$$

$$f_2 = p_2 x + q_2 y + c \tag{23}$$

Layer 1: Every node *i* in this layer is a square node with a node function

$$O_i^1 = \mu_{ai}(x) \tag{24}$$

where *x* is the input node *i*, and A_i is the linguistic label associated with the node function. $O_i{}^1$ is the membership function of A_i and specifies the degree to which the given *x* satisfies the quantifier A_i. Usually $m_{Ai}(x)$ is bell-shaped with a maximum equal to 1 and a minimum equal to 0.

$$\mu_{ai}(x) = \frac{1}{1 + \left[\left(\frac{x - c_i}{a_i}\right)^2\right]^{b_i}} \tag{25}$$

Figure 14. Two input ANFIS architecture

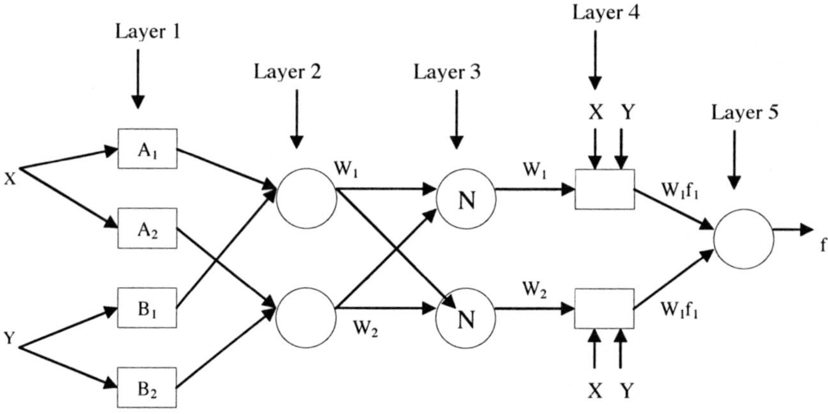

where $\{a_i, b_i, c_i\}$ is the parameter set. As the values of these parameters change, the bell-shaped functions vary accordingly, thus there are various forms of membership function on the linguistic label A_i.

Layer 2: Every node in this layer is a circle node II which multiples the incoming signals and sends the product out.

$$w_i = \mu_{ai}(x) \times \mu_{bi}(y), \quad i = 1,2 \tag{26}$$

Each node output represents the firing strength of a rule. (*T-norm* operators that perform generalized AND can be used at the node function in this layer.)

Layer 3: Each node in this layer is a circle node labelled N. The *i-th* node calculates the ratio of the *i-th* rule's firing strength to the sum of all rule's firing strengths as given below.

$$\overline{w} = \frac{w_i}{w_1 + w_2} \tag{27}$$

The output of this layer is referred to as the *normalized firing strength.*

Layer 4: Every node i in this layer is a square node with a node function

$$O_i^4 = \overline{w_i} f_i = \overline{w_i}(p_i x + q_i y + r_i) \tag{28}$$

where $\overline{w}_i$ is the output of the layer 3, and $\{p_i, q_i, r_i\}$ is the parameter set. The parameters in this layer will be referred to as the *consequent parameters.*

Layer 5: The single node in this layer is a circle node S that computes the overall output as the summation of all incoming signals, that is:

$$O_i^5 = \sum_i \overline{w_i} f_i = \frac{\sum_i w_i f_i}{\sum_i w_i} \tag{29}$$

Figure 15. Inputs/Output of the ANFIS in the IMPACT-ANALYZER component

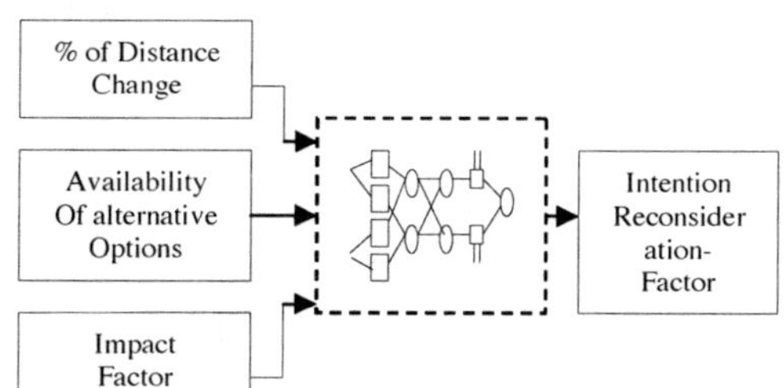

State values produced with the reinforcement learning based INTENTION-DRIVER are passed to the five-layered ANFIS in the IMPACT-ANALYZER component for making the final decision on the intention reconsideration of the *h*-BD[I] model. Figure 15 shows the three input parameters - Percentage of distance change (Ω), Available other options for achieving the agent desire (λ), and Criticality of the distance change (ψ) — and the output variable Intention Reconsideration Factor (IRF).

The new reward, or the distance computed, with the execution of plan *p* at state *s* reflecting the environmental changes, is given as $A_{s,p}^{I,t+1}$ or $d_{s,p}^{I,t+1}$ for the committed intention *I*. Similarly, it is possible to compute the new reward values for other alternative options identified in the *h*-BD[I] model. The percentage of distance change (Ω_s^I) due to the observation of all events occurring in the current environment is given in Equation 30. The total distance from a state *s* to goal state g for an intention *I* at a given time *t* is $D_{s,g}^{I,t}$.

$$\Omega_s^I = \left| \frac{\left(D_{s,g}^{I,t} - D_{s,g}^{I,t+1}\right)}{D_{s,g}^{I,t}} \right| \times 100 \qquad \textbf{(30)}$$

Next, the *"Impact-Factor"* (ψ) is defined to identify the influence of the environmental change towards achieving the goal of the agent.

$$\Psi^I = \begin{cases} \Psi_+^I & if \ \left(D_{s,g}^{I,t+1} - D_{s,g}^{I,t}\right) > 0 \\ \Psi_-^I & if \ \left(D_{s,g}^{I,t+1} - D_{s,g}^{I,t}\right) < 0 \end{cases} \qquad \textbf{(31)}$$

where Ψ_+^I and Ψ_-^I indicate the positive and negative impact of the environmental change at $t+1$ for an intention *I*. The range of values from 1 to 5 has been defined to indicate the importance of the impact factor.

If β_x is the maximum reward expected for x number of steps in achieving the agent's intention, the number of steps is an indication of how many plans an agent has to execute before reaching the final goal state g. The availability of other options ($\lambda_s^{I_0}$) in achieving the agent's desire can be computed as:

$$\lambda_s^I = \left[\frac{\left(D_s^{Io} - D_s^I \right)}{\beta_x} \right] \times 100 \tag{32}$$

where D_s^{Io} and D_s^I are the total distance from state s to the goal state for an alternative option I_o and for the committed intention I. A test case scenario is described in the next section.

Test Case Scenario of a Berthing Application

Vessel berthing data at the main container terminal (JCT) in Port Colombo has been used in our experiments which are based on the new *h*-BD[I] architecture proposed in the paper. Event "*ETA-received()*" from the EVENT-COMPOSER is received at the INTELLIGENT-DELIBERATOR component to produce suitable berths for the incoming vessel. A set of beliefs used for training the neural network in the INTELLIGENT-DELIBERATOR is shown in Table 1 and Table 2.

The "day" field in Table 1 indicates the vessel's arrival day. Since the terminal plans for three days scheduling, the possible values for "day" field is either "1" or "2" or "3." For example, the *etc-B1* in Table 1 shows that the vessel at berth Jct1 finishes its operations at 11:00 a.m. and the vessel in berth Jct4 completes its operations at 3:30 p.m. The terminal can berth the next vessel in the queue if and only if the berth satisfies the conditions mentioned in the "Distance Required for Vessel Berthing and Sailing" section above, or after the existing vessel has sailed out from the berth. The vessels scheduled to arrive at the outer-harbor are shown in Table 2. For simplicity, we have shown a few of the randomly selected test data sets used in our experiments in Table 2.

Table 1. Information available in the vessel declaration (beliefs)

ETA	VBD	VSD	VCR	NOB	DAY	ETC-B1	ETC-B2	ETC-B3	ETC-B4
10;00	11.00	12.00	12.00	349	01	11:00	09:00	04:00	15:30

GBP-B1	GBP-B2	GBP-B2	GBP-B4	BDR-B1	BDR-B2	BDR-B3	BDR-B4	COB-B1	COB-B2
35	40	48	36	11.3	12.3	14.00	14.00	12.00	13.00

COB-B3	COB-B4	NOV-B1	NOV-B2	NOV-B3	NOV-B4	GAP-B1	GAP-B2	GAP-B3	GAP-B4
16.00	18.00	1	1	1	2	1	1	0	1

Table 2. The expected time of arrival of few vessels

Vessel Name	ETA	VBD	VSD	VCR	NOB	CTY
SN1	09:45	13.90	14.00	16.00	784	'N'
MS1	07:00	13.50	13.50	13.00	123	'N'
TG1	10:00	11.00	11.30	13.00	345	'N'
MS2	11:00	11.00	11.20	14.00	456	'N'
HN1	02:00	11.00	11.30	12.00	234	'N'
EG1	05.00	11.20	11.30	12.00	400	'N'
EG2	10.00	14.00	14.00	18.00	356	'N'

Table 3. Values produced indicating the probable berths for incoming vessels

Vessels	Berths			
	JCT 1	JCt2	JCT 3	JCT 4
SN1	0.002345	0.101611	0.441767	0.308158
MS1	0.001245	0.086262	0.280557	0.316147
TG1	0.072562	0.286501	0.002312	0.190276
MS2	0.001232	0.051727	0.070530	0.413108
HN1	0.269970	0.202104	0.172020	0.002311
EG1	0.098996	0.392972	0.426556	0.003212
EG2	0.002312	0.056544	0.137296	0.466352

Three months data of the beliefs given in Table 1 and Table 2 have been used for the training of the neural network based Intelligent Deliberator. Based on the data we randomly selected, the results obtained from the trained Intelligent-Deliberator for those vessels are given in Table 3.

A value between zero and one has been produced by the Intelligent-Deliberator to indicate the possible berths for incoming vessels. The berths with larger values always guarantee a better and faster service than the berths with lower values. For example, berth JCT3 has recorded the highest value compared with other berths for the incoming vessel "SN1," which indicates that the best berth to serve the vessel "SN1" is the berth JCT3. It is noted that vessel "SN1" cannot be berthed at JCT1 as the length of the cranes in the berth is not enough to reach all the boxes in the vessel. Because of the above limitation in JCT1, the INTELLIGENT-DELIBERATOR has assigned a very low value for the berth JCT1. The difficulties in filtering the desirable options have been minimized by the introduction of the intelligent tools in the agent deliberation process.

The graph plotted in Figure 16 indicates the possible berthing options selected by the INTELLIGENT-DELIBERATOR. The berth with the highest value at a given time is the most suitable for the vessel. Hence, it is considered as the intention of the agent. The size of the option-control-factor (θ) described in the algorithm in Figure 10 controls the selection of the number of alternative berthing options in our model. Assume that the expected time of completion of the vessels currently at berths are those given in the Table 4 and consider the effect of environmental changes on the agent's present commitments. For example, the agent has committed to assign the vessel "SN1" to berth JCT3: *I= [Assign—berth (jct3)],* as it has secured the highest value among all the berths. This is the intention of the agent. The possible alternative option is to assign the vessel "SN1" to berth JCT4: I^o_1 = *[Assign—berth (jct4)* because it has recorded the second largest value in Table 3. The other two berth options have been dropped in the filtering process with

Figure 16. Possible options (berths) generated from the intelligent-deliberator for different time periods

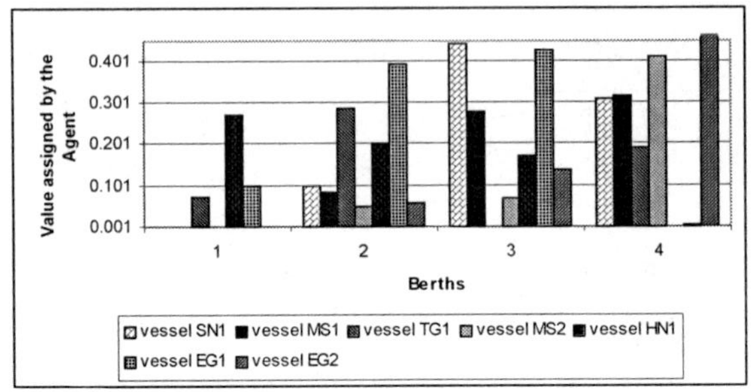

Table 4. The expected time of completions of the vessel at the berths

	Berths in the Terminal			
	JCT1	JCT2	JCT3	JCT3
etc	07:20	08:15	10:15	12:34

Table 5. Estimated state values for the agent intention and other option

	Rewards	
Plans	*I*	*I^o*
P1 : Berth-drafts ( )	0.03	0.03
P2 : Carne-outreach-requirements ( )	0.40	0.40
P3 : Waiting-time-vessels ( )	0.006	0.0012
P4 : Average-crane-productivity ( )	0.826	0.609
P5 : Get-expected-operations-time ( )	0.296	0.24
Value - state to goal D_s	1.558	1.280

the *Option control factor* (θ). The initial reward values computed with the execution of plans for I and $I^0{}_I$ are shown in Table 5.

The required data set or the beliefs in the reinforcement learning for the execution of the above plans are: nob^v, vbd^v, vsd^v vcr^v, bdr_b, $len^i{}_{bj}$, $gcp^v{}_{i,j}$ eta^v, $etc^v{}_b$ $odl_b{}^v$ and $eot^v{}_b$. In a continuously changing environment, an agent cannot be over-committed to its original option at all times. Therefore, the agent should reconsider its committed intentions to find the optimal solutions. Table 6 indicates a few events recorded in the event queue at a given time.

We consider three different cases to explain the improved intelligent behavior of our *h*-BD[I] model in handling this type of scenario. *Case I: (Local view with the immediate event).* The agent considers only the immediate event in the intention reconsideration process. *Case II: (Local view with many events).* In this case, the agent considers the effects of all the relevant events in the intention reconsideration process, that is, the effects of the events E1, E6 and E8 are taken into consideration in the intention reconsideration process. *Case III (Global view):* The effects of all the events and the availability of the other alternative options are considered in the intention reconsideration process. Rewards and the new state values, computed using the *n-step* back method in temporal difference learning are given in Table 7.

Table 6. Events in the event queue at a given time

Time	Event No	Event-Name	Effect of the event on the intention and other option (yes/no)
T1	E1	Vessel-delay(SN1, eta:11:00)	Yes
T2	E2	Change-in-etc(jct2, etc:09:20)	No
T3	E3	Crane-breakdown(jct1: etc:13:00)	No
T4	E4	Crane-productivity(jct1,acp:30mph)	No
T5	E5	Crane-productivity(jct2,acp:36mph)	No
T6	E6	Crane-productivity(jct3, acp:15pmh)	Yes
T7	E7	Vessel-arrival(MS2, eta::08:00)	No
T8	E8	Berth-draft-change(jct3, bdr=13m)	Yes

Table 7(a). New state values and rewards due to event E1

Case I : Only E1 is considered			
	Intention I:" assign-berth(Jct3)"		
Sates	Estimated Value	New Value	Reward
S1	1.5580	1.6520	0.03
S2	1.5280	1.6220	0.40
S3	1.1280	1.2220	0.10
S4	1.1220	1.1220	0.826
S5	0.2960	0.2960	0.2960

Table 7(b). New state values and rewards due to events E1, E6, E8

Case II : Events E1,E6 and E8 are considered			
	Intention I:" assign-berth(Jct3)"		
Sates	Estimated Value	New Value	Reward
S1	1.5580	0.9831	0.0001
S2	1.5280	0.9830	0.40
S3	1.1280	0.5830	0.10
S4	1.1220	0.4830	0.187
S5	0.2960	0.2960	0.2960

Table 7(c). New state values and rewards computed for the intention I *and other alternative option* I^0 *due to events E1, E6 and E8*

Case III: considered events E1,E6 and E8 for Intention I and other option I^0						
	Intention I: "assign-berth(Jct3)"			Other option I^0: "assign-berth(Jct4)"		
States	Estimated values	New value	Reward	Estimated value	New value	Reward
S1	1.5580	0.9831	0.0001	1.2802	1.2843	0.030
S2	1.5280	0.9830	0.40	1.2502	1.2543	0.40
S3	1.1280	0.5830	0.10	0.8502	0.8543	0.0053
S4	1.1220	0.4830	0.187	0.8490	0.8490	0.609
S5	0.2960	0.2960	0.2960	0.2400	0.2400	0.240

In case *I*, the agent computes the new state values due to the immediate event E1 (shown in Table 7(a)). That is, the agent only considers the immediate event: *E1-"vessel-delay (SN1,eta:Mon:11:00)"* in the reward calculation process. In this case, the new value in s1 is greater than the previous value estimated, which implies that the environmental change has a positive impact on achieving the committed intention at this point in time. Therefore the agent proceeds with the next available plan in the intention structure. The agent is not allowed to look forward to changes that could occur due to the other events in the event queue until that state is reached.

In case *II*, the agent's ability to observe all the relevant events before the execution of a plan is demonstrated in Table 7(b). For example, the environmental changes due to events E1, E6 and E8 are considered before the execution of the next plan. It is noted that the new value computed for state s1 is now lower than estimated, which is an indication that the earlier commitment is not the optimal option in the present environment. In this case, the agent has a completely different data set in the intention reconsideration process compared to the earlier situation. But still the agent does not have any idea of the other alternative options if the current intention is no longer valid.

In case *III*, the limitation of not having any knowledge of alternative options in the intention reconsideration process has been removed in our *h*-BD[I] agent model. That is, the effects of the environment change on *I* and I^0 are computed here. The new state values computed for the committed intention and for the alternative option are shown in Table 7(c). In reality, it is important to know the availability of alternative options before we decide whether we are going to continue or drop the current intention. Sometimes, we find that there is a better option than the earlier one in the present environment, and then it is obvious to go ahead with that option. This is the kind of information we have introduced to improve the adaptive and dynamic behavior of our proposed model.

The next step is to use the above results in our ANFIS-based intention reconsideration process to make the final decision about whether to pursue the current intention or not. The decision surfaces produced from the ANFIS based IMPACT-ANALYZER component are shown in Figure 17.

The intention reconsideration decision from the ANFIS-based Impact-Analyzer is shown in Table 8. The *IRF* for the case *I* in Table 8 is recorded as 12.3%, which implies that there is no reason to reconsider the present intention and therefore the agent can proceed with the execution of the next plan in the plan library. The limited knowledge of the future effects of the events on the environment leads the agent to carry out other plans.

In case *II*, the new state values computed have different values compared to the earlier case because the agent looked forward and observed the effect of all the events in the event queue. The *IRF* for case *II* in Table 8 is shown as 67.1%. That is, the ANFIS-based Impact-Analyzer has recommended that it reconsider the current intention, as it has found that the earlier commitment to assign the vessel to JCT3 is not the optimal option at present. But still, on this occasion, the agent does not have any idea of the availability of any alternative berths for the calling vessel. If the agent knows that there are other alternative options available in the present environment, then its confidence in the decisions it makes can be further strengthened. In case *III*, *IRF* has recorded the highest value (70.2%) which says the possibility of reconsidering the current intention is very high. The above vessel berthing example demonstrates the improved adaptive behavior of the proposed *h*-BD[I] agent in a complex, dynamic real-time environment.

Figure 17(a). Decision surface for percentage of distance change and impact-factor

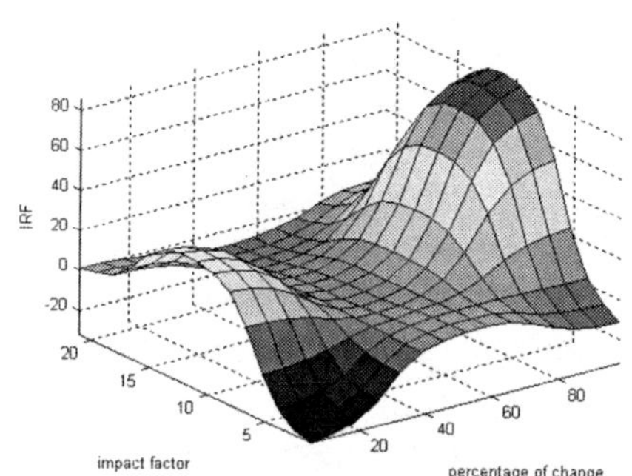

Figure 17(b). Decision surface for percentage of distance change and available of other options

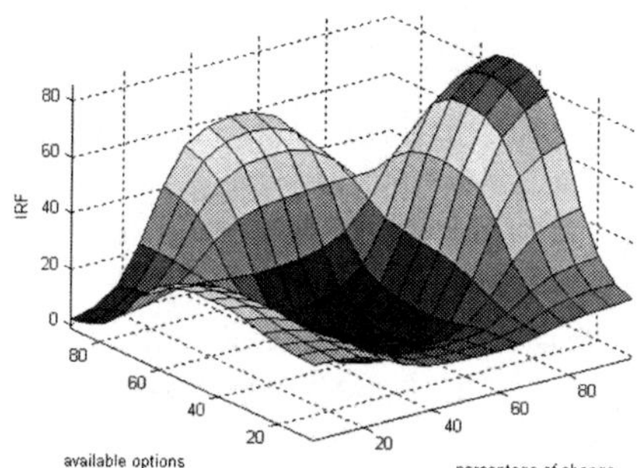

Figure 17(c). Decision surface for available of other options and impact-factor

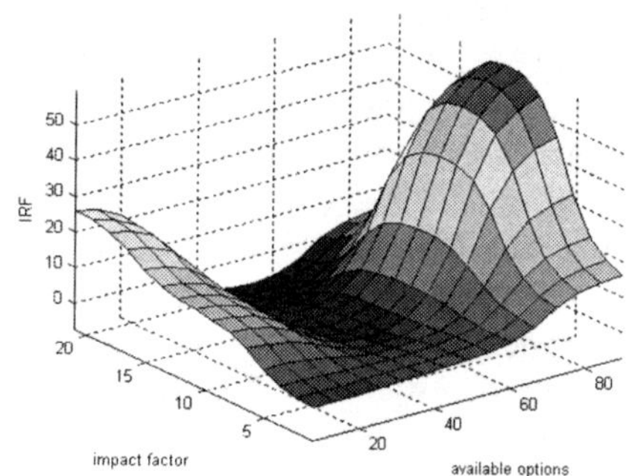

Table 8. Intention reconsideration decision produced from the ANFIS based IMPACT-ANALYZER component

Cases :	Case I	Case II	Case III
Intention/s considered	Only I	Only I	I and I^o
Event/s observed	Only E1	E1,E6 and E8	E1,E6 and E8
Percentage of distance change : Ω_s^I	6.0%	36.89%	36.89%
Available other options : $\lambda_s^{I_o}$	Not applicable	Not applicable	6.024%
Criticality or the impact factor of the distance change (Ψ)	Very low (1-2)	Very high (4-5)	Very high (4-5)
ANFIS output- Intention-reconsideration- factor (IRF)	12.3%	67.1%	70.2%

Conclusion

In this chapter we presented a new hybrid model for BDI agents known as *h*-BD[I] that enables the use of computational intelligence and interactive learning methods to handle multiple events and intentions in the intention reconsideration process. The Neural network-based INTELLIGENT-DELIBERATOR produces many options for an agent to select in achieving the final goal. This is very important, as the agent is updated with the available alternative options if the selected intention is no longer valid in the present environment. The selection of a number of alternative options can also be controlled with the use of an option-control-factor (ϑ). Most importantly, in our model, the agent never forgets the alternative options selected at the beginning of the deliberation. We apply the same environmental changes to these options at every state to compute the new state values. Knowledge of the possible options at every state helps the agent to compare and switch between options quickly if the current intention is no longer valid.

Decision-making is improved as the process computes the effects of the future state changes on the current state. The distance change from the estimated state is then calculated at the current state using ANFIS to decide the action. The next plan is not executed unless a positive answer is produced from the ANFIS-based IMPACT-ANALYZER. As in human reasoning, the agent considers the number of positive or negative effects in the committed intention and also looks to see whether there are any better options available to achieve the final goal. This information may be fuzzy or not clearly defined. Therefore, ANFIS uses this knowledge in making the final decision about whether to drop the current intention or to continue. Finally, the dynamic behavior demonstrated in the hybrid model always assures that the optimal berth is found for incoming vessels. The optimal berth always assures the earliest completion time for the calling vessel. Hence, the productivity of the terminal is enhanced with the introduction of the hybrid intelligent agent system.

References

Anderson, C. W. (1988). *Strategy learning with multilayer connectionist representation.* GTE Labs TR 87-509.3. Waltham, MA: GTE Labs.

Barnard, E. (1993). Temporal-difference methods and Markov models. *IEEE Transactions on Systems, Man and Cybernetics, 23*, 357-365.

Bratman, M. E. (1987). *Intentions, plans and practical reason.* Cambridge, MA: Harvard University.

Bratman, M. E, Israel, D., & Pollack, M. E. (1988). Plans and resources bounded practical reasoning. *Computational Intelligence, 4*, 349-355.

Bratman, M. E, Israel, D., & Pollack, M. E. (1998). Plans and resource-bounded practical reasoning. *Philosophy and AI* (pp. 1-22). Cambridge, MA: MIT.

Brown, G. G., Lawphongpanich, S., &Thurman, K. P. (1994). Optimizing ship berthing. *Naval Research Logistics*, *41*, 1-15.

Chia, J. T., Lau, H. C., & Lim, A. (1999). Ant colony optimization for ship berthing problem. In P. S. Thiagarajan & R. H. C. Yap (Eds.), *Proceedings of the Fifth Asian Computing Science Conference on Advances in Computing Science (ASIAN99), LNCS 1742* (pp. 359-370). London: Springer-Verlag.

Crites, R. H., & Barto, A. C. (1996). Improving elevator performance using reinforcement learning. In D. Touretzky, M. Mozer, & M. Haselmo (Eds.), *Advances in neural information processing systems 8* (pp.1017-1023). Cambridge, MA: MIT.

Georgeff, M., Pell, B., Pollack, M. E., & Wooldridge, M. (1998). *The belief-desire-intention model of agency*. London: Springer.

Georgeff, M. P., & Ingrand, F. F. (1989). Decision making in an embedded reasoning system. In N.S. Sridharan (Eds.), *Proceedings of the Eleventh International Joint Conference on Artificial Intelligence* (pp. 972-978). Detroit, MI: Morgan Kaufmann.

Jang, J. S. R. (1993). ANFIS: Adaptive network based fuzzy inference systems. *IEEE Transactions on Systems, Man and Cybernetics*, *23*, 665-685.

Kim, K. H., & Moon, K. C. (2003). Berth scheduling by simulated annealing. *Transportation Research Part B*, *37*, 541-560.

Li, C. L., Cai, X., & Lee, C. Y. (1998). Scheduling with multiple-job-on-one-processor pattern, *IIE Transactions*, *30*, 45-60.

Lim, A. (1998). On the ship berthing problem. *Operational Research Letters*, *22*(2-3), 105-110.

Ljungberg, M., & Lucas, A. (1992). The OASIS air traffic management system. In K. Y. Wohn & Y. T. Byun (Eds.), *Proceeding of the Second Rim International Conference on Artificial Intelligence, PRICAI,* Seoul, Korea (pp. 15-18). Korea: Centre for Artificial Intelligence Research.

Lokuge, D. P. S., & Alahakoon, L. D. (2004a). Homogeneous neuro-BDI agent architecture for berth scheduling in container terminals. *Journal of Marine Design and Operations Part B*, *6*, 17-27.

Lokuge, D. P. S., & Alahakoon, L. D. (2004b). Hybrid BDI Agents with improved learning capabilities for adaptive planning in a container terminal application. In N. Zhong, J. Bradshaw, S. K. Pal, D. Talia, J. Liu, & N. Cercone (Eds.), *Proceedings of IEEE/WIC/ACM International Conference on Intelligent Agent Technology (IAT)* (pp. 120-126). CA: IEEE Computer Society.

Lokuge, D. P. S., & Alahakoon, L. D. (2004c). A motivation based behaviour in hybrid intelligent agents for intention reconsideration process in vessel berthing application. In M. Ishikawa et al. (Eds.), *Proceedings of the Fourth International Conference on Hybrid Intelligent Systems (HIS-2004)* (pp. 124 -129). CA: IEEE Computer Society.

Muller, J. P. (1996). *The design of intelligent agents: A layered approach*. Berlin: Springer-Verlag.

Rao, A. S., & Georgeff, M. P. (1992). An abstract architecture for rational agents. In C. Rich, W. Swartout, & B. Nebel (Eds.), *Proceedings of the Knowledge Representation and Reasoning Conference (KR&R-92)* (pp. 439-449). Berlin: Springer-Verlag.

Russell, S., & Wefald, E. (1992). Principle of meta-reasoning. *Artificial Intelligence, 49*(1-3), 361-395.

Ryan, N. K. (1998). The future of maritime facilities design and operations. In D. J. Medeiros, E. F. Watson, J. S. Carson, & M. S. Manivannan (Eds.), *Winter Proceedings of the Simulation Conference* (pp. 1223-1227). CA: IEEE Computer Society.

Schut, M. C., & Wooldridge, M. (2000). Intention reconsideration in complex environments. In M. Gini & J. Rosenschein (Eds.), *Proceedings of the Fourth International Conference on Autonomous Agents (Agents 2000),* Barcelona, Spain (pp. 209-216). Spain: ACM.

Schut, M. C., & Wooldridge, M. (2001). Principles of intention reconsideration. In J. P. Mueller, E. Andre, S. Sen, & C. Frasson (Eds.), *Proceedings of the Fifth International Conference on Autonomous Agents, AGENTS'01,* Montreal, Canada (pp. 340-347). ACM.

Sutton, R. S., & Barto, A. G. (1988). *Reinforcement learning: An introduction.* London: MIT.

Tesauro, G. (1995). Temporal difference learning and TD-Gammon. *Communications of the ACM, 38*(3), 58-68.

Wooldridge, M. (2000). *Reasoning about rational agents.* London: MIT.

Wooldridge, M. (2002). *An introduction to multi-agent systems.* New York: John Wiley.

Chapter X

Optimization Using Horizon-Scan Technique: A Practical Case of Solving an Industrial Problem

Ly Fie Sugianto, Monash University, Australia

Pramesh Chand, Monash University, Australia

Abstract

This chapter introduces a new Computational Intelligence algorithm called Horizon Scan. Horizon Scan is a heuristic based technique designed to search for optimal solution in non-linear space. It is a variant of the Hill-Climbing technique and works in contrary to the temperature-cooling scheme used in Simulated-Annealing. Initial experiments on the application of Horizon Scan to standard test cases of linear and non-linear problems have indicated promising results (Chand & Sugianto, 2003a; Chand & Sugianto, 2003b; Chand & Sugianto, 2004). In this chapter, the technique is described in detail and its application in finding the optimal solution for the Scheduling-Pricing-Dispatch problem in the Australian deregulated electricity market context is demonstrated. It is hoped that the proposed approach will enrich the existing literature on Computational Intelligence, in particular to solve optimization problems, such as those that exist in the deregulated electricity industry around the globe.

Introduction

The objective of this chapter is to introduce a heuristic Computational Intelligence (CI) algorithm called Horizon Scan (HS). Horizon Scan is a new heuristic-based global search technique for optimizing non-linear problems. In demonstrating the application of this algorithm, the chapter depicts an industrial problem in today's competitive electricity market environment that exhibits an auction process.

The chapter begins with a discussion on the optimization problem, its characteristics, the classification of linear and non-linear problems, as well as conventional techniques to deal with each class of problem. It also introduces the notion of optimal value for several possible solutions. Next, it describes the concept, the algorithm and the characteristics of the Horizon Scan technique, including the intelligence in its search mechanism, alternative scanning methods and the search termination criteria. In this chapter, the proposed technique has been applied to optimize the energy market in the current Australian National Electricity Market (NEM) setting. The chapter also presents several case examples depicting simplified market models with non-linear constraints.

Optimization Problem

Optimization is often understood as a procedure to obtain the optimal (best) solution to a problem. An optimization problem is characterized by the fact that there exists more than one possible solution and that the solution cannot be identified simply by inspection. A small subset of problem modelling that exhibits a linear relationship between the objective function and the constraints can be solved with Linear Programming. With the available computing power today, such a numerical procedure of optimization can yield an optimal solution in a very short time. However, solutions obtained in such cases are accurate and satisfactory only in very limited circumstances. This is because most practical problems do not fall into the linear category. A substantial proportion of phenomena and problems in real life fall into the non-linear category.

Non-Linear Programming deals with the optimization of non-linear functions subjected to linear and/or non-linear constraints. When more constraints are modelled into the problem, it becomes harder for feasible solutions to be identified. Classical non-linear optimization methods have centered on gradient functions. These involve the calculation of first-order derivatives and in some cases the second-order derivatives of the objective functions. The Newton and its variant methods use Taylor's expansion to approximate the derivates. These techniques gained popularity because of their ability to approximate solutions using the first and second derivates. However, the convergence of the solution is not always guaranteed (Taha, 1997).

For a range of non-linear optimization problems (Al-Turki, 2001; Anderson, 1996; Baykasolmagelu, 2001; Bertsekas 1999; Glover & Laguna, 1993; Lewis, 2000; Pham & Karaboga, 2000; Pirlot, 1996; Rutenbar, 1989; Youssef, 2001), there exists a class of techniques known as heuristic-based techniques, such as Hill Climbing, Simulated

Figure 1. The notion of optimal value

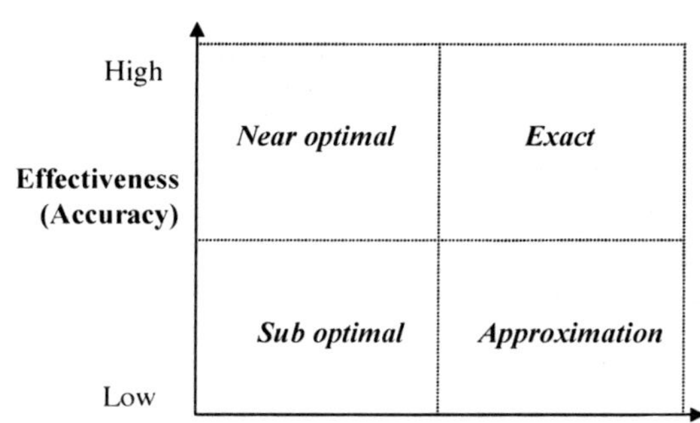

Annealing and Tabu Search. Heuristic-based techniques may not provide optimal solutions, as the search ends upon some conditions being satisfied. Such non-optimal solutions are undesirable. For example, the dispatch-scheduling problem, which will be explained in the next section, requires a highly optimized solution for each of its optimisation runs. This is primarily due to the large number of transactions (funds) involved. Sub-optimal solutions would therefore result in unfair and unwarranted losses and gains by market players.

An example for understanding an optimal solution in a non-linear problem is illustrated in Figure 1. The optimal solution is characterized using two extended criteria, namely the solution's efficiency in processing time and its effectiveness in satisfying a pre-set threshold value. Such a notion is useful, for example, when the processing time to achieve an optimal solution (in the *exact* sense) becomes too costly — hence, a compromise needs to be drawn by setting a satisfactory threshold value to accept feasible solutions. A solution is said to be *near optimal* if it is of high quality and sufficient for practical application. Below the threshold value, there exist only approximate solutions and sub-optimal solutions.

Using this notion, it is fair to conclude that heuristic techniques generally do not produce *exact* solutions. In fact, heuristic techniques may at times fail to produce exact solutions, although this may be acceptable if in a significant number of times the technique produces quality results, especially when the problem is complex in nature and that there is no easy way to find a solution.

Adopting the above notion, the subsequent sections will demonstrate the performance of Horizon Scan in obtaining *near optimal* solutions for complex problems. Although it is not ideal to merely achieve near optimal solutions, these feasible solutions are generally accepted and CI techniques can therefore be beneficial in industrial and business settings.

Horizon Scan

Concept, Algorithm, and its Characteristics

Premature convergence in optimisation is an undesired characteristic. In most heuristic techniques, schemes are employed at the early stages of the algorithm to avoid premature convergence, in order to prevent the algorithm being caught in a local optimum. However, the assumptions used to avoid premature convergence disregard the possibility that the global optima could be found in the early stages of the search. Premature convergence in optimisation is often perceived as an impediment, such as the gravitational force is to a spacecraft. But, if the impeding force could be used beneficially, then there is a way for premature convergence to be positively applied in searching for global optima. This insight provides the foundation for the development of the Horizon Scan technique.

Unlike most other heuristic techniques, HS does not try to avoid local optima or prevent premature convergence. It seeks to encourage any convergence whether it is to a global optimum or a local one. In HS, the premature convergence to an optimum point is used to direct its search and find solutions that are more optimal if such solution exists. The conceptual design of HS borrows its idea from the exploration of uncharted terrain. Parallels can be drawn between the process of optimisation and the explorations of uncharted land and mountainous terrain.

Consider an unexplored mountainous terrain that is accessible only by land. An explorer would not know the location of the highest peak if the mountain range was extensive. A quick visual inspection would reveal the location of the highest peak from the explorer's current point of view. Peaks behind the visible ones may be higher but obscured from view due to the elevation of the explorer's point of view. The explorer would decide on a strategy to inspect the terrain further either by climbing the closest peak or the highest visible peak. This would depend on which move is more cost effective for the explorer. Having chosen a peak, the explorer would climb to the summit so that some of the previously obscured parts of the terrain would become visible. A 360° look-about of the horizon from the summit would reveal higher peaks. Depending on the strategy, the explorer would then move to the higher peaks to explore them further. The explorer does not have to advance all the way to the summit of the peak to identify higher and previously obscured peaks. Obscured peaks could be identified from any higher point on a view deck. However, not all obscured peaks may be visible from there. The explorer would stop ascending the current peak at this new view deck. Having identified peaks higher than the current one, the explorer would advance towards the newly identified peaks. This process would allow charting of an uncharted mountain terrain and eventually, identification of the highest peak.

Similar to the exploration process, the concept of optimisation in Horizon Scan proceeds to the closest optimum point by adopting the Hill Climbing technique and allowing premature convergence to take place. The reached optimum is referred to as the *view-deck*. Then, the optimisation process continues by scanning the horizon. This is analogous to that of the explorer's 360° look-about. Scanning the horizon reveals *scan-points* that may be higher in utility than the current view deck. A new scan-point with a higher utility value indicates the current view deck is a local optimum. Therefore, it provides a new point to restart the hill climb, thereby breaking out of the local optimum. Applying Hill Climbing to the new scan-point allows the optimisation to proceed to a new view deck. The process of scanning and hill climbing continues until no more scan-points can be found.

In short, Horizon Scan is an iterative two-stage optimisation process: using Hill Climbing to reach local optimum and employing Goal Programming (GP) to advance the search beyond the current optimum. Hill Climbing is a fast and simple technique but does not necessarily produce global optimum. Goal Programming is a subset technique in optimisation with the objective to find a feasible solution, again, not necessarily a global one. In HS, the algorithm starts by using the fast Hill Climbing to attain some form of optimality. The solution may be sub-optima or even the global optimum (although it would not be known at this stage whether or not the solution is the global optimum). The test of whether or not the existing solution is the global optimum (and that no other solution with better utility is found) is performed using GP. The objective of the GP step is to break out of the local optimum to find a solution with a utility that is incrementally better than the utility of the current solution. When such solution is found, the GP objective is achieved — the current optimum is deemed to be sub-optimal. The new solution provides a stepping stone to the next optima and a means for breaking out of the local optimum. The iterative step of Hill Climbing will then move the new solution point (scan-point) to a new optimum (view-deck). The new optimum is tested by the iterative GP step for global optimality. If further solutions with better utility are found, the process iterates.

The two-step algorithm in HS implies the employment of two kinds of operators. The Hill Climbing operator is used in the first stage to advance the new scan-point to its view-deck. The scan operator is used in Goal Programming to scan horizons and identify regions that are more optimal than the current view-deck. In doing so the operators create an implicit Tabu list or a *no-go* region where no better results can be found.

The complete formulation of the algorithm is as follows:

- **Generate an Initial Solution:** the initial values assigned to the solution have to be within the dimension bounds, either at the lower bound, upper bound, randomly selected or constraint based.
- **Ensure Solution Feasibility:** since the search always proceeds towards solution with higher utility, the initial solution needs to be feasible. An infeasible initial solution would allow solutions with higher utility to be accepted, but the new solutions would not be feasible either. An alternative approach would be to allow solutions with less utility to be accepted until feasibility is achieved.
- **Initial Hill Climb:** once a feasible solution is found, the Hill Climbing technique is applied to reach the initial view deck (local or global optimum).
- **Determine the Horizon:** the horizon is determined based on the combination of two dimensions. Iteratively all dimensions are paired together and the scan proceeds through each of the horizons.

- **Scan the Horizon (iterative-step):** this is the GP strategy used to find better solutions. Each horizon is scanned until there are no further better solutions (lookouts) from a particular horizon.

In summary, the characteristics of Horizon Scan can be described as:

- **Heuristic based:** HS uses the concept of terrain exploration to guide the search.
- **Non-linear solution space:** HS allows for non-linear objective and constraint functions as well as linear functions. While linear solution spaces can be handled, a linear program would outperform this algorithm.
- **Dimension boundaries:** HS requires an upper and a lower bound on every dimension. Practical scheduling problems are of this nature and would present no hurdles. Mathematical function optimisation may not be suitable if there are no upper and lower bounds.
- **Allows premature convergence:** unlike most techniques, HS does not avoid local optimum. Once a local optimum is found, regions below it are considered sub-optimal and therefore forbidden to traverse.
- **Requires feasible starting position:** the algorithm requires each view deck or lookout point to be a feasible point. This implies the initial position has to be a feasible point as well. In the case of a randomly generated solution where the initial point is not feasible, an adjustment is made to reach a feasible solution despite a loss in the utility value.
- **Discrete/Continuous solution space:** both integer and real number representations can be modelled using this technique.
- **Consistent solution quality:** since the technique breaks out of local optimum, it would be able to do so during each of its independent solutions of the same problem. Thus, near-optimal solutions as results should be of similar quality.

Scanning Methods

Standing at the top of a hill (*view-deck*) and taking a 360° turn enables us to see higher hills. One does not have to be at a summit to be able to do this, but the closer one is to the summit, the better the view of other peaks would be. Such is the analogy employed in the scanning process. Comparison studies of various scanning methods have been reported in Chand and Sugianto (2004). There are several scanning methods that can be utilized in HS, as described in Chand and Sugianto (2003a) and Chand and Sugianto (2004). In the concentric rings scanning method (see Figure 2a), concentric rings of radius r_i form the *scan disks*. Lines originating from the view-deck and at angles that are multiples of a predetermined value q intersects with the radius of the disks giving the next scan point. There are two variations of the concentric rings method:

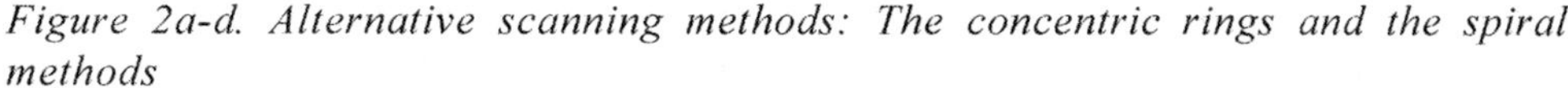

Figure 2a-d. Alternative scanning methods: The concentric rings and the spiral methods

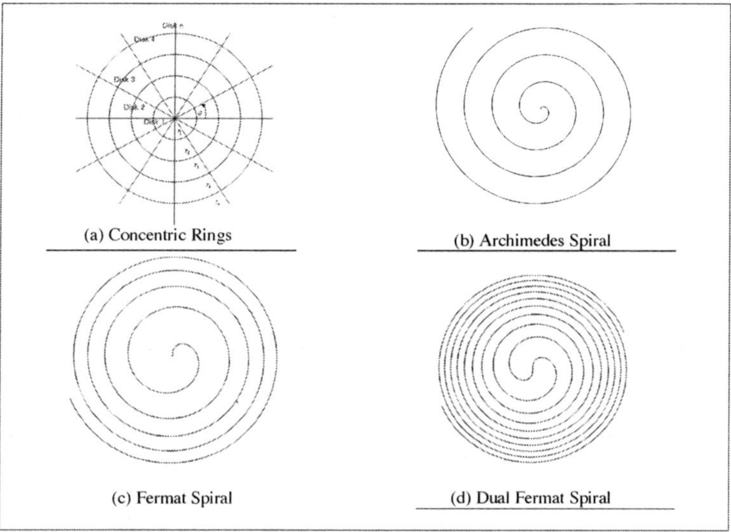

- Scan points at the intersection of the incremental angle and the incremental circular path, namely at any radius of any circular path, r_i.
- Scan points at random angles greater than the previous angle and less than or equal to the next incremental angle.

In the spiral scanning method, the path is not disjoint as in the concentric ring method. An explicit Tabu list can be created to forbid scanning of regions that have been visited previously in order to save some processing time. As well as the regions, the angles of the horizon can also be made forbidden once a particular direction has been visited. Each scan ends with the evaluation of a new solution point.

The scanning process is terminated when either one of these four conditions is satisfied:

1. a solution with a higher utility is found.
2. a solution with a utility value that is higher than the algebraic product of the current utility value and a utility increment factor is found. This factor can be dynamically scaled down if a large incrementing factor does not result in a higher utility value.
3. a group of *k* solutions are found and the best amongst them is chosen. The value of *k* could be an arbitrary value, or one of the numbers of steps taken in one angle view of the horizon, or the number of angles evaluated in the 360° scans.
4. the utility incrementing factor and group solution is applied as a combination.

Once the scanning process is completed and a higher utility value is obtained, the algorithm proceeds to a new solution point and applies Hill Climbing to find a new view-deck. The process of scanning continues in the same horizon plane. When the scan does not find any higher view-decks in the horizon plane, it proceeds to the next horizon and continues with the scanning process. The iteration is terminated when there are no more horizons to scan.

Comparison of results produced by Horizon Scan on benchmark cases have been documented in Chand and Sugianto (2003b). Earlier experiments on test cases indicated that Horizon Scan produced more quality solutions compared to other non-linear optimisation techniques.

Scheduling-Pricing-Dispatch Problem

Optimizing the Energy Market

The electricity industry around the globe has undergone a period of restructuring over the last couple of decades. The motivation was to replace the traditional vertically integrated structure with a competitive market environment. This initiative was based on the fact that the consumption of electricity has shown a consistent increase and that the industry must ensure efficient use of resources and cheaper electricity prices for consumers.

In Australia, the electricity industry has progressively moved towards deregulation and privatization since 1991. Competition was introduced in the generation and retail supply sector while the transmission and distribution sectors remained regulated as monopolies. There are two ways of trading electricity in this market structure: through bilateral contract or agreement, or through the competitive market. This chapter only focuses on the latter.

The principles of competitive market economics are applied to trade electricity like other market commodity such as stocks, shares, oil, and gold. However, electricity cannot be stored. The electricity market is constrained by the technical requirements of simultaneous consumption and supply of electricity. Therefore, the market characteristics are not the same as purely commodity-based market products.

In the competitive market structure, electricity is traded through the *spot market* (see Figure 3). The spot market involves the trading of electricity via *the electricity pool* where the spot price for the electricity is calculated for each half-hour period during the day. An independent system operator employs a centrally coordinated dispatch process to manage the operation of the electricity pool. The generators competing in the electricity market provide dispatch offers, detailing the price and supply quantity, while market customers submit dispatch bids, detailing the price and demand they wish to be scheduled, to the central dispatch coordinator. The central coordinator then dispatches the scheduled generation and demand with the objective of minimizing the cost of

Figure 3. Logical representation of the spot market (Chand, Sugianto, & Smith, 2002)

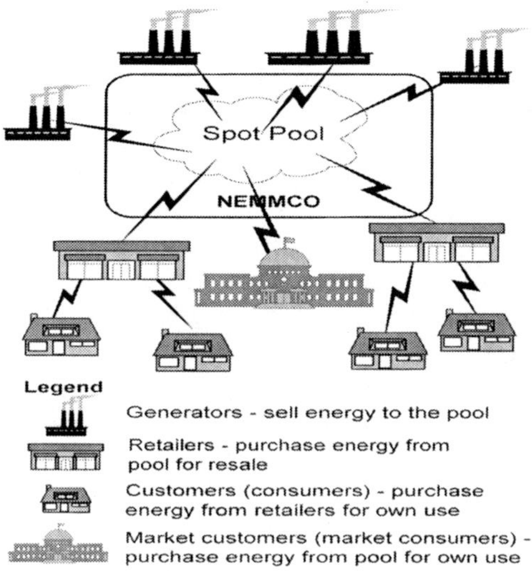

meeting electricity demand based on the offer and bid prices. The clearing price to match supply and demand is defined as the spot price.

In the Australian National Electricity Market (NEM), a trading day consists of 48 trading intervals. The trading commences at 4 a.m. and repeats every 30 minutes until 4 a.m. of the next day. Each of the 30-minute periods is called the trading interval. This is the interval during which settlement of fund transfers occurs between the suppliers and the retailers or market consumers.

In the Australian energy market, each generating company (or supplier) submits ten increasing bands of bid with each bid consisting of a supply price and the additional power output it is offering. The new power output level (level at the start of the dispatch interval plus the additional power output) has to be reached by the end of the particular dispatch interval. Generators may at times bid below zero price to ensure they get scheduled to supply a self-determined minimum level of generation (unit commitment). This implies the generator will pay the market, rather than get paid to keep itself running as this is the cheaper alternative to shutting-down and restarting at a later time. In reality this may not happen, but its implication is a lowering of the wholesale price.

Non-Linearity in the Problem

Non-linear characteristics in the spot market are caused by a number of factors, such as loop flow, network loss, physical limitations of the power plant, and changing market structure. In this chapter, we will not include all these aspects as constraints, but model the loop flow and ramp rates as part of the constraints. The implication of these constraints on the solution is described in a later section.

The Objective Function and the Constraint Functions

The problem of optimizing the Scheduling-Pricing-Dispatch in the deregulated energy market is complex in nature, because it involves fitting the characteristics of physical systems into an economic model. The operation of the physical system, including the generation and transmission of electricity, must be modelled appropriately and accurately — often involving some form of constraint functions. The main objective of the optimisation is to configure the trade quantity schedule that results in the most economical wholesale cost of procuring energy supply for a given demand. In other words, the objective function aims to minimize the *Cost of Supply (COS)* while maintaining the required supply for a *Known Demand Quantity (KDQ)*. The objective function is given in Equation (1).

$$\textit{Minimize:} \quad \sum_{k=1}^{z} c_k q_k \qquad \textbf{(1)}$$

where k: energy bid band, z: total number of bands, c_k: a constant — cost associated with bid band k, q_k: a variable — scheduled quantity for bid band k.

A band refers to a single bid component of a Participant Unit (PU). Although a PU can be a supplier or a load unit, in this chapter the PU is a supplier unit. Each PU has a set of ten bands that are in increasing order of price. The objective function can be redefined by grouping a PU's bands together. Equation (2) shows this definition:

$$\textit{Minimize:} \quad \sum_{i=1}^{n} \sum_{j=1}^{m} c_{(i,j)} q_{(i,j)} \qquad \textbf{(2)}$$

where i: participant unit (PU), n: total number of PU, j: bid band, m: total number bid bands per PU (Note: In NEM, m = 10. In this chapter, for simplicity, m = 4), $c_{(i,j)}$: a constant - cost associated with bid band j of PU i, $q_{(i,j)}$: a variable - scheduled quantity for bid band j of PU i.

The value of c is a constant and reflects the price the PU bids for the scheduled quantity q. The value of q is determined by the optimizer constrained by the maximum q a PU is willing to supply at the price c. The bid band consists of a combination of c and q.

Since the objective is to minimize the procurement cost of supply, it is intuitive that the optimizer needs to schedule the lower-priced bands of a PU before the higher-priced bands. The optimizer using the Horizon Scan algorithm should eventually find the combination, such that the lower bands are allocated first. However, this may take unnecessary steps through the search space and therefore degrade the performance time of the optimisation process. A solution to this is to define a set of constraints that ensure the lower-priced bands are scheduled before the subsequent higher-priced ones. Defining a set of constraints to enforce a simple sequencing operation can also degrade the performance time. Therefore, where applicable, this model considers alternatives to defining constraints. The required constraint on the objective function in Equation (2) can be eliminated by a simple rearrangement of the equation. The rearrangement is represented in Equations (3a), (3b), (4a), (4b) and (5).

Let:

$$Q(i) = \sum_{j=1}^{m} q_{(i,j)} \quad \textbf{(3a)}$$

$$Q(i) = Q_i \quad \textbf{(3b)}$$

$$cf(Q_i) = \sum_{j=1}^{m} c_{(i,j)} q_{(i,j)} \quad \textbf{(4a)}$$

$$\begin{aligned} q_{(i,1)} &= \min(Q_i, s_{(i,1)}) \\ q_{(i,2)} &= \min(Q_i - q_{(i,1)}, s_{(i,2)}) \\ q_{(i,3)} &= \min(Q_i - q_{(i,1)} - q_{(i,2)}, s_{(i,3)}) \\ q_{(i,j)} &= \min(Q_i - \sum_{k=1}^{j-1} q_{(i,k)}, s_{(i,j)}) \end{aligned} \quad \textbf{(4b)}$$

Minimize:

$$\sum_{i=1}^{n} cf(Q_i) \quad \textbf{(5)}$$

where $Q(i)$: function to sum $q(i,j)$ for PU i, Q_i: a variable - replaces $q(i,j)$ *for quantity* allocated by the optimizer to a PU, $Q(i)$ is assigned this value to be distributed over $q(i,j)$ for a PU, $s_{(i,j)}$: a constant — represents the upper limit on $s_{(i,j)}$. It is the maximum quantity that a PU offers at price $c_{(i,j)}$, $cf(Q_i)$: cost function for individual PU, i: participant unit (PU), n: total number of PU, j: bid band j, m: total number bid bands per PU, $c_{(i,j)}$: a constant—cost associated with bid band j of PU i, $q_{(i,j)}$: a variable — scheduled quantity for bid band j of PU i; replaced by Q_i in Equation (5).

In the above rearrangement, the optimizer decision variable $q(i,j)$ is replaced by a new decision variable Q_i. This represents a single quantity for a PU instead of j number of quantities for each PU. The replacement causes *"i * j"* number of variables to be replaced by only *"i"* number of variables. This reduction by the size of j implies a reduction in the problem size and complexity by a factor of j. In the NEM case, this is a reduction by a factor of ten.

Case Studies

This section presents five case studies and their variations. Various constraints based on the NEM regional model are also introduced in these case studies. One hundred simulation runs are performed independently for each case. The results presented include the best case, worst case and average case results from the 100 independent simulation runs using Horizon Scan. The results are analysed and discussed in relation to the constraints.

Constraints in the Single Region Model

- **Band Limit constraint:** Equation (6) is introduced to ensure that the allocated quantity $q_{(i,j)}$ is not greater than the maximum offer.

$$q_{(i,j)} \leq s_{(i,j)} : \forall q_{(i,j)} (i \geq 1 \wedge i \leq n \wedge j \geq 1 \wedge j \leq m) \quad \textbf{(6)}$$

- **Non-Negative constraint:** Equation (7) is introduced to ensure that the scheduled quantity $q_{(i,j)}$ is greater than zero.

$$q_{(i,j)} \geq 0 : \forall q_{(i,j)} (i \geq 1 \wedge i \leq n \wedge j \geq 1 \wedge j \leq m) \quad \textbf{(7)}$$

- **Total Offer constraint:** Since the optimizer allocates the Q_i values and the allocation should not exceed the sum of all quantities in each of the bands of the respective PU, Equation (8) is introduced to ensure the feasibility of the solution.

$$Q_i \leq \sum_{j=1}^{m} s_{(i,j)} : \forall Q_i (i \geq 1 \wedge i \leq n) \quad \textbf{(8)}$$

- **System Demand constraint:** The system demand is the term for the total demand quantity encompassing all participating areas in the trading market. In a single region model the regional demand is the same as the system demand. Therefore, the demand is the same as RDQ. The RDQ is a constant and provides a limit that needs to be imposed during demand-supply balancing (see Equation (9)).

$$\sum_{i=0}^{n} Q_i = RDQ \quad \textbf{(9)}$$

Since the demand needs to be balanced by an equivalent amount of supply, the above limit is regarded as an equality constraint. However, due to the nature of the optimizer, it is easier to implement this constraint as an inequality as presented in Equation (10). Experiments indicated that modifying the model in this way does not produce inaccuracies.

$$\sum_{i=1}^{n} Q_i \geq KDQ \tag{10}$$

Case 1: Meeting System Demand (Single Region Model)

Figure 4 depicts the single region model in which both loads and generators are located in the same region. This implies that there are no transfer limits between the physically separated and interconnected regions. Therefore, there are no considerations for inter-regional flows and losses. The two generating units submit four band offers (see Table 1). In this case study, all the constraints discussed in the previous section are implemented. The demand *(KDQ)* is set to 800 MW and total supply offer is 1,000 MW. All losses occurring in the physical system are considered as part of the demand as is the case in the NEM. Therefore, since there is more supply than demand, there exists a set of feasible solutions for this problem. From this set of solutions, an optimal solution can be found.

As can be seen from Table 2, there is no difference between the best, worst and average case results. The algorithm attempts to find the same optimal solution for each simulation. The results also show that offers were scheduled in an increasing order of offer prices. The objective function value of $20,300 is the lowest cost of procuring an 800 MW supply.

Figure 4. Single region model

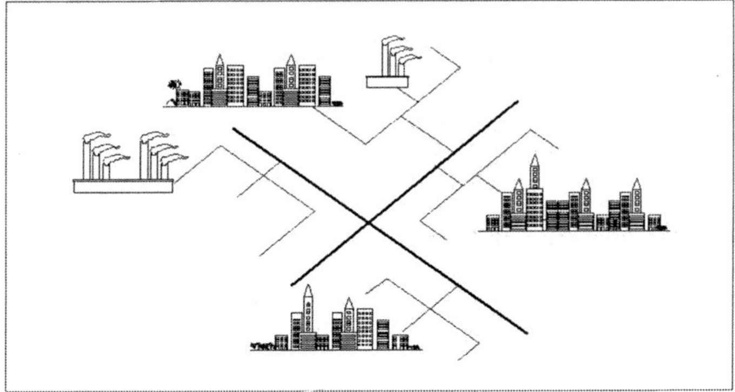

Table 1. PU input for case study 1

PU	Band No.	Quantity-MW	Price-$
i	j	$s_{(i,j)}$	$c_{(i,j)}$
1	1	50	2
	2	200	28
	3	100	30
	4	50	45
2	1	200	15
	2	100	29
	3	200	38
	4	100	85

Table 2. Results of Case Study 1

PU	Band No.	Best Case			Worst Case			Average Case		
i	j	Q_i	$q_{(i,j)}$	$\sum_{i=1}^{n} cf(Q_i)$	Q_i	$q_{(i,j)}$	$\sum_{i=1}^{n} cf(Q_i)$	Q_i	$q_{(i,j)}$	$\sum_{i=1}^{n} cf(Q_i)$
1	1	350	50	$20300	350	50	$20300	350	50	$20300
	2		200			200			200	
	3		100			100			100	
	4		0			0			0	
2	1	450	200		450	200		450	200	
	2		100			100			100	
	3		150			150			150	
	4		0			0			0	

Case 2: Negative Offer in The Bid Band (Single Region Model)

In this case study, negative prices are introduced. The NEM model does not constrain the model by Unit Commitment (UC). UC levels are self imposed and managed by PUs. In this arrangement, PUs that require a UC level would offer prices that are low enough to ensure the minimum supply is maintained. In some cases, PUs would offer negative prices in order to guarantee offer acceptance. This case study presents a similar bidding state as in Table 1, except that the first offer of each of the generators in Table 1 is changed to give negative prices. On inspection, the schedule presented in Table 3 is similar to that of Table 2. The objective function values are different, but this is as expected, since lower offer prices would yield lower cost.

Table 3. Results of Case Study 2

PU	Band No.	Quantity-MW	Price-$	Results		
i	j	$s_{(i,j)}$	$c_{(i,j)}$	Q_i	$Q_{(i,j)}$	$\sum_{i=1}^{n} cf(Q_i)$
1	1	50	-2	350	50	$14100
	2	200	28		200	
	3	100	30		100	
	4	50	45		0	
2	1	200	-15	450	200	
	2	100	29		100	
	3	200	38		150	
	4	100	85		0	

Case 3: Ramp Rates (Single Region Model)

Ramp rates are physical limits on generating units. This places a constraint on the change in magnitude when generating electricity. Both the increase as well as the decrease in magnitude for a given period (in NEM: 5 minutes) is constrained. To enforce this constraint, two parameters are included in the model, namely the current state or initial output ($Q_{(i,currentPeriod)}$) in MW and the ramp rate of each PU.

The initial output defines the output level of a PU at the start of a new trading period. This value reflects the target schedule of the previous trading period. Based on the initial value, the Ramp Rate defines the achievable minimum and maximum output. Ramp Rates in the NEM are quoted for 60-minute periods.

$$Q_{(i,newPeriod)} \geq Q_{(i,currentPeriod)} - RR_i / 12 : \forall i (i \geq 1 \wedge i \leq n) \quad \textbf{(11)}$$

$$Q_{(i,newPeriod)} \leq Q_{(i,currentPeriod)} + RR_i / 12 : \forall i (i \geq 1 \wedge i \leq n) \quad \textbf{(12)}$$

In this case study, KDQ is assumed at 600 MW. The results are presented in Table 4. As can be observed, the Q_i values are different. The more expensive offer of $30 from PU_1 is scheduled even though there is supply capacity in the cheaper offer of $29 from PU_2. The constraint therefore enforces physical limitations due to the current output level.

Constraints in the Two Regions Model

Figure 6 depicts the two-regions model. Although the two regions operate separately, they have an interconnecting (IC) transmission line. Electrical energy is transferred across the lines. The direction of the flow (f) is determined by the supply imbalance in each region.

Table 4. Results of Case Study 3

KDQ = 600								
PU	Band No.	Initial Q_i	Ramp Rate (MW)	Quantity-MW	Price ($)	Re-Run Case 2		
i	j			$S_{(i,j)}$	$c_{(i,j)}$	Q_i	$q_{(i,j)}$	$\sum_{i=1}^{n} cf(Q_i)$
1	1	300	1200	50	-2	350	50	$6950
	2			200	28		200	
	3			100	30		100	
	4			50	45		0	
2	1	200	600	200	-15	250	200	
	2			100	29		50	
	3			200	38		0	
	4			100	85		0	

Some constraints applied to the two regions model include regional demand, maximum regional supply, flow limits, and flow calculation.

- Equation (13) has been introduced to model the Regional Demand Constraint. In the two-regions model, each region has its own Regional Known Demand Quantity (*RKDQ*). Therefore, the total system demand (KDQ) is the sum of all RKDQ:

$$KDQ = \sum_{r=1}^{R} RKDQ \quad \textbf{(13)}$$

where *r*: region id, *R*: number of regions, *RKDQ*: Regional Known Demand Quantity.

- The two-regions model alters the system dynamics since it implies current flow from one region to the next. In an AC interconnector, current flow is controlled by increasing or decreasing supply in one of the regions. The magnitude of the flow is also limited by the physical thermal limits of the line. In short, there are two limits on the line: the interconnector physical limit — no additional current flow is possible beyond this limit; and the interconnector logical limit, which defines the safe operating limit of the line. There are two possible directional flows, namely the *from-region* and the *to-region* (see Figure 5). Equations (14) and (15) define the limits as constraint equations.

$$f \le IFL : f \ge 0 \quad \textbf{(14)}$$

$$-f \le ITL : f < 0 \quad \textbf{(15)}$$

Figure 5. Interconnector flows in the two region model

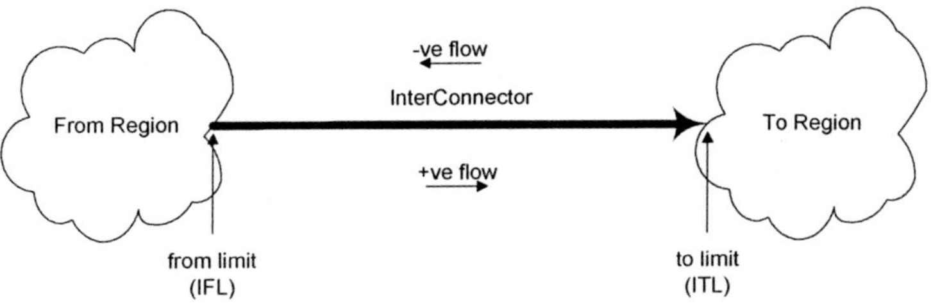

Figure 6. Two region model

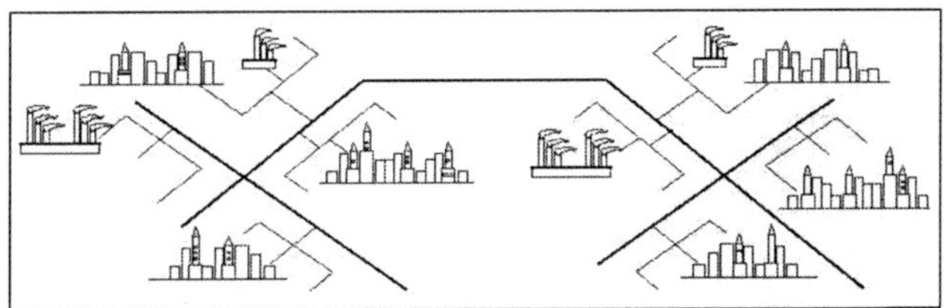

where f: flow on interconnector i, IFL: logical *from* limit on interconnector i, ITL: logical *to* limit on interconnector i.

- In the two-regions model, the objective function will also depend on the magnitude and direction of the flow across the interconnector. Limits discussed in the preceding section will contribute towards the flow magnitude. Therefore, much like Q_i, the flow between the two regions is also a decision variable. To find the optimal solution, the optimiser needs to consider both decision variables. Assuming there is a system-wide balance between demand and supply, any excess generation in a region will flow to the interconnected region. The magnitude of the flow *from the region* is equal to the excess of supply in the region. The value of flow *to the region* is therefore equivalent to inadequacy of supply. This can be formalized as shown in Equations (16) and (17).

$$f_{fromRegion} = \sum_{k=1}^{nf} Q_{(k,fromRegion)} - RKDQ_{fromRegion} \quad \textbf{(16)}$$

$$f_{toRegion} = \sum_{k=1}^{nt} Q_{(k,toRegion)} - RKDQ_{toRegion} \quad \textbf{(17)}$$

where $f_{fromRegion}$: flow value as calculated from the *from region* side of the interconnector, $f_{toRegion}$: flow value as calculated from the *to region* side of the interconnector, k: participant unit (PU), nf: total number of PU in *from region*, nt: total number of PU in *to region*, $RKDQ$: Regional Known Demand Quantity. Since there is a system-wide balance, flow values calculated from both ends must agree in both magnitude and direction. Therefore, Equation (17) is rearranged into Equation (18).

$$f_{toRegion} = RKDQ_{toRegion} - \sum_{k=1}^{nt} Q_{(k,toRegion)} \quad \textbf{(18)}$$

- Regional Supply constraint also needs to be modelled to keep the system balanced. It is defined in terms of balanced flows as shown in Equations (19) to (21). Equation (19a) and (19b) represent the supply demand balance.

$$\sum_{k=1}^{nf} Q_{(k,fromRegion)} + \sum_{k=1}^{nt} Q_{(k,toRegion)} = RKDQ_{fromRegion} + RKDQ_{toRegion} \quad \textbf{(19a)}$$

$$\sum_{k=1}^{nf} Q_{(k,fromRegion)} - RKDQ_{fromRegion} = RKDQ_{toRegion} - \sum_{k=1}^{nt} Q_{(k,toRegion)} \quad \textbf{(19b)}$$

but: $$\sum_{k=1}^{nf} Q_{(k,fromRegion)} - RKDQ_{fromRegion} = f_{fromRegion} \quad \textbf{(20)}$$

$$RKDQ_{toRegion} - \sum_{k=1}^{nt} Q_{(k,toRegion)} = f_{toRegion} \quad \textbf{(21)}$$

therefore: $$f_{fromRegion} = f_{toRegion} \quad \textbf{(22)}$$

Each regional balance is represented by Equations (23) and (24).

$$\sum_{k=1}^{nf} Q_{(k,fromRegion)} = RKDQ_{fromRegion} + f_{fromRegion} \quad \textbf{(23)}$$

$$\sum_{k=1}^{nt} Q_{(k,toRegion)} = RKDQ_{toRegion} - f_{toRegion} \quad \textbf{(24)}$$

Since flows are dependent variables, their values are defined by regional supply, and therefore cannot be used against the supply as constraints. However, the value of the supply can be constrained by the flow limits. This causes the supply to have a lower and an upper limit as modelled by Equations (25) and (26) respectively.

$$\sum_{k=1}^{nf} Q_{(k,fromRegion)} \geq RKDQ_{fromRegion} - ITL \quad (25)$$

$$\sum_{k=1}^{nt} Q_{(k,toRegion)} \leq RKDQ_{toRegion} + IFL \quad (26)$$

Case 4: Independent Regions and Interconnected Regions (Two Regions Model)

The case study discussed here depicts two variations. The first one assumes two independent regions with no interconnection. So, both regions are self-contained and are unable to trade with each other. The second case is an interconnected case but has no transfer limits. Both cases consist of two regions, each with two PUs. The bids of each PU consist of four bands. All offer prices are positive as shown in Table 5. The system demand is 1,200 MW represented by the individual RKDQ in the table. The tabulated results compare the case where the interconnector is non-constrained as well as constrained.

Results show the constraint case to be less optimal than the non-constrained case. In Case 4 (with interconnector), since there is no limit on the flow, the PUs are scheduled according to the cheapest price offers. Regional supply-demand balance is not maintained, unlike in case 4 (without interconnector), where all supplies were scheduled from within the region. Flow from interconnected regions allows the selection of cheaper cost supply from the interconnected region. The resulting price is cheaper than that of the former case. The direction of the flow is consistent with the *from-to* designation on the interconnector. The direction is determined by the schedule offers. The region with surplus would therefore be exporting. The magnitude of the flow is also dependent on the surplus or deficit, however there is a limit on the total flow. The next case study examines this.

Case 5: Imposing Limits on Interconnected Regions (Two-Regions Model)

In the following case studies, limits are imposed on the interconnected regions. An import limit of 100 MW and an export limit of 150 MW are imposed on the interconnector. The second case increases the demand in the first region to allow flow in the negative direction (reversed flow). Parameters and results are presented in Table 6 and pictorially represented in Figure 7 and Figure 8.

The introduction of the flow limit constraint has noticeably changed the value of the flow and the cost. The flow is limited to 100 MW which is the maximum import value of the interconnector. The export limit is not binding. Export of quantity up to the export limit will not be possible. Any amount exported must also be imported at the other end of the

Table 5. Results of Case Study 4

RKDQ = 1200; No Import Limit; No Export Limit										
Region	*PU*	*Band No.*	*Quantity (MW)*	*Price ($)*	*Non-Interconnected Results*			*Interconnected Results*		
r	*i*	*j*	$s_{(i,j)}$	$c_{(i,j)}$	Q_i	$q_{(i,j)}$	$\sum_{i=1}^{n} cf(Q_i)$	Q_i	$q_{(i,j)}$	$\sum_{i=1}^{n} cf(Q_i)$
A	1	1	50	2	350	50	$41730	372.13	50	$40540.45
		2	200	28		200			200	
		3	100	30		100			100	
		4	50	45		0			22.13	
	2	1	200	15	450	200		500	200	
		2	100	29		100			100	
		3	200	38		150			200	
		4	100	85		0			0	
B	3	1	30	39	280	30		211.91	30	
		2	300	60		250			181.91	
		3	50	130		0			0	
		4	20	155		0			0	
	4	1	20	13	120	20		120	20	
		2	100	50		100			100	
		3	80	65		0			0	
		4	100	90		0			0	

interconnector. Since the import limit is binding, transfer up to the export limit will not be possible to achieve. If the export limit was binding then the import would also be constrained by this.

The difference between these two cases is the reversed flow in the second case. The *to-side* of the interconnector is exporting flow instead of importing. Therefore, the *to-side* of the interconnector needs to be imposed with an export limit as opposed to the import limit under normal circumstances. It should be noted that the results of these two cases should not be compared because the demand for Region A in the second case is larger, hence there is a higher dispatch cost for the reversed flow case.

Conclusion

An optimisation problem is characterized by the fact that there exists more than one possible solution and that the solution cannot be identified simply by inspection. In order to solve an optimisation problem, the objective function and the constraints associated with the problem must first be modelled. An optimal solution can be described as a state when the decision variables satisfy the constraints whilst the objective function is at its optimal value.

Table 6. Results of Case Study 5

Case 5 (Constrained Results): RKDQ: [A = 800, B = 400]
Case 5 (Reversed Flow): RKDQ: [A = 1000, B = 400]
For both cases: Import Limit 100; Export Limit 150

Region	*PU*	*Band No.*	*Quantity (MW)*	*Price ($)*	*Constrained Results*			*Reversed Flow Results*		
r	i	j	$s_{(i,j)}$	$c_{(i,j)}$	Q_i	$q_{(i,j)}$	$\sum_{i=1}^{n} cf(Q_i)$	Q_i	$q_{(i,j)}$	$\sum_{i=1}^{n} cf(Q_i)$
A	1	1	50	2		50			50	
		2	200	28	350	200		400	200	
		3	100	30		100			100	
		4	50	45		0			50	
	2	1	200	15		200			200	
		2	100	29	454.	100		599.	100	
		3	200	38	28	154.28	$41641.24	76	200	$54374
		4	100	85		0			99.76	
B	3	1	30	39		30			30	
		2	300	60	275.	245.81		280.	250.14	
		3	50	130	81	0		14	0	
		4	20	155		0			0	
	4	1	20	13		20			20	
		2	100	50	120	100		120	100	
		3	80	65		0			0	
		4	100	90		0			0	

Figure 7. Flow diagram for Case 5 (constrained)

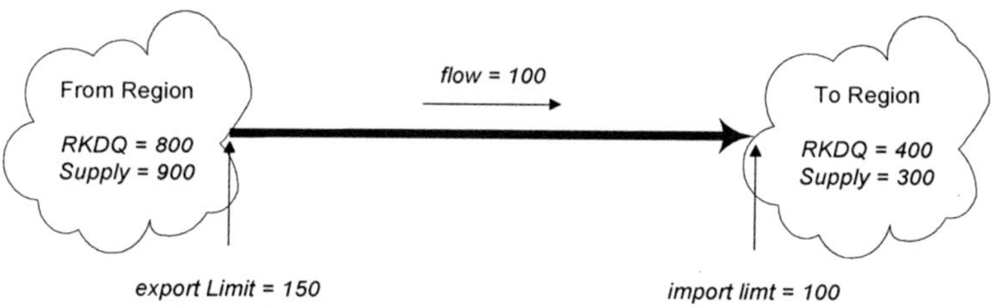

Figure 8. Flow diagram for Case 5 (reversed flow)

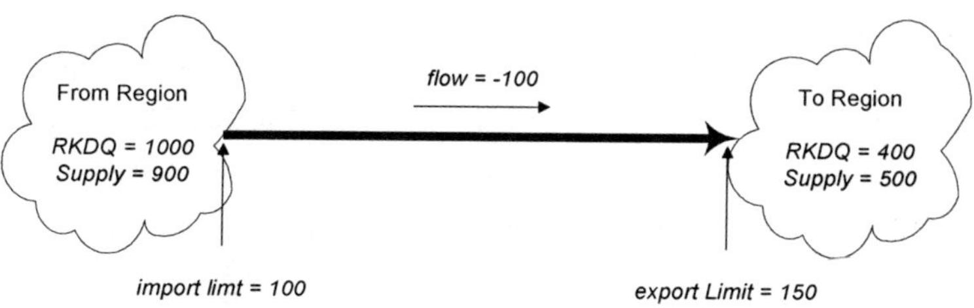

This chapter proposes a heuristic-based search technique called Horizon Scan. The Horizon Scan search strategy has been designed to cope with a non-linear, multi-dimensional search space. In this chapter, Horizon Scan has been applied to solve the Scheduling-Pricing-Dispatch problem in a deregulated electricity market. A number of case studies have been developed to test the performance of Horizon Scan. The case studies include several non-linear constraints that make it more complicated for conventional optimisation techniques to solve. In all case studies presented in the previous sections, Horizon Scan has demonstrated its effectiveness in obtaining near optimal solutions that are consistent and acceptable for the single-region and two-regions models. Simulations of more complex models, that is up to a six-regions model, are being developed and tested. Other non-linear constraints, such as loop flow and network losses, will also be included in future work. Other aspects in relation to the Horizon Scan technique, such as multi-dimension search strategy, iterative step size and scanning methods have been reported in previous work (Chand & Sugianto, 2003b).

In conclusion, it should be pointed out that the proposed technique is universal in application. Although in this chapter the case studies have focussed on economically optimizing bidding resolution in an auction process, the technique can also be applied in many other complex business problems that are non-linear in nature and require rigorous search in multi-dimensional space.

Acknowledgments

The work described in this chapter is part of a project funded by the Australian Research Council Strategic Partnerships with Industry — Research and Training (ARC-SPIRT) grant. The authors would like to thank the industrial partner NEMMCO for its support and technical assistance in many aspects of this project.

References

Al-Turki, U., Fedjki, C., & Andijani, A. (2001). Tabu search for a class of single-machine scheduling problems. *Computers and Operations Research, 28*(12), 1223-1230.

Anderson, E. J. (1996). Mechanisms for local search. *European Journal of Operational Research, 88*(1), 139-151.

Baykasolu, A., & Gindy, N. Z. (2001). A simulated annealing algorithm for dynamic layout problem. *Computers and Operations Research, 28*(14), 1403-1426.

Bertsekas, D. (1999). *Nonlinear programming* (2nd ed.). Nashua, NH: Athena Scientific.

Chand, P., & Sugianto, L. F. (2003a). Horizon scan - A heuristic search technique. In A. Abraham, M. Köppen & K. Franke (Eds.), *Proceedings of the Third Hybrid*

Intelligent Systems Conference, 14-16 December 2003, Melbourne (pp. 291-300). The Netherlands: IOS Press.

Chand, P., & Sugianto, L. F. (2003b, December 17-19). A non-linear approach to scheduling and pricing electricity in the deregulated energy market. In P. Santiprabhob & H. T. Nguyen (Eds.), *Proceedings of the Fourth International Conference on Intelligent Technologies,* Chiang Mai, Thailand (pp. 187-196). Chiang Mai, Thailand: Institute for Science and Technology Research and Development, Chiang Mai University.

Chand, P., & Sugianto, L. F. (2004, March 1-3). A comparative study in alternate scan techniques in horizon scan. In M. H. Hamza (Ed.), *Proceedings of the IASTED Conference in Simulation and Modelling,* Marina Del Ray, Los Angeles (pp. 469-474). Calgary, Canada: ACTA Press.

Chand, P., Sugianto, L. F., & Smith, K. A. (2002, Sept 30-Oct 2). An overview of the Australian national energy market and ancillary services. In A. Zahedi (Ed.), *Proceedings of the Australasian Universities Power Engineering Conference AUPEC2000,* Melbourne, Australia. CDROM. Australia: Monash University.

Glover, F., & Laguna, M. (1993). Tabu search. In C. R. Reeves (Ed.), *Modern heuristic techniques for combinatorial problems* (pp.70-150). Oxford: Blackwell Scientific.

Lewis, R. M., Torczon, V., & Trosset, M.W. (2000). Direct search methods: Then and now. *Journal of Computational and Applied Mathematics, 24*(1-2), 191-207.

Pham, D. T., & Karaboga, D. (2000). *Intelligent optimisation techniques.* New York: Springer-Verlag.

Pirlot, M. (1996). General local search methods. *European Journal of Operational Research, 92*(3), 493-511.

Rutenbar, R. A. (1989). Simulated annealing algorithms: An overview. *IEEE Circuits and Devices Magazine, 5*(1), 19-26.

Taha, H. A. (1997). Classical optimization theory. In H. A. Taha (Ed.), *Operations research: An introduction* (pp.745-780). Englewood Cliffs, NJ: Prentice Hall.

Youssef, H., Sait, S. M., & Adiche, H. (2001). Evolutionary algorithms, simulated annealing and Tabu search: A comparative study. *Engineering Applications of Artificial Intelligence, 14*(2), 167-181.

Section IV

Data Mining Applications

Chapter XI

Visual Data Mining for Discovering Association Rules

Kesaraporn Techapichetvanich, The University of Western Australia, Australia

Amitava Datta, The University of Western Australia, Australia

Abstract

Both visualization and data mining have become important tools in discovering hidden relationships in large data sets, and in extracting useful knowledge and information from large databases. Even though many algorithms for mining association rules have been researched extensively in the past decade, they do not incorporate users in the association-rule mining process. Most of these algorithms generate a large number of association rules, some of which are not practically interesting. This chapter presents a new technique that integrates visualization into the mining association rule process. Users can apply their knowledge and be involved in finding interesting association rules through interactive visualization, after obtaining visual feedback as the algorithm generates association rules. In addition, the users gain insight and deeper understanding of their data sets, as well as control over mining meaningful association rules.

Introduction

In this chapter, we discuss the role of visualization in data analysis and in mining association rules from large databases. We describe reviews of works on visualization techniques in five categories, as well as problems related to visualization. A new visualization technique, called hierarchical dynamic dimensional visualization (HDDV) (Techapichetvanich, Datta, & Owens, 2004) was designed to overcome some of these problems. We present a brief overview of this technique. In addition, we discuss how visual data mining can be performed using the HDDV technique. Our main aim is to design a visualization process for mining association rules of a certain type called *market basket association rules*. This type of association rule is used for analyzing trends and correlations in shopping patterns of customers in supermarkets or other retail outlets. Finally, we discuss future trends in visualization and its application into other research areas related to business data analysis.

Background

Researchers in many disciplines such as science, statistics, finance, medical research, and mathematics have developed a variety of multidimensional visualization techniques to support visual representation of massive data sets. In the business world, managers need tools that help them understand their key business, in order to make quick and precise decisions, and to improve their management strategies. Visualization plays an important role in enabling users to explore and gain insight into their data, through visual or graphical images, rather than textual forms such as spreadsheet or tables. Visualization helps users to extract important information such as trends, correlations, or relationships between the variables or dimensions.

In recent years, various visualization methodologies have been developed to support interpreting and representing characteristics and relationships of large multidimensional data sets. Some research areas focus only on visualization techniques, while some apply visualization techniques to data mining to gain insight into large amounts of data such as databases and data warehouses and to discover trends, patterns, and relationships. The research areas of visualization can be categorized into five groups.

First, *geometric* techniques (Cleveland, 1993; Inselberg & Dimsdale, 1987; Kandogan, 2001; D. Keim, 1996) such as the Scatterplot Matrix, Parallel Coordinates, and Star Coordinates involve geometric transformation and projection of data. For the Scatterplot Matrix, individual variables are arranged along the diagonal of a matrix and each display panel illustrates relationships or correlations between variables. For the Parallel Coordinates technique, the dimensions are represented by parallel vertical lines, which are perpendicular to and uniformly distributed along a horizontal line, rather than by data points plotted on two orthogonal axes. Each variable or dimension is assigned to each parallel axis and each line across the axes represents a data item. The relationship between closed axes or dimensions is easy to perceive. In Star Coordinates, axes emanating from a center point represent attributes of the data set. In contrast to the Parallel Coordinates technique, the Star Coordinates technique transforms each data item and displays it as a point.

Second, *iconographic* techniques use the features of icons or glyphs to represent data variables and each icon represents a data item. Some examples are Chernoff-faces (Chernoff, 1973) and Stick-figure icons (Pickett & Grinstein, 1988). Chernoff-faces represent multidimensional data in the form of a human face. Stick-figure icons represent data elements by five connected line segments. Four are limbs and the other is the body of the icon. The first four variables or dimensions from the data can be mapped onto the four limbs, with each value controlling the angle of a limb. The last dimension controls the orientation of the body. In addition, colors, thickness, or length can be encoded to the limbs and body to represent higher dimensionality.

The third group is known as *hierarchical* techniques (Keim, 1996). These techniques map variables into different recursive levels: Worlds within Worlds (Beshers & Feiner, 1993) and Hierarchical Axis (Mihalisin, Timlin, & Schwegler, 1991a, 1991b). The Worlds within Worlds technique visualizes multidimensional data by placing one coordinate space inside another in a hierarchical manner. The height field or vertical axis of the inner worlds represents the value of a function and all remaining variables, and is used to code the constant value of the outer world (at most, three variables at each level). The Hierarchical Axis method uses one-dimensional subspace embedding and aims at visualizing high dimensionality on two-dimensional graphics space. Dependent variables are mapped on the vertical axis, and independent variables are recursively mapped onto a single horizontal axis.

The fourth group is *pixel-based* techniques (Keim, 2000; Keim, Hao, & Dayal, 2002; Keim & Kriegel, 1994) such as VisDB and Pixel Bar Charts. The techniques in this group aim to represent as many data items as possible. Each data value is mapped onto a pixel and each pixel is colored from a fixed range of colours according to its value, so that its value falls into each attribute range. These techniques also incorporate the Pixel-Oriented technique into data mining through queries and visual feedback. In VisDB, there are two main techniques: Query Independent and Query Dependent. The Query Independent technique employs line ordering or column ordering using *space-filling curves* and *recursive pattern* approaches to order data items based on an attribute. On the other hand, the Query Dependent technique arranges the closest results from queried data items, mapping them to colours in a color ramp onto the center of the display. Pixel Bar Charts is a technique that applies Pixel-Oriented and x-y plotting into traditional bar charts. The bars are used to represent categorical data while x-y plotting and color coding inside the bars are used to represent numerical data.

The last group is *table-based* techniques including Table Lens (Ramana & Card, 1994) and Polaris (Stolte, Tang, & Hanrahan, 2002). Table Lens is a visualization technique based on Focus+Context or a fisheye technique to display multidimensional data in tabular style. This technique displays a data set by applying bar charts and a Focus+Context technique onto a table rather than in a text form. Each bar chart represents a data attribute along a table column and Focus+Context allows users to focus on the details of each bar chart. Similar to Table Lens, FOCUS represents attributes along rows and data items along columns of the table. The object-attribute table combines a

Focus+Context and a hierarchical outliner to display a particular selected area in more detail and to overview the table.

Visualization has been integrated into many applications and research areas, such as data mining, to leverage interpretation and extraction of hidden patterns in data. Data mining is a core process of knowledge discovery in databases (Fayyad, Piatetsky-Shapiro, & Smyth, 1996), used to extract the knowledge or information from a huge amount of data sources without human guidance. The usefulness of extracted knowledge varies for users in different areas. The integration of visualization into data mining is known as *visual data mining*. The integration combines the human ability of exploration with the computer task of analytical processing. Visual data mining helps users to discover knowledge by employing data mining algorithms and representing the knowledge patterns through visualization in understandable ways. Visual data mining can be categorized into three categories based on how the visualization is integrated into the data mining process.

The first group of visual data mining is pre-applying visualization into data mining for exploring data sets. Visualization is used as an exploration tool in which data are firstly displayed to generate initial views before applying data mining algorithms to extract knowledge. MineSet (SGI) is an example of applications in this category.

The second group is post-applying visualization into data mining for conveying the mining results. The data mining algorithms extract patterns in data and then the extracted patterns are visualized. Most of visual data mining research belongs to this category. An example of this category is visualization of association rules over relational DBMSs (Chakravarthy & Zhang, 2003).

The last group is application of visualization into the mining process itself. During the mining process, users can apply their domain knowledge to guide the process to extract useful knowledge. Users can understand the data deeply while mining patterns and associations. This approach can be considered as a tight coupling between visualization and data mining (Wong, Whitney, & Thomas, 1999), while the first two categories are considered as loose coupling. For instance, visual classification (Ankerst, Elsen, Ester, & Kriegel, 1999; Ankerst, Ester, & Kreigel, 2000) is a tightly integrated visual data-mining process for classification purposes and visual mining of market basket association rules (Techapichetvanich & Datta, 2004) is an example tool for mining of association rules in a tightly coupled environment.

Since mining processes in visual data mining rely on data-mining algorithms, most of the mining tasks are similar from an algorithmic point of view. Data-mining tasks have different targets for both gaining insight into data and/or predicting trends in the data sets. The data-mining tasks such as association rules, cluster analysis, and classification have different goals and performance according to the kind of knowledge to be mined. For example, if a store manager wants to study purchasing behaviors of his or her customers in his or her store, he or she needs to identify important associations for further exploration.

The size of databases, such as transaction records in supermarkets, telecommunication companies, e-marketing and credit card companies, has been growing rapidly and it is difficult to extract meaningful information from such large databases. Analysts need a tool to transform large amounts of data into interpretable knowledge and information, and to help in making decisions, predicting trends, and discovering relationships and patterns. Association-rule mining is one of the most important data mining processes. It is a powerful tool that helps analysts to understand and discover the relationships in their data. Market-basket analysis is an example of mining association rules which help marketing analysts to analyze customer behavior to improve their marketing strategies. To increase the number of sales, one such marketing strategy could be placing associated items in the same area of the floor so that customers can access, or place the items in their market baskets, easily. For example, placing items such as bread and cheese that are frequently purchased together in close proximity may increase sales because customers who buy bread may also buy cheese when they see cheese on a nearby shelf. Furthermore, sales promotions of items frequently purchased together on the store catalogs may increase sales of those items.

Mining association rules is a well-researched area within data mining (Han & Kamber, 2001). There are many algorithms for generating *frequent itemsets* and *mining association rules* (Agrawal & Imielinski, 1993; Savasere, Omiecinski, & Navathe, 1995; Srikant & Agrawal, 1995). Such algorithms can mine association rules that have *confidence* and *support* higher than a user-supplied level. However, one of the drawbacks of these algorithms is that they mine all rules exhaustively and many of these rules are not interesting in a practical sense. Too many association rules are difficult to analyze and it is often difficult for an analyst to extract a (usually small) meaningful set of association rules. Hence there is a need for human intervention during the mining of association rules (Agrawal & Srikant, 1994; Wang, Jiang, & Lakshmanan, 2003) so that an analyst can directly influence the mining process and extract only a small set of the interesting rules.

Association Rules

An association rule (Agrawal & Srikant, 1994) is a rule of the type A => B where A is an item set called *antecedent, body*, or *left-hand side* (LHS) and B is an item set called *consequent*, *head*, or *right-hand side* (RHS). The rule implies that if A appears in a transaction, there is a high probability that B will also appear in the same transaction. Each item set consists of items in a transactional database. Items existing in the antecedent are not in the consequent. In other words, an association rule is of the form A => B where $A, B \subset I$ and A) B = $\cap$. $I = \{i_1, i_2,..., i_n\}$ is a set of items in the transaction database where i_j, $1 \leq j \leq n$, is an item in the database that may appear in a transaction. The two common measures of interestingness are *support* and *confidence*. The rule A => B has support s if s is the percentage of transactions that contain both A and B. The same rule A=>B has confidence c if c is the percentage of transactions containing A that also contain B. An example of the association rule is {camera} => {battery, bag}. If this rule has a support of 60% and a confidence of 45%, they show that all items {camera, battery, bag} appear together in 60% of all transactions and 45% of all customers who buy a camera also buy a battery and bag at the same time. A term, *frequent item set* (Han & Kamber, 2001) is used to define an item set whose number of co-appearing items in database is greater than a user specified support. In a database of store transactions, a frequent itemset is a set of items frequently purchased together. For instance, if the user specifies minimum support as 25% and an item set {camera, battery, bag} appears in 48% of all transactions, then the item set is called a frequent item set.

Overview of a New Visualization Technique

Most of the visualization techniques encounter the problems of screen clutter and occlusion when large amounts of data are visualized. For example, lines being plotted along parallel axes of Parallel Coordinates generate bands or clutters when visualizing large amounts of data. Data records being projected and plotted to the same position in the Scatterplot Matrix and Star Coordinates techniques generate occlusion. Both of the problems reduce the capability of visualization and the ability of users to interpret useful information from data sets. In iconographic techniques, a glyph represents a data record. To visualize large data sets, a large enough space is needed to display all data records. However, when data records are spread over the display, it reduces the capability of users to compare distant glyphs or dimensional axes and to extract the trends and correlation from data sets. In addition, most previous work in visualizing large multidimensional data sets has been designed to use static dimensional visualization, where data items are mapped to coordinate system axes in the transformation process. The reconfigurations of assigning attributes to axes are not allowed after the transformation.

We briefly introduce a new technique, called Hierarchical Dynamic Dimensional Visualization (HDDV) (Techapichetvanich et al., 2004). This technique has been designed to address these problems and support a dynamic dimensional approach. The general idea of HDDV is to generate both hierarchical bars in which data of each selected dimension is arranged, and dynamic visualization that is capable of handling large amounts of data. The goals of HDDV are to discover relationships, correlation, distributions, and trends in large data sets, to overcome the limitation of the static dimensional technique and the occlusion of the screen space, and to work effectively without extensive training. The dimensional axes in a dynamic dimensional system can be adjusted and regenerated without fixing the assigned attributes to the axes after mapping data to graphical representation and rendering processes.

In HDDV, a term, *barstick*, has been introduced to represent a data dimension. Users can set up queries by selecting each dimension of interest. Data records in a specified range are mapped into the barstick of that selected dimension. Each data record is arranged into a block in the barstick in ascending order and is displayed by colored vertical lines or vertical blocks based on the number of data records in the data set. Data records of a new selected dimension are transformed to a new barstick based on the previous barsticks and their specified ranges in a hierarchical fashion. The color of the vertical block represents the density of data records falling into a specified range. The darker color means a higher density of data in a block.

Integrating Visualization into Mining Process

Information visualization has been a growing area of research in recent years (Fayyad, Grinstein, & Wierse, 2002). It is much easier to visualize and analyze a large database in a graphical form than in a textual form. There are many methods for visualizing higher dimensional databases on standard graphics displays (Keim & Kriegel, 1994; SGI, n.d.; Stolte et al., 2002). Recently, several researchers have investigated the visualization of association rules (Hofmann, Siebes, & Wilhelm, 2000; Ong, Ong, Ng, & Lim, 2002; Wong et al., 1999). The main motivation behind this research is to identify interesting association rules from a large number of rules mined by using an existing algorithm. Hence, visualizing results of association rules does not directly address the issue of meaningful intervention so that an algorithm mines only interesting association rules.

We feel that it is important for an analyst to participate in the mining process in order to identify meaningful association rules from a large database through his/her guidance and knowledge, as well as to change setting parameters anytime, and easily to access the information of interest. Any such participation should be easy from an analyst's point of view. Hence, visualizing association-rule mining seems to be a natural way of directing the mining process. We have integrated and modified the visualization technique with barsticks for helping an analyst to mine association rules.

A Model for Interactive Association Rule Mining

Our technique can be divided into three stages, *identifying frequent item sets*, *mining association rules* and *visualizing* the mined association rules as shown in Figure 1. Each step has been designed to enhance the ability of the users to interact in the mining process. To effectively handle user interaction, an interactive tool must deal with many human factors (Foley, Dam, Feiner, & Hughes, 1997). Our interactive technique takes into account some principles of interactive designs such as consistency, providing feedback, reducing memorization, and ease of use or simplicity without extensive training. In addition, the analyst has complete control on deciding on the antecedents and consequents of each rule and the whole process is intuitively simple for an analyst. Though a complete visual mining process is slow compared to an automated process, it has the advantage of exploring only interesting association rules. As we have mentioned before, an automated process can mine many association rules that are not meaningful practically. Our visualization tool is extremely simple to use and avoids screen clutter. This makes it an attractive option to use both for small and large databases.

In the first stage of our visual mining technique, the user can first find a suitable frequent itemset. In most data mining algorithms, the selection of a frequent item set is done automatically. Any item that has an occurrence above the user specified support is chosen as the member of the frequent item set. Though this method is efficient for identifying all the frequently occurring items, the subsequent association-rule mining quite often discovers a large number of association rules involving these frequently

Figure 1. A model of our technique to mine association rules

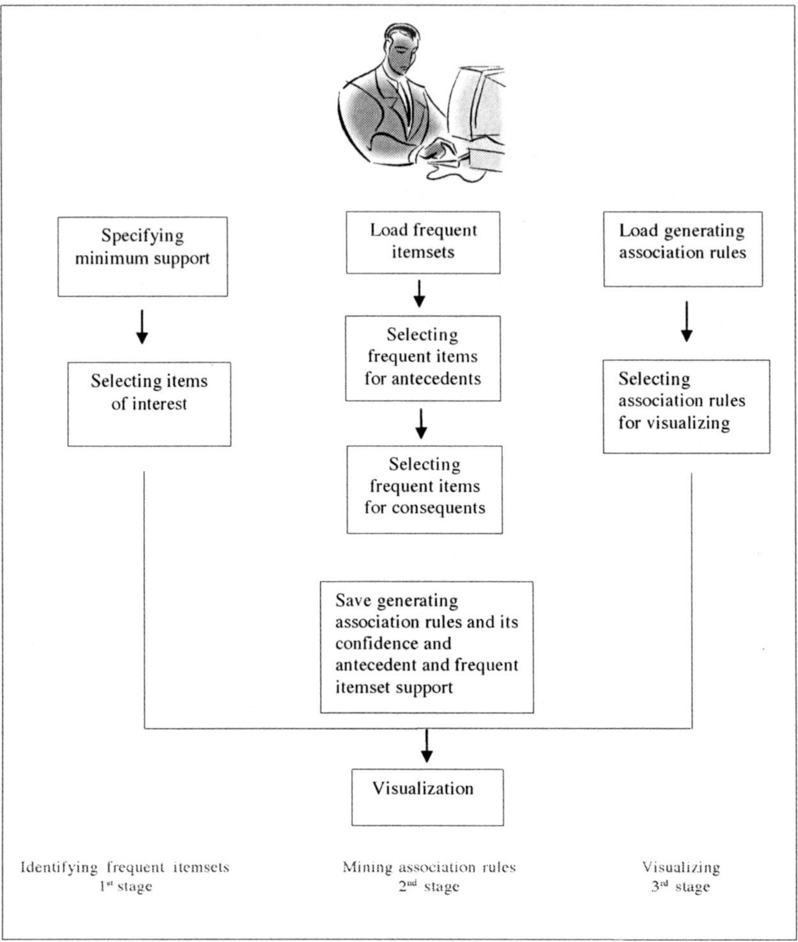

occurring items. In our technique, we give the user complete control over choosing the frequent item set.

In the second stage, the user can mine interesting association rules by specifying the antecedents and consequents of each rule from the frequent itemset chosen in the first stage. The user can experiment with different combinations of antecedents and consequents and save a rule if it is interesting.

Finally, in the third stage, the user can visualize all the discovered rules saved during the second stage. Our technique helps filter out the uninteresting frequent item sets and uninteresting association rules by employing human knowledge.

In our application, we split an application window into two areas: left and right panels. The left panel is a user control panel which allows the user to input parameters. The right

Figure 2. The right drawing space represents each selected item as a barstick with the numbers of purchases from all transactions. The control tab represents combobox for each selected item and the list of its co-existing items.

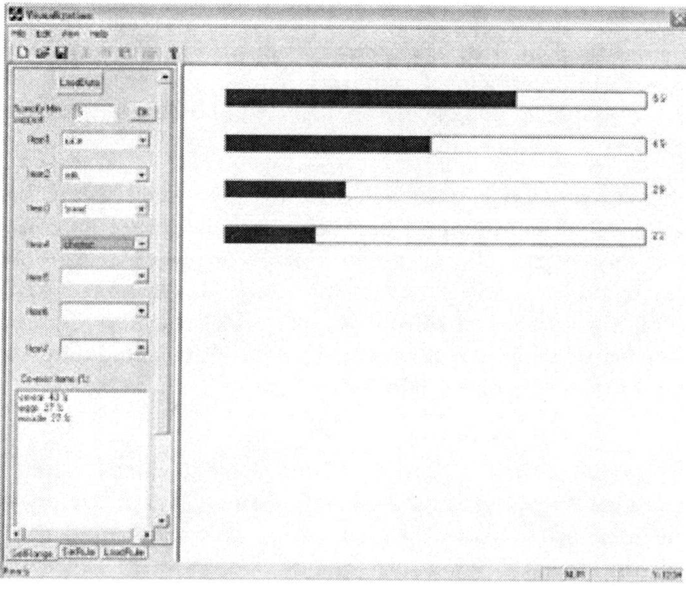

panel is a visualizing panel that displays results responding to the setting parameters of the left panel.

Identifying Frequent Item Sets. This part of our system assists the analyst to search for frequent item sets based on a user-specified minimum support. The analyst can provide the minimum support to filter only items that they are interested in. After specifying the minimum support, all items exceeding the threshold are loaded and sorted in descending order of their support. Analysts can use the sorted list as a guide in selecting each item in the frequent item set. Each selected item is represented by a barstick with the percentage of its support. After the first selection of an item, the system generates a list of items that co-exist with the first selected item. All the items in this co-existing item list have support greater than the user-specified minimum support. The co-existing item list is also generated each time a subsequent item is chosen. The percentage of support is calculated by comparing the numbers of the first and second selected items appearing together with the total number of appearance of the first selected item. At each step, the bar sticks are displayed using the modification of the HDDV technique discussed earlier. This technique helps analysts to find items that tend to appear together in the transactions. In addition, the system has user interaction to support the detail of each selected item. When the analyst clicks in each bar, the percentage of each item in the co-existing item list and its support are displayed to help analysts make decision and compare selected interesting items and their supports. As shown in Figure 2, the display window is divided into two sub-windows. The left panel comprises the specified minimum support, lists of the items through combo-boxes, and the list of co-existing selected items with their supports in descending order. For example, the co-existing item list of cheese consists of 47% of cereal, 27% of eggs, and 27% of noodle. The right panel visualizes selected items with the numbers of purchases from all transactions as hierarchical barsticks. Juice, milk, bread, and cheese are selected in order as items of interest.

The user can change a previously chosen item at any stage. Each item in the set is chosen from a drop-down list of items and the user can resize the frequent itemset by deleting the last item at any stage. The user can change any previously chosen item by successively reselecting any item from the drop-down list. Once the user has chosen the frequent item set, it can be saved for the later stages of the mining process. We have shown only seven items in Figure 2. However, it is possible to include any number of items in the left panel through a scrolling window.

Selecting Interesting Association Rules. In this stage, the selected frequent item set from the first stage is used to generate the association rules. Again, we provide complete freedom to the user in choosing the association rules including the items in the antecedent and consequent of each rule. The number of items in the antecedent and

Figure 3. The right drawing space represents two barsticks. The first bar shows the proportion of antecedent of the association rule. The second bar shows the consequent based on the selected antecedent. The control tab on top of the left hand side is to input the antecedent and consequent of the rule. The bottom of the tab displays the confidence, the antecedent support, and the itemset support.

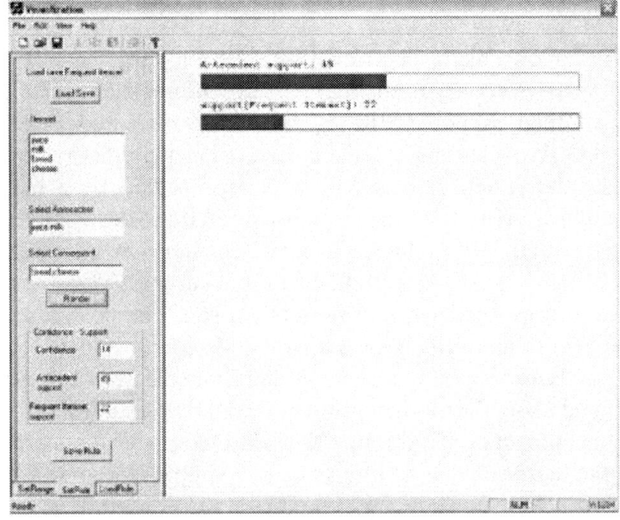

Figure 4. Illustration for deriving interesting association rules from the selection of the rules in Figure 3. The two bars and the texts represent each rule and its properties.

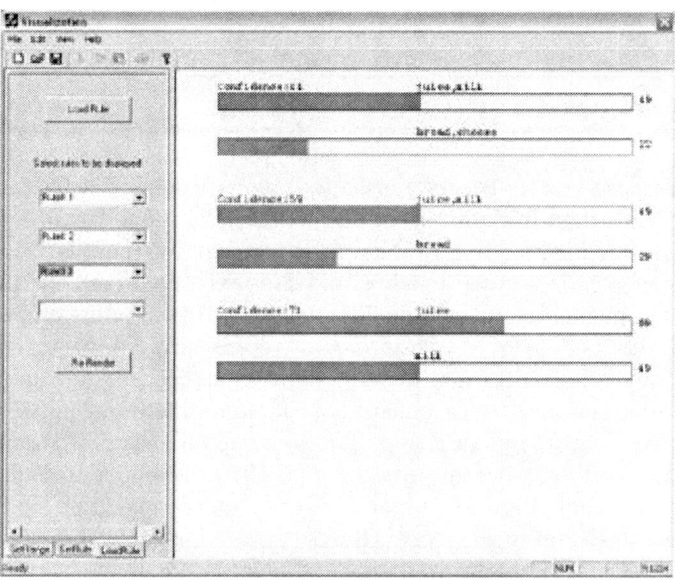

consequent of an association rule is not limited only to one-to-one relationships. The system supports many-to-many relationship rules as well. In Figure 3, the left panel shows the selected frequent item set of interest including juice, milk, bread, and cheese from the first stage. The user is allowed to generate a many-to-many relationship rule, namely juice and milk as antecedent and bread and cheese as consequent, or any other combination of antecedent and consequent.

In the right panel, the first colored bar illustrates the proportion of selected items, juice and milk for an antecedent. The second colored bar represents all selected items of an association rule, in other words it shows the proportion of the consequent items, bread and cheese, appearing together with the antecedent of the rule. In the left control panel, the system shows the support of the antecedent, the support of the selected itemset, and the confidence of the association rule.

Visualizing Association Rules. This part deals with visualization of the mined association rules in the second stage. The visualization allows analysts to view and compare the mined association rules generated from the first two steps. Among the selected interesting rules, the visualization bars allow analysts to obtain the most significant and interesting rules. Figure 4 represents three association rules. For example, the first rule shows the relationship of the antecedent: juice and milk and the consequent: bread and cheese. The confidence, the antecedent support, and the itemset support of this rule are 44, 49, and 22, respectively.

For the second rule, the first bar, with support 49, represents the antecedent: juice and milk and the second bar, with support 29, represents bread. The confidence is 59. The antecedent support of the last rule is 69, the frequency of item set is 49, and the confidence is 71.

Data Structures Used in Our System

Our algorithm scans a market-basket transaction database twice. The first scan is to count the support of each item in the transaction records. The second scan is to generate a bitwise table to store the item lists of the original transaction records. We use a bitwise operation in representing both existing and non-existing items. In the first stage identifying the frequent item set, an item identification list including non-existing items of each transaction is converted to a bit-vector representation, where 1 represents an existing item and 0 represents a non-existing item in the record. For example, suppose a market basket transaction database consists of four items including milk, bread, cheese, and cereal in ascending order of item identifications and a transaction contains two items: milk and cheese. A bit-vector of this transaction is 1010. Hence, the associated items can be retrieved by applying a bitmask operation to each transformed item list. Each bitmask is generated by transforming all selected items to bits which are set to 1. After selecting each interesting item from a menu list in the first stage, an associated item list is generated to support the user's search for the next interesting item. To reduce searching time of associated items in each transaction, the associated item list contains only the indexes of transactions with all selected items appearing together. Each transaction index is linked to the bitwise table so that all associated items in that transaction can be retrieved.

This technique can support a large number of items in a transaction database. Though the bitwise technique needs some preprocessing time to convert the transaction records to a bitwise table, it is more efficient and effective to search the existing and associated items at run time.

User Study

Experimental Methodology

To evaluate the efficiency of our system components for further improvement, we conducted an experiment of a user study with seven postgraduate students from the computer science department by asking them to perform data analysis tasks and report their findings for the assigned tasks. The experiment was run on two data sets and all participants had to complete four main tasks in each data set as follows.

- **Task1:** Identify (name) the first two maximum and two minimum numbers of items sold.

- **Task2:** Identify four items that have the highest percentage of being purchased together and provide an association rule which qualifies the support and confidence threshold provided. (Assume that the support > 70 and confidence > 70 are the possible association of items purchased together).
- **Task3:** Identify three association rules of items A, B, and C including support and confidence of each rule. Which rule do you think contain items that customers are likely to purchase together?
- **Task4:** Do you think it is possible that the items X and Y are frequently purchased together? (Assume that the support > 70 and confidence > 70 are the possible association of items purchased together).

The variable A, B, C, X, and Y were varied to represent different items in each data set. The first data set was derived from UCI Machine Learning Repository and the items are number. The other was from Data Mining II (DMII) with the item names for each transaction. Before starting an experiment, each participant was provided terminologies and descriptions of how to interpret an association rule and frequent itemsets and how to use the system tool. An example of a data set was also shown to the participant. During the time to complete each task, we also investigated the interaction of users for analysis. At the end of the experiment, they were required to complete a brief usability questionnaire partly deriving from Stasko (2000) and Marghescu and Rajanen (2005).

Results

The participants were asked about their experience in data analysis and visualization. All of the participants had no experience in data analysis and only three participants had some experience in using visualization tools. The results for usability, visualization, interaction, and information are presented in Figure 5. A total of 57% of participants found that parameters shown in the tool are understandable and the tool is easy to be used, although 29% of participants did not agree that the tool is easy to use. The tool was found easy to learn (29% strongly agree, 43% agree, and 28% fair). An equal number of participants (43%) provided agree and average points for easily completing the tasks with the tool, although 14% of participants did not agree. For the visualization question, the positive feedback from all participants were provided in identifying the most and least often bought item. Greater than 55% of participants found that they could identify the maximum and minimum percentage of items purchased together and appreciated the clarity of visual representation, although about 14% of participants did not agree. For the interaction question, most provided properties (i.e., ability to change the selection of items, to explore data, to use parameters, and to direct search for data of interest) had positive feedback. A total of 86% of participants both agreed and strongly agreed that they were able to correct their mistakes, although 14% of participants did not agree. Moreover, most users provided positive feedback for all features for the information question.

In Figure 6, the participants spent more time completing the second and third task of Data set1 than Data set2. This result shows that they can search for frequent item sets and

Figure 5. Represents participant opinions in scale ranking

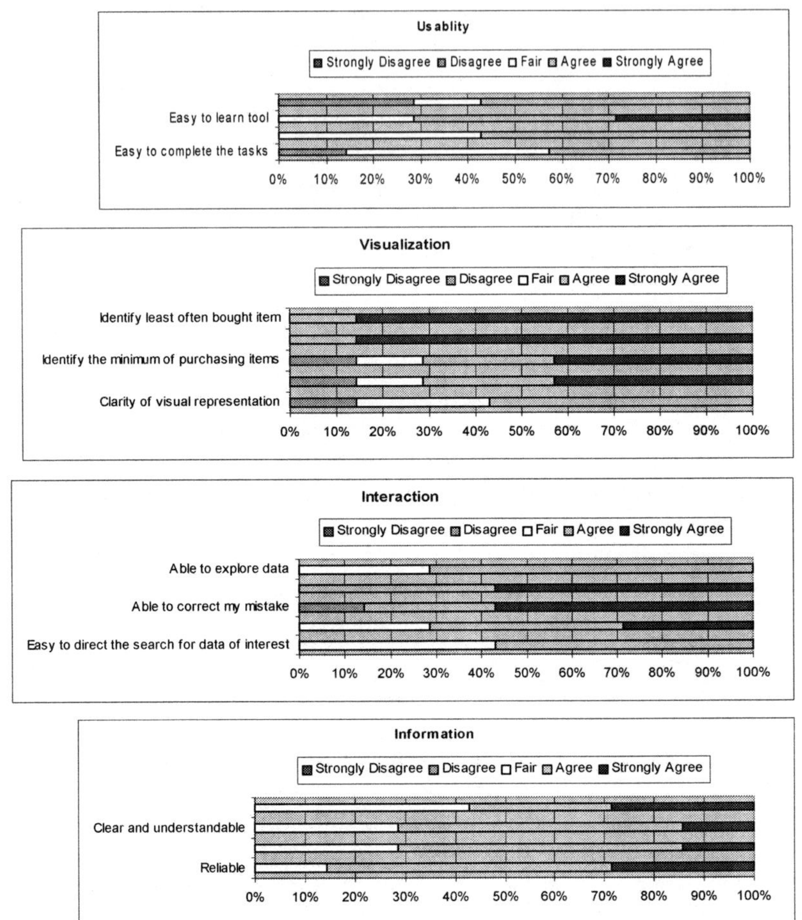

association rules of interest faster after gaining experience from the previous task. For observation, a participant who spent time completing the second task of Data set1 tried to search for the best association rule by making combinations of each items of interest. For correctness, the performance of participants seemed to improve in Task 4 and no one had a problem completing all the first three tasks. From the questionnaire, results of assigned tasks, and observation, the participants were able to learn how to use the tool easily and also learn how to correct their mistake efficiently. However, our user study is limited in number and in the characteristics of the participants, all of whom had no experience in data analysis.

Figure 6. (a) Represents mean time of completing each task (b) Represents the correctness of each task in each data set

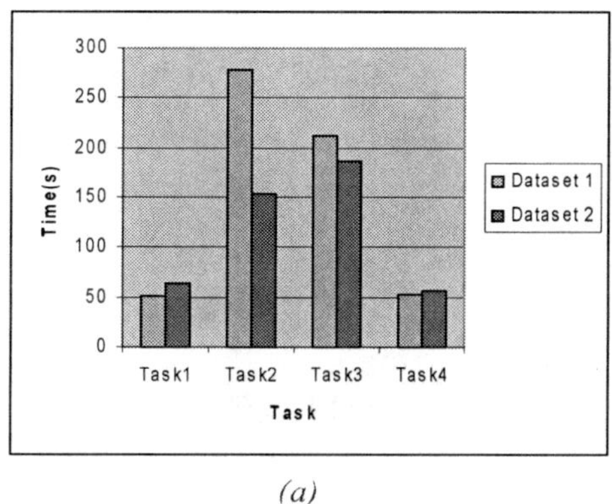

(a)

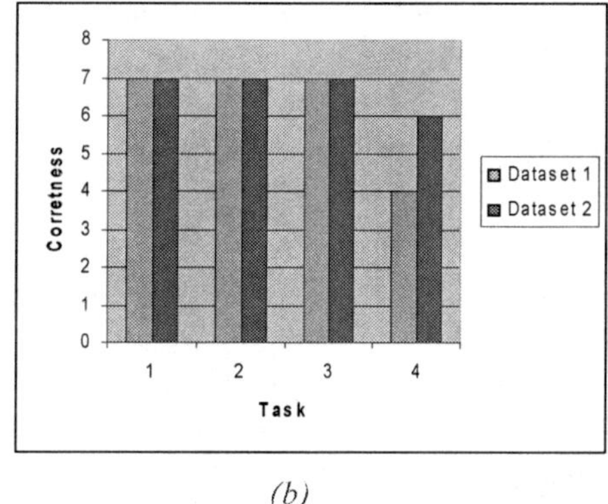

(b)

Conclusion and Future Direction

Visualization techniques have been widely researched and integrated into many applications involving data analysis tasks, including data mining, in order to increase human abilities to understand data and extract hidden patterns from large data sets. However, currently association-rule mining algorithms have some shortcomings. Most of these algorithms usually mine a large number of association rules and some of these rules are not practically interesting. Moreover, visualization techniques for displaying data sets or mining results have problems of screen clutter and occlusion.

We have introduced a novel visualization technique for large multidimensional data sets. This visualization technique has overcome the problems of screen clutter and occlusion, which hinder the extraction of useful information in visualizing huge amounts of data sets. This visualization technique has been integrated and modified to use in a mining process of market-basket association rules, so that users can obtain visual feedback and flexibly apply their knowledge and guidance in the mining process. Furthermore, the integration of both visualization and mining processes help users to understand and gain insight into their data. We presented the three main steps of our model in visual mining of market basket association rules and the design of interactive techniques satisfying minimum requirements for human computer interaction, including an evaluation of usability. In addition, we plan to improve our system tool by integrating the automatic generation of all possible association rules from the frequent item set of interest and also by adding a new technique of visualizing mined association rules.

References

Agrawal, R., & Imielinski, T. (1993). Mining association rules between sets of items in large databases. In P. Buneman & S. Jajodia (Eds.), *Proceedings of the 1993 ACM SIGMOD International Conference on Management of Data,* Washington, DC (pp. 207-216). New York: ACM.

Agrawal, R., & Srikant, R. (1994). Fast algorithms for mining association rules in large databases. In J. B. Bocca, M. Jarke, & C. Zaniolo, C. (Eds.), *Proceedings of the Twentieth International Conference on Very Large Data Bases* (pp. 487-499). San Francisco: Morgan Kaufmann.

Ankerst, M., Elsen, C., Ester, M., & Kriegel, H.-P. (1999). Visual classification: An interactive approach to decision tree construction. In *Proceedings of the Fifth International Conference on Knowledge Discovery and Data Mining (KDD'99),* San Diego, CA (pp. 392-396). New York: ACM.

Ankerst, M., Ester, M., & Kreigel, H.-P. (2000). Towards an effective cooperation of the user and the computer for classification. *Proceedings of the Sixth ACM SIGKDD International Conference on Knowledge Discovery and Data Mining,* Boston (pp. 179-188). New York: ACM.

Beshers, C., & Feiner, S. (1993). AutoVisual: Rule-based design of interactive multivariate visualizations. *Computer Graphics and Applications*, *13*(4), 41-49.

Chakravarthy, S., & Zhang, H. (2003). Visualization of association rules over relational DBMSs. In *Proceedings of the 2003 ACM Symposium on Applied Computing,* Melbourne, FL (pp. 922-926). New York: ACM.

Chernoff, H. (1973). The use of faces to represent points in k-dimensional space graphically. *Journal of the American Statistical Association*, *68*, 361-368.

Cleveland, W. S. (1993). *Visualizing data.* Summit, NJ: Hobart Press Summit.

Fayyad, U., Grinstein, G. G., & Wierse, A. (2002). *Information visualization in data mining and knowledge discovery.* San Francisco: Morgan Kaufmann.

Fayyad, U., Piatetsky-Shapiro, G., & Smyth, P. (1996). From data mining to knowledge discovery in databases. *AI Magazine*, *17*, 37-54.

Foley, J. D., Dam, A. von, Feiner, S. K., & Hughes, J. F. (1997). *Computer graphics: Principles and practice in C* (2nd ed.). Addison Wesley.

Han, J., & Kamber, M. (2001). *Data mining concepts and techniques*. San Francisco: Morgan Kaufmann.

Hofmann, H., Siebes, A. P. J. M., & Wilhelm, A. F. X. (2000). Visualizing association rules with interactive mosaic plots. In R. Ramakrishnan, S. Stolfo, R. Bayardo, & I. Parsa (Eds.), *Proceedings of the Sixth ACM SIGKDD International Conference on Knowledge Discovery and Data Mining,* Boston (pp. 227-235). New York: ACM.

Inselberg, A., & Dimsdale, B. (1987). Parallel coordinates for visualizing multi-dimensional geometry. In T. L. Kunii (Ed.), *CG International '87 on Computer Graphics 1987* (pp. 25-44). New York: Springer-Verlag.

Kandogan, E. (2001). Visualizing multi-dimensional clusters, trends, and outliers using star coordinates. In *Proceedings of the Seventh ACM SIGKDD International Conference on Knowledge Discovery and Data Mining,* San Francisco (pp. 107-116). New York: ACM.

Keim, D. A. (1996). Databases and visualization. *Tutorial, Proceedings of ACM SIGMOD International Conference on Management of Data (SIGMOD'96),* Montreal, Canada (p. 543).

Keim, D. A. (2000). Designing pixel-oriented visualization techniques: Theory and applications. *IEEE Transactions on Visualization and Computer Graphics*, *6*(1), 59-78.

Keim, D. A., Hao, M. C., & Dayal, U. (2002). Hierarchical pixel bar charts. *IEEE Transactions on Visualization and Computer Graphics*, *8*(3), 255-269.

Keim, D. A., & Kriegel, H.-P. (1994). VisDB: database exploration using multidimensional visualization. *Computer Graphics and Applications*, *14*(5), 40-49.

Marghescu, D., & Rajanen, M. J. (2005). Assessing the use of the som technique in data mining. In M. H. Hamza (Ed.), *Proceeding of the Twenty-Third IASTED International Multi-Conference Databases and Applications,* Innsbruck, Austria (pp. 181-186). Calgary, Canada: Acta.

Mihalisin, T., Timlin, J., & Schwegler, J. (1991a). Visualization and analysis of multivariate data: A technique for all fields. In *Proceedings of the IEEE Conference on Visualization '91* (pp. 171-178,421). Los Alamitos, CA: IEEE Computer Society.

Mihalisin, T., Timlin, J., & Schwegler, J. (1991b). Visualizing multivariate functions, data, and distributions. *Computer Graphics and Applications*, *11*(3), 28-35.

Ong, K.-H., Ong, K.-L., Ng, W.-K., & Lim, E.-P. (2002). CrystalClear: Active visualization of association rules. In *International Workshop on Active Mining (AM-2002), in conjunction with IEEE International Conference On Data Mining,* Maebashi City, Japan.

Pickett, R. M., & Grinstein, G. G. (1988). Iconographic displays for visualizing multidimensional data. In *Proceedings of the 1988 IEEE International Conference on Systems, Man, and Cybernetics, 1988,* University of Lowell (pp. 514-519).

Ramana, R., & Card, S. K. (1994). The table lens: Merging graphical and symbolic representations in an interactive focus+context visualization for tabular information. In B. Adelson, S. Dumais, & J. Olson (Eds.), *Proceedings of the SIGCHI Conference on Human Factors in Computing Systems,* Boston (pp. 318-322). New York: ACM.

Savasere, A., Omiecinski, E., & Navathe, S. B. (1995). An efficient algorithm for mining association rules in large databases. In U. Dayal, P. M. D. Gray, & S. Nishio (Eds.), *Proceedings of the Twenty-First International Conference on Very Large Data Bases* (pp. 432-444). San Francisco: Morgan Kaufmann.

SGI. (n.d.). Silicon Graphics Computer Systems, SGI MineSet. Retrieved December 30, 2003, from http://www.sgi.com/software/mineset.html

Srikant, R., & Agrawal, R. (1995). Mining generalized association rules. In U. Dayal, P. M. D. Gray, & S. Nishio (Eds.), *Proceedings of the Twenty-First International Conference on Very Large Databases,* Zurich, Switzerland (pp. 407-419). San Francisco: Morgan Kaufmann.

Stasko, J. (2000). An evaluation of space-filling information visualizations for depicting hierarchical structures. *International Journal of Human-Computer Studies, 53*(5), 663-694.

Stolte, C., Tang, D., & Hanrahan, P. (2002). Polaris: A system for query, analysis, and visualization of multidimensional relational databases. *IEEE Transactions on Visualization and Computer Graphics, 8*(1), 52-65.

Techapichetvanich, K., & Datta, A. (2004). Visual mining of market basket association rules. In A. Laganà et al. (Eds.), *Proceedings of the 2004 International Conference on Computational Science and its Applications* (pp. 479-488). Berlin: Springer-Verlag.

Techapichetvanich, K., Datta, A., & Owens, R. (2004). HDDV: Hierarchical dynamic dimensional visualization for multidimensional data. In M. H. Hamza (Ed.), *Proceedings of IASTED International Conference on Databases and Applications (DBA 2004),* Innsbruck, Austria (pp. 157-162). Calgary, Canada: Acta.

Wang, K., Jiang, Y., & Lakshmanan, L. V. S. (2003). Mining unexpected rules by pushing user dynamics. In *Proceedings of the Ninth ACM SIGKDD International Conference on Knowledge Discovery and Data Mining* (pp. 246-255). New York: ACM.

Wong, P. C., Whitney, P., & Thomas, J. (1999). Visualizing association rules for text mining. In *Proceedings of the 1999 IEEE Symposium on Information Visualization* (pp. 120-123,152). Washington, DC: IEEE Computer Society.

Chapter XII

Analytical Customer Requirement Analysis Based on Data Mining

Jianxin (Roger) Jiao, Nanyang Technological University, Singapore

Yiyang Zhang, Nanyang Technological University, Singapore

Martin Helander, Nanyang Technological University, Singapore

Abstract

This chapter applies data-mining techniques to help manufacturing companies analyze their customers' requirements. Customer requirement analysis has been well recognized as one of the principal factors in product development for achieving success in the marketplace. Due to the difficulties inherent in the customer requirement analysis process, reusing knowledge from historical data suggests itself as a natural technique to facilitate the handling of requirement information and the tradeoffs among many customers, marketing and engineering concerns. This chapter proposes to apply data-mining techniques to infer the latent information from historical data and thereby improve the customer requirement analysis process.

Introduction

Over the years, the philosophy has developed that the customer is the key to the success of product development. The ability to address customer wants and needs by rapidly bringing new and different high quality products to market has been viewed as a major source of competitive advantage for the business organizations in the global market over the past decade (Womack, Jones, & Roos, 1990). For example, the ability to analyze customers' requirements has made Toyota a world-class exemplar among the global automotive producers.

One of the key tasks for a business organization is the production operation. The main challenge facing a business organization is how to provide the right products to meet the consumers' requirements. As shown in Figure 1, the product development process involves information processing in four distinct domains according to the domain framework in axiomatic design (Suh, 2001). Product development in general encompasses three consecutive stages: (1) product definition — mapping of customer needs (CNs) in the customer domain to functional requirements (FRs) in the functional domain; (2) product design — mapping of FRs in the functional domain to design parameters (DPs) in the physical domain; and (3) process design — mapping of DPs in the physical domain to process variables (PVs) in the process domain. Within the context of mass customization, product design and process design are embodied in the respective product and process platforms. Customer requirement analysis is embodied in the product definition phase, characterized by mapping the customer requirements to product functional specifications, which in turn becomes the input to the downstream design activities, and is propagated to product and process platforms in a coherent fashion. The practice of translating customer requirements into products by simultaneously designing the product and manufacturing processes is a notable characteristic of companies that seek a competitive edge (Clark & Fujimoto, 1991). Thus, subjective customer requirements are translated into objective specifications from which engineers can start to design products. Timely, complete and accurate information is important for business organizations to meet diverse customer requirements in today's competitive global market (Pugh, 1991).

Consistent with the product development process, customer requirement analysis involves a tedious elaboration process conducted among customers, marketing practitioners, and designers. First, the customer requirements are normally qualitative and tend to be imprecise and ambiguous due to their linguistic origins. Second, the interrelationships (i.e., mapping) between CNs and FRs are often unclear in the early stage of design. Third, the specification of requirements results from not only the transformation of customer requirements from potential end-users, but also consideration of many engineering concerns, involving internal customers, downstream of the design team along the product realization process (Du, Jiao, & Tseng, 2003). In practice, product development teams must keep track of a myriad of requirement information derived from different perspectives of the product life-cycle, such as product technologies, manufacturability, reliability, maintainability, and environmental safety, to name but a few (Prudhomme, Zwolinski, & Brissaud, 2003).

Figure 1. Product development process

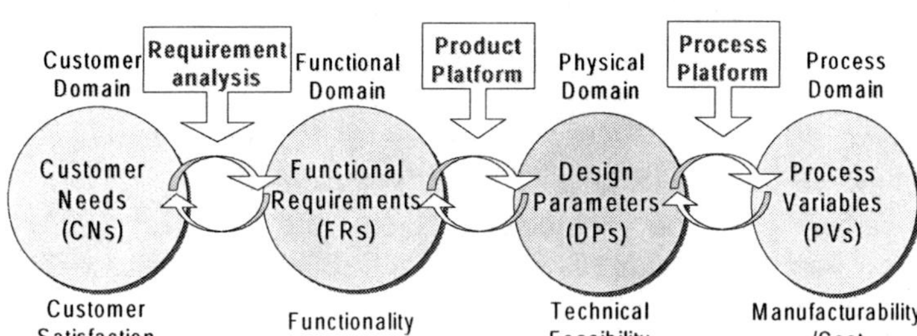

Towards this end, this chapter suggests that customer requirement analysis entails a mapping process from customer needs in the customer domain to functional requirements in the functional domain. Data-mining techniques are adopted to help customer requirement analysis, and a case study of vibration motors for mobile phones is reported.

Background Review

Approaches to defining product specifications by capturing, analyzing, understanding, and projecting customer requirements, sometimes called the Voice of the Customer (VoC), have received a significant amount of interest in recent years (McKay, de Pennington, & Baxter, 2001). A method used for transforming the VoC to product specifications was developed by Shoji, Graham, and Walden (1993), in which semantics methods, such as the Kawakita Jiro (KJ) method (i.e., affinity diagram) and multi-pickup method (MPM), were applied as the basis for discovering underlying facts from affective language. Kano, Seraku, Takahashi, and Tsuji (1984) proposed a diagram to categorize different types of customer requirements for product definition.

On this subject, market researchers have emphasized customer profiling by applying regression analysis to compare customers' characteristics and to determine their overall ranking in contributing towards profitability (Jenkins, 1995). Traditionally, market analysis techniques are adopted for investigating customers' responses to design options. For example, conjoint analysis is widely used to measure preferences for different product profiles and to build market simulation models (Green & DeSarbo, 1978). Louviere, Anderson, White, and Eagle (1990) used discrete choice experiments to predict customer choices pertaining to design options. Turksen and Willson (1993) employed fuzzy systems to interpret the linguistic meaning contained in customer preferences, as an alternative to conjoint analysis. Others have taken a qualitative approach and used focus groups to provide a reality check on the usefulness of a new product design

(LaChance-Porter, 1993). Similar techniques include one-on-one interviews and similarity-dissimilarity attribute rankings (Griffin & Hauser, 1992). While these types of methods are helpful for discovering the VoC, it is still difficult to obtain design requirement information because marketing practitioners do not know what engineers need to know. It is difficult to apply the VoC alone to achieve a synergy of marketing and engineering concerns in developing product specifications (Veryzer, 1993).

From an engineering design perspective, Hauge and Stauffer (1993) developed a taxonomy of product requirements to assist in traditional qualitative market research. To elicit knowledge from customers (ELK), a taxonomy of customer requirements is deployed as an initial concept graph structure in the methodology for question probing — a method used in the development of expert systems. While ELK aims at making customer information more useful to the designer, the taxonomy developed for ELK is too general to be a domain-independent framework (Tseng & Jiao, 1998). A key component of Quality Function Deployment (QFD) (Clausing, 1994) is the customer requirements' frame, which aids the designer's view in defining product specifications. While QFD excels in converting customer information to design requirements, it is limited as a means of actually discovering the VoC (Hauge & Stauffer, 1993). To empower QFD with market aspects, Fung and Popplewell (1995) proposed to pre-process the VoC prior to its being entered as customer attributes into the House of Quality. In this process, the VoC is categorized using an affinity diagram (KJ method). Fung, Popplewell, and Xie (1998) further adopted the Analytic Hierarchy Process (AHP) (Saaty, 1980) to analyze and prioritize customer requirements. Fung, Tang, Tu, and Wang (2002) extended their QFD-based customer requirement analysis method to a non-linear fuzzy inference model. Fukuda and Matsuura (1993) also proposed to prioritize the customer's requirements by AHP for concurrent design. Researchers at IBM have applied structured brainstorming techniques to build customer requirements into the QFD process (Byrne & Barlow, 1993). McAdams, Stone, and Wood (1999) proposed a matrix approach to the identification of relationships between product functions and customer needs.

In summary, most approaches assume product development starts from a clean sheet of paper. In practice, most new products evolve from existing products (i.e., so-called variant design). Therefore, product definition should effectively preserve the strength of product families to obtain significant cost savings in tooling, learning curves, inventory, maintenance, and so on. This demands a structured approach to product definition and to capturing a gestalt of requirement information from previous designs as well as existing product and process platforms.

Problem Description

Figure 2 illustrates the principle of customer requirement analysis based on association-rule mining. In general, customer requirements can be described as a set of features or attributes, $A \equiv \{a_1, a_2, \cdots, a_M\}$. Each feature, $a_i \mid \forall i \in [1, \cdots, M]$, may take on one out of a finite set of options, $A_i^* \equiv \{a_{i1}^*, a_{i2}^*, \cdots, a_{in_i}^*\}$. That is, $a_i =:: a_{ij}^* \mid \exists a_{ij}^* \in A_i^*$, where $j = 1, \cdots, n_i$, denotes the j-th option of a_i. Suppose all customers comprise a set, $C \equiv \{c_1, c_2, \cdots, c_S\}$, where S denotes the total number of customers. The population of customers' needs become a set, $A^* \equiv \{\overline{a_1^*}, \overline{a_2^*}, \cdots, \overline{a_S^*}\}$, which characterizes the customer domain.

In the functional domain, the functionality of each product is characterized by a set of FRs, $V \equiv \{v_1, v_2, \cdots, v_N\}$. Each FR, $v_q \mid \forall q \in [1, \cdots, N]$, possesses a few possible values, $V_q^* \equiv \{v_{q1}^*, v_{q2}^*, \cdots, v_{qn_q}^*\}$. That is, $v_q =:: v_{qr}^* \mid \exists v_{qr}^* \in V_q^*$, where $r = 1, \cdots, n_q$, denotes the r-th possible value of v_q. Suppose all existing products comprise a set, $P \equiv \{p_1, p_2, \cdots, p_T\}$, where T refers to the total number of products. The requirement specification of a particular product, $p_t \in P \mid \exists t \in [1, \cdots, T]$, can be represented as a vector of certain FR values of those FRs. All the instances of FRs (i.e., FR values) in the functional domain constitute a set, $V^* \equiv \{\overline{v_1^*}, \overline{v_2^*}, \cdots, \overline{v_T^*}\}$.

In order to take advantage of commonality in product family design, existing instances of FRs should be analyzed and clustered according to their similarity (Tseng & Jiao, 1998). The result is a few FR clusters, noted as $X = \{\chi_1, \chi_2, , \chi_L\}$. As a result, all FR instances can be represented by the mean value of these FR instances, $\mu_l \equiv [x_1^l, x_2^l, \cdots, x_N^l]$, and the variation range of these FR instances within χ_l, $\Delta_l \equiv [\delta_1^l, \delta_2^l, \cdots, \delta_N^l]$.

Figure 2. Requirement analysis based on association rule mining

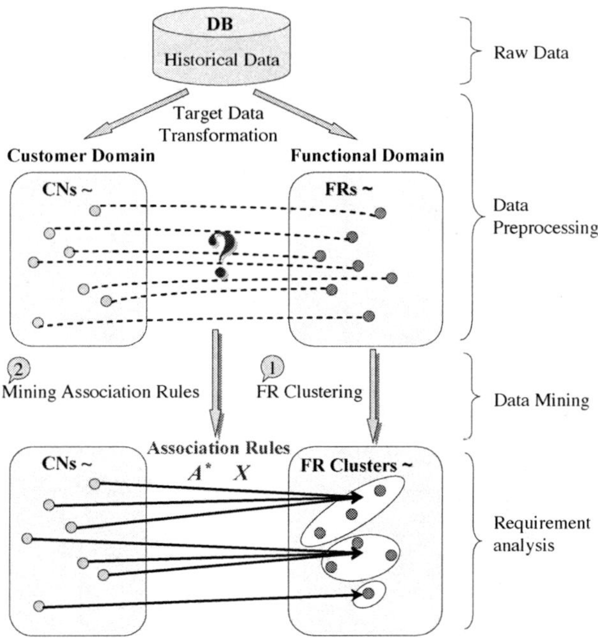

Subsequently, these identified FR clusters become the functional specification of product offerings that can be derived from common product platforms and are supposed to be able to accommodate all the customer needs (Du, Jiao, & Tseng, 2001). At this stage, data-mining techniques can be applied to figure out the mapping relationship between CNs and FR clusters, noted as $A^* \Rightarrow X$, where an association rule, $\Rightarrow$, indicates an inference from the precedent (A^*) to the consequence (X). As a result, a product portfolio specification, Λ, consists of two elements: FR clusters and mappings from CNs to FR clusters, namely, $\Lambda = \langle X, \Rightarrow \rangle$.

Arms Architecture and Implementation

Knowledge discovery for CN-FR mapping mechanisms is an interactive and iterative process. Based on association-rule mining, an inference system can be constructed for effective customer requirement analysis. Figure 3 illustrates the architecture of such an association-rule mining system (ARMS). The system involves four consecutive stages interacting to achieve the goals, namely: data pre-processing, FR clustering, association-rule mining, and rule evaluation and presentation. First, historical data are selected and transformed to proper target data sets, which are further analyzed and pre-processed for

Figure 3. ARMS architecture

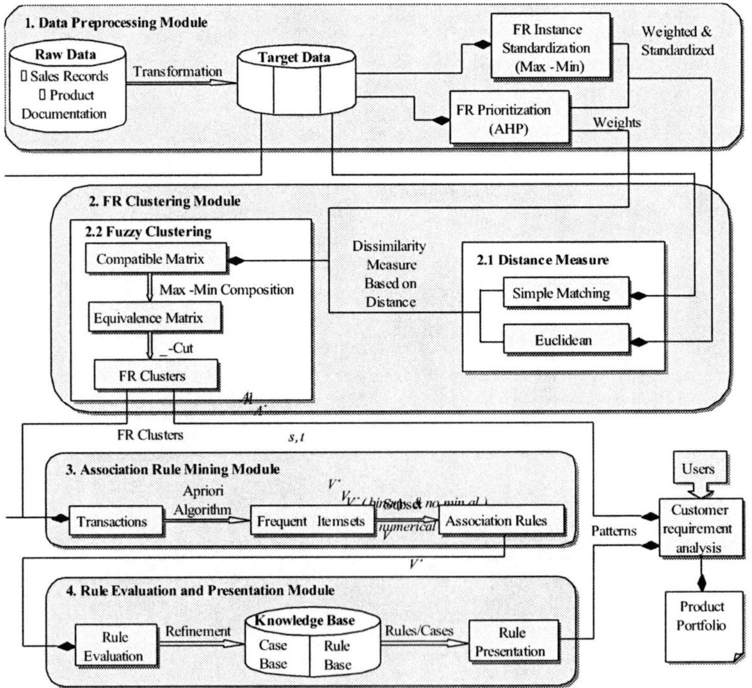

Figure 4. Entity relationships of target data sets

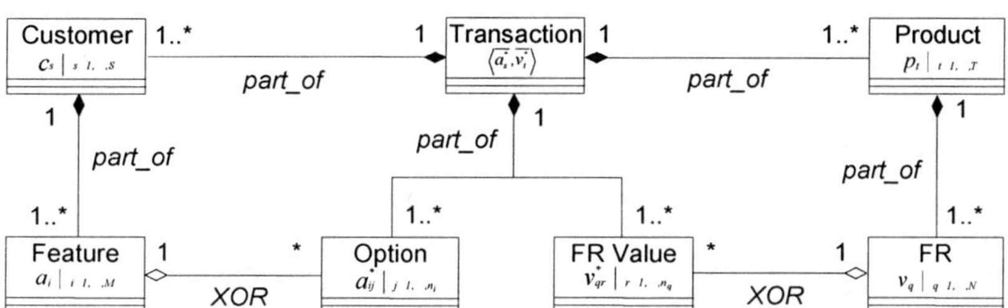

subsequent mining procedures. The data-mining procedure then starts to search for interesting patterns using the clustering module and rule-mining module. After the mining of association rules, the work of rule evaluation is performed to eliminate any weak rules under the initial criteria predefined by the system. The useful rules are stored with different presentation styles in the knowledge base that may be in the forms of case bases, rule bases, and others. Equipped with such knowledge about the patterns of CNs, FRs and their mappings, the system can provide better recommendations and high-degree predictions to improve customer requirement analysis.

Data Pre-Processing Module

Before proceeding to rule mining of data sets, raw data must be pre-processed in order to be useful for knowledge discovery. Three tasks are involved at this stage:

1. **Target data transformation:** Within the ARMS, sales records and product documentation are transformed into transaction data (TID). Transaction data consists of customer records (C) and their ordered products (P). Each customer is described by his or her choices of certain options (A^*) for some functional features (A). The product ordered by this customer is described by specific values (V^*) of related FRs (V). The results of CN-FR mappings, that is, $\langle \overline{a_s^*}, \overline{v_t^*} \rangle$, are embodied in the transaction records ($\langle C, P \rangle$). Figure 4 shows the entity relationships among these target data sets.
2. **Prioritization of FR variables:** The specification of FRs involves multiple variables. These FR variables contribute to the overall functionality of a product differently — some may play more roles than others. Hence, FR variables should be prioritized to differentiate their different effects, in particular those important ones. For the ARMS, the AHP (Saaty, 1980) is adopted for the prioritization of FR variables, owing to its advantages in maintaining consistency among a large number of variables through pair-wise comparisons.

3. **Standardization of FR values:** Prior to clustering analysis of FR instances, all V^* data need to be transformed into standard forms because FR variables may involve different metrics and ranges of values. To avoid dependence on the choice of different metrics or dominance of certain variables over others, those FR instances that are of numerical type should be standardized to become dimensionless. The ARMS adopts the max-min normalization method.

FR Clustering Module

Within the ARMS, FR clustering includes two steps, namely distance measure and fuzzy clustering.

1. **Distance measure.**

In general, each FR instance may involve three types of FR variables: numerical, binary, and nominal FRs. The distance between any two FR instances indicates the dissimilarity between them and thus is measured as a composite distance of three distance components corresponding to these three types of FR variables.

Numerical FRs — The ARMS employs the weighted Euclidean distance. It is computed as the following:

$$d_{numerical}\left(\overline{v_i^*},\overline{v_j^*}\right)=\sqrt{\sum_{q=1}^{Q}\left(w_q\left(N\_v_{qi}^*-N\_v_{qj}^*\right)\right)^2}, \tag{1}$$

where $d_{numerical}\left(\overline{v_i^*},\overline{v_j^*}\right)$ indicates the numerical distance between two FR instances, $\overline{v_i^*}$ and $\overline{v_j^*}$, w_q is the relative importance of the q-th numerical FR variable, Q represents the total number of numerical FR variables among the total size-N FR variables ($Q \le N$), and $N\_v_{qi}^*$ and $N\_v_{qj}^*$ denote the normalized values of original v_{qi}^* and v_{qj}^*.

Binary FRs — A binary variable assumes only two states: 0 or 1, where 0 means the variable is absent and 1 means it is present. The ARMS uses a well-accepted coefficient for assessing the distance between symmetric binary variables, called the simple matching coefficient (Han & Kamber, 2001). It is calculated as the following:

$$d_{binary}\left(\overline{v_i^*}, \overline{v_j^*}\right) = \frac{\alpha_2 + \alpha_3}{\alpha_1 + \alpha_2 + \alpha_3 + \alpha_4}, \qquad (2)$$

where $d_{binary}\left(\overline{v_i^*}, \overline{v_j^*}\right)$ indicates the binary distance between two FR instances, $\overline{v_i^*}$ and $\overline{v_j^*}$, α_1 is the total number of binary FR variables in V that equal to 1 for both $\overline{v_i^*}$ and $\overline{v_j^*}$, α_2 is the total number of binary FR variables that equal to 1 for $\overline{v_i^*}$ but 0 for $\overline{v_j^*}$, α_3 is the total number of binary FR variables that equal to 0 for $\overline{v_i^*}$ but 1 for $\overline{v_j^*}$, and α_4 is the total number of binary FR variables that equal to 0 for both $\overline{v_i^*}$ and $\overline{v_j^*}$.

Nominal FRs — A nominal variable can be regarded as a generalization of a binary variable in that it can take on more than two states. This type of variables cannot be expressed by numerical values but by qualitative expressions with more than one option. Therefore, the simple matching coefficient can also be used here to measure the nominal distance between two FR instances containing nominal FR variables (Han & Kamber, 2001):

$$d_{nominal}\left(\overline{v_i^*}, \overline{v_j^*}\right) = \frac{\beta - \gamma}{\beta}, \qquad (3)$$

where $d_{nomical}\left(\overline{v_i^*}, \overline{v_j^*}\right)$ indicates the nominal distance between two FR instances, $\overline{v_i^*}$ and $\overline{v_j^*}$, γ means the total number of nominal FR variables in V that assume the same states for $\overline{v_i^*}$ and $\overline{v_j^*}$, and β is the total number of nominal variables among total size-N FR variables ($\beta \leq N$).

A composite distance can thus be obtained by the weighted sum:

$$d\left(\overline{v_i^*}, \overline{v_j^*}\right) = W_{numerical} d_{numerical}\left(\overline{v_i^*}, \overline{v_j^*}\right) + W_{binary} d_{binary}\left(\overline{v_i^*}, \overline{v_j^*}\right) + W_{nominal} d_{nominal}\left(\overline{v_i^*}, \overline{v_j^*}\right), \qquad (4)$$

$$\sum \left(W_{numerical} + W_{binary} + W_{nominal}\right) = 1, \qquad (5)$$

where $W_{numerical}$, W_{binary} and $W_{nominal}$ refer to the relative importance of numerical, binary and nominal distances, respectively.

2. **Fuzzy clustering.**

The first step of fuzzy clustering is to define a fuzzy compatible relation, R, for a given set of FR instances, $V^* = \left\{\overline{v_1^*}, \overline{v_2^*}, \cdots, \overline{v_T^*}\right\}$. The R is constructed in a matrix form, that is,

$R = \left[\rho\left(\overline{v_i^*}, \overline{v_j^*}\right)\right]_{T\times T} \mid \forall\left(\overline{v_i^*}, \overline{v_j^*}\right) \in V^* \times V^*$, where $\left(\overline{v_i^*}, \overline{v_j^*}\right)$ suggests pair-wise relationships among FR instances. Within the context of FR clustering, R is called the compatible matrix. A matrix element $\rho\left(\overline{v_i^*}, \overline{v_j^*}\right)$ indicates the similarity grade between any two FR instances, $\overline{v_i^*}$ and $\overline{v_j^*}$. As a measure of similarity, it can be derived from the aforementioned dissimilarity measure that is determined by the distance between FR instances. The second step is to construct a fuzzy equivalence relation for V^* with transitive closure of the fuzzy compatible relation defined above. The fuzzy compatible matrix R is a fuzzy equivalence matrix if and only if the transitive condition can be met, that is,

$$\rho\left(\overline{v_i^*}, \overline{v_j^*}\right) \geq \max\left\{\min\left\{\rho\left(\overline{v_i^*}, \overline{v_z^*}\right), \rho\left(\overline{v_z^*}, \overline{v_j^*}\right)\right\} \mid \forall \overline{v_i^*}, \overline{v_z^*}, \overline{v_j^*} \in V^*\right\}. \quad (6)$$

The third step is to determine λ-cut of the equivalence matrix. The λ-cut is a crisp set, R_λ, that contains all the elements of the universe, V^*, such that the similarity grade of R is no less than λ. The ARMS applies a netting method (Yang & Gao, 1996) to identify partitions of FR instances with respect to a given equivalence matrix.

Association Rule Mining Module

FR clustering can separate data items into clusters of items but cannot explain the clustering results specifically. Knowledge is usually represented in the form of rules. Therefore, the approach described in this chapter employs association rules to explain the meaning of each FR cluster as well as the mapping of CNs to each cluster.

In the ARMS scenario, rule mining involves two different item sets, that is, $Z \subseteq A^*$ and $Y \subseteq V^*$, corresponding to the customer and functional domains, respectively. Based on the clustered FR instances, association rules reporting the mappings between individual A^* and V^* turn out to be the association-rules mapping A^* to FR clusters, X, that is, $A^* \Rightarrow X$. Therefore, the ARMS's transaction data comprises these two item sets, that is, $DB \sim \langle A^*, X\rangle$, where $A^* = \left\{a_s^* \mid \forall s = 1, \cdots, S\right\}$ and $X = \left\{\chi_l \mid \forall l = 1, \cdots, L\right\}$. As a result, the general form of an association rule in the ARMS is given as the following:

$$\alpha_1 \wedge \alpha_2 \cdots \wedge \alpha_e \cdots \wedge \alpha_E \Rightarrow \beta_1 \wedge \beta_2 \cdots \wedge \beta_f \cdots \wedge \beta_F \quad [Support = s\%; Confidence = c\%], \quad (7)$$

where $\exists \alpha_e \in \left\{a_{ij}^*\right\}_{\sum_{i=1}^{M} m_i} \mid \forall e = 1, \cdots, E \leq M$, $\exists \beta_f \in \left\{\left(x_q^l, \delta_q^l\right)\right\}_{N\times L} \mid \forall f = 1, \cdots, F \leq N$, and $s\%$ and $c\%$ refer to the support and confidence levels for this rule, respectively. They are calculated based on the following:

$$s\% = \frac{count(\alpha_1 \wedge \alpha_2 \cdots \wedge \alpha_E \wedge \beta_1 \wedge \beta_2 \cdots \wedge \beta_F)}{count(DB)} \times 100\%, \quad (8)$$

$$c\% = \frac{count(\alpha_1 \wedge \alpha_2 \cdots \wedge \alpha_E \wedge \beta_1 \wedge \beta_2 \cdots \wedge \beta_F)}{count(\alpha_1 \wedge \alpha_2 \cdots \wedge \alpha_E)} \times 100\%, \quad (9)$$

where $count(\alpha_1 \wedge \alpha_2 \cdots \wedge \alpha_E \wedge \beta_1 \wedge \beta_2 \cdots \wedge \beta_F)$ is the number of transaction records in *DB* containing all items α_1, α_2,..., and α_E as well as β_1, β_2,..., and β_F, *count*(*DB*) is the total number of data records contained in *DB*, and $count(\alpha_1 \wedge \alpha_2 \cdots \wedge \alpha_E)$ is the number of transaction records in *DB* containing all items α_1, α_2,..., and α_E. The association rule in Equation (7) means that the data occurrence of α_1, α_2,..., and α_E will most likely (at a *s%*-support and with a *c%*- confidence) associate with the data occurrence of β_1, β_2,..., and β_F.

Rule Evaluation and Presentation Module

Based on all the association rules created, the evaluation and presentation module comes into play to measure the performance of the inference system. The difficulty in association-rule mining measurement arises from the need for determining appropriate thresholds for the support and confidence levels. If the support and confidence thresholds are planned with low values, useful information may be overwhelmed by excessive rules. Alternatively, certain relationship patterns that are of interest may be ignored if the support and confidence criteria are specified too strictly. Efficient rules should cover the

Table 1. List of CNs

Feature		Option		
$a_i \mid \forall i = 1,\cdots,M$	Description	$a^*_{ij} \mid \forall j = 1,\cdots,n_i$	Code	Description
a_1	Feel of vibration	a^*_{11}	A11	Feel the vibration very strongly
		a^*_{12}	A12	Alarmed by vibration without vibrating suddenly
		a^*_{13}	A13	Sensitive to the vibration
a_2	Price	a^*_{21}	A21	Buy an expensive mobile phone with desire for a long time use
		a^*_{22}	A22	Catch up the mobile phone style occasionally at a low price
		a^*_{23}	A23	Try latest fashion of mobile phones at a moderate price
a_3	Size	a^*_{31}	A31	Portable
		a^*_{32}	A32	Comfortable to hold
		a^*_{33}	A33	Not easy to lose
a_4	Volume of sound	a^*_{41}	A41	Little noise
		a^*_{42}	A42	Alarmed independent of vibration
		a^*_{43}	A43	Alarmed by both vibration and sound
a_5	Material	a^*_{51}	A51	Green material for environment friendliness
a_6	Weight	a^*_{61}	A61	As light as possible

Table 2. List of FRs

FR			FR Value		
$v_q \mid \forall q = 1,\cdots,N$	Description	Type	$v^*_{qr} \mid \forall r = 1,\cdots,n_q$	Code	Description
v_1	Current	Numerical	v^*_{11}	V11	100 mA
			v^*_{12}	V12	80 mA
			v^*_{13}	V13	60 mA
v_2	Pbfree	Binary	v^*_{21}	V21	1 (Yes)
			v^*_{22}	V22	0 (No)
v_3	Length	Numerical	v^*_{31}	V31	8 mm
			v^*_{32}	V32	12 mm
			v^*_{33}	V33	10 mm
v_4	Diameter	Numerical	v^*_{41}	V41	5 mm
			v^*_{42}	V42	4 mm
			v^*_{43}	V43	6 mm
v_5	Coating	Nominal	v^*_{51}	V51	Au
			v^*_{52}	V52	Alloy
			v^*_{53}	V53	None
v_6	Angle	Numerical	v^*_{61}	V61	40°
			v^*_{62}	V62	55°
v_7	Strength	Numerical	v^*_{71}	V71	7 Kg
			v^*_{72}	V72	4 Kg
v_8	Weight	Numerical	v^*_{81}	V81	2 g
			v^*_{82}	V82	3 g
v_9	Hardness	Numerical	v^*_{91}	V91	40 HB
			v^*_{92}	V92	70 HB

Table 3. Transaction database

Record (TID)	CNs ($\overline{a^*_s} \mid \forall s = 1,\cdots,S$)	FRs ($\overline{v^*_t} \mid \forall t = 1,\cdots,T$)
T001	A11, A21, A31, A43, A51, A61	V11, V21, V31, V42, V53, V62, V71, V82, V92
T002	A11, A21, A43, A51	V11, V21, V31, V41, V51, V61, V71, V81, V92
T003	A12, A22, A33, A61	V12, V21, V33, V43, V51, V61, V72, V82, V91
…	…	…
T028	A13, A22, A33, A41, A61	V13, V22, V31, V42, V52, V61, V72, V81, V91
T029	A11, A21, A31, A43, A51, A61	V12, V22, V33, V43, V52, V62, V72, V81, V92
T030	A12, A22, A33, A42, A61	V11, V22, V33, V42, V53, V61, V72, V82, V91

right product portfolio which creates the maximal profitability. In this regard, we introduce a performance measure of association-rule mining, based on the ratio of utility and the variable cost, as follows:

$$\Psi^{AR} = \sum_{i=1}^{I} \sum_{j=1}^{J} \frac{U_{ij}}{C_j^V}, \tag{10}$$

Figure 5. Result of distance measures for numerical FR instances

0																													
.076	0																												
.534	.557	0																											
.332	.272	.2	0																										
.194	.285	.271	.315	0																									
.485	.508	.2	.24	.309	0																								
0	.076	.534	.332	.194	.485	0																							
.121	.113	.58	.453	.398	.532	.12	0																						
.453	.476	.08	.121	.352	.118	.453	.5	0																					
.194	.285	.271	.154	.161	.309	.194	.398	.19	0																				
.157	.08	.476	.191	.366	.588	.157	.193	.4	.2	0																			
.16	.235	.374	.492	.192	.487	.159	.122	.455	.353	.316	0																		
.39	.397	.076	.193	.279	.275	.39	.352	.157	.279	.316	.23	0																	
.158	.234	.375	.335	.191	.488	.158	.279	.456	.352	.315	.156	.23	0																
.157	.081	.476	.191	.366	.588	.157	.193	.396	.2	0	.316	.316	.315	0															
.149	.157	.316	.115	.2	.192	.149	.27	.235	.2	.238	.309	.24	.152	.238	0														
.341	.348	.275	.231	.316	.076	.341	.304	.194	.316	.429	.342	.2	.343	.43	.116	0													
.265	.272	.35	.31	.079	.313	.265	.385	.431	.24	.353	.263	.274	.262	.353	.196	.237	0												
.277	.352	.257	.217	.234	.456	.276	.397	.338	.234	.272	.274	.113	.118	.272	.195	.312	.23	0											
.27	.361	.195	.235	.237	.072	.27	.317	.115	.237	.442	.272	.2	.273	.442	.12	.08	.316	.316	0										
.348	.508	.335	.375	.309	.137	.348	.395	.255	.309	.588	.27	.275	.35	.588	.192	.076	.313	.319	.07	0									
.411	.35	.122	.079	.394	.16	.411	.374	.042	.232	.27	.413	.115	.414	.27	.913	.152	.389	.296	.157	.297	0								
.23	.238	.235	.195	.12	.273	.23	.35	.316	.28	.318	.228	.16	.072	.318	.08	.197	.115	.115	.2	.273	.274	0							
.237	.161	.395	.272	.285	.669	.237	.274	.476	.285	.08	.235	.236	.234	.08	.318	.509	.272	.191	.522	.669	.35	..238	0						
.446	.385	.238	.194	.353	.2	.446	.409	.157	.192	.305	.448	.23	.604	.305	.309	.192	.274	.411	.272	.337	.115	.389	.385	0					
.238	.397	.296	.179	.273	.334	.238	.442	.215	.112	.317	.4	.235	.24	.371	.157	.273	.352	.122	.193	.197	.257	.237	.397	.372	0				
.445	.384	.239	.2	.191	.2	.445	.566	.319	.352	.465	.443	.23	.287	.465	.152	.193	.112	.255	.273	.338	.277	.07	.384	.318	.377	0			
.273	.197	.36	.394	.246	.397	.273	.152	.44	.407	.277	.114	.2	.27	.277	.279	.238	.158	.313	.326	.397	.315	.198	.197	.275	.519	.27	0		
.296	.235	.238	.355	.192	.35	.296	.259	.318	.353	.316	.137	.23	.293	.316	.309	.342	.263	.411	.272	.487	.276	.228	.235	.311	.534	.306	.114	0	
.252	.191	.282	.081	.234	.158	.252	.372	.2	.234	.272	.411	.274	.255	.272	.03	.15	.23	.298	.155	.295	.159	.115	.352	.274	.259	.118	.313	.274	0 $_{30\ 30}$

where the resulted product portfolio comprises $j = 1, \cdots, J$ products that are offered to meet a target market segment with $j = 1, \cdots, I$ customers, U_{ij} denotes the utility of the i-th customer with respect to the j-th product, and C_j^V is the related variable cost of producing this product variant.

Case Study

The potential of ARMS has been tested in an electronics company that produces a large variety of vibration motors for major world-leading mobile phone manufacturers. The data have been collected from market surveys and analysed based on natural language processing. The customers' requirements are summarized in Table 1. Those CNs listed in Table 1 provide the ground for the diverse requirements of different mobile phone users. Based on existing product documentation and consultation with design engineers, we know that the functional specification of vibration motors is described by a set of FRs and their values, as shown in Table 2.

Based on the sales records, target data arc identified and organized into a transaction database, as shown in Table 3. For illustrative simplicity, only 30 out of hundreds of transaction records are used in the case study here. As shown in Table 3, each customer order indicates the customer's choice of certain feature options of mobile phones. Corresponding to the 30 customers (end-users of mobile phones), there are 30 vibration motors provided, whose requirement information are described as particular instances of the FR vector.

Figure 6. Result of distance measures for binary FR instances

$$
\begin{bmatrix}
0 \\
0 & 0 \\
0 & 0 & 0 \\
0 & 0 & 0 & 0 \\
1 & 1 & 1 & 1 & 0 \\
0 & 0 & 0 & 0 & 1 & 0 \\
1 & 1 & 1 & 1 & 0 & 1 & 0 \\
0 & 0 & 0 & 0 & 1 & 0 & 1 & 0 \\
0 & 0 & 0 & 0 & 1 & 0 & 1 & 0 & 0 \\
0 & 0 & 0 & 0 & 1 & 0 & 1 & 0 & 0 & 0 \\
1 & 1 & 1 & 1 & 0 & 1 & 0 & 1 & 1 & 1 & 0 \\
0 & 0 & 0 & 0 & 1 & 0 & 1 & 0 & 0 & 0 & 1 & 0 \\
0 & 0 & 0 & 0 & 1 & 0 & 1 & 0 & 0 & 0 & 1 & 0 & 0 \\
0 & 0 & 0 & 0 & 1 & 0 & 1 & 0 & 0 & 0 & 1 & 0 & 0 & 0 \\
1 & 1 & 1 & 1 & 0 & 1 & 0 & 1 & 1 & 1 & 0 & 1 & 1 & 1 & 0 \\
0 & 0 & 0 & 0 & 1 & 0 & 1 & 0 & 0 & 0 & 1 & 0 & 0 & 0 & 1 & 0 \\
0 & 0 & 0 & 0 & 1 & 0 & 1 & 0 & 0 & 0 & 1 & 0 & 0 & 0 & 1 & 0 & 0 \\
1 & 1 & 1 & 1 & 0 & 1 & 0 & 1 & 1 & 1 & 0 & 1 & 1 & 1 & 0 & 1 & 1 & 0 \\
0 & 0 & 0 & 0 & 1 & 0 & 1 & 0 & 0 & 0 & 1 & 0 & 0 & 0 & 1 & 0 & 0 & 1 & 0 \\
0 & 0 & 0 & 0 & 1 & 0 & 1 & 0 & 0 & 0 & 1 & 0 & 0 & 0 & 1 & 0 & 0 & 1 & 0 & 0 \\
0 & 0 & 0 & 0 & 1 & 0 & 1 & 0 & 0 & 0 & 1 & 0 & 0 & 0 & 1 & 0 & 0 & 1 & 0 & 0 & 0 \\
0 & 0 & 0 & 0 & 1 & 0 & 1 & 0 & 0 & 0 & 1 & 0 & 0 & 0 & 1 & 0 & 0 & 1 & 0 & 0 & 0 & 0 \\
0 & 0 & 0 & 0 & 1 & 0 & 1 & 0 & 0 & 0 & 1 & 0 & 0 & 0 & 1 & 0 & 0 & 1 & 0 & 0 & 0 & 0 & 0 \\
0 & 0 & 0 & 0 & 1 & 0 & 1 & 0 & 0 & 0 & 1 & 0 & 0 & 0 & 1 & 0 & 0 & 1 & 0 & 0 & 0 & 0 & 0 & 0 \\
1 & 1 & 1 & 1 & 0 & 1 & 0 & 1 & 1 & 1 & 0 & 1 & 1 & 1 & 0 & 1 & 1 & 0 & 1 & 1 & 1 & 1 & 1 & 1 & 0 \\
1 & 1 & 1 & 1 & 0 & 1 & 0 & 1 & 1 & 1 & 0 & 1 & 1 & 1 & 0 & 1 & 1 & 0 & 1 & 1 & 1 & 1 & 1 & 1 & 0 & 0 \\
0 & 0 & 0 & 0 & 1 & 0 & 1 & 0 & 0 & 0 & 1 & 0 & 0 & 0 & 1 & 0 & 0 & 1 & 0 & 0 & 0 & 0 & 0 & 0 & 1 & 1 & 0 \\
0 & 0 & 0 & 0 & 1 & 0 & 1 & 0 & 0 & 0 & 1 & 0 & 0 & 0 & 1 & 0 & 0 & 1 & 0 & 0 & 0 & 0 & 0 & 0 & 1 & 1 & 0 & 0 \\
0 & 0 & 0 & 0 & 1 & 0 & 1 & 0 & 0 & 0 & 1 & 0 & 0 & 0 & 1 & 0 & 0 & 1 & 0 & 0 & 0 & 0 & 0 & 0 & 1 & 1 & 0 & 0 & 0 \\
0 & 0 & 0 & 0 & 1 & 0 & 1 & 0 & 0 & 0 & 1 & 0 & 0 & 0 & 1 & 0 & 0 & 1 & 0 & 0 & 0 & 0 & 0 & 0 & 1 & 1 & 0 & 0 & 0 & 0
\end{bmatrix}_{30 \times 30}
$$

Figure 7. Result of distance measures for nominal FR instances

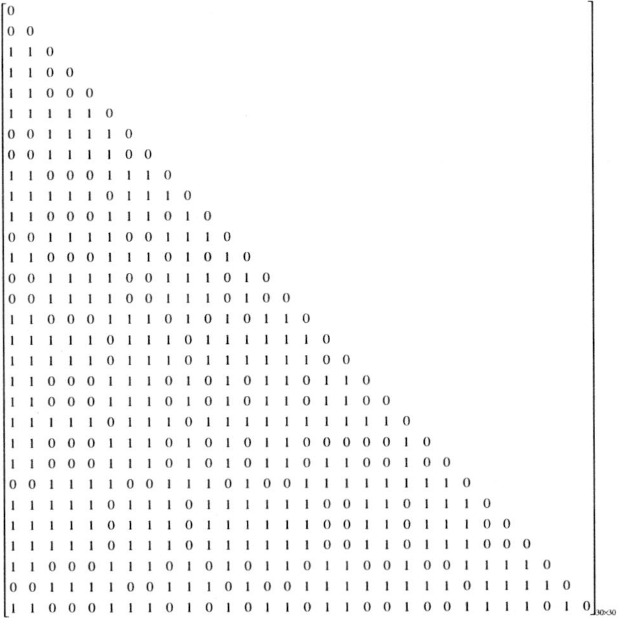

$$
\begin{bmatrix}
0 \\
0 & 0 \\
1 & 1 & 0 \\
1 & 1 & 0 & 0 \\
1 & 1 & 0 & 0 & 0 \\
1 & 1 & 1 & 1 & 1 & 0 \\
0 & 0 & 1 & 1 & 1 & 1 & 0 \\
0 & 0 & 1 & 1 & 1 & 1 & 0 & 0 \\
1 & 1 & 0 & 0 & 0 & 1 & 1 & 1 & 0 \\
1 & 1 & 1 & 1 & 1 & 0 & 1 & 1 & 1 & 0 \\
1 & 1 & 0 & 0 & 0 & 1 & 1 & 1 & 0 & 1 & 0 \\
0 & 0 & 1 & 1 & 1 & 1 & 0 & 0 & 1 & 1 & 1 & 0 \\
1 & 1 & 0 & 0 & 0 & 1 & 1 & 1 & 0 & 1 & 0 & 1 & 0 \\
0 & 0 & 1 & 1 & 1 & 1 & 0 & 0 & 1 & 1 & 1 & 0 & 1 & 0 \\
0 & 0 & 1 & 1 & 1 & 1 & 0 & 0 & 1 & 1 & 1 & 0 & 1 & 0 & 0 \\
1 & 1 & 0 & 0 & 0 & 1 & 1 & 1 & 0 & 1 & 0 & 1 & 0 & 1 & 1 & 0 \\
1 & 1 & 1 & 1 & 1 & 0 & 1 & 1 & 1 & 0 & 1 & 1 & 1 & 1 & 1 & 1 & 0 \\
1 & 1 & 1 & 1 & 1 & 0 & 1 & 1 & 1 & 0 & 1 & 1 & 1 & 1 & 1 & 1 & 0 & 0 \\
1 & 1 & 0 & 0 & 0 & 1 & 1 & 1 & 0 & 1 & 0 & 1 & 0 & 1 & 1 & 0 & 1 & 1 & 0 \\
1 & 1 & 0 & 0 & 0 & 1 & 1 & 1 & 0 & 1 & 0 & 1 & 0 & 1 & 1 & 0 & 1 & 1 & 0 & 0 \\
1 & 1 & 1 & 1 & 1 & 0 & 1 & 1 & 1 & 0 & 1 & 1 & 1 & 1 & 1 & 1 & 1 & 1 & 1 & 1 & 0 \\
1 & 1 & 0 & 0 & 0 & 1 & 1 & 1 & 0 & 1 & 0 & 1 & 0 & 1 & 1 & 0 & 0 & 0 & 0 & 0 & 1 & 0 \\
1 & 1 & 0 & 0 & 0 & 1 & 1 & 1 & 0 & 1 & 0 & 1 & 0 & 1 & 1 & 0 & 1 & 1 & 0 & 0 & 1 & 0 & 0 \\
0 & 0 & 1 & 1 & 1 & 1 & 0 & 0 & 1 & 1 & 1 & 0 & 1 & 0 & 0 & 1 & 1 & 1 & 1 & 1 & 1 & 1 & 1 & 0 \\
1 & 1 & 1 & 1 & 1 & 0 & 1 & 1 & 1 & 0 & 1 & 1 & 1 & 1 & 1 & 1 & 0 & 0 & 1 & 1 & 0 & 1 & 1 & 1 & 0 \\
1 & 1 & 1 & 1 & 1 & 0 & 1 & 1 & 1 & 0 & 1 & 1 & 1 & 1 & 1 & 1 & 0 & 0 & 1 & 1 & 0 & 1 & 1 & 1 & 0 & 0 \\
1 & 1 & 1 & 1 & 1 & 0 & 1 & 1 & 1 & 0 & 1 & 1 & 1 & 1 & 1 & 1 & 0 & 0 & 1 & 1 & 0 & 1 & 1 & 1 & 0 & 0 & 0 \\
1 & 1 & 0 & 0 & 0 & 1 & 1 & 1 & 0 & 1 & 0 & 1 & 0 & 1 & 1 & 0 & 1 & 1 & 0 & 0 & 1 & 0 & 0 & 1 & 1 & 1 & 1 & 0 \\
0 & 0 & 1 & 1 & 1 & 1 & 0 & 0 & 1 & 1 & 1 & 0 & 1 & 0 & 0 & 1 & 1 & 1 & 1 & 1 & 1 & 1 & 1 & 0 & 1 & 1 & 1 & 1 & 0 \\
1 & 1 & 0 & 0 & 0 & 1 & 1 & 1 & 0 & 1 & 0 & 1 & 0 & 1 & 1 & 0 & 1 & 1 & 0 & 0 & 1 & 0 & 0 & 1 & 1 & 1 & 1 & 0 & 1 & 0
\end{bmatrix}_{30 \times 30}
$$

Figure 8. Result of R^4

$$
\begin{bmatrix}
1 \\
.7 & 1 \\
.64 & .74 & 1 \\
.52 & .82 & .8 & 1 \\
.7 & .62 & .85 & .85 & 1 \\
.75 & .71 & .76 & .76 & .78 & 1 \\
.7 & .7 & .56 & .648 & .78 & .79 & 1 \\
.88 & .88 & .73 & .71 & .58 & .71 & .9 & 1 \\
.76 & .76 & .92 & .88 & .58 & .76 & .53 & .71 & 1 \\
.78 & .78 & .8 & .83 & .58 & .79 & .7 & .78 & .85 & 1 \\
.7 & .62 & .58 & .6 & .78 & .51 & .82 & .6 & .52 & .6 & 1 \\
.84 & .84 & .82 & .75 & .58 & .75 & .7 & .78 & .75 & .78 & .6 & 1 \\
.76 & .75 & .92 & .8 & .52 & .78 & .59 & .75 & .82 & .81 & .8 & .75 & 1 \\
.84 & .74 & .8 & .75 & .58 & .79 & .7 & .84 & .76 & .78 & .6 & .84 & .76 & 1 \\
.7 & .62 & .58 & .62 & .78 & .56 & .84 & .62 & .53 & .78 & .82 & .62 & .62 & .62 & 1 \\
.83 & .83 & .8 & .78 & .58 & .89 & .7 & .83 & .78 & .83 & .83 & .83 & .81 & .83 & .62 & 1 \\
.68 & .82 & .79 & .79 & .58 & .72 & .64 & .71 & .86 & .79 & .81 & .76 & .75 & .83 & .62 & .79 & 1 \\
.7 & .62 & .56 & .49 & .79 & .89 & .78 & .58 & .59 & .56 & .71 & .65 & .59 & .59 & .73 & .59 & .59 & 1 \\
.74 & .8 & .89 & .81 & .58 & .79 & .7 & .73 & .84 & .78 & .72 & .76 & .78 & .75 & .62 & .83 & .8 & .59 & 1 \\
.83 & .82 & .8 & .8 & .58 & .81 & .7 & .71 & .8 & .76 & .6 & .75 & .8 & .75 & .62 & .79 & .91 & .59 & .8 & 1 \\
.79 & .79 & .78 & .79 & .58 & .86 & .7 & .73 & .82 & .78 & .68 & .73 & .78 & .79 & .56 & .86 & .76 & .59 & .71 & .76 & 1 \\
.77 & .71 & .78 & .8 & .63 & .86 & .62 & .73 & .78 & .83 & .7 & .75 & .78 & .75 & .62 & .88 & .82 & .59 & .78 & .78 & .82 & 1 \\
.83 & .82 & .8 & .8 & .58 & .79 & .7 & .76 & .8 & .8 & .71 & .76 & .8 & .81 & .62 & .83 & .78 & .58 & .78 & .88 & .79 & .8 & 1 \\
.84 & .84 & .74 & .71 & .61 & .73 & .7 & .74 & .74 & .76 & .88 & .76 & .75 & .76 & .62 & .82 & .74 & .62 & .79 & .74 & .73 & .74 & .79 & 1 \\
.71 & .71 & .71 & .71 & .63 & .56 & .77 & .7 & .74 & .74 & .76 & .88 & .76 & .75 & .76 & .62 & .82 & .74 & .62 & .79 & .74 & .73 & .74 & .79 & 1 \\
.7 & .62 & .59 & .56 & .71 & .59 & .74 & .58 & .89 & .59 & .74 & .59 & .56 & .59 & .74 & .59 & .59 & .71 & .59 & .59 & .59 & .59 & .59 & .62 & .66 & 1 \\
.83 & .75 & .78 & .78 & .6 & .8 & .6 & .71 & .8 & .78 & .6 & .75 & .78 & .75 & .6 & .79 & .8 & .89 & .78 & .8 & .8 & .8 & .83 & .74 & .59 & .59 & 1 \\
.78 & .83 & .8 & .81 & .58 & .75 & .7 & .78 & .8 & .72 & .7 & .76 & .8 & .76 & .62 & .88 & .78 & .73 & .8 & .8 & .71 & .8 & .8 & .78 & .7 & .57 & .75 & 1 \\
.84 & .76 & .75 & .75 & .58 & .74 & .7 & .76 & .74 & .71 & .6 & .76 & .75 & .76 & .62 & .76 & .75 & .69 & .75 & .75 & .71 & .75 & .76 & .76 & .71 & .59 & .75 & .86 & 1 \\
.83 & .82 & .85 & .92 & .58 & .8 & .7 & .79 & .88 & .83 & .71 & .76 & .81 & .76 & .62 & .78 & .84 & .71 & .78 & .84 & .82 & .82 & .8 & .79 & .71 & .59 & .8 & .78 & .76 & 1
\end{bmatrix}_{30\times30}
$$

Figure 9. Result of a λ-cut with λ=0.84

$$
\begin{bmatrix}
1 \\
0 & 1 \\
0 & 0 & 1 \\
0 & 0 & 0 & 1 \\
0 & 0 & 1 & 1 & 1 \\
0 & 0 & 0 & 0 & 0 & 1 \\
0 & 0 & 0 & 0 & 0 & 0 & 1 \\
1 & 1 & 0 & 0 & 0 & 0 & 1 & 1 \\
0 & 0 & 1 & 0 & 0 & 0 & 0 & 0 & 1 \\
0 & 0 & 0 & 0 & 0 & 0 & 0 & 0 & 1 & 1 \\
0 & 0 & 0 & 0 & 0 & 0 & 0 & 0 & 0 & 0 & 1 \\
1 & 1 & 0 & 0 & 0 & 0 & 0 & 0 & 0 & 0 & 0 & 1 \\
0 & 0 & 1 & 0 & 0 & 0 & 0 & 0 & 0 & 0 & 0 & 0 & 1 \\
1 & 0 & 0 & 0 & 0 & 0 & 0 & 1 & 0 & 0 & 0 & 1 & 0 & 1 \\
0 & 0 & 0 & 0 & 0 & 0 & 1 & 0 & 0 & 0 & 0 & 0 & 0 & 0 & 1 \\
1 & 0 & 0 & 0 & 0 & 1 & 0 & 0 & 0 & 0 & 0 & 0 & 0 & 0 & 0 & 1 \\
0 & 0 & 0 & 0 & 0 & 0 & 0 & 0 & 1 & 0 & 0 & 0 & 0 & 0 & 0 & 0 & 1 \\
0 & 0 & 0 & 0 & 0 & 1 & 0 & 0 & 0 & 0 & 0 & 0 & 0 & 0 & 0 & 0 & 0 & 1 \\
0 & 0 & 1 & 0 & 0 & 0 & 0 & 0 & 1 & 0 & 0 & 0 & 0 & 0 & 0 & 0 & 0 & 0 & 1 \\
1 & 0 & 0 & 0 & 0 & 0 & 0 & 0 & 0 & 0 & 0 & 0 & 0 & 0 & 0 & 0 & 1 & 0 & 0 & 1 \\
0 & 0 & 0 & 0 & 0 & 1 & 0 & 0 & 0 & 0 & 0 & 0 & 0 & 0 & 0 & 1 & 0 & 0 & 0 & 0 & 1 \\
0 & 0 & 0 & 0 & 0 & 1 & 0 & 0 & 0 & 0 & 0 & 0 & 0 & 0 & 0 & 1 & 0 & 0 & 0 & 0 & 0 & 1 \\
0 & 0 & 0 & 0 & 0 & 0 & 0 & 0 & 0 & 0 & 0 & 0 & 0 & 0 & 0 & 0 & 0 & 0 & 0 & 1 & 0 & 0 & 1 \\
1 & 1 & 0 & 0 & 0 & 0 & 0 & 0 & 0 & 0 & 1 & 0 & 0 & 0 & 0 & 0 & 0 & 0 & 0 & 0 & 0 & 0 & 0 & 1 \\
0 & 0 & 0 & 0 & 0 & 0 & 0 & 0 & 0 & 0 & 0 & 0 & 0 & 0 & 0 & 0 & 0 & 0 & 0 & 0 & 0 & 1 & 0 & 0 & 1 \\
0 & 0 & 0 & 0 & 0 & 0 & 0 & 0 & 1 & 0 & 0 & 0 & 0 & 0 & 0 & 0 & 0 & 0 & 0 & 0 & 0 & 0 & 0 & 0 & 0 & 1 \\
0 & 0 & 0 & 0 & 0 & 0 & 0 & 0 & 0 & 0 & 0 & 0 & 0 & 0 & 0 & 0 & 1 & 0 & 0 & 0 & 0 & 0 & 0 & 0 & 0 & 0 & 1 \\
0 & 0 & 0 & 0 & 0 & 0 & 0 & 0 & 0 & 0 & 0 & 0 & 0 & 0 & 0 & 1 & 0 & 0 & 0 & 0 & 0 & 0 & 0 & 0 & 0 & 0 & 0 & 1 \\
1 & 0 & 0 & 0 & 0 & 0 & 0 & 0 & 0 & 0 & 0 & 0 & 0 & 0 & 0 & 0 & 0 & 0 & 0 & 0 & 0 & 0 & 0 & 0 & 0 & 0 & 0 & 1 & 1 \\
0 & 0 & 1 & 1 & 0 & 0 & 0 & 0 & 1 & 0 & 0 & 0 & 0 & 0 & 0 & 0 & 1 & 0 & 0 & 1 & 0 & 0 & 0 & 0 & 0 & 0 & 0 & 0 & 0 & 1
\end{bmatrix}_{30\times30}
$$

Table 4. Result of FR clustering

FR Cluster			Clustered FR Instances
χ_l	Mean Value (μ_l)	Variation Range (Δ_l)	$(\{\overline{v_t^*} \sim \chi_l \mid \forall t = 1, \cdots, n_l \leq T\})$
χ_1	$\begin{bmatrix} 100, Y, 9.2, 4.5, Au, \\ 44.5, 6.7, 2.4, 49 \end{bmatrix}$	[0, 0, 1.2, 0.5, 0, 10.5, 2.7, 0.6, 21]	$\{\overline{v_1^*}, \overline{v_2^*}, \overline{v_7^*}, \overline{v_8^*}, \overline{v_{11}^*}, \overline{v_{12}^*}, \overline{v_{14}^*}, \overline{v_{15}^*}, \overline{v_{24}^*}, \overline{v_{29}^*}\}$
χ_2	$\begin{bmatrix} 78.3, Y, 11.17, 5.5, Alloy, \\ 47, 4.5, 2.42, 57.5 \end{bmatrix}$	[21.7, 0, 1.17, 0.5, 0, 8, 2.5, 0.58, 17.5]	$\{\overline{v_3^*}, \overline{v_4^*}, \overline{v_5^*}, \overline{v_9^*}, \overline{v_{10}^*}, \overline{v_{13}^*}, \overline{v_{17}^*}, \overline{v_{19}^*}, \overline{v_{20}^*}, \overline{v_{23}^*}, \overline{v_{26}^*}, \overline{v_{30}^*}\}$
χ_3	$\begin{bmatrix} 67.5, Y, 10.75, 5.13, None, \\ 42.5, 5.13, 2.38, 47.5 \end{bmatrix}$	[12.5, 0, 1.25, 0.87, 0, 12.5, 1.87, 0.62, 22.5]	$\{\overline{v_6^*}, \overline{v_{16}^*}, \overline{v_{18}^*}, \overline{v_{21}^*}, \overline{v_{22}^*}, \overline{v_{25}^*}, \overline{v_{27}^*}, \overline{v_{28}^*}\}$

Table 5. Specification of vibration motor portfolio based on FR clusters

FR Variable	FR Value	
	Base Value	Variation Range
Current (mA)	100	±0
	78.3	±21.7
	67.5	±12.5
Pbfree	1 (Yes)	±0
Length (mm)	9.2	±1.2
	11.17	±1.17
	10.75	±1.25
Diameter (mm)	4.5	±0.5
	5.5	±0.5
	5.13	±0.87
Coating	Au	±0
	Alloy	±0
	None	±0
Angle (°)	44.5	±10.5
	47	±8
	42.5	±12.5
Strength (Kg)	6.7	±2.7
	4.5	±2.5
	5.13	±1.87
Weight (g)	2.4	±0.6
	2.42	±0.58
	2.38	±0.62
Hardness (HB)	49	±21
	57.5	±17.5
	47.5	±22.5

Due to different metrics used for FR variables, all FR instances in Table 3 are standardized based on the max-min normalization method. The pair-wise measures of distances are presented as a 30×30 matrix. The normalized distance measures of numerical FR instances are presented in a matrix form, $\left[N\_d_{numerical}\left(\overline{v_i^*}, \overline{v_j^*}\right)\right]_{30\times30}$, as shown in Figure 5. The results of distance measures for binary and nominal FR instances, $\left[N\_d_{binary}\left(\overline{v_i^*}, \overline{v_j^*}\right)\right]_{30\times30}$ and

$\left[N\_d_{nominal}\left(\overline{v_i^*},\overline{v_j^*}\right)\right]_{30\times30}$, are shown in Figures 6 and 7, respectively. By AHP, the weights associated with numerical, binary and nominal distance components are determined as $W_{numerical} = w_1 + w_3 + w_4 + w_6 + w_7 + w_8 + w_9 = 0.677$, $W_{binary} = w_2 = 0.304$ and $W_{nominal} = w_5 = 0.019$, respectively.

The result of fuzzy equivalence matrix $-R^A$ is shown in Figure 8. Based on R^A, the λ-cut is derived with a similarity threshold setting at 0.84. The result of the λ-cut is shown in Figure 9.

With the obtained λ-cut, 3-clusters of FR instances are identified. The mean value and variation range for each FR cluster are given in Table 4.

The resulted FR clusters comprise an item set, $X = \{(x_q^l, \delta_q^l) \mid \forall q \in [1,9], \exists l \in [1,3]\}$, as shown in Table 5. The characteristics of each FR cluster denotes the specification of a product platform — a set of base values together with the related variation ranges, and therefore can be used to suggest standard settings for vibration motor portfolios. These items are added to the transaction database. The link of each customer order to a FR instance is then replaced with the link to the items of the FR cluster that this FR instance belongs to.

To determine mining rules between item sets A^* and X, the data-mining tool, Magnum Opus (Version 2.0, http://www.rulequest.com/), is employed. All data are extracted from the transaction database and input as a text file into Magnum Opus. The Magnum Opus

Table 6. Result of association rule mining

Rule 1: Green material for environment friendliness\=>pf_y\[Support=0.882; Strength=1.000];
Rule 2: Alarmed independent of vibration\&Not easy to lose\&Catch up the mobile phone style occasionally at a low price\=>h_57.5[±17.5]\[Support=0.265; Strength=0.900];
Rule 3: Alarmed independent of vibration\&Try latest fashion of mobile phones at a moderate price\&Not easy to lose\=> c_78.3[±21.7]\[Support=0.265; Strength=0.900];
.
.
Rule 15: Feel the vibration very strongly\&Portable\=> l_9.2[±1.2]\[Support=0.206; Strength=0.875];
Rule 16: Feel the vibration very strongly\=>c_100[±0]\[Support=0.206; Strength=0.875];
Rule 17: Feel the vibration very strongly\&As light as possible\=>d_4.5[±0.5]\[Support=0.265; Strength=0.750];
Rule 18: As light as possible\=>a_42.5[±12.5]\[Support=0.206; Strength=0.875];
.
.
Rule 22: Alarmed by the vibration without vibrating suddenly\=>l_11.17[±1.17]\[Support=0.294; Strength=0.833];
Rule 23: Portable\&As light as possible\=>d_4.5[±0.5]\[Support=0.265; Strength=0.818];
Rule 24: Portable\&Feel the vibration very strongly\=>l_9.2[±1.2]\[Support=0.265; Strength=0.818];
Rule 25: Portable\=>a_44.5[±10.5]\[Support=0.294; Strength=0.833];
Rule 26: Sensitive to the vibration\=>d_5.13[±0.87]\[Support=0.235; Strength=0.800];
.
.
Rule 36: Try latest fashion of mobile phones at a moderate price\=>d_5.5[±0.5]\[Support=0.206; Strength=0.700];
Rule 37: Try latest fashion of mobile phones at a moderate price\=>co_Alloy\[Support=0.294; Strength=0.833];

Figure 10. Performance analysis of ARMS with respect to minimum support and confidence levels

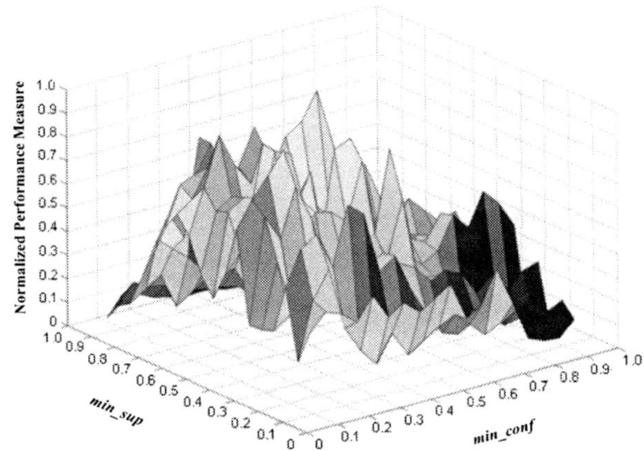

provides five association metrics: leverage, lift, strength, coverage, and support, each of which is supported by a search mode. The case study only uses the support and strength modes for the handling of support and confidence measures, respectively. This is because the coverage, lift and leverage criteria are not considered in the *a priori* algorithm. Under either search mode, the Magnum Opus finds a number of association rules specified by the user. The search guarantees that only those rules with the highest values on the specified metric are found according to user specified search settings. In this case, the minimum leverage, minimum lift, minimum strength, minimum coverage, and minimum support are set as 0, 1.0 (default value required by the system), 0.6, 0, and 0.5, respectively.

At the end of mining, the system generates 37 association rules, a selection of which are shown in Table 6. These rules serve as the basis of knowledge discovery. The possibility of some rule combinations can be considered to discover more implicit rules. For example, Rules 15, 16 and 17 together with Rules 23, 24 and 25 can generate ideas to optimize the size of motors. In addition to such rule refinement, the characteristics of each FR cluster and implicit relationships among them are explored to gain more understanding of vibration motor design specifications, so as to identify prominent settings of particular FR variables, to analyze the tradeoffs between different customer perceptions on mobile phones and the relevant FR values of vibration motors, and so on. All the identified patterns of CNs, FRs and the mapping are built into the knowledge base and are utilized to assist customer requirement analysis.

To analyze the performance of ARMS, a total number of 18×18=324 runs of ARMS are set up by enumerating all combinations of the *min_sup* and *min_conf* values, where both the *min_sup* and *min_conf* values are changed from 0.05 to 0.95 with an increment of 0.05. Using utility data and process data of vibration motors derived from the survey, the result of performance analysis is obtained. As shown in Figure 10, the performance measure in Equation (10) is presented as a normalized comparison. The result of performance analysis suggests that the optimal criteria of association-rule mining are given as the support and confidence thresholds of 0.5 and 0.6, respectively.

Conclusion

This chapter presents a domain-independent inference system for analyzing and organizing requirement information to support product portfolio identification. The methodology is based on the mining of association rules so as to provide an integration of requirement information from both customer and design viewpoints within a coherent framework.

Customer-requirement analysis entails a mapping process from customer needs in the customer domain to functional requirements in the functional domain. The specification of product offerings is embodied in a set of functional requirement clusters in conjunction with a set of associations of customer needs and the clusters. Each functional requirement cluster performs as a functional platform to satisfy a group of customers by enabling a certain range of variation with respect to a base value. For most variant product designs, where market segments have been established and product platforms have been installed, the association-rule mining methodology can improve the efficiency and quality of customer requirement analysis by alleviating the tedious, ambiguous and error-prone process of requirement analysis enacted among customers, marketing staff, and designers. Generating the portfolio based on knowledge discovery from past data serves to maintain the integrity of existing product and process platforms, as well as the continuity of the infrastructure and core competencies, hence leveraging existing design and manufacturing investments. The application of data mining opens opportunities for incorporating experts' experiences into the projection of customer requirement patterns from historical data, thereby enhancing the ability to explore and utilize domain knowledge more effectively.

References

Byrne, J. G., & Barlow, T. (1993). Structured brainstorming: A method for collecting user requirements. In *Proceedings of the Thirty-Seventh Annual Meeting of the Human Factors and Ergonomics Society* (pp. 427-431). Seattle, WA: Human Factors and Ergonomics Society.

Clark, K. B., & Fujimoto, T. (1991). *Product development performance*. Cambridge, MA: Harvard Business School.

Clausing, D. (1994). *Total quality development: A step-by-step guide to world class concurrent engineering*. New York: ASME.

Du, X., Jiao, J., & Tseng, M. M. (2001). Architecture of product family: Fundamentals and methodology. *Concurrent Engineering: Research and Application*, *9*, 309-325.

Du, X., Jiao, J., & Tseng, M. M. (2003). Identifying customer need patterns for customization and personalization. *Integrated Manufacturing Systems*, 14, 387-396.

Fukuda, S., & Matsuura, Y. (1993). Prioritizing the customer's requirements by AHP for concurrent design. *Proceedings of Design for Manufacturability*, *52*, 13-19.

Fung, R. T. K., & Popplewell, K. (1995). The analysis of customer requirements for effective rationalization of product attributes in manufacturing. In *Proceedings of the Third International Conference on Manufacturing Technology* (pp. 287-296). Hong Kong: HKCU.

Fung, R. Y. K., Popplewell, K., & Xie, J. (1998). An intelligent hybrid system for customer requirements analysis and product attribute targets determination. *International Journal of Production Research*, *36*, 13-34.

Fung, R. Y. K., Tang, J., Tu, Y., & Wang, D. (2002). Product design resources optimization using a non-linear fuzzy quality function deployment model. *International Journal of Production Research*, *40*, 585-599.

Green, P. E., & DeSarbo, W. S. (1978). Additive decomposition of perceptions data via conjoint analysis. *Journal of Consumer Research*, *5*, 58-65.

Griffin, A., & Hauser, J. R. (1992). The voice of the customer. *Marketing Science*, *12*, 1-27.

Han, J., & Kamber, M. (2001). *Data mining: Concepts and techniques*. San Francisco: Morgan Kaufmann.

Hauge, P. L., & Stauffer, L. A. (1993). ELK: A method for eliciting knowledge from customers. *Design and Methodology*, *ASME*, *53*, 73-81.

Jenkins, S. (1995, July 13). Modelling a perfect profile. *Marketing*, *6*.

Kano, N., Seraku, N., Takahashi, F., & Tsuji, S. (1984). Attractive and must-be quality (in Japanese). *Hinshitsu*, *14*, 39-48.

LaChance-Porter, S. (1993). Impact of user focus groups on the design of new products. In M. Williams (Ed.), *Proceedings of the Fourteenth National On-line Meeting* (pp. 265-271). Medford, NJ: Learned Information.

Louviere, J., Anderson, D., White, J. B., & Eagle, T. C. (1990). Predicting preferences for new product configurations: A high-tech example. In M. Carnevale, M. Lucertini, & S. Nicosia (Eds.), *Proceedings of the IFIP TC 7 Conference, Modeling the Innovation: Communications, Automation and Information Systems* (pp. 53-61). Rome, Italy: North-Holland.

McAdams, D. A., Stone, R. B., & Wood, K. L. (1999). Functional interdependence and product similarity based on customer needs. *Research in Engineering Design*, *11*, 1-19.

McKay, A., de Pennington, A., & Baxter, J. (2001). Requirements management: A representation scheme for product. *Computer-Aided Design*, *33*, 511-520.

Prudhomme, G., Zwolinski, P., & Brissaud, D. (2003). Integrating into the design process the needs of those involved in the product life-cycle. *Journal of Engineering Design, 14*, 333-353.

Pugh, S. (1991). *Total design: Integrated methods for successful product engineering.* Workingham, MA: Addison-Wesley.

Saaty, T. (1980). *The analytic hierarchy process.* New York: McGraw-Hill.

Shoji, S., Graham, A., & Walden, D. (1993). *A new American TQM.* Portland, OR: Productivity.

Suh, N. P. (2001). *Axiomatic design - Advances and applications.* New York: Oxford University.

Tseng, M. M., & Jiao, J. (1998). Computer-aided requirement management for product definition: A methodology and implementation. *Concurrent Engineering: Research and Application, 6*, 145-160.

Turksen, I. B., & Willson, I. A. (1993). Customer preferences models: Fuzzy theory approach. In *Proceedings of the SPIE — International Society for Optical Engineering* (pp. 203-211). Boston: SPIE.

Veryzer, R. W. (1993). Aesthetic response and the influence of design principles on product performance. In L. McAllister & M. Rothschild (Eds.), *Advances in consumer research* (pp. 224-231). Provo, UT: Association for Consumer Research.

Womack, J. P., Jones, D. T., & Roos, D. (1990). *The machine that changed the world.* New York: Rawson.

Yang, L., & Gao, Y. (1996). *Fuzzy mathematics: Theory and applications.* China: Huadong Technological University.

Chapter XIII

Visual Grouping of Association Rules by Clustering Conditional Probabilities for Categorical Data

Sasha Ivkovic, University of Ballarat, Australia

Ranadhir Ghosh, University of Ballarat, Australia

John Yearwood, University of Ballarat, Australia

Abstract

We demonstrate the use of a visual data-mining tool for non-technical domain experts within organizations to facilitate the extraction of meaningful information and knowledge from in-house databases. The tool is mainly based on the basic notion of grouping association rules. Association rules are useful in discovering items that are frequently found together. However in many applications, rules with lower frequencies are often interesting for the user. Grouping of association rules is one way to overcome the rare item problem. However some groups of association rules are too large for ease of understanding. In this chapter we propose a method for clustering categorical data based on the conditional probabilities of association rules for data sets with large numbers of attributes. We argue that the proposed method provides non-technical users with a better understanding of discovered patterns in the data set.

Introduction

Traditional manual data analysis is becoming impractical in many domains as data volume grows exponentially. Depending on the type of analysis, several Knowledge Discovery in Databases (KDD) methods such as classification, regression, clustering and association rules use automated artificial intelligence, and mathematical and statistical techniques for the task. Frawley, Piatetsky-Shapiro, and Matheus (1992, p. 57) define KDD as "the non-trivial extraction of implicit, previously unknown and potentially useful information from the data." The overall process of finding and interpreting patterns from data involves repeated application of the following steps — data selection, data preprocessing, data transformation, data mining, discovery interpretation / evaluation. KDD is a process involving human interactions. There are traditionally two human roles in any KDD process — a domain expert role and a data miner role. A data miner is someone who primarily uses sophisticated KDD technology in conjunction with existing data sources as the basis for discovering useful patterns in the data. A domain expert is a person with a comprehensive knowledge of a certain domain. However, some domain experts are non-data miners (e.g., data analyst and database administrator) and some are data miners (e.g., external KDD specialist).

A data miner can gather knowledge either from the domain expert or from a domain knowledge repository. However the domain expert is fully dependent on the data miner. One of the reasons that exploitation of KDD technology is not fully implemented within organizations is that the majority of KDD tools currently available are expensive and complex adjuncts to database management systems. Their operation typically requires specialist operators. Furthermore the countless data-mining techniques function in such different ways that even KDD experts cannot be expected to be proficient with all approaches. The specialist knowledge required and the cost of KDD tools militate against their use for non-technical domain experts. We argue that by implementing a balanced relationship between the domain expert and the data miner, the organization will benefit by exploiting its KDD technology at all organizational levels. To explain this further we consider the implementation of KDD technology in an organization.

Goebel and Gruenwald (1999) investigated the use of almost all mainstream commercial KDD products and reported that deploying KDD technology in an organization is traditionally implemented through the following three phases:

1. First, KDD studies are performed by the data-mining specialists (external consultants). (See Figure 1.)
2. Once the profitability of KDD is proven, data-analysis experts apply the KDD techniques (possibly with the help of a domain expert who has strong domain knowledge). (See Figure 2.)

Figure 1. KDD implementation — Phase I

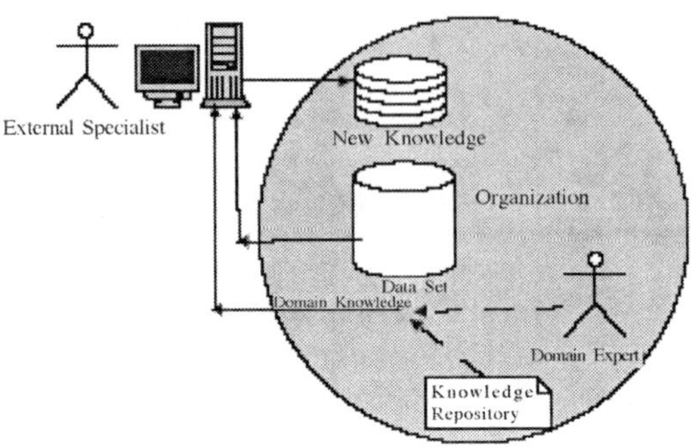

Figure 2. KDD implementation — Phase II

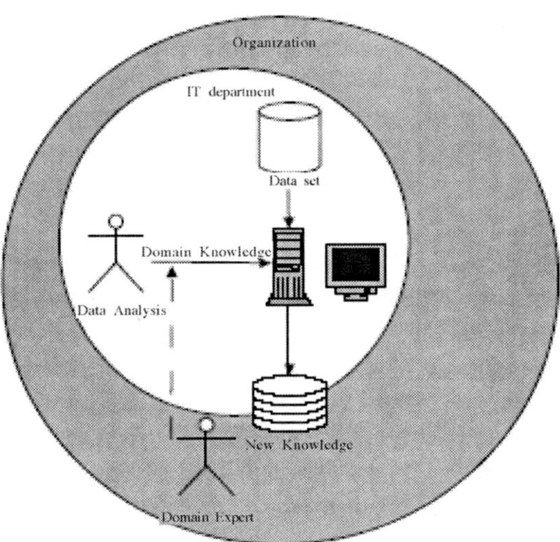

3. When full exploitation of KDD technology occurs within the organization, domain experts are enabled to perform their own KDD analysis according to their individual needs. Although not yet widely implemented, the necessity for this stage is clearly recognized. (See Figure 3.)

Stage Three shows that an organization needs an effective KDD tool for its non-technical domain experts. The role of the new KDD tools is not to replace the use of data-miner-driven "heavy-duty" tools but to provide an additional set of "pure" domain knowledge driven tools that will meet his or her simpler day-to-day requirements.

Figure 3. KDD implementation — Phase III

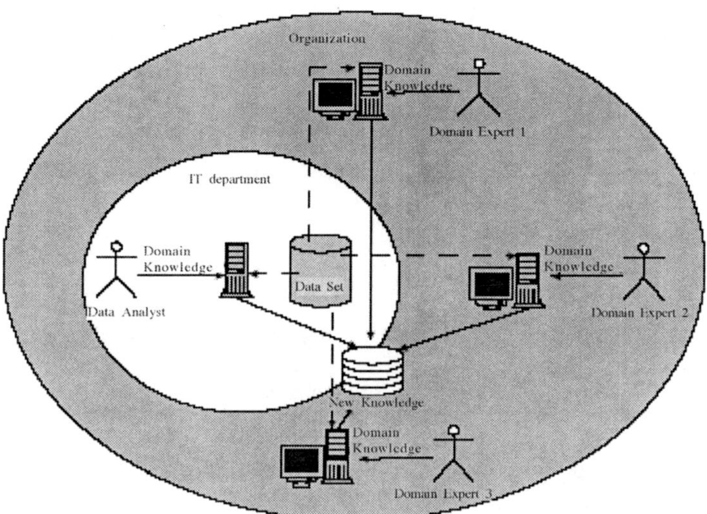

In this study we present a KDD method that can be used by non-technical domain experts with minimal training, to discover and interpret patterns they find useful for their role within the organization. The proposed KDD tool can automatically identify and provide a description of patterns in clusters. The aims of this chapter are as follows:

1. To create a visual tool for the non-technical domain expert based on the basic notion of association rules.
2. To provide a solution to the problem of clustering categorical data.
3. To extract interesting rules involving attributes with a large number of distinct values and provide useful cluster description.

According to Brachman, Khabaza, Kloesgen, Piatetsky-Shapiro, and Simoudis (1996), an increasing trend in KDD shows that companies rely on the analysis of large amounts of data to gain a competitive advantage. Many organizations use discovered knowledge to gain competitive advantage, increase efficiency, or provide more valuable services to customers.

As outlined above, there are usually three stages in deploying KDD technology in an organization (Goebel & Gruenwald, 1999). The initial stage involves the organizational use of KDD through an external KDD specialist (external consultant). In this stage, an organization approaches a third-party company that is a specialist in KDD. The KDD specialist uses domain knowledge, either through a domain expert or a domain knowledge repository, in order to select and pre-process the data set. The second stage involves the organizational use of KDD through an internal KDD specialist or team of analyst experts (e.g., database administrators and data analysts). In this stage, the organization purchases a KDD technology (hardware and software), which should meet the analysis requirements of the organization. The last stage involves the full exploitation of KDD technology within the organization. It includes the use of KDD by enabling domain experts (e.g., lawyers, managers, medical professionals) to perform their own analysis according to their individual needs. This step does not eliminate the use of KDD in any previous stage. Moreover, it enhances the use of KDD within an organization by allowing domain users to search for useful knowledge that would potentially improve their everyday tasks.

Tools for the Non-Technical Domain Expert

The majority of KDD tools require a prohibitive amount of training before being useful, and discovered patterns are often difficult to interpret. One can argue that training non-technical domain experts would overcome this problem. However, most non-technical domain experts are usually not interested in using advanced technology, except for getting clear, rapid answers to their everyday business questions (Goebel & Gruenwald, 1999). Non-technical domain experts require simple-to-use tools that efficiently solve their business problems.

In this chapter we present a KDD method that can be used by non-technical experts with minimal training to discover and interpret patterns that they find useful for their role within an organization. The approach generates association rules and then displays them by grouping rules together and visually depicting deviations between groups.

Frequency Based Interestingness and its Problem

Association rules were introduced by Agrawal and Imielinski (1993), and originated with the problem of supermarket basket analysis. An association rule (AR) is an expression of the form X→Y [support, confidence], where X and Y are sets of items that are often found together in a given collection of data. The attribute group on the left-hand side of the arrow is called the antecedent and the group of attributes on the right-hand side of the arrow is called the consequent. The support and confidence measures, introduced by Agrawal and Imielinski, are used as the pruning methods to reduce the number of discovered rules. The support is the percentage of transactions in the databases containing both X and Y. The confidence is the conditional probability of Y given X, e.g., confidence = $P(Y \mid X)$. If both support and the confidence values are greater than the threshold, the AR is considered interesting. We call this type of interestingness "frequency-based interestingness."

A problem with the threshold-filtering approach is that many analysts do not know what an ideal threshold setting should be (Andritos, Tsaparas, Miller, & Serveik, 2003). If the threshold is set too high, useful rules may be missed. If it is set too low, the user may be overwhelmed by many irrelevant rules. In many real-life applications some items appear very frequently in the data, while others rarely appear. If the threshold is set too low, those rules that involve rare items will not be found. This dilemma is called the "rare item problem." Another common problem with the user specified support measure is that not all high support rules are interesting. Lin, Tseng and Su (2002) and Liu, Hsu, and Ma (1999) argue that most of the rules with higher support are obvious and well known, and it is the rules with low support that provide interesting new insights. For example, a domain expert may already be familiar with the rule R1 "sex Male→law type Criminal [support 47%, confidence 76%]. It is very unlikely that those experts will be satisfied with merely prevalent patterns because presumably the organization is already exploiting that knowledge (Chakrabarti, Sarawagi, & Dom, 1998).

From Frequency-Based to Content-Based Interestingness

Liu, Hsu and Ma (2001) claim that the problem of interestingness is not due to the large number of discovered association rules. The main limitation is with the user's inability to organize and present the rules in such a way that they can be easily analyzed. One promising approach is to organize and present generated AR by grouping rules and measuring differences between groups. Interestingness measures based on group differences have been used by a number of authors (Bay & Pazzani, 2000, 2001; Duda & Hart, 1973; Duda, Hart & Stork, 2001; Liu et al., 1999, 2001). Bay and Pazzani (2000) and Duda and Hart (1973) use contrast sets in order to find differences between groups (subsets). However, contrast sets are not based on AR. Liu et al. (2001) organize association rules by grouping the related rules together and finding differences and similarities between groups. For example, generated association rules:

* R2 "country of birth England→legal aid refused Yes [support 8%, confidence 13.7%]"
* R3 "country of birth Italy→legal aid refused Yes [support 0.5%, confidence 26.7%]"
* R4 "country of birth Greece→legal aid refused Yes [support 1.8%, confidence 23.6%]"
* R5 "country of birth Vietnam→legal aid refused Yes [support 6%, confidence 8.2%]"

are organized by separating the discovered rules into rule sets. Each rule set contains association rules that share a common consequent (R2, R3, R4 and R5 share "legal aid refused = Yes") and different antecedent (R2 "England," R3 "Italy," R4 "Greece," and R5 "Vietnam") belonging to the same attribute "country of birth." If the discrepancy between the confidence values of any group is substantially high, these groups are considered different, otherwise the groups are considered similar on the basis of " legal aid refused = Yes." By grouping related association rules into rule sets (AR with a common consequent but different antecedent), we are able to visually display grouped AR.

Figure 4. Group differences for "legal aid refused = Yes"

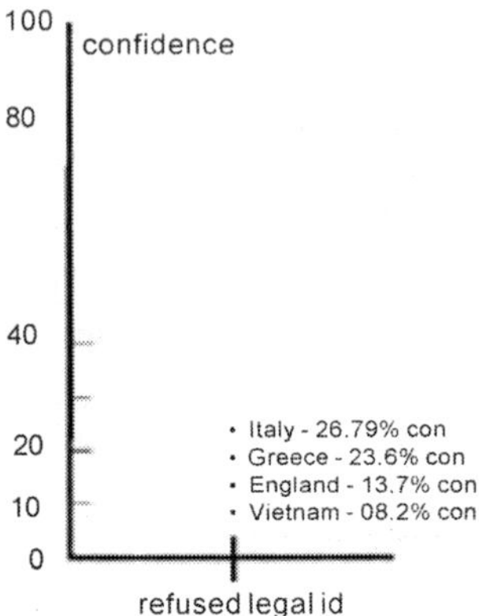

Figure 4 shows that 26.7% of Italian-born applicants were refused aid. An analyst could find the difference in the refusal rate interesting. We call this approach "content based interestingness" because the grouping of AR is based on their content.

Association Rule Visualization

Visualization is the process of transforming data, information and knowledge into a visual form, making use of a human's natural visual capabilities (Gershon, Eick, & Card, 1998). According to Grinstein and Thuraisingham (1996), there are three kinds of visualization categories in KDD. The first category presents the findings obtained from the data-mining step, the second category visualizes the data before applying data-mining algorithms, and the last category uses visualization to complement the data-mining techniques. In our work we focus on the first visualization category, which aims to visually present findings to the user. Furthermore we focus on visualization techniques that display findings generated by AR-based algorithms. More advanced visualization techniques use a 2-D matrix for representing AR. This technique is used by SGI (Silicon Graphics International) in their data-mining software MineSet. The AR are represented as a 2-D matrix where user selected attribute-values are displayed on both axes. One axis is labeled as the left-hand side and the other as the right-hand side. The grid intersection between two axes is displayed as the height of a bar and represents the confidence of the rule corresponding to the left-hand side (LHS) and right-hand side (RHS) labels. The support value is represented as a disk attached to the bar and the expected probability as the color of the bar. All of these three representations are configurable. The limitation of this approach is that MineSet is only able to visually display rules that have single left-hand and right-hand sides. Although MineSet tried to overcome this problem by

Figure 5. Multi item AR representation by SGI MineSet

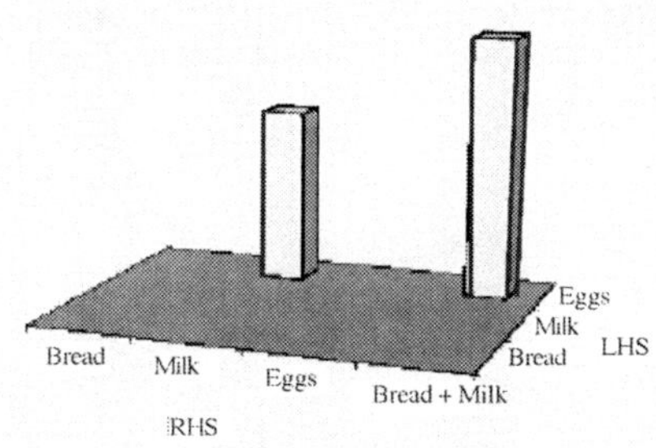

allowing rules that have multiple LHS and RHS, as shown in Figure 5, the limitations are obvious when the number of items in the LHS or RHS is greater than a couple.

Despite visualization limitations by MineSet, the ability of MineSet to adjust the visual display by resizing, rotating and flipping is advanced. However, we find this item-to-item 2-D matrix approach unsuitable because it does not clearly identify deviations.

The limitation of 2-D matrix graphs that show AR mapped as item-to-item resulted in other 3-D visualization techniques (Wong, Whitney, & Thomas, 1999). They represent a rule-to-item approach that shows rows as items and columns as AR rules. The LHS and RHS of a rule are distinguished by two different color bars. Confidence and support values are displayed by the height of the bar placed at the end of the matrix. In Figure 6,

Figure 6. 3D Association Rule visualization

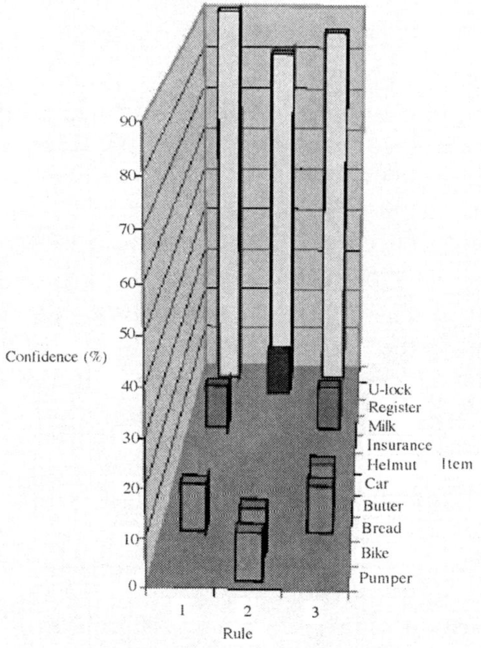

Figure 7. Group differences for country groups

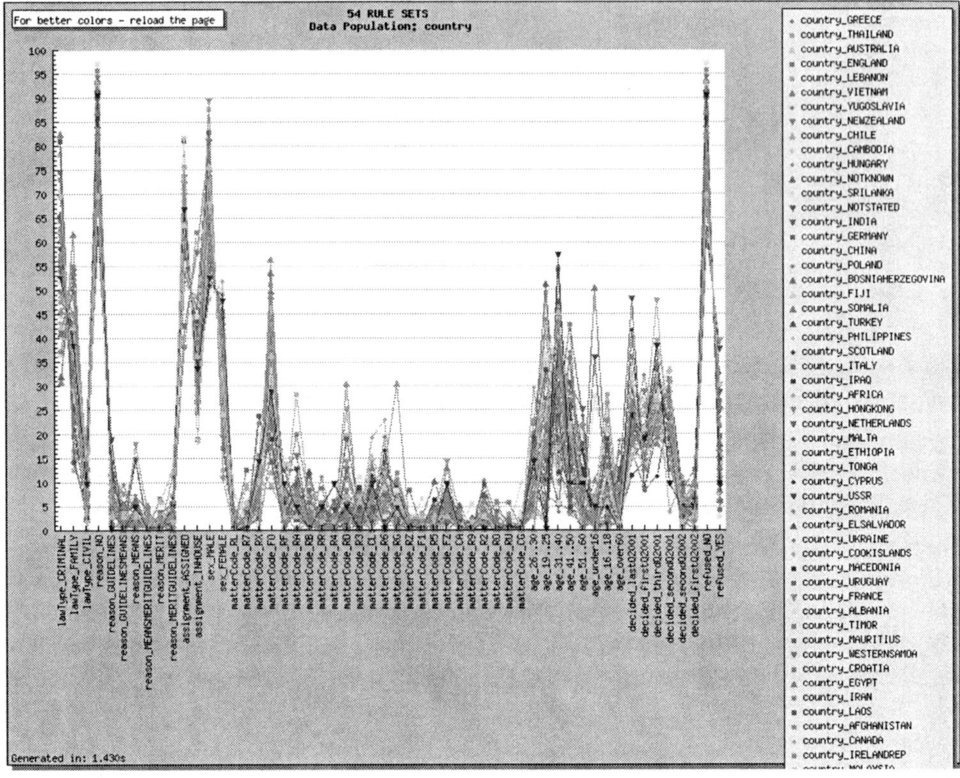

association rule number 3 shows the 3-D AR presentation for the rule Milk => Bread AND Butter (confidence 84%)

The approach suggested by Wong et al. (1999) is best for an AR that has multiple RHS and single LHS. That is, the rule body has only one item. When the LHS has more than one item, the matrix floor is covered with many blocks. We don't find this approach suitable for the representation of deviations because it does not clearly identify deviations between groups of rules with the same consequent.

However with the "content-based interestingness," a problem arises when a user is interested in an attribute that has a large number of distinct values. For example in our Victorian Legal Aid data set the "country of birth" attribute has 143 possible values. The graphical representation of grouped association rules in this case is very hard to understand. We demonstrate this in Figure 7.

Proposed Two-Step Methodology to Create an Effective Visual Tool

Creating an effective visual tool involves two sets of problems. The first problem is to transform the categorical data for an effective clustering method. The second problem

Figure 8. Clustered country groups

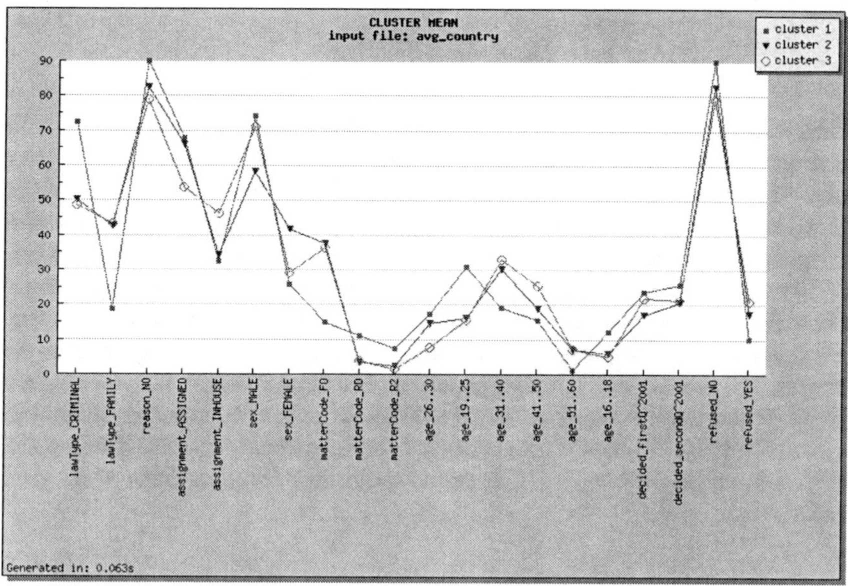

is to cluster the transformed data set in a meaningful way. Transforming the categorical data can be solved using a 2-D conditional probability matrix (**A**). Each row of the **A** matrix denotes the attribute(s) appearing in the antecedent and each column denotes the consequent. The element of the matrix $\mathbf{A}_{rc}$ denotes the conditional probability of P(column | row).

In the next step, this data matrix is clustered using a hierarchical two-layer abstraction technique. The first level of abstraction is achieved using Kohonen's Self Organizing Map (SOM) and the final level of abstraction is achieved using a non-linear optimization approach. The centers of the discovered clusters are then plotted in a graph against all variable values to identify the properties of each cluster. This leads to useful descriptions of the data set from the perspective of the chosen variable. In the next section we discuss the rationale behind transforming categorical data into a conditional probability matrix. In Figure 8 we show the clarity of the improved graphical representation of the same rules after clustering.

Clustering is an important problem in data mining. Most early work on clustering focussed on numeric attributes, which have a natural ordering on their attribute values. In this work clustering data with categorical attributes, whose attribute values do not have a natural ordering, is considered. Many clustering algorithms do not give a formal description of the clusters they discover.

Given *n* data points in a d-dimensional space, a clustering algorithm partitions the data points into *k* clusters such that the data points in a cluster are more similar to each other than data points in different clusters. Clustering algorithms developed in the literature can be classified into partition clustering and hierarchical clustering (Ester, Kriegel, Sander, & Xu, 1996; Ivkovic, 2004). Partition clustering algorithms, as the name suggests, divide the point space into *k* clusters that optimize a certain criterion function. The most commonly used criterion function for metric spaces is:

$$f(x,k) = \sum_{i=1}^{k} \sum_{x \in C_i} d(x, c_i)$$

In the above equation, c_i is the centroid of cluster C_i while $d(x, c_i)$ is usually the Euclidean distance between x and c_i. Intuitively, this criterion function attempts to minimize the distance of every point from the centre of the cluster to which the point belongs. Minimization of the criterion function is frequently carried out using an iterative, local optimization technique. For example, starting with k initial partitions, data points are moved from one cluster to another to improve the value of the criterion function. A hierarchical clustering is a nested sequence of partitions. Agglomerative, hierarchical clustering starts by placing each point in its own cluster and then merges these clusters into larger and larger clusters until all points are in a single cluster. Divisive, hierarchical clustering reverses the process by starting with all points in a cluster and subdividing into smaller pieces. While the use of this criterion function often gives satisfactory results for numeric attributes, it is not appropriate for data sets with categorical attributes.

Categorical Data

Categorical attributes do not have a continuous range of values and are not limited to the binary values 0 and 1, but can be any arbitrary finite set of values. An example of a categorical attribute is color, whose domain includes values such as red, green, black, white, etc. Most previous work in clustering focused on numerical data whose inherent geometric properties can be exploited usually in the form of a naturally defined distance function between the points. However many data sets consists of categorical attributes on which distance functions cannot so naturally be applied. Recently the problem of clustering categorical data started receiving interest (Andritos et al., 2003; Guha, Rastogi, & Shim, 2000; Kohonen, 1982). The ROCK clustering algorithm proposed in Guha et al. (2000) is a hierarchical clustering technique that is based on links to measure the similarity/proximity between a pair of data points. It utilizes the information about links between points when making decisions on the points to be merged into a single cluster and is very robust. The algorithm described in Guha et al. (2000) is based on an iterative process for assigning and propagating weights on the categorical values in a table. It generalizes the powerful methodology of spectral graph partitioning to produce a clustering technique applicable to arbitrary collections of sets. Those authors note that approaches that rely on co-occurrence of attribute values for the similarity metric are limited. A vehicle database example they use identifies Toyotas and Hondas as similar, not because they share common properties but because a disproportionate number of each are sold in the month of August. Ghua et al. (2000) discount the use of association rules in categorical clustering because of the association rules' emphasis on similarity of properties. In the approach presented here association rules are not used to cluster raw data. Instead, raw data is transformed to sets of conditional probabilities of multiple combinations of attribute values. The conditional probabilities are then clustered. In this way, the similarities between Toyotas and Hondas with respect to August sales can be captured. Information theoretic metrics for similarity have been used by Andritos et al. (2003). The similarity metrics employed are entropy-based metrics based on the Gini index and Shannon Entropy. There are similarities to conditional probabilities. Genetic algorithm operators are used to derive the partitions that are used in the entropy functions. In the approach advanced here, the conditional probability formulation is not embedded in an entropy-based similarity metric, but is made explicit by its use in transforming raw data to conditional probabilities. This has the advantage of enabling the data to be more immediately accessible to the user for manual discovery of interesting patterns and also enables the application of standard clustering algorithms to be considered. The categorical clustering algorithm CACTUS described in Gibson, Kleinberg, and Raghavan (2000) is based on generalizing a definition of cluster for numerical attributes. It requires two scans for the data set and it can find clusters in subsets of all attributes. Ganti, Gehrke, and Ramakrihnan (1999) propose a clustering method for large databases that is based on randomized search. Each cluster is represented by its mediod or the most centrally located point in the cluster and the objective is to find the best medoids. Bay and Pazzani (2000) use the R*-tree to improve the I/O efficiency on a large database.

Creation of 2-D Conditional Probability Matrix

The raw categorical data of the data set is converted to conditional probabilities as follows:

A particular variable with a reasonable number of values (categories) is chosen. The conditional probabilities of all other variable:value pairs given the values of this selected variable are computed using an SQL (Structured Query Language) query. The result is a matrix of conditional probabilities that are amenable to clustering. This table of probabilities (AR confidences) is clustered using a Self-Organizing Map. This clustering approach does not reveal clusters. A second level of clustering based on an optimization approach that makes use of the weights attached to points in the SOM map is used as described below. The input for the SOM algorithm is provided by calculating the conditional probabilities. The conditional probabilities are obtained by using SQL queries to count frequencies. For example, in order to count the conditional probability of refused YES given a country, we determined frequencies for each country by executing SQL query:

Q1: SELECT COUNT(country), country FROM VLA GROUP BY country.

We get the second frequency count by executing SQL query:

Q2: SELECT count(*) FROM VLA WHERE country=vector[ii] AND refused='refused YES'.

Table 1. SOM input — Conditional probabilities for X given country

	Refused YES	Refused NO	Sex MALE	Property..n
ITALY	26.7	73.3	77	
AUSTRALIA	10.7	89.3	65	
GREECE	24.5	75.5	73	
Country..n				

Finally we calculate conditional probabilities for each country by dividing the second count (Q2) by the first count (Q1). The conditional probabilities are stored in a file with appropriate column and row headings. Table 1 illustrates part of the input for the SOM algorithm.

Rationale Behind the Two Level Abstraction for Clustering

Kohonen's (1982) Self-Organizing Map (SOM) is a well known clustering algorithm. It is an unsupervised learning clustering algorithm that creates a map (discrete lattice) relationship from the patterns. During training, the output node with the minimum Euclidean distance is found. This will indicate the node (class) to which the input pattern belongs. The training is performed using a winner-take-all algorithm. The basic idea behind the winner-take-all algorithm is that if neurons are located on a discrete lattice, the competitive learning can be generalized. The neurons represent the inputs with reference vectors $\boldsymbol{m}_i$, the components of which correspond to synaptic weights. The unit with index c, whose reference vector is nearest to the input x is the winner of the competition:

$$c = c(x) = \arg\min_i \left\{ \| x - m_i \|^2 \right\}$$

Usually the Euclidian metric is used. The winning unit and its neighbors adapt to represent the input by modifying their reference vector. The amount the units lean is governed by a neighborhood kernel h, which is a decreasing function of the distance of the units from the winning lattice. Thus:

$$h_{ij}(t) = h\left(\| r_i - r_j \|; t \right)$$

where t denotes time, and r_i and r_j represent the location of units i and j respectively. During leaning, reference vectors are changed according to the following adaptation rule

$$m_i(t+1) = m_i(t) + h_{c_i}(t)[x(t) - m_i(t)]$$

where c is the index of the reference vector.

In the beginning of the learning process the neighboring kernel is chosen wide and is decreased over time. It has been shown that in the case of a discrete data set and a fixed neighborhood size, there exists a potential function for the SOM, which can be represented by

$$E = \sum_k \sum_i h_{c_i} \|x_k - m_i\|^2$$

where index c depends on x_k and the reference vector $\boldsymbol{m}_i$.

The learning rule corresponds to a gradient descent step in minimizing the sample function

$$E_1 = \sum_i h_{c_i} \|x(t) - m_i\|^2$$

obtained by selecting randomly a sample $\boldsymbol{x(t)}$ at iteration t. Locally, if the index does not change for any x_k, the gradient step can be considered as valid. It is also shown that SOM follows the distribution of the data set in the input space. For vector quantization, density of the reference vector approximates the density of the input vectors for high dimensional data set. In a one-dimensional case this density can be expressed as $p(x)^{2/3}$ where $p(x)$ is the probability density function.

The cost function of the SOM in the case of discrete data can be represented as

$$E = \sum_k \|x_k - n_c\|^2 + \sum_i \sum_j h_{ij} N_i \|n_i - m_j\|^2$$

where n_i denotes the number of data items which are closest to reference vector i and

$$n_i = 1/N_i \sum_{x_k \in Vi} x_k$$

where V_k is Voronoi region corresponding to m_i. The approximation can be made with the assumption that the SOM partitions the input space into convex Voronoi regions, each of which corresponds to one unit of the map. The Voronoi region of a map unit i is the union of all vectors **X** to which it is the closest one:

$$V_i = \{x|\ \|m_i - x\| < \|m_j - x\|, i \neq j\}$$

In the Voronoi region the reference vector can be shown to be placed according to the local conditional expectation of the data weighted by the neighborhood kernel:

$$m = \frac{\int h_{ci} p(x) x dx}{\int h_{ci} p(x) dx}$$

$\sum_j h_{ij} = 1$ for all i, which holds exactly for toroidal maps when the kernel h has the same shape for all i and also away from borders on a non-toroidal map if the kernel differs from zero locally. The first term in the cost-function equation above is equivalent to the cost function of the K-means cluster algorithm. The second term, can be interpreted as governing the ordering of the reference vector. At a fixed point

$$m_i = \sum_k h_{c(x_k)i} x_k / \sum_k h_{c(x_k)i}$$

which is closer to n_i the more the neighborhood kernel h_{ci} is centered around c.

However there are two major problems with the self-organizing map. Both of these problems exist when we consider the raw cluster points from the SOM. The standard SOM model requires a predefined map structure, which affects the projection from one high dimensional system into two dimensions. If points on SOM are to be considered as individual clusters then one of the major problems is that the complete learning process has to be repeated if the size of the map is very small, and the classification error for every pattern can be very high, resulting in dissimilar vectors being assigned to the same unit or similar vectors can being assigned to different units. One solution to the existing problem could be using a growing SOM, where a small grid size is initially trained and is made bigger until such time as the error is greater than some threshold value. However this also has its own disadvantage of using repetitive training of the SOM. If we define the confidence of a point on the map as the number of vectors that are projected into the map, then within an acceptable range of map size and a proper training this confidence value of points will be proportional to the map size. Thus finding clusters from the set of these maps considering confidence values of each point can be considered as an optimization problem. This serves a two-fold purpose, firstly the problem of finding clusters using optimization techniques applied to the original high dimensional data set can be reduced to a two-dimensional problem. And finally, further clustering the points on the map reduces the sensitivity problem for the SOM with the map size. Also, the curse of many cluster points in the SOM could be solved. Thus we can say that the SOM could be a useful tool for clustering for the initial abstraction level to form some prototypes for the clustering.

Figure 9 illustrates the two levels of abstraction from the original data set. In this figure, we can see that the original data set is first transformed into a two-dimensional SOM plane to form **M** cluster prototypes. From these prototypes we compute the confidence of each point according to the frequency of the original data that have been mapped into a cluster prototype, and then finally the optimization technique used to find **C** different clusters. The confidence for prototype $\mathbf{M}_i$ can be calculated using the following formula

$$M_i = \sum_{j=1}^{N} A_j \text{; } where$$

$$A_j = \begin{Bmatrix} 1, A_j \in M_i \\ 0, A_j \notin M_i \end{Bmatrix}$$

Data Set

The Victorian government created a body called Victorian Legal Aid (VLA) with the objective of providing legal aid in the most effective, economic and efficient manner to those in the community with the greatest need. To get legal aid in the format of legal costs or cost-free lawyers, a client provides his or her personal, financial and case details. In order to measure to what extent their objectives have been met, VLA experts have to analyze their data set. Furthermore, the experts need to monitor their financial resources (e.g., where was the money spent) as well as human resources (e.g., lawyer's assignments). All these details are stored in a VLA database. The VLA cases shown in this study are real examples showing some everyday tasks of the VLA domain experts. VLA domain experts selected nine variables that were important and interesting for data analysis. The selected variables were:

Sex (2 possible values), Age group (8 possible values), reason for refusal (10 pre-specified VLA refusal codes), lawType (civil, family, criminal), refused (aid granted or not granted), assignment (assigned - external lawyer or in-house - VLA lawyer), country (country of birth, 134 possible values), decided (date of decision).

Figure 9. Levels of abstractions used to form cluster from the original data set

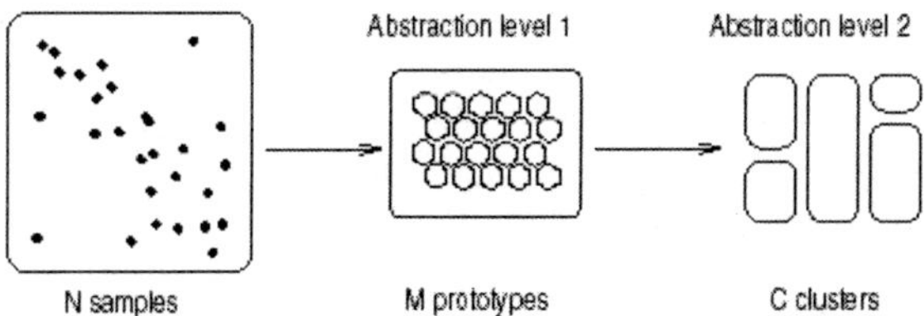

Sample Solution

Our results show many meaningful rule sets and provide a lot of insight for the domain expert. We discuss here only the results from clusters based on conditional probabilities with the conditional variable of country. We have obtained three distinct clusters and a description of the clusters is given below (see Figure 10).

- **Cluster 1:** A very high proportion of the applicants in cluster 1: (a) applied for criminal matters, (b) are males, (c) were approved legal aid, (d) are younger applicants, (e) applied for drug-related matters, (f) applied for motor car theft-related matters.
- **Cluster 2:** The applicants: (a) almost equally applied for criminal and family matters, (b) have proportion of females higher than any other clusters, (c) applied for family matters more than any other matters, (d) are mostly middle-aged applicants, (e) were approved legal aid less than applicants from countries in cluster 1.
- **Cluster 3:** The applicants: (a) almost equally applied for criminal and family matters, (b) have high proportion of males, (c) are slightly older applicants, (d) were approved legal aids less than applicants from countries in clusters 1 and 2.

Figure 10. Clusters formed from Victorian Legal Aid data set

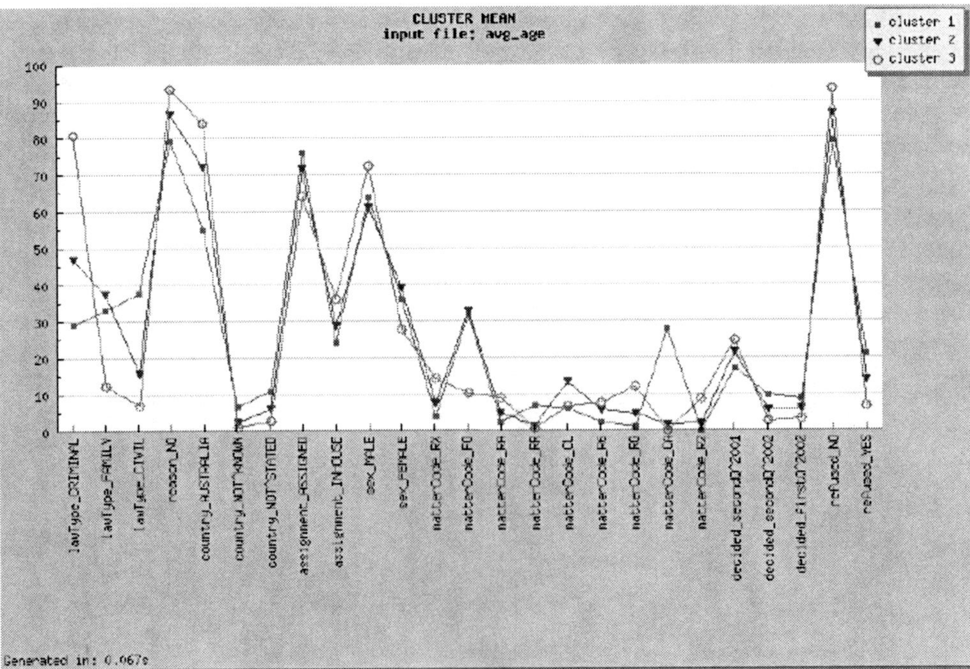

Conclusion

In this chapter, we have proposed a new visual tool for non-technical domain experts within organizations to further facilitate the extraction of meaningful information and knowledge from in-house databases. The tool is mainly based on the basic notion of grouping association rules. We achieved this by first creating a 2-D probability matrix of conditional probability from the categorical data and finally by clustering the confidence values. We applied the proposed methodology to the Victorian Legal Aid data set. Middle- to senior-level management found the ability to visualize the results of this knowledge discovery process very useful and the knowledge discovered was meaningful for the organization.

References

Agrawal, R., & Imielinski, T. (1993). Mining association rules between sets of items in large databases. In P. Buneman & S. Jajodia (Eds.), *Proceedings of the 1993 ACM SIGMOD International Conference on Management of Data,* Washington, DC (pp. 207-216). New York: ACM.

Andritos, P., Tsaparas, P., Miller, R. J., & Serveik, K. C. (2003). *LIMBO: A linear algorithm to cluster categorical data.* Technical report CSRG-467, Department of Computer Sciences, University of Toronto.

Bay, S. D., & Pazzani, M. J. (2000). Discovering and describing category differences: What makes a discovered difference insightful? In *Proceedings of the Twenty Second Annual Meeting of the Cognitive Science Society.*

Bay, S. D., & Pazzani, M. J. (2001). Detecting group differences: Mining contrast sets. *Data Mining and Knowledge Discovery*, *5*(3) 213-246.

Brachman, R. J., Khabaza, T., Kloesgen, W., Piatetsky-Shapiro, G., & Simoudis, E. (1996). Mining business databases. *Communications of the ACM*, *39*(11), 42-48.

Chakrabarti, S., Sarawagi, S., & Dom, B. (1998). Mining surprising patterns using temporal description length. In *Proceedings of the Twenty-fourth International Conference on Very Large Data Bases* (pp. 606-617). San Francisco: Morgan Kaufmann.

Duda, R. O., & Hart, P .E. (1973). *Pattern classification and scene analysis.* New York: John Wiley.

Duda, R. O., Hart, P. E., & Stork, D. G. (2001). *Pattern classification.* New York: John Wiley.

Ester, M., Kriegel, H.-P., Sander, J., & Xu, X. (1996, August). A density-based algorithm for discovering clusters in large spatial database with noise. In *Proceedings of the International Conference on Knowledge Discovery in Databases and Data Mining (KDD-96),* Montreal, Canada.

Frawley, W., Piatetsky-Shapiro, G., & Matheus, C. (1992, Fall). Knowledge discovery in databases — an overview. *AI Magazine*, *13*, 57-70.

Ganti, V., Gehrke, J., & Ramakrishnan, R. (1999). CACTUS—clustering categorical data using summaries. In *Proceedings of the Fifth ACM SIGKDD International Conference on Knowledge Discovery and Data Mining* (pp. 73-83). New York: ACM.

Gershon, N. Eick, S. G., & Card, S. (1998). Information visualization. *ACM Interactions*, *5*(2), 9-15.

Gibson, D., Kleinberg, J., & Raghavan (2000). Clustering categorical data: An approach based on dynamical systems. *Proceedings of the Twenty-fourth Very Large Databases Conference*, *8*(3/4), 222-236.

Goebel, M., & Gruenwald, L. (1999). A survey of data mining and knowledge discovery tools. *SIGKDD Explorations*, *1*(1), 20-33.

Grinstein G., & Thuraisingham, B. (1996), Data mining and data visualization. In *Proceedings of the Second Workshop on Database Issues for Data Visualization*, LNCS 1138 (pp. 54-56). Berlin: Springer-Verlag.

Guha, S., Rastogi, R., & Shim, K. (2000). ROCK: A robust clustering algorithm for categorical attributes. *Information Systems*, *25*(5), 345-366.

Ivkovic, S. (2004). *Visual grouping of association rules for hypothesis suggestion.* Masters Thesis, School of Information Technology and Mathematical Sciences, University of Ballarat.

Kohonen, T. (1982). Self organizing formation of topologically correct feature maps. *Biological Cybernatics*, *43*, 59-69.

Lin, W.-Y., Tseng, M.-C., & Su, J.-H. (2002). A confidence-lift support specification for interesting association mining. In *Proceedings of the PAKDD International Conference on Knowledge Discovery and Data Mining* (pp. 148-158). Berlin: Springer-Verlag.

Liu, B., Hsu, W., & Ma, Y. (1999). Mining association rules with multiple minimum supports. In *Proceedings of the Fifth ACM SIGKDD International Conference on Knowledge Discovery and Data Mining* (pp. 337-341). New York: ACM.

Liu, B., Hsu, W., & Ma, Y. (2001). Identifying non-actionable association rules. In *Proceedings of the Seventh ACM SIGKDD International Conference on Knowledge Discovery and Data Mining* (pp. 329-334). New York: ACM.

Wong, P. C., Whitney, P., & Thomas, J. (1999). Visualizing association rules for text mining. In *Proceedings of the 1999 IEEE Symposium on Information Visualization* (pp. 120-123,152). Washington, DC: IEEE Computer Society.

Chapter XIV

Support Vector Machines for Business Applications

Brian C. Lovell, NICTA & The University of Queensland, Australia

Christian J. Walder, Max Planck Institute for Biological Cybernetics, Germany

Abstract

This chapter discusses the use of Support Vector Machines (SVM) for business applications. It provides a brief historical background on inductive learning and pattern recognition, and then an intuitive motivation for SVM methods. The method is compared to other approaches, and the tools and background theory required to successfully apply SVM to business applications are introduced. The authors hope that the chapter will help practitioners to understand when the SVM should be the method of choice, as well as how to achieve good results in minimal time.

Introduction

Recent years have seen an explosive growth in computing power and data storage within business organisations. From a business perspective, this means that most companies now have massive archives of customer and product data and more often than not these archives are far too large for human analysis. An obvious question has therefore arisen, "How can one turn these immense corporate data archives to commercial advantage?" To this end, a number of common applications have arisen, from predicting which products a customer is most likely to purchase, to designing the perfect product based on responses to questionnaires. The theory and development of these processes has grown into a discipline of its own, known as Data Mining, which draws heavily on the related fields of Machine Learning, Pattern Recognition, and Mathematical Statistics.

The Data Mining discipline is still developing, however, and a great deal of sub-optimal and ad hoc analysis is being done. This is partly due to the complexity of the problems, but is also due to the vast number of available techniques. Even the most fundamental task in Data Mining, that of inductive inference, or making predictions based on examples, can be tackled by a great many different techniques. Some of these techniques are very difficult to tailor to a specific problem and require highly skilled human design. Others are more generic in application and can be treated more like the proverbial "black box." One particularly generic and powerful method, known as the Support Vector Machine (SVM) has proven to be both easy to apply and capable of producing results that range from good to excellent in comparison to other methods. While application of the method is relatively straightforward, the practitioner can still benefit greatly from a basic understanding of the underlying machinery.

Unfortunately most available tutorials on SVMs require a very solid mathematical background, so we have written this chapter to make SVM accessible to a wider community. This chapter comprises a basic background on the problem of induction, followed by the main sections. In the first section we introduce the concepts and equations on which the SVM is based, in an intuitive manner, and identify the relationship between the SVM and some of the other popular analysis methods. In the second section we survey some interesting applications of SVMs on practical real-world problems. Finally, the third section provides a set of guidelines and rules of thumb for applying the tool, with a pedagogical example that is designed to demonstrate everything that the SVM newcomer requires in order to immediately apply the tool to a specific problem domain. The chapter is intended as a brief introduction to the field that introduces the ideas, methodologies, as well as a hands-on introduction to freely available software, allowing the reader to rapidly determine the effectiveness of SVMs for their specific domain.

Background

SVMs are most commonly applied to the problem of inductive inference, or making predictions based on previously seen examples. To illustrate what is meant by this, let us consider the data presented in Tables 1 and 2. We see here an example of the problem of inductive inference, more specifically that of supervised learning. In supervised learning we are given a set of input data along with their corresponding labels. The input data comprises a number of examples about which several attributes are known (in this case, age, income, etc.). The label indicates which class a particular example belongs to. In the example above, the label tells us whether or not a given person has a broadband

Table 1. Training or labelled set

Age	Income	Years of Education	Gender	Broadband Home Internet Connection?
30	$56,000 / yr	16	male	Yes
50	$60,000 / yr	12	female	Yes
16	$2,000 / yr	11	male	No
35	$30,000 / yr	12	male	No

The dataset in Table 1 contains demographic information for four randomly selected people. These people were surveyed to determine whether or not they had a broadband home internet connection.

Table 2. Unlabelled set

Age	Income	Years of Education	Gender	Broadband Home Internet Connection?
40	$48,000 / yr	17	male	unknown
29	$60,000 / yr	18	female	unknown

The dataset in Table 2 contains demographic information for people who may or may not be good candidates for broadband internet connection advertising. The question arising is, "Which of these people is likely to have broadband internet connection at home?"

Internet connection to their home. This is called a binary classification problem because there are only two possible classes. In the second table, we are given the attributes for a different set of consumers, for whom the true class labels are unknown. Our goal is to infer from the first table the most likely labels for the people in the second table, that is, whether or not they have a broadband Internet connection to their home.

In the field of data mining, we often refer to these sets by the terms test set, training set, validation set, and so on, but there is some confusion in the literature about the exact definitions of these terms. For this reason we avoid this nomenclature, with the exception of the term training set. For our purposes, the training set shall be all that is given to us in order to infer some general correspondence between the input data and labels. We will refer to the set of data for which we would like to predict the labels as the unlabelled set.

A schematic diagram for the above process is provided in Figure 1. In the case of the SVM classifier (and most other learning algorithms for that matter), there are a number of parameters which must be chosen by the user. These parameters control various aspects of the algorithm, and in order to yield the best possible performance, it is necessary to make the right choices. The process of choosing parameters that yield good performance is often referred to as model selection. In order to understand this process, we have to consider what it is that we are aiming for in terms of classifier performance. From the point of view of the practitioner, the hope is that the algorithm will be able to make true predictions about unseen cases. Here the true values we are trying to predict are the class labels of the unlabelled data. From this perspective it is natural to measure the performance of a classifier by the probability of its misclassifying an unseen example.

Figure 1. Inductive inference process in schematic form (Based on a particular training set of examples with labels, the learning algorithm constructs a decision rule which can then be used to predict the labels of new unlabelled examples.)

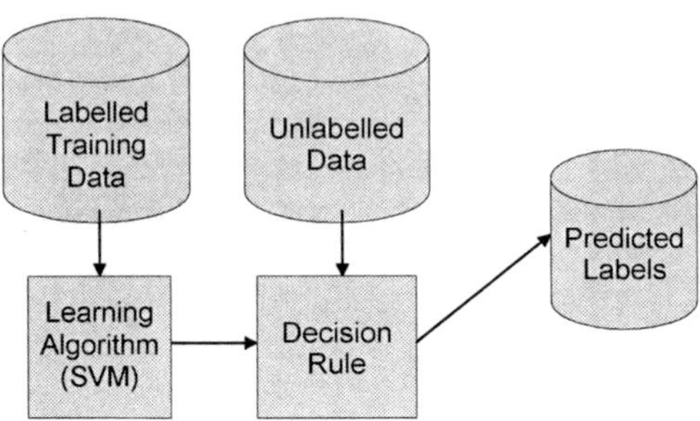

It is here that things become somewhat less straightforward, however, due to the following dilemma. In order to estimate the probability of a misclassification, we need to know the true underlying probability distributions of the data that we are dealing with. If we actually knew this, however, we wouldn't have needed to perform inductive inference in the first place! Indeed knowledge of the true probability distributions allows us to calculate the theoretically best possible decision rule corresponding to the so-called Bayesian classifier (Duda, Hart, & Stork, 2001).

In recent years, a great deal of research effort has gone into developing sophisticated theories that make statements about the probability of a particular classifier making errors on new unlabelled cases — these statements are typically referred to as generalization bounds. It turns out, however, that the research has a long way to go, and in practice one is usually forced to determine the parameters of the learning algorithm by much more pragmatic means. Perhaps the most straightforward of these methods involves estimating the probability of misclassification using a set of real data for which the class labels are known — to do this one simply compares the labels predicted by the learning algorithm to the true known labels. The estimate of misclassification probability is then given by the number of examples for which the algorithm made an error (that is, predicted a label other than the true known label) divided by the number of examples that were tested in this manner.

Some care needs to be taken, however, in how this procedure is conducted. A common pitfall for the inexperienced analyst involves making this estimate of misclassification probability using the training set from which the decision rule itself was inferred. The problem with this approach is easily seen from the following simple decision rule example. Imagine a decision rule that makes label predictions by way of the following procedure (sometimes referred to as the notebook classifier):

The notebook classifier decision rule: We wish to predict the label of the example X. If X is present in the training set, make the prediction that its label is the same as the corresponding label in the training set. Otherwise, toss a coin to determine the label.

For this method, while the estimated probability of misclassification on the training set will be zero, it is clear that for most real-world problems the algorithm will perform no better than tossing a coin! The notebook classifier is a commonly used example to illustrate the phenomenon of overfitting — which refers to situations where the decision rule fits the training set well, but does not *generalize* well to previously unseen cases. What we are really aiming for is a decision rule that generalizes as well as possible, even if this means that it cannot perform as well on the training set.

Cross-validation: So it seems that we need a more sophisticated means of estimating the generalization performance of our inferred decision rules if we are to successfully guide the model selection process. Fortunately there is a more effective means of estimating the generalization performance based on the training set. This procedure, which is referred to as *cross-validation* or more specifically *n-fold cross-validation*, proceeds in the following manner (Duda et al., 2001):

1. Split the training set into n equally sized and disjoint subsets (partitions), numbered 1 to n.
2. Construct a decision function using a conglomerate of all the data from subsets 2 to n.
3. Use this decision function to predict the labels of the examples in subset number 1.
4. Compare the predicted labels to the known labels in subset number 1.
5. Repeat steps 1 through 4 a further (n-1) times, each time testing on a different subset, and always excluding that subset from training.

Having done this, we can once again divide the number of misclassifications by the total number of training examples to get an estimate of the true generalization performance. The point is that since we have avoided checking the performance of the classifier on examples that the algorithm had already "seen," we have calculated a far more meaningful measure of classifier quality. Commonly used values for n are 3 and 10 leading to so called *3-fold* and *10-fold* cross-validation.

Now, while it is nice to have some idea of how well our decision function will generalize, we really want to use this measure to guide the model selection process. If there are only, say, two parameters to choose for the classification algorithm, it is common to simply evaluate the generalization performance (using cross validation) for all combinations of the two parameters, over some reasonable range. As the number of parameters increases, however, this soon becomes infeasible due to the excessive number of parameter combinations. Fortunately one can often get away with just two parameters for the SVM algorithm, making this relatively straightforward model selection methodology widely applicable and quite effective on real-world problems.

Now that we have a basic understanding of what supervised learning algorithms can do, as well as roughly how they should be used and evaluated, it is time to take a peek under the hood of one in particular, the SVM. While the main underlying idea of the SVM is quite intuitive, it will be necessary to delve into some mathematical details in order to better appreciate why the method has been so successful.

Main Thrust of the Chapter

The SVM is a supervised learning algorithm that infers from a set of labeled examples a function that takes new examples as input, and produces predicted labels as output. As such the output of the algorithm is a mathematical function that is defined on the space from which our examples are taken. It takes on one of two values at all points in the space, corresponding to the two class labels that are considered in binary classification. One of the theoretically appealing things about the SVM is that the key underlying idea is in fact extremely simple. Indeed, the standard derivation of the SVM algorithm begins with possibly the simplest class of decision functions: linear ones. To illustrate what is meant by this, Figure 2 consists of three linear decision functions that happen to be correctly classifying some simple 2D training sets.

Linear decision functions consist of a decision boundary that is a hyperplane (a line in 2D, plane in 3D, etc.) separating the two different regions of the space. Such a decision function can be expressed by a mathematical function of an input vector **x**, the value of which is the predicted label for **x** (either +1 or -1). The linear classifier can therefore be written as

$$g(\mathbf{x}) = sign(f(\mathbf{x}))$$
$$\text{where } f(\mathbf{x}) = <\mathbf{w}, \mathbf{x}> +b.$$

In this way we have parameterized the function by the weight vector **w** and the scalar b. The notation <w,x> denotes the inner or scalar product of **w** and **x**, defined by

Figure 2. A simple 2D classification task, to separate the black dots from the circles (Three feasible but different linear decision functions are depicted, whereby the classifier predicts that any new samples in the gray region are black dots, and those in the white region are circles. Which is the best decision function and why?)

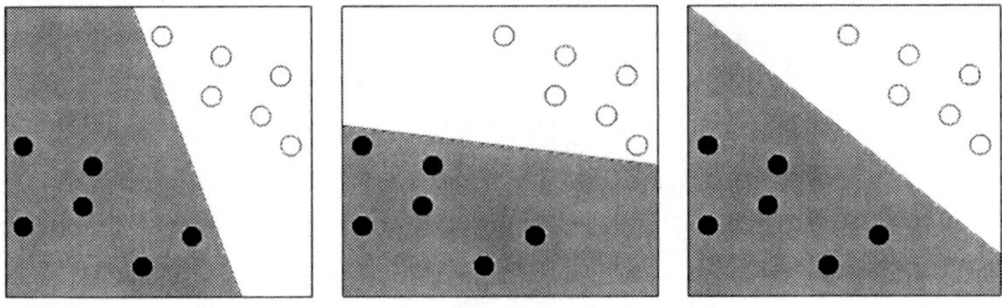

$$< \mathbf{w}, \mathbf{x} > = \sum_{i=1}^{d} w_i x_i$$

where d is the dimensionality, and w_i is the i-th component of **w**, where **w** is of the form $(w_1, w_2, \ldots w_d)$. Having formalized our decision function, we can now formalize the problem that the linear SVM addresses:

*Given a training set of vectors $\mathbf{x}_1, \mathbf{x}_2, \ldots \mathbf{x}_n$ with corresponding class membership labels $y_1, y_2, \ldots y_n$ that take on the values +1 or -1, choose parameters **w** and b of the linear decision function that generalizes well to unseen examples.*

Perceptron Algorithm: Probably the first algorithm to tackle this problem was the Perceptron algorithm (Rosenblatt, 1958). The Perceptron algorithm simply used an iterative procedure to incrementally adjust **w** and b until the decision boundary was able to separate the two classes of the training data. As such, the Perceptron algorithm would give no preference between the three feasible solutions in Figure 2 — any one of the three could result. This seems rather unsatisfactory, as most people would agree that the rightmost decision function is the superior one. Moreover, this intuitive preference can be justified in various ways, for example by considering the effect of measurement noise on the data — small perturbations of the data could easily change the predicted labels of the training set in the first two examples, whereas the third is far more robust in this respect. In order to make use of this intuition, it is necessary to state more precisely why we prefer the third classifier:

We prefer decision boundaries that not only correctly separate two classes in the training set, but lie as far from the training examples as possible.

This simple intuition is all that is required to lead to the linear SVM classifier, which chooses the hyperplane that separates the two classes with the maximum *margin*. The margin is just the distance from the hyperplane to the nearest training example. Before we continue, it is important to note that while the above example shows a 2D data set, which can be conveniently represented by points in a plane, in fact we will typically be dealing with higher dimensional data. For example, the example data in Table 1 could easily be represented as points in four dimensions as follows:

$$
\begin{array}{llllllll}
\mathbf{x}_1 = [& 30 & 56000 & 16 & 0 & 1]; & & y_1 = +1 \\
\mathbf{x}_2 = [& 50 & 60000 & 12 & 1 & 0]; & & y_2 = +1 \\
\mathbf{x}_3 = [& 16 & 2000 & 11 & 0 & 1]; & & y_3 = -1 \\
\mathbf{x}_4 = [& 35 & 30000 & 12 & 0 & 1]; & & y_4 = -1
\end{array}
$$

Figure 3. Linearly separable classification problem

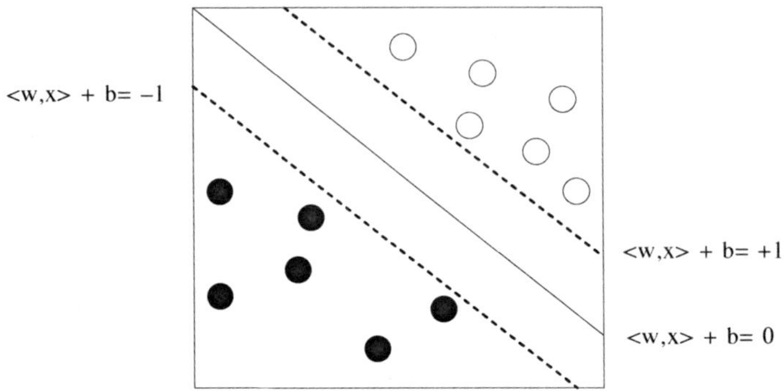

Actually, there are some design decisions to be made by the practitioner when translating attributes into the above type of numerical format, which we shall touch on in the next section. For example here we have mapped the male/female column into two new numerical indicators. For now, just note that we have also listed the labels y_1 to y_4 which take on the value +1 or −1, in order to indicate the class membership of the examples (that is, $y_i = 1$ means that $\mathbf{x}_i$ has a broadband home Internet connection).

In order to easily find the maximum margin hyperplane for a given data set using a computer, we would like to write the task as an *optimization problem*. Optimization problems consist of an objective function, which we typically want to find the maximum or minimum value of, along with a set of constraints, which are conditions that we must satisfy while finding the best value of the objective function. A simple example is to minimize x^2 subject to the constraint that $1 \leq x \leq 2$. The solution to this example optimization problem happens to be x = 1. To see how to compactly formulate the maximum margin hyperplane problem as an optimization problem, take a look at Figure 3.

The figure shows some 2D data drawn as circles and black dots, having labels +1 and −1 respectively. As before, we have parameterized our decision function by the vector **w** and the scalar b, which means that, in order for our hyperplane to correctly separate the two classes, we need to satisfy the following constraints:

$$< \mathbf{w}, \mathbf{x}_i > +b > 0, \text{for all } y_i = 1$$
$$< \mathbf{w}, \mathbf{x}_i > +b < 0, \text{for all } y_i = -1$$

To aid understanding, the first constraint above may be expressed as: "**<w, x$_i$>** + b must be greater than zero, *whenever y_i is equal to one.*" It is easy to check that the two sets of constraints above can be combined into the following single set of constraints:

$$(<\mathbf{w},\mathbf{x}_i>+b)y_i>0, i=1...n$$

However meeting this constraint is not enough to separate the two classes optimally — we need to do so with the maximum margin. An easy way to see how to do this is the following. First note that we have plotted the decision surface as a solid line in Figure 3, which is the set satisfying:

$$<\mathbf{w},\mathbf{x}>+b=0.$$

The set of constraints that we have so far is equivalent to saying that these data must lie on the correct side (according to class label) of this decision surface. Next notice that we have also plotted as dotted lines two other hyperplanes, which are the hyperplanes where the function $<\mathbf{w},\mathbf{x}>+b$ is equal to -1 (on the lower left) and +1 (on the upper right). Now, in order to find the maximum margin hyperplane, we can see intuitively that we should keep the dotted lines parallel and equidistant to the decision surface, and maximize their distance from one another, while satisfying the constraint that the data lie on the correct side of the dotted lines associated with that class. In mathematical form, the final clause of this sentence (the constraints) can be written as:

$$y_i(<\mathbf{w},\mathbf{x}_i>+b)>1, i=1...n.$$

All we need to do then is to maximize the distance between the dotted lines subject to the constraint set above. To aid in understanding, one commonly used analogy is to think of these data points as nails partially driven into a board. Now we successively place thicker and thicker pieces of timber between the nails representing the two classes until the timber just fits — the centreline of the timber now represents the optimal decision boundary. It turns out that this distance is equal to $2/\sqrt{<\mathbf{w},\mathbf{w}>}$, and since maximizing $2/\sqrt{<\mathbf{w},\mathbf{w}>}$ is the same as minimizing $<\mathbf{w},\mathbf{w}>$, we end up with the following optimization problem, the solution of which yields the parameters of the maximum margin hyperplane. The term ½ in the objective function below can be ignored as it simply makes things neater from a certain mathematical point of view:

$$\min_{\mathbf{w},b} \frac{1}{2}\mathbf{w}\cdot\mathbf{w}$$

$$\text{such that } y_i(\mathbf{w}\cdot\mathbf{x}_i+b)\geq 1 \quad \textbf{(1)}$$

$$\text{for all } i=1,2,...n$$

Figure 4. Linearly inseparable classification problem

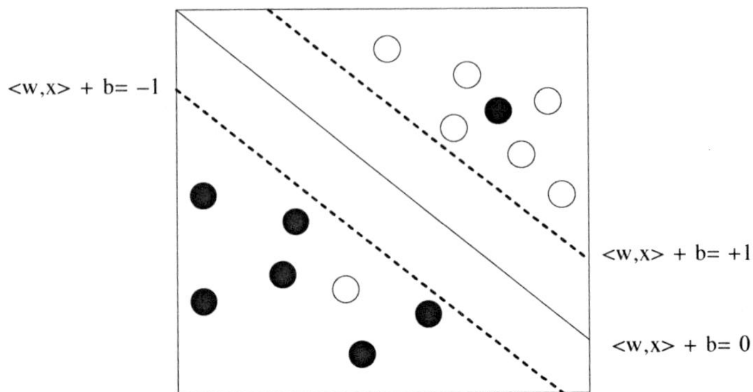

The previous problem is quite simple, but it encompasses the key philosophy behind the SVM — maximum margin data separation. If the above problem had been scribbled onto a cocktail napkin and handed to the pioneers of the Perceptron back in the 1960s, then the Machine Learning discipline would probably have progressed a great deal further than it has to date! We cannot relax just yet, however, as there is a major problem with the above method: What if these data are not *linearly separable*? That is if it is not possible to find a hyperplane that separates all of the examples in each class from all of the examples in the other class? In this case there would be no combination of **w** and b that could ever satisfy the set of constraints above, let alone do so with maximum margin. This situation is depicted in Figure 4, where it becomes apparent that we need to *soften* the constraint that these data lie on the correct side of the +1 and -1 hyperplanes, that is we need to allow some, but not too many data points to violate these constraints by a preferably small amount. This alternative approach turns out to be very useful not only for data sets that are not linearly separable, but also, and perhaps more importantly, in allowing improvements in generalization.

Usually when we start talking about vague concepts such as "not too many" and "a small amount," we need to introduce a parameter into our problem, which we can vary in order to balance between various goals and objectives. The following optimization problem, known as the 1-norm *soft margin* SVM, is probably the one most commonly used to balance the goals of maximum margin separation, and correctness of the training set classification. It achieves various trade-offs between these goals for various values of the parameter C, which is usually chosen by cross-validation on a training set as discussed earlier.

$$\min_{\mathbf{w},b,\xi} \frac{1}{2}\mathbf{w}\cdot\mathbf{w} + C\sum_{i=1}^{m}\xi_i$$

$$\text{such that } y_i(\mathbf{w}\cdot\mathbf{x}_i + b) + \xi_i \geq 1 \qquad * \qquad \textbf{(2)}$$

$$\text{for all } i = 1,2,\ldots n.$$

The easiest way to understand this problem is by comparison with the previous formulation that we gave, which is known as the *hard margin* SVM, in reference to the fact that the margin constraints are "hard," and are not allowed to be violated at all. First note that we have an extra term in our objective function that is equal to the sum of the ξ_i's. Since we are minimizing the objective function, it is safe to say that we are looking for a solution that keeps the ξ_i values small. Moreover, since the ξ term is added to the original objective function after multiplication by C, we can say that as C increases we care less about the size of the margin, and more about keeping the ξ's small. The true meaning of the ξ_i's can only be seen from the constraint set, however. Here, instead of constraining the function $y_i(<\mathbf{w},\mathbf{x}_i> + b)$ to be greater than 1, we constrain it to be greater than $1 - \xi_i$. That is, we allow the point $\mathbf{x}_i$ to violate the margin by an amount ξ_i. Thus, the value of C trades between how large of a margin we would prefer, as opposed to how many of the training set examples violate this margin (and by how much).

So far, we have seen that the maximally separating hyperplane is a good starting point for linear classifiers. We have also seen how to write down the problem of finding this hyperplane as an optimization problem consisting of an objective function and constraints. After this we saw a way of dealing with data that is not linearly separable, by allowing some training points to violate the margin somewhat. The next limitation we will address is in the form of solutions available. So far we have only considered very simple linear classifiers, and as such we can only expect to succeed in very simple cases. Fortunately it is possible to extend the previous analysis in an intuitive manner, to more complex classes of decision functions. The basic idea is illustrated in Figure 5.

The example in Figure 5 shows on the left a data set that is not linearly separable. In fact, the data is not even close to linearly separable, and one could never do very well with a linear classifier for the training set given. In spite of this, it is easy for a person to look at the data and suggest a simple elliptical decision surface that ought to generalize well. Imagine, however, that there is a mapping Φ, which transforms these data to some new, possibly higher dimensional space, in which the data is linearly separable. If we knew Φ then we could map all of the data to the *feature space*, and perform normal SVM classification in this space. If we can achieve a reasonable margin in the feature space,

Figure 5. An example of a mapping Φ to a feature space in which the data become linearly separable

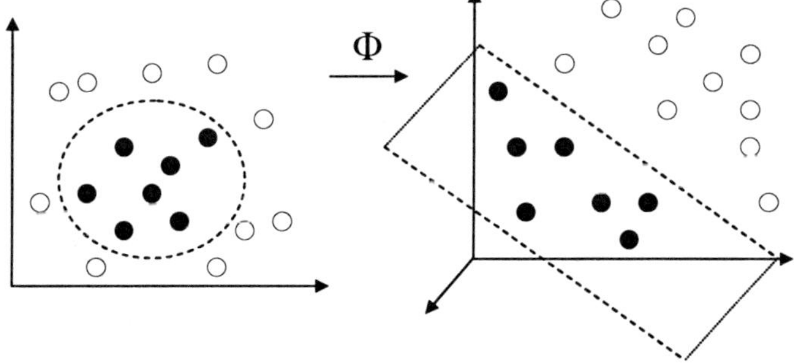

then we can expect a reasonably good generalization performance, in spite of a possible increase in dimensionality.

The last sentence of the previous paragraph is far deeper than it may first appear. For some time, Machine Learning researchers have feared the *curse of dimensionality*, a name given to the widely-held belief that if the dimension of the feature space is large in comparison to the number of training examples, then it is difficult to find a classifier that generalizes well. It took the theory of Vapnik and Chervonenkis (Vapnik, 1998) to put a serious dent in this belief. In a nutshell, they formalized and proved the last sentence of the previous paragraph, and thereby paved the way for methods that map data to *very* high dimensional feature spaces where they then perform maximum margin linear separation. Actually, a tricky practical issue also had to be overcome before the approach could flourish: if we map to a feature space that is too high in dimension, then it will become impossible to perform the required calculations (that is, to find **w** and b) — that is, it would take too long on a computer. It is not obvious how to overcome this difficulty, and it took until 1995 for researchers to notice the following elegant and quite remarkable possibility.

The usual way of proceeding is to take the original soft margin SVM, and convert it to an equivalent *Lagrangian dual problem*. The derivation is not especially enlightening, however, so we will skip to the result, which is that the solution to the following *dual* or equivalent problem gives us the solution to the original SVM problem. The dual problem, which is to be solved by varying the α_i's, is as follows (Vapnik, 1998):

$$\begin{aligned} &\min_{\boldsymbol{\alpha}} \frac{1}{2}\sum_{i,j=1}^{m} y_i y_j \alpha_i \alpha_j (\mathbf{x}_i \cdot \mathbf{x}_j) - \sum_{i=1}^{m} \alpha_i \\ &\quad \text{such that } \sum_{i=1}^{m} y_i \alpha_i = 0 \\ &\quad 0 \le \alpha_i \le C,\ i = 1, 2, \dots, m. \end{aligned} \tag{3}$$

The α_i's are known as the *dual variables*, and they define the corresponding *primal variables* **w** and b by the following relationships:

$$\mathbf{w} = \sum_{i=1}^{m} \alpha_i y_i \mathbf{x}_i$$

$$\alpha_i (y_i (<\mathbf{w}, \mathbf{x}_i> + b) - 1) = 0$$

Note that by the linearity of the inner product (that is, the fact that **<a+b,c>** = **<a,c>** + **<b,c>**), we can write the decision function in the following form:

$$f(\mathbf{x}) = < \mathbf{w}, \mathbf{x} > +b = \sum_{i=1}^{m} \alpha_i y_i < \mathbf{x}_i, \mathbf{x} > +b$$

Recall that it is the sign of f(**x**) that gives us the predicted label of **x**. A quite remarkable thing is that in order to determine the optimal values of the α_i's and b, and also to calculate f(**x**), we do not actually need to know any of the training or testing vectors, we only need to know the scalar value of their inner product with one another. This can be seen by noting that the vectors only ever appear by way of their inner product with one another. The elegant thing is that rather than explicitly mapping all of the data to the new space and performing linear SVM classification, we can operate in the original space, provided we can find a so-called *kernel* function k(.,.) which is equal to the inner product of the mapped data. That is, we need a kernel function k(.,.) satisfying:

$$k(\mathbf{x}, \mathbf{y}) = < \Phi(\mathbf{x}), \Phi(\mathbf{y}) >$$

In practice, the practitioner need not concern him or herself with the exact nature of the mapping Φ. In fact, it is usually more intuitive to concentrate on properties of the kernel functions anyway, and the prevailing wisdom states that the function k(**x**,**y**) should be a good measure of the similarity of the vectors **x** and **y**. Moreover, not just any function k can be used — it must also satisfy certain technical conditions, known as Mercer's conditions. This procedure of implicitly mapping the data via the function *k* is typically often called the *kernel trick* and has found wide application after being popularized by the success of the SVM (Schölkopf & Smola, 2002). The two most widely used kernel functions are the following.

Polynomial Kernel $\quad k(x, y) = (< x, y > +1)^d$

The polynomial kernel is valid for all positive integers $d \geq 1$. The kernel corresponds to a mapping Φ that computes all degree d monomial terms of the individual vector components of the original space. The polynomial kernel has been used to great effect on digit recognition problems.

Gaussian Kernel $\quad k(x, y) = \exp(-\frac{\| \mathbf{x} - \mathbf{y} \|^2}{\sigma^2})$

The Gaussian kernel, which is similar to the Gaussian probability distribution from which it gets its name, is one of a group of kernel functions known as radial basis functions (RBFs). RBFs are kernel functions that depend only on the geometric distance between **x** and **y**. The kernel is valid for all non-zero values of the kernel width σ, and corresponds to a mapping Φ into an infinite dimensional and therefore somewhat less interpretable, feature space. Nonetheless, the Gaussian is probably the most useful and commonly used kernel function.

Now that we know the form of the SVM dual problem, as well as how to generalize it using kernel functions, the only thing left is to see is how to actually solve the optimization problem, in order to find the α_i's. The optimization problem is one example of a class of problems known as Quadratic Programs (QPs). The term program, as it is used here, is somewhat antiquated and in fact means a "mathematical optimization problem," not a computer program. Fortunately there are many computer programs that can solve QP's such as this, these computer programs being known as Quadratic Program (QP) solvers. An important factor to note here is that there is considerable structure in the QP that arises in SVM training, and while it would be possible to use almost any QP solver on the problem, there are a number of sophisticated software packages tailored to take advantage of this structure, in order to decrease the requirements of computer time and memory.

One property of the SVM QP that can be taken advantage of is its sparcity — the fact that in many cases, at the optimal solution most of the α_i's will equal zero. It is interesting to see what this means in terms of the decision function $f(\mathbf{x})$: those vectors with $\alpha_i = 0$ do not actually enter into the final form of the solution. In fact, it can be shown that one can remove all of the corresponding training vectors before training even commences, and get the same final result. The vectors with non-zero values of α_i are known as the *Support Vectors*, a term that has its root in the theory of convex sets. As it turns out, the Support Vectors are the "hard" cases — the training examples that are most difficult to classify correctly (and that lie closest to the decision boundary). In our previous practical analogy, the support vectors are literally the nails that support the block of wood! Now that we have an understanding of the machinery underlying it, we will soon proceed to solve a practical problem using the freely available SVM software package libSVM written by Hsu and Lin (Chang & Lin, 2001).

Relationship to Other Methods

We noted in the introduction that the SVM is an especially easy-to-use method that typically produces good results even when treated as a processing "black box." This is indeed the case, and to better understand this it is necessary to consider what is involved in using some other methods. We will focus in detail on the extremely prevalent class of algorithms known as artificial neural networks, but first we provide a brief overview of some other related methods.

Linear Discriminant Analysis (Hand, 1981; Weiss & Kulikowski, 1991) is widely used in business and marketing applications, can work in multiple dimensions, and is well-grounded in the mathematical literature. It nonetheless has two major drawbacks. The first is that linear discriminant functions, as the name implies, can only successfully classify linearly separable data thus limiting their application to relatively simple problems. If we extend the method to higher-order functions such as quadratic discriminators, generalization suffers. Indeed such degradation in performance with increased numbers of parameters corroborated the belief in the "curse of dimensionality" finally disproved by Vapnik (1998). The second problem is simply that generalization performance on real problems is usually significantly worse than either decision trees or artificial neural networks (e.g., see the comparisons in Weiss & Kulikowski, 1991).

Decision Trees are commonly used in classification problems with categorical data (Quinlan, 1993), although it is possible to derive categorical data from ordinal data by introducing binary valued features such as "age is less than 20." Decision trees construct a tree of questions to be asked of a given example in order to determine the class membership by way of class labels associated with leaf nodes of the decision tree. This approach is simple and has the advantage that it produces decision rules that can be interpreted by a human as well as a machine. However the SVM is more appropriate for complex problems with many ordinal features.

Nearest Neighbor methods are very simple and therefore suitable for extremely large data sets. These methods simply search the training data set for the *k* examples that are closest (by the criteria of Euclidean distance for example) to the given input. The most common class label that associated with these *k* is then assigned to the given query example. When the training and testing computation times are not so important, however, the discriminative nature of the SVM will usually yield significantly improved results.

Artificial Neural Network (ANN) algorithms have become extremely widespread in the area of data mining and pattern recognition (Bishop, 1995). These methods were originally inspired by the neural connections that comprise the human brain — the basic idea being that in the human brain many simple units (neurons) are connected together in a manner that produces complex, powerful behavior. To simulate this phenomenon, neurons are modeled by units whose output y is related to the input x by some *activation function* g by the relationship $y = g(x)$. These units are then connected together in various *architectures*, whereby the output of a given unit is multiplied by some constant *weight* and then fed forward as input to the next unit, possibly in summation with a similarly scaled output from some other unit(s). Ultimately all of the inputs are fed to one single final unit, the output of which is typically compared to some threshold in order to produce a class membership prediction. This is a very general framework that provides many avenues for customization:

- Choice of activation function.
- Choice of network architecture (number of units and the manner in which they are connected).
- Choice of the "weights" by which the output of a given unit is multiplied to produce the input of another unit.
- Algorithm for determining the weights given the training data.

In comparison to the SVM, both the strength and weakness of the ANN lies in its flexibility — typically a considerable amount of experimentation is required in order to achieve good results, and moreover since the optimization problems that are typically used to find the weights of the chosen network are non-convex, many numerical tricks are required in order to find a good solution to the problem. Nonetheless, given sufficient skill and effort in engineering a solution with an ANN, one can often tailor the algorithm very specifically to a given problem in a process that is likely to eventually yield superior results to the SVM. Having said this, there are cases, for example in handwritten digit recognition, in which SVM performance is on par with highly engineered ANN solutions (DeCoste & Schölkopf, 2002). By way of comparison, the SVM approach is likely to yield a very good solution with far less effort than is required for a good ANN solution.

Practical Application of the SVM

As we have seen, the theoretical underpinnings of the SVM are very compelling, especially since the algorithm involves very little trial and error, and is easy to apply. Nonetheless, the usefulness of the algorithm can only be borne out by practical experience, and so in this sub-section we survey a number of studies that use the SVM algorithm in practical problems. Before we mention such specific cases, we first identify the general characteristics of those problems to which the SVM is particularly well-suited. One key consideration is that in its basic form the SVM has limited capacity to deal with large training data sets. Typically the SVM can only handle problems of up to approximately 100,000 training examples before approximations must be made in order to yield reasonable training times. Having said this, the training times depend only marginally on the dimensionality of the features — it is often said that SVM can often defy the so-called *curse of dimensionality* — the difficulty that often occurs when the dimensionality is high in comparison with the number of training samples. It should also be noted that, with the exception of the string kernel case, the SVM is most naturally suited to ordinal features rather than categorical ones, although as we shall see in the next section, it is possible to handle both cases.

Before turning to some specific business and marketing cases, it is important to note that some of the most successful applications of the SVM have been in image processing - in particular handwritten digit recognition (DeCoste & Schölkopf, 2002) and face recognition (Osuna, Freund & Girosi, 1997). In these areas, a common theme of the application of SVM is not so much increased accuracy, but rather a greatly simplified design and implementation process. As such, when considering popular areas such as face recognition, it is important to understand that very simple SVM implementations are often competitive with the complex and highly tuned systems that were developed over a longer period prior to the advent of the SVM. Another interesting application area for SVM is on string data, for example in text mining or the analysis of genome sequences (Joachims, 2002). The key reason for the great success of SVM in this area is the existence of "string kernels" — these are kernel functions defined on strings that elegantly avoid many of the combinatoric problems associated with other methods, whilst having the advantage over generative probability models such as the Hidden Markov Model that the SVM learns to *discriminate* between the two classes via the maximization of the margin. The practical use of text categorization systems is extremely widespread, with most large enterprises relying on such analysis of their customer interactions in order to provide automated response systems that are nonetheless tailored to the individual. Furthermore, the SVM has been successfully used in a study of text and data mining for direct marketing applications (Cheung, Kwok, Law, & Tsui, 2003) in which relatively limited customer information was automatically supplanted with the preferences of a larger population, in order to determine effective marketing strategies. SVMs have enjoyed success in a number of other business related applications, including credit rating analysis (Huang, Chen, Hsu, Chen, & Wu, 2004) and electricity price forecasting (Sansom, Downs, & Saha, 2002). To conclude this survey note that while the majority of the marketing teams do not publish their methodologies, since many of the important data mining software packages (e.g., Oracle Data Mining and SAS Enterprise Miner) have incorporated the SVM, it is likely that there will be a significant and increasing use of the SVM in industrial settings.

A Worked Example

In "A Practical Guide to Support Vector Classification" (Hsu, Chang, & Lin, 2003) a simple procedure for applying the SVM classifier is provided for inexperienced practitioners of the SVM classifier. The procedure is intended to be easy to follow, quick, and capable of producing reasonable generalization performance. The steps they advocate can be paraphrased as follows:

1. Convert the data to the input format of the SVM software you intend to use.
2. Scale the individual components of the data into a common range.
3. Use the Gaussian kernel function.
4. Use cross-validation to find the best parameters C (margin softness) and σ (Gaussian width).
5. With the values of C and σ determined by cross-validation, retrain on the entire training set.

The above tasks are easily accomplished using, for example, the free libSVM software package, as we will demonstrate in detail in this section. We have chosen this tool because it is free, easy to use and of a high quality, although the majority of our discussion applies equally well to other SVM software packages wherein the same steps will necessarily be required. The point of this chapter, then, is to illustrate in a concrete fashion the process of applying an SVM. The libSVM software package with which we do this consists of three main command-line tools, as well as a helper script in the python language. The basic functions of these tools are summarized here:

- **svm-scale:** This simple program simply rescales the data as in step 2 above. The input is a data set, and the output is a new data set that has been rescaled.
- **grid.py:** This function can be used to assist in the cross validation parameter selection process. It simply calculates a cross validation estimate of generalization performance for a range of values of C and the Gaussian kernel width σ. The results are then illustrated as a two dimensional contour plot of generalization performance versus C and σ.
- **svm-train:** This is the most sophisticated part of libSVM, which takes as input a file containing the training examples, and outputs a "model file" — a list of Support Vectors and corresponding α_i's, as well as the bias term and kernel parameters. The program also takes a number of input arguments that are used to specify the type of kernel function and margin softness parameter. As well as some more technical options, the program also has the option (used by grid.py) of computing an n-fold cross-validation estimate of the generalization performance.
- **svm-predict:** Having run svm-train, svm-predict can be used to predict the class labels of a new set of unseen data. The input to the program is a model file and a data set, and the output is a file containing the predicted labels, sign(f($\mathbf{x}$)), for the given data set.

Detailed instructions for installing the software can be found on the libSVM Web site (Chang & Lin, 2001). We will now demonstrate these three steps using the example data set at the beginning of the chapter, in order to predict which customers are likely to be home broadband Internet users. To make the procedure clear, we will give details of all the required input files (containing the labelled and unlabelled data), the output file (containing the learned decision function), and the command line statements required to produce and process these files.

Preprocessing (svm-scale)

All of our discussions so far have considered the input training examples as numerical vectors. In fact this is not necessary as it is possible to define kernels on discrete quantities, but we will not worry about that here. Instead, notice that in our example training data in Table 1, each training example has several individual features, both numerical and categorical. There are three numerical features (age, income and years of education), and one categorical feature (gender). In constructing training vectors for the SVM from these training examples, the numerical features are directly assigned to individual components of the training vectors

Categorical features, however, must be dealt with slightly differently. Typically, if the categorical feature belongs to one of m different categories (here the categories are male and female so that our m is 2), then we map this single categorical feature into m individual binary valued numerical features. A training vector whose categorical feature corresponds to feature n (the ordering is irrelevant), will have all zero values for these into binary valued numerical features, except for the n-th one, which we set to 1. This is a simple way of indicating that the features are not related to one another by relative magnitudes. Once again, the data in Table 1 would be represented by these four vectors, with corresponding class labels y_i:

$$
\begin{array}{lllllll}
\mathbf{x}_1 = [& 30 & 56000 & 16 & 0 & 1]; & y_1 = +1 \\
\mathbf{x}_2 = [& 50 & 60000 & 12 & 1 & 0]; & y_2 = +1 \\
\mathbf{x}_3 = [& 16 & 2000 & 11 & 0 & 1]; & y_3 = -1 \\
\mathbf{x}_4 = [& 35 & 30000 & 12 & 0 & 1]; & y_4 = -1
\end{array}
$$

In order to use the libSVM software, we must represent the above data in a file that is formatted according to the libSVM standard. The format is very simple, and best described with an example. The above data would be represented by a single file that looks like this:

```
+1 1:30 2:56000 3:16 5:1
+1 1:50 2:60000 3:12 4:1
-1 1:16 2:2000 3:11 5:1
-1 1:35 2:30000 3:12 5:1
```

Each line of the training file represents one training example, and begins with the class label (+1 or -1), followed by a space and then an arbitrary number of index:value pairs. There should be no spaces between the colons and the indexes or values, only between the individual index:value pairs. Note that if a feature takes on the value zero, it need not be included as an index:value pair, allowing data with many zeros to be represented by a smaller file.

Now that we have our training data file, we are ready to run **svm_scale**. As we discovered in the first section, ultimately all our data will be represented by the kernel function evaluation between individual vectors. The purpose of this program is to make some very simple adjustments to the data in order for it to be better represented by these kernel evaluations. In accordance with step 3 above we will be using the Gaussian kernel, which can be expressed by

$$k(x,y) = \exp(-\frac{\|\mathbf{x}-\mathbf{y}\|^2}{\sigma^2}) = \exp(-\sum_{d=1}^{D}\frac{(x_d - y_d)^2}{\sigma^2}).$$

Here we have written out the D individual components of the vectors **x** and **y**, which correspond to the ($D = 5$) individual numerical features of our training examples. It is clear from the summation on the right, that if a given feature has a much larger range of variation than another feature it will dominate the sum, and the feature with the smaller range of variation will essentially be ignored. For our example, this means that the income feature, which has the largest range of values, will receive an undue amount of attention from the SVM algorithm. Clearly this is a problem, and while the Machine Learning community has yet to give the final word on how to deal with it in an optimal manner, many practitioners simply rescale the data so that each feature falls in the same range, for example between zero and one. This can be easily achieved using **svm_scale**, which takes as input a data file in libSVM format, and outputs both a rescaled data file and a set of scaling parameters. The rescaled data should then be used to train the model, and the same scaling (as stored in the scaling parameters file) should be applied to any unlabelled data before applying the learnt decision function. The format of the command is as follows:

```
svm-scale –s scaling_parameters_file training_data_file > rescaled_training_data_file
```

In order to apply the same scaling transformation to the unlabelled set, svm_scale must be executed again with the following arguments:

```
svm-scale –r scaling_parameters_file unlabelled_data_file >
        rescaled_unlabelled_data_file
```

Here the file unlabelled_data_file contains the unlabelled data, and has an identical format to the training file, aside from the fact that the labels +1 and -1 are optional, and will be ignored if they exist.

Parameter Selection (grid.py)

The parameter selection process is without doubt the most difficult step in applying an SVM. Fortunately the simplistic method we prescribe here is not only relatively straightforward, but also usually quite effective. Our goal is to choose the C and σ values for our SVM. Following the previous discussion about parameter or model selection, our basic method of tackling this problem is to make a cross-validation estimate of the generalization performance for a range of values of C and σ, and examine the results visually. Given the outcome of this step, we may either choose values for C and σ, or conduct a further search based on the results we have already seen.

The following command will construct a plot of the cross-validation performance for our scaled data set:

```
grid.py –log2c -5,5,1 –log2g -20,0,1 –v 10 rescaled_training_data_file
```

The search range of the C and σ values are specified by the –log2c and –log2g commands respectively. In both cases the numbers that follow take the form begin,end,stepsize to indicate that we wish to search logarithmically using the values

Figure 6. A contour plot of cross-validation accuracy for a given training set as produced by grid.py

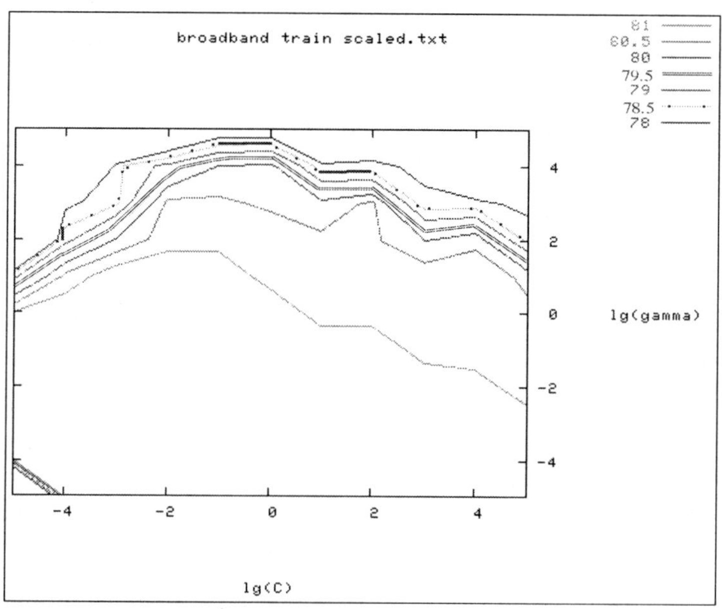

$$2^{begin}, 2^{begin+stepsize} \ldots 2^{end}.$$

Specifying "-v n" indicates that we wish to do n-fold cross-validation (in the above command n = 10), and the last argument to the command indicates which data file to use. The output of the program is a contour plot, saved in an image file of the name rescaled_training_data_file.png. The output image for the above command is depicted in Figure 6.

The contour plot indicates with various line colors the cross-validation accuracy of the classifier, as a function of C and σ — this is measured as a percentage of correct classifications, so that we prefer large values. Note that óð is in fact referred to as "gamma" by the libSVM software — the variable name is of course arbitrary, but we choose to refer to it as σ for compatibility with the majority of SVM literature.

Given such a contour plot of performance, as stated previously there are generally two conclusions to be reached:

1. The optimal (or at least satisfactory) values of C and σ are contained within the plotting region.
2. It is necessary to continue the search for C and σ, over a different range than that of the plot, in order to achieve better performance.

In the first case, we can read the optimal values of C and óð from the output of the program on the command window. Each line of output indicates the best parameters that have been encountered up to that point, and so we can take the last line as our operating parameters.

In the second case, we must choose which direction to continue the search. From Figure 6 it seems feasible to keep searching over a range of smaller σ and larger C. This whole procedure is usually quite effective, however, there can be no denying that the search for the correct parameters is still something of a black art. Given this, we invite interested readers to experiment for themselves, in order to get a basic feel for how things behave. For our purposes, we shall assume that a good choice is $C = 2^{-2} = 0.25$ and $\sigma = 2^{-2} = 0.25$, and proceed to the next step.

Training (svm-train)

As we have seen, the cross-validation process does not use all of the data for training — at each iteration some of the training data must be excluded for evaluation purposes. For this reason it is still necessary to do a final training run on the entire training set, using the parameters that we have determined in the previous parameter selection process. The command to train is:

svm-train –g 0.25 –c 0.25 rescaled_training_data_file model_file

This command sets C and σ using the –c and –g switches, respectively. The other two arguments are the name of the training data, and finally the file name for the learnt decision function or model.

Prediction (svm-predict)

The final step is very simple. Now that we have a decision function, stored in the file model_file as well as a properly scaled set of unlabelled data, we can compute the predicted label of each of the examples in the set of unlabelled data by executing the command:

svm-predict rescaled_unlabelled_data_file model_file predictions_file

After executing this command, we will have a new file of the name predictions_file, Each line of this file will contain either "+1" or "–1" depending on the predicted label of the corresponding entry in the file rescaled_unlabelled_data.

Summary

The general problem of induction is an important one, and can add a great deal of value to large corporate databases. Analyzing this data is not always simple, however, and it is fortunate that methods that are both easy to apply and effective have finally arisen, such as the Support Vector Machine.

The basic concept underlying the Support Vector Machine is quite simple and intuitive, and involves separating our two classes of data from one another using a linear function that is the maximum possible distance from the data. This basic idea becomes a powerful learning algorithm, when one overcomes the issue of linear separability (by allowing margin errors), and implicit mapping to more descriptive feature spaces (through the use of kernel functions).

Moreover, there exist free and easy to use software packages, such as libSVM, that allow one to obtain good results with a minimum of effort. The continued uptake of these tools is inevitable, but is often impeded by the poor results obtained by novices. We hope that this chapter is a useful aid in avoiding this problem, as it quickly affords a basic understanding of both the theory and practice of the SVM.

References

Bishop, C. (1995). *Neural networks for pattern recognition*. Oxford: Oxford University.

Chang, C.-C., & Lin, C.-J. (2001). *LIBSVM: A library for support vector machines* [Computer software and manual]. Retrieved May 11, 2005, from http://www.csie.ntu.edu.tw/~cjlin/libsvm

Cheung, K.-W., Kwok, J. T., Law, M. H., & Tsui, K.-C. (2003). Mining customer product ratings for personalized marketing. *Decision Support Systems*, *35*(2), 231-243.

DeCoste, D., & Schölkopf, B (2002). Training invariant support vector machines. *Machine Learning*, *45*(1-3), 161-290.

Duda, R. O., Hart, P. E., & Stork, D. G. (2001). *Pattern classification*. New York: John Wiley.

Hand, D. J. (1981). *Discrimination and classification*. New York: John Wiley.

Hsu, C.-W., Chang, C.-C., & Lin, C.-J. (2003). *A practical guide to support vector classification*. Retrieved May 11, 2005, from http://www.csie.ntu.edu.tw/~cjlin/papers/guide/guide.pdf

Huang, Z., Chen, H., Hsu, C.-J., Chen, W.-H., & Wu, S. (2004). Credit rating analysis with support vector machines and neural networks: A market comparative study. *Decision Support Systems*, *37*(4), 543-558.

Joachims, T. (2002). *Learning to classify text using support vector machines: Methods, theory and algorithms*. Norwell, MA: Kluwer Academic.

Osuna, E., Freund, R., & Girosi, F. (1997). Training support vector machines: An application to face detection. In *Proceedings of the 1997 Conference on Computer Vision and Pattern Recognition — CVPR'97* (pp. 130-138). Washington, DC: IEEE Computer Society.

Quinlan, R. (1993). *C4.5: Programs for machine learning.* San Francisco: Morgan Kaufmann.

Rosenblatt, F. (1958, November). The Perceptron: A probabilistic model for information storage and organization in the brain, *Psychological Review*, *65*, 386-408.

Sansom, D. C., Downs, T., & Saha, T. K. (2002). Evaluation of support vector machine based forecasting tool in electricity price forecasting for Australian National Electricity Market participants. *Journal of Electrical and Electronics Engineering Australia*, *22*(3), 227-233.

Schölkopf, B., & Smola, A. (2002). *Learning with kernels: Support vector machines, regularization, optimization, and beyond.* Cambridge, MA: MIT.

Vapnik, V. N. (1998). *Statistical learning theory.* New York: Wiley.

Weiss, S. A., & Kulikowski, C. A. (1991). *Computer systems that learn: Classification and prediction methods from statistics, neural nets, machine learning, and expert systems.* San Mateo, CA: Morgan Kaufmann.

Chapter XV

Algorithms for Data Mining

Tadao Takaoka, University of Canterbury, New Zealand

Nigel K. Ll. Pope, Griffith University, Australia

Kevin E. Voges, University of Canterbury, New Zealand

Abstract

In this chapter, we present an overview of some common data mining algorithms. Two techniques are considered in detail. The first is association rules, a fundamental approach that is one of the oldest and most widely used techniques in data mining. It is used, for example, in supermarket basket analysis to identify relationships between purchased items. The second is the maximum sub-array problem, which is an emerging area that is yet to produce a textbook description. This area is becoming important as a new tool for data mining, particularly in the analysis of image data. For both of these techniques, algorithms are presented in pseudo-code to demonstrate the logic of the approaches. We also briefly consider decision and regression trees and clustering techniques.

Introduction

Data mining is often used to extract useful information from vast volumes of data, typically contained within large databases. In this context "useful information" usually means some interesting information that realistically can only be found by analyzing the database with a computer and identifying patterns that an unaided human eye would be unable to ascertain. Applications of data mining occur in a wide variety of disciplines — the database could contain the sales data of a supermarket, or may also be image data such as a medical x-rays. Interesting information could then be customers' purchasing behavior in the sales database, or some abnormality in the medical image. As the size of these databases is measured in gigabytes and they are stored on disk, algorithms that deal with the data must not only be fast, but also need to access the disk as few times as possible.

One of the oldest and most widely used data mining techniques involves the identification of association rules. For example, mining an association rule in a sales database can involve finding a relationship between purchased items that can be expressed in terms such as: "A customer who buys cereal is likely to buy milk." In the following discussion we use a simple example to illustrate a number of issues with association rule mining and to assist in the outline of data mining algorithms. Figure 1 illustrates a simple record of sales at a food supermarket, including a list of items purchased by specific customers, as well as some known attributes of the customers.

Figure 1. Example transaction and customer databases

Transactions

Customer	Items	Total amount spent
1	ham, cheese, cereal, milk	$42
2	bread, cheese, milk	$22
3	ham, bread, cheese, milk	$37
4	bread, milk	$12
5	bread, cereal, milk	$24
6	ham, bread, cheese, cereal	$44

Customers

Customer	Name	Gender	Age	Annual income	Address
1	Anderson	female	33	$20000	suburb A
2	Bell	female	45	$35000	suburb A
3	Chen	male	28	$25000	suburb B
4	Dickson	male	50	$60000	suburb B
5	Elias	male	61	$65000	suburb A
6	Foster	female	39	$45000	suburb B

In the first part of the figure, the numbers correspond to specific customers. In a real database, each line would be a transaction, as the same customers may return several times. It may be possible, in some circumstances, to link a specific customer to a specific transaction. The second part of the figure shows the attributes of those customers. Given databases with this type of structure, we want to analyze and predict a purchaser's behavior. The size of a database is usually measured by the number of transactions, N, which is six in the above example. But in real-world applications the number could easily be a few million. As Figure 1 shows, four out of five customers who bought "bread" also bought "milk," so we can specify an association rule "bread→milk". The probability of this rule is 4/5, or 80%, or 0.80. This value is referred to as the "confidence" or "confidence level" of the association rule. This type of analysis based on list of purchased items is sometimes called "basket analysis."

There are many different data-mining algorithms, and there is already a comprehensive literature on the subject (Adriaans & Zantinge, 1996; Berry & Linoff, 2004; Chen, 2001; Han & Kamber, 2000; Witten & Frank, 1999). It is not possible to do justice to this comprehensive literature within the space of a chapter, so we will concentrate on selected specific algorithms and problems. The next section presents an overview of one of the most fundamental areas in data mining, that of association rules. The third section introduces the maximum sub-array problem, which is an emerging area that is yet to produce a textbook description. This area is becoming important as a tool for data mining, particularly in the analysis of image data. The fourth section provides a brief overview of two other data-mining algorithms, covering decision and regression trees, and clustering. In the final section, we briefly consider other issues that need to be addressed in the development of any data-mining system, including parallel and distributed processing, privacy and security concerns, and the user interface.

Algorithms in this chapter are given in pseudo-C code. The codes for mining association rules are rather informal, intended to communicate the basic concepts, whereas those for the maximum sub-array problem are more technical and detailed, ready for use. The full implementations of code, which can be modified and adapted to the reader's various applications, are available via a Web site and the address is given in the Appendix.

Association Rules

In this section we introduce the concept of association rules and introduce a fast algorithm for finding promising association rules developed by Agrawal and Imielinski (1993) and Mannila, Toivonen, and Verkamo (1994). We also discuss possible extensions such as negative and hierarchical rules. A number of general discussions on association rules are available (Berry & Linoff, 2004; Han & Kamber, 2000; Hand, Mannila, & Smyth, 2001; Witten & Frank, 1999).

Mining Association Rules

Suppose a manager wants to identify some rule that indicates that if a customer buys item X, he or she is likely to buy item Y. We denote this rule, usually called an association rule, by X →Y, where X is called the antecedent and Y the consequence. Our confidence in the rule is given by the formula:

$$\text{conf}(X \rightarrow Y) = \text{support}(X, Y)/\text{support}(X)$$

where support(X, Y) is the number of transactions that include both X and Y, and support(X) is the number of transactions that include X. For most practical cases, there needs to be some minimum level of support for the occurrences of X and Y in the transaction database. The minimum support level is written either as a fraction or as an absolute value. Usually X and Y are sets of items rather than individual items.

The basic data-mining problem is how to efficiently find a rule X→Y with the maximum possible confidence and at least the minimum support level. Decision makers need a minimum support level, because in most situations they cannot take an action based on a rule derived from just a few examples. There are exceptions to this situation of course, where the decision maker may be trying to identify an event with a low level of occurrence, but which is still significant. The decision maker sets minimum support (and confidence) levels as part of the data-mining process. Setting the support level to lower levels requires that more candidate transactions have to be analyzed in order to find promising association rules. As database sizes are usually measured in gigabytes, fast algorithms for discovering these rules are essential.

An anecdote that surfaces in most data-mining discussions and textbooks concerns a U.S. retail store chain that found the association rule "nappy→beer" particularly for Friday night shopping. The suggested explanation was that male shoppers, stocking up on baby requisites, also stocked up on their own weekend requisites. While the story is apocryphal, it serves a useful purpose in demonstrating that often the association rules found through the data-mining process can be counter-intuitive. Such findings can obviously help with managerial decision-making, and presumably with store profitability. A true example, from a UK supermarket, found that high-income customers tended to buy luxurious cheese. The association rule had a high confidence level, but rather low support. However, if the supermarket had stopped selling this type of cheese due to low levels of sales, they might have lost those valuable customers who clearly are in a position to purchase many other items.

In the example shown in Figure 1, all three customers who bought "cheese" also bought "ham," and thus conf(ham→cheese) = 3/3 = 1, with support(ham, cheese) = 1/2. This is obviously the highest possible confidence level. However this rule would only be found if the minimum support was set at 1/2 (as a fraction), or 3 (in absolute value). If the minimum support was set at 2/3, the rule with the highest confidence would have been "bread→milk" with conf(bread→milk) = 4/5.

Mining Association Rules with Numerical Attributes

Many customer attributes are numerical, such as age or income, as distinct from categorical, such as gender or suburb. We may want to use numerical attributes to analyze purchasers' behavior (Srikant & Agrawal, 1996). Specifically, we use numerical attributes in the antecedent. In our example, if we use the condition "age < 40" for the antecedent, then conf(age < 40→ham) = 1. However, if we set the condition to "age ≤ 50", however, then conf(age < 50→ham) = 3/5. The decision-making implication is that an advertisement for "ham" would be best sent to customers younger than 40.

Brief Aside: Generating Words in Lexicographic Order

Lexicographic order means the order that the words appear in a dictionary. Expressed more formally, if $\mathbf{a} = a_1a_2...a_n$ and $\mathbf{b} = b_1b_2...b_n$ are words of length n, we define $\mathbf{a} < \mathbf{b}$, if for some i ($1 \leq i \leq n$), $a_1 = b_1, ..., a_{i-1} = b_{i-1}$, and $a_i < b_i$, where order "<" (for words) is defined by the alphabetic order. For example, all words of length 3 consisting of the letters "A" and "B" are listed in Figure 2 in lexicographic order.

We can associate the words as the leaves of the tree. Labels A and B are attached to nodes in the tree in such a way that A and B are attached to the two children of each node in order. Each word attached to a leaf can be identified by the path from the root to the leaf. Similar tree structures are used when we wish to generate item sets in lexicographic order in the section after next.

Formal Definition of Association Rules

An association rule in database D is given in the form:

$$X_1, X_2, ..., X_m \rightarrow Y_1, Y_2, ..., Y_n,$$

antecedent → consequence

Figure 2. Lexicographic order

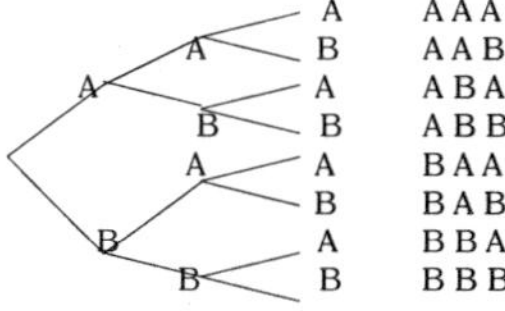

Figure 3. Simplified transaction database

Customer	Items
1	A, C, D, E
2	B, C, E
3	A, B, C, E
4	B, E
5	B, D, E
6	A, B, C, D

This rule means that a person who buys $X_1, \ldots, X_m$ is likely to buy $Y_1, \ldots, Y_n$.

The degree of confidence "conf" is defined by:

$$\text{conf} = \text{support}(X_1, \ldots, X_m, Y_1, \ldots, Y_n) / \text{support}(X_1, \ldots, X_m),$$

where support($Z_1, \ldots, Z_k$) is the number of transactions that include $Z_1, \ldots, Z_k$ in database D.

We define support(empty) = N. Thus if the left hand side is empty, "conf" is the proportion of support($Y_1, \ldots, Y_n$) in all transactions.

A k-tuple is an ordered set of k items (e.g., A,B,C is a 3-tuple). A set of items, or simply item set, is expressed by a k-tuple if it has k items arranged in alphabetic order. Thus the item set {B,C,A} is expressed by a 3-tuple (A,B,C). We express by C_k the set of candidate k-tuples for analyzing the database, for example, C_2 = {(A,B), (A,C), (B,C)} We express by L_k the set of frequent k-tuples, which appear in transactions at least the number of times given by the minimum support. We call the number of times a tuple occurs in all transactions its frequency. A frequent tuple is called a large item set in some literature. We denote the minimum support in ratio form by "minsup."

Figure 3 shows a simplified version of the transaction database in Figure 1, using letter symbols for purchased items. Analyzing this transaction database, we obtain the following results for k-tuples for k = 1 to k = 3, The frequency is shown in the brackets ( ). We set minsup = 0.5, n = 6, and minimum frequency = 0.5*6 = 3.

The 1-tuples (k = 1) are: A(3), B(5), C(4), D(3), E(5)

The 2-tuples (k = 2) are: (A,C)(3), (B,C)(3), (B,E)(4), (C, E)(3)

The 3-tuples (k =3) are: (B,C,E)(2).

The 3-tuple is not considered for rule extraction, because it appears 2 times, below the minimum frequency. For the rule (B→E), we obtain conf(B→E) = 4/5 with support 4. For the rule (A→C), we obtain conf(A→C) = 1 with support 3.

Generating Frequent Item Sets

We use the following lemma to avoid many unnecessary item sets:

Lemma 1. Let S and T be item sets. Then we have $T \supseteq S \Rightarrow support(T) \leqq support(S)$.

For a large database with millions of transaction records and thousands of items, if we generate all k-tuples and check their frequencies in the database, as we did in the previous section, we experience what is called a combinatorial explosion, which can be very time consuming. To generate frequent item sets from large databases, we can make use of Lemma 1, and we can proceed from the k-th stage to the (k+1)-th stage by generating (k+1)-tuples that include only k-tuples generated at the k-th stage. The algorithm for achieving this is presented below. To avoid confusion in the following, we use "minfreq" to express the minimum support as an absolute number, not a fraction. Also, "c.count" is the counter for the tuple "c" used to count the number of times tuple "c" appears in the database. We call the work of this algorithm the tuple generation phase. The maximum size of tuples becomes M at the end. The smaller the value of "minfreq," the larger the value of M. Note that the algorithm tries to minimize the number of times the database residing on disk space needs to be accessed. At line 4, we make access to database D to get transaction t, and we process C_k and L_k in internal memory. Thus scanning the database occurs M times.

```
Algorithm Apriori(D,minfreq){
1.    Insert all the single items into C_1
2.    Set k=1
3.    While C_k is not empty, do{
4.          For all the transactions t in D, do{
5.                Extract into C all k-tuples in C_k that appear in t
6.                For all tuples c in C, increment the count of c, c.count
7.          }
8.          Extract all the tuples whose count is greater than or equal to minfreq into L_k
9.          Generate the set C_k+1 of tuples of size k+1 using Apriori_Gen(L_k)
10.         Set M = k
11.         Increment k
12.   }
13.   Return the union of L_1, ..., L_M
14. }
```

The function Apriori_Gen is used to generate candidate (k+1)-tuples from L_k based on the left longest match as illustrated in the following example: When we generate C_{k+1} from L_k, we pick up a k-tuple, x, from L_k, and scan the list for k-tuple y that has the same (k–1)-tuple as that of x from position 1 to k-1. We call the common (k–1)-tuple a common prefix. Then we concatenate the last element of y to the end of x, resulting in a new (k+1)-tuple for C_{k+1}. Let last(x) be the last element of x.

In the following algorithm, $prefix_{k-1}(p)$ is the prefix of length k-1 of k-tuple p. In the concatenation phase we use the lexicographic order in tuples. For example we have (A, B, C)<(A, B, D). In line 4, items in p and q match except for the last ones. The removal phase is understood from the fact that if (A, B, C, D) is made for C_4, and (B, C, D) is not frequent, (A, B, C, D) is not needed for the future generation of frequent tuples (Lemma 1).

```
Algorithm Apriori_Gen(L_k){
1. /* concatenation phase */
2.     Empty C_k+1
3.     For each p and q in L_k such that prefix_k-1(p) = prefix_k-1(q) and p<q, do{
4.         Let c be (k+1)-tuple of (p, last(q))
5.         Add c to C_k+1
6.     }
7. /* removal phase for unnecessary tuples */
8.     For each tuple p in C_k+1,do{
9.         For each k-tuple s that is a sub-tuple of p, do{
10.            If s is not in L_k, delete p from C_k+1
11.        }
12.    }
13.}
```

If we run the algorithms on the simplified data set (Figure 3), we obtain the following result:

Frequencies are in parentheses following tuples. Let minsup=1/2.

C_1 = (A), (B), (C), (D), (E),

L_1 = (A)(3), (B)(5), (C)(4), (D)(3), (E)(5)

C_2 = (A,B), (A,C), (A,D), (A,E), (B,C), (B,D), (B,E), (C,D), (C,E), (D,E),

L_2 = (A,C)(3), (B,C)(3), (B,E)(4), (C,E)(3)

C_3 = (B,C,E)(2),

L_3 = φ (empty), M=3

Figure 4. Tree structure for "Apriori_Gen"

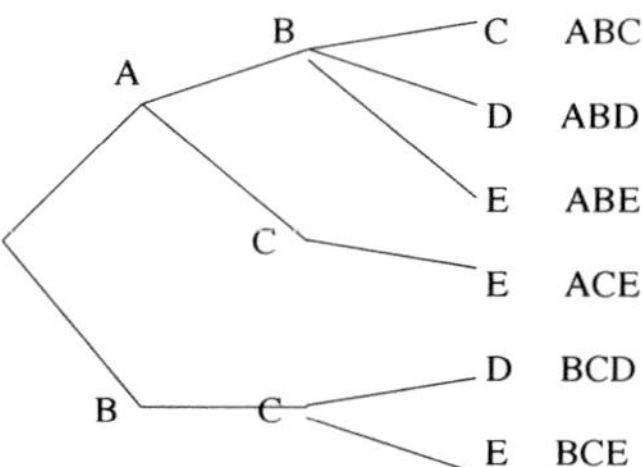

From L_1 to C_2, we generate all ten possibilities. From L_2 to C_3, (B,C) and (B,E) have the common prefix of B. Thus we create (B,C,E).

When we create C_{k+1} from L_k we repeatedly scan the list L_k, which can be time consuming. If we store the lists in tree form, "Apriori_Gen" can be implemented efficiently. When we have a list of k-tuples, L_k, we store them at the leaves of a tree. Each node has branches to child nodes. Each branch corresponds to an item, and the path from the root to a leaf corresponds to the k-tuple represented by the leaf. To illustrate, let L be given by {(A,B,C), (A,B,D), (A,B,E), (A,C,E), (B,C,D), (B,C,E)}. (Note that this example is different from our ongoing example derived from Figure 3). The tree shown in Figure 4 can implement list L.

Empty branches are not shown in this figure. When we traverse this tree from the root in depth-first manner, and reach a leaf, we can append the last items of the sibling leaves to the k-tuple at the leaf, and we can carry on for other leaves. In this example, we generate ((A,B,C,D), (A,B,C,E), (A,B,D,E), (B,C,D,E)). The first two are generated from ABC and the two siblings ABD and ABE. The third is by ABD and ABE, etc. The last two are discarded by line 10.

Generating Association Rules

The next step in this process is to obtain association rules from the list of frequent tuples of items. We use the following lemma in the algorithm.

Lemma 2. For disjoint item sets S and T, and item X included in S, and not in T, we have $conf(S \rightarrow T) \geq conf(S - X \rightarrow T + X)$. X can be generalized to an item set. The meaning is that if $S \rightarrow T$ does not have enough confidence, neither does $S - X \rightarrow T + X$. [1]

This lemma can be used for generating association rules efficiently. Suppose an item set w of size k is frequent. We divide w into two disjoint subsets S and T, and see if $conf(S \rightarrow T)$ is at least "minfreq." We increase the size of T by one each time. Such T's are maintained in H_1, H_2, ... in the following algorithm. Specifically in line 6, we can go to H_{m+1} using apriori_gen. Also we can exclude an item set in line 10, if it is not in the right-hand side of a confident rule. Lemma 2 supports both these steps. We call the work of the algorithm the rule generation phase.

```
Algorithm for association rules{
1.    For k from 2 upto M, do{
2.          For each frequent tuple w in L_k, do {
3.                Let H_1 be a set of items h, where conf(w-h→h) ≥ minconf
4.                Set m=1
5.                While m ≤ k-2, do{
6                       Construct the set H_m+1 from H_m using Apriori_Gen(H_m)
7.                      For each tuple h in H_m+1, do{
8.                            Calculate confidence by conf=support(w)/support(w-h)
9.                            If conf e•minconf, then output the rule (w-h '! h)
10.                           Otherwise, remove h from H_m+1
11.                     }
12.                     Increment m
13.               }
14.         }
15.   }
16.}
```

Two example traces show how this algorithm works on the transaction example.

First trace with minsup = 1/2 and minconf = 2/3

k = 2

L_2 = (A,C), (B,C), (B,E), (C,E). For each w in L_2, we have the following.

H_1 = (A,B,C,E) given by the union of the following :

{A, C}, obtained from C→A (3/4) and A→C (1)

{B}, obtained from C→B (3/4),

{B, E}, obtained from E→B (4/5), and B→E (4/5)

{E}, obtained from C→E (3/4)

k = 3. C_3 = (B,C,E), L_3 = empty

Second trace with minsup = 1/3 and minconf = 2/3. L_2 has all 10 pairs.

L_3 = {(A,B,C) (2), (A,C,D) (2), (A,C,E) (2), (B,C,E) (2)}

Let us trace only for w = (A,B,C).

H_1 = {A,B,C}, obtained from B,C→A (2/3), A,C→B (2/3), and A,B→C (1)

H_2 = {(A,B), (A,C), (B,C)}, only A→B,C (2/3) is output.

C_4 = {(A,C,D,E)}, L_4 = empty

Negative Rules

Suppose conf(A→C) < conf(A, –B→C). This means that a purchaser who buys A and not B is more likely to buy C than the purchaser who buys just A. We call an association rule with negative notation such as –B a negative rule. Negative notation can appear in either the left-hand side or the right-hand side of an association rule. We can use the previous algorithms to find association rules with negative items by simply introducing –X for each X. But this approach will potentially produce 2^k tuples for each k-tuple, and thus is not very efficient. We can use the following lemma to reduce the number of tuples, and also produce association rules with sufficient confidence. We explain using small examples, but the results can be extended to larger tuples.

Lemma 3.

support(A, B) + support(A, –B) = support(A).

conf(A→B) + conf(A→–B) = 1

We can use the first formula to assess support(A, –B) by support(A) – support(A, B) during the generation of frequent item sets phase - if it is smaller than "minfreq" we can discard it. We can use the second formula in the generation of association rules phase in a similar way. In real applications, the first formula does not contribute very much to the speed-up, since support(A, –B) is much greater than support(A, B). For the second formula, normally we can assume the minimum confidence is at least 1/2. Then if conf(A→ B) >1/2, we can discard the generation process for conf(A→ –B). This heuristic based on the second formula leads to some speed-ups during the rule generation phase.

For practical applications we generate (A, –B) only when (A, B) has minimum support. This has no particular mathematical grounding, but has some logic from a management point of view - only when (A, B) has enough support can we talk about (A, -B). Also we can generate tuples with only one negative item, such as (A, –B, C), and examine rules, such as (A, –B→C), or (A, C→–B), etc. We are interested in questions such as: "If a purchaser does not buy an item, can it influence his or her purchasing pattern for other items?" or "If he or she buys an item, is he or she unlikely to buy some other item?" Even one negative item may give us a potential marketing strategy. A discussion on negative rules can be found in Wu, Zhang and Zhang (2004).

Hierarchical Rules

In many sales databases, commodities can be classified by category. For example a "jacket" may have a hierarchical structure of (clothes: jacket), and "spinach" may have (food: vegetable: spinach). Here "jacket" and "spinach" exist as bottom items. If we cannot find a useful rule regarding the bottom items due to lack of support, we may be able to find one if we go up the hierarchy one or more steps.

We can express this hierarchy by a number of trees. The roots of the trees correspond to the broadest categories, such as "clothes" and "food." We can expand the database so that we have records of transactions with those upper items. If we simply use the previous algorithms on the expanded database, we may have frequent item sets such as (clothes, jacket), from which we generate a redundant rule such as "jacket ' clothes." The simplest approach is to generate all possible rules including upper items and remove those redundant rules that include ancestors and descendants. But this method may generate too many redundant rules, and is not very efficient. To prevent this, we remove item sets that include ancestors and descendants at the tuple generation phase and the rule generation phase. Systematic approaches to hierarchical rules can be found in Han and Fu (1995) and Srikant and Agarwal (1995).

We can have a mixed association rule with negative and hierarchical items. In many cases, for the bottom items A and B, there is not a significant difference between conf(→B) where the left-hand side is empty, and conf(-A→B), because support(-A) is close to the entire set of transactions. If A is higher in the hierarchy, however, the sensitivity of –A could be higher.

Removal of Redundant Rules

Suppose we have a rule A→B with a high level of confidence. If purchases of A and B are nearly independent, this rule cannot give us an effective estimation as to the behavior of purchasers of B. We call such rules redundant. We need to remove such redundant rules from the set of confidence rules. As the concept of an association rule is similar to that of conditional probability, we can use a similar strategy. Namely, if conf(→B) = support(B) is close to conf(A→B), that is, support(A)support(B) is close to support(A, B), we can discard A→B from the set of confidence rules if it is present. In other words, A is not sensitive to the purchase of B, if A and B are nearly independent. We can perform stricter statistical tests on the independence of A and B if we treat them as random variables.

Maximum Sub-Array Problem

The maximum sub-array problem is used to find the consecutive portion of an array that maximizes the sum of array elements in that portion. In most applications, one-dimen-

Figure 5. One-dimensional maximum subarray problem

The following are the monthly sales figures of beer for one year, where units are in thousands, and the bottom symbols indicate months starting from January.

298	143	154	235	631	345	879	743	298	241	198	252
J	F	M	A	M	J	J	A	S	O	N	D

At the moment, all the values are positive, so the obvious (and trivial) solution is the whole array. However, if we subtract the mean value 368, we have a more meaningful trend as to which season is the most promising for the sale of beer.

–70	–225	–214	–133	263	–23	511	375	–70	–127	170	–116
J	F	M	A	M	J	J	A	S	O	N	D

From this, we can see that the maximum subarray is the May to August season. Using the original array figures, the total sales amount is (631+345+879+743) = 2598.
By identifying the season, we can decide for example, to hire more staff, or offer incentives in the "off" months to increase sales.

Figure 6. Two-dimensional maximum subarray problem

For this example, the mean value has already been subtracted from each array element.
Co-ordinates are given by (x, y) where x is the row number and y is the column number.

0	3	-2	6	-3	-7	4	-2
3	-3	-5	-7	13	-4	51	2
3	-2	9	-8	13	6	-51	2
1	-3	5	-6	18	-2	21	-6

The maximum subarray (with the value 16) is given by the rectangle defined by the upper left corner (2, 5) and the lower right corner (4, 7).
If this table showed the sales figures of some commoditywith the rows and columns age groups and income levels. The maximum subarray given above may, for example, correspond to senior age groups and above-average income groups.
If the table showed pixel values of an image file, the maximum subarray might correspond to the brightest part of the image.

sional and two-dimensional arrays are used. This problem was first introduced by Bentley (1984a, 1984b) as a programming example, and has recently attracted some attention in relation to data mining (Takaoka, 2002; Tamaki & Tokuyama, 1998). Figure 5 shows an example of a one-dimensional maximum sub-array problem and Figure 6 shows an example of a two-dimensional maximum sub-array problem.

Relationship between Association Rules and Maximum Sub-Arrays

Suppose each purchase (e.g., beer) has an attribute of time of purchase. The rule "A→B" could be interpreted as follows: If a purchase occurs at a time between month *l* and month r, the purchase is likely to include beer. Let M be the number of all items purchased during month 1 to month n. Let θ be the ratio of beer among purchased items. Then the maximum confidence for "A→B" is defined by:

$$\operatorname*{Max}_{1 \le l \le r \le n}\{\sum_{i=l}^{r}(a[i] - \theta(M/n)\}$$

We can use the one-dimensional maximum sub-array problem when the antecedent A can be described by maximizing the interval in a numerical attribute such as time (or age, income, etc.). If we have two numerical attributes, we can use the two-dimensional maximum sub-array problem (see Figure 6).

Kadane's Algorithm

This algorithm scans the given one-dimensional array, accumulating a tentative sum in t, and if t>s for the current maximum sum s is updated by t. If t becomes negative, it is reset to 0. The variables k and *l* keep track of the beginning and ending positions of the sub-array whose sum is s. The situation is illustrated in Figure 7.

The algorithm follows. If all values are negative, we allow the empty sub-array with s=0 for the solution. In this case (k,*l*) = (0,0) will not change.

```
1.    (k,l)=(0,0); s=0; t=0; j=1;
2.    for (i=1; i<=n; i++) {
3.          t=t+a[i];
4.          if (t>s) { (k,l)=(j,i); s=t; }
5.          if (t<0){ t=0; j=i+1; }
6.    }
```

As can be seen from this algorithm, the computing time is O(n) (linear). This is the optimal situation because we need to look at every array element. If the time was O(f(n)), it would be proportional to f(n) where f(n) is a function of input size n.

Figure 7. Illustration of Kadane's algorithm (one dimension)

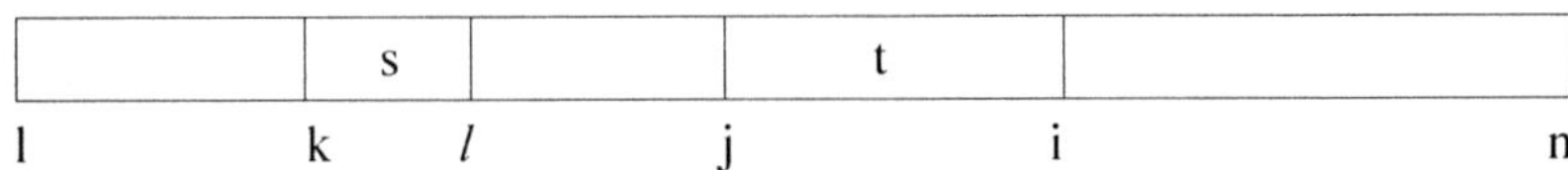

Figure 8. Illustration of Kadane's algorithm (two dimensions)

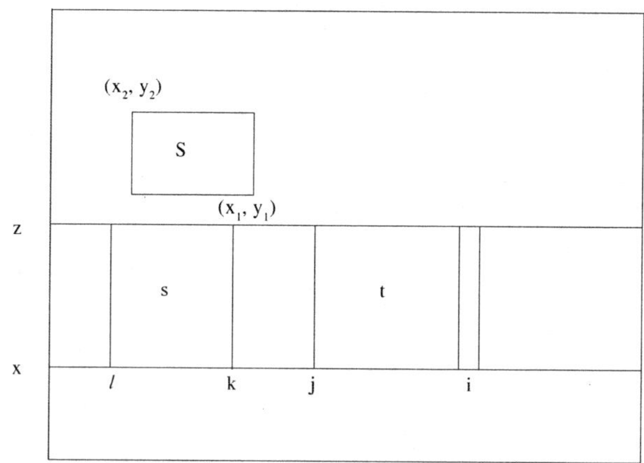

We can extend Kadane's algorithm into two dimensions. We perform the one–dimensional Kadane's algorithm for the strip defined by row x and row z as shown in Figure 8. The rectangle defined by (x_1, y_1) and (x_2, y_2) at the bottom-right and top-left corner is a tentative one for the solution, while the rectangle defined in the strip from *l* to k is a tentative one for this particular one-dimensional case defined by x and z. As we solve the one-dimensional Kadane by changing x and z, the computing time of this algorithm is $O(m^2n)$ in total. The value of column[x][i] is the sum of a[z .. x][i], that is, the sum of the i-th column of array a from row z to row x.

The algorithm follows. This algorithm takes $O(m^2n)$ time

```
1.    ((x1,y1),(x2,y2))=((0,0),(0,0));
2.    S=0;
3.    for(z=1;z<=m;z++){
4.            /** initialize clolumn[][] **/
5.            for(i=1;i<=n;i++)column[z–1][i]=0;
6.            for(x=z;x<=m;x++){
7.                    t=0; s=0; (k,l)=(0,0);
8.                    j=1;
9.                    for(i=1;i<=n;i++){
10.                           column[x][i]=column[x][i–1]+a[x][i];
11.                           t=t+column[x][i];
12.                           if(t>s){s=t; (k,l)=(i,j); }
13.                           if(t<0){t=0; j=i+1; }
```

```
14.                 }
15.                 if(s>S){S=s; x1=x; y1=k; x2=z; y2=l; }
16.         }
17.  }
```

Algorithm by Prefix Sum

The prefix sum of array a at position i, denoted by sum[i], is the sum of a[1], ..., a[i]. The prefix sum array "sum" is computed in O(n) time as follows:

```
sum[0]=0;
for(i=1;i<=n;i++) sum[i]=sum[i–1]+a[i];
```

The prefix sum at position (i, j) of a two-dimensional array a is the sum of array portion a[1..i][1..j]. Using the data structure of "column" given above, we have the following algorithm for array "sum" with O(mn) time, that is, linear time, in two dimensions.

```
1.  /** initialize column[][] **/
2.  for(j=1;j<=n;i++)column[0][j]=0;
3.  /** main iteration **/
4.  for(i=1;i<=m;i++){
5.          for(j=1;j<=n;j++){
6.                  column[i][j]=column[i–1][j]+a[i][j];
7.          sum[i][j]=sum[i][j–1]+column[i][j];
8.          }
9.  }
```

Using the concept of prefix sum, we can develop algorithms for the maximum sub-array problem in the following.

Algorithm for one-dimensional case. In the following "min_prefix" is the minimum prefix sum at the end of iteration i, and "k_{min}" holds the position for it.

```
1.  min_prefix=0; s=–999; k=0; l=0; kmin=0;
2.  for(i=1;i<=n;i++){
3.          if(sum[i]–min_prefix>s) {s=sum[i]–min_prefix; l=i; k=kmin;}
4.          if(sum[i]<min_prefix) {min_prefx=sum[i]; kmin=i;}
5.  }
```

Figure 9. Illustration of algorithm by prefix sum (one dimension)

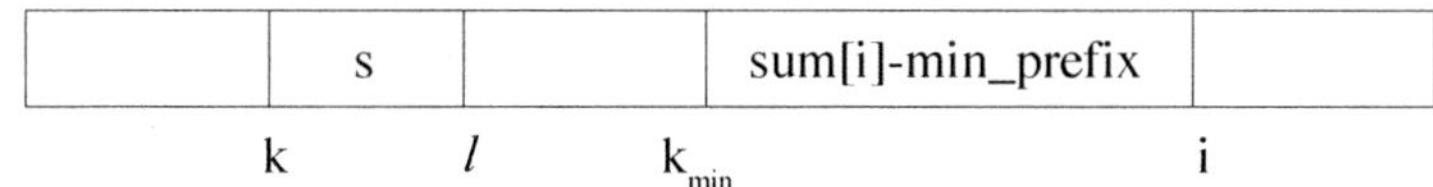

Figure 9 illustrates the computation.

Algorithm for two-dimensional case. In the following we solve the one-dimensional problem repeatedly for the strip bounded by row z and row x in a similar way to the two-dimensional Kadane algorithm. This algorithm takes $O(m^2n)$ time

```
1.  ((x1,y1),(x2,y2))=((0,0),(0,0));
2.  S=0;
3.  for(z=1;z<=m;z++){
4.        for(x=z;x<=m;x++){
5.            t=0; s=0; (k,l)=(0,0); kmin=0; min_prefix=0;
6.            for(i=1;i<=n;i++){
7.                 t=sum[x][i]–sum[z–1][i]–min_prefix;
8.                 if(t>s){s=t; k=kmin; l=i; }
9.                 if(sum[x][i]–sum[z–1][i]<min_prefix){
10.                    min_prefix=sum[x][i]–sum[z–1][i];
11.                    kmin=i;
12.                }
13.           }
14.           if(s>S){S=s; x1=x; y1=l; x2=z; y2=k+1; }
15.       }
16. }
```

The algorithms based on prefix sums are not as efficient as Kadane's algorithms in terms of time and space, but they can be starting points for further speed-up and generalizations.

k-Maximum Sub-array Problem

In many applications we need to find the maximum sub-array, the second maximum, the third maximum, etc., down to the k-th maximum. For example, suppose the database contains a geographical distribution of customers, and we need to post flyers to the most loyal customers. The identified rectangle region for posting may not be very suitable due to road construction, etc. Then we need the second or third alternative. As usual, we start from the one-dimensional case.

The algorithm based on prefix sum is modified. The variable min_prefix is extended to a one-dimensional array of size k. Array portion min_prefix[1 .. k] holds k minima of sum[1], ..., sum[i] at the end of iteration i in the following algorithm. Also the solution variable "s" is extended to an array of size k, s[1], ..., s[k], representing the maximum, the second maximum, ..., the k-th maximum. At the end of the iteration i, s[1..k] represents the k-maxima for the array portion a[1..i].

In the following, the function "max" is used to merge array s[1..k] and (sum[i]–min_prefix[1], ..., sum[i]–min_prefix[k]), and take the first k elements. The function "insert" is used to insert the element "sum[i]" into the sorted list of "min_prefix[1..k]." If it is smaller than "min_prefix[k]," it is abandoned. Obviously those two operations take O(k) time. Thus total time for the algorithm is O(kn). We omit the maintenance of positions for the possible k-maxima.

```
1.    min_prefix[1..k]=(0,...,0); s[1..k]=(0,...,0);
2.    for(i=1;i<=n;i++){
3.            s[1..k]=max(s[1..k], sum[i]–min_prefix[1..k]);
4.            insert sum[i] into min_prefix[1..k];
5.    }
```

We can easily extend the above algorithm into two dimensions, as we did for the ordinary maximum (1-maximum) sub-array problem. This result is reported in Bae and Takaoka (2004) with time complexity of $O(km^2n)$ for an (m, n)-array. An efficient hardware implementation method is reported in the same literature. In many applications, such as graphic images, the found k-maximum regions heavily overlap, that is, the algorithm finds k maxima by only changing co-ordinates slightly from the found portion. The following algorithm for the disjoint problem is often more useful.

Divide-and-Conquer Algorithm

For a square array of size (n, n), we have so far developed $O(n^3)$ time algorithms, which we call cubic. We show in this section that we can do better than cubic - that is, subcubic (Takaoka, 2004). The main weapon in this section is the idea of "divide-and-conquer," a major tool in algorithm design.

Because of space consideration, we will only consider the one-dimensional case. Divide the given array into two halves. We name the maximum sub-array in the left half, right half, and the one stretching over the center by "left.max," "right.max," and "center." Then the solution must be the maximum of those three. To obtain "left" and "right," we go recursively. To obtain "center," we need the concept of the maximum prefix sum and minimum prefix sum, which we call "max_prefix" and "min_prefix." We use the struct type named "triple" which consists of three integers "max," "min_prefix," and "max_prefix."

Figure 10. Illustration of subcubic algorithm (one dimension)

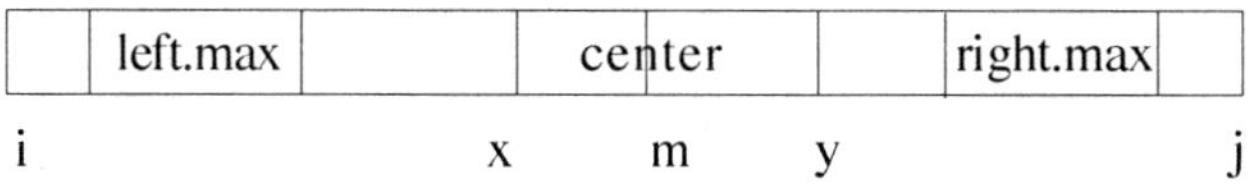

	left.max		center		right.max	

i x m y j

The recursive function returns those values obtained from interval [i, j]. Let us assume the prefix sum array "sum" is already available. Figure 10 illustrates the situation, where sum[x] is the min_prefix in the left half and sum[y] is the max_prefix in the right half. The algorithm follows.

```
1.   struct triple maxsubarray(int i, int j) {
2.   struct triple sol; int m, center;
3.   if(i==j){sol.max=sum[i]; sol.min_prefix=sum[i–1]; sol.max_prefix=sum[i];
4.        return sol;
5.   }
6.   else {
7.        m=(i+j–1)/2;
6.        left=maxysubarray(i,m);
8.        right=maxsubarray(m+1,j);
9.        center=right.max_prefix–left.min_prefix;
10.       sol.min_prefix=min(left.min_prefix, right.min_prefix);
11.       sol.max_prefix=max(left.max_prefix, right.max_prefix);
12.       sol.max=max(max(left.max, right.max), center);
13.       return sol;
14   }
15.}
```

In the main program, we compute the prefix sum array "sum," and call "maxsubarray(1,n)." In lines 10-12, min(a, b) is the minimum of a and b, and max(a, b) is the maximum. At lines 4 and 13, the value of the solution values, minimum prefix sum, and maximum prefix sum for array portion sum[i..j] are brought back to the calling site in variable "sol." Variable "m" is to show the mid-point. The key observation is that the value of "center" can be computed by right.max_prefix - left.min_prefix, and those minimum and maximum prefix sum values are brought through recursion.

If we extend the idea of divide-and-conquer to two dimension and use a fast distance matrix multiplication algorithm, we can solve the maximum subarry problem for an (n,n) array in subcubic time.

Other Data Mining Algorithms

We have discussed two representative areas in data mining; association rules and the maximum sub-array problem. The following is an overview of some areas not covered. The examples use the sales data from Figure 1.

Decision Tree/Regression Tree

As an example, we want to make a decision tree that can answer a question such as "Is a customer who is female and age 40 or greater likely to buy milk?" A decision tree is a binary tree such that at each node we make a binary decision, and go down one of the two branches depending on the outcome of the question until we reach a leaf (see Figure 11a). In our example, we are guided to the "female branch" and the prediction that she buys milk is 2/3. At the next node, we are guided to the branch with "no" for "age < 40" and the prediction that she buys milk is 1/1. Obviously a realistic tree based on a large database would lead to more precise predictions.

If we ask a question such as "How much in total is spent by a customer?" we can attach to each leaf the average amount spent. Using the tree in Figure 11(b), we can predict a customer who is male and not younger than 40 will be spending about $18. If the predicted value at the leaves is a numerical value, the tree is called a regression tree. The database on which the tree is constructed is called the training set. The problem of how to organize the tree so that the prediction is accurate and the number of questions asked is minimal is described in Quinlan (1993), Witten and Frank (1999), Han and Kamber (2000), and Berry and Linoff (2004).

Figure 11. Decision tree example

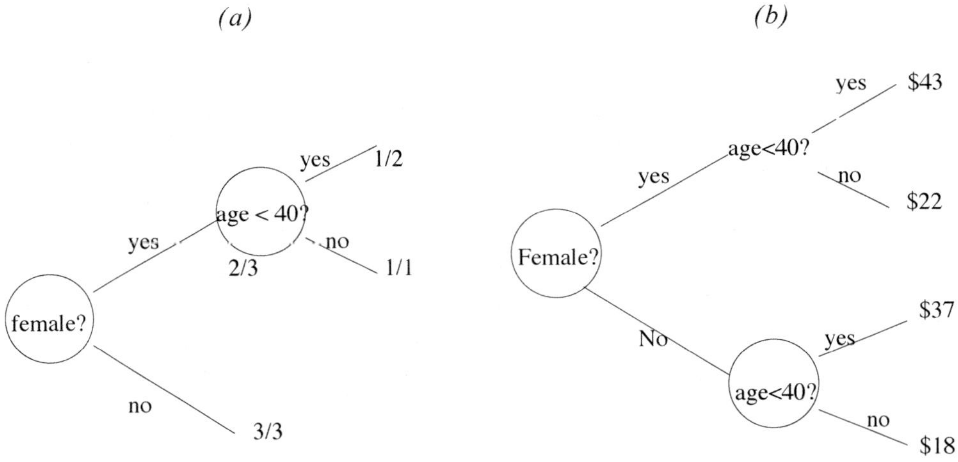

Clustering

Clustering is used to classify data items into several categories so that items in each category are close to each other according to some criterion of closeness based on selected attribute values. Suppose we wish to send brochures to customers. If we send brochures for daily items and luxurious items separately, we can classify the customers into two groups according to a closeness measure based on their age and annual income. Then we may classify them into the junior/low income group {1, 3} to receive the daily items' brochure and the senior/high income group {2, 4, 5, 6} to receive the luxurious items brochure. If we used suburbs as the closeness measure (for ease of delivery) we would classify the customers into {1, 2, 5} and {3, 4, 6}. In general, we can classify customers into k groups with various measures of closeness. Several methods are described in Kaufman and Rousseeuw (1990), Witten and Frank (1999), Han and Kamber (2000), and Hand, Mannila and Smyth (2001).

Conclusion

To illustrate the algorithms developed in this chapter, using the C programs available (see Appendix), a sales database of a supermarket in Japan was analyzed. The size parameters and performance measurements are summarized in Table 1. As the sales database is from a food supermarket, the rules mined were not unexpected - "miso" and "tofu" are the main ingredients for making "miso soup" in Japanese cooking.

In addition to the topics discussed above, the following issues need to be addressed for practical applications of data-mining algorithms.

- **Parallel/distributed processing:** As the amount of data processed is large, we may be able to speed up the processing time using many computers that cooperate with each other. Also data may be gathered from various sites through the Internet. Various techniques developed in parallel/distributed computing should be used in data mining.

Table 1. Sample run of Japanese supermarket sales database

Total number of transactions : 88303
Total number of different items : 459
Average number of items per transaction : 16.3

Experiment with minsup = 0.06, minconf = 0.7
Processing time for association rules : 1 min 28 sec
Among high confidence rule "Miso Tofu" has conf=0.7
Time for one query given above : 0.65 sec

- **Privacy/security:** The database normally includes sensitive client data that must be protected from leakage. This is especially so in medical databases. The leakage can occur in the data acquisition phase through the network, or by unauthorized access to the database. Control of passwords, data encryption and authentication need to be rigorous. If data mining is going to be accepted by general society, the issue of privacy must be addressed.
- **User interface:** Useful information extracted from the database must be shown for human consumption, preferably using some visual method.

Acknowledgment

The authors are very thankful to two students, Bae Sung Eun and Kiyoyuki Nakagaki, who implemented and tested the C programs given in this chapter. They are also grateful to anonymous referees, whose constructive comments greatly improved the chapter.

References

Adriaans, P., & Zantinge, D. (1996). *Data mining*. Harlow, UK: Addison Wesley.

Agrawal, R., & Imielinski, T. (1993). Mining association rules between sets of items in large databases. In P. Buneman & S. Jajodia (Eds.), *Proceedings of the 1993 ACM SIGMOD International Conference on Management of Data,* Washington, DC (pp. 207-216). New York: ACM.

Bae, S. E., & Takaoka, T. (2004). Algorithms for the problem of K maximum sums and a VLSI algorithm for the K maximum subarrays problem. In *Proceedings of the International Symposium on Parallel Architectures, Algorithms and Networks ISPAN'04* (pp. 247-253). IEEE.

Bentley, J. (1984a). Programming pearls: Algorithm design techniques. *Communications of the ACM, 27*, 865-871.

Bentley, J. (1984b). Programming pearls: Perspective on performance. *Communications of the ACM, 27*, 1087-1092,

Berry, M. J. A., & Linoff, G. S. (2004). *Data mining techniques*. New York: John Wiley.

Chen, Z. (2001). *Data mining and uncertain reasoning*. New York: John Wiley.

Han, J., & Fu, Y. (1995). Discovery of multiple-level association rules from large databases. In *Proceedings of the Twenty-first International Conference on Very Large Databases,* Zurich, Switzerland (pp. 420-431).

Han, J., & Kamber, M. (2000). *Data mining: Concepts and techniques*. San Francisco: Morgan Kaufmann.

Hand, D., Mannila, H., & Smyth, P. (2001). *Principles of data mining*. Cambridge, MA: MIT.

Kaufman, L, & Rousseeuw, P. J. (1990). *Finding groups in data: An introduction to cluster analysis*. New York: John Wiley.

Mannila, H., Toivonen, H., & Verkamo, A. I. (1994). Efficient algorithms for discovering association rules. In *Proceedings of KDD-94, AAAI-94 Workshop on Knowledge Discovery in Databases*, Seattle, WA (pp. 181-192). American Association for Artificial Intelligence.

Quinlan, J. R. (1993). *C4.5: Programs for machine learning*. San Mateo, CA: Morgan Kaufmann.

Srikant, R., & Agarwal, R. (1995). Mining generalized association rules. In *Proceedings of the Twenty-first International Conference on Very Large Data Bases* (pp. 407-419). San Francisco: Morgan Kaufmann.

Srikant, R., & Agrawal, R. (1996, June). Mining quantitative association rules in large relational tables. In *Proceedings of the 1996 ACM SIGMOD International Conference on Management of Data (SIGMOD '96)*, Montreal, Canada.

Takaoka, T. (2002, January). Efficient algorithms for the maximum subarray problem by distance matrix multiplication. *Electronic Notes in Theoretical Computer Science*, *61*, 191-200.

Takaoka, T. (2004). A faster algorithm for the all–pairs shortest path problem and its application. In *Proceedings of the Tenth International Conference on Computing and Combinatorics, COCOON2004, LNCS3106* (pp. 278-289). Berlin: Springer-Verlag.

Tamaki, H., & Tokuyama, T. (1998). Algorithms for the maximum subarray problem based on matrix multiplication. In *Proceedings of the Ninth Annual ACM-SIAM Symposium on Discrete Algorithms* (pp 446-452). Society of Industrial and Applied Mathematics.

Witten, I., & Frank, E. (1999). *Data mining: Practical machine learning tools and techniques with java implementations*. San Francisco: Morgan Kaufman.

Wu, X. D., Zhang, C., & Zhang, S. (2004, July). Efficient mining of both positive and negative association rules. *ACM Transactions on Information Systems*, *22*, 381-405.

Endnotes

[1] **Proof:** The lemma follows directly from the definition as follows:

conf(S→T) = support(S, T)/support(S)

conf(S – X→T + X) = support(S, T)/support(S – X)

Appendix

A Guide to Program Source Lists

We provide the source lists of C programs for algorithms used in this chapter. From the association rule section, we list two source programs. The first is the extraction of association rules with minimum support and confidence in source list A. The C program will prompt you to give several parameters. The size of the database measured by the number of transactions is stored in variable "num_transaction", and the number of all possible different items the supermarket can sell is stored in variable "num_items." The user is also prompted to give the minimum support and minimum confidence by variables "minsup" and "minconf." The program is designed to run with random numbers. For practical databases, the portion commented out in the main function should be invoked, and the portion using the random number generator should be commented out. The database file can consist of up to NUM_TRANSACTION lines. Each line consists of a number of items given by integers. Thus the database needs to be prepared from the original sales database in such a way that each item is converted to a unique integer. We assume there are NUM_ITEMS items that the supermarket sells.

We also provide a program that can handle a specific inquiry to the database. A typical enquiry is "A→ B?" This enquiry will give the support of the rule and its confidence. This is given in source list B. The actual enquiry form is "A > B."

For the two-dimensional maximum sub-array problem, we list two C programs. The first is the two-dimensional Kadane's algorithm in source list C. The other is based on the prefix sum approach in source list D. Both are run on random numbers in the range of 0 - 99. Each value is reduced by 50, rather than the mean value. The user is prompted to give the value of "m" and "n," which define the size of the given two-dimensional array.

These source programs are available at http://cosc.canterbury.ac.nz/~tad/mining/.

Section V

Management Applications

Chapter XVI

A Tool for Assisting Group Decision-Making for Consensus Outcomes in Organizations

Faezeh Afshar, University of Ballarat, Australia

John Yearwood, University of Ballarat, Australia

Andrew Stranieri, University of Ballarat, Australia

Abstract

This chapter introduces an approach, ConSULT (Consensus based on a Shared Understanding of a Leading Topic), to enhance group decision-making processes within organizations. ConSULT provides a computer-mediated framework to allow argumentation, collection and evaluation of discussion and group decision-making. This approach allows for the articulation of all reasoning for and against propositions in a deliberative process that leads to cooperative decision-making. The chapter argues that this approach can enhance group decision-making and can be used in conjunction with any computational intelligence assistance to further enhance its outcome. The approach is particularly applicable in an asynchronous and anonymous environment.

Introduction

Current computer-mediated communication (CMC) systems allow for informal interaction of two or more people with limited computational intelligence (CI) support. Alternatively, computational intelligence systems facilitate only elementary collaboration. The objective of this chapter is to describe the development of a CMC system that integrates computational techniques into normal social interactions so that participants are an integral part of the problem-solving process and automation of an outcome is not merely the result of inferences by an automated system.

There is no suggestion that the use of automated reasoning in decision-making is not appropriate, but rather the choice of what to automate should take into account human capabilities as well as limitations. We agree with Woods (1986) that desired systems are those where humans have clear authority, can intervene flexibly, and are engaged actively in informal decision-making. This is particularly the case with decisions that involve consensus among people within an organisational context.

Consensus decision-making in organisations is regularly conducted through discussion and debate, yet underlying assumptions and reasoning invested, is often lost, implicit, or not expressed clearly. Often problem definition, implicit assumptions, and varying approaches as to the determination of a resolution, are some of the causes of conflict in decision-making. This could strongly influence both the decision-making process and its outcome.

This chapter describes a framework called ConSULT. The framework derives from argumentation theories and is used to assist groups within organizations to reach consensus decisions. Further, the framework provides a natural structure for the meaningful inclusion of computational intelligence techniques that support participants in formulating their views and enables observers such as managers to track the discussion to discover reasoning trends.

Reaching a *consensus* decision based on *shared understanding* in ConSULT occurs through the articulation of all reasoning for and against all propositions in a deliberative argumentation process that allows free participation and contribution in a *cooperative decision-making environment.* ConSULT allows the level of consensus to be specified and uses a Borda count calculation of votes to determine a consensus outcome.

Group meetings are an important aspect of decision-making in any organization. Among the many reasons for this are those listed by Drucker (1989) as the sharing of information by participants, and learning from the knowledge, experience and expertise of others in the group. Turoff and Hiltz (1996) also found that decision-making is enhanced if the views of more than one individual are considered. Ocker, Hiltz, Turoff, and Fjermestad (1995) found that the contribution of knowledge of the various group members can have a positive impact on outcome decisions.

Siegel, Dubrovsky, Kiesler, and McGuire (1986) suggest that increased participation in discussion and arguments present different viewpoints, which lead to greater modification in the opinions of the individuals. In an environment in which free participation is encouraged and all contributions are valued, the interaction of open and creative ideas could trigger new thoughts and lead to better decisions. The term "*consensus*" has been used in many group decision-making activities for centuries. It is becoming a popular democratic form of decision-making. A consensus decision is usually the outcome solution that starts as proposals are initially put forth and evolves to become an outcome that needs to be accepted by the whole group. Consensus decision-making is a central element of the ConSULT framework and is discussed in some detail in the next section.

Consensus Decision-Making

Consensus is based on *compromise* and the ability to find *common ground*, which should take into account and validate each participant's point of view (Habermas, 1990). Habermas' Discourse Ethics distinguishes the following requirements for a consensus in determining norms:

- **Principle of universalisation:** This sets the conditions for the equality of rights and freedom for all the participants in the discussion of proposed norms.
- **Equality of influence.** Participants to a group discussion are equally influential. This also assumes that those affected can accept the consequences of their decisions.
- **Concern for the common good:** Decisions are made by taking into consideration the needs, interests, and feelings of all others influenced by the norm.
- **Reasoning focus:** The focus of discussion should be on giving reasons for and against proposed norms (Habermas, 1987).

In his Discourse Ethics, Habermas (1993) demands consideration of the viewpoints of all people affected by certain decisions. He further stresses that participation in a discourse should be with full awareness of the other people's perspectives and interpretations. Therefore, a consensus process needs to be in an environment which provides equal opportunities for every individual in the group to share their opinions, suggestions, assertions, supporting or opposing reasons to propositions, and evaluation. This proposition is affirmed by Butler and Rothstein (1991).

There are two main types of consensus, unanimous and non-unanimous consensus. In unanimous consensus, there is complete agreement and acceptance of a decision. Although agreement in its own right is considered as an important group outcome (Whitworth & Felton, 1998), decisions cannot always attract everyone's complete agreement. Since cooperation is necessary to make any decision work, any non-unanimous consensus decision needs to be accepted by all in order to be implemented successfully. Studies show that independent of any kind of outcome, acceptance and agreement increases group unity and participants' commitment to group decisions (Boje & Murnighan, 1982). In order that everyone at least accepts the outcome, there should be no one who has any disagreement who has not been valued and considered in the outcome decision.

Nemeth and Wachtler (1983) indicate that unresolved concerns of minorities often promotes resentment, conflict and lack of motivation to act willingly on the implementation of the final decision. Yet, simply allowing a concern to be expressed often helps a resolution of these negative consequences. The explicit articulation of a minority's concerns could also help to expand group perspectives, resulting in increased levels of creativity that could lead to possible new solutions. However, there are times when individuals themselves keep quiet and do not express their opinions due to some social or psychological factors, such as avoiding the stress caused by confrontation, shyness or lack of status indicated by Maass and Clark (1984). The lack of expression of disagreement in face-to-face meetings could cause a false assumption of unanimity, that is to say, if any individual is silent, he or she is in full agreement with what others are saying. This assumption could lead to an illusionary consensus. Yet, people are often inactive in participating in decision-making processes because they feel that their viewpoints are not going to be considered, and they have no power or role in the ultimate decisions made.

Turoff and Hiltz (1996) assert that many barriers to freedom of participation in group decision-making processes derive from face-to-face communication barriers. Barriers to consensus in face-to-face include:

- Individuals are sometimes reluctant to initiate their opinions in case these opinions turn out not to be suitable.
- Higher ranked or well-known participants, if their identity is known to the group, can be reluctant to suggest ideas or opinions that they are not certain will prove to be correct.
- The association of the participants' names with their opinions assumes a commitment that makes it difficult for them to reject or change their minds over time.
- Participants' consideration of suggestions may be biased by the identity of the originator of the suggestion, if it is known.
- The apparent or actual opinions of a group may bias the opinions of individuals within the group, either unconsciously or consciously, and impact on the decisions made.

In summary, consensus decisions need to be reached by group interaction that promotes participation, gives everyone power to express their opinions, encourages people to listen to each other, considers concerns rather than ignoring them, and eliminates the possibility of the choice of only one or a few individuals determining a proposal. This environment should encourage cooperation, trust, respect, unity of purpose, and detachment.

Clark and Brennan (1991) and Altman, Valenzi, and Hodgetts (1985) have found that, most of our activities, communications, and arguments are often based on implicit underlying assumptions and reasoning. Misunderstandings can undermine consensus, so the clear articulation of views and reasons is important. The concept of shared understanding is introduced to refer to the knowledge of the reasoning and views held by others. In addition to consensus, shared understanding is a central principle in ConSULT and is discussed next.

Shared Understanding

Individuals often assume that their contributions to discussion are understandable and should be understood by others because it is common sense or because of the assumption that others hold the same belief as they do. They fail to realise that what they see as common sense might not seem that way to others. Ross, Greene and House (1977) use the term "*false consensus*" for this assumption that everyone else is sharing one's beliefs. "*False consensus*" is referred to as the "*tacit assumption of the universal validity of our claims*" by Habermas (1993). He asserts that *communicative action* is fundamental to the process of presenting supportive or critical reasons for accepting or rejecting particular claims.

Different perceptions or mental models, if allowed to be shared by explicit articulation of the underlying assumptions and reasoning, could enrich the participants' perspectives and promote a deeper understanding of the situation which could lead to resolution of conflicts and a more effective outcome decision. Without explicit articulation and shared understanding, individuals may interpret and assume different common understanding for the same suggestion in a discussion.

The concept of shared understanding could be viewed from two perspectives. Cole (1991) in defining the word "*shared*," distinguishes two distinct meanings, to *possess in common*, and to *distribute*. He explains that:

- To *possess in common* refers to receiving, using, and experiencing in common with others.
- To *distribute* refers to sharing something between oneself and others.

While shared understanding from the distribution perspective occurs through conversations, listening, and reading and writing, understanding of implicit viewpoints of others needs to be based on the first meaning given by Cole as *common understanding*, which is also referred to as *common ground* or *mutual beliefs*. Common ground is the only concept that usually is associated with shared understanding. Yet, Clark and Brennan (1991) indicate that the success of a conversation is dependent on shared information, assumptions and beliefs. Shared information, or common ground, requires the process of *grounding*, in which the contributors in the discussion constantly ground the content of their conversation. Grounding is therefore the process of seeking and establishing understanding based on reasoning in conversation. This requires explicitly sharing or *distributing* the underlying understanding and reasons in order to establish the common ground or common understanding.

Consensus and shared understanding have been identified as two central objectives of a group discussion to be supported by a computational intelligence framework. Two well known approaches that have been used to enhance the quality of decisions that result from group decision making are approaches based on IBIS (Kunz & Rittel, 1970) and on Delphi. Delphi was originally established by Olaf Helmer and Norman Dalkey in 1933 and developed in the 1960's by Turoff and Hiltz (1996) as a technique for technological forecasting and corporate planning. Since then its area of application has expanded to include many other contexts. Essentially, Delphi can now be seen as a method for structuring group communication so that the process is effective in allowing a group to deal with a complex problem. Delphi is limited in that it is essentially a paper-and-pencil technique that does not accommodate computational intelligence.

The Delphi method is a structured process for acquiring and capturing knowledge from a group of pre-selected individuals by utilization of a paper-and-pencil communication process, in which repeated rounds of questionnaires, together with controlled feedback, are sent to the participants. The technique requires facilitators to collect, interpret and summarise the content of the discussion to help its participants to systematically explore and present their solutions to complex problems. These questionnaires are designed to help experts develop their responses to a problem by refining their views according to the responses of the group. The members should reach a consensus on the solution that is most acceptable to the group as a whole. This process may be conducted several times before the facilitator feels a sense of agreement and a certain degree of consensus is reached (Ziglio, 1996).

The similarities between the ConSULT approach and Delphi include some of those features of Delphi described by Dalkey (1975). The goals of both methods are:

- Facilitating the communication of a group.
- Providing feedback.
- Providing guaranteed anonymity of the members of the group.
- Providing asynchronous communication of participants.
- Acquiring knowledge or opinions from experts or individuals.

Although some of the features adopted in the ConSULT approach are supported and justified by the research into the Delphi method, we have avoided many of its disadvantages and shortcomings. There are a few very important aspects included in the ConSULT approach that overcome some of the issues related to the practices used by Delphi (Afshar, 2004). These include issues such as:

- The authority fallacy in argumentation.
- The role of the facilitator, particularly with the collection and summarisation of suggestions.
- The formation and subsequent alteration of questionnaires.
- The evaluation approach to the suggestions.
- The voting technique.

The ConSULT approach is presented in the next section.

Figure 1. ConSULT process

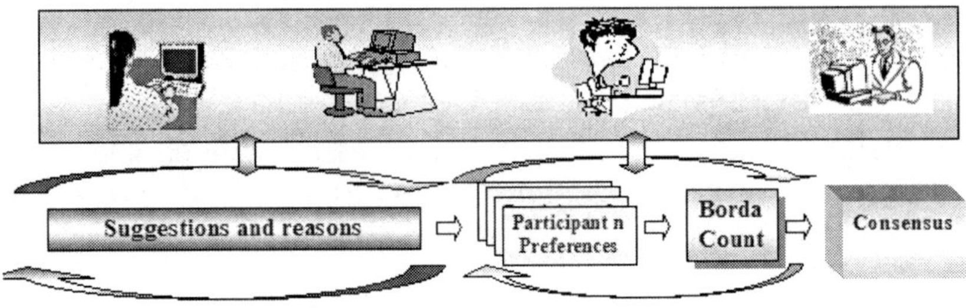

The ConSULT Process

ConSULT (an acronym for *Con*sensus based on a *S*hared *U*nderstanding of a *L*eading *T*opic) is an approach to facilitate consensus decision-making.

Participants in a ConSULT process advance through three phases in determining consensus and a shared understanding.

1. Deliberation and collection of all contributions in the discussion.
2. Anonymous and independent evaluation and voting by participants.
3. Re-evaluation through an iterative voting process only this time with the knowledge of collective trends in previous rounds.

Each phase is discussed below. Figure 1 illustrates the ConSULT approach in the collection of suggestions and reasons, and voting towards a consensus. The computational intelligence techniques that directly underpin the ConSULT approach derive from argumentation, voting and information communication technologies and are discussed in the fourth section.

Phase 1: Deliberation and Collection of Contributions

This phase involves an iteration of two levels of deliberation used in discussion by participants.

- The first level of deliberation involves participants adding suggestions that are not already presented. The reasons underlying each suggestion need to be provided by the participant presenting the suggestion. The strength of reasoning is to allow participants to clarify and justify their points of view. This means a suggestion should not be added if an entry already exists that could represent the participant's perspective. This eliminates redundant suggestions and the need for summariza-

Figure 2. An issue, its description, and deliberation of a suggestion

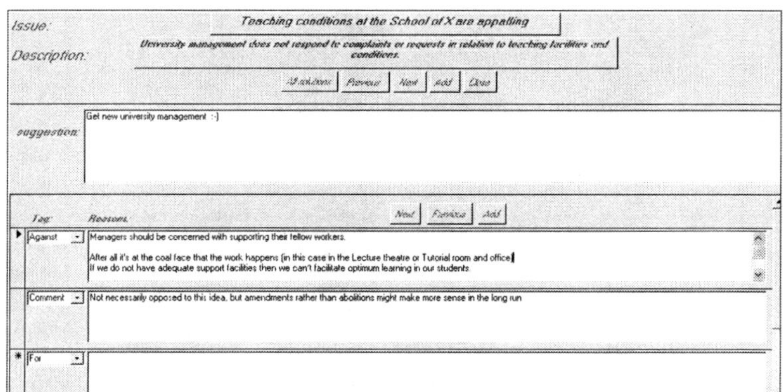

tion. Participants may enter a proposition or other alternatives. Propositions could be actions, goals, solutions or decisions. The purpose of this stage is to distribute ideas in the group and to include as many suggestions and points of view into the discussion as possible.

- The second level of deliberation is more analytical, in which all presented points of view are systematically evaluated by each participant. If differences of opinion appear, their reasoning should be investigated and if desired, other possible reasons for or against each suggestion could be provided. A reason should not be added if an entry already exists that could represent the participant's reasoning. This eliminates duplication of reasons and the need for summarisation.

Figure 2 shows an issue (teaching conditions at the School of X are appalling) drawn from an actual study. The description, entered by the participant that advanced the issue, explains more about the issue and in this case relates to teaching facilities and conditions. A suggestion offered by another participant reads as a solution: Get new university management. A rationale tagged (by the participant advancing the rationale) as a *Comment* suggests that abolition of management is too extreme. Another, tagged as *Against* refers to a quasi-moral stance that managers should be concerned about supporting workers.

Phase 1 terminates at a scheduled time. During Phase 1, participants are free to contribute as much or as little as they wish. There is no facilitation or moderation.

Phase 2: Independent Evaluation

The evaluation and voting allows individuals to provide their preferences for contributions based on the evaluation of the strengths and weaknesses of the reasons for and against a given proposition. We found strong support for this perspective in Habermas' Discourse Ethics (Habermas, 1987).

Figure 3. An independent evaluation and voting on a suggestion and its four reasons

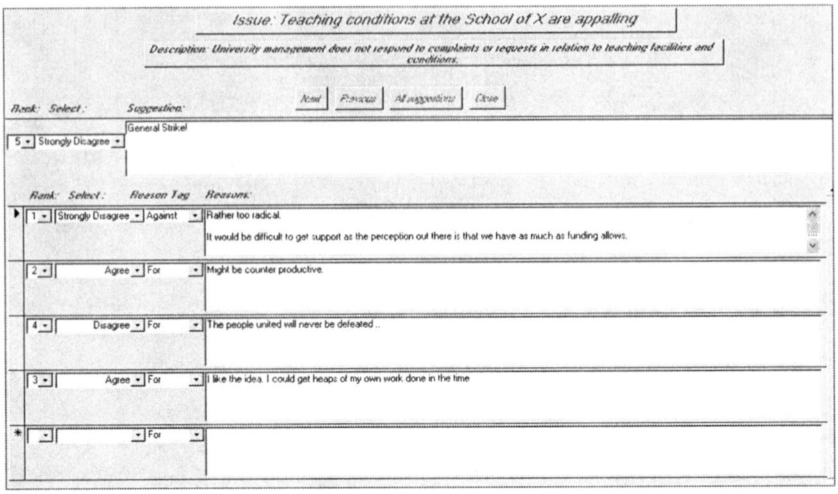

This phase involves the analytical evaluation of all suggestions made to analyse critical issues. Participants may have conscious or unconscious reasons for their opinions that, if not explicitly articulated, may not be realised by others to be used in their evaluation of the opinions. Participants must note that opinions are not arguments, because they cannot possibly be evaluated. Therefore, to evaluate a suggestion one must know the arguments underlying it. Figure 3 illustrates different reasons for the same suggestion. There is one reason tagged as *Against* the suggestion and three reasons tagged as *For*. This figure also illustrates an ordering or ranking that a participant has applied to the reasons to describe his or her level of agreement with each reason.

This stage involves allowing participants to rank their preferences with each option and select a level of agreement from a five-point scale (Strongly Disagree, Disagree, Neutral, Agree, Strongly Agree). Participants are encouraged to first evaluate the reasons for each suggestion and rank them, and then based on the reasons, rank the suggestions. Figure 3 shows the independent evaluation and voting on a suggestion and its four reasons by one of the participants in the case study.

Figure 4 illustrates an evaluation and voting on all suggestions by a participant. Phase 2 terminates at a scheduled time, or when everyone is finished with his or her contributions. In this phase, the contributions of the participants are necessary to capture their consensus preferences. The time required is entirely dependent on the amount of reflection they need for voting.

Analysis of the Votes

The preferendum is a means by which people could achieve a result which all regard either as the best possible compromise or the shared understanding on an argument. The latter is what we desire. It is expected that all participants would rank all options. By doing so, they would have full influence on the outcome, whereas if they participate partially in the process, they would have only exercised partial influence, resulting in an inequitable and undemocratic outcome.

The analysis would follow as:

- The analysis of ranking is made automatically according to the Borda count calculations and scaling by the average of numerical agreements.
- The level of consensus for each option is considered as the percentage of the total score from the maximum possible score (i.e., if the maximum possible score is 80 and the total score for a suggestion is 60, the consensus level is considered to be 60/80=75%).
- Finally, in the analysis, ConSULT will automatically determine the consensus decision(s) and consensus shared understanding (reasons), as well as the level of agreements for each option.
- If two options have an equal rating, ConSULT looks at the total ranking of the reasons supporting it to select the higher one. If this too yields the same result, the facilitator asks the participants to re-vote for the conflicting options.
- ConSULT can help to prepare a summary of the results, showing the level of consensus and agreement for each option.

We suggest the outcome decision, as a consensus decision when reached by the implementation of the above conditions, is more likely to be accepted and adopted by the group. However, organisations should define the level of agreement they require on the consensus outcome, thus the degree of the consensus in our approach needs to be determined by the group using it.

Phase 3: Re-Evaluation

This phase of the voting is proposed to increase the level of consensus and agreement for the winning suggestion(s) by allowing the modification of votes with consideration of the collective trends based on the re-evaluation of reasons. Each winning suggestion, reason, or participant's position and collective voting results could be presented back to the participants to find out if a greater consensus could be achieved. Each participant therefore is allowed to view collective outcome of votes and his or her previous position for each option. This allows participants to further evaluate their votes against the consensus trends. After all the re-votes are in, participants again can see their previous position against the collective outcome of votes, indicating the group position on each consensus option. This process can be repeated as long as the group desires a higher level of consensus and agreement.

Figure 5 shows a collective voting outcome (*Consensus Rank and Agreement*) is provided as a feedback for re-evaluation of options by participants to help reach a higher consensus. Participants if they wish, can modify their ranks and agreements towards reaching a higher consensus or even unanimity.

Figure 4. Evaluation and voting on all suggestions by a participant

Rank:	Select:	Suggested Solution:
6	trongly Disagree	Get new university management :-)
1	Strongly Agree	Rotate the position of assistant manager through the workers. Why not have a system where the workers take on some of the duties of manager on a rotational basis. So for 6 months or so each of us in turn takes on the role of co-manager ie co-head of school co-vice chancelor ??
5	trongly Disagree	General Strike!
4	trongly Disagree	What about the Union could they help?
2	Agree	We need to find a way to be assertive about our needs so we aren't at end of line as it now appears.
3	Strongly Agree	We need to respond to this issue more collectively and collaboratively as a staff.

Hoffman and Maier (1961) indicate that there is evidence that once the group is seen to reach a commonly understood threshold level for a given option, members assume that the group has made its decision and they adjust their positions accordingly. This has been proven in Delphi methodology to improve the level of consensus.

The group decision-making literature suggests that increased participation, discussion, and arguments lead to greater changes in the opinions of individuals (Myers & Lamm, 1976). Moreover based on their experiment Scheibe, Skusch, and Schofer (1975, p. 272) suggest that "most participants are both interested in the opinions of the other members of the group and desirous of moving closer to the perceived consensus." They refer to the studies of the psychology of small groups and indicate that highly confident participants usually are not influenced by group pressure and move less towards the consensus, the opposite has been observed by participants with low confidence. Popper (1959) in (Linstone & Turoff, 1975) also indicates that one of the mechanisms for self-correction is the ability to re-evaluate arguments. A participant presented with all the suggestions and their reasons has more information to accept or reject even his own suggestions. This would provide an outcome that could reflect a richer, better, fairer, and more precise decision (Linstone & Turoff, 1975).

This phase can be iterated for the participants to modify their votes as many times as the group considers it as a positive move towards achieving a higher level of consensus, or as long as there is a conflict between two or more options with the same ranking or agreement level, or a higher level of agreement is required. Everyone votes on all the items or only the conflicting options, to uncover the group position. In the Delphi method the desired changes usually occur within three iterations. The highest ranking preferences and agreed upon suggestions and reasons are selected by ConSULT to represent a consensus decision and its shared understanding.

If there is any conflict between options by having the same rank, the agreement scale is evaluated. The option with the highest agreement score is selected. If the conflict still exists, the option with the highest agreed upon reasoning is selected. In the case of unresolved issues, ConSULT will tag them for further evaluation and voting by the participants.

The consensus based on a shared understanding in ConSULT is reached through both the decision-making process and the outcome decision:

- The decision-making process allows participants to share their opinions, suggestions, assertions, supporting or opposing reasons to propositions, evaluation and voting, in an environment which provides equal opportunities and power for every individual in a group.
- The *outcome decision* is determined by a calculation method of finding the highest preference of opinions, suggestions, assertions and their supporting reasons.

Finally, based on requirement for consensus decision-making and shared understanding, the ConSULT approach allows:

1. Individuals to have their own unique mental models and perceptions of their surrounding environments. Consequently, this diversity of thought would enrich the expected outcomes of their decision-making.
2. Each and every participant to have the opportunity to voice his or her opinion.
3. Participants to have freedom in the deliberation of their propositions and to express their perspective, including concerns, and supporting and opposing reasons. The deliberation should be in the spirit of collaboration, rather than persuasion or negotiation.
4. Each participant to express and elaborate his/her reasoning and rationale in favour or against any raised point.
5. Only the "strength" or the "weaknesses" of the reasoning of an individual participant to be considered in the "participants' preferences."
6. The outcome of voting to include every participant's preferences including extreme agreements and disagreements.
7. Consensus decision-making reflects the ideas and thoughts of all participants. Reaching a consensus ensures that decisions are explored thoroughly and both strong agreements and disagreements are considered.

Consensus is a decision that is acceptable to everyone, not unanimity. The outcome may not be everyone's first choice, nor a majority vote, yet acceptable to everyone.

Figure 5. The voting feedback to help reaching a higher Consensus

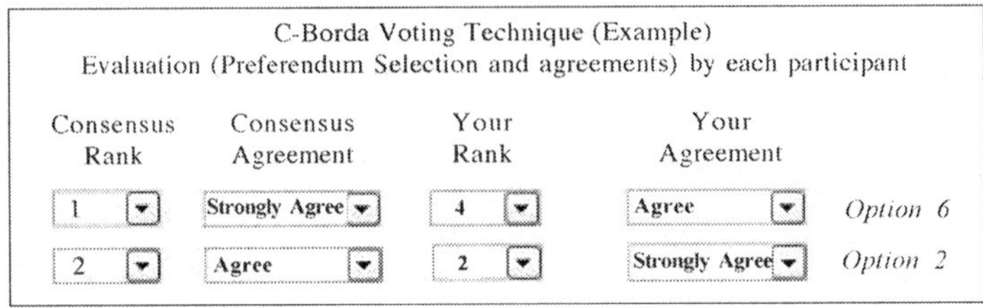

Argumentation and Computational Intelligence

ConSULT's suggestions and reasons phase has elements from both Toulmin and IBIS argumentation structures. Its procedural features resemble some of Delphi's, and its outputs resemble a variation of the Toulmin argumentation framework. Figure 6 illustrates the conceptual phases of the ConSULT approach: Argumentation, Deliberation and Voting. Each phase will be discussed independently in the following sections.

Toulmin Argumentation Structure and ConSULT

In group decision-making, ConSULT uses a variation of the Toulmin Argumentation Structure, C-TAS. The Toulmin argumentation structure provides a tool to identify the parts of an argument. Toulmin's model of argument consists of six elements that he

Figure 6. Overall process of ConSULT

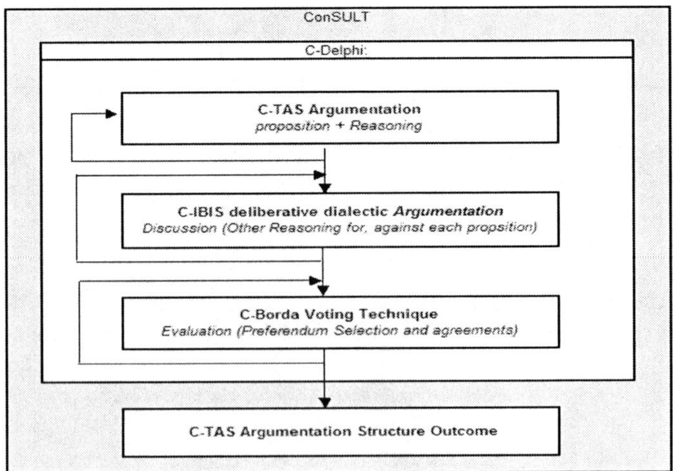

Figure 7. Toulmin argumentation model

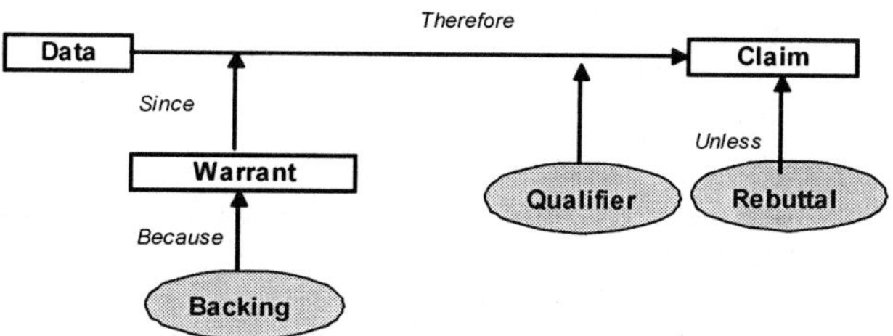

believed were common to any field. His model enhanced the traditional premises-conclusion, or data-claim model of arguments by distinguishing additional aspects, like warrant, backing and rebuttal. He believed that subject content of arguments may change from one field to another, yet the parts of the argument will remain the same. Toulmin described the six aspects of an argument to be: Claim, Data, Warrant, Qualifier, Backing, and Rebuttal (illustrated in Figure 7).

Forming an argument with this model as it is shown in Figure 7 can be described as: Given Data, and since Warrant and because of Backing, therefore Qualified Claim holds, unless specific Rebuttals exist that weakens or causes the reasoning to fail. However according to Toulmin (1958), an arguer might not need to provide all parts of the layout. For example, a group making a decision might only use justification (warrants) for the proposals (data) to address an issue, or a problem (claim). Nevertheless, in some cases such as arguments in the domain of law, the arguments might require a rigorous warranting and backing, which makes the arguer provide all of the parts of the structure in TAS to give maximum validity and credibility.

In making a policy, researchers such as Mitroff, Mason, and Barabba (1982) and Hamalainen, Hashim, Holsapple, Suh, and Whinston (1992) have suggested that Toulmin's premise-warrant-claim model should be used. The claim and data in the Toulmin structure is mainly adapted in ConSULT by following the Turoff, Hiltz, Bieber, Fjermestad and Rana (1999) description. They described that in a given situation depending on the nature of a claim (topic), data (suggestion) could be almost anything: actions, goals, criteria, requirements, solutions, decisions, etc. Figure 6 shows the use of C-TAS in the initial elicitation of suggestions.

Consequently, ConSULT uses C-TAS (a variation of the Toulmin argumentation structure) to allow the participants to provide supporting reasons for any given suggestions to make the underlying understanding, reasons, and assumptions explicit.

The output that results from the implementation of the ConSULT method represents a variation of the Toulmin argument structure in that for the claim (topic), one or more consensus data (proposition, suggestion) must be provided, that are supported by one or more consensus warrants (reasons) justifying the data. The consensus approach in ConSULT finally presents the warrants that are most preferred and agreed upon and, since they reflect a consensus belief of all the participants, they can be more effective and valuable in supporting the consensus propositions. Each warrant could be backed by one or more consensus backings (optional). If backing is used in ConSULT, a consensus backing would be selected for each consensus warrant. Rebuttals are derived from the preference ranking of the opposing reasons. So, when an option is rejected, the highest reason ranked against that option is to be considered as its consensus rebuttal.

The TAS qualifier in ConSULT (C-Qualifier) is derived from the calculation of the preferences of participants. Every consensus element of the argument could be associated with two modal factors called C-Qualifier: Qualifier preference and Qualifier agreement, indicating the level of preferences and agreement on each selection:

- C-Qualifier for preference indicates the level of consensus on each option. It measures the level of preference in the consensus selection in comparison with the highest possible preference.
- C-Qualifier for agreement or confidence qualifier reveals the collective agreement on an option. In our approach, the C-Qualifier for consensus reasoning is referred as the level of shared understanding for that element. The C-Qualifiers are determined by the calculation of the collective agreements and preferences of the participants on each element of the consensus outcome. This includes consensus C-Data(s) supporting C-Claim.

Although it would be desirable to achieve a qualifier that is 100% or a unanimous consensus for each selection, this situation is unlikely. Each element is selected according to the highest qualifier, which also determines the level of consensus. In addition, ConSULT also provides a level of consensus agreement on each proposition, which could be considered as an additional collective agreement factor. Therefore we can say there are two kinds of qualifier to be used in ConSULT, one is the qualifier element of rank in consensus selection to show the level of preference in comparison with the other options, and the other is the qualifier element of agreement to reveal the collective agreement on an option.

However, since the qualifier usually establishes that the argument does not have a 100% agreement among the participants, the other element of the Toulmin model, the rebuttal, could explain why. ConSULT is intended to encourage all the reasons for and against a reason or proposition to be shared by the participants' deliberations in a spirit of common goals and collaboration. The reasoning against each proposition is considered as that proposition's C-Rebuttal. When an option is rejected, the highest ranked reason against that proposition is considered to be its consensus C-Rebuttal. In this context, ConSULT represents Toulmin's rebuttal as the most preferred reason against each proposition.

While ConSULT is intended to assist users to provide their premises to support a claim, it is not designed to either provide a mechanism to inherently test the validity and soundness of premises that is required, for example, by syllogisms in analytical reasoning, or the deductive inference mechanism to infer a conclusion based on the premises. The CI underpinnings of ConSULT involve the structuring of the discussion space and the communication technologies that make this possible. However, CI techniques that aim to automate inferences can be added as an optional tool for participants to use to derive or evaluate suggestions. For example, in the use of ConSULT for the resolution of property issues following divorce, participants may access a neural network that has been trained from past Family Court of Australia decisions to offer an outcome prediction to inform their own suggestions. Embedding the automated inference into the architecture of ConSULT goes against the spirit of consensus decision-making based on shared understanding and involves viewing the CI inference as an oracle.

In accordance with the requirement of Habermas' Discourse Ethics (Habermas 1993) the ConSULT use of argumentation is intended to allow participants to freely bring all their points of view, however diverse, to the discussion. It encourages participants to put forth information in a well-organized, well-reasoned way and, in contrast to face to face discourse, enables participants to address the group rather than another individual. Participants are required to provide facts, evidence or other information to back up their suggestions. Proposals are produced through an impersonal approach based on anonymous arguments. Behaviours such as overconfidence of participants are less prevalent because proposals are based on arguments, not on personal feelings.

In cooperative decision-making, there are a number of possible intuitive functions made by argumentation in the decision procedure. Baker (1999) has categorised these functions as "*additive function,*" "*subtractive function,*" "*verification function,*" and "*clarification function.*" He describes:

- The additive function is where argumentation is used in cooperative decision-making to add a decision as common-ground knowledge.
- The subtractive function is the opposite of additive in that by using argumentation, a previously mutually believed proposition is removed from common-ground knowledge through a cooperative decision by the participants.
- The verification function is where argumentation is used to better verify a given proposition.
- Finally, the clarification function of argumentation is when it is used for participants to collaborate in reaching a more clarified proposition.

The ConSULT structure could allow the organisation of a constructive debate about a topic. The results achieved will be the consensus decision based on the collective group insights into alternative desirable resolutions that are based on shared understanding. This approach, as a group decision support technique, could have a positive effect on the outcome of the process. The argument-based approach we use is inherently adaptive to support a variety of needs from consensus resolution of an issue to helping in the construction of a consensus knowledge base according to various elements needed in decision-making and its outcome (Afshar, Yearwood, & Stranieri, 2002).

Consensus in group decision-making is an agreement derived from multiple points of view. While the approach of Toulmin's argumentation structure has been the motivation for many recent formal systems that attempt to promote opinion exchange and joint decision-making, its structure is so rigid and defined that even though it can represent knowledge in many domains, it cannot represent ill-structured problems or allow the discussion of multiple viewpoints. These limitations have given way to another argumentation model. Kunz and Rittel (1970) designed an alternative argumentation method called the *Issue Based Information Systems (IBIS)* model which allows problems to be explored and framed.

The initial argument presented by C-TAS in ConSULT by one participant is prone to disagreement by other participants. This is required to allow free discussion of agreements and disagreements and their evaluation to lead to a consensus. In ConSULT, all the reasoning for and against any C-Data is required to be shared with the participants involved in the deliberation in the pursuit of a common goal and collaboration. For the presentation of reasoning for or against the suggestions (C-Data), a variation of IBIS called C-IBIS (ConSULT-IBIS) is used to allow deliberation of further reasoning.

IBIS and ConSULT

Group participants intentionally or unintentionally bring with them different assumptions, backgrounds, and agendas, which can create conflict. The presence of multiple perspectives should allow the challenge of satisfying multiple, often competing viewpoints. Argumentation systems may assist a decision-maker to deal with problems that are difficult to define, and to support the group discussion required to capture and share various points of view, information and expertise that will lead towards the solution of the problem (Rittel & Webber, 1984).

Kunz and Rittel (1970) state that their IBIS model starts with a topic. According to different positions taken to address the topic, issues are brought up and disputed. In defending or opposing the different positions, as shown in Figure 8, arguments are constructed until the issue is either settled by convincing all parties, or determined by a formal decision procedure.

ConSULT uses a variation of IBIS (C-IBIS) by using dialogue deliberation to allow each participant to provide reasons for and against every suggestion. C-IBIS is illustrated in Figure 8. Kraus, Sycara, and Evenchik (1998) generalise argument as a means of persuasion used by a persuader to dynamically change the preferences, action and thoughts of the persuadee to cooperate. The ConSULT approach is not intended to use argument as a means of persuasion. It encourages the focus on the reasoning for and against the propositions rather than persuasion to a specific position. The aim of discussions in ConSULT is to allow the shared deliberation of participants towards reaching a mutual decision.

In ConSULT, the strength of reasoning is encouraged to be the maximum power applied by the participants to decide to accept or reject a proposition. Therefore, the validity and the soundness of the reasoning should be the only determinant factors used to reach a consensus. This is one of the main reasons that ConSULT greatly emphasises that participants deliberate any concern or support by providing reasons for each suggestion.

The utilisation of some of the characteristics of IBIS in ConSULT, (C-ConSULT), allows this *deliberation* in a dialectical argumentation to support or oppose the propositions. This allows the consensus to be based on the participants' preferences of the issues,

Figure 8. The IBIS Model

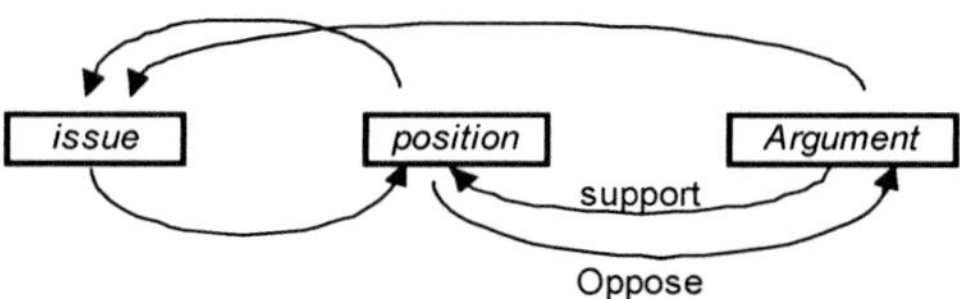

Figure 9. The use of C-IBIS in discussion by providing reasons for and against each suggestion

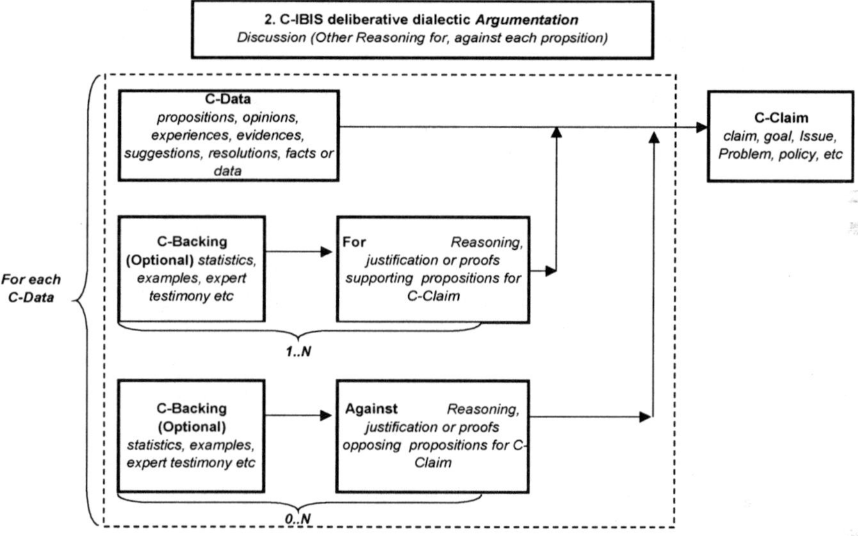

reasons, and the assumptions made. Figure 9 shows the use of C-IBIS in discussion by providing reason for and against each suggestion.

Using C-IBIS, reasoning manifests as the *for* or *against* statements to address a suggestion (C-data). Any attempt to argue about reasons rather than suggestions should be avoided in the ConSULT approach. It is the evaluation and preferences based on the strength or the weaknesses of these reasons that help to determine the preferences of the suggestions. Thus, if a reason seems to be weak in supporting a suggestion, a stronger reason needs to be provided rather than demoting that reason. Also, if the reasons are not convincing in their support, a stronger reason to support or oppose the suggestion needs to be provided rather than discussing the strengths or weaknesses of reasons themselves. This approach does not allow negotiation, persuasion or debate, and provides the freedom of deliberation in a collaborative environment in accordance with the Habermas' Discourse Ethics (Habermas, 1987).

The ConSULT approach is intended to facilitate the collection of all suggestions and reasons and to allow participants to vote on each suggestion and reason. This approach has some similarities with the Delphi method in the collection of all the contributions that will be used in evaluation.

Voting and ConSULT

In decision-making, one of the ways to choose between at least two options and take their supporting or opposing arguments into account is to use a voting technique. One of the most practiced forms of group decision-making, that often overlooks the role of democratic participation of each individual, is the use of majority-rule systems. These systems often impose a decision, reached by the majority vote, on a minority whose concerns were overlooked, or whose preferences were not considered. Nemeth (1986) indicates that in majority-rule systems often the opinions of the minority are assumed incorrect and are not taken seriously. This assumption is based on the belief that the majority is infallible, that there is nothing to learn from the minority, and that the minority can simply be disregarded by being outvoted. This would mean that, only the most persistent of minorities could make the majority reconsider their behaviour and assumptions.

While there are not many other systems of decision-making which are as consistent and efficient as majority rule, this system, by disregarding the opinions of the unhappy minority and not reflecting the preferences of all the people involved in the decision-making, causes injustice and creates dissention (Nemeth, 1986). Other consensus processes are often informal, vague, and follow very inconsistent structures.

Arrow's theorem (Arrow, 1963) demonstrates that when there are more than two alternatives, it is impossible to construct a perfect system of voting which can satisfy all four desirable fairness properties. One of the factors usually considered necessary for a voting system is its consistency and fairness. For many years, mathematicians and others interested in voting theory searched for a voting system that would satisfy a reasonable set of fairness criteria. Kenneth J. Arrow (1963), one of the 20th century's leading mathematical economists, first specified precise criteria for what he considered an ideal election method, and then he proved that those criteria are mutually exclusive. What Arrow was able to prove mathematically is that there is no method or rule for establishing collective or social preferences from individual preferences. Arrow's work, for which he won the Nobel Prize in 1972, ended the efforts of mathematicians to find the ideal election method when he showed such a search was in vain and that an ideal election method does not exist. What was even more important is that Arrow's theorem was not limited to only pure mathematics, but it is applicable to areas such as economics and political science.

Exploring various voting systems, their strengths and weaknesses (especially based on Arrow's fairness criteria), we adopted a preferential voting method called the Borda count or its modern name the Borda Preferendum. Borda Count voting is among the most prominent alternatives to simple majority voting systems. However, in the Borda Count system the fourth fairness condition is violated. The violation of the "*independence from irrelevant alternatives*" in Borda Count system occurs because it takes into account not only the number of voters for a preference, but also the distance between choices. However, this violation has been noted as an advantage of the model (List & Pettit, 2002).

Comparing the Borda Count with some other methods of voting reveals that the Borda Count has several compelling advantages over other voting procedures commonly used in elections. One of the advantages of the Borda Count is that it provides the ability to consider all options. For instance, if there is no strong preference for one option, participants can express this fact by assigning higher preferences to all options they find more acceptable. This helps the strongest option to win. In systems that allow voting only for one option, if the option most preferred by a given voter has little chance of winning, that voter has no chance of determining a second preferred option to be considered. This is overcome by the Borda Count which gives minority options their proper consideration as these options tend to receive votes which reflect their true level of support. The Borda Count is a decision-making methodology that is not majoritarian and is usually fair.

In reaching a consensus decision, it is essential that any suggestion given by the participants be evaluated based on the arguments supporting or opposing it and not only based on the expertise of the participants. The validity and the soundness of the contents and the reasoning of arguments determine if a suggestion should be accepted as a final solution or not. This is one of the main reasons that ConSULT greatly emphasizes the provision of reasons supporting or opposing each suggestion. The voting, according to the Borda method, eliminates the limitations imposed by a majority vote. The strength of reasons is the only force permitted for participants to justify their points of view.

Therefore, the process of voting in ConSULT is through C-Borda Count, which is an adaptation of the Borda Count technique. This technique captures the preferences of the participants, reflecting all of their preferences including both extreme agreement and disagreement positions of the participants. In the iterative process of voting, participants view the collective preferences and agreements towards all the suggestions and reasoning which gives feedback to the group to allow them the opportunity to respond to earlier judgments and, if required, to alter their preferences after reflection to agree with the better supported reasons.

In ConSULT, the Borda Count's ranking method is used for participants to vote on suggestions and supporting or opposing reasoning in the voting process. While the ranking method requires that participants rank the suggestions from the most desirable to the least, and rank the reasons, which are more unstructured open-ended statements. The same rank could be given to two or more reasons supporting or opposing a suggestion. This could improve the flexibility of ranking.

In the Borda Count method for *n* options the participants should enter 1 for their most preferred option (first is the best), 2 for their next favourite, 3 points for the third preference, and so on down to *n* points for their last preference. The counting method is the first place is ranked 1 but it is worth is *n* points, the second place is ranked 2 but its worth is *n-1* points, down to an nth-ranked place being worth 1 point. An option core is the sum of the number of points it received. The highest-scoring option is selected as a consensus outcome. To be able to assign the first-placed preference which has the largest number of points in the group of options, the points need to be calculated using

Figure 10. The use of C-Borda and agreement scale in the evaluation of each suggestion and reason

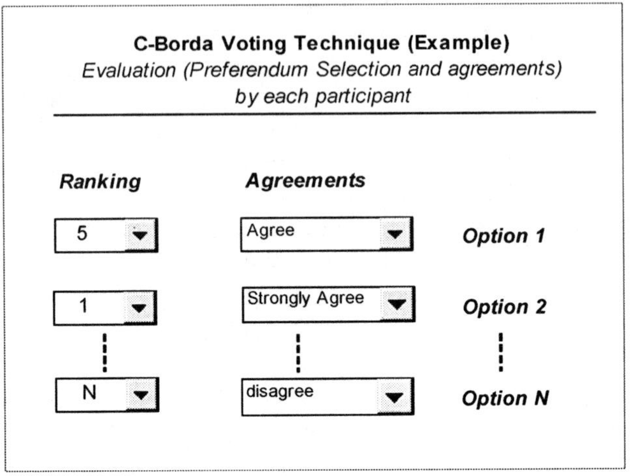

this formula: $p = n+1-r$, in which "p" is the calculated preference, "n" the number of options, and "r" is the rank chosen by the participants for each option. The sums of all the calculated preferences are referred to as the "*Borda Total Ranks (BTR)*" in the headings of the following tables. In circumstances where more than one option can be selected as a consensus, any preferences with a total of points over a predetermined threshold (for example over 50% of the total possible votes) are selected as consensus outcomes. In other circumstances where only one consensus outcome is desired, the option with the highest collective preference within the threshold is selected. If no option reaches the threshold, the voting is repeated. Figure 10 shows preferences and agreements on each option.

By applying the Borda Count voting technique, ConSULT addresses the need identified by Hwang and Lin (1987) of a method of voting that allows the voter to indicate not only which of the options he would most desire to see elected, but also in what order of preference he would place the other options. This was advocated by Hwang and Lin as the natural and correct method that should always be used when more than two candidates compete for a single place and was supported by Saari (1995) as the unique method to represent the "true wish of the voters."

C-Borda allows ConSULT to determine the highest collective preferences of the participants. This is used in ConSULT to achieve the consensus view and shared understanding of the participants in their decision-making. More than one reason could be selected to support suggestions.

Computational Intelligence for Evaluating Discussions

Computational intelligence techniques that derive from argumentation underpin the design of ConSULT. Furthermore, CI techniques that automate inferences, whilst not embedded in the ConSULT framework to preserve consensus and shared understanding, can be deployed as a tool to help a participant evaluate suggestions. There is a third way that computational intelligence can be deployed to facilitate deliberative discussions. Automated techniques can be deployed to provide performance indicators of participants and of the quality of the discussion as whole.

Computational intelligence based on statistical calculations reveal each participants percentage of preferred as well as agreed-upon suggestions and reasons. This could be used by the organisation for promotion or other incentives to encourage motivation towards more collaborative and productive contributions. This will help to recognise individual capability in terms of motivation, reasoning and their contributions towards decision-making.

For determining the percentage of the total preferences acquired by each participant for their suggestions:

$$\% W_i = \sum_1^i P_i \times 100 / \sum_1^n P_n$$

Where

W_i represents the percentage weight of preference for each participants contribution

P_i represents the consensus preference for each suggestion by a participant

P_n represents the sum of all consensus preferences by all participants

$$\% U_i = \sum_1^i P_i \times \sum_1^i W_i \times 100 / (\sum_1^n P_n \times \mathrm{W}_n)$$

Where

$\% U_i$ represents the percentage worth of the total contribution of a participant

For determining the percentage of the total agreements acquired by each participant for their suggestions:

$$\% W_i = \sum_1^i A_i \times 100 / \sum_1^n A_n$$

Where

W_i represents the percentage weight of agreements on reasons for each participants contribution

A_i represents the consensus agreements for each suggestion by a participant

A_n represents the sum of all consensus agreements for all suggestions by all participants

$$\% A_i = \sum_1^i A_i \times \sum_1^i W_i \times 100 / \sum_1^n A_n \times W_n$$

Where

$\% A_i$ represents the percentage worth of the total agreements for the suggestions contribution of a participant

The same calculations are done to determine the percentage of the preferences on all reasons contributions by each participant.

ConSULT has been implemented as a Web-based tool in PHP with a mySQL database that allows asynchronous participation in discussions. It has undergone limited testing where positive results were reported. A case study was used to explore the use of the ConSULT approach in facilitating group discussions and determining consensus outcomes in both the selection and resolution of issues based on the participants' shared understanding.

The participants were four out of ten randomly selected staff from a university department. The ConSULT approach to consensus decision-making was studied through an interpretive content analysis approach on the data collected in the case study. The data was collected from the contributions of the participants in reaching a consensus decision towards selecting and resolving an issue. The process, content and outcome of the case study were used to explore how ConSULT approach could support and represent the discussions and resolution.

The participants using ConSULT may form dynamically with a particular purpose and time limitation, and may not be composed of people in the same geographic space. Some of the complexities that could surround this kind of scenarios are: the availability and level of expertise, and the commitment of the participants to the process. A brief scan of the journal and conference literature shows that there are very rare instances of careful empirical evaluation of systems in terms of sound measurements for processes and outcomes of group decision-making. It is even very difficult to choose efficiency measures that often are the focus of information technology evaluation (Sproull & Kiesler, 1991). One of the reasons for this complexity is that changing the participants could change the information environment and, as a result, measures which made sense for one group of participants may not be applicable for the new one, making the comparison impossible.

However, a prototype implementation of the ConSULT approach, *aConSULT*, exceeded the expectations of the participants during their process of discussion and decision-making, leading to a consensus decision based on a shared understanding. A questionnaire was conducted based on evaluations of the participants experiences on: their agreement with the outcome, their anonymity and asynchronous communication, the role of deliberation of reasons in their decision-making, the effectiveness of the process, and the use of extra resources. The following summarises the findings (Afshar, 2004):

- The capability of the ConSULT approach in facilitating a consensus selection of an issue and its description was confirmed.
- The capability of the ConSULT approach in facilitating a consensus resolution of an issue based on the participants' shared understanding was also confirmed.
- The feedback from the participants has shown a relatively high level of agreement on effectiveness of the ConSULT approach in reaching consensus.
- The feedback from the participants has shown support for effectiveness of the ConSULT approach in reaching shared understanding. However, participants found the exercise of providing reasoning as being intellectually demanding and slowing the process down.
- The feedback from the participants has shown support for effectiveness of the anonymity and asynchronous communication in their deliberation and decision-making

Conclusion

Considering the assumptions and principles underlying effective group discussions and necessary for moving group discussions towards a consensus decision based on a shared understanding, our research suggests an approach in an environment which:

- Prevents the influence of social barriers in communication.
- Helps participants in a discussion with equal opportunities to contribute suggestions without interrupting other members.
- Allows free expression of different ideas and opinions.
- Handles disagreements more respectfully.
- Encourages individuals to address the group rather than another individual.
- Allows the provision of new information or insights for suggestions.
- Allows transparency through deliberation on underlying reasons for each suggestion.

- Encourages participants to thoughtfully explore differences and conflicts and provide as many alternative suggestions as possible.
- Minimises the involvement of any kind of external interpretation and mediation.

Face-to-face communication situations in group decision-making often fail to provide such an environment. To overcome some of the barriers in communication in the process of consensus decision-making, we propose an approach that allows equal participation and support group decision-making in a cooperative environment.

Computer-mediated communication allows *distributed, asynchronous* and *anonymous* group discussion. Distributed communication allows the discussion of participants to take place *from different locations*. Asynchronous communication allows participants to contribute to discussion in *their own convenient time*. Anonymous communication allows *anonymity of discussions* to free participants from some of the problems associated with individual and social communication barriers related to some psychological issues.

In the process of consensus decision-making, computer-mediated communication is employed by ConSULT to address some of the issues relating to face-to-face decision-making situations. Computer-mediated communication allows distributed, asynchronous and anonymous group discussion. The ConSULT use of argumentation:

- Encourages discussions that focus on collaborative deliberation.
- Facilitates the deliberation of structured arguments to provide reasons to support or oppose propositions to achieve justified decisions.
- Invites the discussions of differences of opinions based on the construction, justification and criticism of arguments.

The ConSULT framework provides a certain amount of structure to the discussion which makes it more difficult to deviate from the decision-making cycle and make incomplete or premature decisions. The group has more concentrated discussions based on reasoning, and they may stay more focused on the issues throughout their communication.

Some of the benefits of the application of ConSULT in general, in any decision-making situation are:

- The ease with which individuals can contribute to the group decision-making.
- The assistance provided to participants in handling disagreements respectfully and to freely express different ideas and opinions.
- The freedom of the participants to choose the sequence in which they desire to examine suggestions.
- The opportunity to contribute and provide suggestions without interrupting other members, and encourages the expression of differing viewpoints. It requires

participants to thoughtfully explore differences and conflicts and provide as many alternative suggestions as desired.

- Avoidance of the influence of body language, facial expressions, domination, debate between individuals, and suppression of differences.

In particular Consult provides a model that is designed to allow groups to reach a level of consensus and provides computational advice about the consensus choice and the level of consensus achieved.

References

Afshar, F. (2004). *A computer-mediated framework to facilitate group consensus based on a shared understanding — ConSULT.* Master's Thesis, ITMS, University of Ballarat, Victoria, Australia.

Afshar, F., Yearwood, J., & Stranieri, A. (2002). Capturing consensus knowledge from multiple experts. In M. A. Bramer, A. Preece, & F. Coenen (Eds.), *The Twenty-Second SGAI International Conference on Knowledge Based Systems and Applied Artificial Intelligence* (pp. 253-265). Cambridge: Springer.

Altman, S., Valenzi, E., & Hodgetts, R. M. (1985). *Organizational behavior: Theory and practice.* New York: Academic.

Arrow, K. J. (1963). *Social choice and individual values.* New York: Wiley.

Baker, M. J. (1999). The function of argumentation dialogue in cooperative problem-solving. In F. H. van Eemeren, R. Grootendorst, J. A. Blair, & C. A. Willard (Eds.), *Proceedings of the Fourth International Conference on Argumentation of the International Society for the Study of Argumentation* (pp. 27-33). Amsterdam: SIC SAT.

Boje, D. M., & Murnighan, J. K. (1982). Group confidence pressures in iterative decisions. *Management Science, 28*(10), 1187-1197.

Butler, C. T., & Rothstein, A. (1991). *On conflict and consensus, a handbook on formal consensus decision-making.* Cambridge, MA: Foods Not Bombs.

Clark, H. H., & Brennan, S. E. (1991). Grounding in communication. In L. B. Resnick, J. M. Levine, & S. D. Teasley (Eds.), *Perspectives on socially shared cognition* (pp. 127-149). Washington, DC: American Psychological Association.

Cole, M. (1991). Conclusion. In L. B. Resnick, J. M. Levine, & S. D. Teasley (Eds.), *Perspectives on socially shared cognition* (pp. 398-417). Washington, DC: American Psychological Association.

Dalkey, N. C. (1975). Toward a theory of group estimation. In H. A. Linstone & M. Turoff (Eds.), *The Delphi method, Techniques and applications* (pp. 236-261). London: Addison-Wesley.

Drucker, P. F. (1989). *The new realities.* New York: Harper and Row.

Habermas, J. (1987). *The theory of communicative action: Reason and the rationalization of society* (T. McCarthy, Trans.). Boston: Beacon.

Habermas, J. (1990). Justice and solidarity: On the discussion concerning Stage 6. *Philosophical Forum: A Quarterly, 21*(1-2), 32-52.

Habermas, J. (1993). *Justification and application: Remarks on discourse ethics* (C. Cronin, Trans.). Cambridge: Polity.

Hamalainen, M., Hashim, S., Holsapple, C. W., Suh, Y., & Whinston, A. B. (1992). Structured discourse for scientific collaboration: A framework for scientific collaboration based on structured discourse analysis. *Journal of Organizational Computing, 2*(1), 1-26.

Hoffman, L. R., & Maier, N. R. F. (1961). Quality and acceptance of problem solutions by members of homogenous and heterogenous groups. *Journal of Abnormal and Social Psychology, 62*, 401- 407.

Hwang, C. L., & Lin, M. J. (1987). *Group decision making under multiple criteria: Methods and applications.* Berlin: Springer-Verlag.

Kraus, S., Sycara, K., & Evenchik, A. (1998). Reaching agreements through argumentation: a logical model and implementation. *Artificial Intelligence Journal, 104*(1-2), 1-69.

Kunz, W., & Rittel, H. (1970). *Issues as elements of information systems.* Working paper 131, Institute of Urban and Regional Development, University of California, Berkeley.

Linstone, H. A., & Turoff, M. (1975). *The Delphi method, techniques and applications.* London: Addison-Wesley.

List, C., & Pettit, P. (2002). Aggregating sets of judgments: Two impossibility results compared. *Economics and Philosophy, 18*, 89-110.

Maass, A., & Clark, R. D. (1984). Hidden impact of minorities: Fifteen years of minority influence research. *Psychological Bulletin, 95*, 428-450.

Mitroff, I. I., Mason, R. O., & Barabba, V. P. (1982). Policy as argument — a logic for ill-structured decision problems. *Management Science, 28*(12), 1391-1404.

Myers, D. G., & Lamm, H. (1976). The group polarization phenomenon. *Psychological Bulletin, 83*(4), 602-627.

Nemeth, C. J. (1986). Differential contributions of majority and minority influence. *Psychological Review, 94*, 23-32.

Nemeth, C. J., & Wachtler, J. (1983). Creative problem solving as a result of majority vs. minority influence. *European Journal of Social Psychology, 13*, 45-55.

Ocker, R., Hiltz, S. R., Turoff, M., & Fjermestad, J. (1995). Computer support for distributed asynchronous software design teams: Experimental results on creativity and quality. In *Proceedings of the Twenty-Eighth Annual Hawaii International Conference on System Sciences* (pp. 4-13). Hawaii.

Popper, K. R. (1959). *The logic of scientific discovery.* New York: Harper and Row.

Rittel, H. J., & Webber, M. M. (1984). Planning problems are wicked problems. In N. Cross (Ed.), *Developments in design methodology* (pp. 135-144). Chichester, UK: John Wiley.

Ross, L., Greene, D., & House, P. (1977). The false consensus phenomenon: An attributional bias in self-perception and social perception processes. *Journal of Experimental Psychology, 13*, 279-301.

Saari, D. G. (1995). *Basic geometry of voting*. Berlin: Springer.

Scheibe, M., Skusch, M., & Schofer, J. (1975). Experiments in Delphi methodology. In H. A. Linstone & M. Turoff (Eds.), *The Delphi method, techniques and applications* (pp. 262-288). London: Addison-Wesley.

Siegel, J., Dubrovsky, V., Kiesler, S., & McGuire, T. W. (1986). Group processes in computer-mediated communication. *Organizational Behavior and Human Decision Processes*, 37, 157-197.

Sproull, L., & Kiesler, S. (1991). *Connections: New ways of working in the networked organization*. Cambridge, MA: MIT.

Toulmin, S. E. (1958). *The uses of argument*. Cambridge, UK: Cambridge University.

Turoff, M., & Hiltz, S. R. (1996). *Computer based Delphi processes*. Retrieved August 4, 2002, from http://eies.nJit.edu/~turoff/Papers/delphi3.html

Turoff, M., Hiltz, S. R., Bieber, M., Fjermestad, J., & Rana, A. (1999). Collaborative discourse structures in computer mediated group communications. *Journal of Computer-Mediated Communication, 4*(4). Retrieved from http://jcmc.huji.ac.il/

Whitworth, B., & Felton, R. (1998). Measuring disagreement in groups facing limited choice problems. *The Database for Advances in Information Systems, 30*(3&4), 22-33.

Woods, D. D. (1986). Cognitive technologies: The design of joint human machine cognitive systems. *AI Magazine, 6*, 86-92.

Ziglio, E. (1996). The Delphi method and its contribution to decision-making. In M. Adler & E. Ziglio (Eds.), *Gazing into the oracle: The Delphi method and its application to social policy and public health* (pp. 3-33). London: Jessica Kingsley.

Chapter XVII

Analyzing Strategic Stance in Public Services Management: An Exposition of NCaRBS in a Study of Long-Term Care Systems

Malcolm J. Beynon, Cardiff University, UK

Martin Kitchener, University of California, USA

Abstract

This chapter describes the utilization of an uncertain reasoning-based technique in public services strategic management analysis. Specifically, the nascent NCaRBS technique (developed from Dempster-Shafer theory) is used to categorize the strategic stance of each state's public long-term care (LTC) system to prospector, defender or reactor. Missing values in the data set are termed ignorant evidence and withheld in the analysis rather than transformed through imputation. Optimization of the classification of states, using trigonometric differential evolution, attempts to minimize ambiguity in their prescribed stance but not the concomitant ignorance that may be inherent. The graphical results further the elucidation of the uncertain reasoning-

based analysis. This method may prove a useful means of moving public management research towards a state where LTC system development can be benchmarked and the relations between strategy processes, content, and performance examined.

Introduction

In public services research, strategy scholarship remains relatively under-developed even though reform programs in countries such as the United States (U.S.) and United Kingdom rest on assumptions that "management matters" (Meier & O'Toole, 2001; Thompson, 2000). It has been argued that progress in specifying and measuring public services strategy content has been hampered by the limited applicability of extant frameworks to public-sector contexts. To address this issue, Boyne and Walker (2004) present a classification scheme of public services strategy content that comprises two dimensions the authors suggest are conflated in existing work: (1) the relatively enduring nature of strategic stance towards innovation (the extent to which an organization is a prospector, defender or reactor) and (2) strategic action (the relative emphasis on changes in markets, services, revenues, external relationships and internal characteristics). While this framework offers a promising development towards the goal of specifying and examining relations among public-service strategy and performance, the authors provide little indication of how to assess strategic stance.

This chapter elucidates an approach to analyzing strategic stance in public services. The context of this exposition is a study of the ways that the 51[1] U.S. states' Medicaid long-term care (LTC) agencies address the policy goal of achieving a better balance between traditionally dominant institutional provision (e.g., in nursing homes) and alternative services provided in the home and community (HCBS), such as home health care. Specifically, this classification problem involves using selected concomitant state LTC system characteristics to allocate each state to one of the three classic groupings of strategic stance towards innovation: (1) prospector (pioneering), (2) defender (late adopter), and (3) reactor (adjusts only when forced to).

The classification technique elucidated here is the NCaRBS system (N state Classification and Ranking Belief Simplex), a development of the CaRBS system that was originally able to classify objects to one of only two different classes (Beynon, 2005; Beynon & Buchanan, 2004). This exposition of NCaRBS classifies objects (states) to the described three strategic stance groupings. The mathematical foundation of NCaRBS is through Dempster-Shafer Theory (DST), introduced in the work of Dempster (1968) and Shafer (1976). As such, NCaRBS operates within the domain of uncertain reasoning, particularly here in the presence of "ignorance" (see Smets, 1991). The ignorance involved in this exposition includes incomplete data and uncertainty in the evidential support of characteristics to the final classification of the states. A methodological concern relevant to the strategy stance application here is the issue of missing values. This chapter demonstrates that NCaRBS is able to uniquely manage their presence by considering them as ignorant values. This process removes the need to falsely transform the data set in any way.

The process of matching the states to their known adopted grouping, using NCaRBS, is here defined to be a constrained optimization problem (COP), with the incumbent control variables required to be assigned values within their known domains. Here, this COP is solved using the nascent evolutionary algorithm Trigonometric Differential Evolution (TDE), introduced in Storn and Price (1997) and Fan and Lampinen (2003). Central to this optimization process is the defined objective function (OB), to quantify the difference between the known and estimated classifications of the states. Within NCaRBS, the OB adopted attempts to sequentially minimize the level of ambiguity between the possible classification of each state and their compliment, without forcing the level of concomitant ignorance to also be reduced. This approach using the defined OB is a direct feature of the utilization of DST within NCaRBS and is a novel illustration of the issue of uncertain reasoning in the area of strategic management in public services.

Background

For more than three decades, general management research has matured to specify and examine relationships among organizational environments, strategic processes, strategy content, and organizational performance (Pettigrew, Thomas, & Whittington, 2001; Whittington, 2000). Following the trend for public-policy practitioners and researchers to (unquestioningly) adopt concepts and models from general management, there has been increased importance to notions of strategy and performance. In fields such as large U.S. hospital systems, there has been considerable conceptual and empirical analysis of organizational strategy (Zajac & Shortell, 1989). By contrast, policy innovations and assumptions concerning strategy have developed ahead of conceptual and empirical analysis in LTC, a field in which fully public organizations (variously named state agencies) are the primary strategic units (Beynon & Kitchener, 2005).

For more than 20 years, a central (espoused) goal of LTC policy has been to redress the systematic bias for treatment in institutions such as nursing homes that reduces the opportunities for the elderly and disabled to remain integrated within their communities (Kitchener & Harrington, 2004). The joint federal-state Medicaid program for the poor is central to this policy effort for two reasons. First, it is the single largest payer of LTC spending — an estimated $132 billion in 2002 (Kitchener, Ng, & Harrington, 2005). Second, the persistent institutional bias within the Medicaid LTC systems in most U.S. states is evidenced by the fact that 70% of Medicaid LTC spending in 2002 was consumed by facilities such as nursing homes rather than alternative HCBS. As with other contemporary public policies, attempts to "rebalance" state Medicaid LTC systems have been premised on suggestions from management research that organizational strategy can be identified, that it does "matter" in terms of performance, and can be influenced (Whittington, 2000). These assumptions persist even though it is known that the defining features of state Medicaid LTC systems (publicness, state funding, and political constraints) confound standard managerial specifications and analysis of strategy (Kitchener & Harrington, 2004).

Recognizing the need to develop more contextually appropriate models for the study of strategy content in public contexts such as Medicaid LTC, Boyne and Walker (2004) present a framework that distinguishes among two dimensions of organizational strategy content that are often conflated: (1) strategic stance, the (relatively enduring) orientation towards innovation (expressed as prospector, defender, or reactor); and (2) strategic action, the (more malleable) efforts toward achieving specific goals pursued through changes in markets, services, revenues, external relationships and internal characteristics. Together, strategic stance and actions constitute an organization's strategy content which, following management theory, influences performance.

Boyne and Walker's analytical frame recognizes that while state LTC systems may have the same general orientation towards innovation (prospector, analyzer, or reactor), they may pursue various combinations of strategic actions (changes in markets, services, and prices) directed towards specific policy areas (e.g., Medicaid LTC, garbage disposal, education). While this framework displays potential for moving public management research towards a state where relations between strategy and performance can be assessed, little attention has been given to methods of assessing either strategic stance or content.

Although previous studies recognize the importance of state LTC agencies (as primary payers and regulators of LTC providers), none has explicitly considered strategic stance. They do, however, provide three forms of analysis (Crisp, Eiken, Gerst, & Justice, 2003; Fox-Grage, Coleman, & Folkemer, 2004): (1) statistical analyses of factors associated with individual measures such as HCBS participation or expenditures, (2) qualitative case studies of innovative or laggard states as defined by researchers, and (3) national studies of policy implementation such as the use of Certificate of Need/Moratoria to restrict nursing home bed supply. Drawing insights from that work, here the NCaRBS system is employed to identify (what is conceived to be) the relatively enduring characteristic (Boyne & Walker, 2004) of a state's strategic stance towards LTC.

This analysis begins with an experienced researcher's assignment of each U.S. state's stance towards long-term care strategy into one of the three groupings presented in Boyne and Walker's model: (1) prospector (*Pr*), (2) defender (*Df*), and (3) reactor (*Rc*). Each state is described by the following six concomitant "LTC system innovation" characteristics:

1. Medicaid HCBS participants (waiver, home health and personal care programs) per 1,000 state population in 2002 (HPTS),
2. Medicaid HCBS expenditures (waiver, home health and personal care programs) per 1,000 state population in 2002 (HXPS),
3. Nursing home beds per 10,000 state population in 2002 (NHBp),
4. Number of persons reported to be on a waiting list for waiver services in 2002 (WVRL),
5. Financial eligibility criteria used for Medicaid HCBS waiver programs (FELG),
6. Dollar value of Federal Systems Change Grants awarded to states 2001-03 (SCGs).

Table 1. Descriptive details of state LTC characteristics

Characteristic	HPTS	HXPS	NHBp
Mean	7.458	12061.22	64.877
St. dev.	3.973	5796.34	23.364
Missing	0	0	0
Characteristic	WVRL	FELG	SCGs
Mean	3347.06	1.825	2786.02
St. dev.	10807.33	0.380	1070.35
Missing	4	11	0

These six characteristics were selected from those most commonly used within the research literature in studies of innovation in state LTC system development (e.g., Crisp et al., 2003; Fox-Grage et al., 2004; Kitchener & Harrington, 2004). In brief, both the standardized measures of state Medicaid HCBS program development (participants and expenditures) would indicate more innovative LTC systems. Similarly, LTC system innovation is associated with lower rates of institutional bed supply (sometimes arising from regulation policies), smaller numbers of persons held on waiting lists for HCBS, and the use of discretion allowed within the Medicaid program to operate "more generous" eligibility criteria for a specific HCBS expansion program called "waivers." Finally, following generic management research, the value of competitive research and demonstration grants awarded is used as an indicator of an innovative organizational stance.

Due to non-responses to national research surveys used to collect data for some characteristics, the data set includes missing values. A description of these characteristics is given in Table 1, with respect to their individual mean and standard deviation values. Table 1 also displays the number of missing values present in the WVRL and FELG characteristics (from among the 51 U.S. states). The majority of ignorance (missing values) concerning WVRL arises from a "do not know" response to a survey of responsible state officials concerning (somewhat complex) program eligibility criteria. It is possible that ignorance arising from non-responses to a survey question concerning waiting lists for waiver programs may arise from a reluctance to report such politically sensitive information (Kitchener & Harrington, 2004).

Of course, missing data are common within public services' research and other fields. Because this issue cannot be avoided in this or many other fields of social enquiry, the management of missing values must be considered explicitly and reported within analyses (Schafer & Graham, 2002; West, 2001). Despite this, many data analysis techniques are still not designed to handle aspects of ignorance such as the presence of missing values (*ibid.*). Their incumbency in a problem is often mitigated by the utilization of imputation (Carriere, 1999; Huisman, 2000), whereby they are replaced by some surrogate value (very often the mean value). However, this approach alters the data set being considered and subsequently the findings that accrue. In NCaRBS, their presence is managed by their unique prescription as an ignorant value, with no imputation necessary. The subsequent analysis operates on the original data set, conferring more confidence in the identified results.

The rudiments of the NCaRBS system is within the area of uncertain reasoning, more particularly, the Dempster-Shafer theory of evidence (DST) introduced in the work of Dempster (1967) and Shafer (1976). In summary, it is a methodology for evidential reasoning, manipulating uncertainty and is capable of representing partial knowledge (Haenni & Lehmann, 2002; Kulasekere, Premaratne, Dewasurendra, Shyu, & Bauer, 2004; Scotney & McClean, 2003). The perception of DST as a generalization of Bayesian theory (Shafer & Pearl, 1990), identifies its subjective view, simply, the probability of an event indicates the degree to which someone believes it.

The general terminology inherent within DST starts with a finite set of hypotheses Θ (frame of discernment). A *basic probability assignment* (*bpa*) or mass value is a function m:$2^{\Theta}\rightarrow[0,1]$ such that: $m(\emptyset) = 0$ and $\sum_{A\in 2^{\Theta}} m(A) = 1$ (2^{Θ} the power set of Θ). Any $A\in 2^{\Theta}$, for which $m(A)$ is non-zero is called a focal element and represents the exact belief in the proposition depicted by A. From one source of evidence, a set of focal elements and their mass values can be defined a body of evidence (BOE). To collate two or more sources of evidence (e.g., BOEs $m_1(\cdot)$ and $m_2(\cdot)$), DST provides a method to combine them, using Dempster's rule of combination. If $m_1(\cdot)$ and $m_2(\cdot)$ are independent BOEs, then the function $m_1 \oplus m_2$: $2^{\Theta} \rightarrow [0, 1]$ is defined by:

$$[m_1 \oplus m_2](y) = \begin{cases} 0 & y = \emptyset \\ (1-k)^{-1}\sum_{A\cap B=y} m_1(A)m_2(B) & y \neq \emptyset \end{cases}$$

where $k = \sum_{A\cap B=\emptyset} m_1(A)m_2(B)$, is a mass value associated with $y \subseteq \Theta$. The term $(1 - k)$, can be interpreted as a measure of conflict between the sources. It is important to take this value into account for evaluating the quality of combination: when it is high, the combination may not make sense and possibly lead to questionable decisions (Murphy, 2000).

Efforts have been made to transform a BOE into the more familiar (traditional) probability values. Moreover here, a BOE is partitioned into a set of pseudo probability values, one value for each identified focal element in the frame of discernment. For this, the pignistic probability function (BetP($\cdot$)) is utilized (see Denœux & Zouhal, 2001), which transforms a BOE into a (Bayesian) probability distribution, given by:

$$\mathrm{BetP}(F_i) = \sum_{F_j\subseteq\Theta,\, F_j\neq\emptyset} m(F_j)\frac{|F_i \cap F_j|}{|F_j|},$$

for a $F_i \subseteq \Theta$. In the case of only single hypotheses considered, their BetP($\cdot$) values are found from the sum of all the focal elements which contain the hypothesis, each divided by the number of hypotheses in the focal element.

To demonstrate the utilization of DST, the example of the murder of Mr. Jones is considered, where the murderer was one of three assassins, Peter, Paul or Mary, hence frame of discernment $\Theta = \{\text{Peter, Paul, Mary}\}$. There are two witnesses. Witness 1 is 80% sure that it was a man, the concomitant BOE, defined $m_1(\cdot)$, includes $m_1(\{\text{Peter, Paul}\}) = 0.800$. Since we know nothing about the remaining mass value it is allocated to Θ, $m_1(\{\text{Peter, Paul, Mary}\}) = 0.200$. Witness 2, is 60% confident that Peter was leaving on a jet plane when the murder occurred, a BOE defined $m_2(\cdot)$, includes $m_2(\{\text{Paul, Mary}\}) = 0.600$ and $m_2(\{\text{Peter, Paul, Mary}\}) = 0.400$.

The aggregation of these two sources of information, using Dempster's combination rule, is based on the intersection and multiplication of focal elements and mass values from the BOEs $m_1(\cdot)$ and $m_2(\cdot)$. Defining this BOE $m_3(\cdot) = m_1 \oplus m_2$, it can be found (with $k = 0$ in this case); $m_3(\{\text{Paul}\}) = m_1(\{\text{Peter, Paul}\}) \times m_2(\{\text{Paul, Mary}\}) = 0.800 \times 0.600 = 0.480$, $m_3(\{\text{Peter, Paul}\}) = 0.320$, $m_3(\{\text{Paul, Mary}\}) = 0.120$ and $m_3(\{\text{Peter, Paul, Mary}\}) = 0.080$. This combined evidence has a more spread-out allocation of mass values to varying subsets of Θ. Further, there is a general reduction in the level of ignorance associated with the combined evidence.

The transformation of the combined BOE $m_3(\cdot)$ into a series of probability values is found using the BetP($\cdot$) formulation. In the case of the individual assassins; Peter, Paul and Mary, they are BetP(Peter) = $m_3(\{\text{Peter, Paul}\})/2 + m_3(\{\text{Peter, Paul, Mary}\})/3 = 0.320/2 + 0.080/3 = 0.160 + 0.027 = 0.187$, similarly BetP(Paul) = $0.480/1 + 0.320/2 + 0.120/2 + 0.080/3 = 0.480 + 0.160 + 0.060 + 0.027 = 0.727$ and BetP(Mary) = $0.120/2 + 0.080/3 = 0.060 + 0.027 = 0.087$. From these values it is possible to identify that the most probable assassin was Paul.

Main Thrust of the Chapter

This section undertakes an analysis using the NCaRBS system (Beynon, 2005) based on the strategic stance problem described previously. Here, the NCaRBS system works on n_O states o_i ($i = 1, \ldots, 51 = n_O$), each described by n_C characteristics $c_1, \ldots, c_{n_C}$ (= 6), and classified to one of n_S strategic stance groups $s_1, \ldots, s_{n_S}$ (= 3, hypotheses, which make up the frame of discernment $\Theta = \{s_1, s_2, s_3\}$). For a state o_i and its hth characteristic value c_h, the dyadic comparison between its classification to a group s_j and its compliment defined $\neg s_j$ (not group s_j) is quantified in a *constituent* BOE, denoted by $m_{i,h,j}(\cdot)$, with *mass* values defined in the vector form $[m_{i,h,j}(\{s_j\}), m_{i,h,j}(\{\neg s_j\}), m_{i,h,j}(\Theta)]$. In the context of the strategic stance problem, an example would be the comparison of a states' possible assignment as being either: a prospector or not a prospector (either a defender or a reactor). Following Safranek, Gottschlich, and Kak (1990), the values assigned to the focal elements of a constituent BOE $m_{i,h,j}(\cdot)$ are given by:

$$m_{i,h,j}(\{s_j\}) = \frac{B_{h,j}}{1 - A_{h,j}} cf_{h,j}(v) - \frac{A_{h,j} B_{h,j}}{1 - A_{h,j}}, \quad m_{i,h,j}(\{\neg s_j\}) = \frac{-B_{h,j}}{1 - A_{h,j}} cf_{h,j}(v) + B_{h,j}$$

and $m_{i,h,j}(\Theta) = 1 - m_{i,h,j}(\{s_j\}) - m_{i,h,j}(\{\neg s_j\})$,

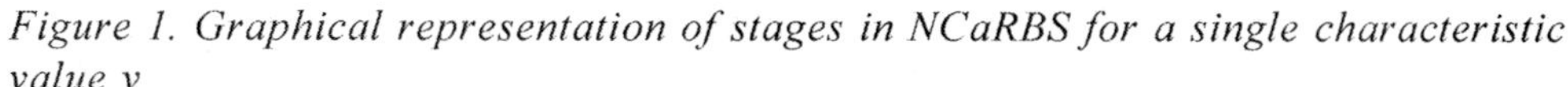

Figure 1. Graphical representation of stages in NCaRBS for a single characteristic value v

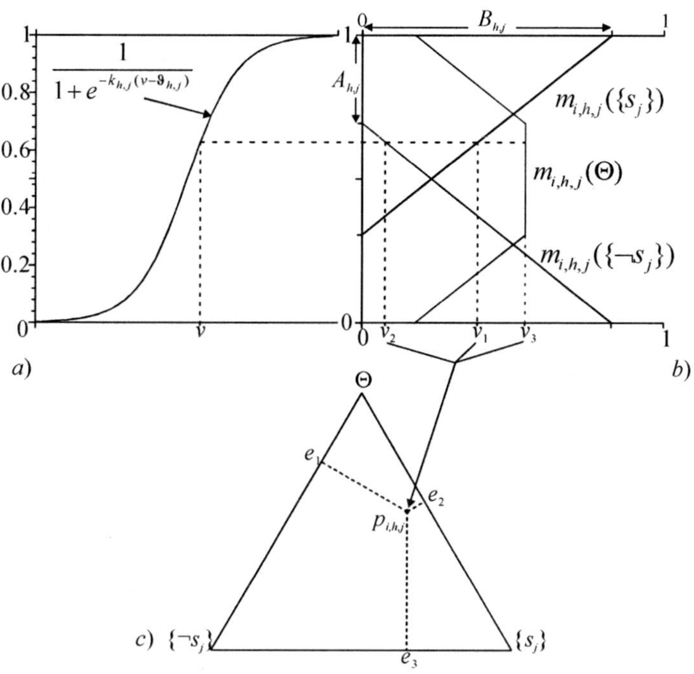

where $cf_{h,j}(v) = \frac{1}{1+e^{-k_{h,j}(v-\theta_{h,j})}}$ is a confidence factor (transforms characteristic value v to a value between 0 and 1) and $k_{h,j}$, $\theta_{h,j}$, $A_{h,j}$ and $B_{h,j}$ are the incumbent control variables present in the NCaRBS system. Importantly, if either $m_{i,h,j}(\{s_j\})$ or $m_{i,h,j}(\{\neg s_j\})$ are negative they are set to zero, and the $m_{i,h,j}(\Theta)$ value then calculated. Figure 1 presents the progression from a characteristic value v to a constituent BOE and its representation as a single simplex coordinate in a simplex plot. This offers a clear visual presentation of the support each characteristic offers to an object's classification (intermediate and final). In Figure 1, a characteristic value v is first transformed into a confidence value (Figure 1*a*), and then deconstructed into its constituent BOE (Figure 1*b*). The constituent BOE is represented as a single simplex coordinate $p_{i,h,j}$ in a simplex plot (Figure 1*c*). Within NCaRBS, the BOEs are represented as points in a simplex plot.

The set of constituent BOEs $\{m_{i,h,j}(\cdot) \mid h = 1, \ldots, n_C\}$ (from all characteristics) associated with an individual state o_i and its possible classification to a group s_j and $\neg s_j$ can be combined using Dempster's combination rule into a *group* BOE, defined $m_{i,-,j}(\cdot)$, see the background section. An analogous set of values could be found based on combining the constituent BOEs found from the same characteristics, over comparisons to the different groups, defined $m_{i,h,-}(\cdot)$, $j = 1, \ldots, n_S$. For an object o_i, a set of group BOEs $\{m_{i,-j}(\cdot), j = 1, \ldots, n_S\}$ are constructed (similarly $m_{i,h,-}(\cdot)$). Since these are BOEs, they can be combined to construct a (final) *object* BOE, defined $m_i(\cdot)$, for object o_i (short form for $m_{i,-,-}(\cdot)$), which contains mass values to sets of groups (power set of Θ). To elucidate a final classification of a state o_i to a single strategic group, the respective $\text{BetP}_i(s_j)$ ($j = 1, \ldots, n_S$) values associated with each state are constructed. For a single state o_i, the largest of its $\text{BetP}_i(\cdot)$ values identifies its final strategic stance classification.

The classification of the states to the n_S groups using NCaRBS depends on the assignment of values to the incumbent control variables ($k_{h,j}$, $\theta_{h,j}$, $A_{h,j}$ and $B_{h,j}$, $h = 1, \ldots n_C$ and $j = 1, \ldots, n_S$). Defined as a constrained optimization problem over a continuous parameter space, this study utilizes Trigonometric Differential Evolution (TDE) to assign values to the control variables (Fan & Lampinen, 2003; Storn & Price, 1997), which minimizes a defined objective function (OB). The OB utilised here directly attempts to reduce ambiguity, but not the inherent ignorance, by mitigating the similarity in the $m_{i,-j}(\{s_j\})$ and $m_{i,-j}(\{\neg s_j\})$ mass values. Moreover, for objects in the equivalence classes $E(s_j)$ and $E(\neg s_j)$, the optimum solution is to maximize the difference values ($m_{i,-j}(\{s_j\}) - m_{i,-j}(\{\neg s_j\})$) and ($m_{i,-j}(\{\neg s_j\}) - m_{i,-j}(\{s_j\})$), respectively (no attempt to minimize the respective $m_{i,-j}(\Theta)$ mass values). The subsequent OB associated with their discernment to the group s_j and its compliment $\neg s_j$, defined OB_j, is given by:

$$\frac{1}{4}\left(\frac{1}{|E(s_j)|}\sum_{o_i \in E(s_j)}(1 - m_{i,\cdot,j}(\{s_j\}) + m_{i,\cdot,j}(\{\neg s_j\})) + \frac{1}{|E(\neg s_j)|}\sum_{o_j \in E(\neg s_j)}(1 + m_{i,\cdot,j}(\{s_j\} - m_{i,\cdot,j}(\{\neg s_j\}))\right)$$

In the limit, each difference value can attain –1 and 1, then $0 \leq \text{OB}_j \leq 1$. The definition of the OB highlights that there is one (OB_j) for each group (s_j) and their discernment from their respective compliment ($\neg s_j$). Each of these OB_j are optimized separately so that the evidence from each grouping is independent, a prerequisite for the utilisation of Dempster's combination rule.

The first stage of the NCaRBS analysis is the assignment of values to the incumbent control variables $k_{h,j}$, $\theta_{h,j}$, $A_{h,j}$ and $B_{h,j}$ ($h = 1, \ldots 6, j = 1, \ldots 3$). To remove bias in their evaluation they were identified using standardized characteristic values. Consistent domains of the control variables were then given as $-2 \leq k_{h,j} \leq 2$, $-1 \leq \theta_{h,j} \leq 1$, $0 \leq A_{h,j} \leq 1$ and $B_{h,j} = 0.4$ (the assignment of 0.4 to each $B_{h,j}$ is based on the analysis from Beynon (2005) and Beynon and Buchanan (2004)). The TDE technique was run five times[2] and the best results subsequently used, reported in Table 2 (now replacing s_1, s_2 and s_3 with *Pr*, *Df* and *Rc*, respectively).

It is the control variables presented in Table 2 that allow the respective constituent, group and object BOEs to be calculated. To illustrate the utilisation of the control variables, the state of Illinois (IL) is considered with respect to the construction of the group BOE $m_{\text{IL},-,Pr}(\cdot)$, which attempts to discern the state's possible classification to $\{Pr\}$ and $\{\neg Pr\} = \{Df, Rc\}$ (its compliment). (See Table 3.)

The results in Table 3 highlight how each BOE (constituent or group) is made up of three mass values, which sum to one. A description of the construction process of an

Table 2. Control variables of the six characteristics in the state LTC data set

Char.	HPTS	HXPS	NHBp	WVRL	FELG	SCGs
$k_{h,Pr}$	2.000	−2.000	−2.000	2.000	2.000	2.000
$\theta_{h,Pr}$	0.327	−0.306	−0.616	−0.843	0.998	−0.054
$A_{h,Pr}$	0.250	0.789	0.975	0.903	0.746	0.794
$k_{h,Df}$	−2.000	2.000	2.000	−2.000	2.000	−2.000
$\theta_{h,Df}$	0.705	0.209	0.027	−0.206	0.998	−0.198
$A_{h,Df}$	0.312	0.370	0.881	0.448	0.746	0.868
$k_{h,Rc}$	−2.000	−2.000	−2.000	−2.000	−2.000	−2.000
$\theta_{h,Rc}$	−0.126	−0.102	−0.079	−0.360	−0.246	−0.072
$A_{h,Rc}$	0.240	0.318	0.895	0.873	0.196	0.774

Table 3. Constituent and group BOEs for IL with respect to its classification to Pr *or* ¬Pr

BOE	St. value v	$m_{\text{IL},j,Pr}(\{Pr\})$	$m_{\text{IL},j,Pr}(\{\neg Pr\})$	$m_{\text{IL},j,Pr}(\Theta)$
HPTS	−0.702	0.000	0.340	0.660
HXPS	−0.798	0.000	0.000	1.000
NHBp	0.985	0.000	0.000	1.000
WVRL	−0.310	0.000	0.000	1.000
FELG	-	0.000	0.000	1.000
SCGs	−1.715	0.000	0.332	0.668
Group BOE		0.000	0.559	0.440

individual constituent BOE is given for the SCG's characteristic. This starts with the calculation of the confidence value $cf_{\text{SCGs},Pr}(v)$, with $v = -1.715$ (standardized characteristic value), given by:

$$cf_{\text{SCGs},Pr}(\text{-}1.715) = \frac{1}{1+e^{-k_{SCGs,\text{Pr}}(v-\vartheta_{SCGs,\text{Pr}})}} = \frac{1}{1+e^{-(2.000)(-1.715-(-0.054))}} = \frac{1}{1+27.739} = 0.035.$$

The subsequent mass values of the constituent BOE $m_{\text{IL,SCGs},Pr}(\cdot)$; $m_{\text{IL,SCGs},Pr}(\{Pr\})$, $m_{\text{IL,SCGs},Pr}(\{\neg Pr\})$ and $m_{\text{IL,SCGs},Pr}(\Theta)$, are then found, given by:

$$m_{\text{IL,SCGs},Pr}(\{Pr\}) = \frac{B_{SCGs,\text{Pr}}}{1-A_{SCGs,\text{Pr}}} cf_{SCGs,\text{Pr}}(v) - \frac{A_{SCGs,\text{Pr}} B_{SCGs,\text{Pr}}}{1-A_{SCGs,\text{Pr}}} = -1.478 < 0 \text{ so} = 0.000,$$

$$m_{\text{IL,SCGs},Pr}(\{\neg Pr\}) = \frac{-B_{SCGs,\text{Pr}}}{1-A_{SCGs,\text{Pr}}} cf_{SCGs,\text{Pr}}(v) + B_{SCGs,\text{Pr}} = -0.068 + 0.4 = 0.332,$$

subsequently

$$m_{\text{IL,SCGs},Pr}(\Theta) = 1 - 0.000 - 0.332 = 0.668.$$

This constituent BOE is combined with the other BOEs reported in Table 3 (using Dempster's combination rule) to produce the concomitant group BOE, defined $m_{\text{IL},-,Pr}(\cdot)$. It follows, the combination of the group BOEs $m_{\text{IL},-,Pr}(\cdot)$,$m_{\text{IL},-,Df}(\cdot)$ and $m_{\text{IL},-,Rc}(\cdot)$, similarly produces the final object BOE for Illinois, defined $m_{\text{IL}}(\cdot)$, made up of mass values associated with subsets of the frame of discernment $\Theta = \{Pr, Df, Rc\}$, given by:

$$m_{\text{IL}}(\{Pr\}) = 0.000, m_{\text{IL}}(\{Df\}) = 0.234, m_{\text{IL}}(\{Rc\}) = 0.549, m_{\text{IL}}(\{Pr, Df\}) = 0.000,$$
$$m_{\text{IL}}(\{Pr, Rc\}) = 0.038, m_{\text{IL}}(\{Df, Rc\}) = 0.100 \text{ and } m_{\text{IL}}(\Theta) = 0.079.$$

The final classification to a particular strategic stance uses the pignistic probability function, for IL it is defined $\text{BetP}_{\text{IL}}(\cdot)$, and for the case of Pr its value is given by:

$$\text{BetP}_{\text{IL}}(Pr) = m_{\text{IL}}(\{Pr\}) + m_{\text{IL}}(\{Pr, Df\})/2 + m_{\text{IL}}(\{Pr, Rc\})/2 + m_{\text{IL}}(\Theta)/3$$
$$= 0.000 + 0.000 + 0.019 + 0.026 = 0.045,$$

similarly, $\text{BetP}_{\text{IL}}(Df) = 0.310$ and $\text{BetP}_{\text{IL}}(Rc) = 0.645$. With $\text{BetP}_{\text{IL}}(Rc)$ the largest of these values, it is this strategic stance that the state IL is classified to (the correct classification in this case). Each individual BOE (constituent, group and object) can be represented as a point in a simplex plot, the standard domain for the analysis of any of the 51 US states. To illustrate, the state of Illinois (IL) is further considered (see Figure 2).

In Figure 2, the three simplex plots 2*a* ($Pr, \neg$Pr), 2*b* ($Df, \neg Df$) and 2*c* ($Rc, \neg Rc$) show the evidence from the characteristics to the classification of the state IL to each of the strategic stances (Pr, Df, Rc) and their respective compliments ($\neg Pr, \neg Df, \neg Rc$). In each of these simplex plots, the base vertices are the points where there exists certainty in the evidence towards a specific strategic stance or its compliment, the top vertex signifying concomitant ignorance. The shaded region denotes the domain that each constituent BOE can exist in (constrained by the $B_{h,j}$ control variables). The vertical dashed lines identify the boundary between which the evidence from a characteristic supports more the classification of the state to a particular strategy stance (right) or its compliment (left).

For the state IL, the characteristics HPTS and SCGs support more its classification to $\neg Pr$, whereas the other characteristics are at the top Θ vertex indicate no supportive evidence (ignorance) from them (see Figure 2*a*). The position of FELG in the simplex plot is because it was a missing value and is considered an ignorant value, whereas the others at the Θ vertex are a consequence of the control variables utilised. The evidence from the characteristics support more its classification to $\neg Pr = \{Df, Rc\}$, based on the position of the group BOE ($m_{\text{IL},-,Pr}(\cdot)$) to the left of the vertical dashed line (which includes Rc, which is the state's known classification). In Figures 2*b* and 2*c*, the evidence from the group BOEs ($m_{\text{IL},-,Df}(\cdot)$ and $m_{\text{IL},-,Rc}(\cdot)$) supports more its classification to Df and Rc, respectively.

Figure 2. Simplex plots containing evidence towards the classification of state Illinois (IL)

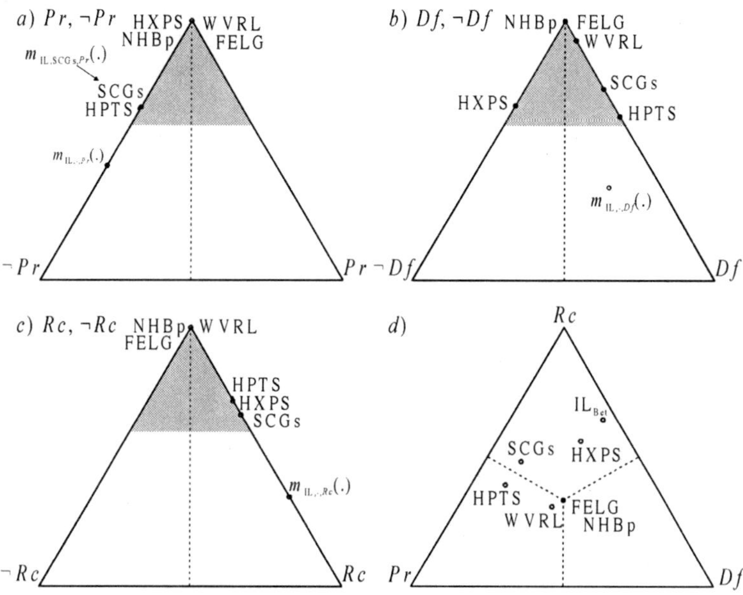

In Figure 2*b*, this is incorrect classification evidence, but near the vertical dashed line, hence inherently ambiguous. In Figure 2*c*, this is strong correct classification evidence.

The final classification of the state IL to one of the *Pr*, *Df* and *Rc* strategic stances is with respect to the pignistic values $\text{BetP}_{\text{IL}}(Pr)$, $\text{BetP}_{\text{IL}}(Df)$ and $\text{BetP}_{\text{IL}}(Rc)$, presented as a point (labelled IL_{Bet}) in the simplex plot in Figure 2*d*. The vertices in this simplex plot each represent one of the three strategic stances considered. The position of IL_{Bet} in Figure 2*d* indicates it is nearest the *Rc* vertex, hence correct classification (the dashed boundary lines presented indicates the region's association with each strategic stance). Also shown in Figure 2*d* are points showing the level of support from each characteristic value (using the $m_{i,h,-}(\cdot)$ BOEs, mentioned previously). The results presented in these figures are the standard domains to interpret the evidence from the individual characteristics to the classification of a U.S. state.

The sets of pignistic values $\text{BetP}_i(Pr)$, $\text{BetP}_i(Df)$ and $\text{BetP}_i(Rc)$ for each state can be found and represented as points in a simplex plot (see Figure 3).

In Figure 3, each point (set of $\text{BetP}_i(\cdot)$ values) is represented by the standard two letter abbreviation for that state (see case of state IL). Those underlined signify incorrect classification (with their known classification given here — smaller font size), it is thus found that there is 74.51% correct classification of states. Amongst these results it is noted all *Pr* and all but one *Rc* defined states were correctly classified.

Figure 3. Simplex plot showing $BetP_i(\cdot)$ based points for each US state LTC system

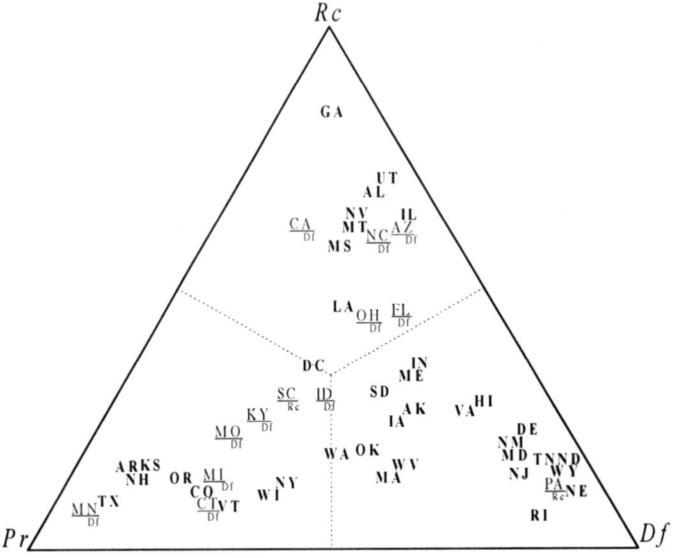

The spread of the state labels over the simplex plot is relatively uniform, the exception being the sparsely populated area midway between the *Pr* and *Rc* vertices. The reason for this is that these strategic stances are at the extremes of the stance a state can hold (crudely stated as: *Pr* best, *Rc* worst and with *Df* in between them). Hence even with dyadic comparisons that grouped *Pr* and *Rc*, the final evidence does not suggest overly ambiguous classification of a state to these diverse stances.

Future Trends

The mode of data analysis reported here is still developing at a pace equivalent to the increase in the worldwide availability of data. An important future consideration is how analysis techniques react to the variations in the quality of the data considered. One direction worth considering is within the area of uncertain reasoning, with methodologies (including Dempster-Shafer theory and fuzzy set theory) that specifically accommodate for a level of ignorance in the data as well as the presented results.

Within the area of public services management, although the issue of ignorance is a real and present incumbency to fruitful analysis, it is often overlooked. Such ignorance is well illustrated by the imprecision and incompleteness of characteristics used here to allocate the strategic stance of state agencies to one of three classic groupings. It is evident then that analysts need to acknowledge this incumbency so their findings can be viewed with confidence. It is expected that in time, analysts will turn progressively to those "uncertain reasoning"-based techniques. In the case of the presence of missing values, it may mean the demise of the imputation (management) required for the utilisation of more traditional techniques such as multivariate discriminant analysis and neural networks. Instead, and as illustrated here, there may be some potential in movement towards the realistic management of ignorance (including missing values).

Conclusion

For the purposes of public services strategic management research, the method of analyzing strategic stance elucidated here may prove a useful means of moving the field towards a state where relations between strategy processes, content, and performance can be assessed (Boyne & Walker, 2004). More specifically, this chapter addresses the widely acknowledged need to develop broader classification and measurement approaches to help benchmark progress towards state LTC rebalancing and identify case sites of better and worse practice (Kitchener & Harrington, 2004). The analytical findings presented here may also have two specific uses within the development of Boyne and Walker's framework: (1) as the dependent variable within analyses of the predictors of state's strategic stance towards LTC, and (2) as an independent variable within investigations of relations among strategic stance, strategic action (after appropriate measurement techniques have been determined), and eventually outcomes.

In terms of practical application, using NCaRBS, the utilisation of simplex plots to report the evidential support of the state characteristics and final classification of states offers the fullest opportunity for policymakers and others to interpret and judge the relevant findings. This mitigates the need to encumber themselves with mathematical notation and formulation. It is also of interest to theoreticians who will have the opportunity to further elucidate strategy analysis within the area of uncertain reasoning.

References

Beynon, M. J. (2005). A novel technique of object ranking and classification under ignorance: An application to the corporate failure risk problem. *European Journal of Operational Research*, *167*(2), 493-517.

Beynon, M. J., & Buchanan, K. L. (2004). A novel approach to gender classification under ignorance: The case of the European barn swallow (Hirundo Rustica). *Expert Systems With Applications*, *27*(3), 403-415.

Beynon, M. J., & Kitchener, M. (2005). Ranking the 'balance' of states long-term care systems: A comparative exposition of the SMARTER and CaRBS techniques. *Healthcare Management Science, 8*, 159-168.

Boyne, G., & Walker, R. (2004). Strategy content and public service organizations. *Journal of Public Administration Research and Theory*, *14*(2), 231-252.

Carriere, K. C. (1999). Methods for repeated measures data analysis with missing values. *Journal of Statistical Planning and Inference*, *77*, 221-236.

Crisp, S., Eiken, S., Gerst, K., & Justice, D. (2003). *Money follows the person and balancing long-term care systems: State examples*. A report for the US Department of Health and Human Services, Centers for Medicare and Medicaid Services, Disabled and Elderly Health Programs Division. Washington, DC: Medstat.

Dempster, A. P. (1968). A generalization of Bayesian inference (with discussion). *Journal of the Royal Statistical Society — Series B*, 30, 205-247.

Denoeux, T., & Zouhal, L. M. (2001). Handling possibilistic labels in pattern classification using evidential reasoning. *Fuzzy Sets and Systems*, *122*(3), 47-62.

Fan, H.-Y., & Lampinen, J. (2003). A trigonometric mutation operation to differential evolution. *Journal of Global Optimization*, *27*, 105-129.

Fox-Grage, W., Coleman, B., & Folkemer, D. (2004). *The States response to the Olmstead decision: 2004 update.* Washington, DC: National Conference of State Legislatures.

Haenni, R., & Lehmann, N. (2002). Resource bounded and anytime approximation of belief function computations. *International Journal of Approximate Reasoning*, *31*, 103-154.

Huisman, M. (2000), Imputation of missing item responses: Some simple techniques. *Quality & Quantity*, *34*, 331-351.

Kitchener, M., & Harrington, C. (2004). U.S. long-term care: A dialectic analysis of institutional dynamics. *Journal of Health and Social Behavior, 45*, 87-101.

Kitchener, M., Ng, T., & Harrington, C. (2005). Medicaid home and community-based services: National program trends. *Health Affairs*, *24*(1), 206-212.

Kulasekere, E. C., Premaratne, K., Dewasurendra, D. A., Shyu, M-L., & Bauer, P. H. (2004). Conditioning and updating evidence. *International Journal of Approximate Reasoning*, *36*, 75-108.

Meier, K. J., & O'Toole Jr., L. (2001). The dynamics of multi-organizational partnerships: An analysis of changing modes of governance. *Journal of Public Administration Research and Theory*, *11*, 271-93.

Murphy, C. K. (2000). Combining belief functions when evidence conflicts. *Decision Support Systems*, *29*, 1-9.

Pettigrew, A., Thomas, H., & Whittington, R. (2001). *The handbook of strategy and management.* London: Sage.

Safranek, R. J., Gottschlich, S., & Kak, A. C. (1990). Evidence accumulation using binary frames of discernment for verification vision. *IEEE Transactions on Robotics and Automation*, *6*, 405-417.

Scotney, B., & McClean, S. (2003). Database aggregation of imprecise and uncertain evidence. *Information Sciences*, *155*, 245-263.

Schafer, J. L., & Graham, J. W. (2002). Missing data: Our view of the state of the art. *Psychological Methods*, *7*(2), 147-177.

Shafer, G. A. (1976). *Mathematical theory of evidence*. Princeton: Princeton University.

Shafer, G., & Pearl J., (1990). *Readings in uncertain reasoning*. San Mateo, CA: Morgan Kaufman.

Smets, P. (1991). Varieties of ignorance and the need for well-founded theories. *Information Sciences*, 57-58, 135-144.

Storn, R., & Price, K. (1997). Differential evolution – A simple and efficient heuristic for global optimization over continuous spaces. *Journal of Global Optimization, 11*, 341-359.

Thompson, J. R. (2000). Reinvention as reform: Assessing the National Performance Review. *Public Administration Review*, *60*, 508-550.

West, S. G. (2001). New approaches to missing data in psychological research: Introduction to the special section. *Psychological Methods*, *6*(4), 315-316.

Whittington, R. (2000). *What is strategy – and does it matter*? London: Thomson.

Zajac, E. J., & Shortell, S. M. (1989). Changing generic strategies: Likelihood, direction and performance implications. *Strategic Management Journal*, *10*, 413-430.

Endnotes

[1] Administratively, Washington, D.C. is considered a state, making 51 states in total.

[2] The parameters utilised for the operation of TDE are: Amplification control F = 0.99, Crossover constant CR = 0.85, Trigonometric mutation probability Mt = 0.05 and Number of parameter vectors NP = 135.

Chapter XVIII

The Analytic Network Process – Dependence and Feedback in Decision-Making: Theory and Validation Examples

Thomas L. Saaty, University of Pittsburgh, USA[1]

Abstract

Simple multi-criteria decisions are made by deriving priorities of importance for the criteria in terms of a goal and of the alternatives in terms of the criteria. Often one also considers benefits, opportunities, costs and risks and their synthesis in an overall outcome. The Analytic Hierarchy Process (AHP) with its independence assumptions, and its generalization to dependence among and within the clusters of a decision — the Analytic Network Process (ANP), are theories of prioritization and decision-making. Here we show how to derive priorities from pair-wise comparison judgments, give the fundamental scale for representing the judgments numerically and by way of validation illustrate its use with examples and then apply it to make a simple hierarchic decision in two ways: pair-wise comparisons of the alternatives and rating the alternatives with respect to an ideal. Network decisions are discussed and illustrated with market share examples. A mathematical appendix is also included.

Introduction

The material in this chapter is an outgrowth of the author's work over a long period of time in multi-criteria decision-making. It contains some of the basic ideas together with a modicum of the mathematics of the Analytic Hierarchy Process (AHP) with a structure that descends from a goal to criteria, subcriteria, stakeholders and their objectives, the groups affected and the alternatives of the decision. It also contains information about the generalization of the AHP to dependence and feedback, the Analytic Network Process (ANP), along with some elementary applications to determine the market share of different companies in relative form. In the ANP one identifies clusters of elements that influence each other and influence and are influenced by elements in other clusters. The ANP allows considerable flexibility (but requires more work) and frees us from having a fixed structure to follow, as in a hierarchy. In addition the ANP makes it possible to analyze influence separately according to many factors: political, economic, social, business and trade, etc., and then combine them into a single outcome. It can even include interdependence among these factors themselves according to higher order values. Numerical priorities are derived from comparisons made mostly on intangible attributes used to study the influences of individuals, companies or governments with respect to these attributes. The outcome is then compared with the actual money market shares for validation purposes so the method can be applied with greater confidence to cases where the answers are not already known.

Decision-making involves criteria and alternatives to choose from. The criteria usually have different importance and the alternatives in turn differ in our preference for them on each criterion. To make such trade-offs and choices we need a way to measure. Measuring needs a good understanding of methods of measurement and different scales of measurement. Figueira, Greco, and Ehrgott (2005), in their overview of decision-making, include a chapter on the AHP/ANP. This approach differs from other theories of decision-making in that, instead of interval scale numbers normally used by other theories, the AHP/ANP approach uses absolute scale numbers (invariant under the identity transformation). These numbers cannot be changed to other numbers to have any meaning, like Fahrenheit to Celcius as interval scale numbers or pounds to kilograms as ratio scale numbers. It is primarily a descriptive (rather than a prescriptive) psycho-physical theory. There are two ways to deal with the measurement of intangibles. One relies on questioning a person relative to his/her preferences among things and deriving a general utility function for that person to be used as representative of their values in general. The assumption is that people have a utility function which many people question. The other is to rely on people's *tacit knowledge* about a problem and use pair-wise comparisons to determine numerically, according to the strength of feelings or judgments, as to what may be more preferred, more important or more likely for that particular decision and then derive priorities from these judgments. To have confidence that such a process leads to accurate outcomes and is much better representative of how the mind of a person works in practice to make decisions, it needs validation by checking the results obtained against existing percentages and other measurements put in relative form when there are such measurements. Usually the purpose is not to legislate what is a good decision, but to make sure that a best decision also survives the hazards it faces after it is made. Such hazards are included under risks, for example, but can also be later combined with benefits, opportunities, and costs to produce a single overall outcome. It is often said in the multi-criteria decision-making literature that the AHP is the most widely used method around the world to make decisions. For example, in China there is widespread knowledge and use of the method by municipalities and by the central government. We would be glad to provide the reader with a chapter prepared by a military official in Beijing about uses of the AHP known to him in China. Criteria for comparing different decision-making methods and the actual comparison of such methods have been undertaken by Peniwati (2005).

Many people think that measurement needs a physical scale with a zero and a unit to apply to objects or phenomena. That is not true. Surprisingly enough, we can also derive accurate and reliable relative scales that do not have a zero or a unit by using our understanding and judgments that are, after all, the most fundamental determinants of why we want to measure something. In reality we do that all the time and we often do it subconsciously. Physical scales help our understanding and use of the things that we know how to measure. After we obtain readings from a physical scale, they still need to be interpreted according to what they mean and how adequate or inadequate they are to satisfy some need we have. But the number of things we don't know how to measure is infinitely larger than the things we know how to measure, and it is highly unlikely that we will ever find ways to measure everything on a physical scale with a unit. Scales of measurement are inventions of a technological mind. The brain is an electrical device of neurons whose firings and synthesis must perform measurement with great accuracy to give us all the meaning and understanding that we have to enable us to survive and reach out to control a complex world. Can we rely on our minds to be accurate guides with their judgments? The answer depends on how well we know the phenomena to which we apply measurement and how good our judgments are to represent our understanding. In our own personal affairs we are the best judges of what may be good for us. In situations involving many people, we need the judgments from all the participants. In general we think that there are people who are more expert than others in some areas, and their judgments should have precedence over the judgments of those who know less. In fact this is often the case in practice.

Judgments expressed in the form of comparisons are fundamental in our biological makeup. They are intrinsic in the operations of our brains and that of animals and one might even say of plants since, for example, they control how much sunlight to admit. We all make decisions every moment, consciously or unconsciously. Decision-making is a fundamental process that is integral in everything we do. How do we do it? The Harvard psychologist Arthur Blumenthal tells us that there are two types of judgment: "Comparative judgment which is the identification of some relation between two stimuli both present to the observer, and absolute judgment which involves the relation between a single stimulus and some information held in short-term memory about some former comparison stimuli or about some previously experienced measurement scale using which the observer rates the single stimulus" (Blumenthal, 1977, p. 95). We shall illustrate the use of both of these modes by an example given below involving a decision regarding the best city to get married in (for a friend of the author).

When we think about it, both these processes involve making comparisons. Comparisons imply that all of the things we know are understood in relative terms to other things. It does not seem possible to know an absolute in itself independently of something else that influences it or that it influences. The question then is how do we make comparisons in a scientific way and derive from these comparisons scales of relative measurement? When we have many scales with respect to a diversity of criteria and subcriteria, how do we synthesize these scales to obtain an overall relative scale? Can we validate this process so that we can trust its reliability? What can we say about other ways people have proposed to deal with judgment and measurement, how do they relate to this fundamental idea of comparisons, and can they be relied on for validity? These are all questions we need to consider in making a decision. It is useful to remember that there are many people in the world who only know their feelings and may know nothing about numbers, but who can still make good decisions. How do they do it? It is unlikely that guessing at numbers and assigning them directly to the alternatives to indicate order under some criterion will yield meaningful priorities, because the numbers are arbitrary. Even if they were taken from a scale for a particular criterion, how would we combine them across the criteria, as they would likely be from different scales? Our answer to this conundrum is to derive a relative scale for the criteria with respect to the goal and to derive relative scales for the alternatives with respect to each of the criteria and use a weighting and adding process that will make these scales alike. The scale we derive under each criterion is the same priority scale that measures the preference we have for the alternatives with respect to each criterion, and the importance we attribute to the criteria in terms of the goal. As we shall see below, the judgments made use absolute numbers and the priorities derived from them are also absolute numbers that represent relative dominance. The AHP was used by IBM as part of its quality improvement strategy to design its AS/400 computer, and consequently win the prestigious Malcolm Baldrige National Quality Award.

Deriving a Scale of Priorities from Pairwise Comparisons

The AHP/ANP takes the descriptive rather than the normative or prescriptive approach to making decisions. In general it does not say one *must* do this or that but rather it helps people to lay out their perceptions in an organized way and provide their judgments as they do naturally. It is being used in practical applications in many places, such as, in making major national policy decisions, some military and government decisions, and in corporations where project prioritization and resource allocation are pressing issues.

The AHP/ANP uses a reciprocal matrix to represent judgments expressed on a fundamental scale of absolute numbers. The AHP uses only absolute scale numbers for judgments and for their resulting priorities. Judgments are of necessity inconsistent because new knowledge changes judgments about old relations. In the consistent case adding the entries in any column of the judgment matrix, and then dividing each entry in that column by its sum, or dividing the sum of each column by their total sum, gives the priorities as the principal right eigenvector of the matrix. Since each judgment is expressed as an absolute number from the fundamental scale, so also are the sum, product and quotient of such judgments. When normalized, each column gives the same vector of priorities because of consistency. In the inconsistent case one solves a system of linear homogeneous equations that have coefficients that belong to an absolute scale to obtain the principal right eigenvector for the priorities, and hence the solution also belongs to an absolute scale, which on normalization or idealization becomes a relative scale of absolute numbers, like probabilities and percentages that sum to one but have no unit. The smaller of two elements in a paired comparison serves as a unit for that comparison. Priorities are then derived from all the comparisons.

Suppose we wish to derive a scale of relative importance according to size (volume) of three apples A, B, C shown in Figure 1. Assume that their volumes are known respectively as S_1, S_2 and S_3. For each position in the matrix the volume of the apple at the left is compared with that of the apple at the top and the ratio is entered. A matrix of judgments $A=(a_{ij})$ is constructed with respect to a particular property the elements have in common. It is reciprocal; that is, $a_{ji} = 1/a_{ij}$, and $a_{ii} = 1$. For the matrix in Figure 1, it is necessary to make only three judgments with the remainder being automatically determined. There are $n(n-1)/2$ judgments required for a matrix of order n. Sometimes one (particularly an expert who knows well what the judgments should be) may wish to make a minimum set of judgments and construct a consistent matrix defined as one whose entries satisfy $a_{ij}a_{jk} = a_{ik}$, $i, j, k = 1, ..., n$. To do this one can enter $n-1$ judgments in a row or in a column, or in a spanning set with at least one judgment in every row and column, and construct the rest of the entries in the matrix using the consistency condition. Redundancy in the number of judgments generally improves the validity of the final answer because the judgments of the few elements one chooses to compare may be more biased.

Note that to recover the scale values from the matrix of comparisons $A = (S_i/S_j)$ we can multiply A on the right by the vector $S=(S_1, S_2, S_3)^T$ that is, an eigenvalue problem. Here the T indicates the transpose of the vector. In general instead of S used for convenience

Figure 1. Reciprocal structure of pairwise comparison matrix for apples

Pairwise Comparisons

Size Comparison	Apple A	Apple B	Apple C
Apple A	S_1/S_1	S_1/S_2	S_1/S_3
Apple B	S_2/S_1	S_2/S_2	S_2/S_3
Apple C	S_3/S_1	S_3/S_2	S_3/S_3

Figure 2. Pairwise comparison matrix for apples using judgments

Pairwise Comparisons

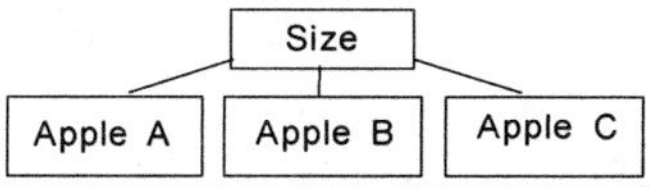

Size Comparison	Apple A	Apple B	Apple C	Resulting Priority
Apple A	1	2	3	6/10
Apple B	1/2	1	3	3/10
Apple C	1/6	1/3	1	1/10

to indicate the size of apples we shall use $w = (w_1, ..., w_n)^T$ to indicate an arbitrary vector of priorities derived from paired comparison judgments.

Assume that we know the volumes or sizes of the apples so that the values we enter in Figure 2 are consistent. Apple A is twice as big in volume as apple B, and apple B is three times as big as apple C, so we enter a 2 in the (1,2) position, and so on. Ones are entered on the diagonal by default as every entity equals itself on any criterion. Note that in the (2, 3) position we can enter the value 3 because we know the judgments are consistent as they are based on actual measurements. We can deduce the value this way: from the first row A = 2B and A = 6C, and thus B = 3C.

If we did not have actual measurements, we could not be certain that the judgments in the first row were accurate, and we would not mind estimating the value in the (2, 3) position directly by comparing apple B with apple C. We are then very likely to be inconsistent. How inconsistent can we be before we think it is intolerable? Later we give an actual measure of inconsistency and argue that a consistency of about 10% is considered acceptable.

We obtain from the consistent pair-wise comparison matrix above a vector of priorities showing the relative sizes of the apples. Note that we do not have to go to all this trouble to derive the relative volumes of the apples. We could simply have normalized the actual measurements. The reason we did so is to lay the foundation for what to do when we have no measures for the property in question. When judgments are consistent as they are here, this vector of priorities can be obtained in two ways: dividing the elements in any column by the sum of its entries (normalizing it), or by summing the entries in each row to obtain the overall dominance in size of that alternative relative to the others and normalizing the resulting column of values. Incidentally, calculating dominance plays an important role in computing the priorities when judgments are inconsistent, for then an alternative may dominate another by different magnitudes by transiting to it through intermediate alternatives. Thus the story is very different if the judgments are inconsistent, and we need to allow inconsistent judgments for good reasons. In sports, team A beats team B, team B beats team C, but team C beats team A. How would we admit such an occurrence in our attempt to explain the real world if we do not allow inconsistency? Most theories have taken a stand against such an occurrence with an axiom that assumes transitivity and prohibits intransitivity, although one does not have to be intransitive to be inconsistent in the values obtained. Others have wished it away by saying that it should not happen in human thinking. But it does, and we offer a theory below to deal with it.

Fundamental Scale of the AHP for Making Comparisons with Judgments

In general when we make comparisons, we would estimate the ratios as numbers using the Fundamental Scale of the AHP, shown in Table 1, which can be derived analytically from stimulus response theory. A judgment is made on a pair of elements with respect to a property they have in common. The smaller element is considered to be the unit and one estimates how many times more important, preferable or likely, more generally "dominant," the other is by using a number from the fundamental scale. Dominance is often interpreted as importance when comparing the criteria and as preference when comparing the alternatives with respect to the criteria. It can also be interpreted as likelihood as in the likelihood of a person getting elected as president, or other terms that fit the situation (Saaty, 2000).

The set of objects being pair-wise compared must be homogeneous. That is, the dominance of the largest object must be no more than 9 times the smallest one (this is the widest span we use for many good reasons discussed elsewhere in the AHP literature). Things that differ by more than this range can be clustered into homogeneous groups and dealt with by using this scale. If measurements from an existing scale are used, they can simply be normalized without regard to homogeneity. When the elements being compared are very close, they should be compared with other more contrasting elements, and the larger of the two should be favored a little in the judgments over the smaller. We have found this approach to be effective to bring out the actual priorities of the two close elements. Otherwise we have proposed the use of a scale between 1 and 2 using decimals and similar judgments to the Fundamental Scale above. We note that human judgment is relatively insensitive to such small decimal changes.

Table 3 shows how an audience of about 30 people, using consensus to arrive at each judgment, provided judgments to estimate the *dominance* of the consumption of drinks in the United States (which drink is consumed more in the US and how much more than another drink?). Each judgment was debated openly according to the verbal scale value that describes it best. A compromise intermediate value was agreed upon in case of sharp differences. In a more formal setting the geometric mean of the judgments is used if experts are involved and only after some debate. The geometric mean has been shown to be the only way to synthesize different judgments when their reciprocal values are also involved. When the participants are not present in the same room, one often sends a

Table 1. Fundamental scale of absolute numbers

Intensity of Importance	Definition	Explanation
1	Equal Importance	Two activities contribute equally to the objective
2	Weak or slight	
3	Moderate importance	Experience and judgment slightly favor one activity over another
4	Moderate plus	
5	Strong importance	Experience and judgment strongly favor one activity over another
6	Strong plus	
7	Very strong or demonstrated importance	An activity is favored very strongly over another; its dominance demonstrated in practice
8	Very, very strong	
9	Extreme importance	The evidence favoring one activity over another is of the highest possible order of affirmation
Reciprocals of above	If activity i has one of the above nonzero numbers assigned to it when compared with activity j, then j has the reciprocal value when compared with i	A reasonable assumption
Rationals	Ratios arising from the scale	If consistency were to be forced by obtaining n numerical values to span the matrix
From 1.1 to 1.9	To compare things that are very close	One can use the same kind of verbal descriptions as above. It is usually better to compare close alternatives with widely contrasting ones and make some distinction between the close alternatives by using the 1-9 scale.

questionnaire asking them to indicate their judgments on each pair of factors that range on a line from a value of 9 when one factor is preferred to the other factor gradually decreasing to one according to the scale values and then increasing to 9 in the direction of the other factor.

The vector of relative consumption derived and the actual vector, obtained by normalizing the consumption given in official statistical data sources, are shown at the bottom of the table.

If the objects are not homogenous they may be divided into groups that are homogeneous. If necessary, additional objects can be added merely to fill out the intervening clusters to move from the smallest object to the largest one. Figure 3 shows how this process works in comparing a cherry tomato with a watermelon, which appears to be two orders of magnitude bigger in size, by introducing intermediate objects in stages.

Table 2. Relative consumption of drinks

Which Drink is Consumed More in the U.S.?
An Example of Estimation Using Judgments

Drink Consumption in the U.S.	Coffee	Wine	Tea	Beer	Sodas	Milk	Water
Coffee	1	9	5	2	1	1	1/2
Wine	1/9	1	1/3	1/9	1/9	1/9	1/9
Tea	1/5	2	1	1/3	1/4	1/3	1/9
Beer	1/2	9	3	1	1/2	1	1/3
Sodas	1	9	4	2	1	2	1/2
Milk	1	9	3	1	1/2	1	1/3
Water	2	9	9	3	2	3	1

The derived scale based on the judgments in the matrix is:

Coffee	Wine	Tea	Beer	Sodas	Milk	Water
.177	.019	.042	.116	.190	.129	.327

with a consistency ratio of .022.

The actual consumption (from statistical sources) is:

.180	.010	.040	.120	.180	.140	.330

Figure 3. Clustering to compare non-homogeneous objects

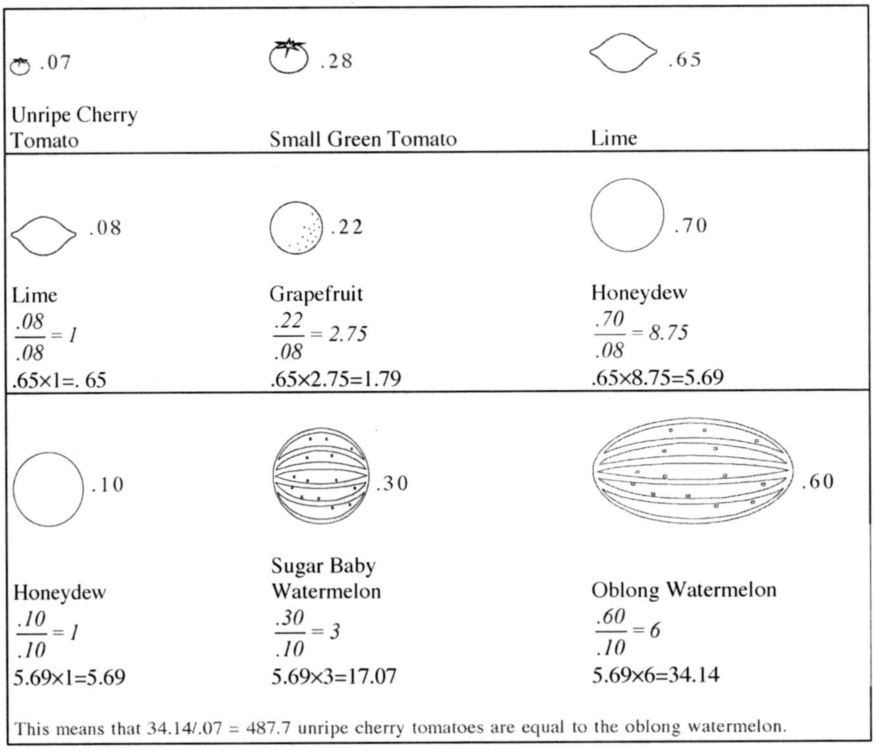

.07 Unripe Cherry Tomato	.28 Small Green Tomato	.65 Lime
.08 Lime $\frac{.08}{.08} = 1$ .65×1=. 65	.22 Grapefruit $\frac{.22}{.08} = 2.75$ .65×2.75=1.79	.70 Honeydew $\frac{.70}{.08} = 8.75$ .65×8.75=5.69
.10 Honeydew $\frac{.10}{.10} = 1$ 5.69×1=5.69	.30 Sugar Baby Watermelon $\frac{.30}{.10} = 3$ 5.69×3=17.07	.60 Oblong Watermelon $\frac{.60}{.10} = 6$ 5.69×6=34.14

This means that 34.14/.07 = 487.7 unripe cherry tomatoes are equal to the oblong watermelon.

A Simple Three-Hierarchic Decision Illustrative Example: Where Best to Get Married

A friend of the author had the dilemma of what city of three possibilities to choose to get married in. Thus her goal was is to determine a location to get married. Her criteria are the things that influence her decision. These include: money, convenience, fun, family stress, and family presence. The alternatives are the Caribbean, the Hometown, and Las Vegas. [1]

A simple hierarchy was used to display the analysis of this decision. The goal of "where to get married" was represented as a node at the top of the hierarchy. Below the goal there is a level called "criteria" that included the nodes: convenience, family presence, family stress, fun, and money.

The alternative cities: Caribbean, Hometown and Las Vegas occupied the third or bottom level of the hierarchy. Arrows are drawn form the goal to each criterion. More arrows are drawn from each criterion to each alternative in the third level, all to indicate how important an element in a lower level is to the element in the level above it. Here for economy we use a single arrow from a level to the level below it in order not to crowd the picture in Figure 4.

It was thought desirable to get married in a location that is convenient for the bride and possibly also for her family members. It would have been desirable to have most of the family members there, but that would have added family stress as a factor influencing the decision because if they came to the wedding, there would be stress and arguments. Fun is an aspect that she valued highly. One could argue that a wedding should be a celebration and celebrations should be fun. Money is something that unfortunately had to be considered. There was little interest in having a large wedding or in having very expensive accessories (string quartet, $2,000 dress, etc.).

As we shall see below, as the bride-to-be had expected, fun and family stress received the highest priority values of 0.4507 and 0.1944, so they were weighted heavily in comparison with the other criteria. It seemed that Las Vegas was consistently the ideal place to get married, with the Caribbean a close second. That was because Las Vegas is less costly than getting married in the Caribbean and more fun. While family would all likely attend a wedding in the Hometown, it would be more costly than Las Vegas, more stressful and not as much fun. Hometown was thought to be less convenient due to all of the planning that would have to go into a church wedding and reception.

Node comparisons shown in Table 3 were made. The criteria were compared with one another using the fundamental scale, by answering the question, "Which criterion is more important in deciding on the best place to get married, and how much more important is it?"

The inconsistency of these judgments is 0.096 which is below 10% and therefore generally acceptable. Where the inconsistency was high for a judgment it was thought through and revised the earlier estimate aided by the software superdecisions (www.superdecisions.com/~saaty).

Figure 4. Where to get married

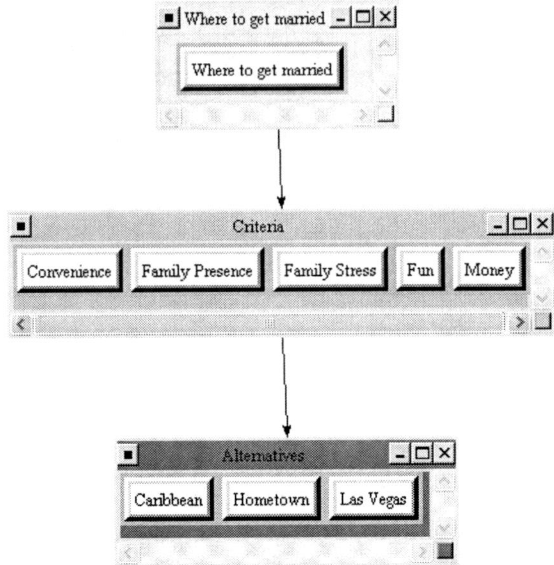

Table 3. Paired comparisons of the criteria

Criteria with Respect to Goal						**Priorities of Criteria with Respect to the Goal**	
	Convenience	Family Presence	Family Stress	Fun	Money	Normalized	Idealized
Convenience	1.0000	0.5000	4.0000	0.3333	0.3333	**0.1199**	0.0833
Family Presence	2.0000	1.0000	2.0000	0.3333	2.0000	**0.1944**	0.5000
Family Stress	0.2500	0.5000	1.0000	0.1667	0.2500	**0.0558**	0.0625
Fun	3.0000	3.0000	6.0000	1.0000	4.0000	**0.4507**	1.0000
Money	3.0000	0.5000	4.0000	0.2500	1.0000	**0.1792**	0.2500

The three alternative places were then compared in a separate matrix with respect to each criterion as in Tables 4 to 8. In the case of Money (more money less desirable), Hometown was thought to be more expensive because the family lives there and one would have to have an expensive elaborate wedding. Similarly for Family Stress, the less stress the more desirable and in the Hometown with all the relatives around, the stress would be high. Then the priorities were weighted, each vector of priorities by its corresponding criterion priority and added the values thus obtained the weighted (normalized) sum for each alternative. The priorities of the alternatives were also idealized for each criterion by dividing each one by the largest value among them and then weighted each by the

Table 4. Comparisons of the alternatives with respect to convenience of location

Convenience of Location				Priority Vectors for Alternatives Under Criteria	
	Caribbean	Hometown	Las Vegas	Normalized	Idealized
Caribbean	1.0000	0.2000	0.3333	**0.1047**	0.1644
Hometown	5.0000	1.0000	3.0000	**0.6370**	1.0000
Las Vegas	3.0000	0.3333	1.0000	**0.2583**	0.4055

Table 5. Comparisons of the alternatives with respect to family presence

Family Presence				**Priorities**	**Priorities**
	Caribbean	Hometown	Las Vegas	**Normalized**	Idealized
Caribbean	1.0000	0.2000	0.3333	**0.1095**	0.1882
Hometown	5.0000	1.0000	2.0000	**0.5816**	1.0000
Las Vegas	3.0000	0.5000	1.0000	**0.3090**	0.5313

Table 6. Comparisons of the alternatives with respect to family stress

Family Stress				**Priorities**	**Priorities**
	Caribbean	Hometown	Las Vegas	**Normalized**	Idealized
Caribbean	1.0000	7.0000	3.0000	**0.6586**	1.0000
Hometown	0.1429	1.0000	0.2500	**0.0786**	0.1194
Las Vegas	0.3333	4.0000	1.0000	**0.2628**	0.3989

priorities of its criterion and the sum taken. These two operations yielded the final priorities of the alternatives in Table 9. It is useful to idealize in many decisions when the alternatives are assumed not to influence each other according to quality or number and thus adding more alternatives would not influence the relative ranks of the old ones provided that the new alternatives are compared with the ideal and allowed to take their place above it (with a priority value greater than one) if they are preferred to it. Otherwise one uses normalization.

It seems that Las Vegas is consistently the ideal place for the marriage. While the family could easily attend a wedding in the Hometown, it would be more costly than Las Vegas, more stressful, and not as much fun.

Rating the alternative cities with respect to the criteria is the other way to obtain the priorities for the alternatives by putting them in categories of excellence with respect to each criterion. These categories had to be compared according to their relative importance for their criterion their priorities derived and divided by the largest value among them. Each alternative is then assigned a category and weighting the priority of

Table 7. Comparisons of the alternatives with respect to fun

Fun				Priorities	Priorities
	Caribbean	Hometown	Las Vegas	**Normalized**	Idealized
Caribbean	1.0000	4.0000	0.3333	**0.2706**	0.4200
Hometown	0.2500	1.0000	0.1667	**0.0852**	0.1323
Las Vegas	3.0000	6.000	1.0000	**0.6442**	1.0000

Table 8. Comparisons of the alternatives with respect to money

Money				Priorities	Priorities
	Caribbean	Hometown	Las Vegas	Normalized	Idealized
Caribbean	1.0000	3.0000	0.1667	**0.1618**	0.2010
Hometown	0.3333	1.0000	0.1111	**0.0679**	0.0882
Las Vegas	6.0000	9.0000	1.0000	**0.7703**	1.0000

Table 9. Synthesis of the alternatives with respect to the criteria

			SYNTHESIS of ALTERNATIVES			Priorities	Priorities
			Criteria				
	Convenience	*Family Presence*	*Family Stress*	*Fun*	*Money*		
	0.1199	*0.1944*	*0.0558*	*0.4507*	*0.1793*	Normalized	Idealized
Caribbean	0.1047	0.1095	0.6586	0.2706	0.16175	0.2215	0.4148
Hometown	0.6370	0.5816	0.0786	0.0852	0.0679	0.2444	0.4576
Las Vegas	0.2583	0.3090	0.2628	0.6442	0.7703	0.5341	1.0000

its category for a criterion by the priority of that criterion and adding over the criteria gives its overall priority.

To assess convenience of location, the categories of very, moderately, and not very convenient are used. Family presence was a yes or no category. Family stress was rated as high, moderate, or low. Fun was rated as a lot or a little. Money was rated as a low, moderate, or high cost. Tables 10-14 exhibit the comparisons. Table 15 shows the ratings and Table 16 gives the final outcome.

Again Las Vegas came out the first although here much closer to Caribbean. Ratings give a cruder outcome because one is limited to choosing from the categories. In general the two outcomes obtained by comparing the alternatives and by rating them can be very different. Comparisons are more scientific than ratings that depend on experience and the standards derived for it that can be limited and biased.

Let us note that most decision problems need more than a three-level hierarchy to represent all the different levels of influence, and these must be arranged in an appropriate order to capture the flow of influence from the most general set of elements

Table 10. Convenience categories comparisons

Convenience of Location	Very	Moderately	Not very	Ideal Priorities
Very	1	4	7	1.0000
Moderately	1/4	1	3	0.2992
Not very	1/7	1/3	1	0.1194

Table 11. Family presence stress categories comparisons

Family Presence	Very likely	Likely	Not Likely	Ideal Priorities
Very likely	1	4	7	1.0000
Likely	1/4	1	3	0.2992
Not Likely	1/7	1/3	1	0.1194

Table 12. Family stress categories comparisons

Family Stress	High	Moderate	Low	Ideal Priorities
High	1	1/4	1/7	0.1194
Moderate	4	1	1/3	0.2992
Low	7	3	1	1.0000

Table 13. Fun categories comparisons

Fun	A lot	A little	Ideal Priorities
A lot	1	4	1.0000
A little	1/4	1	0.2500

Table 14. Money categories comparisons

Money	Low	Moderate	High	Ideal Priorities
Low	1	4	7	1.0000
Moderate	1/4	1	4	0.2992
High	1/7	1/4	1	0.1194

Table 15. Rating the wedding locations for each criterion

Ratings	Convenience 0.1199	Family presence 0.1944	Family stress 0.0558	Fun 0.4507	Money 0.1793
Las Vegas	Very	Yes	Moderate	A lot	Low
Caribbean	Very	No	Moderate	A lot	Moderate
Hometown	Moderately	Yes	High	A little	High

Table 16. Final ratings priorities

Name	Results from ratings	Ideals
Caribbean	0.3516	0.9346
Hometown	0.2722	0.7236
Las Vegas	0.3762	1.000000

in a level to the next level that falls below it representing a somewhat more specific set of elements. The literature of the subject has a very large number of such examples (Saaty, 2000; Saaty & Alexander, 1989; Saaty & Forman, 1993).

Network Decisions

In making a decision, we need to distinguish between the goal-oriented hierarchic structures and the holistic and interactive network structures that we use to represent that decision problem. In a hierarchy we have levels arranged in a descending order of importance. The elements in each level are compared according to dominance or influence with respect to the elements in the level immediately above that level. The arrows descend downwards from the goal pointing to where the influence originates from, which is a kind of service. The elements in lower levels contribute to or influence the well-being and success of elements in higher levels. We can interpret the downward pointing of the arrows as a process of stimulating the influence of the elements in the lower level on those in the level above. In a network (Saaty, 2006), the components (counterparts of levels in a hierarchy) are not arranged in any particular order, but are connected as appropriate in pairs with directed lines. Again an arrow points from one component to another to stimulate the influence of the elements of the second component on those in the first. The pair-wise comparisons of elements in a component are made according to the dominance of influence of each member of a pair on an element in the same or in another component. Influence may be evaluated in terms of importance, preference or likelihood.

In addition, in a network, the system of components may be regarded as elements that interact and influence each other with respect to a criterion or attribute with respect to which the influences occurs. That attribute itself must be of a higher order of complexity than the components and a fortiori of higher order than the elements contained in the components. We call such an attribute a control criterion. Thus even in a network, there is a hierarchic structure that lists control criteria above the networks. For each of the four benefits, opportunities, costs and risks, known for brevity as BOCR, merits we have a system of control criteria that we use to assess influence. The result is that such control criteria and/or their subcriteria serve as the basis for all comparisons made under them, both for the components and for the elements in these components. In a hierarchy one does not compare levels according to influence because they are arranged linearly in a predetermined order from which all influence flows downwards. In a network, the effect of the influence of different clusters of elements can differ from cluster to cluster, and hence they need to be weighted to incorporate the proportionality of their contributions. The criteria for comparisons are either included in a level, or more often implicitly replaced by using the idea of "importance, preference or likelihood" with respect to the goal, without being more finely detailed about what kind of importance it is. The control criteria for comparisons in a network are intended to be explicit about the importance of influence that they represent.

In a hierarchy, we ask the question for making a comparison, which of two elements is more dominant or has more influence (or in the opposite sense is influenced more) with respect to a certain element in the level above? In a network we ask, which of two elements is more dominant in influencing another element in the same or in another component with respect to a control criterion? In both hierarchies and networks the sense of having influence or being influenced must be maintained in the entire analysis. The two should not be mixed together.

The ANP frees us from the burden of ordering the components in the form of a directed chain as in a hierarchy. We can represent any decision as a directed network. While the AHP has a visibly better structure that derives from a strict understanding of the flow of influence, the ANP allows the structure to develop more naturally, and therefore is a better way to describe faithfully what can happen in the real world. These observations lead us to conclude that hierarchic decisions, because of imposed structure are likely to be less accurate in representing a problem because it ignores dependence. By including dependence and feedback and by cycling their influence with the supermatrix, the ANP is more objective and more likely to capture what happens in the real world. It does things that the mind cannot do in a precise and thorough way. Putting the two observations together, the ANP is likely to be a strongly more effective decision-making tool in practice than the AHP.

In all we have a three-phase structure of complex decisions: (1) *The BOCR merits* of the decision, their criteria and subcriteria known as control criteria in terms of which influence is evaluated, (2) *The hierarchies or networks of influences* and "objective" facts that make one alternative of the decision more desirable than another for each of the BOCR, and finally, (3) *The system of strategic criteria* in terms of which the top alternative of each of the BOCR merits must be rated by itself and whose ratings are then used to combine the weights of each alternative under all the four merits and obtain an overall synthesis. In each of these phases there are major concerns that are subdivided into less major ones and these in turn into still smaller ones. The entire set of three levels may sometimes be structured into a single network as we have done in some decision problems. Due to space limitations, we summarize the outcomes of two of the simplest applications of the ANP.

Applications (Single Network)

Market Shares for the Cereal Industry

The following is one of numerous validation examples that use the Superdecision software. This example estimates market shares for the Ready-to Eat breakfast cereal industry. To see how good the assumptions were, one compares the calculated results with the market shares of 2001. First one creates the model. Six major competitors were identified in the ready-to-eat cereal market, Kellogg, General Mills, Post, Quaker, Nabisco, and Ralston as the alternatives. There were more companies in this market having an actual cumulative market share of roughly about 6% that it turned out later had been left out. Since one is only concerned with deriving relative values, the relative shares of other residual companies do not matter.

Major impacts on the companies' market share are:

- Price of the products offered (named cost for the consumer)
- Advertising/Sales Ratio (how much money is spend for advertising)
- Shelf Space (places where the products are located in the stores)
- Tools (selling tools used to increase sales and market shares)
- Distribution/Availability (major distribution channels used to sell the product)

These five major impacts (clusters) are further divided into the following nodes:

- Tools: (coupons, trade dealing, in-pack premiums, vitamin fortifications)
- Distribution: (supermarket chains, food stores, mass merchandiser)
- Shelf Space: (premium space, normal space, bad space)
- Cost: (expensive, normal, cheap)
- Advertising: (<15%,<14%,<13%,<12%,<11%,<5%)

Their interactions are depicted in Figure 5. Second, comparisons and calculations were made to obtain the final result (see later). Finally one compares the calculated market shares with the real market shares for 2001. Table 18 lists estimated market share values and the actual ones taken from the Web site of the International Data Corporation.

Compatibility index value: 1.01403 (very good). It is obtained by multiplying element-wise the matrix of ratios of one set of data, by the transpose of the matrix of ratios of the other set, adding all the resulting entries and dividing by n^2 and requiring that this ratio not be more than 1.1.

Let us describe the calculations needed to derive the result in the "Estimated" column of Table 17. From the pair-wise comparison judgments a supermatrix is constructed, done automatically by the software superdecisions. Then the blocks of the supermatrix are weighted by the corresponding entries from the matrix of priority vectors of paired comparisons of the influence of all the clusters on each cluster with respect to market share shown in Table 18. This yielded the weighted supermatrix that is now stochastic as its columns add to one. It was then raised to limiting powers to obtain the overall priorities of all the elements in Figure 6.

Market Shares for the Airline Industry

Here is another example of the market share of eight U.S. airlines. Nowhere were numerical data used, but only knowledge of the airlines and how good each performed relative to the others on the factors mentioned below. Note that in three of the clusters there is an

Figure 5. Cereal industry market share

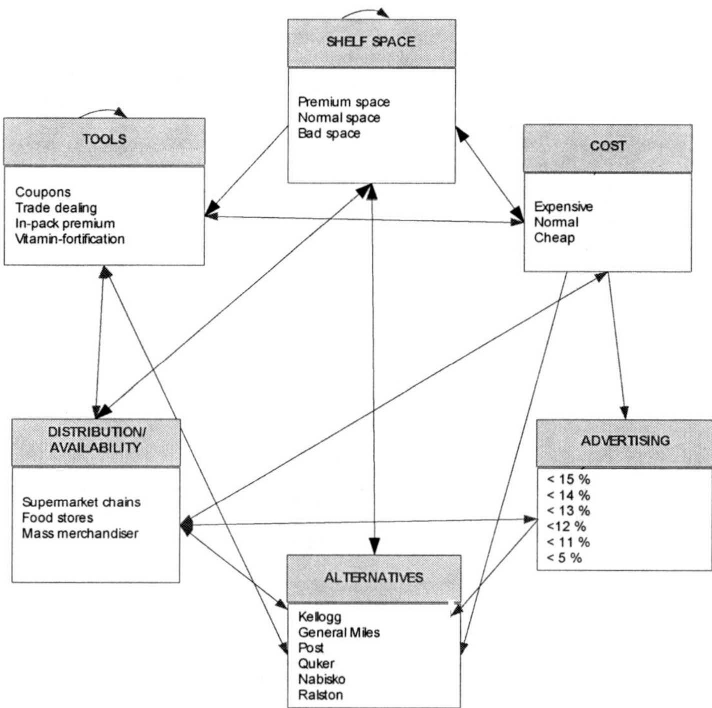

Table 17. Overall results — Estimated and actual

Alternatives	Kellogg	General Mills	Post	Quaker	Nabisco	Ralston
Estimated	0.324	0.255	0.147	0.116	0.071	0.087
Actual	0.342	0.253	0.154	0.121	0.057	0.073

inner dependence loop that indicates that the elements in that cluster depend on each other with respect to market share. Figure 6 shows the clusters and their inner and outer dependence connections. Table 19 gives the final estimated and the actual relative values that are again very close. A person who was a frequent traveler provided the judgments. Personal experience and perception of consumer sentiment towards the airlines to make the comparison were needed. The results are surprisingly close to the actual relative market share values. In fact, one initially questioned how they could be so close. Much has changed in the industry since the 9/11 tragedy in 2001.

Table 18. Cluster priority matrix

	Advertising	Alternatives	Cost	Distrib./ Availability	Shelf Space	Tools
Advertising	0.000	0.184	0.451	0.459	0.000	0.000
Alternatives	0.000	0.000	0.052	0.241	0.192	0.302
Cost	0.000	0.575	0.000	0.064	0.044	0.445
Distribution / Availability	0.000	0.107	0.089	0.000	0.364	0.159
Shelf Space	0.000	0.071	0.107	0.084	0.297	0.000
Tools	0.000	0.062	0.302	0.152	0.103	0.095

Figure 6. Airline model from the ANP super decisions software

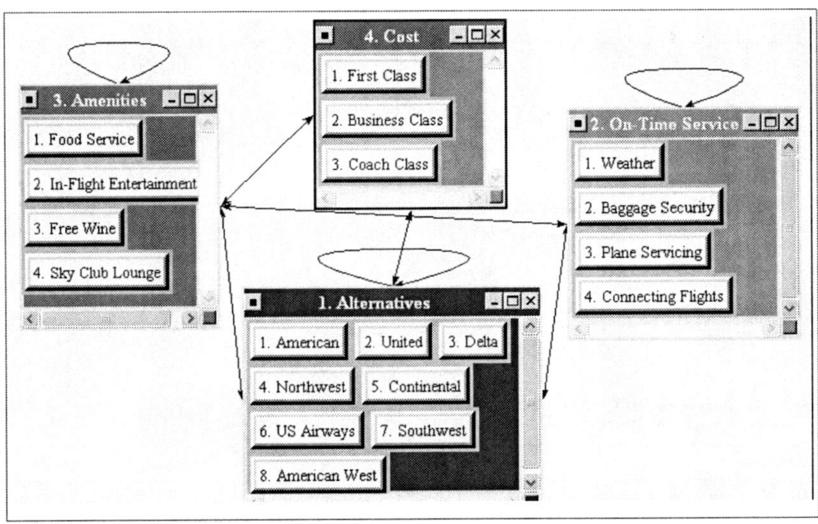

Table 19. Market shares of airlines — Actual and predicted

American	23.9	24.0
United	18.7	19.7
Delta	18.0	18.0
Northwest	11.4	12.4
Continental	9.3	10.0
US Airways	7.5	7.1
Southwest	5.9	6.4
American West	4.4	2.9

Actual (yr 2000) Model Estimate

Conclusion

There is a natural way in which people make decisions that is more or less independent of what one does in the academic world with its diverse and changing techniques. By learning to use and apply the simple approach to prioritization given above we obtain better organization of our ideas and understanding. The framework has found many applications in planning and forecasting and also in conflict resolution because it makes it possible for one to measure intangible criteria in relative terms. Examples of complex decisions in the context of benefits, opportunities, costs and risks are given in Saaty (2006).

The process must rely on the knowledge and judgments of knowledgeable people particularly when dealing with group, corporate and governmental decisions. It is not guaranteed that a person or a group without knowledge and experience can mechanically obtain a good outcome for their decision by going through the motions of imitating the examples shown here. Where is the greatest limitation of this process? It lies in our ability to practice learning to use it to be more systematic in structuring our judgments and gaining adequate knowledge and information about a decision before plunging into arithmetic technicalities. It also has its limits in dealing with conflict problems where the parties are unwilling to cooperate. Yet it is possible to work out potential solutions of a conflict if for no other reason than to show what is possible and what is not to the different sides. This author has written a book on conflict resolution and participated in the resolution of some conflicts by using the process described above (see Saaty & Alexander, 1989).

References

Blumenthal, A. (1977). *The process of cognition*. Englewood Cliffs, NJ: Prentice-Hall.

Figueira, J., Greco, S., & Ehrgott, M. (Eds.). (2005). *Multiple criteria decision analysis: State of the art surveys*. Berlin: Springer.

Frazer, R. A., Duncan, W. J., & Collar, A. R. (1955). *Elementary matrices*. London: Cambridge University Press.

Horn, R.A., & Johnson, C.R. (1985). *Matrix analysis*. New York: Cambridge University Press.

Peniwati, K. (2005). *Criteria for evaluating group decision-making methods*. PPM Graduate School of Management, Jakarta, Indonesia.

Saaty, T. (2000). *Decision-making for leaders: The Analytical Hierarchy Process for decisions in a complex world* (Rev. ed.). Pittsburgh, PA: RWS.

Saaty, T. (2006). *Theory and Applications of the Analytic Network Process*. Pittsburgh, PA: RWS.

Saaty, T., & Alexander, J. (1989). *Conflict resolution: The Analytic Hierarchy Process*. New York: Praeger.

Saaty, T., & E. Forman, E. (1993). *The Hierarchon — A dictionary of hierarchies*, Pittsburgh, PA: RWS.

Endnote

[1] I am grateful to Kristen Sonon, Stephanie Gier, Florian John, and James Nagy for their help and contribution with this and the following examples.

Appendix

Some Mathematics of Paired Comparisons

We learn from the consistent case $Aw = nw$ that the vector on the right is proportional to the same vector on the left transformed by the judgment matrix A. This says that weighting the entries of the matrix by the importance of their corresponding elements yields an outcome that is proportional to the original vector. This has to be true of a priority vector, otherwise one gets an infinite number of vectors that would be different on successive re-weightings, leading to the problem of finding stable priorities. Thus in general we seek proportionality between the left and the right side of our equation. Our general problem with inconsistent judgments takes the form as in Table A1:

Table A1. General mathematical formulation

$$Aw = \begin{bmatrix} 1 & a_{12} & \cdots & a_{1n} \\ 1/a_{12} & 1 & \cdots & a_{2n} \\ \vdots & \vdots & \vdots & \vdots \\ 1/a_{1n} & 1/a_{2n} & \cdots & 1 \end{bmatrix} \begin{bmatrix} w_1 \\ w_2 \\ \vdots \\ w_n \end{bmatrix} = c \begin{bmatrix} w_1 \\ w_2 \\ \vdots \\ w_n \end{bmatrix}$$

This homogeneous system of linear equations $Aw = cw$ has a solution w if c is the principal eigenvalue of A. That this is the case can be shown using an argument that involves both left and right eigenvectors of A. Two vectors $x = (x_1, ..., x_n), y = (y_1, ..., y_n)$ are orthogonal if their scalar product $x_1y_1 + ... x_ny_n$ is equal to zero. It is known that any left eigenvector of a matrix corresponding to an eigenvalue is orthogonal to any right eigenvector corresponding to a different eigenvalue. This property is known as biorthogonality (Horn & Johnson, 1985).

Theorem: For a given positive matrix A, the only positive vector w and only positive constant c that satisfy $Aw = cw$, is a vector w that is a positive multiple of the principal eigenvector of A, and the only such c is the principal eigenvalue of A.

Proof: We know that the right principal eigenvector and the principal eigenvalue satisfy our requirements. We also know that the algebraic multiplicity of the principal eigenvalue is one, and that there is a positive left eigenvector of A (call it z) corresponding to the principal eigenvalue. Suppose there is a positive vector y and a (necessarily positive) scalar d such that $Ay = dy$. If d and c are not equal, then by biorthogonality y is orthogonal to z, which is impossible since both vectors are positive. If d and c are equal, then y and w are dependent since c has algebraic multiplicity one, and y is a positive multiple of w. This completes the proof.

Priorities Derived from Dominance

The study of the transitivity of order takes us to the concept of transition in the form of preference or dominance of one alternative over another through intermediate alternatives. This preference that expresses dominance can be represented by a directed graph with the alternatives as its nodes and directed arcs joining two alternatives indicating the intensity of dominance of one alternative over another. A directed graph can have paths between its nodes. The product of the intensities along the arcs in a path from a node to another represents the dominance of the starting node over the terminal node along that path. From this follows the representation of dominance with a matrix, known as the path matrix, and its powers to compute dominance along paths of length equal to each power. For each such matrix the dominance of an alternative is given by the sum of the entries in its corresponding row divided by the total sum of the rows—a normalization operation. Finally, we sum all the dominances.

Let us write this in matrix notation by using the vector $e = (1, \dots 1)^T$ with T indicating the transpose vector. All other vectors are column vectors. A consistent matrix A of order n satisfies the relation $a_{ij} = a_{ik} / a_{jk}$ for all $i, j, k = 1, \dots, n$. Thus $A^m = n^{m-1}A$. Note that a consistent matrix is reciprocal with $a_{ji} = 1 / a_{ij}$. Because a consistent matrix is always of the form $A = (w_i / w_j)$, we immediately have

$$\lim_{k\to\infty} \frac{\sum_{m=1}^{k} A^m e}{\sum_{m=1}^{k} e^T A^m e} = \lim_{h\to\infty} \frac{Ae}{e^T Ae} = cw$$

where because A has rank one, n is its principal eigenvalue and $w = (w_1, \dots, w_n)$ is its corresponding principal right eigenvector and c is a positive constant.

For an inconsistent matrix, the sum of all the dominances along paths of length 1, 2, and so on has a limit determined as a Cesaro sum. That limit is the principal eigenvector of the matrix of preferences. Let us develop these ideas in some detail.

Let a_{ij} be the relative dominance of A_i over A_j. To simplify the notation, let the matrix corresponding to the reciprocal pairwise relation be denoted by $A = (a_{ij})$. The relative dominance of A_i over A_j along paths of length k is given by

$$\frac{\sum_{j=1}^{n} a_{ij}^{(k)}}{\sum_{i=1}^{n}\sum_{j=1}^{n} a_{ij}^{(k)}}$$

where $a_{ij}^{(k)}$ is the (i,j) entry of the kth power of the matrix (a_{ij}). The total dominance $w = (A_i)$ of alternative i over all other alternatives along paths of all lengths is given by the infinite series

$$w(A_i) = \sum_{k=1}^{\infty} \frac{\sum_{j=1}^{n} a_{ij}^{(k)}}{\sum_{i=1}^{n}\sum_{j=1}^{n} a_{ij}^{(k)}}$$

whose sum is the Cesaro sum

$$\lim_{M \to \infty} \frac{1}{M} \sum_{k=1}^{M} \frac{\sum_{j=1}^{n} a_{ij}^{(k)}}{\sum_{i=1}^{n}\sum_{j=1}^{n} a_{ij}^{(k)}}.$$

Now we give some detail. Note that the sums of different sets with k numbers in each determine their ranks according to their total value. The average of each sum is obtained by dividing by k. The averages give the same ranks because they only differ by the same constant from the original sums. Often the sum of an infinite series of numbers is infinite but if we form the average, that average as k tends to infinity may converge. In that case it converges to the same limit as that of the kth term of the infinite sum. Thus taking the limit of the averages gives us a meaningful ranking of the objects. This is a profound observation proved by the Italian Mathematician Ernesto Cesaro (1859-1906).

Cesaro Summability: Let us prove that if a sequence of numbers converges then the sequence of arithmetic means formed from that sequence also converges to the same limit as the sequence.

Proof: Let s_n denote the nth term of the sequence and let $\sigma_n = \frac{s_1 + ... + s_n}{n}$, if $\lim_{n\to\infty} \sigma_n = S$, then S is called the Cesaro sum of s_n.

Let $t_n = s_n - S, \tau_n = \sigma_n - S$, and thus $\tau_n = \frac{t_1 + ... + t_n}{n}$. We prove that $\tau_n \to 0$ as $n \to \infty$. Choose $a > 0$, so that each $|t_n| < a$. Given $\varepsilon > 0$, choose N so that for $n > N, |t_n| < \varepsilon$. Now for $n > N$, $|\tau_n| \le \frac{|t_1| + ... + |t_N|}{n} + \frac{|t_{N+1}| + ... + |t_n|}{n} < \frac{Na}{n} + \varepsilon$. Since ε is arbitrary, it follows that $\lim_{n\to\infty} |\tau_n| = 0$ and $\sigma_n \to S$.

Cesaro' summability ensures that

$$w(A_i) = \sum_{k=1}^{\infty} \frac{\sum_{j=1}^{n} a_{ij}^{(k)}}{\sum_{i=1}^{n}\sum_{j=1}^{n} a_{ij}^{(k)}} = \lim_{M\to\infty} \frac{1}{M} \sum_{k=1}^{M} \frac{\sum_{j=1}^{n} a_{ij}^{(k)}}{\sum_{i=1}^{n}\sum_{j=1}^{n} a_{ij}^{(k)}} = \lim_{k\to\infty} \frac{\sum_{j=1}^{n} a_{ij}^{(k)}}{\sum_{i=1}^{n}\sum_{j=1}^{n} a_{ij}^{(k)}}$$

This approach to the idea of derived overall dominance is a variant of the well-known theorem of Oskar Perron for positive matrices in which it is demonstrated that the limit converges to the principal right eigenvector of the matrix. Thus a reciprocal pair-wise comparison's reciprocal matrix $A = (a_{ij})$ satisfies the system of homogeneous equations $\sum_{j=1}^{n} a_{ij} w_j = \lambda_{\max} w_i, i = 1,...,n$, where $\lambda_{\max}$ is the principal eigenvalue of the matrix A and w is its corresponding principal right eigenvector.

Mathematics of the Analytic Network Process

The Supermatrix of a Feedback System

Assume that we have a system of N clusters or components, whereby the elements in each component interact or have an impact on or are themselves influenced by some or all of the elements of that component or of another component with respect to a property governing the interactions of the entire system, such as energy or capital or political influence (Saaty, 2006). Assume that component h, denoted by C_h, $h = 1, ..., N$, has n_h elements, that we denote by $e_{h_1}, e_{h_2}, ..., e_{h_{n_h}}$. A priority vector derived from paired comparisons in the usual way represents the impact of a given set of elements in a component on another element in the system. When an element has no influence on another element, its influence priority is **assigned** (not derived) as zero.

The priority vectors derived from pair-wise comparison matrices are each entered as a part of some column of a supermatrix. The supermatrix represents the influence priority of an element on the left of the matrix on an element at the top of the matrix. A supermatrix along with an example of one of its general entry i, j blocks are shown in Figure A1 The component C_i alongside the supermatrix includes all the priority vectors derived for nodes that are "parent" nodes in the C_i cluster. Figure A2 gives the supermatrix of a hierarchy along with its supermatrix. The entry in the last row and column of the supermatrix of a hierarchy is the identity matrix I.

Figure A1. Supermatrix of a network and detail of a matrix in it

$$W = \begin{array}{c} \\ C_1 \begin{array}{c} e_{11} \\ e_{12} \\ \vdots \\ e_{1n_1} \end{array} \\ C_2 \begin{array}{c} e_{21} \\ e_{22} \\ \vdots \\ e_{2n_2} \end{array} \\ \vdots \\ C_N \begin{array}{c} e_{N1} \\ e_{N2} \\ \vdots \\ e_{Nn_N} \end{array} \end{array} \begin{array}{c} \begin{array}{cccc} C_1 & C_2 & \cdots & C_N \\ e_{11} e_{12} \cdots e_{1n_1} & e_{21} e_{22} \cdots e_{2n_2} & & e_{N1} e_{N2} \cdots e_{Nn_N} \end{array} \\ \begin{bmatrix} W_{11} & W_{12} & \cdots & W_{1N} \\ W_{21} & W_{22} & \cdots & W_{2N} \\ \vdots & \vdots & \cdots & \vdots \\ W_{N1} & W_{N2} & \cdots & W_{NN} \end{bmatrix} \end{array}$$

$$W_{ij} = \begin{bmatrix} W_{i1}^{(j_1)} & W_{i1}^{(j_2)} & \cdots & W_{i1}^{(jn_j)} \\ W_{i2}^{(j_1)} & W_{i2}^{(j_2)} & \cdots & W_{i2}^{(jn_j)} \\ \vdots & \vdots & \cdots & \vdots \\ W_{in_i}^{(j_1)} & W_{in_i}^{(j_2)} & \cdots & W_{in_i}^{(jn_j)} \end{bmatrix}$$

Figure A2. Structure and supermatrix of a hierarchy

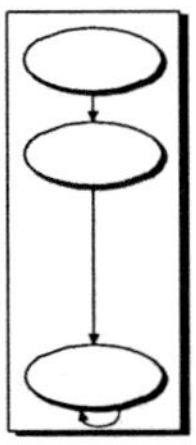

$$W = \begin{bmatrix} 0 & 0 & 0 & \cdots & & \bullet & 0 & 0 \\ W_{21} & 0 & 0 & \cdots & & \bullet & 0 & 0 \\ 0 & W_{32} & 0 & \cdots & & \bullet & 0 & 0 \\ \vdots & \vdots & \vdots & \vdots & & \vdots & \vdots & \vdots \\ \bullet & \bullet & \bullet & \cdots & W_{n-1,n-2} & & \bullet & \bullet \\ 0 & 0 & 0 & \cdots & & \bullet & W_{n,n-1} & I \end{bmatrix}$$

The Need for Powers of the Supermatrix to Represent Transitivities of All Order

According to Cesaro summability we only need to raise the supermatrix to limiting powers to capture the overall priorities of the elements. But there are different forms of the limit depending on the multiplicity of its principal eigenvalue, which as we shall see below must be equal to one or is a complex root of one, and on whether the matrix is reducible and cycles or not. We do not have sufficient room here to detail all of these cases. It is sufficient to say that mostly the Cesaro sum is taken for the limits when they are not unique. The following is well known in algebra (Horn and Johnson, 1985). According to J. J. Sylvester (Frazer, Duncan, & Collar, 1955) one can represent an entire function of a (diagonalizable) matrix W whose characteristic roots are distinct as: $f(W)=\sum_{i=1}^{n} f(\lambda_i)Z(\lambda_i)$, where $Z(\lambda_i)=\prod_{j\neq i}(\lambda_j I - W)/\prod_{j\neq i}(\lambda_j - \lambda_i)$. The $Z(\lambda_i)$ can be shown to be complete orthogonal idempotent matrices of W; that is, they have the properties $\sum_{i=1}^{k} Z(\lambda_i)=I,\ Z(\lambda_i)Z(\lambda_j)=0,\ i\neq j,\ Z^2(\lambda_i)=Z(\lambda_i)$, where I and 0 are the identity and null matrices, respectively. Thus for example if one raises a matrix to arbitrarily large powers, it is enough to raise its eigenvalues to these powers and form the above sum involving the sum of polynomials in W. Because the eigenvalues of a stochastic matrix are all less than or equal to one, when raised to powers they vanish except when they are equal to one or are complex conjugate roots of one. Because here the eigenvalues are assumed to be distinct, we have the simplest case to deal with, that is $\lambda_{max} = 1$ is a simple eigenvalue. Formally, because the right-hand side is a polynomial in W multiplying both sides by W^{∞} each term on the right would be a constant multiplied by W^{∞} and the final outcome is also a constant multiplied by W^{∞}. Because we are only interested in the relative values of the entries in W^{∞} we can ignore the constant and simply raise W to very large powers which the computer program *Superdecisions* does in this case of distinct eigenvalues.

Next we consider the case where $\lambda_{max} = 1$ is a multiple eigenvalue. For that case we have what is known as the confluent form of Sylvester's theorem:

$$f(W)=\sum_{j=1}^{k} T(\lambda_i)=\sum_{i=1}^{k}\frac{1}{(m_i-1)!}\frac{d^{m_i-1}}{d\lambda^{m_i-1}} f(\lambda)(\lambda I - W)^{-1}\left.\frac{\prod_{i=1}^{n}(\lambda-\lambda_i)}{\prod_{i=m_{i+1}}^{n}(\lambda-\lambda_i)}\right|_{\lambda-\lambda_1}$$

where k is the number of distinct roots and m_i is the multiplicity of the root λ_i. However, as we show below, this too tells us that to obtain the limit priorities it is sufficient to raise W to arbitrarily large powers to obtain a satisfactory decimal approximation to W^{∞}.

The only possible non-zero survivors as we raise the matrix to powers are those λ's that are equal to one or are roots of one (Horn & Johnson, 1985). If the multiplicity of the largest real eigenvalue λ_{max} is n_1, then we have

$$W^{\infty} = n_1 \left. \frac{\dfrac{d^{(n_1-1)}}{d\lambda^{(n_1-1)}}\left[(\lambda I - W)^{-1}\Delta(\lambda)\right]}{\Delta^{(n_1)}(\lambda)} \right|_{\lambda=1}$$

where one takes derivatives of the characteristic polynomial of the matrix W, and $\Delta(\lambda) = \det(\lambda I - W) = \lambda^n + p_1\lambda^{n-1} + ... + p_n$. Also $(\lambda I - W)^{-1} = F(\lambda) / \Delta(\lambda)$ and $F(\lambda) = W^{n-1} + (\lambda + p_1)W^{n-2} + (\lambda^2 + p_1\lambda + p_2)W^{n-3} + ... + (\lambda^{n-1} + p_1\lambda^{n-2} + ... + p_{n-1})I$ is the adjoint of $(\lambda I - W)$.

Now the right side is a polynomial in W. Again, if we multiply both sides by W^{∞}, we would have on the right a constant multiplied by W^{∞} which means that we can obtain W^{∞} by raising W to large powers.

For the cases of roots of one when $\lambda_{max} = 1$ is a simple or a multiple root let us again formally see what happens to our polynomial expressions on the right in both of Sylvester's formulas as we now multiply both on the left and on the right first by $(W^c)^{\infty}$ obtaining one equation and then again by $(W^{c+1})^{\infty}$ obtaining another and so on c times, finally multiplying both sides by $(W^{c+c-1})^{\infty}$. We then sum these equations and take their average on both sides. The left side of each of the equation reduces to W^{∞} and the average is $\frac{1}{c}W^{\infty}$. On the right side the sum for each eigenvalue that is a root of unity is simply a constant times the sum $(W^c)^{\infty} + (W^{c+1})^{\infty} + ... + (W^{c+c-1})^{\infty}$. Also, because this sum is common to all the eigenvalues, it factors out and their different constants sum to a new constant multiplied by $(1/c)$. This is true whether one is a simple or a multiple eigenvalue because the same process applies to accumulating its constants. In the very end we simply have:

$$\frac{1}{c}\left[\left(W^c\right)^{\infty} + \left(W^{c+1}\right)^{\infty} + \cdots + \left(W^{c+c-1}\right)^{\infty}\right] = \frac{1}{c}\left(1 + W + \cdots + W^{c-1}\right)\left(W^c\right)^{\infty} \quad c \geq 2,$$

which amounts to averaging over a cycle of length c obtained in raising W to infinite power. The cyclicity c can be determined, among others, by noting the return of the form of the matrix of powers of W to the original form of blocks of zero in W.

Section VI

Financial Applications

Chapter XIX

Financial Classification Using an Artificial Immune System

Anthony Brabazon, University College Dublin, Ireland

Alice Delahunty, University College Dublin, Ireland

Dennis O'Callaghan, University College Dublin, Ireland

Peter Keenan, University College Dublin, Ireland

Michael O'Neill, University of Limerick, Ireland

Abstract

Recent years have seen a dramatic increase in the application of biologically-inspired algorithms to business problems. Applications of neural networks and evolutionary algorithms have become common. However, as yet there have been few applications of artificial immune systems (AIS), algorithms that are inspired by the workings of the natural immune system. The natural immune system can be considered as a distributed, self-organizing, classification system that operates in a dynamic environment. The mechanisms of natural immune systems, including their ability to distinguish between self and non-self, provides a rich metaphorical inspiration for the design of pattern-recognition algorithms. This chapter introduces AIS and provides an example of how an immune algorithm can be used to develop a classification system for predicting corporate failure. The developed system displays good classification accuracy out-of-sample, up to two years prior to failure.

Introduction

Classification problems abound in business. Examples include decisions as to whether or not to invest in a firm, whether to extend trade credit to a new customer, or whether to extend a bank loan. In each of these scenarios the possibility of financial loss exists if a firm is incorrectly classified as being financially healthy when in fact it is not. This chapter introduces a novel methodology for classification purposes, the negative selection algorithm.

The negative selection algorithm is drawn from the literature of *artificial immune systems* (AIS), which in turn are inspired by the workings of the natural immune system (de Castro & Timmis, 2002). The natural immune system is a highly complex system, comprised of an intricate network of specialized tissues, organs, cells and chemical molecules. The natural immune system can recognize, destroy, and remember an almost unlimited numbers of pathogens (foreign objects that enter the body, including viruses, bacteria, multi-cellular parasites, and fungi). To assist in protecting the organism, the immune system has the capability to distinguish between self and non-self. Notably, the system does not require exhaustive training with negative (non-self) examples to make these distinctions, but can identify items that it has never before encountered as non-self.

The most commonly applied AIS can be grouped into three categories (see Figure 1), based on distinct features of the natural immune system. In this chapter we focus on the negative-selection algorithm. The object in designing and applying AIS is not to produce exact models of the natural immune system. Rather the objective is to extract ideas and metaphors from the workings of the natural immune system that can be used to help solve real-world problems. Artificial immune systems represent a relatively new class of algorithms and, as yet, few business applications of these algorithms have been developed. This chapter introduces AIS, and demonstrates their application by creating a classification system to distinguish between failing and non-failing companies.

The rest of this chapter is organized as follows. The next section provides an overview of the literature on corporate failure, followed by a section that introduces the natural immune system. We then outline the data set and methodology utilized in implementing the negative selection algorithm. The remaining sections provide the results of the study, followed by a number of conclusions.

Corporate Failure Prediction

Corporate failure can impose significant private costs on multiple parties including shareholders, providers of debt finance, employees, suppliers, customers and auditors. All of these stakeholders have an interest in being able to identify whether a company

Figure 1. A taxonomy of AIS

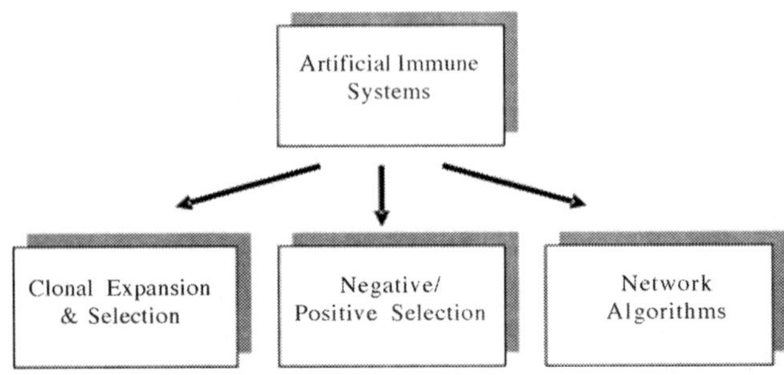

is on a trajectory that is tending towards failure. Early identification of such a trajectory would facilitate intervention to avert potential disaster.

Research into the prediction of corporate failure has a long history (Fitzpatrick, 1932; Horrigan, 1965; Smith & Winakor, 1935). Early statistical studies such as Beaver (1966) adopted a univariate methodology, identifying which accounting ratios had greatest classification accuracy in separating failing and non-failing firms. Although this approach did demonstrate classification power, it suffers from the shortcoming that a single weak financial ratio may be offset (or exacerbated) by the strength (or weakness) of other financial ratios. Altman (1968) addressed this issue by developing a multivariate linear discriminant analysis (LDA) model and this was found to improve the accuracy of the classification models. Altman's discriminant function had the following form:

$$Z = 0.012X_1 + 0.014X_2 + 0.033X_3 + 0.006X_4 + 0.999X_5$$

where

X_1 = working capital to total assets

X_2 = retained earnings to total assets

X_3 = earnings before interest and taxes to total assets

X_4 = market value of equity to book value of total debt

X_5 = sales to total assets

Altman's original Z-Score model was modified by Altman, Haldeman, and Narayanan (1977), using a larger data set than Altman's original 33 failed and 33 non-failed companies. This model (the ZETA model) had the following financial variables:

X_1 = return on assets (EBIT/Total Assets)

X_2 = stability of earnings

X_3 = debt service (EBIT / Total Interest)

X_4 = cumulative profitability (Retained Earnings / Total Assets)

X_5 = liquidity (Current Assets / Current Liabilities)

X_6 = capitalization (Equity / Total Capital)

X_7 = firm size (Total Assets)

The coefficients used in this study were not disclosed. Since these early studies, a vast range of methodologies have been applied for the purposes of corporate failure prediction including, logit and probit regression models (Gentry, Newbold, & Whitford, 1985; Ohlson, 1980; Zmijewski, 1984). In more recent times, as the field of biologically inspired computing has flourished, the methodologies applied to the domain of corporate failure prediction have expanded to include artificial neural networks (Serrano-Cinca, 1996; Shah & Murtaza, 2000; Tam, 1991; Wilson, Chong, & Peel, 1995), genetic algorithms (Brabazon & Keenan, 2004; Kumar, Krovi, & Rajagopalan, 1997; Varetto, 1998), and grammatical evolution (Brabazon & O'Neill, 2003, 2004). Other methodologies applied to this problem include support vector machines (Fan & Palaniswami, 2000) and rough sets (Zopounidis, Slowinski, Doumpos, Dimitras, & Susmaga, 1999). Review studies covering much of the above literature can be found in Dimitras, Zanakis, and Zopounidis (1996) and Morris (1997). The potential for applying AIS to anticipate corporate failure was noted by Chen (2002), but has yet attracted little attention.

Results from Prior Studies

Generally, the results from prior studies indicate that a significant deterioration in financial ratios occurs between the third and second years prior to eventual failure, although there is also evidence that indicators of impending bankruptcy can be detected up to five years prior to its occurrence. In Altman (1968), the developed LDA model correctly identified (in-sample) 95% of failing firms one year prior to failure. The classification accuracy fell to 72% and 48% in the second and third year prior to failure. Wilson et al. (1995) report in-sample classifications of 98.7% for a neural network model, one year prior to failure, and 95% for a logit model on the same data. Varetto (1998) reports in-sample classification accuracy for a GA-based model of approximately 97%, one year prior to failure. In-sample classification accuracies provide a limited assessment of model generalizability. Hence, in this study, developed models are assessed based on classification performance on out-of-sample data.

The Natural Immune System

The natural immune system is comprised of numerous cells and molecules, which interact in complex ways. In this section we provide a simplified description of the system's

Table 1. Key immune system terms

Pathogens	Foreign bodies including viruses, bacteria, multi-cellular parasites, and fungi
Antigens	Foreign molecules expressed by a pathogen that triggers an immune system response
Leukocytes	White blood cells, including phagocytes and lymphocytes (B and T cells) for identifying and killing pathogens
Antibodies	Glyco-protein (protein + carbohydrate) molecules secreted into the blood in response to an antigenic stimulus that neutralize the antigen by binding specifically to it

workings, and only consider a subset of its components and their interactions. Readers requiring a detailed introduction to the immune system are referred to Janeway, Travers, Walport, and Shlomchik (2004) or Goldsby, Kindt, Kuby, and Osborne (2002).

Innate vs. Acquired Immunity

Humans possess two main types of immunity, *innate* or natural immunity, and acquired or *adaptive* immunity. Both the innate and acquired immune systems are comprised of a variety of molecules, cells and tissues. The most important cells are *leukocytes* (white blood cells), which can be divided into two major categories: *phagocytes,* and *lymphocytes*. The first group belongs to the innate immune system while the latter group mediate adaptive immunity. The innate immune system is present at birth and it does not adapt over a person's lifetime. The innate immune system includes a variety of physical barriers (such as skin, nasal hairs, and mucus) and biochemical barriers (such as a rapid change in pH level in the gut and the lysozyme enzyme in tears). If an infectious agent penetrates these defences they meet a second set of barriers, the phagocytes, a subset of white blood cells. Phagocytes can engulf many pathogens including bacteria and fungi, destroying them in the process. The innate immune system uses several reliable signatures of non-self. An example of such a pattern is the mannose carbohydrate molecule that is found in many bacteria but not in mammals. These patterns have remained stable for long periods of time and are encoded in the genome of our immune systems (Chao & Forrest, 2003). If the innate immune system fails to deal with an invading pathogen, then the adaptive immune system takes over.

Adaptive Immune System

The adaptive immune system responds to specific chemical triggers called antigens. If the immune system encounters an antigen for the first time, a *primary response* is provoked in the adaptive immune system, and the organism will experience an infection while the immune system learns to recognize the antigen. In response to the invasion, a large number of antibodies will eventually be produced by the immune system that will help eliminate the associated pathogen from the body. After the infection is cleared, a memory of the successful receptors is maintained to allow much quicker *secondary response* when the same or a similar antigen is encountered in the future. The secondary response is characterized by a much more rapid and more abundant production of the relevant antibody, than the primary response.

In the adaptive immune system, lymphocytes play a critical role. These circulate constantly through the blood, lymph, lymphoid organs and tissue spaces. A significant portion of the population of lymphocytes is made up of B and T cells. These cells are capable of recognizing and responding to certain antigenic patterns presented on the surface of pathogens. A major role in the recognition process for antigens is played by molecules of the *major histocompatibility complex* (MHC) (Hofmeyer & Forrest, 2000). These molecules act to transport peptides (fragments of protein chains) from the interior regions of a cell and "present" these peptides on the cell's surface. This mechanism enables roving T cells of the immune system to detect infections inside cells, without having to penetrate a cell's membrane.

Adaptive immunity can be divided into two branches: *humoral immunity*, controlled by B cells, and *cellular immunity,* controlled by T cells. Humoral immunity is mediated by specially designed proteins and *antibodies*, and it involves, for example, the interaction of B cells with antigens. Cellular immunity is cell-mediated, and plays an important role in the killing of virus-infected cells and tumors. Figure 2 provides a diagram of the immune system architecture, which shows both the innate and the adaptive immune system. The arrows indicate the different levels of penetration of various different pathogens.

Figure 2. Diagram of the immune system architecture

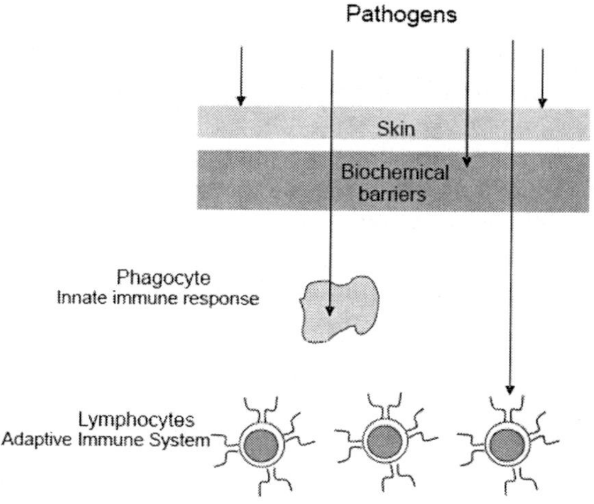

B Cells and T Cells

B cells and T cells have receptors on their surfaces that are capable of recognizing antigens via a binding mechanism. The surface of a B cell contains Y-shaped receptors (or antibodies). Antibodies possess two *paratopes* (corresponding to each arm of the Y-shaped receptor), which are used to match or identify molecules. The regions on the antigen that a paratope can attach to are called the *epitopes*. Identification of an antigen by the immune system is achieved by a complementary matching between the paratope of the antibody and the epitope of the antigen. The match between the paratope and epitope need not be perfect. To increase the number of pathogens that the immune system can detect, individual lymphocytes can bind to a variety of antigens. This enhances the power of the immune system, as multiple lymphocytes will bind to invading pathogens. This ensures that there will be multiple "signals" created in the immune system, indicating that an invader has been detected. The closer the match between paratope and epitope, the stronger the molecular binding between the antibody and the antigen, and the greater the degree of *stimulation* of the B cell.

T Cell-Dependent Humoral Immune Response

When an antibody of a B cell binds to an antigen, the B cell becomes stimulated. The level of stimulation depends on the closeness or *affinity* of the match between the antibody and the antigen. Once a threshold level of stimulation is reached, the B cell is *activated*. Before activation takes place, the B cell must be *co-stimulated* with the help of a variant of the T cell population called *helper T cells*. When helper T cells recognize and bind to an antigen, they secrete cytokines, which are soluble proteins that are used to provide signalling between the cells of the Immune System. In addition to the cell-to-cell interaction where the T cell can bind to a B cell, the secreted cytokines can act on B cells to co-stimulate them.

Once the stimulation level of a B cell has reached a threshold level, the B cell is transformed into a *blast cell* and completes its maturation in the lymph nodes where a clonal *expansion and affinity maturation* process occurs. The object of the clonal expansion process is to generate a large population of antibody secreting plasma cells and memory B cells, which are specific to the antigen. In the lymph nodes, activated B cells begin to clone at a rate proportional to their affinity to the antigen that stimulated them. These clones undergo a process of affinity maturation, in order to better tune B cells to the antigen that initiated the immune system response. When new B cells are generated, the DNA strings that encode their receptors are subject to recombination, mutation and insertion processes, and new forms of receptors are constantly created. When a tailor-made detector is required for a specific novel antigen, then the immune system must generate diversity. This is achieved by means of a high mutation rate in the cloning process, for the genes that encode the B cell's Y-shaped receptors (this process is known as somatic hypermutation), and the differential selection of the clones that best match the antigen. The evolutionary process of creating diversity, and the subsequent selection of the variants of lymphocyte that become increasingly specific to an antigen, is referred to as *clonal selection.*

T Cell Tolerogenesis

A major challenge for the immune system is to ensure that only foreign, or misbehaving-self cells, are targeted for destruction. The system must be able to differentiate between self, (proteins and molecules which are native to the organism) and non-self (cells and molecules which are foreign). In the normal creation of T cells, their receptors are randomly generated, and so could potentially bind to either self or non-self. To avoid autoimmune reactions where the immune system attacks its host organism, it is theorized that the cells must be *self-tolerized.* In the case of T cells, this process of tolerogenesis takes place in the thymus. One mechanism that can be used to confer self-tolerance as the lymphocytes are maturing is that they are exposed to a series of self-proteins. Any lymphocyte that binds to self-proteins is killed, and only self-tolerized cells are allowed into the circulation system for lymphocytes. This represents a negative selection process, as only non self-reactive T cells are permitted to survive.

Adaptive Immune System Response to an Invader

Following from the above, the T cell-dependent humoral immune response is a series of complex immunological events. It commences with the interaction of B cells with antigens. The B cells that bind to the antigen are co-stimulated by helper T cells, leading to proliferation and differentiation of the B cells to create B plasma and memory cells. The new B plasma cells secrete antibodies (immunoglobulins) that circulate in the organism and "mark" the antigens by binding to them. These antigens and the associated pathogen are then targeted by the immune system for destruction. The steps in the process can be summarized as follows:

1. Antigen-secreting pathogen enters the body.
2. B-cells are activated by the foreign antigen.
3. With help of T cells, B cells undergo cloning and mutation.
4. Plasma B cells secrete immunoglobulins which attach to the antigen.
5. "Marked" antigens are attacked by immune system.
6. Memory of the antigen is maintained by B memory cells.

Summary

Even from the brief description of the natural immune system, it is apparent that the system is intricate. However, the system can be considered as a sophisticated information-processing system, which possesses powerful pattern-recognition and classification abilities. Artificial Immune Algorithms (AIA) draw metaphorical inspiration from the workings of the natural immune system, or theories of the workings of this system, in order to design algorithms to solve computational problems. AIA typically use a limited number of components, often only a single lymphocyte and a single form of antigen. For each application, a similarity or affinity measure and a fitness measure are defined. Although a multitude of metaphors could be drawn from natural immune systems for the purposes of designing AIA, we will focus on one, the negative selection algorithm. The next section describes two variants of this algorithm and outlines its application for corporate failure prediction.

Methodology

This section describes the methodology adopted in constructing the corporate failure classification model. Initially, the data set used in the example is outlined. This is followed by a description of two forms of the negative selection algorithm, the canonical negative selection algorithm and the variable size detector negative selection algorithm. A classification model is constructed using each algorithm.

Data for Corporate Failure Example

A total of 178 firms were selected judgementally (89 failed, 89 non-failed), from the Compustat Database. The criteria for selection of the failed firms were:

(i) Inclusion in the Compustat database in the period 1991-2000

(ii) Existence of required data for a period of three years prior to entry to Chapter VII or Chapter XI

(iii) Sales revenues must exceed $1M

The first criterion limits the study to publicly quoted U.S. corporations. For every failing firm, a matched non-failing firm is selected. The firms are matched using both industry sector and sales revenue three years prior to failure. The definition of corporate failure adopted in this example is the court filing of a firm under Chapter VII or Chapter XI of the U.S. Bankruptcy code. The selection of this definition provides an objective benchmark, as the occurrence (and timing) of either of these events can be determined through examination of regulatory filings. Chapter VII of the U.S. Bankruptcy code covers corporate liquidations and Chapter XI covers corporate reorganizations, which usually follow a period of financial distress.

A selection of explanatory variables is collected for each firm for the three years prior to entry into Chapter VII or Chapter XI. The choice of explanatory variables is hindered by the lack of a clear theoretical framework that explains corporate failure (Argenti, 1976; Dimitras et al., 1996; Wilson et al., 1995). Most empirical work on corporate failure adopts an ad-hoc approach to variable selection. If attention is restricted to ratios drawn from the financial statements of companies, five groupings are usually given prominence in the literature of corporate failure, namely: liquidity, debt, profitability, activity, and size (Altman, 2000). Liquidity refers to the availability of cash resources to meet short-term cash requirements. Debt measures focus on the relative mix of funding provided by shareholders and lenders. Profitability considers the rate of return generated by a firm in relation to its size, as measured by sales revenue and/or asset base. Activity measures consider the operational efficiency of the firm in collecting cash, managing stocks and controlling its production or service process. Firm size provides information on both the sales revenue and asset scale of the firm and acts as a proxy metric on firm history (Levinthal, 1991). A range of individual financial ratios can represent the groupings of potential explanatory variables, each with slightly differing information content. The groupings are interconnected, as weak (or strong) financial performance in one area will impact on another. For example, a firm with a high level of debt may have lower profitability due to high interest costs. Prior to the selection of the explanatory variables for this example, a total of ten previous studies were examined (Altman, 1968; Altman et al., 1977; Back, Laitinen, Sere, & van Wezel, 1996; Beaver, 1966; Dambolena & Khoury, 1980; Kahya & Theodossiou, 1996; Moody, 2000; Ohlson, 1980; Serrano-Cinca, 1996; Sung, Chang, & Lee, 1999). These studies employed a total of 58 distinct ratios. From these the following eight ratios were judgementally chosen:

1. EBIT / Sales
2. Return on Investment
3. Cash from Operations to Total Liabilities
4. Working Capital to Total Assets
5. Sales to Total Assets
6. Inventory to Working Capital
7. Total Liabilities to Total Assets
8. Interest / EBIT

Negative Selection Algorithm

Forrest, Perelson, Allen, and Cherukuri (1994) developed a negative selection algorithm analogous to the negative selection process for T cell tolerogenesis in the thymus. This early form of the negative selection algorithm used a binary string representation for encoding data and detectors, partly because the focus of the early development of the algorithm was the construction of computer virus detection systems. The binary version of the algorithm was subsequently extended to include a real-valued representation by Gonzalez and Dasgupta (2003).

Figure 3. Flowchart of the creation of a population of valid detectors in the canonical negative selection algorithm

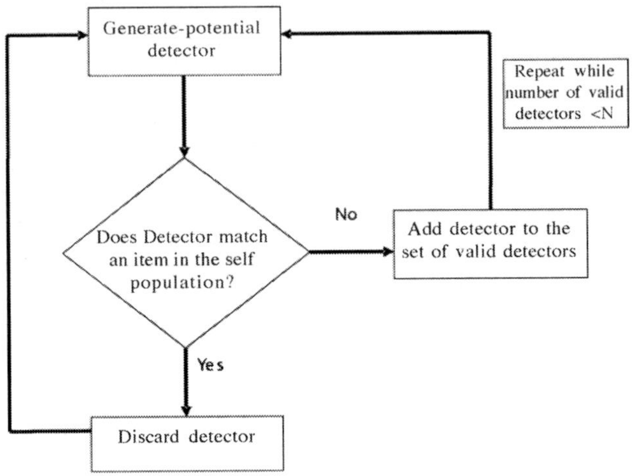

Canonical Real-Valued Negative Selection Algorithm

The canonical real-valued negative selection algorithm is outlined in Figure 3.

Initially a pre-determined number of detectors are created randomly. During the training (tolerogenesis) process any detector that falls within a threshold distance r_s (usually measured using Euclidean distance) of any elements of the set of self-samples is discarded and replaced by another randomly generated detector. The replacement detector is also checked against the set of self-samples. The process of detector generation is iterated until the required number of valid detectors is generated. All of the resulting detectors are potentially useful detectors of non-self. The pseudo-code for the algorithm is as follows (S is the set of self-samples, r_s is a pre-defined threshold distance, and it is assumed that the search-space is bounded by an n-dimensional (0,1) hypercube):

Detector set (D) is empty

Repeat

Create a random vector **x** drawn from $(0,1)^n$

For every $\mathbf{s}_i$ **in** $S = \mathbf{s}_i : i=1,2, ...,m$

  Calculate the Euclidean distance (d) between $\mathbf{s}_i$ and **x**

If $d > r_s$ **then** Add **x** (a valid non-self detector) to set D

Until D contains the required number of detectors

Once the required number of detectors has been created, they can be used to classify new data observations. To do this the new data vector is presented to the population of detectors, and if it does not fall within $\boldsymbol{r}_s$ of any of them, the data vector is deemed to be self, as it did not trigger any of the non-self detectors, otherwise the new data vector is deemed to be non-self.

In an application of the algorithm for the purposes of predicting corporate failure, self can be defined as a healthy or non-failing company, and the objective is to correctly identify failing companies. Each company is defined by a vector of its accounting ratios. When developing the classification system, the non-self detectors are initially located randomly in the self/non-self space. The distance between each detector and each self company in the training sample being used to construct the classifier is calculated, and if a detector is within the threshold distance of any self vector, it is discarded and a new detector is randomly created to replace it. More technically, in the implemented algorithm, detectors are discarded where the median distance of a detector to its *k*-nearest self vectors is less than the threshold distance. The use of *k*-nearest neighbors makes the algorithm less susceptible to noise in the input data (Gonzalez & Dasgupta, 2003). In our experiments K is set at 5. When the full population of detectors has been generated, they can be exposed to new (out-of-sample) data, and then used to predict whether these companies will fail or not. New data vectors that are similar to a detector (which have characteristics similar to failing companies) are classed as unhealthy companies. Otherwise the vector is classed as a healthy company. As in the training process, the detection of whether a detector has been triggered is determined by finding the Euclidean distance between a detector and a test data vector. Any vector (company) in the out-of-sample test set that is within a threshold distance of any detector is deemed to be a non-self or unhealthy company.

Figure 4 provides a graphical representation of the model at the end of the training process, where the area covered by detectors corresponds to an "unhealthy zone" of financial ratios. For ease of display, only two ratios are considered, the debt equity ratio and the return on assets metric. Both measures have been normalized into the range (0,1), and figure 3 suggests that companies with high debt ratios and low return on assets are more likely to be unhealthy. Any company outside the zone of the detectors is classed as a healthy company.

The algorithm requires that the modeler specifies both the number of detectors to be created, and the size of the threshold distance. Following experimentation on the corporate failure data set, 40% of the self data was used to train the detectors, the number of detectors was set at 500, and a threshold distance of 0.80 was applied. Intuitively, the number of detectors and the size of the threshold distance determine the degree of coverage of the self/non-self space by the detectors. As the number of detectors and their threshold distance increases, the model will tend to mis-identify healthy companies as being unhealthy. Conversely, if there are very few detectors, and/or they have a small threshold distance, the model will tend to mis-identify unhealthy companies as being healthy. In the real-valued fixed detector algorithm 500 detectors was found to be the optimal number of detectors to obtain a balance between the prediction accuracy and the number of healthy companies that are incorrectly identified as unhealthy. Using 1,000 detectors for example causes a greatly increased percentage of healthy companies to be classified as unhealthy.

Figure 4. Example of location of detectors for corporate failure model after training. Axes correspond to two financial ratios.

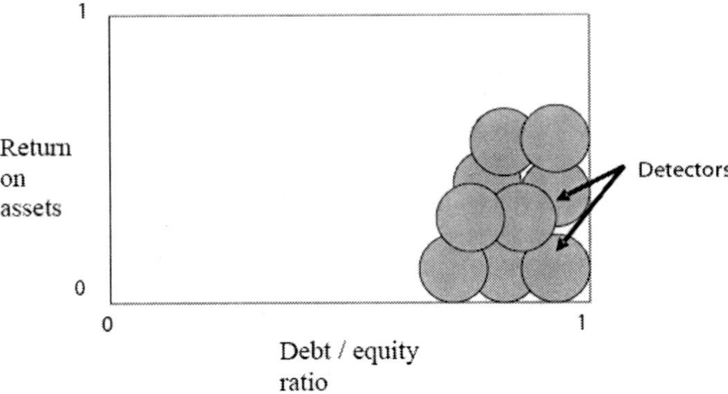

Variable Size Detector Algorithm

Ji and Dasgupta (2004a, 2004b) developed the variable-size detector algorithm as an alternative to the canonical real-valued negative selection algorithm. In the canonical real-valued negative selection algorithm described in the previous section, the detectors have a fixed radius of detection, and hence are all the same size. In the variable detector algorithm, the size of each detector is permitted to differ. During the training or model-building process, the radius of detection for each detector is determined by the distance between that detector and the closest self vector. Detectors which are a long way from any training self vectors are given a large radius of detection. Detectors which are close to self vectors get a small radius of detection. This allows areas of non-self which are removed from any self vectors to be covered with a relatively small number of large radius detectors, and also allows for the insertion of smaller detectors to cover any gaps or holes in the non-self space between the large detectors (see Figure 5). The variable size algorithm allows the modeler to set the approximate degree of "coverage" of the non-self space by the generated detectors. The greater the degree of coverage required, the more detectors the algorithm generates.

As for the canonical negative selection algorithm, the variable-size detector algorithm requires that the modeler specify the value of a number of parameters: the number of detectors to be created, the size of the self-radius distance for each detector, and the expected coverage. Following experimentation, 40% of the self data was used to train the detectors, the number of detectors was set at 500, and the expected coverage was set at 99% in line with the recommendation of Ji and Dasgupta (2004a).

Figure 5. Variable size detectors vs. fixed size detectors

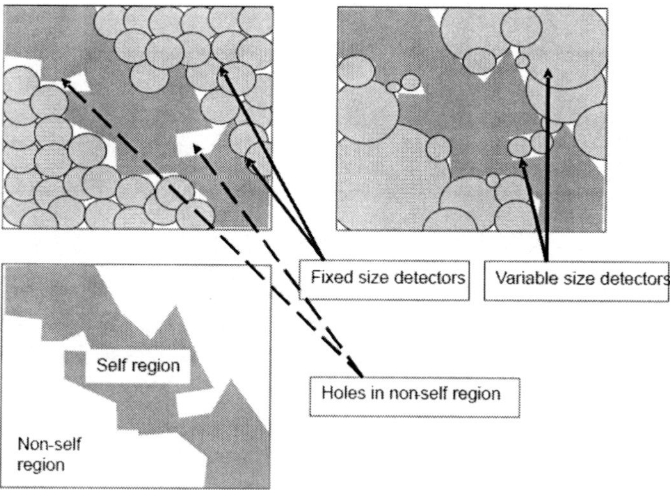

Results/Discussion

Classification models were developed using data drawn from each of the three years prior to failure (T-3, T-2 and T-1 are three, two and one year prior to failure respectively). For both versions of the negative selection algorithm, all ratios were normalized into the range (0,1) after clipping outliers. Therefore the self/non-self space is an eight dimensional hypercube, where each dimension corresponds to an individual financial ratio. In order to train the detectors, a percentage of the self data (healthy companies) was randomly chosen. The remaining matched pairs were used as out-of-sample test data.

Accuracy of the developed models was assessed based on their overall classification accuracy on the out-of-sample data sets. All reported results are averaged over three recuts of the data set between training and test data. Summarized classification accuracies are provided in Table 2. The classification accuracies for T-1 and T-2 are notably better than random chance, and calculation of Press's Q statistic (Hair, Anderson, Tatham, & Black, 1998) for the results from both of these algorithms for T-1 and T-2 rejects a null hypothesis, at the 5% level, that the out-of-sample classification accuracies are not significantly better than chance. By T-3, the accuracy of the developed classifiers drops off markedly. This is not unexpected, as results from earlier studies (Altman, 1968; Altman et al., 1977; Back et al., 1996; Dambolena & Khoury, 1980) have indicated that the classification accuracy of failure models increases rapidly as the date of final failure approaches. Generally, prior results indicate that a significant deterioration in financial ratios occurs between the third and second years prior to eventual failure, and this is also evident in the results obtained by the two negative selection algorithms.

Table 2. Classification accuracies for the canonical negative selection algorithm vs variable size detector algorithm, where 40% of the non-fail data is used to train the detectors. All results are averaged over three recuts.

Results	Canonical Negative Selection Algorithm Out-of-Sample	Variable Size Detector Algorithm Out-of-Sample
T-1	74.12%	75.88%
T-2	65.44%	64.21%
T-3	37.88%	39.40%

The results produced by the two forms of the negative selection algorithm are quite similar, indicating that, in spite of the potential advantages of the variable-size detector algorithm in providing better coverage of non-self space (by closing "holes"), this did not make a marked difference on this data set.

This corporate failure data set was also used by Brabazon and Keenan (2004) to compare conventional LDA with an approach where the inputs and structure of a neural network (NN) model are automatically selected by means of a genetic algorithm (GA). The AIS approach used in this chapter outperformed LDA in periods T-1 and T-2 in the identification of companies likely to fail. AIS performed less well than the relatively sophisticated GA/NN technique. However, AIS has advantages over these techniques. To achieve an effective level of prediction, LDA and NN techniques require both good and bad exemplars in the training dataset. AIS does not require to be exposed to bad exemplars, it can be trained on non-failed companies alone. This is an important advantage as "normal" data will generally be readily available, but special cases are by definition scarce.

Conclusion

In this chapter a novel methodology inspired by the workings of the natural immune system was introduced and applied for the purposes of prediction of corporate failure. The developed classifier was found to be able to accurately distinguish between failing and non-failing firms using a small number of financial ratios drawn from those companies. The classifier was shown to perform as well as widely used LDA methods on data that had been pre-processed to favor the LDA technique. AIS have potential for use without this need for pre-processing of data. It is noted that the negative selection algorithm has general utility for classification and it can be applied to a wide-variety of business settings beyond the corporate failure example developed in this chapter. Examples of potential applications include credit rating, bond rating, fraud detection, and customer database segmentation. Self could be generally defined as any normal pattern of activity, or as the stable behavior of a system of interest. Dasgupta and Forrest (1996) provide an example of how the negative selection algorithm could be applied to detect unusual patterns in time-series data.

This chapter provides a demonstration of how the negative selection algorithm could be applied to develop a classifier, and the initial results from the application of this novel methodology suggest that negative selection algorithms can be applied to construct quality classifiers. A number of improvements could be implemented to further improve the efficiency of the algorithm. Unlike the scenario faced by natural immune systems, historic examples of failed companies (non-self) exist. These could be used to seed the process of creating valid detectors in order to speed it up. The task of generating a population of valid detectors grows rapidly as the size of self increases. Therefore seeding could be particularly useful when developing classification systems for high-dimensional business applications. Another possibility is to automate the selection of parameters such as the number of detectors. Recent work by Gonzalez and Cannady (2004) demonstrates the potential of a hybrid AIS system which embeds an evolutionary algorithm, for the purposes of automating parameter selection. Just as hybrid evolutionary-NN methodologies can improve on basic NN techniques (Brabazon & Keenan, 2004), these hybrid evolutionary-AIS methodologies could improve the performance of AIS approaches.

References

Altman, E. (1968). Financial ratios, discriminant analysis and the prediction of corporate bankruptcy. *Journal of Finance, 23*(1), 589-609.

Altman, E. (2000). *Predicting financial distress of companies: Revisiting the Z-score and Zeta models*. Retrieved October 30, 2001, from http://www.stern.nyu.edu/~ealtman/Zscores.pdf

Altman, E., Haldeman, R., & Narayanan, P. (1977). ZETA analysis: A new model to identify bankruptcy risk of corporations. *Journal of Banking and Finance, 1*(1), 29-54.

Argenti, J. (1976). *Corporate collapse: The causes and symptoms*. London: McGraw-Hill.

Back, B., Laitinen, T., Sere, K., & van Wezel, M. (1996). *Choosing bankruptcy predictors using discriminant analysis, logit analysis and genetic algorithms*. Technical Report no. 40, Turku Centre for Computer Science, Turku School of Economics and Business Administration.

Beaver, W. (1966). Financial ratios as predictors of failure. *Journal of Accounting Research — Supplement: Empirical Research in Accounting*, 71-102.

Brabazon, A., & Keenan, P. (2004). A hybrid genetic model for the prediction of corporate failure. *Computational Management Science, 1*(3/4), 293-310.

Brabazon, A., & O'Neill, M. (2003). Anticipating bankruptcy reorganisation from raw financial data using grammatical evolution. In G. Raidl et al. (Eds.), *Proceedings of EvoIASP 2003: Applications of Evolutionary Computing, LNCS 2611* (pp. 368-378). Berlin: Springer-Verlag.

Brabazon, A., & O'Neill, M. (2004). Diagnosing corporate stability using grammatical evolution. *International Journal of Applied Mathematics and Computer Science, 14*(3), 363-374.

Chao, D., & Forrest, S. (2003). Information immune systems. *Genetic Programming and Evolvable Machines*, *4*(4), 311-331.

Chen, J. (2002). A heuristic approach to efficient production of detector sets for an artificial immune algorithm-based bankruptcy prediction system. *Proceedings of the Congress on Evolutionary Computation*, *1*, 932-937.

Dambolena, I., & Khoury, S. (1980). Ratio stability and corporate failure. *Journal of Finance*, *35*(4), 1017-1026.

Dasgupta, D., & Forrest, S. (1996). Novelty detection in time series data using ideas from immunology. In F. C. Harris (Ed.), *Proceedings of the Fifth International Conference on Intelligent Systems* (pp. 82-87). Cary, NC: ISCA.

de Castro, L., & Timmis, J. (2002). *Artificial immune systems: A new computational intelligence approach*. London: Springer.

Dimitras, A., Zanakis, S., & Zopounidis, C. (1996). A survey of business failures with an emphasis on prediction methods and industrial applications. *European Journal of Operational Research*, *90*(3), 487-513.

Fan, A., & Palaniswami, M. (2000, May). A new approach to corporate loan default prediction from financial statements. In S. Ferris et al. (Eds.), *Proceedings of Computational Finance / Forecasting Financial Markets Conference (CF/FFM-2000)*, London.

Fitzpatrick, P. (1932). *A comparison of the ratios of successful industrial enterprises with those of failed companies*. Washington: The Accountants' Publishing Company.

Forrest, S., Perelson, A. Allen, L., & Cherukuri, R. (1994). Self-nonself discrimination in a computer. In *Proceedings of the 1994 IEEE Symposium on Research in Security and Privacy* (pp. 202-212). Los Alamitos, CA: IEEE Computer Society.

Gentry, J., Newbold, P., & Whitford, D. (1985). Classifying bankrupt firms with funds flow components. *Journal of Accounting Research*, *23*(1), 146-160.

Goldsby, R., Kindt, T., Kuby, J., & Osborne, B. (2002). *Immunology* (5th ed.). New York: W. H. Freeman.

Gonzalez, L., & Cannady, J. (2004). A self-adaptive negative selection approach for anomaly detection. *Proceedings of the Congress on Evolutionary Computation*, 2 (pp. 1561-1568).

Gonzalez, F.A., & Dasgupta, D. (2003). Anomaly detection using real-valued negative selection. *Genetic Programming and Evolvable Machines*, *4*, 383-403.

Hair, J., Anderson, R., Tatham, R., & Black, W. (1998). *Multivariate data analysis*. Upper Saddle River, NJ: Prentice Hall.

Hofmeyer, S., & Forrest, S. (2000). Architecture for an artificial immune system. *Evolutionary Computation*, *8*(4), 443-473.

Horrigan, J. (1965, July). Some empirical bases of financial ratio analysis. *The Accounting Review*, 558-568.

Janeway, C., Travers, P., Walport, M., & Shlomchik, M. (2004). *Immunobiology* (6th ed.). New York: Garland.

Ji, Z., & Dasgupta, D. (2004a). Augmented negative selection algorithm with variable-coverage detectors. *Proceedings of the Congress on Evolutionary Computation*, 1 (pp. 1081-1088).

Ji, Z., & Dasgupta, D. (2004b). Real-valued negative selection algorithm with variable-sized detectors. In K. Deb et al. (Eds.), *GECCO2004: Genetic and Evolutionary Algorithm Conference — LNCS 3103* (pp. 287-298). Berlin: Springer-Verlag.

Kahya, E., & Theodossiou, P. (1996). Predicting corporate financial distress: A time-series CUSUM methodology. *Review of Quantitative Finance and Accounting*, *13*, 71-93.

Kumar, N., Krovi, R., & Rajagopalan, B. (1997). Financial decision support with hybrid genetic and neural based modelling tools. *European Journal of Operational Research*, *103*(2), 339-349.

Levinthal, D. (1991). Random walks and organisational mortality. *Administrative Science Quarterly*, *36*(3), 397-420.

Moody (2000). *RiskCalc For private companies: Moody's default model*. Retrieved July 30, 2001, from http://riskcalc.moodysrms.com/us/research/crm/56402.pdf

Morris, R. (1997). *Early warning indicators of corporate failure: A critical review of previous research and further empirical evidence*. London: Ashgate.

Ohlson, J. (1980). Financial ratios and the probabilistic prediction of bankruptcy. *Journal of Accounting Research*, *18*(1), 109-131.

Serrano-Cinca, C. (1996). Self organizing neural networks for financial diagnosis. *Decision Support Systems*, *17*(3), 227-238.

Shah, J., & Murtaza, M. (2000). A neural network based clustering procedure for bankruptcy prediction. *American Business Review*, *18*(2), 80-86.

Smith, R., & Winakor, A. (1935). *Changes in the financial structure of unsuccessful corporations*. University of Illinois, Bureau of Business Research, Bulletin No. 51.

Sung, T., Chang, N., & Lee, G. (1999). Dynamics of modelling in data mining: Interpretative approach to bankruptcy prediction. *Journal of Management Information Systems*, *16*(1), 63-85.

Tam, K. (1991). Neural network models and the prediction of bank bankruptcy. *Omega*, *19*(5), 429-445.

Varetto, F. (1998). Genetic algorithms in the analysis of insolvency risk. *Journal of Banking and Finance*, *22*(10), 1421-1439.

Wilson, N., Chong, K., & Peel, M. (1995). Neural network simulation and the prediction of corporate outcomes: Some empirical findings. *International Journal of the Economics of Business*, *2*(1), 31-50.

Zmijewski, M. (1984). Methodological issues related to the estimation of financial distress prediction models. *Journal of Accounting Research-Supplement*, 59-82.

Zopounidis, C., Slowinski, R, Doumpos, M., Dimitras, A., & Susmaga, R. (1999). Business failure prediction using rough sets: A comparison with multivariate analysis techniques. *Fuzzy Economic Review*, *4*(1), 3-33.

Chapter XX

Development of Machine Learning Software for High Frequency Trading in Financial Markets

Andrei Hryshko, University of Queensland, Australia

Tom Downs, University of Queensland, Australia

Abstract

Foreign exchange trading has emerged in recent times as a significant activity in many countries. As with most forms of trading, the activity is influenced by many random parameters, so that the creation of a system that effectively emulates the trading process will be very helpful. This chapter presents a novel trading system using Machine Learning methods of Genetic Algorithms and Reinforcement Learning. The system emulates trader behavior on the Foreign Exchange market and finds the most profitable trading strategy.

Introduction

In spite of many years of debate between economists and financiers, the question of whether financial markets are predictable remains open. Numerous tests with financial data have been conducted by researchers but these have tended to support both sides of the issue. In our view, the best evidence of predictability of financial markets would be the development of a strategy or an algorithm which is capable of consistently gaining a profit from the financial market. In this chapter we demonstrate that machine learning techniques are capable of performing this task.

The use of machine learning and optimization methods in finance has become a fairly common practice amongst financiers and researchers. With the continuous deregulation and increasing volatility of financial markets, competition in the financial industry is getting stronger and new techniques are being developed to provide efficient trading for financial institutions and the public.

At the present time, millions of people trade in financial markets and even more wish to become involved. The main problems they face are how to trade and how to develop a profitable strategy. Usually it takes several years to become a successful trader and sometimes success remains elusive.

Trading usually takes place through a broker who provides software for the trader to buy and sell assets on a financial market. This software provides information to the trader such as current and past share prices, exchange rate, market indicators, etc. Based on this data, a trader can decide when to sell and when to buy a particular stock or currency. Choosing these actions in order to maximize profit is a difficult task, not just for beginners, but also for experienced traders. The market is constantly changing so that different rules and concepts apply in different situations. It is not uncommon that a trader's strategy that works well at a given time performs poorly two hours later. Hence the trader has to determine the times at which a strategy should be changed and to identify the changes that should be made. Another problem for the trader is that different strategies are successful for different financial markets. Thus, a strategy should be tailored to a particular situation in a particular market.

To deal with these problems, the issue of market information analysis needs to be addressed, not only theoretically but also practically. In this chapter, we describe our investigations into this issue and how they can be used to develop a software system capable of operating in the manner of a human trader.

Some related studies have previously been carried out, but the question of how to combine theoretical investigations with practical trading requires further attention. Existing methods (at least those in the open literature) are examined and are considered not capable of generating significant profits and therefore cannot be applied to online trading.

Figure 1. EUR/USD prices and volumes for October, 2004

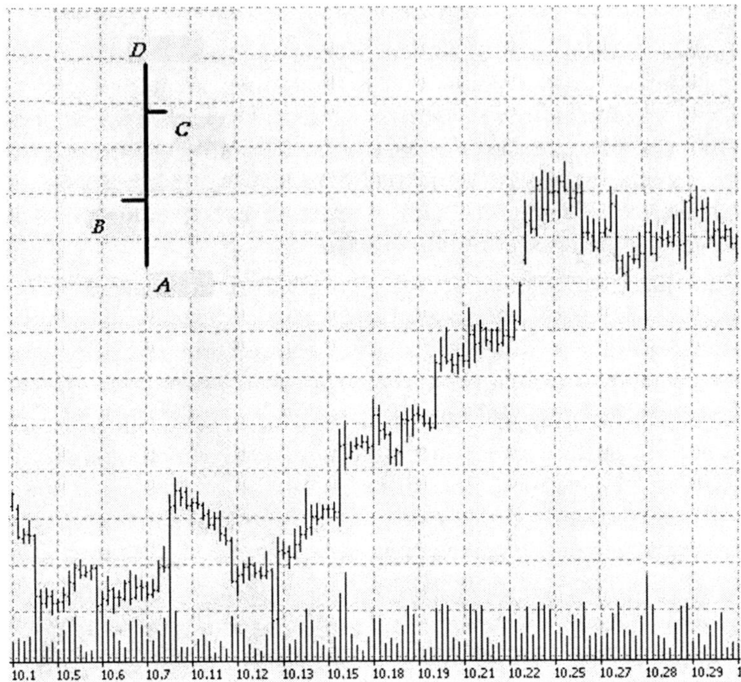

The Foreign Exchange Market

The Foreign Exchange (FX) Market is an interbank market that was created in 1971 when international trade began using floating rather than fixed exchange rates. The FX Market was an integration of deregulated domestic stock markets in leading countries. Since the time of its creation, currency rates have been determined based on supply and demand with regard to each currency (Carew & Slatyer, 1989). Figure 1 displays a sequence of four-hour prices and volumes for the Euro/US dollar market during October 2004.

Each element of the upper curve has the structure shown at the upper left of the figure. In this structure, points A and D indicate the lowest and highest rates achieved in a four-hour period, and points B and C indicate the opening and closing prices, respectively, for the four-hour period. The histogram-like plot along the bottom of the figure indicates the volume of transactions over each four-hour period.

It is our view that the FX market is a good basis for testing the efficiency of the prediction system because:

1. Historical data on exchange rates of currencies is readily available.
2. The FX market is easily accessible. It is open to individual investors and doesn't require large deposits.
3. The FX market provides freedom to open and close positions of any size at any time at the current market rate.
4. The FX market is open 24 hours a day, five days a week. This means that at each moment of time every time zone (London, New York, Tokyo, Hong Kong, Sydney) has dealers who can quote prices for currencies.
5. A trader can define a period of time for his position on the FX market. This means that his position is kept open until that time has elapsed.

Statistical Approach to Technical Analysis

There are two basic approaches to market analysis: fundamental analysis and technical analysis.

Fundamental analysis focuses on the economic forces of supply and demand and determines whether prices move higher, lower or stay almost the same. It examines all relevant factors affecting the price in order to determine the intrinsic value of the market. Intrinsic value means worth based on the law of supply and demand. Technical analysis is the practice of trying to forecast market prices by examining trading patterns and comparing the shape of current charts to those from the past.

Both of these approaches to market forecasting try to solve the same problem, that is, to determine in what direction prices will move. The difference between fundamental and technical analyses is that the first one explores the causes of movements on the market and the second one explores the effect of these movements.

Fundamental analysis is generally concerned with longer-term trends than technical analysis. So given that most traders on the FX market are intra-day traders they use just technical analysis and do not take into consideration the fundamental method. The main instrument employed by technical analysts is the set of available indicators, which helps traders to discover trends, reversals of trends and other fluctuations.

An indicator makes use of a set of mathematical formulae that may, for instance, be derived from past prices or from other market data such as trade volumes. Different indicators play different roles in the analysis. Some indicators work better when the market has a strong trend, and some when the market is neutral. The Machine Learning system described here makes use of ten commonly used indicators.

The simplest indicator we use is the Moving Average (MA) that shows the average value of prices during a defined period of time. The n-day MA is calculated using the simple formula:

$$MA = \frac{P_1 + ... + P_n}{n}$$

where P_i is the price *i*-1 days previously.

Buy and sell signals are generated according to the behavior of moving averages in the short and longer term. A buy signal is produced when the short average crosses above the longer one. When the short average moves below, a sell signal is generated. This technique is called the *double crossover method.*

The 10 commonly used indicators that we have employed in this work are detailed in Appendix 1.

Methodology

Genetic Algorithms

Genetic Algorithms (GA) were introduced by Holland (1975) as a general model of adaptive processes and have been widely applied as an optimization technique. They were inspired by natural genetic processes and employ a population of "chromosomes" (represented by binary strings) that are analogous to the DNA of a natural organism. Unlike traditional optimization methods that require well-defined mathematical representations of the objective, GA can solve optimization problems that are far less well described mathematically. This makes them very useful for trading models, which cannot easily be expressed in terms of mathematical formulas and functions.

In the original GA formulation, a population of possible solutions is encoded as a set of bit strings (known as parameter strings), each of the same fixed length. The fitness of each string in the population is estimated and the basic GA operators are then applied as described below. This provides a second generation population whose average fitness is greater than that of the initial population. The GA operators are now applied to the second generation population and the process is repeated, generation after generation, until some stopping criterion is met. The string with maximum fitness in the final population is then selected as the solution.

In applying a GA to FX trading, each string represents a possible solution for the trader — adopt a short, long or neutral position.

Decisions made by the trader are based upon the values of a set of market indicators. These values can be incorporated into the GA bit strings as binary variables. For instance, in the case of the double-crossover method mentioned in the previous section, the indicator generates a sell signal when the short average moves below the longer one. The indicator corresponding to this signal is called "MASell" and it takes on the binary value 1 when the condition for the sell signal is met. It has the value 0 otherwise.

Table 1. A sell rule and its associated bit string

MASell	Connective	MomSel	Connective	StochBuy	Sell
1	0	1	1	0	0

Table 2. An example of an exit

RSI Buy	Connect	Mom Sell	Connect	LW Sell	Connect	PO Sell
1	0	1	0	1	1	0

An example of a rule employing this and two other indicators (described in the Appendix) is shown in Table 1. This rule instructs the trader to adopt a short position (i.e., sell) and is encoded as a bit string in the table. The rule states "IF MASell = 1 OR (MomentumSell =1 AND StochasticBuy = 0) THEN adopt a short position." Thus the connectives in the table are the Boolean operators AND and OR which have binary values 1 and 0 respectively.

Note that the instruction to sell in this rule is encoded as a zero at the right-hand end of the bit string. Rules that instruct the trader to adopt a long position (i.e., to buy) have a "1" in this position.

Rules for adopting a short or long position are called *entry* rules because they instruct the trader to participate actively in the market. There are also exit rules under which the trader returns to a neutral position. An example is shown in Table 2. Note that there is no explicit binary value for the instruction to exit. No such value is necessary because the exit action is always the same — that is, to return to a neutral position.

The rule in Table 2 rule states "IF RSIBuy = 1 OR (MomentumSell = 1 OR (Larry WilliamsSell = 1 AND Price OscillatorSell = 0) THEN adopt a neutral position."

The rules and their binary strings are obviously significantly longer than these, when a large number of indicators have to be coded.

The rules in Tables 1 and 2 together can be considered as a *strategy*. This strategy states that if the trader enters under the rule in Table 1, the rule for exiting is the one in Table 2. Our objective is to use machine learning methods to determine the best possible strategy for given market conditions.

In a typical implementation, a population of 150 rules of each type (entry and exit) is generated randomly. Then out of these 300 rules we randomly combine 150 pairs consisting of one entry rule and one exit rule. This therefore gives us 150 trading strategies. These strategies are ranked according to their profitability and are then stochastically chosen to participate in the creation of a new population. Those strategies with greater profitability (or *fitness*) are more likely to be selected to participate. The process of generating a new population employs rules that are analogous to processes involved in natural reproduction. The exchange of genetic material is reflected in the *crossover* operation which combines a pair of rules to form two "children" by swapping sub-strings. A form of *mutation* is also occasionally applied in order to broaden the mix of bit strings. This is implemented by simply inverting bit values. A low probability is used for this so that bit values are only infrequently inverted.

Crossover and mutation are applied only to rules of the same type (entry or exit). If rules derived in this way are unique (differing from all other rules in the population), they are used to replace low-ranked rules. This is done in such a way that the number of rules in the population remains constant. The process is continued until a stopping criterion is met upon which the best pair of rules (the best strategy) is chosen to be the output of the genetic algorithm. The best strategy is the one that gives maximum profitability.

Reinforcement Learning

Another Machine Learning framework that is helpful in the implementation of a financial market model is reinforcement learning. The general reinforcement learning problem addresses the following: an agent must explore its environment and make decisions in different situations based on incomplete knowledge about this environment. The only feedback that the agent receives from the environment is a scalar reinforcement signal which is positive if its actions are beneficial and negative otherwise. The objective of the agent is to choose its actions so as to increase the long-term sum of the reinforcement signals (Kaelbling & Littman, 1996). Besides the reinforcement signal the agent also receives information on the current state of the environment (in the form of a vector of observations). On the FX market a trader (machine or human) has insufficient knowledge about the environment to choose the times at which buy and sell decisions should be made in order to maximize profit. The only information available is the gain (positive or negative) generated by trading decisions and this provides the reinforcement signal that drives our system.

Figure 2 illustrates the principles of reinforcement learning (RL). At time t the agent receives inputs x_t (a vector of observations) and r_t (a reinforcement signal) and based on these it chooses an action, a_t. The action a_t changes the state of the environment from s_t to s_{t+1}. The process then repeats.

For our software implementation, we have developed an RL-engine based on the Q-learning algorithm proposed by Watkins (1989) for partially observable Markov decision processes. The Q-learning algorithm, which can be used online, was developed for the optimization of a strategy based upon experience gained from the unknown environment.

In general, the Q-learning algorithm works as follows. The value $Q(s, a)$ is defined to be the expected discounted sum of future reinforcement signals when action a is taken in state s and an optimal policy is then followed. The state s belongs to S, the discrete set of states of the environment and the action a belongs to the set A of possible agent actions. Once we have the $Q(s, a)$ values, the optimal action from any state is the one with the highest Q-value. This means that we obtain the policy by executing the action with the highest Q-value. At the first step we initialize $Q_0(s_0, a_0)$ by arbitrary numbers and improved estimates of the Q-values are then obtained from incoming signals using the following procedure:

Figure 2. Reinforcement learning cycle

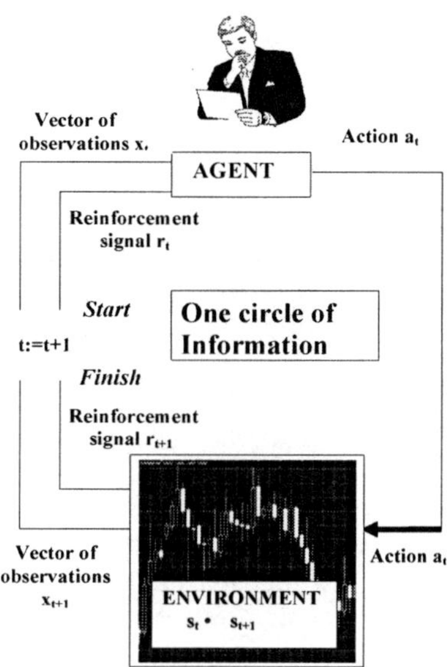

1. From the current state s_t, select an action a_t. This takes us to the next state s_{t+1} and provides the reinforcement signal $r_{t+1.}$
2. Update $Q_t(s_t, a_t)$ based on this experience:

$$Q_{t+1}(s_t, a_t) := Q_t(s_t, a_t) + \alpha\left(r_{t+1} + \gamma \max_a Q_t(s_{t+1}, a) - Q_t(s_t, a_t)\right) \quad (1)$$

   where $\alpha (0 < \alpha \leq 1)$ is a learning-rate parameter and 0 < ãð < 1 is the discount factor used to place more emphasis on reinforcement signals that are received earlier.

3. Go to 1.

Note that we have to store each value $Q(s,a)$ for all $s \in S$ and $a \in A$. They are stored in a table called a Q-table. An illustration of Q-learning algorithm is given in Appendix 2.

The objective of the agent is to find the optimal policy $\pi(s) \in A$ for each state of the environment to maximize the long-run total reward. The Q-learning algorithm uses optimal Q-values $Q^*(s_t, a_t)$ for states s and actions a. The optimal Q-value function satisfies Bellman's optimality equation:

$$Q^*(s_t, a_t) := \sum_{s_{t+1}} P(s_t, a_t, s_{t+1}) \left[R(s_t, a_t, s_{t+1}) + \gamma \max_{a'} Q^*(s_{t+1}, a') \right] \quad (2)$$

where $P(s_t, a_t, s_{t+1})$ is the probability of a transition from state s_t to s_{t+1} with action a_t is taken. $R(s_t, a_t, s_{t+1})$ is an immediate reward obtained from taking action a_t when the environment state changes s_t to s_{t+1}.

$\gamma (0 \leq \gamma \leq 1)$ is a discount factor to weight future rewards.

Given the optimal Q-values $Q^*(s,a)$ it is possible to choose the best action:

$$a^* = \arg\max_a (Q^*(s,a))$$

A major advantage of using Q-learning is that there is no need to know the transitive probabilities $P(s_t, a_t, s_{t+1})$. The algorithm can find the $Q^*(s,a)$ in a recursive manner. The Q-values are adjusted according to equation (1).

If equation (1) is repeatedly applied for each pair (s_t, a_t) and the learning rate α is gradually reduced toward 0 over time, then $Q(s,a)$ converges with probability 1 to $Q^*(s,a)$.

A Hybrid Trading System

Our hybrid system involves a combination of the two techniques of machine learning described in the previous section.

Combining the Two Techniques

It is important to realize that, because of the vast number of combinations of indicator values and connectives, the GA is unable to search the whole space of strategies to find the optimum. To see this, note that if we have m indicators per rule and N indicators in total, the number of possible rules is $P(N, m)*2^{m-1}$, where $P(N, m)$ is the number of permutations of N objects taken m at a time. In our system, the ten indicators we use are applied to both buying and selling, giving a total of 20 indicators in all. Our average rule length is eight indicators, so the above formula gives the approximate number of possible rules as 6.5×10^{11}.

To illustrate our procedure a little further, suppose that the strategy given by Table 1 has been selected by the GA as the most profitable one. (Note that this could only occur in a market where prices are falling.) Because of the combinatorial complexity, the GA will, with very high probability, have only considered one set of instantiations for the indicators and connectives making up this rule (i.e., the ones in Tables 1 and 2). And this is where reinforcement learning comes in.

The fact that the GA identified this strategy as a profitable one shows that the indicators used in the strategy are capable of making useful market predictions. Because of this, it is worthwhile to consider the other possible instantiations of the rule values in the strategy, and this is the role of the Q-learning algorithm. Figure 3 shows the basic structure of the system. Once we have the set of the most useful indicators, they can be used to represent states of the environment and in this way we can take into account all possible combinations of the indicators.

Consider the theoretical situation where the GA module has identified the two indicators RSIBuy and CCISell as useful predictors. They provide the following set of states of the environment

$$\begin{cases} s_1 = \text{RSIBuy} = 1, \text{CCISell} = 1 \\ s_2 = \text{RSIBuy} = 1, \text{CCISell} = 0 \\ s_3 = \text{RSIBuy} = 0, \text{CCISell} = 1 \\ s_4 = \text{RSIBuy} = 0, \text{CCISell} = 0 \end{cases}$$

At each moment of time the trader has to make a decision whether take a short, long or neutral position. Thus, the set of actions is {buy, neutral, sell}.

This set of indicators and actions gives a Q-table of the form in Table 3. The entries in this table contain Q-values that are calculated and updated using the method explained in the Reinforcement Learning section. A detailed example is given in Appendix 2.

Since a trader on the FX Market tries to maximize profit, the reinforcement signal r_t is set to the difference between portfolio values at times t "1 and t. For instance, if at time t "1

Figure 3. The hybrid system

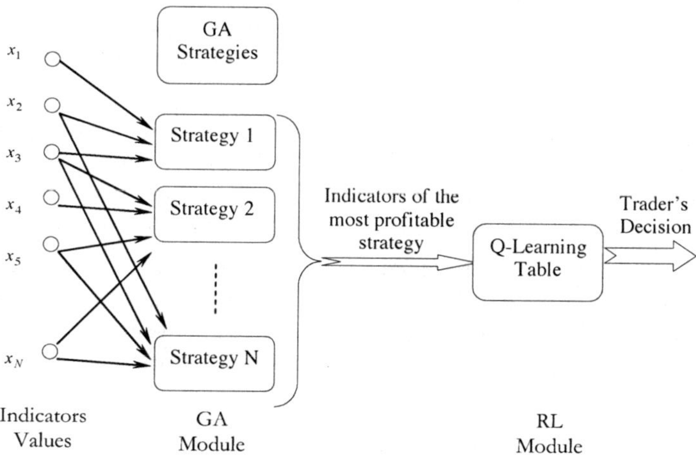

Table 3. Q-learning table consisting of 3 actions and 2^N states where N — number of indicators

	RSIBuy=1 CCISell=1	RSIBuy=1 CCISell=0	RSIBuy=0 CCISell=1	RSIBuy=0 CCISell=0
Buy				
Neutral				
Sell				

the trader took a long position, and then it was found that the portfolio at time t has a lower value than at time t"1, the reinforcement signal would be negative. This provides the basic mechanism for adopting long and short positions. But the third position, the neutral position, must also be properly dealt with. This requires the allocation of a threshold to avoid spurious shifts from the neutral position caused by minor market fluctuations. The major effect of this is to avoid the cost of insignificant transactions.

Related Methods

Previous work with similar objectives includes Dunis, Gavridis, Harris, Leong and Nacaskul (1998) who used a genetic algorithm (GA) to optimize indicator parameters. Their trading model was based on two indicator — *viz.* the Momentum Oscillator and the Relative Strength Index (both are described in the Appendix). Their data covered only a relatively brief trading period. Many experiments were carried out and their best results were 7.1% of the annualized return for the period 20/3/1996 – 20/5/1996. This is approximately equal to the interest rate at that time and so the gains were not particularly impressive.

Yao and Tan (2000) used Neural Networks to perform technical forecasting on the FX. The only technical indicators they used were moving averages of different orders and these were employed as inputs to the neural network. The best results achieved were 8.4% annualised return trading the USD/CHF exchange rate.

Dempster, Payne, Romahi and Thompson (2001) used a method based on an ensemble of indicators. They compared genetic algorithms and reinforcement learning to a simple linear program characterizing a Markov decision process and a heuristic. The best result achieved for trading over a 15-minute interval was around a 5% return.

Dempster and Romahi (2002) introduced a hybrid evolutionary reinforcement learning approach to constrain inputs to the RL system. The GA here aims to choose an optimal subset of indicators and then feeds them to the RL module. The annualised return gained from the implementation of this approach varied from 5% to 15% at a 15-minute trading frequency.

Moody and Saffell (2001) proposed the use of *recurrent* reinforcement learning to optimize risk-adjusted investment returns. Their system is based on price series returns rather than technical indicators. The recurrent RL trading system achieves an annualised

15% return on the USD/GBP exchange rate and they concluded that the recurrent RL system is superior to Q-Learning.

Note that although these results appear excellent, one must be careful in extrapolating them to real trading. Note also that Q-learning on its own is very susceptible to over-fitting but, as will become clear below, it can perform very well in a hybrid system.

The Software

The human trader makes use of online data to take a short, neutral or long position. Usually traders start with a set of concepts based upon indicators and then turn those concepts into a set of rules. The rule creating process requires a subjective choice to be made of which indicators to rely on and further subjectivity is needed in order to define rules for interpretation of the indicator signals. The trader then has to program the rules to create software for technical analysis. This is a difficult task, even for experienced traders. The market is changing all the time so that different rules and concepts work in different situations. Hence a trader has to determine the times at which the program should be changed, and obviously program modifications cannot be made online. Another problem for the trader is that different indicators are successful on different financial markets. For example, indicators that are profitable on one set of exchange rates could lead to catastrophic losses on another. Therefore a trader's strategy must be tailored to a particular situation. A software system that is able to adapt automatically to changing conditions avoids most of these problems and therefore has the potential to outperform a human in online trading. Our hybrid approach provides such an automated adaptive system and Figure 4 provides a snapshot of our system in operation.

Figure 4. Software for trading on the FX market

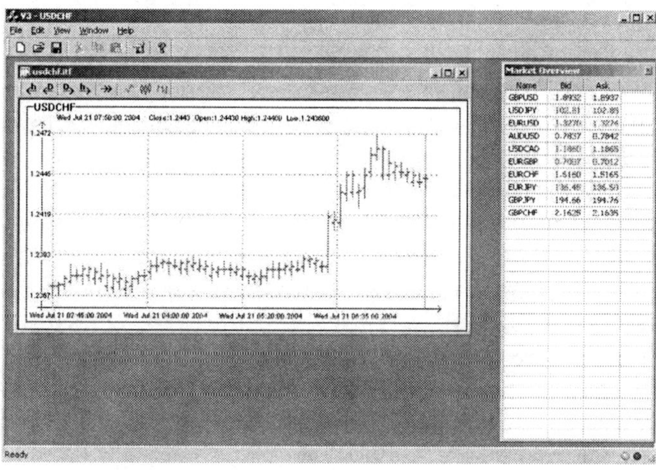

When a trader uses our system, the software automatically connects to the broker's server, downloads data from the server and analyses the situation in the market. When using the "online trading" mode the trader does not require any knowledge of the state of the market " the software system automatically sells and buys assets and follows the market whilst updating system parameters. In the "off-line trading" mode, the trader can himself (or herself) place orders to sell or buy based upon analysis and advice provided by the system. When the software connects to the server at the first time, initial learning based on historical data occurs and then one of the modes can be selected.

The engine of the software consists of a genetic algorithm module and a reinforcement learning module based on Q-learning as described above. This system draws upon available information to determine the optimum strategy for the trader. Unlike the human trader, it is capable of working online and around the clock so its parameters are updated continuously over time to achieve the highest returns. Our system makes its decisions and predicts the future market using a combination of different market models. It recognizes the state of the market by simultaneously examining signals from each market indicator (rather than examining indicator signals one–by-one).

The fitness evaluation, crossover and mutation mechanisms are repeated until the fitness function cannot be improved any longer or a maximum number of iterations is reached. The fitness function is considered maximized if the average performance of the most profitable ten pairs of rules does not change more than 3% over several iterations. When the GA module is finished we feed the indicators from the most profitable strategy to the RL module.

Our method of choosing the indicators to feed to the RL module is an improvement on the one in Dempster & Romahi (2002) where the RL algorithm is itself employed to determine which of the indicators have the greatest fitness. This is computationally much more demanding than our method in which the fitness function is simply calculated in terms of the Sharpe ratio (Sharpe, 1966).

Main Results

The data employed for testing our system is the intra-day Foreign Exchange (FX) rate EUR/USD. This currency pair is highly liquid since it is traded by a large number of market participants in all time zones. The data we employ relate to the period from 02 June 2002 to 31 December 2002 with a five-minute frequency 'off-line trading' mode and were obtained from the CQG Data Factory (www.cqg.com). They consist of 43,700 intra-day records with each daily record containing seven data fields. Figure 5 illustrates a sample of this data.

The first row of entries in the table in Figure 5 indicates that in the five-minute period commencing 1600 on 02 June 2002 the rate was 1 EURO = 0.9238 USD and at 1605 it was 1 EURO = 0.9331 USD. The highest and lowest rates in this period were 0.9335 USD and 0.9222 USD respectively. There were 41 trades between 1600 and 1605. A typical plot of the EUR/USD exchange rate that would provide a data entry identical to the first row of Figure 5 is shown in Figure 6.

Figure 5. Samples of 5 minute EUR/USD data extracted from 2 June 2002

Date	Time	Open	High	Low	Close	# Ticks
20020602	1600	9328	9335	9322	9331	41
20020602	1605	9324	9334	9320	9330	30
20020602	1610	9326	9334	9320	9333	32
20020602	1615	9323	9334	9320	9330	46

Figure 6. Illustration of the first row of Figure 5

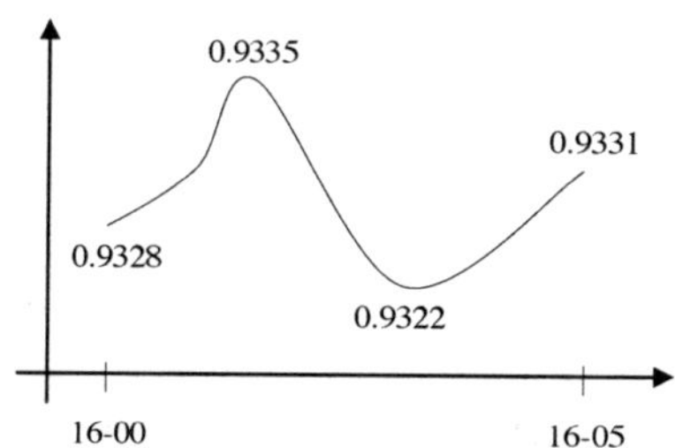

Using historical data our system learns to implement online trading. New training data is provided every five minutes and using this, the system learns to take a position - buy, sell or neutral.

Note that the software is able to work in any financial market where generally accepted market rules are applicable. Transaction cost here is 2 pips per trade where a pip is the minimum unit of currency movement in the FX market. The initial trading capital was 10,000 Euros. Following training on 2.5 months of data the system achieved a profitability of about 6% on 3.5 months of test data. The annualised return achieved was therefore about 20%, which is clearly superior to the results quoted above for other approaches.

Concluding Remarks

A hybrid GA-RL system has been described that is aimed at optimizing trading strategies in the FX market. The system was trained and tested on historical data and was shown to be capable of achieving moderate gains over the tested period. Based on this system, real-time software has been designed that is capable of replacing a human trader. There are still some important features that are to be designed in future versions of the system. Some of these include stop-losses, different contract sizes, and the possibility of trading through different brokers simultaneously.

References

Carew, E., & Slatyer, W. (1989). *Forex: The techniques of foreign exchange.* Sydney: Allen and Unwin.

Dempster, M., & Romahi, Y. (2002). Intraday FX trading: An evolutionary reinforcement learning approach. In H. Yin et al. (Eds.), *Intelligent Data Engineering and Automated Learning: Proceedings of the IDEAL 2002 International Conference* (pp. 347-358). Berlin: Springer Verlag.

Dempster, M., Payne, T., Romahi, Y., & Thompson, G. (2001). Computational learning techniques for intraday FX trading using popular technical indicators. *IEEE Transactions on Neural Networks, 4*(12), 744-754.

Dunis, C., Gavridis, M., Harris, A., Leong, S., & Nacaskul, P. (1998). An application of genetic algorithms to high frequency trading models: A case study. In C. Dunis & B. Zhou (Eds.), *Nonlinear modelling of high frequency financial time series* (pp. 247-278). New York: Wiley.

Holland, J. (1975). *Adaptation in natural and artificial systems.* Ann Arbor: University of Michigan.

Kaelbling, L., & Littman, M. (1996). Reinforcement learning: A survey. *Journal of Artificial Intelligence Research, 4*, 237-285.

Moody, J., & Saffell, M. (2001). Learning to trade via direct reinforcement. *IEEE Transactions on Neural Networks*, *4*(12), 875-889.

Murphy, J. (1999). *Technical analysis of the financial markets: A comprehensive guide to trading methods and applications.* Englewood Cliffs, NJ: Prentice Hall.

Sharpe, W. (1966). Mutual fund performance. *Journal of Business*, *39*, 119-138.

Watkins, C. (1989). *Learning with delayed rewards.* PhD thesis. Cambridge University, UK.

Watkins, C., & Dayan, P. (1992). Technical note. Q-learning. *Machine Learning*, *8*, 279-292.

Yao, J., & Tan, C. (2000). A case study on using neural networks to perform technical forecasting of Forex. *Neurocomputing*, *34*, 79-98.

Appendix 1: The Indicators

Besides the Moving Average (MA) indicator described in the Statistical Approach to Technical Analysis section, our system employs nine other indicators as described below. Here we add a little technical detail to the description of the MA indicator before detailing the other nine. All ten indicators provide the two signals: buy and sell. We consider standard indicator parameters that are usually used in the calculation by traders as advised in Murphy (1999).

Moving Average (MA)

The nine-day and 40-day moving averages can be written

$$MA_9(n) = \frac{1}{9}\sum_{i=0}^{9} C(n-i)$$

$$MA_{40}(n) = \frac{1}{40}\sum_{i=0}^{40} C(n-i)$$

where $C(n)$ is the latest closing price.

$\text{MABuy}(n) = 1$ if $(\text{MA}_9(n\text{-}1) < \text{MA}_{40}(n\text{-}1))$ AND $(\text{MA}_9(n) > \text{MA}_{40}(n))$.

$\text{MASell}(n) = 1$ if $(\text{MA}_9(n\text{-}1) > \text{MA}_{40}(n\text{-}1))$ AND $(\text{MA}_9(n) < \text{MA}_{40}(n))$.

Moving Average Convergence/Divergence (MACD)

The MACD is one of the most popular indicators. Two lines are used in its calculation. The MACD line is the difference between two exponentially smoothed moving averages of closing prices and responds very quickly to trend movements. The signal line is the exponentially smoothed average of the MACD line and it responds more slowly to trend movements. To calculate the MACD we need to compute 12 and 26 period Exponential Moving Averages (EMA).

$$EMA_{12}(n) = \frac{2}{12+1}C(n) + (1 - \frac{2}{12+1})EMA_{12}(n-1)$$

$$EMA_{26}(n) = \frac{2}{26+1}C(n) + (1 - \frac{2}{26+1})EMA_{26}(n-1)$$

$$MACD(n) = EMA_{12}(n) - EMA_{26}(n)$$

$$EMA_{12}(1) = EMA_{26}(1) = C(1)$$

The Signal Line is given by the nine-day exponentially smoothed average of the MACD line.

$$SignalLine(n) = \frac{2}{9+1} MACD(n) + (1 - \frac{2}{9+1}) SignalLine(n-1) \quad SignalLine(1) = MACD(1)$$

Signals:

MACDBuy = 1 if (MACD(n-1) < SignalLine(n-1)) AND (MACD(n) > SignalLine(n))

MACDSell = 1 if (MACD(n-1) > SignalLine(n-1)) AND (MACD(n) < SignalLine(n))

The Stochastic (Slow Stochastic)

This is based on the observation that as prices go up, closing prices tend to be closer to the upper end of the price range and vice versa when trend goes down the closing price tends to be near the lower end of the range. The Stochastic consists of two lines: the %K line and the %D line.

$$\%K(n) = 100 * \frac{C(n) - L14(n)}{H14(n) - L14(n)}$$

where

L14(n) – the lowest low for the last 14 periods

L14(n) = min (Low(n), Low(n-1), ..., Low(n - 13))

H14(n) – the highest high for the same 14 periods

H14(n) = max (High(n), High(n - 1), ..., High(n - 13))

where Low and High are respective components of price bar in Figure 5.

%D is a three-period moving average of the %K

$$\%D(n) = \frac{1}{3} \sum_{i=0}^{2} \%K(n-i)$$

%Dslow is a three-period moving average of the %D

$$\%Dslow(n) = \frac{1}{3} \sum_{i=0}^{2} \%D(n-i)$$

Signals:

StochasticBuy(n) = 1 if (%D(n) < 20) AND (%Dslow(n) < 20) AND (%D(n - 1) < %Dslow(n - 1)) AND (%D(n) > %Dslow(n)).

StochasticSell(n) = 1 if (%D(n) > 80) AND (%Dslow(n) > 80) AND (%D(n - 1) > %Dslow(n - 1)) AND (%D(n) < %Dslow(n)).

Relative Strength Index (RSI)

This is considered to be a very powerful and popular indicator among traders. It is used to identify overbought and oversold market conditions.

$$RSI(n) = 100 - \frac{100}{1 + RS(n)}$$

$$RS(n) = \frac{\left[(Average\ Gain(n-1)) * 13 + Current\ Gain(n)\right] / 14}{\left[(Average\ Loss(n-1)) * 13 + Current\ Loss(n)\right] / 14}$$

where

Current Gain(n) = max (C(n) – C(n - 1), 0)

Current Gain(n) = max (C(n - 1) – C(n), 0)

$$Average\ Gain(n) = \frac{1}{14}\sum_{i=0}^{13} \max(C(n-i) - C(n-i-1), 0)$$

$$Average\ Loss(n) = \frac{1}{14}\sum_{i=0}^{13} \max(C(n-i-1) - C(n-i), 0)$$

Signals:

RSIBuy(n) = 1 if (RSI(n - 1) < 30) AND (RSI(n) > 30))

RSISell(n) = 1 if (RSI(n - 1) > 70) AND (RSI(n) < 70))

Commodity Channel Index (CCI)

This was designed to identify cyclical turns in exchange rates movements.

Most traders use CCI as an overbought/oversold oscillator. CCI is based upon the comparison the current price with a moving average over a selected time frame.

$$TypicalPrice(n) = \frac{C(n) + High(n) + Low(n)}{3}$$

$$SMATP(n) = \frac{1}{20}\sum_{i=0}^{19} TypicalPrice(n-i)$$

$$MeanDeviation(n) = \frac{\sum_{i=0}^{19} abs(SMATP(n) - TypicalPrice(n-i))}{20}$$

$$CCI(n) = \frac{TypicalPrice(n) - SMATP(n)}{0.015 * MeanDeviation(n)}$$

Signals:

CCIBuy(n) = 1 if (CCI(n - 1) < 100) AND (CCI(n) > 100))

CCISell(n) = 1 if (CCI(n - 1) > -100) AND (CCI (n) < -100))

Momentum Oscillator

Momentum measures velocity of price changes as opposed to the actual price level.

$$Momentum(n) = C(n) - C(n-10)$$

Signals:

MomentumBuy(n) = 1 if (Momentum(n - 1) < 0) AND (Momentum(n) > 0)

MomentumSell(n) = 1 if (Momentum(n - 1) > 0) AND (Momentum(n) < 0)

Price Oscillator

This is based upon the difference between two moving averages. The moving averages can be exponential, weighted or simple. Here, we consider the exponential moving average. Averages are calculated based on closing prices.

$$PO(n) = \frac{EMA_{10}(n) - EMA_{20}(n)}{EMA_{20}(n)}$$

where EMA_k is calculated using the same principle as for MACD calculation.

Signals:

POBuy(n) = 1 if (PO(n - 1) < 0) AND (PO(n) > 0)

POSell(n) = 1 if (PO(n - 1) > 0) AND (PO(n) < 0)

Larry Williams

This is an indicator that works similarly to the Stochastic Indicator and is especially popular for identifying overbought and oversold markets.

$$LW(n) = -100 * \frac{H14(n) - C(n)}{H14(n) - L14(n)}$$

L14(n) = min (Low(n), Low(n - 1), ..., Low(n - 13)

H14(n) = max (High(n), High(n - 1), ..., High(n - 13)).

Signals:

LWBuy(n) = 1 if (LW(n - 1) < -80) AND (LW(n) > -80)

LWSell(n) = 1 if (LW(n - 1) > -20) AND (LW(n) < -20)

Bollinger Bands

This is based on two trading bands placed around a moving average. Upper and lower bands are three standard deviations above and below the moving average.

$$UpperBand(n) = Average\Pr ice(n) + 3 * StDev(n)$$

$$LowerBand(n) = Average\Pr ice(n) - 3 * StDev(n)$$

$$AveragePrice(n) = \frac{1}{20} \sum_{i=0}^{19} C(n-i)$$

$$StDev(n) = \sqrt{\frac{\sum_{i=0}^{19} \left(C(n-i) - AveragePrice(20)\right)^2}{20}}$$

BBandBuy(n) = 1 if (C(n - 1) < LowerBand(n - 1)) AND (C(n) > LowerBand(n))

BBandSell(n) = 1 if (C(n - 1) > UpperBand(n - 1)) AND (C(n) < UpperLowerBand(n))

On Balance Volume

OBV can be used either to confirm the price trend or notify about a price trend reversal.

$$OBV(n) = OBV(n-1) + \frac{C(n) - C(n-1)}{abs(C(n) - C(n-1))} * V(n)$$

where V(n) is #Ticks component of the price bar in Figure 5.

The direction of OBV is more important than the amplitude. The OBV line should follow in the same direction as the price trend otherwise there is a notification about a possible reversal.

OBVBuy(n) = 1 if (OBV(n - 3) > OBV(n - 2)) AND (OBV(n - 2) < OBV(n - 1)) AND (OBV(n - 1) < OBV(n)) AND (C(n - 3) > C(n - 2)) AND (C(n - 2) > C(n - 1)) AND (C(n - 1) > C(n))

OBVSell(n) = 1 if (OBV(n - 3) < OBV(n - 2)) AND (OBV(n - 2) > OBV(n - 1)) AND (OBV(n - 1) > OBV(n)) AND (C(n - 3) < C(n - 2)) AND (C(n - 2) < C(n - 1)) AND (C(n - 1) < C(n))

Appendix 2: Illustration of Q-Learning

In Figure 7 we consider a real but simplified situation where a trader has two indicators for a financial market and has to make a decision based on the indicator signals. In this simplified situation, we assume that each indicator can advise either to buy or sell only. That is, we ignore the possibility of indicators advising that a neutral position be adopted. Since we have two indicators that can have two values each, we have in total four states of the environment. In any state of the environment a trader can make two decisions - either to buy a security or to sell it. Thus, writing the set of actions available in state i as A(state i), we have A(state i) = {buy, sell}for i = 1,2,3,4. After taking an action the trader makes a transition from one state of the environment to another according to a set of probabilities determined by the market situation.

The state of the environment is determined by the values of the indicators and, whatever the state, the trader must decide whether to buy or sell. To understand the meaning of Figure 7, consider the arrow at the upper-left of the figure. The rectangle attached to this arrow contains the following: "Sell, R.S. = 20, Pr = 12%." What this means is that this particular transition from state 1 to state 2 will take place if the trader, in state 1, decides to sell and that this decision will result in a transition to state 2 with a 12% probability, upon which the trader will receive a reinforcement signal of 20. Note that the decision to sell while in state 1 could also result in a transition to state 4, with probability 88%. Note also that the probabilities of these two transitions add to 100%, indicating that there is zero probability of a decision to sell when in state 1 causing a transition to state 3.

The values of the reinforcement signals and the transition probabilities in Figure 7 have been chosen arbitrarily for the purposes of this illustration. In practice, these values would change due to the non-static nature of the market, but we keep them fixed here so that the key features of Q-learning can be clearly understood. If we did not do this, the origin of some of the numbers in the example would become unclear unless we included frequent updates to Figure 7.

Suppose that the initial values of $Q_0(s, a) = 0$ for all s, a, discount rate $\gamma = 0.85$ and learning rate $\alpha = 0.15$. Also assume that the following sequence has taken place: (state 1, sell) → (state 3, buy) → (state 2, sell) → (state 3, sell) → (state 4, buy) → (state 3, buy)→ (state 2, buy) → (state 1, buy) → (state 2, sell) → (state 3, ...) → ... For this state-action sequence, equation (1) gives the following sequence of Q-value updates:

1) (state 1, sell, 20, state 3)

$$Q_1(state\,1,\ sell) = Q_0(state\,1,\ sell) + 0.15\left[20 + 0.85 \max_a Q_0(state\,3,\ a) - Q_0(state\,1,\ sell)\right] =$$
$$0 + 0.15[20 + 0.85 \max\{0,0\} - 0] = 0 + 0.15 * 20 = 3$$

2) (state 3, buy, 70, state 2)

$$Q_2(state\,3,\ buy) = Q_1(state\,3,\ buy) + 0.15\left[70 + 0.85 \max_a Q_1(state\,2,\ a) - Q_1(state\,3,\ buy)\right] =$$
$$0 + 0.15[70 + 0.85 \max\{0,0\} - 0] = 0 + 0.15 * 70 = 10.5$$

3) (state 2, sell, -30, state 3)

$$Q_3(state\,2,\ sell) = Q_2(state\,2,\ sell) + 0.15\left[-30 + 0.85 \max_a Q_2(state\,3,\ a) - Q_2(state\,2,\ buy)\right] =$$
$$0 + 0.15[-30 + 0.85 \max\{10.5,0\} - 0] = 0 + 0.15 * (-30 + 0.85 * 10.5) = -3.16$$

4) (state 3, sell, 10, state 4)

$$Q_4(state\,3,\ sell) = Q_3(state\,3,\ sell) + 0.15\left[10 + 0.85 \max_a Q_3(state\,4,\ a) - Q_3(state\,3,\ sell)\right] =$$
$$0 + 0.15[10 + 0.85 \max\{0,0\} - 0] = 0 + 0.15 * 10 = 1.5$$

So after the first four steps of the state-action sequence the Q-table looks like:

Table 4. Q-learning table after 4 steps

$Q_4(s, a)$	Buy	Sell
state 1	3	0
state 2	0	-3.16
state 3	10.5	1.5
state 4	0	0

Figure 7. Example of Q-Learning

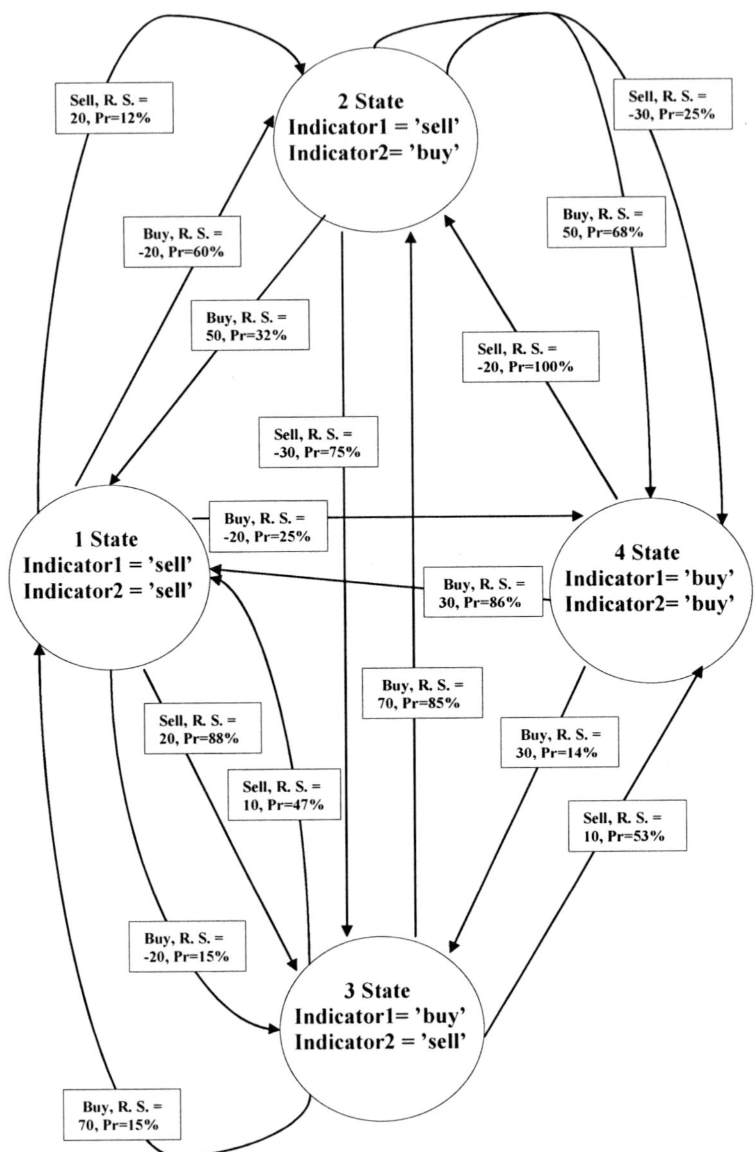

Now consider the remaining values in the sequence:

(state 4, buy) → (state 3, buy) → (state 2, buy) → (state 1, buy) → (state 2, sell) → (state 3, ...) → ...

5) (state 4, buy, 30, state 3)

$$Q_5(state4,\ buy) = Q_4(state3,\ buy) + 0.15\left[30 + 0.85\max_a Q_4(state3,\ a) - Q_4(state4,\ buy)\right] =$$
$$0 + 0.15[30 + 0.85\max\{10.5, 1.5\} - 0] = 0 + 0.15*(30 + 0.85*10.5) = 5.84$$

6) (state 3, buy, 70, state 2)

$$Q_6(state3,\ buy) = Q_5(state3,\ buy) + 0.15\left[70 + 0.85\max_a Q_5(state2,\ a) - Q_5(state3,\ buy)\right] =$$
$$10.5 + 0.15[70 + 0.85\max\{0, -3.16\} - 10.5] = 10.5 + 0.15(70 + 0.85*0 - 10.5) = 19.43$$

7) (state 2, buy, 50, state 1)

$$Q_7(state2,\ buy) = Q_6(state2,\ buy) + 0.15\left[50 + 0.85\max_a Q_6(state1,\ a) - Q_6(state2,\ buy)\right] =$$
$$0 + 0.15[50 + 0.85\max\{3, 0\} - 0] = 0 + 0.15*(50 + 0.85*3) = 7.88$$

8) (state 1, buy, -20, state 2)

$$Q_8(state1,\ buy) = Q_7(state1,\ buy) + 0.15\left[-20 + 0.85\max_a Q_7(state2,\ a) - Q_7(state1,\ buy)\right] =$$
$$3 + 0.15[-20 + 0.85\max\{7.88, -3.16\} - 3] = 3 + 0.15*(-20 + 0.85*7.88 - 3) = 0.55$$

9) (state 2, sell, -30, state 3)

$$Q_9(state2,\ sell) = Q_8(state2,\ sell) + 0.15\left[-30 + 0.85\max_a Q_8(state3,\ a) - Q_8(state2,\ sell)\right] =$$
$$-3.16 + 0.15[-30 + 0.85\max\{19.43, 1.5\} - (-3.16)] = -3.16 + 0.15*(-30 + 0.85*19.43 + 3.16)$$
$$= -4.71$$

After nine steps of the state-action sequence the Q-table looks like

Table 5. Q-learning table after 9 steps

$Q_9(s, a)$	Buy	Sell
state 1	0.55	0
state 2	7.88	-4.71
state 3	19.43	1.5
state 4	5.84	0

And the optimal policy after nine steps is given by equation

$$\pi^*(s) = \arg\max_a Q_9(s, a).$$

Thus, at every state of the environment the trader will be able to determine the appropriate action. It can be shown (Watkins & Dayan, 1992) that the Q-table converges with probability 1 to the optimal set of Q-values.

Chapter XXI

Online Methods for Portfolio Selection

Tatsiana Levina, Queen's University, Canada

Abstract

This chapter overviews recent online portfolio selection strategies for financial markets. These investment strategies achieve asymptotically the same exponential rate of growth as the portfolio that turns out to be best ex post *in the long run and do not require any underlying statistical assumptions on the nature of the stock market. The experimental results, which compare the performance of these strategies with respect to a standard sequence of historical data, demonstrate a high future potential of online portfolio selection algorithms.*

Introduction

The purpose of this chapter is to overview some recent online portfolio selection sequential investment strategies for financial markets. A strategy must choose a portfolio of stocks to hold in each trading period, using information collected from the past history of the market. We consider the case when a portfolio selection strategy achieves asymptotically the same exponential rate of growth as the portfolio that turns out to be best *ex post* in the long run.

One of the most common approaches to adaptive investment strategies is probably the distributional method proposed by Kelly in his work on horse race markets (Kelly, 1956). In mathematical finance literature the resulting portfolio is often called the growth optimal portfolio (Iyengar, 2005; Platen, in press). This approach assumes the existence of an underlying probability distribution of the price relatives and uses Bayes' decision theory to specify the next portfolio. Under different conditions it was established that it is possible to specify a sequence of investment strategies which is growth optimal for ergodic and stationary markets with general assets return (Algoet & Cover, 1988). However, in all these settings the optimal portfolio *depends* on the underlying distribution of the price relatives, which is usually unknown in practice.

In this chapter, we consider portfolio selection strategies that *do **not** depend* upon underlying statistical assumptions (not even a probability distribution) and still achieve asymptotically the same exponential rate of growth as the portfolio that turns out to be best *ex post*. Such an investment strategy was named a universal portfolio since the convergence of the growth rate to the best *ex-post* rate is not done in a stochastic sense but rather uniformly over all strategies that could possibly be optimal for a given market. It was originally discovered in Cover (1991), Vovk (1990), and Helmbold, Schapire, Singer, and Warmuth (1998), and later studied and applied in Cover and Ordentlich (1996), Borodin and El-Yaniv (1998), Vovk and Watkins (1998), Cross and Barron (2003), and others.

Financial institutions use a number of portfolio selection strategies, which, in general, can be classified as passive investing and active investing. Passive investing is based on the idea of market efficiency. A passive investor captures the market rate of return by investing in a well diversified portfolio selected to match the performance of a standard security market index. Passive investors rely on their belief that in the long term the investment will be profitable. These strategies are usually called *buy-and-hold* (BAH). The best *ex post* (also called *optimal off-line*) BAH strategy performs as well as the best security in the market.

Active investing is an attempt to beat the overall returns of the security market by buying and selling securities more frequently. This can be achieved through the purchase of individual securities or actively-managed mutual funds. The active investing approach assumes that there are inefficiencies in the market pricing of securities that can be exploited by knowledgeable investors.

A typical active strategy that is considered in this chapter and is often used in practice is the *constant rebalanced portfolio* (CRP). This strategy fixes a distribution of capital over securities and uses it for every period. Therefore, it may be necessary to buy and sell a security between periods in order to keep the proportion of one's capital in each security constant. For example, suppose we have two securities and the $CRP_{(0.5, 0.5)}$ keeps the same amount of money in both of them in every trading period. Assume that the first security is risk-free, that is, the price of it never changes, and the second security is highly volatile. The price of the second security alternatively doubles and halves on even and odd days respectively. When the second security doubles, the $CRP_{(0.5, 0.5)}$ relative return grows by $\frac{1}{2}+\frac{1}{2}\times 2=\frac{3}{2}$ since half of its money is in this security. When the second security halves, the $CRP_{(0.5,\ 0.5)}$ relative wealth decreases by $\frac{1}{2}+\frac{1}{2}\times\frac{1}{2}=\frac{3}{4}$. Therefore, after two consecutive trading periods the $CRP_{(0.5,\ 0.5)}$ value increases by a factor of $\frac{3}{2}\times\frac{3}{4}=\frac{9}{8}$. At this exponential growth rate the relative wealth will be doubled after 12 trading periods (Cover, 1991; Helmbold et al., 1998; Kalai, 2001). Yet, when the market is changing, the CRP does not always perform very well as we may observe on the following example. Suppose we have two highly volatile securities. The value of the first security increases during the first n trading periods by a factor of 1.5, then it decreases by a factor of 0.25 on each of the subsequent n trading periods. The second security behaves vice versa. The relative price changes of these securities may be described as the following market sequence:

$$\begin{pmatrix} 1.5 \\ 0.25 \end{pmatrix}, \begin{pmatrix} 1.5 \\ 0.25 \end{pmatrix}, \ldots, \begin{pmatrix} 1.5 \\ 0.25 \end{pmatrix}, \begin{pmatrix} 0.25 \\ 1.5 \end{pmatrix}, \begin{pmatrix} 0.25 \\ 1.5 \end{pmatrix}, \ldots, \begin{pmatrix} 0.25 \\ 1.5 \end{pmatrix}.$$

Obviously, the value of the $CRP_{(0.5,\ 0.5)}$ will be dropping exponentially faster, resulting in loss of almost all of the initial investment. However, the CRP that puts everything in the first security for n periods and then invests everything in the second security will make money exponentially (Borodin, El-Yaniv, & Gogan, 2000). Therefore, the best off-line CRP (BCRP), that has an advantage of "seeing" all market moves, will *always* have an exponential return. Note that the performance of the BCRP is always at least as good as that of the best off-line BAH, since BCRP takes an advantage of market fluctuations.

There are many papers concerning online portfolio selection. Cover's work on universal portfolios (UNIV) is often referred to as the pioneer work in this area (Cover, 1991). Cover defines UNIV as the weighted average of all constant rebalanced portfolios, with bigger weights placed on portfolios with larger returns.

Cover and Ordentlich (1996) introduced a UNIV algorithm that has a way of determining a portfolio based on a signal. The signal might include information from inside the investment game (the number of trading periods, the performance of stocks or other advisers, etc.), or from outside the investment game (analysts' reports, economics, statistics, financial reports, etc.). This information may help an investor to identify which stocks are more likely to perform better. However, the significance of this information must be learned by an investor, since he or she only has a sequential knowledge of the stock vector.

Cover's, and Cover and Ordentlich's UNIV strategies are special cases of Vovk's aggregating algorithm (proven in Levina, 2004), which was developed to address the more general problem of combining expert advice (Bousquet & Warmuth, 2002; Cesa-Bienachi, Freund, Haussler, Helmbold, Schapire, & Warmuth, 1997; Herbster & Warmuth, 1998; Littlestone & Warmuth, 1994; Vovk, 1990, 1999). The aggregating algorithm universalizes by averaging, but in general it does not necessarily directly average the moves of the experts. Instead it may combine these moves in such a way that an exponential transform of the gains is averaged. Vovk has formulated conditions under which this produces a winning strategy for the decision maker. An investor wants to switch from one strategy to another from time to time. One of Vovk's most important contributions was to point out that switching can be handled within the aggregating algorithm. Instead of aggregating elementary experts, more complicated experts can be aggregated, each of whom has a different rule for switching. Moreover, it may be unnecessary to construct the more complicated experts explicitly. Instead, we can construct a stochastic rule for switching and then take the expected value. The result can be interpreted as an application of the aggregating algorithm to an underlying pool of deterministic experts, each of whom behaves following a particular realization of the stochastic rule. The strategy produced by the aggregation is also deterministic — it is called the derandomization of the stochastic rule.

Levina explains the aggregating algorithm in the general context of online portfolio selection problem (Levina, 2004). She also shows how the aggregating algorithm is applied to switching strategies for portfolio selection problem and presents a new Gaussian random walk (GRW) strategy, which uses the aggregating algorithm to rebalance a portfolio.

Vovk and Watkins (1998) applied aggregating algorithm to the modification of Cover's UNIV strategy where investors can take short-selling positions. They also generalize Cover's universal portfolio to the case when one of the parameters of the aggregating algorithm, learning rate η, is different from *1* (originally, Cover's universal portfolio coincides with the aggregating algorithm with learning rate $\eta = 1$).

Unfortunately, the strategies presented above cannot be easily computed when more than a few stocks are considered. In a straightforward implementation a multiple dimensional integration is involved, and the computational time grows exponentially in the number of stocks. Blum and Kalai proposed a randomized implementation based on the uniform random sampling of the portfolio simplex for Cover's UNIV strategy (Blum & Kalai, 1998). However, in the worst case, to have a high probability of performing almost as well as UNIV, they require an exponential number of samples. Kalai and Vempala proposed an implementation based on non-uniform random sampling which can be achieved by random walks on the simplex of portfolios (Kalai & Vempala, 2003). They showed that by sampling portfolios from a non-uniform distribution, only a polynomial number of samples is required to have a high probability of performing nearly as well as UNIV strategy.

Helmbold et al. (1998) have developed the exponential gradient algorithm ($EG(\eta)$), which achieves the same wealth as the best CRP determined in hindsight but uses a different approach. It adaptively computes a weighted average of portfolios by gradually increasing the relative weights of the more successful portfolios using a multiplicative update rule. Although the competitive bound proven by Helmbold et al. for ($EG(\eta)$) strategy is weaker then the bound for UNIV strategy, it is easier to implement and the computational time is linear in the number of stocks. Other surveys of online investment strategies include Borodin and El-Yaniv (1998) and El-Yaniv (1998).

The research that focused on developing portfolio selection strategies with asymptotic exponential growth rate and with no underlying statistical assumptions on the nature of the stock market is relatively new (about 15 years), and it remains an active area of research nowadays (Akcoglu, Drineas, & Kao, 2004; Borodin, El-Yaniv, & Gogan, 2000;

Borodin, El-Yaniv, & Gogan, 2004; Cross & Barron, 2003; Levina, 2004). However, due to space limitations, in this chapter we focus only on a subset of the work done in this area. Specifically, we introduce strategies proposed by Cover (1991), Cover and Ordentlich (1996), Helmbold et al. (1998), and the aggregating algorithm in the context of portfolio selection (Levina, 2004).

It is important to note that the portfolio selection problem described here ignores several factors (such as transaction costs, short selling, bid-ask spreads and risk tolerance) which are important in the corresponding real-life problem. We briefly consider the transaction costs in the experimental section of this chapter, but only under the simplified assumption of proportional transaction costs, that is, the investor pays a fraction of the transaction amount to a broker. We also assume that securities units and money are arbitrarily divisible.

It is worth mentioning that practitioners have already started to employ online portfolio selection strategies. The investment firm that utilizes the universal portfolio strategy, *Mountain View Analytics*, was founded a few years ago. Another investment company, *Archetype Risk Advisors* (ARA), started a joint venture partnership with T. Cover in 2004. The ARA Hedged universal portfolio strategy utilizes Cover's algorithm to design and trade a long U.S. cash equity portfolio.

The rest of the chapter is organized as follows. In the next section, we describe the interaction between an investor and the market in which he or she invests as a two-person, perfect-information game. We also consider a more complicated game that includes additional players, who advise the investor. The third section describes the aggregating algorithm in the portfolio selection context. We discuss different online portfolio selection strategies in the fourth section. Finally we look at the numerical results that demonstrate the performance of the strategies considered in the previous section on several standard test problems in the literature.

Investment Protocols

As we explain in this section, the interaction between an investor and the market in which he or she invests can be thought of as a two-person, perfect-information game. We call the two players Investor and Market. Investor decides how to invest at the beginning of each period, and then Market decides how prices change from the beginning of the period to the end. In reality, Market is composed of many players, but when we take the viewpoint of an individual investor and ignore the microstructure of the market, only Market's collective determination of prices matters, and so Market can be regarded as a single player. The fact that the many players who comprise Market cannot really coordinate their actions in playing against Investor is ignored in this formulation, but this is acceptable, because we are interested in worst-case results for Investor. In other words, we are interested in goals that Investor can achieve no matter what Market does.

After introducing notation and formulating a protocol for a game between Investor and Market, we also formulate a more complicated protocol for a game that includes additional players, who advise Investor. In this game, Investor's goal is to outperform all of his advisers: his capital should grow as fast, asymptotically, as it would if he obeyed the adviser whose advice turned out, after the fact, to be the best. Again, we are asking for a worst-case result: Investor should asymptotically match the *best* adviser no matter what Market does or what the advisers say.

The game involving Investor, Market, and a Pool of Advisers might be used to model situations where an investor really does consider the advice of various analysts. But as we have already explained, we are most interested in using it in a more formal way; we assign different strategies, which may use different types of exogenous information, to the different advisers, so that the Investor's goal becomes that of aggregating all the information and asymptotically outperforming all the strategies.

Notation

We write **b** for a *portfolio*—a vector that specifies the proportion of capital that Investor puts into each security during a particular period. If there are m securities, then $\mathbf{b} = (b_1, \ldots, b_m)$, where b_j is the proportion of capital invested in the jth security. The b_j are nonnegative and add to one. We set

$$B := \{\mathbf{b} \in R^m \mid b_j \geq 0, j = 1, \ldots, m, \text{ and } \sum_{j=1}^{m} b_j = 1\}. \quad (1)$$

Let $\mathbf{x}$ be a vector of *price multipliers* for the securities—factors by which they change in price from the beginning to the end of a particular period: $\mathbf{x} = (x_1, \ldots, x_m)$. If v_j is the price of the jth security at the beginning of the period, then $x_j v_j$ is its price at the end of the period. Because securities' prices cannot become negative, the x_j are nonnegative. We set

$$X := \{\mathbf{x} \in R^m \mid x_j \geq 0, \ j = 1, \ldots, m\}.$$

If Investor holds his capital in the portfolio **b** during a period, and **x** is the vector of price multipliers for the period, then his capital is multiplied by

$$\mathbf{b} \cdot \mathbf{x} := \sum_{j=1}^{m} b_j x_j.$$

We need some measure to assess the performance of online algorithms considered in this chapter. For evaluating an online algorithm researches commonly use a competitive ratio, which indicate the worst case performance of the algorithm over all possible sequences of inputs. This approach was first introduced by Sleator and Tarjan (1985), who used it to analyze the List Update Problem. The competitive ratio is the ratio of the cost of an online algorithm to the cost of the optimal off-line algorithm, which has a complete knowledge of the sequence of security prices in advance.

Universalization of an online portfolio algorithm (first introduced by Cover, 1991) may be considered as another evaluation parameter. An online portfolio selection algorithm is *universal*, in the sense that it will achieve asymptotically the same exponential rate of growth as the single constant rebalanced portfolio that turns out to be best *ex post* (Cover, 1991; Cover & Ordentlich, 1996).

The Basic Protocol

Suppose Investor is in the market for T periods. Write $\mathbf{b}^t$ for his portfolio during the tth period, and write $\mathbf{x}^t$ for the price multipliers during this period. Write I^0 for Investor's initial capital, I^t for his absolute wealth and $\Im^t$ for his logarithmic wealth at the end of tth period ($\Im^t = \ln(I^t)$). If we assume that Investor starts with unit capital, so that $\Im^t = 0$, then we obtain the following protocol for the game he is playing:

Players: Investor, Market

Protocol:

$\Im^t = 0$

FOR : $t = 1, 2, \ldots, T$;

Investor chooses $\mathbf{b}^t$ from B.

Market chooses $\mathbf{x}^t$ from X.

$\Im^t = \Im^{t-1} + \ln(\mathbf{b}^t \cdot \mathbf{x}^t)$

This protocol allows Market's move $\mathbf{x}^t$ to be a vector of zeros (all the securities in the market become worthless), so that $\ln(\mathbf{b}^t \cdot \mathbf{x}^t) = -\infty$. Market can also make $\ln(\mathbf{b}^t \cdot \mathbf{x}^t)$ arbitrarily large and positive. If we were to specify a goal for the players — if, for example, we said that Investor is trying to reach a particular level of capital at the end of the game — then this would define a perfect-information, two-player game.

Investor's absolute wealth I^t and logarithmic wealth $\Im^t$ can also be described non-recursively:

$$I^t = \prod_{s=1}^{t} \mathbf{b}^s \cdot \mathbf{x}^s \text{and } \Im^t = \ln(I^t) = \sum_{s=1}^{t} \ln(\mathbf{b}^s \cdot \mathbf{x}^s). \qquad \textbf{(2)}$$

Investment with Advice

One way to specify a goal for Investor is to introduce other investors into the game and to compare Investor's performance to theirs. Alternatively, we can imagine other players who merely make recommendations, and we can compare Investor's performance with how well he would have done following their recommendation.

Let us suppose that Investor has a whole set Θ of advisers, each of whom recommends a portfolio at the beginning of each period. For each $\theta \in \Theta$, we write $\pi^t(\theta)$ for the portfolio recommended by adviser θ in the tth period. Thus, the advisers' moves in the tth period together amount to a mapping π^t from Θ to B. The set Θ may be infinite, and in this case we assume that it is endowed with an σ-algebra F, and we assume that the mapping π^t is measurable. If we write A^t for adviser θ's capital at time t, and A^t for its logarithm, then our protocol takes the form:

Players: Pool of Advisers, Investor, Market
Parameters: (Θ, F)
Protocol:

$A_\theta^0 = 0$ for all $\theta \in \Theta$.

$\mathfrak{I}^0 = 0$.

FOR $t = 1, 2, \ldots, T$:

Pool of Advisers chooses a measurable mapping π^t from Θ to B.

Investor chooses $\mathbf{b}^t$ from B.

Market chooses $\mathbf{x}^t$ from X.

$A_\theta^t = A_\theta^{t-1} + \ln(\pi^t(\theta) \cdot \mathbf{x}^t)$.

$\mathfrak{I}^t = \mathfrak{I}^{t-1} + \ln(\mathbf{b}^t \cdot \mathbf{x}^t)$.

One goal for Investor is that he should do as well, asymptotically, as the most successful of his advisers. As we will see, he can often achieve a version of this goal: in many cases, he can achieve the same asymptotic growth rate for the logarithmic wealth as the most successful of the advisers.

Each adviser's absolute and logarithmic capital can be described cumulatively, just as Investor's capital is described cumulatively by Equation (2):

$$\mathrm{A}_\theta^t = \prod_{s=1}^{t} \pi^s(\theta) \cdot \mathbf{x}^s \text{ and } A_\theta^t = \ln(\mathrm{A}_\theta^t) = \sum_{s=1}^{t} \ln(\pi^s(\theta) \cdot \mathbf{x}^s). \tag{3}$$

As explained earlier, we are mostly interested in the case where each θ represents a strategy — a rule for choosing the move $\pi^t(\theta)$, perhaps as a function of previous moves in the game and other information. The condition that the mapping $\pi^t : \Theta \to B$ is measurable may seem a bit odd in general, since it suggests that the advisers in Θ coordinate their moves to satisfy an intricate mathematical condition. However, this condition is needed to treat $\pi^t : \Theta \to B$ as a random variable. In the next section we define the probability measures on Θ, and then compute the probabilities of the sets of portfolios with respect to these measures. Measurability says that, for any "range" of portfolios, the advisors with recommendations in this range belong to a set which can be assigned a probability. This condition is obviously satisfied when Θ is finite (as in the case where it represents a set of actual advisers). When Θ represents a set of strategies, it is natural to assume that $\pi^t(\theta)$ is measurable both as a function of θ and as a function of the information the strategy uses. Note: we are not making any assumptions about the strategies or the advisers, except the measurability.

Next we present the aggregating algorithm in the portfolio selection context.

The Aggregating Algorithm

In this section, we explain the aggregating algorithm, which simply averages the recommendations of the advisers with respect to some probability distribution. Although theoretically we might apply it to actual advisers, it is more practical to apply it to explicit strategies. In the second half of this section we briefly explain (and give several examples) how Vovk's aggregating algorithm can be applied to a set of strategies for switching, from one trading period to another, between one-period strategies.

Vovk's aggregating algorithm determines a strategy for Investor in the investment game with advice. From an intuitive point of view, this strategy is very simple. Investor basically distributes his capital at the beginning of the game to his different advisers to manage. Then he takes no further action until the end of the game. As we have already indicated, this simple strategy has the remarkable property that under certain conditions it enables Investor to achieve an asymptotic exponential rate of capital growth as good as that of the most successful of the advisers.

Vovk's general theory involves a learning rate η $(0 < \eta < \infty)$ and an additive loss L. His aggregating algorithm aims for a strategy for which $e^{-\eta L}$ is the average of its value for the strategies being aggregated. To apply the theory to portfolio selection, one identifies the loss L with $-\ln H$, where H is the factor by which one's capital is multiplied. Thus, one is averaging $e^{-\eta \ln H} = H^{\eta}$. In this chapter we, just like most work in portfolio selection, take $\eta = 1$(Cover, 1991; Cover & Ordentlich, 1996; Levina, 2004), so that one is merely averaging H.

Aggregating Investment Strategies by Averaging

Investor's Performance

The way Investor initially distributes his capital among his different advisers defines a probability distribution P on the distribution space (Θ, F). Because he leaves the capital and the return earned by each adviser with that adviser for all T periods his performance at the end of period t, where, $t \leq T$ will be the average, with respect to this probability distribution, of the performance of the different advisers:

$$I^t = \int_\Theta \mathrm{A}_\theta^t P(d\theta). \tag{4}$$

(The fraction $P(d\theta)$ of Investor's capital is invested following θ's advice and therefore becomes $\mathrm{A}_\theta^t P(d\theta)$ at the end of period t. Investor's total capital is obtained by adding up $\mathrm{A}_\theta^t P(d\theta)$ over all advisers).

Investor's Move

What is $\mathbf{b}^t$, Investor's move in the tth period, when he follows the aggregating algorithm with a particular probability distribution P?

In order to answer this question correctly, we have to keep in mind that the *fraction* of Investor's capital managed by the different advisers changes as the game is played even though Investor does not move capital from one adviser to another. At the beginning of the game, Investor has unit capital, and the advisers within a neighborhood $d\theta$ of a particular adviser θ are managing the fraction $P(d\theta)$ of it, but after the first $t-1$ periods, this capital $P(d\theta)$ has grown to $\mathrm{A}_\theta^{t-1} P(d\theta)$, which is now the fraction

$$\frac{\mathrm{A}_\theta^{t-1} P(d\theta)}{\int_\Theta \mathrm{A}_\theta^{t-1} P(d\theta)} \tag{5}$$

of Investor's total capital. At the beginning of period t, the advisers near θ distribute their portion over the m securities according to the vector $\pi^t(\theta)$, and so Investor's capital as a whole is distributed over the m securities according to the vector

$$\mathbf{b}^t := \frac{\int_\Theta \pi^t(\theta) A_\theta^{t-1} P(d\theta)}{\int_\Theta A_\theta^{t-1} P(d\theta)}. \tag{6}$$

A strategy for a player in a game is a rule that specifies each of his moves as a function of available information, including the earlier moves of the other players. Equation (6) gives a strategy for Investor in this sense, because $\pi^t(\theta)$ is θ's move in the current period, and A_θ^{t-1} is determined by θ's and Market's moves in earlier periods (see Equation (3)).

Updating the Probability Distribution

Consider the sequence $P^0, P^1, \ldots, P^T$ of probability measures defined by setting P^0 equal to P and defining P^t, for $t = 1, \ldots, T$ by

$$P^t(E) := \frac{\int_E A_\theta^t P(d\theta)}{\int_\Theta A_\theta^t P(d\theta)}. \tag{7}$$

We can put Equation (7) into words by saying that P^t is absolutely continuous with respect to P and that its density with respect to P is $C_t A_\theta^t$, where the constant C_t is chosen to make $P^t(\Theta) = 1$.

In order to have $P^t(\Theta) = 1$ we must, of course, have $C_t = (\int_\Theta A_\theta^t P(d\theta))^{-1}$. We will follow the convention according to which this is expressed by writing

$$P^t(d\theta) \propto A_\theta^t P(d\theta), \tag{8}$$

or, alternatively,

$$P^t(d\theta) := \frac{A_\theta^t P(d\theta)}{\int_\Theta A_\theta^t P(d\theta)}. \tag{9}$$

Since $A^t_\theta = (\pi^t(\theta) \cdot \mathbf{x}^t) A^{t-1}_\theta$, we see that

$$P^t(d\theta) \propto (\pi^t(\theta) \cdot \mathbf{x}^t) P^{t-1}(d\theta), \tag{10}$$

or

$$P^t(d\theta) = \frac{(\pi^t(\theta) \cdot \mathbf{x}^t) P^{t-1}(d\theta)}{\int_\Theta (\pi^t(\theta) \cdot \mathbf{x}^t) P^{t-1}(d\theta)}. \tag{11}$$

This shows that the sequence $P^1, \ldots, P^T$ can be defined recursively. Comparing Equations (6) and (9), we see that:

$$\mathbf{b}^t = \int_\Theta \pi^t(\theta) P^{t-1}(d\theta). \tag{12}$$

This, together with the recursive relation (11), gives us a way of describing the aggregating algorithm:

1. Begin with a probability distribution on (Θ, F).
2. At the end of each period, update the probability distribution by multiplying θ's probability by the factor by which θ's capital has been multiplied during that period and then renormalizing so that the total probability is still one (Equation (11)).
3. At the beginning of each period, average over the advisers' recommendations using the current probability distribution (Equation (12)).

It is important to bear in mind that we have *not* introduced a probability distribution for the moves by Market (the $\mathbf{x}$'s). Nor have we introduced a probability distribution for the exogenous information (economic statistics, for example) that the adviser might use in deciding on their moves.

Universalization

As we have already emphasized, the aggregating algorithm is of interest because under certain conditions the capital it produces has an asymptotic rate of capital growth as good as that of the best, in hindsight, of the advisers being aggregated. We express this by saying that the strategy it produces is *universal* with respect to these advisers. It has been shown (Levina, 2004) that the aggregating algorithm is universal when there is a finite number of advisers, as well as when the space Θ of advisers is finite-dimensional.

Switching Strategies

Market conditions change constantly, so perhaps Investor should switch from one strategy to another from time to time. One of Vovk's most important contributions was to point out that switching can be handled within the aggregating algorithm (Vovk, 1999). Instead of aggregating elementary strategies (e.g., stocks), we can aggregate more complicated strategies each of whom has a different rule for switching. Moreover, it may be unnecessary to construct the more complicated strategies explicitly. Instead, we can construct a stochastic rule for switching — we call it *Stochastic Investor* — and then take the expected value. The result can be interpreted as an application of the aggregating algorithm to an underlying pool of deterministic strategies (or advisers), each of whom behaves following a particular realization of the stochastic rule. The strategy produced by the aggregation is also deterministic. It is called the derandomization of the stochastic rule.

The idea of a switching strategy does not take us outside the theory of the preceding section, which dealt with aggregating investment strategies by averaging them. A switching strategy is merely a way of constructing an investment strategy, and we can average such investment strategies just as we can average any other investment strategies. This was first explained by Vovk in 1999 (Vovk, 1999).

While the idea of a switching strategy does not introduce anything new from a purely abstract point of view, it does expand the scope of Vovk's aggregating algorithm from a practical point of view. For one thing, it leads to investment strategies that we might not have thought of otherwise. For another, it leads to efficiencies in representation and computation. These efficiencies arise for two reasons:

1. Specifying switching strategies can be an efficient way of specifying investment strategies. It is enough to explain when and how to switch. Vovk's aggregating algorithm tells us to average the investment strategies, but we can achieve this by averaging the switching strategies, and so we may not need to specify the investment strategies in a more explicit way.
2. A switching strategy boils down to a sequence of T one-period strategies which tell Investor how to invest in a single period. So specifying and manipulating the probability distribution P required by Vovk's aggregating algorithm boils down to specifying and manipulating a probability distribution for a sequence. We do not need to specify explicitly the probability for each possible sequence. Instead, we specify and work with initial and transition probabilities.

The following examples may help us to better understand the concept of stochastic switching strategies.

Example 1: In this example, the one-period strategies are stocks: $\Phi := \{1, ..., m\}$. Stochastic Investor has a way of choosing a stock at random from the m stocks. (Each stock has probability $1/m$ of being chosen.) He also has a biased coin, which comes up heads with probability α. He chooses at random a stock in which to invest for the first period. At the beginning of each period, he tosses the coin in order to decide whether to stick with the stock in which he invested in the preceding period or to invest in a stock chosen randomly from the other $m-1$.

Example 2: This example is like the preceding one, except that instead of beginning with a coin with a specified bias α, Stochastic Investor first determines the bias α by choosing it randomly from some specified probability distribution on (0,1). This determination is made once, at the beginning of the game.

Example 3: Stochastic Investor behaves as in the preceding example, except that instead of choosing α at random once, at the beginning of the game, he chooses α that depends on the holding time of stock i. The longer he holds stock i the smaller becomes the probability that Investor will invest in a different stock.

The switching strategy can depend not only on Market moves, but also on other information that becomes available in the course of the game. The information can be though of as a signal y from some signal space Y that can include information from inside the investment game (the number of trading periods, the performance of securities or other advisers, etc.), or from outside the investment game (analysts' reports, economics, statistics, financial reports, etc.).

For a complete analysis of the switching strategies and their application to the preceding examples refer to Levina (2004).

Online Portfolio Selection Strategies

In this section we briefly describe several portfolio selection strategies that achieve an asymptotic growth rate as good as the best ex-post strategy without any underlying statistical assumptions on the nature of the stock market. Specifically, we present

- the Gaussian random walk strategy (which was derived using the aggregating algorithm) by Levina (2004),
- the universal portfolio strategy by Cover (1991), Cover and Ordentlich (1996), and
- the $EG(\eta)$ strategy by Helmbold et al. (1998).

The Gaussian random walk and universal portfolio strategies are special cases of Vovk's aggregating algorithm that we described in the previous section. The $EG(\eta)$ strategy introduced by Helmbold et al. uses a slightly different approach.

Stochastic Switching Viewed as a Random Walk

The idea of a Markov stochastic switching strategy considered earlier forms the core of Levina's portfolio selection strategy (2004). Since a Markov switching strategy can be represented as a random walk in the simplex of portfolios, B, we propose a portfolio selection strategy that uses a Gaussian random walk in $\mathbb{R}^m$ and then projects it into the $(m-1)$ – dimensional simplex B using a simple transformation.

To be more precise, if N is the multivariate normal distribution with mean vector 0 and the identity covariance matrix on $\mathbb{R}^m$, then Stochastic Investor makes a Gaussian random walk with steps drawn from N. This means that he randomly chooses one by one a sequence $\tilde{h}^1,...,\tilde{h}^T$ of random vectors from N, each independent of the preceding ones. As he proceeds, he sets $\tilde{z}^0 = \tilde{h}^0$ and $\tilde{z}^t = \tilde{z}^{t-1} + \tilde{h}^t$ for $t = 1,..., T$. Thus, the random walk is defined as $\tilde{z}^0, \tilde{z}^1,...,\tilde{z}^T$. When the random walk is at $\tilde{z}^t$, Stochastic Investor chooses the portfolio $\lambda(\tilde{z}^t) \in B$, where the transformation $\lambda : \mathbb{R}^m \to B$ is defined by

$$\lambda(\tilde{z}_1,...,\tilde{z}_m) = \left(\frac{e^{z_1}}{e^{z_1}+...+e^{z_m}},...,\frac{e^{z_m}}{e^{z_1}+...+e^{z_m}}\right) \text{ for all } (z_1,...,z_m) \in \mathbb{R}^m.$$

Assuming that Investor starts with unit capital, we can represent the GRW strategy as the following protocol:

Strategy for Stochastic Investor

Start at the origin of $\mathbb{R}^m$; set $\mathbf{z}^0 = (0,0,...,0)$, $b^0 = L(\mathbf{z}^0) = \left(\frac{1}{m},\frac{1}{m},...,\frac{1}{m}\right)$.

At the beginning of each period, $t = 1,..., T$

Invest all one's capital in $\mathbf{b}^{t-1}$

Choose a random vector $\mathbf{w}^t$ from N

set $\mathbf{z}^t = \mathbf{z}^{t-1} + \mathbf{w}^t$,

set $\mathbf{b}^t = L(\mathbf{z}^t)$.

The explicit strategy can be written in terms of integrals which are not easy to evaluate, therefore it was implemented using the combination of the rejection sampling with the bootstrap-like resampling (Levina, 2004). The empirical performance of this strategy is explored in the last section.

Universal Portfolio

The basic idea of the aggregating algorithm has become fairly well known in a restrictive form studied by Cover. In the case first considered by Cover and published in 1991, each adviser always recommends the same portfolio. Since the adviser must rebalance to keep his portfolio constant, we say that Cover universalized the constant rebalanced portfolios.

In 1996 Cover and Ordentlich generalized Cover's initial work to the case where each of the strategies being averaged chooses a portfolio based on a signal (Cover & Ordentlich, 1996). If we write Y for the set of possible signals, then the adviser can be identified with a mapping $Y \to B$ that determines his recommended portfolio on the basis of the signal. Little can be done at this level of generality — if Y is too complex and there are too many advisers doing different things with the signal, then it may be difficult to define and implement an interesting distribution P, and we could have little hope of it achieving universalization. However, Cover and Ordentlich (1996) were able to demonstrate a universalization for the case when Y consists of a finite number of possible signals and the space Θ of advisers is finite dimensional.

Cover: Constant Rebalanced Portfolios

Cover's universal portfolio is the investment strategy obtained by applying Vovk's aggregating algorithm to the case where for each possible portfolio there is an adviser who always recommends that portfolio. More precisely, we assume that the advisers are in one-to-one correspondence with the portfolios. Formally, we identify Θ with the set B of portfolios:

$$\Theta := \{\theta \in R^m \mid \theta_j \geq 0, j = 1, \ldots, m, \text{ and } \sum_{j=1}^{m} \theta_j = 1\}.$$

And each adviser recommends the portfolio θ for each period: $\pi^t(\theta) := \theta$ for all t. Although adviser θ always recommends the portfolio θ, this does not mean that he advises Investor to distribute his money over the securities in the proportions defined by θ and then leave his investments unchanged during the T periods. On the contrary, if the relative prices of the securities change during one period, one must buy and sell at the beginning of the next period in order to keep the proportion of capital in security i equal to θ_i. In general, adviser θ recommends selling a fraction of each security that has done well, in order to invest more in those securities that have done less well. His "constant rebalanced portfolio" is therefore a contrarian strategy.

Assuming Investor and every adviser start with unit capital, the strategy for Investor in this game can be described as follows:

Strategy for Investor

Choose a probability distribution over the set of all possible portfolios, P.

At the beginning of each period, $t = 1,\ldots, T$:

Invest all one's capital in $\mathbf{b}^t = \dfrac{\int_\Theta \theta A_\theta^{t-1} P(d\theta)}{\int_\Theta A_\theta^{t-1} P(d\theta)}$

$A_\theta^t = A_\theta^{t-1} + \ln(\theta \cdot \mathbf{x}^t)$ (each adviser's logarithmic wealth)

$\Im^t = \Im^{t-1} + \ln(\mathbf{b}^t \cdot \mathbf{x}^t)$ (Investor's logarithmic wealth) **(13)**

A universal portfolio (UNIV) used in trading day t is the weighted average over all feasible portfolios, where the weight of each portfolio is established based on its past performance, A_θ^{t-1}, as well as the probability distribution on the portfolio simplex, $P(d\theta)$. Cover and Ordentlich considered the uniform (Dirichlet (1, 1,..., 1)) and the Dirichlet (1/2, 1/2, ..., 1/2) distributions on the portfolio simplex, B.

Cover and Ordentlich show that with respect to the performance of the *best* adviser universal portfolio is *universal*. In other words, UNIV strategy achieves asymptotically the same rate of return as the best adviser *ex post*. Cover and Ordentlich prove that UNIV strategy that uses uniform distribution has competitive ratio [1]

$$\frac{I^t}{\mathrm{A}^t_{\theta^t}} \geq \frac{1}{(t+1)^{m-1}}, \text{ or equivalently} \quad \textbf{(14)}$$

$$\frac{\Im^t}{t} \geq \frac{A^t_{\theta^t}}{t} - \frac{(m-1)\log t + 1}{t} \quad \textbf{(15)}$$

Equation (14) tells that UNIV strategy is $\frac{1}{(t+1)^{m-1}}$ competitive with respect to BCRP.

Looking at the daily log-performance (Equation (15)) we see that the difference between Investor's and the best constant adviser's performance quickly goes to zero with time, that is, Investor can achieve the same asymptotic growth rate for the logarithmic wealth as the most successful of the advisers.

Cover and Ordentlich (1996) also show that for the Dirichlet (1/2, 1/2, , 1/2) distribution, the algorithm is universal as well with the following competitive ratio:

$$\frac{I^t}{A^t_{\theta^t}} \geq \frac{1}{2(t+1)^{(m-1)/2}}, \text{ or, equivalently, } \frac{\mathfrak{I}^t}{t} \geq \frac{\mathcal{A}^t_{\theta^t}}{t} - \frac{(m-1)\log(2(t+1))}{2t}.$$

Up to date this is the best competitive bound achieved by an online algorithm in the context of portfolio selection problem with unknown horizons (Borodin et al., 2000).

Cover and Ordentlich: Fixed Signal Spaces

In 1996 Cover and Ordentlich generalized Cover's initial work to the case where each of the strategies being averaged chooses a portfolio based on a signal (Cover and Ordentlich, 1996). They assumed that the signal at the beginning of each period is always a signal from the same fixed finite signal space Y, say $Y := (1, ..., k)$. In this case, the space Θ of advisers is finite dimensional and an adviser θ can be identified with a matrix $\theta = (\theta_1, ..., \theta_k)$, where θ_y, for each $y \in Y$, is the portfolio that θ recommends when the signal is y. Formally, $\Theta = B^k$. If the signal for the first t periods is $y^1, ..., y^t$, then θ recommends the sequence of portfolios $\theta_{y^1}, ..., \theta_{y^k}$, and so its capital at the end of the tth period, A^t_θ, is a function of $y^1, ..., y^t$:

$$A^t_\theta(y^1,...,y^t) = \prod_{s=1}^{t} (\theta_{y^s} \cdot \mathbf{x}^s).$$

It is helpful to break this product into the subproducts accounted for by the different $y \in Y$. We set $A^t_{\mathbf{b},y}(y^1,...,y^t) := \prod\{(\mathbf{b} \cdot \mathbf{x}^s) \mid 1 \leq s \leq t, y^s = y\}$ for all $y \in Y$ and all $\mathbf{b} \in B$, so that

$$A^t_\theta(y^1,...,y^t) = \prod_{y \in Y} A^t_{\theta_y,y}(y^1,...,y^t).$$

Because $\Theta = B^k$, the simplest way to construct a probability distribution P on Θ is to choose a probability distribution Q on B and form its k-fold product: $P := Q^k$. Cover and Ordentlich considered such product measures for two different Q: the uniform and the Dirichlet $(\frac{1}{2},...,\frac{1}{2})$. In both cases, they showed that universalization is achieved and established performance bounds.

When we apply the aggregating algorithm using a product distribution, the integrals in the denominator and the numerator of the right-hand side of the formula for Investor's portfolio in the tth period (Equation (6)), both factor into components for each possible signal:

$$\int_{\Theta} A_{\theta}^{t-1} P(d\theta) = \int_{\Theta} A_{\theta}^{t-1}(y^1,\ldots,y^{t-1}) P(d\theta)$$
$$= \int_{\Theta} \prod_{y \in Y} A_{\theta_y, y}^{t-1}(y^1,\ldots,y^{t-1}) \prod_{y \in Y} Q(d\theta_y)$$
$$= \prod_{y \in Y} \int_{B} A_{\mathbf{b},y}^{t-1}(y^1,\ldots,y^{t-1}) Q(d\mathbf{b}),$$

and

$$\int_{\Theta} \pi^t(\theta) A_{\theta}^{t-1} P(d\theta) = \int_{\Theta} \theta_y A_{\theta}^{t-1}\left(y^1,\ldots,y^{t-1}\right) P(d\theta)$$
$$= \int_{\Theta} \theta_y \left(\prod_{y \in Y} A_{\theta_y, y}^{t-1}\left(y^1,\ldots,y^{t-1}\right) \prod_{y \in Y} Q\left(d\theta_y\right) \right)$$
$$= \int_{B} \mathbf{b} A_{\mathbf{b},y}^{t-1}\left(y^1,\ldots,y^{t-1}\right) \prod_{y \in Y, y \neq y^t} \int_{B} A_{\mathbf{b},y}^{t-1}\left(y^1,\ldots,y^{t-1}\right) Q(d\mathbf{b}).$$

So Equation (6) becomes

$$\mathbf{b}^t = \frac{\int_{B} \mathbf{b} A_{\mathbf{b},y}^{t-1}\left(y^1,\ldots,y^{t-1}\right) Q(d\mathbf{b})}{\int_{B} A_{\mathbf{b},y}^{t-1}\left(y^1,\ldots,y^{t-1}\right) Q(d\mathbf{b})}$$

which is equivalent to Equation (25), page 10 in (Cover & Ordentlich, 1996).

Assuming Investor and every adviser start with unit capital, we describe the strategy for the investor when the side information is present as follows:

Strategy for Investor

Choose a probability distribution over the set of all possible portfolios, $P := Q^k$.

At the beginning of each period, $t = 1, \ldots, T$:

Invest all one's capital in $\mathbf{b}^t = \dfrac{\int_{B} \mathbf{b} A_{\mathbf{b},y}^{t-1}\left(y^1,\ldots,y^{t-1}\right) Q(d\mathbf{b})}{\int_{B} A_{\mathbf{b},y}^{t-1}\left(y^1,\ldots,y^{t-1}\right) Q(d\mathbf{b})}$

$A_{\mathbf{b},y}^{t}\left(y^1,\ldots,y^t\right) = A_{\mathbf{b},y}^{t-1}\left(y^1,\ldots,y^{t-1}\right) + \ln\left(\mathbf{b}^{\mathbf{t}} \cdot \mathbf{x}^{\mathbf{t}}\right)$ (each adviser's logarithmic wealth)

$\Im_y^t\left(y^1,\ldots,y^t\right) = \Im_y^{t-1}\left(y^1,\ldots,y^{t-1}\right) + \ln(\mathbf{b}^t \cdot \mathbf{x}^t)$ (Investor's logarithmic wealth)

When considering the usefulness of Cover and Ordentlich's work, we must remember that the sequence of signals $\{y^1, y^2, ..., y^T\}$ may or may not contain useful information. It may be meaningless noise or, at the opposite extreme it may be an excellent indicator of which investments will do well. We do not assume that Investor knows how to use the signals. He does not know their quality or meaning in advance, and these may change with time. The asymptotic universalization result depends on each signal occurring times, and on every way of using the signal getting a large enough share of Investor's capital that it can make him do well if that way of using it turns out to be best. So we can expect the signal to be helpful only when k, the number of possible signals is very small, so that each signal can recur often and the dimensionality of Θ is not too large (Cover & Ordentlich, 1996; Helmbold et al., 1998).

For the Dirichlet (1/2, 1/2), this strategy is universal, since it achieves the same asymptotically exponential rate of growth as the constant rebalanced portfolio that turns out to be best *ex post*:

$$\frac{\Im_y^t(y^1,...,y^t)}{t} \geq \frac{\mathcal{A}_{\mathbf{b}^t,y}^t(y^1,...,y^t)}{t} - \frac{k(m-1)\log(t+1)}{2t} - \frac{k\log 2}{t}, \quad \text{or}$$

$$\frac{I_y^t(y^1,...,y^t)}{\mathrm{A}_{\mathbf{b}^t,y}^t(y^1,...,y^t)} \geq \frac{1}{2^k(t+1)^{k(m-1)/2}}$$

for all t, $y^t \in \{1,2,...k\}^t$.

$EG(\eta)$ Algorithm

Universal portfolio strategy has some practical disadvantages, including computational difficulties when more than a few stocks are considered (since a multiple dimensional integration is involved). For this strategy the computational time grows exponentially in the number of stocks. Helmbold et al. (1998) suggest the *exponential gradient* strategy ($EG(\eta)$) to overcome this problem. $EG(\eta)$ strategy uses a different approach which is based on techniques from an online regression framework where the goal is to perform as well as the best weighted combination of advisers (Kivinen & Warmuth, 1997). The computational time and storage requirements are linear in the number of stocks.

For $EG(\eta)$ strategy we assume that the advisers are in one-to-one correspondence with the portfolios, thus Θ represents the set B of portfolios: $\Theta := \left\{\theta \in \mathbb{R}^m \mid \theta_j \geq 0, j = 1,...,m, \text{ and } \sum_{j=1}^{m}\theta_j = 1\right\}$. And each adviser θ recommends the portfolio θ for each period: $\pi^t := \theta$ for all t.

This strategy selects the portfolio at t's trading period, $\mathbf{b}^t$, to [approximately] maximize $\eta \log\left(\mathbf{b}^t \cdot \mathbf{x}^t\right) - dist\left(\mathbf{b}^t \| \mathbf{b}^{t-1}\right)$, where $\eta > 0$ is a learning rate and *dist* is a distance measure that operates as a penalty. If the relative entropy is used as the distance, $dist_{RE}\left(\mathbf{b}^t \| \mathbf{b}^{t-1}\right) = \sum_{i=1}^{m} b_i^t \log \frac{b_i^t}{b_i^{t-1}}$, then the $EG(\eta)$ strategy computes the next portfolio as $b_i^t = \frac{b_i^{t-1} \exp\left\{\eta x_i^{t-1} / \mathbf{b}^{t-1} \cdot \mathbf{x}^{t-1}\right\}}{\sum_{i=1}^{m} b_i^{t-1} \exp\left\{\eta x_i^{t-1} / \mathbf{b}^{t-1} \cdot \mathbf{x}^{t-1}\right\}}$. In other words, $EG(\eta)$ strategy computes a weighted average of advisers (which in this case are portfolios) by gradually increasing the relative weights of the more successful stocks using a multiplicative update rule. At the t's period EG strategy adapts to the recent history, while keeping its next portfolio similar to the portfolio at *t-1* trading period (since it pays a penalty (*dist*) from moving far from the previous portfolio).

Let's assume that Investor and every adviser start with unit capital, and the relative entropy is used as a distance measure. Then, we can also represent $EG(\eta)$ strategy as a game protocol:

Strategy for Investor

Start with $\mathbf{b}^0 = \left(\frac{1}{m}, \ldots, \frac{1}{m}\right)$.

At the beginning of each period, $t = 1, \ldots, T$:

Invest all one's capital in $b_i^t = \frac{b_i^{t-1} \exp\left\{\eta x_i^{t-1} / \mathbf{b}^{t-1} \cdot \mathbf{x}^{t-1}\right\}}{\sum_{i=1}^{m} b_i^{t-1} \exp\left\{\eta x_i^{t-1} / \mathbf{b}^{t-1} \cdot \mathbf{x}^{t-1}\right\}}$

$A_\theta^t = A_\theta^{t-1} + \ln(\theta \cdot \mathbf{x}^t)$ (each adviser's logarithmic wealth)

$\mathfrak{I}^t = \mathfrak{I}^{t-1} + \ln(\mathbf{b}^t \cdot \mathbf{x}^t)$ (Investor's logarithmic wealth)

To achieve universality, Helmbold et al. (1998) set the learning parameter η equal to $2x_{\min}\sqrt{2(\log m)/t}$, where $x_{\min}$ is a lower bound on the set of price relatives. Then, $EG(\eta)$ strategy is universal since $\frac{\mathfrak{I}^t}{t} \geq \frac{A_{\theta'}^t}{t} - \sqrt{\frac{\log m}{(2x_{\min}^2 t)}}$, that is, the logarithmic wealth achieved by $EG(\eta)$ strategy is guaranteed to converge to the logarithmic wealth of the best adviser *ex post* as time horizon asymptotically increases. Although the convergence rate of $EG(\eta)$ strategy is worse $\left(O\left(\sqrt{(\log m)/t}\right)\right)$ than the rate proved by Cover and Ordentlich

Figure 1. Cumulative return graphs (starting at 3500 trading day) for the portfolio consisting of Comm.Metals & KinArk Corp. with daily trading. The figure on the top shows returns achieved by various strategies with no transaction costs, and the one on the bottom shows the returns with a presence of 2% transaction cost. Note that the BCRP plot tracks the performance of a single portfolio that maximizes the return on the final day.

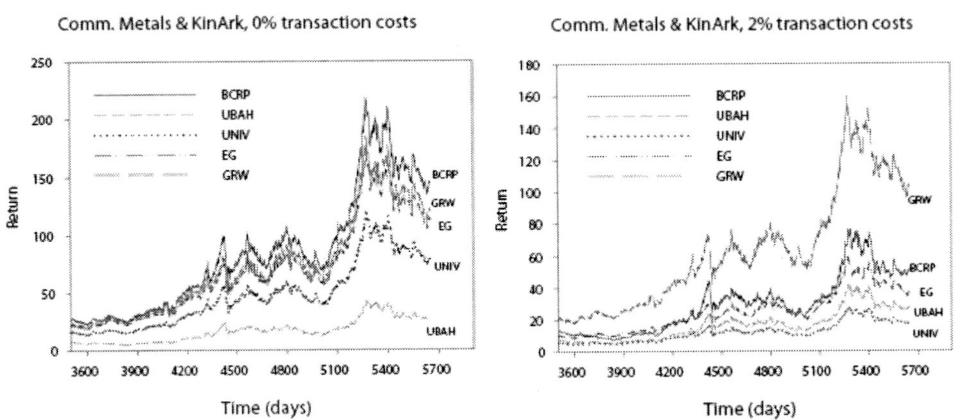

in their 1996 paper $\left(O\left((m \log t)/t\right)\right)$, empirical results show that in some cases $EG(\eta)$ strategy obtains higher returns than UNIV strategy, with the correct choice of the learning rate parameter (which should be a small number to achieve universality).

Numerical Results

We test the investment strategies described in the previous section on three different sets of financial data (notice that we do not require any knowledge of the market). These data sets represent standard test problems used to analyze the performance of different online strategies for portfolio selection. The first data set is the standard set of New York Stock Exchange (NYSE) [2] market data that was initially used by Cover (1991), Cover and Ordentlich (1996), Singer (1997), Helmbold et al. (1998), Blum and Kalai (1998), Borodin, El-Yaniv, and Gogan (2000), Stoltz and Lugosi (2004), Györfi, Lugosi, and Udina (in press) and others. This data set consists of 36 stock prices accumulated over 22 years (5651 days) from July 3rd, 1962 to Dec 31st, 1984. The second data set contains daily prices for 30 stocks composing the Dow Jones Industrial Average (DJIA) index during the period November 1999 to May 2003 (876 days). The final data set contains 3087 daily prices for 95 stocks randomly picked from NASDAQ market for a 12-year period from January 1st, 1991 to March 28, 2003.

Figure 2. Cumulative return graphs (starting at 3500 trading day) for the portfolio consisting of Iroquois & KinArk Corp. with daily trading. The figure on the top shows returns achieved by various strategies with no transaction cost, and the one on the bottom shows the returns with a presence of 2% transaction cost. Note that the BCRP plot tracks the performance of a single portfolio that maximizes the return on the final day.

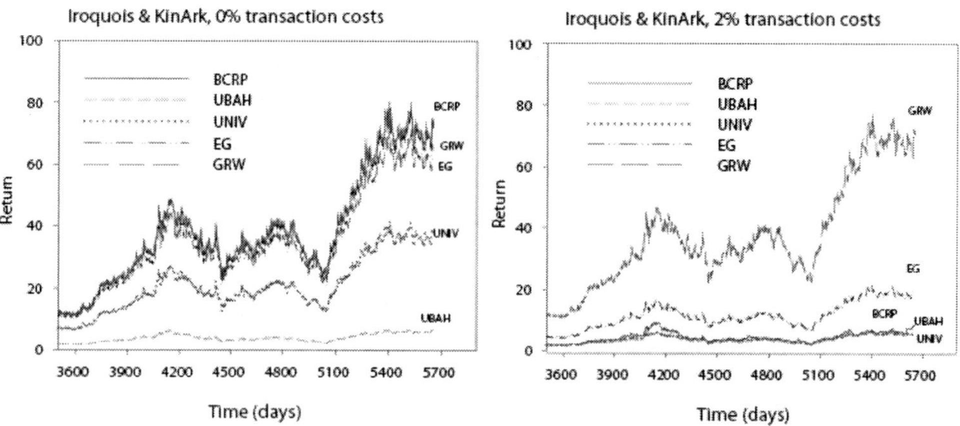

Table 1. Comparison table of the portfolio selection strategies for NYSE data set, with daily trading and different transaction costs. Strategies which outperform UBAH are in bold, and a strategy with the highest return among compared portfolio selection strategies is underlined.

Markets	Benchmark Portfolios			Selection Strategies		
	Best Stock	UBAH	BCRP	UNIV	EG ($\eta = 0.05$)	GRW ($\sigma = 0.005$)
Comm.Metals & KinArk						
0% transaction costs	52.02	28.07	**144.00**	**78.47**	**111.92**	**117.75**
0.1% transaction costs	51.97	28.05	**130.13**	**72.14**	**105.91**	**117.13**
2.0% transaction costs	50.98	27.51	**50.98**	17.98	**37.06**	**105.91**
Comm.Metals & Meicco						
0% transaction costs	52.02	37.49	**102.96**	**73.63**	92.01	**94.49**
0.1% transaction costs	51.97	37.43	**95.51**	**68.64**	**88.51**	**94.12**
2.0% transaction costs	50.98	36.72	**50.98**	26.25	**42.32**	**87.47**
Iroquois & KinArk						
0% transaction costs	8.92	6.52	**73.7**	**39.67**	**69.51**	**70.07**
0.1% transaction costs	8.91	6.51	**65.19**	**34.98**	**62.22**	**69.72**
2.0% transaction costs	8.74	6.39	**8.74**	6.33	**19.52**	**63.42**
IBM & Coca Cola						
0% transaction costs	13.36	12.79	**15.07**	**14.18**	**14.86**	**14.85**
0.1% transaction costs	13.34	12.77	**14.61**	**13.89**	**14.59**	**14.79**
2.0% transaction costs	13.09	12.53	**13.09**	9.55	10.76	**13.59**

Table 2. Volatility for NYSE pairs and correlation between the returns of the constituent stocks

Stocks	Volatility	Correlation
Comm.Metals & KinArk	0.025 0.05	0.041
Comm.Metals & Meicco	0.025 0.031	0.064
Iroquios & KinArk	0.034 0.05	0.067
IBM & Coca Cola	0.013 0.014	0.388

To compare the performance of these three strategies[3] we use three benchmarks: uniform BAH (UBAH), Best Stock and BCRP strategies. The first two benchmarks may be considered as naive, that is, Investor would expect a portfolio selection strategy to do well compare to these benchmarks (Borodin et al., 2000).

The NYSE data are different from the DJIA and NASDAQ data, with respect to the value of stocks. While every stock increased in value in the NYSE data, 14 of the 30 stocks in the DJIA data and 29 of the 95 in the NASDAQ data lost money. The DJIA data has the smallest number of trading periods and NYSE data has the largest number of trading periods. Since we showed earlier that investment strategies considered in this section achieve (at least theoretically) the same growth rate as the best portfolio *ex post asymptotically*, we expect that the online strategies will not beat the BCRP for DJIA data and may be even for NASDAQ data.

Summarizing our results we found that the performance of all compared portfolio selection strategies, not surprisingly, highly depends on the market data and transaction costs. If we ignore transaction costs, then on NYSE stock market data all strategies show a good performance, especially when we, following Cover (Cover, 1991), look at some pairs of stocks (Table 1). As Figures 1 and 2 show, GRW strategy achieves the best performance among compared strategies for these data, and in the presence of transaction costs it even beats the BCRP.

However, the performance of GRW (and other strategies) is not as good for other data sets. One of possible explanations might be the one given earlier, that about half of the stocks in the DJIA data set and about third of the NASDAQ data set lost their money, unlike NYSE data set, where every stock had positive return. Another explanation might be that the time horizon is relatively small for DJIA and NASDAQ data sets. Also, as was mentioned in several previous papers the volatility of used stocks and the correlation between stocks affect the performance of online strategies (Helmbold et al., 1998; Borodin et al., 2000; Borodin et al., 2004). The strategies perform better if a portfolio consists of volatile and loosely correlated stocks.

Table 3. Comparison table of the portfolio selection strategies with daily trading and different transaction costs. Strategies which outperform UBAH are in bold, and a strategy with the highest return among compared portfolio selection strategies is underlined.

Markets	Benchmark Portfolios			Selection Strategies		
	Best Stock	UBAH	BCRP	UNIV	EG ($\eta = 0.05$)	GRW ($\sigma = 0.005$)
NYSE						
0% transaction costs	54.14	14.50	**243.36**	**24.3**	**27.10**	**26.678**
0.1% transaction costs	54.09	14.48	**213.91**	**24.12**	**26.21**	**26.664**
2.0% transaction costs	53.06	14.21	**56.03**	13.61	13.73	**26.301**
DJIA						
0% transaction costs	9.88	1.502	**9.88**	1.327	1.2463	1.2367
0.1% transaction costs	9.87	1.501	**9.87**	1.315	1.2388	1.2361
2.0% transaction costs	9.68	1.472	**9.68**	1.116	1.1031	1.2253
NASDAQ						
0% transaction costs	1815.00	49.43	**4298.70**	22.637	6.96	5.865
0.1% transaction costs	1813.20	49.38	**4276.23**	22.59	6.75	5.848
2.0% transaction costs	1778.70	48.44	**3082.48**	12.58	3.79	5.54

We see in NYSE data (Table 2) that pairs with volatile stocks and loose correlation perform better (CommMetal & KinArk, CommMetals & Meicco, and Iroquous & KinArk) compare to IBM & CocaCola combination with stronger correlation and smaller volatility.

Table 3 presents the return achieved by different portfolio selection strategies for three market types. For the market consisting of all 36 stocks from NYSE data set, none of the considered portfolio selection strategies achieves the return of BCRP, and EG is the only strategy that does slightly better then UCRP. The most challenging for all strategies is a market consisting of NASDAQ stocks. None of these strategies reach the returns obtained by most benchmark portfolio selection strategies (except UCRP).

Transaction Costs

An introduction of transaction costs makes the portfolio selection problem more complex. However, we can not ignore it completely, since in a real market we have to pay commissions for every change in the portfolio. Different types of transaction costs are used in the market. The most popular ones, however, are: (1) proportional, that is, a broker charges a specific fraction, say 3% of the transaction; (2) fixed, that is, an investor pays a fixed amount, say \$15, per transaction. In our experiments we use the proportional transaction cost models. Specifically, we use modest 0.1% and hefty (but more realistic) 2% transaction cost models.

We apply Blum and Kalai's extension of Cover's universal portfolio to the case of proportional percentage transaction costs to obtain a return for UNIV and BCRP strategies (Blum & Kalai, 1998). Previous results (Blum & Kalai, 1998; Borodin et al., 2000; Borodin et al., 2004; Cover, 1991; Helmbold et al., 1998; Levina, 2004) indicate the significant impact of transaction costs (e.g., at 2% rate) on the performance of the strategies. Our numerical results for most portfolio selection strategies (except GRW) confirm this observation. On NYSE data GRW shows a very good performance when there is a transaction cost, especially for the (more realistic) 2% transaction cost (Table 3).

Conclusion and Directions for Future Research

In this chapter we presented an overview of some recent online methods for portfolio selection problems and compared the practical performance of these methods. In particular, we discussed investment strategies that are *universal*, that is, they achieve asymptotically the same exponential rate of growth as the portfolio that turns out to be best *ex post without making any assumptions* about the market. The latter (that is, no statistical assumptions on the nature of the stock market) presents an important difference with widely known notion of growth optimal portfolio. Although the online portfolio selection strategies are not yet widely used, it seems that this is going to change in the near future, since investment companies started to recognize the usefulness of the online portfolios for long term investments.

The strategies considered in the chapter include the universal portfolio (UNIV) (Cover, 1991; Cover & Ordentlich, 1996), Gaussian random walk (GRW) (Levina, 2004), and exponential gradient (EG) (Helmbold et al., 1996). We also explain how Vovk's aggregating algorithm is used in the context of portfolio selection and provided several examples of its application to a set of switching strategies.

The obtained numerical results show that GRW strategy performs almost as well as best constant rebalance portfolio for NYSE stock data, and better compare to other portfolio selection algorithms for other data sets. It achieves significantly better results for everyday trading (compare to all presented portfolio selection strategies, including benchmarks) with a presence of transaction costs (especially for 2% transaction cost). The conducted experiments also suggest that GRW strategy works better for riskier stocks (i.e., more similar to KinArk and Meicco than to IBM and Coca Cola).

One immediate direction for future research is to consider a learning rate parameter different from 1 from general theory of aggregating algorithm. With different learning rate we expect GRW strategy (and other strategies based on the aggregating algorithm) to discover the significant tendencies in the data faster and thus achieve higher returns.

The transaction costs should be explored in more detail. In particular, some experimental results (Blum & Kalai, 1998) suggest that trading periodically (e.g., once a week) may be beneficial.

It would also be interesting to run numerical experiments with signals and try to determine the size of the efficient signal space, and how the signals would affect the performance of the GRW strategy. Other directions for future work may include finding the competitive ratio for GRW strategy, study portfolio selection algorithms utilizing short-selling, and study the risk tolerance of advisers.

Acknowledgments

We would like to acknowledge the anonymous referees for their helpful comments and suggestions.

References

Akcoglu, K., Drineas, P., & Kao, M.-Y. (2004). Fast universalization of investment strategies. *SIAM Journal on Computing, 34*(1), 1-22.

Algoet, P., & Cover, T. M. (1988). Asymptotic optimality and asymptotic equipartition property of log-optimal investment. *Annals of Probability, 16*, 876-898.

Blum, A., & Kalai, A. (1998). Universal portfolios with and without transaction cost. *Machine Learning, 30*(1), 23-30.

Borodin, A., & El-Yaniv, R. (1998). *Online computation and competitive analysis*. New York: Cambridge University.

Borodin, A., El-Yaniv, R., & Gogan, V. (2000). On the competitive theory and practice of portfolio selection. In G. H. Gonnet, D. Panario, & A. Viola (Eds.), *LATIN 2000: Theoretical Informatics, 4th Latin American Symposium, Proceedings: LNCS 1776* (pp. 173-196). Uruguay: Springer.

Borodin, A., El-Yaniv, R., & Gogan, V. (2004). Can we learn to beat the best stock. *Journal of Artificial Intelligence Research, 21*, 579-594.

Bousquet, O., & Warmuth, M. K. (2002). Tracking a small set of experts by mixing past posteriors. *Journal of Machine Learning Research, 3*, 363-396.

Cesa-Bienachi, N., Freund, Y., Haussler, D., Helmbold, D., Schapire, R., & Warmuth, M. K. (1997). How to use expert advice. *Journal of the Association for Computing Machinery, 44*, 427-285.

Cross, J. E., & Barron, A. R. (2003). Efficient universal portfolios for past-dependent target classes. *Mathematical Finance, 13*(2), 245-276.

Cover, T. M. (1991). Universal portfolios. *Mathematical Finance, 1*(1), 1-29.

Cover, T. M., & Ordentlich, E. (1996). Universal portfolios with side information. *IEEE Transactions on Information Theory, 42*(2), 348-363.

El-Yaniv, R. (1998). Competitive solutions for online financial problems. *ACM Computing Surveys, 30*(1), 28-69.

Györfi, L., Lugosi, G., & Udina, F. (in press). Nonparametric kernel-based sequential investment strategies. *Mathematical Finance*.

Helmbold, D., Schapire R., Singer, Y., & Warmuth, M. K. (1998). On-line portfolio selection using multiplicative updates. *Mathematical Finance*, *8*(4), 325-347.

Herbster, M., & Warmuth, M. K. (1998). Tracking the best expert. *Journal of Machine Learning*, 32, 151-178.

Iyengar, G. (2005). Universal investment in markets with transaction costs. *Mathematical Finance*, *15*(2), 359-371.

Kalai, A. (2001). Probabilistic and on-line methods in machine learning. *Dissertation Abstracts International* (UMI No. AAT 3040463).

Kalai, A., & Vempala, S. (2003). Efficient algorithms for universal portfolios. *The Journal of Machine Learning Research, 3*, 423-440.

Kelly, J. (1956). A new interpretation of information rate. *Bell System Technical Journal*, *35*, 917-926.

Kivinen, J., & Warmuth, M. K. (1997). Additive versus exponential gradient updates for linear prediction. *Information and Computation*, *132*(1), 1-64.

Levina, T. (2004). *Using the aggregating algorithm for portfolio selection.* Unpublished doctoral dissertation, Rutgers the State University of New Jersey, Newark.

Littlestone, N., & Warmuth, M. K. (1994). Weighted majority algorithm. *Information and Computation*, *108*, 212-261.

Platen, E. (in press). On the role of the growth optimal portfolio in finance. *Australian Economic Papers*.

Singer, Y. (1997). Switching portfolios. *International Journal of Neural Systems*, *8*(4), 445-455.

Sleator, D. D., & Tarjan, R. E. (1985). Amortized efficiency of list update and paging rules. *Communications of the ACM*, *28*(2), 202-208.

Stoltz, G., & Lugosi, G. (2004). Internal regret in on-line portfolio selection. *Machine Learning*, *59*, 1-35.

Vovk, V. G. (1990). Aggregating strategies. In M. Fulk & J. Case (Eds.), *COLT '90: Proceedings of the Third Annual Workshop on Computational Learning Theory* (pp. 371-383). San Francisco: Morgan Kaufmann.

Vovk, V. G. (1999). Derandomizing stochastic prediction strategies. *Machine Learning*, *35*, 247-282.

Vovk, V. G., & Watkins, C. (1998). Universal portfolio selection. In P. Bartlett & Y. Mansour, (Eds.), *COLT'98: Proceedings of the Eleventh Annual Conference on Computational Learning Theory* (pp. 12-23). New York: ACM.

Endnotes

1. The universality of UNIV was also elegantly proved by Blum and Kalai (1998).
2. This data set was originally generated by Hal Stern. Thanks to Yoram Singer for providing us with the NYSE data.
3. When implementing *EG*(η) strategy we followed Helmbold et al. (1998) and set η=0.05, since a smaller value of η allows Investor to get a better return. For GRW strategy we introduced parameters of the normal distribution and picked σ=0.005.

Section VII

Postscript

Chapter XXII

Ankle Bones, Rogues, and Sexual Freedom for Women: Computational Intelligence in Historical Context

Nigel K. Ll. Pope, Griffith University, Australia

Kevin E. Voges, University of Canterbury, New Zealand

Abstract

In this chapter we review the history of mathematics-based approaches to problem solving. The authors suggest that while the ability of analysts to deal with the extremes of data now available is leading to a new leap in the handling of data analysis, information processing, and control systems, that ability remains grounded in the work of early pioneers of statistical thought. Beginning with pre-history, the paper briefly traces developments in analytical thought to the present day, identifying milestones in this development. The techniques developed in studies of computational intelligence, the applications of which are presented in this volume, form the basis for the next great development in analytical thought.

Introduction

This book is part of a wave of interest in computational methods that is increasing apace. The ability of the computer to handle large amounts of data has had an inordinate effect on the capacity of business to analyse and refer to vast arrays of information. It is possible — indeed, we are certain that it is so — that we are at the beginning of, and part of, the next great development in statistical analysis. In light of that, we feel it is appropriate to place this development in the context of the history of statistical thought. It has been argued that in business as in life, it is impossible to know where one is going if one does not know where one came from. Equally, it could be said that when a discipline becomes interested in its own history it is in a state of decay! No matter. To be interested in this history places us in the company of great personages, as the reader will see from the references to this chapter. We therefore offer this chapter in part as a tribute to those who went before. As we will see, they were fascinating characters.

The argument that the "... foundations of mathematical statistics were laid between 1890 and 1930..." (Porter, 1986, p. 3) is difficult to refute. That was a time when great minds — Weldon, Karl Pearson, Fisher and Gosset to name only a few — began to apply knowledge gained from genetics to the mathematical expression of statistics. But interest had been shown much earlier, as we shall show. The first use of the word "statistics" occurs in 1589 by Girolamo Ghilini (Kendall, 1960). Ghilini principally was speaking in the public policy sense of the word, but we see an interest here in the concept of dealing with large numbers. Crosby (1997) provides a comprehensive and entertaining account of the transition from qualitative to quantitative thinking that occurred in Western Europe in the period 1250 to 1600, the forerunner to many of the issues discussed below.

Much earlier still, we find that interest in probability had been occurring since the most primitive times, though as an empirical art only. It was only far in the future that it became an object of mathematical science. We can be certain that primitive man played games, some of them based on chance and they can be accounted for as either religious in significance, or as a form of pleasure. Evidence for this can be seen in the large number of astragali found in archaeological digs (David, 1955). Now the astragalus is a small bone from the ankle region with no particular use to anyone after its initial owner has passed away. It has no marrow for eating and no surface that can be used for writing or drawing, due to its size. Its only use is as a toy. Such a use has been identified in Egyptian tomb paintings in the board game of Hounds and Jackals (David, 1955). Fortunately for us, there is also evidence that it was used in early forms of dice gaming. Here, we find possibly the earliest example of an intuitive understanding of the nature of probability. It seems that the game of knucklebones, in which four astragali would be balanced on the large knuckles of the back of the hand and then thrown, was scored in such a fashion as to reflect true odds. For example, the four fours — the throw of Euripides — were valued at 40 (David, 1955). A quick calculation will reveal that the actual odds are approximately 1 in 39.

This is an important step in the development of probability and computation. While the use of dice for divination or for personal profit through gambling allowed pleasure and religious value, it lent the individual with an inherent, though crude, understanding of the nature of probability an immense advantage. That advantage could be employed whether one were gambler or priest in exactly the same way as the modern business with access to good computational techniques can apply them to the market place.

The curious can be well rewarded by a visit to Paris' Musée de Louvre, where one can see large numbers of astragali carved to form early, proper dice. In the same exhibits, one can also see that these were later replaced — at least by 3000 BC — by pottery. In an intriguing statement on human nature — and again an early example of an intuitive understanding of probability — we find that by 1000 BC, the first rigged dice (by placing numbers more than once on the cube) were appearing. Much cleverer, by at least the Roman times, the biasing of dice (performed by hollowing out a section) was occurring. Incidentally, to show how closely related were the developments of gambling and mathematics, it is intriguing to note that one of the first applications of the knowledge of the geometry of solid figures was the construction of polyhedral dice in rock crystal by the Ancient Greeks (David, 1955).

One is tempted to ask why it was that the ancient Greeks with their knowledge of geometry and mathematics did not go on to develop a mathematic of probability. This was a people who were able to plot a location by using coordinates, a major advance in its time [the plot of a simple function such as $y = f(x)$ would not occur until the time of Renée Descartes (1596-1650)] yet they did not apply that ability to what must have been an important part of their lives, either for pleasure or worship. The answer lies in the second part of that statement. It seems that, as with the Romans, the use of dice in divination inhibited the examination of chance. Chance was the role and expression of the Gods, and to investigate it would have been sacrilege, a concept that would continue into mediaeval times in the Christian Church (David, 1955; Kendall, 1956).

This did not inhibit the popularity of dice-like games, however. Two Roman emperors, Augustus and Claudius, were each heavy players and gamblers. Claudius even went on to write a text on the topic (David, 1955). In fact, under the Romans, gaming with either dice or knucklebones became so popular that it was banned except at certain periods of the year. Christians of the Dark Ages also — unsuccessfully — tried to outlaw the practice (David, 1955; Kendall, 1956). Germany's Friedrich II and France's Louis IX each banned gambling with dice in the Middle Ages (Kendall, 1956). With the advent of playing cards in the 15th century, England's Henry VIII — something of a moral crusader at one stage, despite his later marital and religious problems — added these to an earlier list of banned games (Kendall, 1956). Soccer was one of those other games and the ban on dice and cards proved just as effective as it did with that sport.

It is now that we begin to see an interest being shown in the mathematical probabilities of gambling. The displaying of possible falls of dice in tabular form had begun by the end of the 15th century, so the more intuitive gambler could begin to calculate some of the vagaries of the game. Then, in the early part of the 16th century the first example of astronomy leading the way in mathematical probability occurred when Calcagnini produced the dissertation *De talorum, tesserarum ac calculorum ludis ex more veterum*. Not long after, in 1556, Tartaglia published his *General Trattato* in 1556, which considered several gaming possibilities. In a wonderful example of how the academic personality seems to be a constant, he also included in it a major lambasting of other teachers of mathematics (Kendall, 1956).

Now, Calcagnini's work did not exhibit any interest in the mathematics of dice as had Tartaglia's, but it is known to have been read by, and to have influenced, that most delicious of libertines, Girolamo Cardano (David, 1955). This delightful character was born in 1501, the bastard son of a Pavian geometrician and jurist. Remember that the role of the scholar in these times was not subject to tenure or other forms of security. Indeed, they were in many ways itinerant workers, dependent on the largesse of a sponsor or on their wit. Similarly, academic codes of conduct were not enforceable and the young Cardano, being the son of such a worker would early have learned the insecurity of the scholar's life. He would also have been in his element. In a fascinating career he was at various times physician, plagiarist, mathematician and astrologer. Significantly, he was always a gambler and very often in trouble with the authorities. At one stage he was imprisoned for casting the horoscope of Jesus Christ, which is odd considering that we know what happened to him. At another, he incurred the wrath of his in-laws, having sold all of his wife's property in order to feed his gambling habit. Unfortunately, we can find no record of the poor woman's reaction, but we do know that his son was executed for murdering his own wife. Having cast his own horoscope that indicated he would live to 75, Cardano took his own life at that age, a possible indication of amazing self-confidence.

Cardano and Tartaglia long disputed the authorship of Cardano's mathematical work and it seems that Tartaglia may have had the right of this. Cardano's treatise on gambling however, *Liber de Ludo Alae*, was published 87 years after his death (1663), and it is from this that we know it was not plagiarized. This work was significant because it was the first to identify that if dice are true then it is possible to calculate the chances of a given number being thrown (David, 1955). It was a major step in the examination of probability.

During Cardano's lifetime, another major figure in mathematics was born in Italy. Galileo-Galilei, the son of a musicographer, was born in Pisa in 1564. He was both astronomer and mathematician. At the age of 70, he recanted his theory of the movement of the earth about the sun when placed under torture by the tender members of the Inquisition – something of a wise move on his part. He had been yielded up to the Inquisition by envious, fellow scholars, a rather pithy illustration of early academic politics. Galileo's treatise *Sopra le Scoperte de I Dadi* deals with some of the same issues as raised by Cardano. Unfortunately, his work on gambling was not published until 1718. Contemporary with Galileo, the French mathematicians Pascal and Fermat were corresponding with regard to probability and from their writing it is clear that by this time the definition and idea of probability were already assumed to be known (David, 1955).

The role of astronomy in the development of a mathematic of probability is significant at this period. Although there is evidence that both Babylonian and Greek astronomers noted discrepancies in the transition of the sun through a particular solstitial point — thereby affecting the length of the year — there is no indication that they were able to translate the calculations they had used (comparison with a mean) into a general principle. This occurred in Tycho Brahe's work on the position of stars in the late 16th century, being a contemporary with Galileo. Brahe was able to use the calculation of the mean to eliminate systematic error. Further advances in the precision of use of the mean occurred over the next 100 years — again in astronomy — and by 1736 we see the French expedition to Lapland under Maupertuis proving that the earth is flattened at the poles by measuring the mean length of a degree of latitude there and comparing it with the similar mean in France (Plackett, 1958). This also marks the end of the Italian period of the great steps in the movement toward mathematical statistics.

We have already noted that the Frenchmen, Pascal and Fermat were corresponding on probability. The Dutchman Christian Huygens arrived in Paris in 1655 and after returning to Holland began a correspondence with Fermat. It was he who successfully distilled the work of these Parisians into a clear theory of probability, based on gambling, with the publication of his *Tractatus de Ratiociniis in Aleae Ludo*, published in 1667 (David, 1955). Things were now moving quickly. The Parisians and Huygens had shown that analysis of games of chance could be used to solve a priori questions. This had become well understood by 1700. Jacob Bernoulli addressed the a posteriori solutions to gaming — and thereby other natural events — by formally showing that the intuitive belief that prior observations can be used to predict future events was correct. His work was further refined by de Moivre, Bayes, and Simpson, who were able to address the problems of precision through the use of the standard deviation (Stigler, 1986). So by the mid- to late-18th century we see in the works of Simpson, de Moivre, and Lagrange, the beginnings of a discrete probability calculus and differential calculus. This allowed for extension from discrete to continuous functions with proper limiting processes, Simpson being the first to consider distribution of error (Kendall, 1961; Plackett, 1958).

It was now time for the mathematicians to repay the favor to the astronomers. In 1805, Legendre published the method of least squares and by 1825 it was in common use in England, Prussia, Italy and France, particularly in the fields of astronomy and geodesics. As Stigler (1986, p. 15) rightly states: "The rapid geographic diffusion of the method and its quick acceptance...is a success story that has few parallels in the history of scientific method." Scholars being what they are, Gauss (1777-1855) naturally would later claim that he had been using the method since 1795 (Stigler, 1986).

At about the same time, we find the concepts of graphical display being developed. It is to William Playfair in about 1800 that we owe justification for the use of a graph to plot money against time: a true business application (Royston, 1956). Playfair also used pie graphs and histograms and was a competent economist. He was also, if not a rogue, at least odd. For example, he claimed to have introduced semaphore to England, which he didn't, and to have warned the government of Napoleon's escape from Elba, which he hadn't. He claimed to be the inventor of what he called linear arithmetic, although it has been suggested that he merely applied it to descriptive statistics, having learnt the method when a draughtsman for the great James Watt (Royston, 1956). But no matter the oddity of Playfair, the use of graphical presentations of data had arrived. Gauss developed the concept of the normal curve early in the 19th century and the Belgian social scientist Quetelet introduced the application to humans from astronomy with his identification of an error law to explain human deviations from the average (Porter, 1986).

We now move to what E. S. Pearson (1967, p. 355), the son of Karl, describes as the formative period of the development of mathematical statistics (he calls it the "English school"): the period 1890-1905. In other writing, he extended the dates:

"Perhaps the two great formative periods in the history of mathematical statistics were the years 1890-1905 and 1915-30. In both, the remarkable leap forward was made in answer to a need for new theory and techniques to help in solving very real problems in the biological field." (E. S. Pearson, 1965, p. 3)

The beginnings of this lie with the brilliant Englishman, Sir Francis Galton. Galton, a cousin of Charles Darwin, contributed to meteorology research, invented the use of finger printing for recognition of criminals and was an early proponent of psychoanalysis (Haldane, 1957). His principal interest however, was the improvement of humankind through selective breeding, a science he named eugenics. In the course of this work in human genetics, Galton developed the concept of regression. He arrived at that point through the idea of measuring correlations in parent and child organ size in the 1880s. Walter Weldon then developed this into the concept of a correlation coefficient that may be constant across species. It was Karl Pearson who expressed this mathematically and was able to extend it into polynomial regression as opposed to problems of measurement error (Seal, 1967). In sum, Weldon and Pearson (K. Pearson, 1920) developed Galton's work into multiple correlation and multiple regression, which culminated in the χ^2 test of goodness of fit (E. S. Pearson, 1967).

In 1911, Galton died and in his will endowed a Chair of Eugenics at University College. Karl Pearson was the first occupant of that chair. In 1920, the Department of Applied Statistics was formally opened. In discussing Karl Pearson, Haldane (1957) likens him to Columbus who sailed for China and found America. Pearson set out to develop theories of evolution and heredity and found multiple regression. Like his mentor Galton, Pearson was a brilliant and multi-talented man. He read for the bar and was admitted in 1881 (his father, too, was a lawyer). He also wrote books attacking Christian orthodoxy and lectured on Marx to drawing room audiences. Indeed, one of his books on Marxism was done the honor of being attacked in writing by Lenin! At age 27, he was appointed Chair of Applied Mathematics at University College, London where, amongst other academic pursuits he founded the "Men's and Women's Club," which avowed sexual freedom for unmarried women. Pearson also diverted considerable time to research into German literature of the medieval and renaissance periods. His great colleague Walter Weldon was a natural scientist who had been profoundly influenced by Francis Galton's work. Both these men were mentored and befriended by Galton.

Of their students, many stand out, but of particular interest is Gosset, often known by his nom-de-plume, Student. It was he who developed the t-test after discovering the distribution of the sample standard deviation. Gosset was a scientist with the Guinness brewery and became a personal friend of Karl Pearson. Like Pearson, he had multiple interests, though not so cerebral. He was reportedly possessed of an inability to be stressed, he grew magnificent pears, toyed with carpentry and loved fishing, sailing (he built his own boats), golf and shooting (McMullen & Pearson, 1939). Gosset, with the ability of his test to deal with small sample sizes, is a wonderful example of the application of statistics to business. His work is, of course, at the other end of the spectrum to matters dealt with in this book.

One of Gosset's great correspondents was Ronald Aylmer Fisher. Fisher was a Cambridge graduate who had worked as a teacher but had begun to publish in the area of statistics. He early on came to the attention of Karl Pearson of whom he is a direct inheritor (E. S. Pearson, 1967). He declined the offer of a position with Pearson at University College and instead joined Sir John Russell at Rothamsted Experimental Station. His major contributions between 1920 and 1940 related to ANOVA, multivariate analysis and experimental design, though he did much other work that was of help in other areas (e.g., *k*-statistics). He was also rude, arrogant, intolerant of criticism (Kendall, 1963) and "...did not like to admit mistakes..." (Bartlett, 1982, p. 45). For unknown reasons, the young Fisher hated the 65-year-old Karl Pearson. This would go on until even 20 years after Pearson's death when Fisher was still attacking his work (Kendall, 1963). Fisher would later become Chair of Eugenics at University College, Pearson's old position, and later Chair of Genetics at Cambridge. It is indeed odd that the greatest statistician of his time never held a chair in statistics, that honor going instead to Pearson's son.

It is here, at the end of E. S. Pearson's "English" period that we leave the great leap. There are many that we have not named (Mahalabanois and Roy, for instance) but our intention is not to provide a comprehensive history of the discipline. That has been done elsewhere. Instead, we seek to place a background to the work presented in this volume: work that seeks to open up new areas of interest and scope for the use of statistical analysis. While those researchers who went before did great things, we have sought to show that they were only human. It was in their failings and foibles that their great strengths lay, for they were able to put these aside in order to bring the discipline to the point at which it is now. That is the work continued by the authors whose contributions appear here.

References

Bartlett, M. S. (1982). Chance and change. In J. M. Gani (Ed.), *The making of statisticians.* New York: Springer-Verlag.

Crosby, A. W. (1997). *The measure of reality: Quantification and Western society.* Cambridge: Cambridge University.

David, F. N. (1955). Dicing and gaming (a note on the history of probability). *Biometrika, 42*, 1-15.

Haldane, J. B. S. (1957). Karl Pearson, 1857-1957. *Biometrika, 44*, 303-313.

Kendall, M. G. (1956). The beginnings of a probability calculus. *Biometrika, 43*, 1-14.

Kendall, M. G. (1957). A note on playing cards. *Biometrika, 44*, 260-262.

Kendall, M. G. (1960). Where shall the history of statistics begin? *Biometrika, 47*, 447-449.

Kendall, M. G. (1961). Daniel Bernoulli on maximum likelihood, introductory note to Daniel Bernoulli, The most probable choice between several discrepant observations and the formation therefrom of the most likely induction. *Biometrika, 48*, 1-18.

Kendall, M. G. (1963). Ronald Aylmer Fisher, 1890-1962. *Biometrika, 50*, 1-15.

McMullen, L., & Pearson, E. S. (1939). William Sealy Gosset, 1867-1937: (1) 'Student' as a man, (2) 'Student' as a statistician. *Biometrika, 30*, 205-250.

Pearson, E. S. (1965). Some incidents in the early history of biometry and statistics. *Biometrika, 52*, 3-18.

Pearson, E. S. (1967). Some reflexions on continuity in the development of mathematical statistics. *Biometrika, 54*, 341-355.

Pearson, K. (1920). Notes on the history of correlation. *Biometrika, 13*, 25-45.

Plackett, R. L. (1958). The principle of the arithmetic mean. *Biometrika, 45*, 130-135.

Porter, T. M. (1986). *The rise of statistical thinking: 1820-1900*. Princeton, NJ: Princeton University.

Royston, E. (1956). A note on the history of the graphical presentation of data. *Biometrika, 43*, 241-247.

Seal, H. L. (1967). The historical development of the Gauss linear model. *Biometrika, 54*, 1-24.

Stigler, S. M. (1986). *The history of statistics: The measurement of uncertainty before 1900*. Cambridge, MA: Belknap.

About the Authors

Kevin E. Voges is a senior lecturer in marketing at the University of Canterbury, New Zealand. Dr. Voges has taught research methods courses in psychology, education, and business. He has consulting experience in education, organizational development, business planning, and market research. His research interests include the application of concepts and techniques from computational intelligence to marketing theory and practice. He has developed a new cluster analysis technique, rough clustering, based on rough sets theory.

Nigel K. Ll. Pope is an associate professor of marketing at Griffith Business School, Australia. His work has appeared in the *Journal of Advertising* and *European Journal of Marketing.* In addition, he is a winner of the Literati Award and the Australian Award for Excellence in Academic Publishing. His research interests include the application of analysis to marketing strategy and planning.

* * *

Faezeh Afshar is a lecturer in the School of Information Technology and Mathematical Sciences, University of Ballarat, Australia. Her research interests are in the fields of knowledge acquisition and representation, argumentation and group decision-making.

Damminda Alahakoon received a BSc (Hons.) in computer science from the University of Colombo, Sri Lanka and a PhD in computer science from Monash University, Australia. He has more than eight years experience in IT and finance industries and is currently a lecturer in the School of Business Systems, Monash University. Before joining Monash, he held positions as accountant, credit officer and data mining specialist in IT and financial organizations in Sri Lanka, Australia, and The Netherlands. His current research interest includes data mining and analysis, artificial neural networks, fuzzy systems, and adaptive intelligent systems.

Malcolm J. Beynon, PhD, is a senior lecturer at the Cardiff Business School, Cardiff University, UK. His research and teaching concentrate on the notion of uncertain reasoning in decision making and data analysis. He has an international reputation for his work using the concomitant techniques: Dempster-Shafer Theory (DST), Rough Set Theory, and Fuzzy Set Theory. Recent papers appear in journals including: *Computers and Operations Research, Economic Systems Research, European Journal of Operational Research, Healthcare Management Science, International Journal of Approximate Reasoning, International Journal of Intelligent Systems, International Journal of Management Science (OMEGA)*, and *Maritime Economics and Logistics*.

Anthony Brabazon lectures at University College Dublin, Ireland. Dr. Brabazon's research interests include mathematical decision models, evolutionary computation, and the application of computational intelligence to the domain of finance. He has in excess of 100 journal, conference, and professional publications, and has been a member of the program committee at multiple conferences on evolutionary computation, as well as acting as reviewer for several journals. He has also acted as consultant to a wide range of public and private companies in several countries.

David Cairns has worked as a researcher and application developer within the field of computational intelligence for more than 15 years. Dr. Cairns has developed and sold neural network based CI systems and has run a consultancy company specializing in CI-based solutions for marketing, financial services, and insurance. Dr. Cairns is a lecturer in the Department of Computing Science at the University of Stirling, Scotland.

David Camacho is an associate professor in the Computer Science Department at the Autonomous University of Madrid, Spain. He received a PhD in computer science (2001) from the Universidad Carlos III de Madrid for his work on coordination of planning heterogeneous agents to solve problems with information gathered from the Web. He received a BS in physics (1994) from the Universidad Complutense de Madrid. His research interests include multi-agent systems, distributed artificial intelligence, Web service technologies, knowledge representation, automated planning and machine learning. He has also participated in several projects about automatic machine translation, optimizing industry processes, multi-agent technologies, and intelligent systems. He is the managing editor of the *International Journal of Computer Science & Applications (IJCSA)*, and has been selected as a chairman and member of the organizing committee for several international conferences.

Pramesh Chand received a Bachelor of Computing (computer science) from Monash University, Australia (1995) and is currently a PhD research scholar at the Faculty of

Information Technology. His areas of interests are energy market and operations research. His current research involves investigation of a nonlinear constraint model of the Australian wholesale energy and ancillary services markets. He has published a number of technical papers on optimizing the Australia market.

Amitava Datta received his MTech (1988) and PhD (1992) degrees in computer science from the Indian Institute of Technology, Madras. He did his postdoctoral research at the Max Planck Institute for Computer Science, University of Freiburg and the University of Hagen. He joined the University of New England, Australia, in 1995 and subsequently the School of Computer Science and Software Engineering at University of Western Australia in 1998, where he is currently an associate professor. He was a visiting professor at the Computer Science Institute, University of Freiburg, Germany in 2001, 2003, and 2005. His research interests are in parallel processing, optical computing, computer graphics, information visualization, bioinformatics and mobile and wireless computing. He has served as a program committee member for several international conferences in these areas including the International Parallel and Distributed Processing Symposium in 2001 and 2005. He is on the editorial board of the *Journal of Universal Computer Science* (Springer) and the *Journal of Pervasive Computing and Communications* (Troubador). He is a member of the IEEE, IEEE Computer Society and the ACM.

Zhao Yang Dong received a PhD in electrical and information engineering from The University of Sydney, Australia (1999). He is now a senior lecturer at the School of Information Technology and Electrical Engineering, The University of Queensland, Australia. His research interest includes power system security assessment and enhancement, electricity market, artificial intelligence and its application in electric power engineering, power system planning and management, and power system stability and control.

Alice Delahunty is a post-graduate student in the Department of Management Information Systems at University College Dublin, Ireland.

Tom Downs earned a bachelor's degree and PhD both in electrical engineering and both from the University of Bradford, UK. His PhD was awarded for work carried out in the Theoretical Sciences Laboratory of the Marconi Company at Baddow, Essex. He joined the Department of Electrical Engineering at The University of Queensland, Australia, as a lecturer in 1973. He was appointed a professor of electrical engineering in 1987 and was head of the department for five years from 1990. He is now located in the recently merged School of Information Technology and Electrical Engineering. His research interests include neural networks, machine learning, and applied probability.

Ranadhir Ghosh completed his BSc in computer science and engineering from Bangalore University, India, then obtained his MSc in IT from Bond University, and later obtained a PhD from Griffith University (2003) with an academic excellence award. He is currently a lecturer in the School of ITMS at the University of Ballarat, Australia. His expertise is in evolutionary neural learning and its applications. He has many publications in various international journals, conferences, and book chapters.

Martin G. Helander is a professor at the School of Mechanical and Aerospace Engineering at Nanyang Technological University, Singapore. He received a PhD from Chalmers University of Technology in Göteborg, Sweden. He has held faculty positions at Luleå University, State University of New York at Buffalo and Linköping University, and visiting appointments at Virginia Tech, MIT and Hong Kong University of Science and Technology. His primary research interests are in human factors engineering and ergonomics. He is the past president of the International Ergonomics Association.

Andrei Hryshko received his 1st Class Honors degree in applied mathematics and computer science from the Belarus State University (2001). He is currently reading for his PhD in the School of Information Technology and Electrical Engineering, University of Queensland, Australia. His research interests include machine learning, evolutionary computation, optimization and finance.

Sasha Ivkovic is currently a lecturer in the school of ITMS at University of Ballarat, Australia. His interests include open source, Linux, and knowledge discovery from databases (data mining — association rules). Mr. Ivkovic completed his BComp (Hons.) and Master of IT (research) from the University of Ballarat. His current research includes the organization of generated association rules and discovery visualization.

Kristina Risom Jespersen received a PhD from Aarhus School of Business, Denmark, on the topic "information and new product development decision-making" and is currently working as an assistant professor at the Department of Marketing, Informatics and Statistics where she is responsible for courses in general statistics and data collection methodologies.

Jianxin (Roger) Jiao is an assistant professor of systems and engineering management with the School of Mechanical and Aerospace Engineering, Nanyang Technological University, Singapore. He received a PhD in industrial engineering from Hong Kong University of Science and Technology. He holds a bachelor's degree in mechanical engineering from Tianjin University of Science and Technology, China, and a master's degree in mechanical engineering from Tianjin University, China. His research interests include mass customization, design theory and methodology, reconfigurable manufacturing systems, engineering logistics, and intelligent systems.

Peter Keenan lectures at University College Dublin, Ireland. Dr. Keenan's research interests include decision support systems, the application of computational intelligence to decision support, geographic information systems in business and their application to decision support, especially in the context of transportation problems. He has published extensively in these areas, as well as acting as a member of the program committee at numerous conferences and has reviewed for a variety of publishers, conferences and scholarly journals.

Martin Kitchener, PhD, MBA, is an associate professor at the University of California, San Francisco (UCSF), USA. His research and teaching concentrate on the organizational analysis of health and social care. He was previously economic and social research council (ESRC) fellow at Cardiff University, UK, and Harkness research fellow at the University of California, Berkeley. Kitchener currently directs a federal government research program on the development of health programs for the disabled. Recent papers appear in edited volumes and journals including: *Organization Studies*, *Organization*, *Health Affairs*, *Healthcare Management Science*, *Inquiry*, *Social Science & Medicine*, and *Journal of Health and Social Behavior*. He is also the co-author of the book, *Residential Children's Care: A Managed Service* (Macmillan, 2004).

Tatsiana Levina is an assistant professor of management science at Queen's School of Business, Canada. She holds an MBA and PhD in management (Rutgers University, 2004). Her current research focuses on the development of new online learning strategies and their applications to portfolio analysis, optimization, and revenue management problems.

Prasanna Lokuge has more than 14 years experience in information systems in both public and private sectors. Since 2003, Lokuge has been an assistant lecturer/lecturer at the School of Business Systems, Monash University, Australia. He obtained his first degree in BSc in 1990. He then completed his post graduate diploma in information technology from the University of Colombo, Sri Lanka (1993) and completed the master's degree in computer science at the University of Colombo, Sri Lanka (1999). He currently is reading for his doctorate at Monash University, Australia, in intelligent agents for the shipping industry. He is a full member of the Australian Computer Society, Computer Society of Sri Lanka and a chartered member of the British Computer Society.

Brian C. Lovell received a BE in electrical engineering (Honors I) in 1982, a BSc in computer science in 1983, and a PhD in signal processing in 1991, all from the University of Queensland (UQ), Australia. Lovell is program director of engineering and research director of the Intelligent Real-Time Imaging and Sensing Research Group in the School of ITEE, UQ. He is president of the Australian Pattern Recognition Society, senior member of the IEEE, fellow of the Institute of Engineers, Australia, and voting member for Australia on the governing board of the International Association for Pattern Recognition.

Dennis O'Callaghan is a post-graduate student in the Department of Management Information Systems at University College Dublin, Ireland.

Michael O'Neill is a lecturer in the Department of Computer Science and Information Systems at the University of Limerick, Ireland. Dr. O'Neill has more than 70 peer-reviewed publications on biologically inspired algorithms including the seminal book on grammatical evolution. Dr. O'Neill is a regular reviewer for the leading evolutionary computation journals and conferences.

Rob Potharst studied applied mathematics at the University of Amsterdam where he received his MSc in 1971. He taught mathematics, statistics and economics at several high schools and colleges until he joined the Computer Science Department, Erasmus University Rotterdam (1987), The Netherlands. Since 1995 he has been involved in research at the cutting edge of applied statistics and artificial intelligence, culminating in a PhD from Erasmus University Rotterdam in 1999. Currently, as an assistant professor at the Econometric Institute of this university, his main interest is in applying methods from the field of computational learning to marketing problems. Potharst has published several articles in international books and journals.

Michiel van Rijthoven obtained his MSc in economics and computer science at the Erasmus University Rotterdam. He is currently an employee of Oracle Netherlands, where he creates J2EE systems with Oracle products.

Thomas L. Saaty is a professor of the Katz Graduate School of Business, University of Pittsburgh, USA, and earned his PhD in mathematics from Yale. He is a member of the National Academy of Engineering. Previously, he was a professor with the Wharton School, University of Pennsylvania, before which he worked at the Arms Control and Disarmament Agency, State Department, Washington, DC, on nuclear arms reduction negotiations with the Soviets in Geneva. He has published 33 books and 250 papers. His latest books include *The Brain: Unraveling the Mystery of How It Works* and *Creative Thinking, Problem Solving & Decision Making*. He developed the analytic hierarchy process (AHP) for decision-making and its generalization to feedback, the analytic network process (ANP).

Tapan Kumar Saha was born in Bangladesh and immigrated to Australia in 1989. He is currently a professor in the School of Information Technology and Electrical Engineering, University of Queensland, Australia. Before joining the University of Queensland, he taught at the Bangladesh University of Engineering and Technology, Dhaka for three and a half years; and then at James Cook University, Australia for two and a half years. His research interests include power systems, power quality, and condition monitoring of electrical plants. Dr. Saha is a fellow of the Institute of Engineers Australia.

Andrew Stranieri is a senior lecturer in the School of Information Technology and Mathematical Sciences, University of Ballarat, Australia, and managing director of a decision support system company, JustSys Pty Ltd. Dr. Stranieri has published more than 30 journal and conference articles on the application of artificial intelligence to law and a text on data mining in law. His current research interests are in the field of narrative for conveying information, knowledge based systems, online dispute resolution and data mining.

Ly Fie Sugianto is currently a senior lecturer at the Faculty of Information Technology, Monash University, Australia. She holds a Bachelor of Computer Systems Engineering (Honors 1) from Curtin University and Doctor of Philosophy in electrical engineering from Monash University. Dr. Sugianto has published more than 50 research papers in optimization technique, fuzzy mathematics, decision support systems and e-commerce. She has also received several grants to conduct research in electricity markets and information systems. Her areas of interest include spot price forecasting, strategic bidding and dispatch optimization.

Kevin Swingler has dedicated his 15-year career to the commercial application of intelligent computing techniques. He started off on research projects for British Telecom and The Ford Motor Company before forming his own company (in partnership with the other author of this chapter) to develop and sell neural network based software. The business served clients in insurance, banking, marketing, publishing and lending. His book, *Applying Neural Networks* (Academic Press) was the first practical guide to applying those techniques in a commercial environment. He now runs a consultancy company that helps universities to find commercial applications for computational intelligence techniques.

Tadao Takaoka is professor of computer science at the University of Canterbury, New Zealand. He obtained his bachelor's, master's, and PhD degrees in applied mathematics and physics at the School of Engineering, Kyoto University, Japan. After working at the NTT Laboratory as a researcher and at Ibaraki University as a professor, he started at Canterbury in 1997. Takaoka's research areas are in theoretical computer science in general and algorithms in particular. He specializes in algorithms for pattern matching, combinatorial generation, shortest paths, data mining, cryptology, and so forth. He co-authored the book, *Fundamental Algorithms* (Iwanami Shoten Pub. Co.), organized the 12th International Symposium on Algorithms and Computation (ISAAC 2001), edited a special issue of *Algorithmica* for ISAAC 2001, and has published more than 70 papers in journals and proceedings of international conferences.

Kesaraporn Techapichetvanich received her Bachelor of Engineering in electronics engineering from King Mongkut Institute of Technology, Ladkrabang, Thailand. She worked as a system engineer in a telecommunication company. She completed a Master of Science in computer science at The University of New South Wales in July 2001. She is currently doing a PhD in computer science and software engineering at the University of Western Australia, Australia. Her research interests include information visualization, data mining, and computer graphics. Her current research projects involve in visual exploration and analysis.

Christian J. Walder received a BE in electrical engineering (Honors I) in 2000 from the University of Queensland. After completing the degree, Walder worked as a research scientist in Telstra Research Laboratories until September 2002. He worked on novel data mining algorithms for the mobile phone customer database, as well as a grammatical inference package (now proprietary). After working at Telstra, he enrolled as a full-time PhD student of the University of Queensland supported by the C. H. Bennett bequest and the German Government DAAD scholarship. He is currently located at the Max Planck Institute in Tübingen, Germany.

Hsiao-Fan Wang has been teaching at the Department of Industrial Engineering and Engineering Management, National Tsing Hua University, Taiwan, ROC after she graduated from Cambridge University in 1981. She has been the head of the Department of IEEM, National Tsing Hua University, president of the Chinese Fuzzy Systems Association, and vice president of the International Fuzzy Systems Association. She has also been awarded the Distinguished Research Award from the National Science Council of Taiwan, ROC and now she is the contracted research fellow of NSC. Her research interests are in multicriteria decision making, fuzzy set theory, and operations research.

Miao-Ling Wang received her PhD in industrial engineering from National Tsing-Hua University (1995). She is now a vice professor with the Department of Industrial Engineering and Management, Minghsin University of Science & Technology, Taiwan, ROC. Her main research interests are in fuzzy set theory and multiobjective linear programming.

Yi Wang currently works as a production engineer at Intel Chengdu, China. He received an MSc in computer integrated manufacturing from Nanyang Technological University, Singapore and a BEng in mechanical engineering from Sichuan University, China. He has worked as a production engineer in Singapore and as a college lecture in China. His research interests include design theory and supply chain management.

Michiel van Wezel received his MSc in computer science from Utrecht University (1994), and his PhD in computer science (artificial intelligence) from Leiden University (1994). He is currently working as an assistant professor at the Econometric Institute of the Erasmus University Rotterdam, The Netherlands where his main research topic is the application of machine learning in marketing, management science and e-business.

Kit Po Wong obtained his MSc, PhD and DEng degrees from the University of Manchester, Institute of Science and Technology (1972, 1974 and 2001, respectively). Professor Wong was with The University of Western Australia since 1974. He is currently chair professor and head of the Department of Electrical Engineering, The Hong Kong Polytechnic University, Hong Kong. Professor Wong received three Sir John Madsen medals (1981, 1982 and 1988) from the Institution of Engineers Australia, the 1999 Outstanding Engineer Award from IEEE Power Chapter Western Australia and the 2000

IEEE Third Millennium Award. His research interests include artificial intelligence and evolutionary computation applications to power system planning and operations. Professor Wong was a co-technical chairman of the IEEE ICMLC 2004 conference and general chairman of IEEE PowerCon2000. He is an honorary editor of the *IEE Proceedings in Generation, Transmission and Distribution* and editor (electrical) of the Transactions of Hong Kong Institution of Engineers. He is a Fellow of IEEE, IEE, HKIE and IEAust

John Yearwood is deputy director of the Centre for Informatics and Applied Optimisation and the leader of the research group in data mining and informatics. As associate professor, he has published and worked extensively in decision support, computational intelligence, and applications of artificial intelligence to health and law. He currently holds an ARC research fellowship working on argumentation and narrative.

Yiyang Zhang is a PhD candidate in the School of Mechanical and Aerospace Engineering, Nanyang Technological University, Singapore. She received her BBA and MBA degrees from the School of Management at Northeastern University, China (1999 and 2002, respectively). Her current research interests are customer decision-making process, product portfolio planning and customer requirement management.

Index

K

L

M

N

O

P

CPSIA information can be obtained at www.ICGtesting.com
Printed in the USA
238212LV00007B/14/P

9 781591 407027